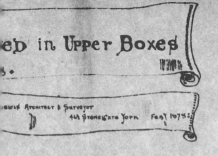

...ed in Upper Boxes

...gewen Architect & Surveyor   4 Stonegate York   Fery 1875:

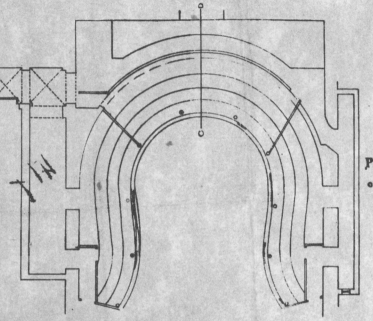

Plan as at Present

of Upper Boxes

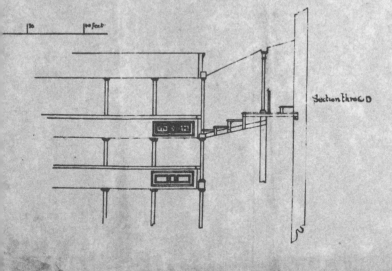

Section thro C D

The York Theatre

Sybil Rosenfeld

THE SOCIETY FOR THEATRE RESEARCH

LONDON

First published 2001

by the Society for Theatre Research,
c/o The Theatre Museum, 1E Tavistock Street,
Covent Garden, London WC2E 7PA

ISBN 085430 066 X

Production by Sarah Cannon Publishing Services, Oxford

Printed and bound by Woolnough Bookbinding,
Church Street, Irthlingborough, Northants.

CONTENTS

ILLUSTRATIONS

Frontispiece

Sybil Rosenfeld, celebrating her ninetieth birthday at
the Garrick Club. *From a photograph by Jennie Walton.*

Between pages 222 and 223

Endpapers

Plan of the interior of the Theatre Royal, York, c.1876.
Reproduced by kind permission of the City of York Council, York Reference Library.

Sybil Rosenfeld, celebrating her ninetieth birthday
at the Garrick Club

A PERSONAL TRIBUTE

I FIRST knew Sybil Rosenfeld when we laboured together in the thickets of theatre research in the 1960s. We were joint editors, with Ifan Kyrle Fletcher completing the trio, of *Theatre Notebook*, the journal of the Society for Theatre Research.

From the start I admired the academic rigour with which Sybil approached whatever material came before us. But it was also impossible to work with her without rapidly becoming a close friend. Above all, I came to cherish her for her extraordinary generosity of spirit. It informed everything she did, and affected everyone she was in contact with, much to the benefit of those involved in studying the history of British theatre.

Sybil invariably had work of her own on the stocks, usually breaking new ground as does *The York Theatre*, but she never let this deter her from helping others. I marvel still at the time she used to take in knocking unwieldy articles into shape for *Theatre Notebook*, or in answering requests from students for often very detailed advice and information.

Yet at the same time none of this was allowed to distract her from her own intense enjoyment of the living theatre, and indeed of all the arts. It is typical that when she died, at the age of ninety-three, she had been that very afternoon to an exhibition at the Royal Academy and had a ticket for a play the following evening.

Without any official academic position, but working to the highest academic standards, Sybil was the essential amateur in every best sense of the word. She loved life and she adored the theatre, past and present alike.

Bamber Gascoigne

PREFACE

THE publication of this book has had a long gestation. Just after the conclusion of the Second World War Sybil Rosenfeld was invited by the York Citizens' Theatre to write the history of the York Theatre, with special reference to the Theatre Royal, York. The work was completed and the manuscript typed in 1948, but at that time, because of other extended commitments, there proved to be insufficient funds to meet the cost of the proposed publication. Miss Rosenfeld then tried to interest the commercial publishing world of the time, but without success: books on theatre history were considered to have neither a potentially large readership nor profitability.

In the event, apart from the copy in the possession of the Citizens' Theatre trustees who had commissioned it, Dr. Rosenfeld, with their permission, donated a copy to the York City Reference Library, with the generous permission that it should be made freely available to future researchers.

In 1998, fifty years after, the Society for Theatre Research, then celebrating its own Golden Jubilee and wishing to commemorate the life of one of its founders, proposed to undertake the publication of this neglected work as a tribute to her memory, and so that in a permanent form it could reach the wider academic world as it had long deserved.

The early chapters of the book summarise the account of the early beginnings of theatre in York, the miracle plays, the Elizabethan period, and supplement the information on the early theatres contained in the author's previously published seminal study, *Strolling Players and Drama in the Provinces 1660–1765* (1939). The main body of the new work, therefore, gives a detailed study of the York Theatre after that period onwards from the first Theatre Royal in 1765, and is based on new research using the unrivalled set of playbills in the York Minster Library, manuscript material in the Corporation Records as well as Tate Wilkinson's account books and letters in the City of York Library and the Harvard Theatre Collection.

The manuscript has, over the years, provided a rich mine of information for subsequent scholars and particularly as a basis for other booklets such as that published by the York Theatre Royal to celebrate its 250th anniversary in 1994.

Many people have helped to bring this initiative of delayed publication to fruition: these are named in the Acknowledgements that follow. In addition the Society has decided to print Sybil Rosenfeld's own Acknowledgements page which she prepared in 1948. Most – probably all – of the names she records are now no longer living, but it seems fitting to remember, across the years, their initial contribution to the evolution of this history.

Finally, as a postscript, it is to be hoped that the appearance of this book may prompt another theatre historian to compile the history of the Theatre Royal and the other York theatres since 1948.

Jack Reading

ACKNOWLEDGEMENTS

MY principal thanks for the making of this book must go to the Governors of the York Citizens' Theatre who conceived the project and generously enabled it to be carried out.

In compiling the facts I have met with much kindness and helpfulness from many people. I am indebted to the late Chancellor Harrison for allowing me to work in the Minster Library at many hours when it was not officially open, and for his long-suffering patience at my constant stream of requests. Mr. Doherty and the York Library Staff have taken unstinting pains in procuring all the volumes of newspapers and playbills, and the authorities at the Guildhall went to much trouble in allowing me to see the Corporation Records and plans of the Theatre. The *York Herald* office generously gave me free access to their excellent files and the use of a room in which to study them in comfort. Dr. van Lennep, Curator of the Harvard College Theatre Collection, made it possible for me to see all the York material in a brief visit. I have to thank the Revd. Angelo Raine for his kindness in allowing me to make use of his notes from the 16th and early 17th century Corporation books and Mr. Ifan Kyrle Fletcher and Sir St. Vincent Troubridge Bt. and Mr. Patrick Waddington for permission to inspect their playbills. The following have all helped me with information: Miss Brunskill, Mr. W. J. Carter, the Revd. R. O. Clark of St. John's Wakefield, the Revd. P. Cowley of St. Mary Castlegate, Mr. Finney formerly of the York Art Gallery, the Chief Librarian at Hull, Miss Foster Leeds Archivist, the Leeds City Librarian, Miss Pauline Letts, Mr. John Parker, Miss Violet Rodgers formerly of the Castle Museum, Mr. P. J. Stead, Mr. Geoffrey Staines, the Revd. I. Spencer of Acomb, and the Revd. F. E. Vokes. Last but by no means least I am indebted to the Cambridge University Press for allowing me to reprint part of my chapters on the York stage in *Strolling Players*.

My labours have been rendered enjoyable by the enthusiasm and interest shown in this history by those whom I troubled on its behalf.

Sybil Rosenfeld, October 1948

FURTHER
ACKNOWLEDGEMENTS

WERE she able to do so I am sure that Sybil Rosenfeld would wish to make posthumous acknowledgements to three friends of hers who have carried this book through to publication: Dorothy Moore, Hilda Schiff and Jack Reading. Without their distinctive contributions it is unlikely that *The York Theatre* would have been published, and I should like to add the thanks of the Society to those which I have presumed to give on behalf of the author. Acknowledgement is also due to Sheila Rosenberg, Helen Groves and Councillor Katherine Carr for their help, and to all the subscribers for their support and patience.

Richard Foulkes, General Editor of Publications
The Society for Theatre Research

ABOUT THE AUTHOR

Sybil Rosenfeld, 1903–1996

WHEN Sybil Rosenfeld completed her first degree in English Literature at the age of 19, at King's College, London (gaining a First and the Goldsmith Prize for the first amid the Firsts of that year), she came under the influence of Allardyce Nicoll who encouraged her to take up research into what was then a very new subject: theatre history.

She followed his lead, and throughout her long life never looked back. Her publications in this field are too numerous to list here, but some of the ground-breaking ones are: *The Letter Books of Sir George Etherege* (Oxford University Press, 1928); *Strolling Players and Drama in the Provinces, 1660–1765* (Cambridge University Press, 1939); *The Theatres of the London Fairs in the Eighteenth Century* (Cambridge University Press, 1960); *A Short History of Scene Design in Great Britain* (Basil Blackwell, Oxford, 1973); *Temples of Thespis: Some Private Theatres and Theatricals in England and Wales, 1700–1820* (Society for Theatre Research, 1978); and *Georgian Scene Painters and Scene Painting* (Cambridge University Press, 1981).

Unlike many of her contemporaries, and deferring to her father's wish, Sybil did not embark on a university teaching career but pursued her scholarly work independently, as an amateur in the true sense of that word. She loved her subject and brought to it not only the highest standards of patient and exacting research but also a wide and deep background in all the arts. It became a byword amongst her friends to say, when at a loss as to who wrote or painted what, 'Ask Sybil'. She was the archetypal cultured person for her day, but wore her learning lightly and with humour.

Yet it was not her way to extrapolate wildly from one field into another or embroider her subject matter beyond what the evidence could support, and thereby gain popular appeal. She focused sharply on her topic, and communicated it clearly and succinctly, with liveliness and driving force. Thus her style seems transparent and the story that emerges from her researches appears to have formulated itself. She was a writer Ranke would have approved of when he said it was the business of the historian not to show how things could or might have been, but how things really were.

This history of the York Theatre displays these attributes. We are fortunate in having recovered the unpublished manuscript when we did. It came to light after Sybil's death, deposited as it was long ago in a cupboard, wrapped up in tattered brown paper and tied with string. It has taken four long years for the manuscript to reach book form. Jack Reading refers in his Preface to how the book was first conceived; here we can give thanks for its safe delivery.

Hilda Schiff

SUBSCRIBERS

John Adrian
Anthony Amberg
I.N. Anderson
Graham J. Bacon
Mrs Jean Napier Baker
Miss Olive Baldwin
Graham F. Barlow
Professor John Barrell
Roger Beacham
Dr Thomas L. Berger
Miss J.A. Beryl
Mrs Fern Bevan
Birmingham City
   Central Library
Alex J.I. Bisset
Mrs Jennie Bisset
Mrs S.M. Blanshard
Marston C.E. Bloom
Steven Blyth
E.G. Bottle
P.R. Boyce
Professor J.S. Bratton
K.W. Brown
Miss Jennifer A.
   Carnell
David F. Cheshire
Bruce Cleave
Miss Margaret Collins
D.G. Corble
M. Cordner
Anthony Cornish
Mrs Eileen Cottis

Graeme Cruickshank
G.C. Davidson
Mrs A. Davinson
Professor Tracy C.
   Davis
Richard Digby Day
Philip M.L. de Grouchy
Professor Joseph W.
   Donohue
Professor Ron W.
   Edwards, CBE
Professor James D. Ellis
J.C. Emes
Mrs Angela Escott
Dr Graeme Feggetter
E.D.M. Forbes
Dr Richard G. Foulkes
Miss Francesca Franchi
Paul M. Furness
Mrs Gorel Garlick
The Garrick Club
Bamber Gascoigne
Dr Todd S. Gilman
Professor Henry
   Goodman
Dr D. Griffiths
Anselm Heinrich
Robert Henderson
A.C. Hessey
Ms Audrey Hickey
Miss M.M. Hobbs
Mrs K. Houghton

Mrs Frances Hughes
Geoff Humphrys
Dr Neville Hunnings
Paul Iles
Professor Madeleine
   Inglehearn
Mrs L.B. Jackson
M.Y. Jones
P.W. Jones
Denis Kelly
Ms H. Kenwright
Professor Edward A.
   Langhans
Mark Lardner
Mrs Helen Leacroft
Brian Lead
Miss M. Leask
Miss M. Leng
Mr & Mrs C. McCarthy
Dr Arthur W.
   McDonald
Miss Dorothy M.
   Moore, MBE
Hugh Murray
A. Naylor
Mrs Lilian Neuberger
Professor P. Nuttgens
Dr Marion O'Connor
M.A. Ostler
Mr & Mrs J. Parker
Mark Pessell
Richard Platt

Dr H.C. Porter
Dr Lois Potter
Miss Jane Pritchard
Dr Paul V. Ranger
Dr M.G. Read
Jack Reading
Jocelyn A. Reilly
Jonathan A. Reynolds
Catherine M.E. Roberts
Sheila K. Rosenberg
D. Savage
John Savident
Hilda Schiff
Lady A.A. Sekers
The Shakespeare
    Birthplace Trust
Barry Sheppard
Mrs Anne Sheridan
Professor Frances
    Shirley
Mrs Sheila Skilleter
Gerald Smith

Miss H.R. Smith
Southern Methodist
    University,
    Dallas, USA
George Speaight
D.J. Spurling
Alan G. Stockwell
Miss Elizabeth M.
    Sutter
Ms Kate Taylor
Mrs Marjorie Tetlow
The Theatre Museum,
    London
The Theatre Royal,
    York
Edward Thompson
Dr Ross Thorne
Thomas Tillery
Gerald E.B. Tyler
Dr Pieter van der
    Merwe
Donald Walker

Professor J. Michael
    Walton
R.W. Waters
Professor Stanley W.
    Wells
Mrs J. Whitehouse
Professor Glynne
    Wickham
Professor Don B.
    Wilmeth
Dr David C. Wilmore
Peter Wood
P.B. Woodroofe
The York City Archives
The York City Art
    Gallery
York City Council
    Leisure Services
York City Council
    Libraries
York University Library
Miss Olive E.B. Youngs

PRELUDE

THE dramatic history of York may be said to start with the great cycle of miracle plays which was performed in the city's streets from about the middle of the 14th century[1] until the 1580s. Of the fifty-seven plays on Old and New Testament subjects forty-eight and a fragment are extant, the greatest number for any one town. They have been fully dealt with elsewhere.[2] Sufficient here to remind ourselves that they formed part of the Corpus Christi celebrations, and were performed on 'pageants' or movable carts by the various guilds at twelve or more stations about the town. They took the livelong summer's day since the complete cycle was given at each station in turn and the actors had to be ready between 4 and 5 a.m.[3] The coming of the Reformation caused alterations to be made in the plays and they were at times looked on with some disfavour as too Catholic. Yet as late as 1580, well into Elizabeth's reign, we find the citizens of York petitioning for the plays which had been performed as recently as the previous year.

In addition to the great cycle there were the Paternoster and Creed plays which have not come down to us but which were performed at intervals. The Paternoster play, which was given at least as early as 1378, was later absorbed by the Holy Trinity guild of mercers and was sometimes presented instead of the cycle. The Creed play was bequeathed to the guild of Corpus Christi in 1446, and in 1495 the guild was given permission to play it that year and every ten years at the Common Hall about Lammastide (August). It thus seems to have been the first play to be performed, not in the streets, but within doors.

A schoolmaster named John Grafton borrowed the pageants and gave some plays at street stations at late as 1584 to 1585 but we have no positive evidence of performances after that.

Twenty years before in 1565 we hear for the first time of the visit of a secular company of players to York. The Chamberlain's Accounts mention payments to four companies of players that year the first being Lord Scrope's in January.[4] They played in the Common Hall, Coney Street and were awarded 13s. 4d. There are no further awards until 1576 when three companies of players, the Earl of Essex's, Lord Stafford's and the otherwise unknown Lancashire men players gave performances in the Minster Close before the Dean and Chapter. Payments of £1 to the two former and 10s.0d. to the last are recorded in the Chamberlain's books in the Zouche chapel.[5] Elizabethan travelling troupes then had two potential audiences and playing places in York, one secular when they were rewarded by the civic authorities, and the other ecclesiastical when they were remunerated by the Dean and Chapter, usually at the rate of £1.2s.0d. Occasionally the same company played in both places. Thus in 1584 the Queen's players had £3.6s.8d. from the City Chamberlain and £2 from the Dean and Chapter. The Earl of Essex's players performed before both in 1587, and Her Majesty's in 1596. The last ecclesiastical entry is for a performance in February 1599. We hear of no further secular performances after 1565 for sixteen years, but that there were some given may be presumed from the resolution of the Lord Mayor's Court on October 22, 1578 'from henseforth that ther shalbe no interludes, playes or other devises for assemblinge of the common people at the Common Hall of this cittie played published or put in exercise ther but onely at such tyme or tymes as the L. Mayors of this Cyttie shalbe presente at the same except speciall lycense be granted therin by the full consent of this court.'[6]

It is not, though, until September 1, 1581 that we hear of a definite visit when an entry in the Corporation Minute Book[7] reads: 'it was agreed by thes presente that my L. of Sussex men being players of Interluds shall play this afternone at the Common Hall at two of the clocke and the said players to have such rewarde as other players have heretofore had in tymes past.'[8]

The following year we come on the first attempt to limit the players' activities: 'players of Interludes now come and comyng from henceforth to this cittie shall play but twise in the common hall of this cyttie viz: once before the L. maior and aldermen and thother before the commons.' (February 3, 1582).[9] Players continued to come in the following years and in 1587 there were no less than seven visiting troupes.

The plague in London in 1592 sent Lord Strange's company on tour and Edward Alleyn[10], in a letter to his wife, mentions York, as one of the towns to which she could address letters. There is no actual record of their visit and it is possible that they were prevented from playing. Alleyn's letter is dated August 1 and on July 24 the Corporation made the following decision: 'And whereas the doores, lockes, keyes, wyndowes, bordes, benches and other buildings of the Common Hall are greatlye impared and hurtt and diverse of the same broken, shakne, lowst and ryven up by the people reparinge thither to se and heare plays. It is theirfore nowe agreed by theis presente that no Players shalbe permitted to playe anye manner of playes, either in the same Common Hall or in St. Anthony's Halle at anye tyme or tymes hereafter.'[11] St. Anthony's Hall, thus first mentioned as an alternative playing place to the Common Hall, is still in existence. The players evidently attracted rough houses, and the damage caused gave a handle to the authorities, to stop performances by shutting the two principal halls of the city in the players' faces. However, six companies visited York the following year though whether the restrictions were relaxed or they found other accommodation we do not know. In 1595 it was 'Agreed that my L. Willowbies players shall play at ther host house or such other house or place within this Citty as they can get for three or four days so it be not in the night tyme nor on the Sabbath daie but not in the Common Hall nether to have any reward of this Citty.'[12] From 1598 we find entries of players who came and 'played not' being given £2 or other sums to go away. An entry in the Minute Books under March 28, 1599[13], for example, reads: 'The Earle of Worsters players shall have xxxs given them and depart and not playe, wch was delivered to Mr. Holcroft.' However the Earl of Pembroke's men in January 1599-1600 were more fortunate and played before the Lord Mayor and Aldermen in the Common Hall for a reward of £2.10s.[14]

That the players sometimes found playing room in a private house is witnessed by an entry on July 15, 1601: 'Aggreed that my Lord Shandoze players shall have libertie to playe at Marmaduke gill howse till Sunday next and they to depart and not to play in the night tyme.'[15] With this may be compared the entry in the ecclesiastical chamberlain's accounts under February 5, 1597/8 'To players in Mr. Doctor Bennitts xvs.'

When James I visited York in April 1603 on his way to ascend his throne in London, Lord Dudley's men entertained him, but in 1607 they were unlucky and were among those who 'played not', for which they however received £1.10s. in comparison with 13s.4d. and £1 when they had played.

This same year, 1607, the Queen's players came with a royal licence that was not to be denied. On September 23 the Council gave their permission as follows: 'And nowe the Queens Mat^ies players have maide suite to this Court that they might be permitted to plaie in this cittie and have showed a licence from her Mat^ie that they maie be permitted to plaie in all Cittyes and Townes corporate it is agreed by thes presente that they shalbe permitted to playe in this cittes [sic] so as they do not plaie on the Sabaoth daies and on the nights.'[16]

York may put in a claim to have had one of the earliest provincial playhouses though it was never used.[17] Unfortunately we know nothing of the kind of building it was, only that it was to be especially erected for the performance of plays. The two entries relating to this playhouse in the Minute Books are under the dates September 22 and December 11, 1609.[18] In the first Richard Middleton and others petitioned for permission 'to erect a Theater or playhouse within this cittie wherein such as have bene borne and brought upp therin should imploye ther laborious expenses for the maintenance therof wch might be a meanes to restrayne the frequent comminge herunto of other Stage plaiers, and they would yeild x li per annum unto this Corporacion.' This skilful appeal to civic pride savoured with the inducements that the detested travelling troupes might thereby be

xix

discouraged from coming to the town, and the corporation have a good income from the venture, won the day, and the court agreed to grant the permission upon certain conditions which were to be laid down later by them. Unhappily this first attempt to found a local company was speedily suppressed when it was discovered that Middleton and his colleagues had gone ahead without further orders: 'And whereas Richard Middleton and others did heretofore of late make suite unto this court that they might be permitted to erect a Theater or playhouse within this cittie, And thys court then takeinge consideracion upon ther requeste did think good that before they should begyn to erect the same playhowse ther should be some condicions considered upon by this court wch they should on ther pte performe, And forasmuch as this court doth understand that they have erected a Theater or playhowse in this cittie, and have not attended this Court to have receyved dyriccions upon what condicions they might have been permitted, And have drawne unto ther companyes straingers that did inhabitt in the countrie, and likewise some of manuell occupacions in this cittie who do intend to give over ther occupacions and fall to an idle course of life, It is nowe thought good and agreed by this court for that they have proceded in suche sorte as aforesaide, that they shalbe discharged for kepeinge of anie play-house in this cittie, as they will answere at their own perells.' If only Middleton had been a little less eager, it may well be that York would have had the first of all city companies instead of an empty and barren playhouse hastily erected only to be deprived of its purpose. Henceforward we hear of very few visiting companies, and most of them were refused permission to play. In 1625 they were turned away without even a reward: 'Wheras two severall companyes of Players have made sute to play it is thought meete that nether of the same Companyes shall play nor have any benevolence' (February 8).[19]

In 1629 another project for forming a York company of players was mooted. On September 18 William Perry was granted a commission 'for making up and keeping a company of players, to present all usual stage plays, by the name of His Majesty's servants for the City of York.'[20] That this was not the mere name of a touring company is proved by a warrant in the Lord Chamberlain's warrant book, dated February 27, 1632/3, for a licence to William Perry and his associates to practise plays in the city of York and elsewhere. Perry's company were also designated players of the private chamber in York when they were in King's Lynn in March, 1633. Perry was manager of the Red Bull company with which the King's travelling company was probably connected.[21] Unfortunately there is no trace of its actually having acted in York. If indeed it did, as seems likely, it was the last recorded one to do so for over fifty years.

The York Theatre

CHAPTER ONE

The Early York Theatres 1705–1764

LITTLE is known about theatrical activity in the provinces during the Restoration period. The Corporation House Books for the second half of the 17th century contain no references to players and we cannot be certain that any visited York. There were, however, at least two instances of proposed visits by London companies. Thomas Shipman, in his *Carolina; or Loyal Poems*, 1683, has a prologue and epilogue for a company of players leaving London for York upon their first appearance, dated 1670. And about 1682 Sir Thomas Player wrote to the Lord Mayor of York (Sir Henry Thompson) and Sir John Newly asking them 'to encourage the dramatist Elkanah Settle in his design to carry John Coysh, who had a company of players which visited provincial towns, and others, to act plays or drolls in York.'[1] We do not know whether Shipman's addresses were ever actually spoken or Settle's plan carried out.

It is not until February 23, 1705 that we find a definite reference to the players in York, in a memorandum in the Minute books of the Merchant Taylors which reads: 'It was then Ordered and Agreed the Day and year above written by us whose names are here unto sett, at the Court then Assembled the said day, That Mr. Gilbert and his Company shall have the use and bennifitt of the Hall to play in and shall pay for the same to the p'sent Master Mr. J_n^o Riveley, for the use of the Company the Sume of Twenty Shillings weekly And it is further Covenanted and Agreed that J_n^o Jackson the Printer and J_n^o Gilbertson Joyner shall Give bond that none of the Sealing or fflower in the said Hall shall in any ways be Damnifyed but shall make good and leave the same in as good order as they now find it; and shall now begin to pay weekly or enter to pay until Thursday next bi the 29th of January.'

The next entry concerning the players is dated July 10, 1711: 'Agreed then with Mr Ager for the use of the Hall with the p'sent Master Mr Geo. Barnatt and he the said Mr Ager is to pay unto the said Master £1.1s.6d. Weekly and is to Enter on tuesday the 16th of this Instant July/10th August.' Thomas Ager was manager of the Duke of Norfolk's players. Either this year or on a subsequent unrecorded visit they performed William Hunt's tragedy

1

The Fall of Tarquin at the Merchant Taylors' Hall.[2] This piece was printed in York and Newcastle in 1713 and the quarto edition gives the names of two members of the cast, William Fieldhouse and Robert Pearson, who thus have the distinction of being the first actors on the York stage whose names we possess. The author William Hunt was a collector of excise at York 'a gentleman adorned with great learning and humanity who had been near twenty years before his death [in 1714] composing a book of Geography.'[3] As for the blank verse tragedy, we can but endorse the opinion of the *Biographia Dramatica* that it is 'a most wretched performance.' The scenes are but episodic snatches and a taste of the bombastic tone of the language may be savoured in

> 'Twas Hero like, to have a ravish'd Crown
> Streaming with Blood, and gorgeously beset
> With Royal Deaths

to which we sympathetically reply with the heroine:

> Oh don't I pray, do not thus wildly rave,
> 'Tis useless all, indeed 'tis all in vain.

The prologue and epilogue, according to a Ms. note in the British Museum copy, were written by Dr. Towne. Inept as the tragedy is, it is noteworthy as being a local production. York started early to produce its own dramatists and is unusual among provincial towns in presenting a number of plays by local playwrights, many of them actors, in succeeding years. Arthur, Yarrow, Peterson and Ward were all members of the York company who wrote comedies which were acted in York and in some instances outside it.[4] A satirical glimpse of the performances at this time is given in a scurrilous production entitled *The Northern Atlantis; or The York Spy*, which was printed in 1713. After an unpleasant description of the odours which emanated from the packed humanity in the playhouse the writer continues: 'We sat not long before the Musick entertain'd us with a Flourish, the Curtain was Drawn, and the strutting Actors Commenc'd their Foolery. I was extremely satisfy'd with their performances; for every Thing was Acted to such a perfectness of Uncouthness, that had so many Dicks and Dolls, as are sold in the French Shop i'th' Minster Yard, been Cloth'd and qualified with Speech, we cou'd not have Laught more heartily at their preposterous, awkward Imitation, everyone looking, notwithstanding his garb, like what he really was, and not what he represented.' We must make allowances for the satirical intent of the pamphlet; even so the performances were probably of a low standard.

The next memorandum concerning the players in the Merchant Taylors' books is dated September 5, 1715 and records the following agreement: 'that Mr. Ager is to have and Enjoy the Hall – Six Weeks at Lent Assize and Six Weeks at Lammas Assize, he paying to the Said Company fforty shillings in each Assize being in part of Six Pounds then payable, And he the Said Mr. Ager is to give the Said Company One Month's Notice before Either of the Said Assizes shall happen to begin or doe fall. And upon failure of the Said Notice to be Given to the Said Company by the Said Mr. Ager then the Said Company shall be free to let the Said Hall to whom they please and the fforty shillings – to be fforfeited by the said Mr. Tho: Ager in his not Coming or Giveing notice as aforesaid.' The players' visits were timed to coincide with the Spring and August assizes when the city was full of company, and thus were inaugurated the two York theatrical seasons which persisted for many years.

Strolling companies were gradually settling down in circuits of towns which became their own particular ports of call. Thus on August 29, 1716, Ager made a more permanent arrangement with the Merchant Taylors by securing a lease of their Hall for seven years for which he was to pay £12 whether he came or no. If he exceeded the six weeks assigned to him at Lent and Lammas he was to pay £1 for every additional week 'provided the Right Honourable the Lord Mayor of this City give him Liberty to Act.' Thus Ager and his company were accepted as York's regular players.

The Merchant Taylors' Hall was, however, not the only place of acting at this time since Mary Davys's comedy *The Northern Heiress: Or, The Humours of York* was given in the Market House in Thursday Market, now St. Sampson's Square, in 1715 or early 1716.[5] This structure had been completed in 1705 and stood on the west side of the square. An engraving of the exterior shows the upper room where plays were acted and the steps leading up to it.[6] Mary Davys, the authoress of the play, was an Irishwoman who had been a correspondent of Swift's. She married a clergyman and after his death kept a coffee house in Cambridge.[7] In the prologue to the comedy she alludes to herself as 'A Female Muse from Northern Clime', and in the preface she relates 'how industrious some of the York Gentlemen were to damn this Play', though their efforts resulted in but two hisses on the opening night. *The Northern Heiress* has a certain interest as a satirical picture of York society at the time, but as a comedy it lacks inventive power, and its heavy style is completely devoid of wit. Who performed it we do not know.

The rough treatment to which the Common Hall had been subjected well over a century before is recalled by the next entry relating to the players in the Merchant Taylors' minute books wherein it was 'ordered by the General Consent of this Court that whatsoever of the Sealing, fflower or Glass Windows which is or Doth in any way appear to be Damnifyed or Broke by the players, the Said Master is to Gett them repaired and that the players shall make Satisfaction for the same before they be Admitted to have the Benefit or use of the said Hall.' This was in 1720 and the next year we find that the Duke of Norfolk's Servants had been taken over by Thomas Keregan who had been a member of the company for ten years.[8] Keregan was acting in Newcastle in 1721 and 1723 and in Leeds in 1722 but we first hear of him in York in 1724. Ager's seven years' contract had expired in

1723 but on March 19, 1724, Keregan obtained a renewal:

> At a Court of Assistants by Speciall Warning Given, it was
> agreed upon that a Lease of the Hall be Granted to Mr.
> Thomas Kerigan for the terme of ten Years to enjoy the
> Same twelve weeks in each Year vizt: Six Weeks about Lent
> Assizes and Six Weeks about Lammas Assizes to commence
> from the building of the stage at each of the same times
> which shall not exceed a Week in building. It was then also
> agreed that if three Sufficient Workmen do agree that in
> Case a Sellar be Sunk in the Hall for the More Conven-
> iency of the acting to no disadvantage to the Hall that leave
> be given to Mr. Kerigan to Sink one at his Own expense,
> he paying half the Charge of the Workmen's View.

Keregan's application for a cellar under his stage means that he intended
to use understage machinery such as traps for the better production of the
plays.

For some reason Keregan did not play at the Merchant Taylors during
the summer season of 1727 and on August 14 'It was unanimously agreed
that Mr. Kerrigan's rent due, in the Months of July and August, 1727 Shall
be remitted him.' His company acted instead at Banks's Cockpit without
Bootham Bar, and a playbill of this season, the earliest York bill of which we
have knowledge, is reproduced by Tate Wilkinson.[9] The date is August
15,[10] the play was Congreve's tragedy *The Mourning Bride*, the cast for which
tells us for the first time the names of several actors and actresses in the
company: King = Orfeur, Gonsalez = Woodward, Garcia = Theo. Lacy,
Perez = Goodfellow, Alonzo = Gibbs, Osmyn = Keregan, Hely = Miller,[11]
Selim = Fuller, Almeria = Mrs. Glassington, Zara = Mrs. Keregan,
Leonora = Mrs Goodshaw. It was Orfeur's benefit, but he was 'debarr'd the
Liberty of paying his Respects and making his Interest on the Account of an
Action in the power of Mr. Huddy from one at London.' He had been
unable, that is, to go round touting tickets and subscriptions towards his
night. In addition to acting in the play, Orfeur recited a Congratulatory
Poem on the Accession of King George which he had written. Dancing and
dialogues set to music by Purcell completed the entertainment which
started at 6 p.m.

Visits to the play are recorded by Darcy Dawes in his account book[12] on
January 19, 21, August 4, 5, 1726; January 6, 11, 19 and August 1, 2, 3, 12,
14, 1727 and March 28, 1728, on which last occasion he paid a boy 6d. to
light him and his companions from the playhouse. His payments for places
were variously 2/-, 2/6, 3/-, 4/-, 5/-, and once 6/-, the last three amounts
being presumably for two seats. On October 2, 1727 Keregan was cited for
not paying church assessment but was indemnified at the Merchant Taylors'
charge. A year later on September 17, 1728 'At a Court of Assistance it was

Ordered that in case the Overseers of the poor of St. Cuthbert in York do distreyn of Mr Kerrigan for the Poor's Tax for the Hall that the Company will vindicate him for not paying the said tax and that Mr Jenkinson, the Master, Two Wardens and two Assistants have Power to get Councell about the Same at the Company's Charges.' This year saw the production of *The Beggar's Opera* in York, soon after it had created such a sensation at Lincoln's Inn Fields in January, with Woodward as Macheath.[13]

In the autumn of 1731 Keregan arranged for an extra winter season as we find by an entry in the minute books under October 5: 'it was unanimously agreed that Mr Kerrigan shall have the use of the Hall from the day of the date hereof till Candlemass day [February 2] next comeing at the rate of ten shillings per Week during the said terme.' A spirited epilogue spoken by Mr. and Mrs. Keregan at the end of this season is printed in *The Gentleman's Magazine*:[14]

Wife: Hold Consort – where's this Epilogue I pray?
You know was promis'd in the Bills toDay.

Hus: Our Poet has deceiv'd us, – and what then? –
D--n his dull Head, and split his venal Pen;
The Price I offer'd might have spurr'd his Wit –

Wife: Rail not on him, 'tis you yourself is bit.
Poor man, I'm sure, he labour'd Day and Night,
And work'd his Brain some mighty thing to write,
'Till tir'd, at last, this Truth he came to know,
No words can paint the Gratitude we owe.

Hus: But something must be said; Why, yes, 'tis true;
And must be spoke by, either me or you.

Wife: Come on then Sir, clear up your cloudy Face,
A Look like that wou'd the best Words disgrace;
We're us'd t'harangue in Verse, faith e'en let's try
Who best can chant Heroicks, you or I.
What! marching – stop for shame, and turn again.
You shall address the Ladies, – I the men.

Hus: Well, since it must be so, – I'll do my best; –
Ladies! – see here a truly grateful Breast,
Which labours now and heaves to think which way
To ease a Debt, it never can repay.
Your favour to our late Subscription shown,
An Obligation we shall ever own
Has rais'd us from the Depth of black Despair,

And made the Winter, as the Summer clear.
What Choice of Blessings ever wait the Dead,
Who cloath the Naked, and the Hungry feed,
Behold these Objects – those your kindness warms,
                         (pointing to his Actors)
Secur'd by you from Winter's fierce Alarms;
Whilst Days and Nights pass cheerfully away,
Pray for their Benefactors – when they pray.
How oft within these Walls has Hamlet dy'd,
With not a cross his Fun'rals to provide?
Mark Anthony has drop'd so very poor,
His Chandler's Bill has took up all his Store.
Nay, the great Cato, we've been forc'd to show
T'an Audience, as his little Senate, few.
But now – this charming Pit and glorious Stage,
So cheers my Heart, as warms me into Rage.
Let Rich and Cibber boast their crouded Seats,
Half fill'd with painted Whores and Bawds, and
                                   Cheats;
Here sit the Northern Stars, and shine so clear
T'out-rival all within the Hemisphere.
Whose darling Beauty strikes the strongest Light,
With sterling Virtue join'd – makes all divinely
                                 bright.

Oh may your Influence another Day,
(For this, alas, is but a parting Ray,)
When next we court your favour, kindly shine,   ⎫
And our best Services, we'll not repine,   ⎬
But offer 'em humbly up at beauty's Shrine.   ⎭

Wife: Well off indeed! – now Gentlemen for you,
To whom an equal Share of Thanks is due,
But don't expect it in his highflown Lays,
Pick'd out from Ends of Verse and Scraps of Plays.
A plain and humble Muse shall speak my Mind;
I'll call you Mortals, – but of gen'rous Kind;
Whose Goodness, to our Company express'd,
Shall dwell for ever in my Grateful Breast. –
But now to end this Struggle for the Bayes,
How shall I gain your Hands t'applaus my Lays?
My Spouse has plac'd your Ladies in the Sky,   ⎫
Pray where must I put you? above 'em – fy!   ⎬
Why then, e'en pluck 'em down again, you cry; ⎭
For, after so extravagant a Sketch,

They seem as gone as ever, – from your Reach.
Such strange Poetick Flights will never bear;
How bright soe'er he's made his Stars appear,
Believe me, they'd look dull enough – were you
                              not here. }

From this epilogue we learn that the season was run on a subscription system, possibly for the first time, and that it had proved a success, rescuing the company from the poverty to which empty benches had reduced them. The winter season was to continue to be a subscription one for many years to come.

Keregan further extended his winter season in September 1732 when he was granted 'liberty to act in the Hall from Martinmas next [November 11] to May day following after at the rate of ten shillings per Week exclusive of the terme limited for Lent Assizes in his Articles.' As the interval between his winter and summer seasons was then only from May to July, he left his stage standing whereupon an order went forth on June 20 1733: 'that from the 12th instant So long as the Stage Stands till Mr. Kerrigan's time of acting by vertue of his Lease that the sd Mr. Kerrigan shall pay Weekly five shillings for His Stage Standing & at every time he shall leave the Hall the Windows and Wainscot shall be in repair.'

Keregan's ten year lease of the Merchant Taylors' Hall was due to expire at the end of 1733, and in January 1733 he applied to the Mayor's Court for permission to build a playhouse. The Court's judgment, given in the House Books[15] dated January 29, 1733, was as follows:

> Mr Thomas Keregan haveing remonstrated to this House that for the Conveniency of the Gentry resorting to this City he purposes to build a playhouse and requesting that some order might be made in his favour. This House being of opinion That the having a commodious playhouse in this City may very much conduce to the Entertainment of the Nobility and Gentry resorting to this City and incourageing them to spend their Winter Seasons here and Mr Keregan having always behaved himself very well in this City. This House dothe approve of the said proposal and resolve to give Mr Keregan all proper Encouragement therein and do hereby recommend it to the present and future Magistracy of this City to prohibit all other Companys of Comedians from playing in this City.

Keregan was fortunate in finding so progressive and far-seeing a corporation.

The company spent the three months between the two York seasons at Scarborough and Newcastle. A visitor to their booth in the former resort pronounced that 'allowing for Scenes and Decorations here, they perform several Plays very well.'[16] This early link between the York and Scarborough theatres, though of short duration, since Scarborough was to pass into the orbit of another circuit, is of interest in view of their recent reunion.

Keregan's new theatre was not ready until October 1734. Like several others from Restoration times onwards it was a converted tennis court and it stood in the grounds of the ruined Archbishop's Palace in Lord Irwin's Yard, Minster Yard, where the Residentiary now stands.[17] At that time it belonged to the Ingram family and from them Keregan rented 'the house and some Ground about it Buck lived in, and Tennis Court' for £12 a year. But it was not without protest and misgivings from the Archbishop of York. On August 29 Thomas Hayter wrote on his behalf to Lord Irwin: 'the Dean tells his Grace that the Tennis Court belonging to his Old Palace in York is going to be turn'd into a Playhouse, That this will occasion many Disorders to be committed within the Jurisdiction of the Church and that therefore he desires his Grace's assistance and direction how to prevent it from going on. His Grace cannot but concur with the Dean in thinking that this Project if pursued will give much offence and upon that account he makes it his Request to your Lordship that you will be so good as consider of some means of putting a stop to it'. The letter is endorsed 'Send this back with a counterpart of Kerregan's lease'.[18] Rent was paid half yearly at Michaelmas and Lady Day. The entries in the rent books show arrears of the first payment due at Michaelmas 1734 which were, however, made up on Lady Day 1735. Keregan was thus established both with a Theatre and a nearby house so that henceforth York became his permanent headquarters and the chief town of the circuit.

In the *York Courant* of September 17, 1734 a reward of 5/- is offered to anyone 'who shall write the best Prologue or Epilogue, for the opening of Mr Keregan's New Theatre in this City.' As an encouragement it was stated that 'the ingenious Mr Maxwell, the celebrated Mr Lashley, and a Reverend Clergyman in the Country have already sent in their Performances' and that authors would be allowed to speak their verses on the stage should they wish to do so. On September 24 the newspaper announces: 'that on Tuesday next [October 1] will be open'd Mr Keregan's fine new Theatre, with a Prologue and Epilogue suitable to the Occasion. It is to be hoped that the Gentry and others of this City will consider the great Charge he has been at for their Diversion, and let him taste a little of their Bounty before the Subscription Plays begin.'

Wilkinson[19] reproduces the playbill for this occasion, at which *Henry IV* was given for Keregan's own benefit: 'it being the only night he desires' of the ladies and gentlemen 'before subscription time, notwithstanding his great Charge for their Reception.' Charges were: boxes and stage 3s., pit 2s., middle gallery 1s. The playbill continues:

> The Play will be all new dress'd with New Scenes, from London, suitable to his House; With a Prologue and

Epilogue. The Musick consists of Overtures, Concertos, Sonatos, and Solos. Three Pieces will be perform'd before the Play begins: The first at five o'Clock, the second at half an hour after five, and the third at six; at the end of which, the Curtain will be drawn up.

It adds that, on Thursday, October 3:

Will begin a Subscription for Twenty-six Plays at Two per week, Box and Stage Tickets a Guinea and a Half each; A Ticket for the Pit One Guinea. Tickets may be transferr'd. Those who don't subscribe, are liable to the above-mention'd Price. As there is no difference made of the Boxes, those who bespeak them first, sending their Names to the Box-Keepers, will have 'em kept for them. N.B. No Servants will be admitted to any part of the House with a Subscription Ticket.

The subscription for twenty-six plays allows for a thirteen weeks' season which in future years was to start at the beginning of January. Saturdays were usually devoted to benefits which were not, of course, included in the subscription series. The *York Courant* of October 8, speaking of the opening night, relates that 'a vast Concourse of Gentry, &c. appeared; and were exceedingly well pleased with the Elegance of the Scenes, and the Performance of the Actors.' The winning prologue, which was written by Maxwell and spoken by Keregan, is the customary well-worn defence of the stage by classic example:

When Athens flourish'd, and the Grecian State,
Submissive, on its great Decrees did wait,
Over their Manners then the Stage did rule,
Approv'd with Wit, condemn'd by Ridicule,
Each virtuous Mind, by just Example form'd;
And show'd how Vice and Folly shou'd be scorn'd.
In Public, Kings, disdain'd not then to shew
Favour to Poets, and to Actors too.
So much they esteem'd all those who did excel,
Either in Writing, or in Speaking well.
Augustus in the Zenith of his Fame,
When suppliant Kings in Adoration came,
Preferr'd a Poet's to a Monarch's Name.
In Public wou'd his Tragedies rehearse.
And dwell with Pleasure on the Charms of Verse.
This shew'd how much Antiquity approv'd

The Buskin'd Muse, how well the Comic lov'd.
While Sophocles, by Turns the Soul alarm'd,
Now chil'd with Terror, now with Pity warm'd,
And polish'd Terence every Audience charm'd
The British muse disdains to stoop her Wing,
No higher soars, but does as sweetly sing.
Whether in Love's delightful Scenes she strays,
Or to severer Virtue points the Ways;
Harmoniously, her numerous Beauties shine,
As if Apollo dictated each Line.
Studious to please, we'll rifle all her Store,
And to Delight unusual Paths explore;
But if the modish Taste so far prevail
That our Attempts to please in this shou'd fail,
Then we'll engage Attention by Surprize,
Make Witches, Ghosts, and frolick Devils rise,
And dance to the hoarse Music of the Skies,
All Ways we'll prove, your Favour to obtain;
Than your Applause, we wish no other Fame.
If You, ye Fair, approve of our Design,
And in this Galaxy vouchsafe to shine?
The Men, compell'd, your Motions will obey,
They must attend, where Beauty leads the Way.

The Epilogue, spoken by Mrs. Keregan, was in lighter vein:

I Think, I've somewhere read in antient Stories,
Of strange Philosophers call'd Pytha-gories.
I'm sure 'tis some such Latin Name they give 'em,
And I, who know no better, must believe 'em.
To these same Men, they say, such Souls were given,
That after Death ne'er went to Hell, nor Heaven,
But liv'd, I know not how, in Beasts, and then
When many Years were past, in Man again.
Methinks, we Play'rs resemble such a Soul,
That, does from Bodies, we from Houses strole,
That Aristotle's Soul, of old that was,
May now be damn'd to animate an Ass;
Or in this very House, for ought we know,
Is doing painful Penance in some Beau.
Our Fate, to whom we've often been a Sport,
At length has toss'd us to a Tennis Court.
These Walls have, some time since, been fill'd with Noise
Of roaring Gamesters, and your Damn-me-Boys.

Then bounding Balls and Rackets they encompass'd;
And now they're fill'd with Jests, and Flights, and Bombast;
But I vow I don't much like this Transmigration,   ⎫
Grant Heaven we don't return to our first Station,   ⎬
Strolling, from Place to Place, about the Nation.   ⎭
I know not what he thinks, but for my Part,
I can't reflect, without an aking heart,
How we shou'd end in our Original – a Cart.
But Providence, we hope, design'd this Place
To be the Players Refuge in Distress;
That, when the Winter comes, we may all flock hither,
As to a Shed, to shield us from the Weather.
For, like Noah's Dove, the Water's yet afloat,
We must return from whence we first set out.
And now we're thus set up, pray don't leave us;
We cannot fear, when you're so good to save us.
For from the past, we hope for future Grace,
I beg it –
And some here know I have a begging Face.
Then pray continue this your kind Behaviour,
For a clear Stage won't do – without your Favour.

Our main souce of information about the years from 1733 onwards is the *York Courant*[20], but unfortunately there is a gap in the files from 1735 to 1738 so that our knowledge of this period is scanty. The Minster Library, however, possess the first known extant York playbill for January 27, 1736.[21]

The Keregans played the leading parts in Shadwell's adaptation of *Timon of Athens*. Mrs. Furnival also played capital parts but in 1737 she was sent for by the Manager of Drury Lane on the recommendation of a person of high birth, and made what was probably her first appearance in London on March 17, 1737.[22] Samuel Crisp, who had only a minor part in *Timon*, was later to become the leading actor in the company until he was ousted from this position by Frodsham. He was a relation of Keregan's and had previously played at Goodman's Fields. He is said to have been well made but awkward. His acting was of the ranting variety and his fellow player Robertson satirically writes of him:

Lo! Nature's direst foe, King Crisp appears,
And with discordance vile torments our ears;
The signal cue when giv'n, the machine moves,
It strikes the same whether it chides or loves;
An octave higher always than the rest;
Sweet harmony ne'er touch'd that callous breast,
A wooden poor Automaton at best;

With toes turn'd in, thumbs cock'd, and bellman's cant,
It scolds, nay whispers always in a rant;
Ended the speech, fix'd to the spot it stands,
Till cue-struck, once again it lifts its hands.

The fault of acting only when you were speaking was a common one in the 18th century and is frequently commented upon by critics.

Mrs. Crisp had been, as Miss Tollett, an actress at Drury Lane where she unfortunately learnt to quaver in imitation of the tragedy queen Mrs. Porter. Wilkinson[23] says 'she was so habituated to sing her speaking with such a monotony, that she could not, if accident intervened, extricate herself with any advantage,' He adds two anecdotes in illustration. Once as Queen Elinor in *King John* she dried up but pronounced 'in the same swelling tone, in high blank verse – "Mr. Wilkinson, go on, go on, go on! I cannot speak a word more." ' On another occasion as the Queen in *Hamlet* 'her enormous hoop and long velvet train caught in the wing; half on, half off the stage, she thundered out with all the grief of Denmark's Queen, – "Stage-keeper, my hoop is fast! I am dis-tress-ed." ' This is incidentally a reminder of the awkwardness of managing contemporary costume, then still used in Shakespearian rôles, on a confined stage. Her assets were her gentility and neatness in dress, indeed Wilkinson considered that she dressed the Nurse in *Romeo and Juliet* better than any other actress he could recollect. Like many before and since she played the young girls too long so bringing on her head the scorn of Robertson who writes of her:

that wither'd antique dame
Murders the youthful parts; oh shame! shame! shame!
Patches and paint in vain their aid supply.
The old crack'd wall tho' varnished o'er we spy.

This was written many years later; in their prime the Crisps were held in high esteem in York.

John Arthur had recently joined the company but was to remain in it only a short while, as he was engaged at Covent Garden for the 1737-8 season. He later became manager of the Bath Theatre until his death in 1772. He was a man of understanding and good observation, a diverting clown and famous in old men's parts.[24] His opera *The Lucky Discovery: or, The Tanner of York* was performed in York[25] and printed by Thomas Gent in 1737. It was cast as follows: Modish = Ware, Bark the Tanner = Marten, Simon = Arthur, Mrs. Modish = Mrs. Keregan, Mrs. Bark = Mrs. Emmett. The piece has a certain liveliness, especially in the cut and thrust dialogue of its opening scene, but Arthur was accused of ridiculing local people and families and suffered some disadvantage as a result. He strenuously denies the allegations in his preface, thanks the town for their kind reception of the opera, and for the good result of his benefit.

Another actor in the company, Joseph Yarrow, published *A Choice Collection of Poetry* in 1738 which included four epilogues spoken to plays given by the York company. Three of these were delivered by Mrs. Furnival: one to Cibber's *The Careless Husband*, the opening line of which is 'York, fam'd for virtuous Wives, and modest Maids'; a second to *Julius Caesar* when her husband played Mark Anthony for his benefit, and a third in the character of Mrs. Clerimont in Steele's *The Tender Husband*. The fourth was spoken by the child Miss Copen in the character of the servant Dicky in *The Constant Couple*. Thus we learn the names of a few of the plays performed by the Company.

Keregan was soon compelled to reduce his pit subscription. Drake[26], who boasts that the comedians were 'allowed to be the best strollers in the kingdom,' puts the subscription at 15s. instead of the original guinea. This was in 1736 from about which time must be dated Keregan's complaint[27] which in telling its own sad story sheds light on the organisation and financial workings of the company:

> The case of Thomas Keregan Proprietor of the Theatre, Humbly address to the Quality, Gentry and Citizens of York.
>
> Having suffered very much of late in my business, and, as I apprehend, by an ill opinion conceived of me for keeping up my subscription tickets at the price they were first given out after the erecting of my new theatre, it having been suggested that they might be afforded at a lower price, but an unreasonable desire of gain to myself had made me reject the advice of my friends in that respect; I thought it my duty, as well as interest, to give the inhabitants of this ancient city the best satisfaction I was able in this affair, by voluntarily laying before them the state of my last quarter's accounts; whereby it will appear, that I was near one hundred pounds a looser by the last quarter's subscription only: And as I never did desire any thing more than a reasonable maintenance for myself and family, I humbly hope, after the great expence I have been at, that I shall not be compelled to remove my Company to some other place for want of encouragement here: I beg leave further to inform the public that notwithstanding I have lowered the pit tickets to sixteen shillings, the advantage I have received by it hath been very small, viz. only the addition of fourteen subscribers, notwithstanding it reduces the pit to *sevenpence halfpenny a night*, which is less than half the price paid to the meanest company of Players in the kingdom. Before I conclude this short representation of my case, I cannot but

take notice, that it hath been insinuated very much to my prejudice, *That neither myself, nor my wife, have been sufficiently thankful for the favours which have been done us in coming to our benefits*: Whereas I can say, with great truth, that no one was ever more sensible of (and thankful for) such favours than we both have always been; however we may have failed in any acknowledgements from the stage; a thing never practised in any theatre but this, it being contrary to the rules of the stage; But as we are now sensible it is expected from us, we shall take care for the future, to the best of our knowledge, to do nothing which may give offence to any of our friends and benefactors.

Money received last Quarter	£.	s.	d.
47 Box tickets, at one guinea and a half each.	74	0	6
34 Pit, at one guinea each	35	14	0
The half of five benefit plays	53	9	9
Chance money taken in time of the subscription	125	9	0

Money paid last Quarter	£.	s.	d.
To sixteen actors and actresses at 12s. and a pit ticket per week.	145	12	0
To Mrs. Evans, and Mrs. Copen's children	1	10	0
For the use of clothes, scenes, properties, &c. four shares or salaries, allowed by the meanest companies abroad.	72	16	0
Getting up two entertainments, with new scenes and clothes &c.	30	0	0
To charges of new people coming from London	10	10	0
31 nights charge, at £4 per night, viz: 5 benefits, and 26 subscription nights	124	0	0
Sum total of expences	384	8	0
Of receipts	288	13	3
Lost last quarter	95	14	0

The persons who take my money, and deliver out all the subscription-tickets, have set their hands to this account; and, if occasion be, are ready to make oath of the same.

William Green

John Emmett.

For a more particular satisfaction, the following account *of the* nightly charges *of* acting, *exclusive of* salaries, &c.

	£.	s.	d.
Music	0	10	6
Office keeper	0	2	6
Wardrobe keeper	0	2	6
Clerk and numberer	0	3	0
Door keepers	0	6	6
Stage keeper	0	3	6
Coals	0	2	0
Tallow, oil, cotton, and candles	0	12	6
Bills one day with another	0	6	0
Incidents one night with another	0	1	0
Rent of the house as now built up	0	1	0
Mr. Chock	0	2	6
Drink to the Doorkeepers	0	0	6
	2	14	0

Besides play books, writing of plays out, and odd parts; for writing out music for entertainments; drink for the music at practice; letters from several players; carpenters and smiths; jobs, often for particular plays; glasses, frequently broke; washing the stock linen; cards, wax, and the printing subscription tickets; and many other little articles that are impossible to remember, which exceed four pounds *per* night.

Tickets delivered for the present quarter are, 32 box tickets at £1.11s.6d. each, is fifteen pence a night. 31 pit tickets, at 16s. each, is sevenpence halfpenny a night; both which in the whole, pay me no more than two pounds sixteen shillings and fivepence a night, for acting, or five pounds twelve shillings and tenpence *per* week; So that I am obliged to stand the favour of the town for £16.7s. per week.

N.B. All those, who are willing to encourage the present box subscription, shall be allowed in proportion for the PLAYS that are past.

The following points may be noted. The company was not run on the sharing system, which prevailed in many country companies at this time, but the actors were paid salaries. The fact that these were the same for all members of the company preserved the equality of the sharing system whilst doing away with its uncertainty. The custom that prevailed in sharing companies by which the manager received four shares for his expenses in connection with scenery, properties and wardrobe was retained by Keregan. He also took half receipts at the benefits. On the other hand he defrayed the expenses of actors journeying from London to join the company, and the cost of getting up new entertainments – £30 for two – which was relatively high. The York audience is seen to be as exigent in these early days as it was in Tate Wilkinson's time, demanding servile gratitude from its servants. A further blow fell on this, as on all provincial companies, by the passing of the Licensing Act in 1737. This outlawed all acting for hire, gain or reward outside London or the place of the King's residence, and reduced itinerant players to the status of rogues and vagabonds, liable to the penalties of the law on information being lodged against them. The law was evaded everywhere and seems to have made but little practical difference, though fear of arrest was now an additional hazard in the players' lives. The usual method of evasion, to advertise a concert between the parts of which the play and afterpiece were given gratis, was adopted by the York company. Whether because of financial difficulties or because of the Licensing Act or from other causes the Theatre in the Minster Yard does not appear to have been used after 1737 though Keregan, and afterwards Mrs. Keregan paid rent up to Ladyday 1744.[28] In 1738 we find a company from Wakefield acting every night during Race Week in August at the Merchant Taylors' Hall.[29] The following spring the regular company also played there. A playbill in the Minster Library for Saturday, April 7, 1739 is for a performance of *The Twin Rivals* for the benefit of Craig. The cast was: Elder Wouldbe = Baker, Young Wouldbe = Peterson, Richmore = Yarrow, Trueman = Crisp, Subtleman = Norris, Balderdan = Pearson, Clearaccount = Burt, Teague = Smith, Constance = Mrs. Pearson, Amelia = Mrs. Crisp, Midnight = Mrs. Yarrow, Steward's Wife = Mrs. Peterson. Entertainments of singing and dancing between the acts were given by Craig, Baker and Smith. The afterpiece was *Flora*: Sir Thos. Testy = Norris, Friendly = Craig, Hob = Baker. Of the several new names the most important is that of Joseph Baker who was to succeed to the management of the company six years later and was to run it for twenty-two years.

Joseph Peterson was the author of an opera entitled *The Raree Show, or The Fox Trapt* which was printed by Gent in 1739. Whether it was acted in York is doubtful as only a designed cast is given which is omitted in the second edition of 1740. On the other hand in addition to the prologue and epilogue there is an epilogue spoken by Peterson at his benefit which would normally have been delivered on the 3rd or author's night, but might also be for Peterson's ordinary benefit night as an actor. *The Raree Show* is an unoriginal piece with the usual comedy stock characters; the contrivance of shutting an obstructive guardian in a raree show box and one passable song are about all the opera has to offer. Peterson left to join the Norwich company in 1746. Henry Norris was also an author who had adapted *The Royal Merchant* in 1706 and published *Poems upon Several Occasions* at Hull in 1740. He was the son of the celebrated comedian known as Jubilee Dicky, whom, however, he resembled only in stature[30] and he came to York late in life after a career on the London and Dublin boards. A more famous comedian was in the company by 1739 for in the baptismal register of Holy Trinity, Goodramgate,[31] we find an entry under February 7, 1739: 'Ann, Daughter of Mr. James Robertson, player, by his wife Frances.' James Robertson was born in Ireland in 1714, and performed for a while at the Smock Alley Theatre, Dublin. He was with the York company for forty years for a large part of which he was its first low comedian. He has given us a picture of himself in a satire he wrote in 1764 on its members.[32]

> See Robertson's poor Merry-Andrew mien,
> The footman's Zany – mar the comic scene;
> He squints, distorts, and aims the scurvy jest;
> An actor he! A mere buffoon at best.

Hitchcock[33] considered that few excelled him in the comic line and Wilkinson[34] pronounced him a comedian of true merit and a great favourite. His talent as well as his popularity are commented upon by Tom Davies[35]: 'To rank a country actor with these gentlemen of the established London theatres may seem bold and unprecedented; but I am not afraid to name, among men of comic genius, Mr. James Robertson of York; a man, like Yorick, *of infinite wit and of most excellent fancy*. What gentleman of the county of York, does not know Jemmy Robertson? What critic so sour as not to be pleased with his sallies of humour – His being a very pleasing actor, and a lively companion, forms but a small part of his character. He is respected for merit of a more durable kind: for his honesty, worth and friendly disposition.' The fact that an etching was made of him in 1798, shortly before his retirement, is further testimony to the popularity he had attained in the circuit. He was another in the list of actor authors and his *Poems on Several Occasions* were published in 1773 and reprinted, with additions and alterations, in 1780 and 1787.

Thomas Keregan of whom we know nothing after 1736, died at the end of December 1740 and was buried in St. Michael-le-Belfry on December 31.[36] By his will[37], dated December 17, 1740 he appointed trustees to dispose of his malt and brewing utensils as he did not wish his widow to continue in the business. On January 13, 1741, the *York Courant* advertises the sale of the brewing vessels, coppers and malt belonging to the late Mr. Keregan about which inquiries were to be made 'of Mrs. Keregan on the Lord Irvine's Walk.' Keregan had owned the Billiard Table Inn in Stonegate at any rate since 1731[38] as well as running the company of comedians. The provisions of the will with regard to the playhouse were as follows: 'my Will is that my said Wife so long as she shall continue my Widow shall be permitted by my said Trustees and Executors to Enjoy to her own Use my Playhouse with the Clothes and Scenes and all other things thereto belonging or usually Used therewith or in the Acting and all the Profits arising therefrom. Upon Condition that she shall out of the Profits arising therefrom allow my Son Patrick for his Acting and Assisting in carrying on and managing the Affairs of the said Playhouse One pound seven shillings a Week being double to his present Allowance and what I so direct him to have to continue so long as he remains a Quiet, and sober good manager for my said Wife and no longer.' His sister Catherine Williams, as long as she was capable 'of attending and managing as usual in and about the Management of the Playhouse' was to have 6/- a week and board and lodging with Mrs. Keregan; if unable to continue she was not to be discharged but her allowance reduced to 4/-; even if totally useless she was to be paid 4/-, or 6/- if she ceased to live with his widow and son. In the event of his widow remarrying, the playhouse was to pass to his son Patrick who, in return, was to pay to his mother and sisters £50 more than before. But Patrick soon followed his father to the grave and was buried in St. Michael-le-Belfry on March 4, 1741.[39] Mrs. Keregan was left alone to carry on the company.[40] John Arthur wished to undertake the management but his offer was rejected. Piqued, he issued from London proposals for a new theatre which are preserved in Wilkinson's *Wandering Patentee* and were as follows:

To the Gentlemen and Ladies of the City of York.

Gentlemen and Ladies,
The present indifferent situation of the PLAY-HOUSE at YORK and your great disposition to promote Theatrical Diversions, encourag'd me, since the death of Mr. *Keregan* and his son to undertake the regulation and improvement of that STAGE: Upon which I apply'd in person to Mrs. *Keregan*, thinking I might, upon reasonable terms, enter upon the management, both with your and her approbation, but to my surprise, instead of meeting with the civility I imagin'd my proposals deserv'd, she treated me in a manner I as little merited as expected. However, finding this usage from Mrs. *Keregan*, I made my design known to some gentlemen of the city, who were pleased to promise me all the encouragement they seemed to think such an

undertaking deserved, and persuaded me to publish my PROPOSALS for a SUBSCRIPTION, not doubting, as I had the good fortune formerly to meet with tolerable success in my theatrical capacity, I should not now fail of it in my present undertaking.

PROPOSALS

I purpose to have a new and commodious Theatre (to be situated in some convenient part of the city) the model of those in *London*. There shall be several complete sets of new Scenes, painted by the best masters in London, with all such properties and machines as are required as well for ornament as use.

The *Orchestra* shall consist of a proper number of hands, to make a complete Band of Music, that may correspond with the rest.

A Wardrobe of such clothes as shall no ways be inferior in shape or trim to those on any stage, the quantity excepted.

The Company shall be made up of several persons from London, the rest to be collected from travelling companies; in which particular care shall be had to their private life, that they may be as social off the stage as entertaining on it. And that I may be enabled to procure such people, I will make an addition to the salary before given, and by that means make up a better company than has been in any city but London.

Every season there shall be got up such Plays, Operas, Farces and Pantomimical Entertainments as are done with any reputation in London, and with the utmost expedition.

There shall be a Quarterly Subscription for the Boxes and Pit, as before has been practised, and at the usual rates, that is to say, One Guinea and an Half the Boxes, and the Pit One Guinea.

Mr. *Keregan*, for several quarters last past, made an abatement in the Subscription, which I believe was occasioned through the barrenness of his diversions, rather than a desire in the Subscribers to reduce the price, I therefore hope it will not be considered as an imposition if I restore the Subscription to what it was, since my expence both as to house and performers will be more considerable, and consequently more agreeable.

The Gentlemen and Ladies who are willing to encourage this undertaking, I hope will excuse my personal application, my business obliging me to attend the theatre in London till the latter end of May; and am

Their most obedient humble servant
JOHN ARTHUR

LONDON, *April* 5
1741.

This ambitious scheme never came to anything, and Mrs. Keregan continued to conduct the company without rivalry.

Joseph Yarrow published three plays in 1742. One of these *Trick upon Trick; or ... Vintner in the Suds* was performed by the York company. It is little more than a droll derived from Betterton's *Vintner Outwitt'd* in its turn taken from Marston's *The Dutch Courtezan*. A second piece *Love at First Sight; or The Wit of a Woman* was dedicated to the gentlemen of Hull and Newcastle but, though a designed cast is written in Ms. in the British Museum copy, there is no actual evidence that it was performed. The musical interlude *Nancy* does not appear to be extant.

Hull was in the circuit by 1743 when the company acted at the New Theatre in Lowgate in September. They had already visited Leeds in May and Beverley in August. By the end of December they were back in York and opened on December 27, as henceforth was customary, with a benefit for the County Hospital at the Merchant Taylors' Hall. The play was Ambrose Philips's tragedy *The Distress'd Mother* with a new prologue and epilogue suitable to the occasion. Box and pit tickets were 2s.6d., gallery 1s., and no-one was admitted without a ticket. The advertisement adds that 'To-morrow will be deliver'd out Tickets for Mrs. Keregan's Subscription; which will be Open'd on Thursday Evening with a Concert of Musick; Between the Two Parts of the Concert will be perform'd (Gratis) a Comedy call'd *Love Makes a Man* – with an Entertainment, as will be express'd in the Bills of the Day.'

Either during this winter season of 1744 or at the beginning of the Race Week season Mrs. Keregan opened her new Theatre in the Mint Yard. Unfortunately most of the newspapers for this year are missing so that we have no record of the Theatre's inaugural night. We first hear of it in use in a playbill of Thursday, August 2.[41] It was built over the cloisters of the united Hospitals of St. Leonard and St. Peter, on ground which belonged to the Corporation. It is shown marked as 'New Theatre' and standing among trees on a contemporary map[42] and was practically on the same site as the present Theatre Royal in which one may still see the vaulted remains of the cloisters.

To return to the playbill – it announces the usual concert of vocal and instrumental music with, gratis, Hill's adaptation of *Henry V*, in which a romantic sub-plot replaced the comic element, never before performed in

20

York, 'With proper Decorations and an Entire New Set of Scenes not inferior to any in England.' The prologue was spoken by Mrs. Keregan, the epilogue by Crisp, and the cast was as follows: K. Henry = Crisp, Dauphin = Stone, King of France = Yarrow, Exeter = Achurch, Bourbon = Ward, Orleans = Oram, Scroope = Crofts, York = Norris, Gray = Robertson, Harriet = Mrs. Robertson, Charlot = Mrs. Crofts, Princess Catherine = Mrs. Crisp. The popular ballad opera *The Devil to Pay* was the afterpiece. Charges, which were to remain constant for several years, were boxes 2s.6d., pit 2s., gallery 1s.; seats on the stage, always a nuisance to the actors and impediments to the performance, were abolished 'As the House is made so Complete and Large'. This last provision could not be enforced and gallants cumbered the stage for many years to come.

Of the cast Henry Ward left the company soon after this to join the Edinburgh one. Advertising the forthcoming publication of his comedies by subscription[43], he says: 'As I have left Mrs. Keregan I shall very soon make my personal Application. The Gentlemen and Ladies &c. of York, Doncaster, Leeds and Wakefield, have generously encouraged this Undertaking beyond Expectation.' This volume of Ward's *Works* contains a ballad farce *The Happy Lovers* and two farces, *The Petticoat Plotter* and *The Widow's Wish*, all of which were performed at York.

Two other actors in the cast of whom we first hear, were Achurch and Oram who both remained with the company for the rest of their careers. Oram, according to Wilkinson[44], was 'an unhappy-tempered man, either on or off the stage, a self-tormentor.' Robertson's description of him is as follows:

> Next marches Oram, with slow labour'd pace,
> Right reverend air, and consequential face;
> His ivory look, work, motion, all declare
> Those looks, words, motions, all pre-studied were.
> Like Sysiphus, he rolls the pond'rous stone,
> Like Sysiphus, he still may roll it on;
> He toils, he moils, he labours up the hill,
> Strive as you please, poor man! 'Tis labour, labour, still.

In 1782 Oram was obliged to quit the stage owing to ill-health and was one of those actors to whom Wilkinson gave an annual benefit until his death in 1791.

The company spent the months from September until the end of December in Hull, which became the second most important town in the circuit. Sometime about then Mrs. Keregan must have retired or died since Joseph Baker had taken over the management when the company re-opened in York for their winter season on December 26, 1744. *Macbeth* was played 'With new Cloaths, Scenes, Machines and other Decorations proper for this Play and never used before,' for the benefit and towards the furnishing of the New County Hospital. The city waits and others gave their services and the Bakers handed 'upwards of £55' to the good cause. The subscription was for twenty-six plays for which box tickets cost £1.5s., pit tickets 18s. Benefits were given on Saturday nights, and were usually advertised in the *York Courant*. Subscription nights were rarely advertised, neither were performances during the summer season when benefits were not given. Command or bespeak performances were few. Several pieces new to York were put on in 1745. Thomson's *Tancred and Sigismunda* came out at the Giffards' benefit with Mr. and Mrs. Giffard[45] in the title rôles, Tancred being 'new dressed'. The tragedy was followed by a new pantomime entitled *Harlequin Restor'd*, 'Containing the Imprisonment, Release, Adventures and Death of Harlequin. The whole concluding with the Grand Scene of his Monument and Restoration to Life by the Power of Magick.' A notice was appended: 'As there are a number of new Deceptions in the Entertainment, and their Performance so greatly depends on the Stage being kept entirely clear, 'tis hoped no Gentlemen will insist on coming "behind the Scenes".' Crofts was Harlequin, Robertson Pantaloon, Cartwright Pierrot and Mrs. Crofts Columbine. The chief ingredients of these early pantomimes were mime, dancing, acrobatics and tricks, though some of them also contained dialogue and singing. Harlequin and Columbine were always dancers and Harlequin had to be something of an acrobat as well. Other new plays were Hughes's popular tragedy *The Siege of Damascus*, Otway's *Cheats of Scapin*, Edward Phillips's ballad opera, *Britons Strike Home* and Ambrose Philips's tragedy *The Briton* which had a local flavour as depicting 'the Overthrow of the Romans in three successive Battles near the River Ouze.'

The *Beggar's Opera* was revived with Cartwright as Macheath, Achurch as Peachum, Robertson as Mrs. Slamakin and Mrs. Robertson as Polly. After the opera Cartwright danced Harlequin and Mrs. Giffard Columbine in another new pantomime *Pygmalion, or Harlequin Triumphant*.[46] Congreve's *Mourning Bride* was also revived 'With a new magnificent Scene of the Tomb of Anselmo.' This tomb scenery, like altar and banquet scenes, was to do duty in many plays. The company advertised, as we have seen in the case of Tancred, when a character was newly dressed, other members of the cast having to make shift with stock costumes.

Lord Kingsland had a command performance on May 4 for the benefit of Miss Yarrow for which *The Distress'd Mother* was chosen. Soon after this the company went to Leeds where they advertised that most of their scenes and clothes were new.[47]

We know little of the season of 1746 since only two advertisements are available. Two pieces new to York, Dryden's *Don Sebastian* and Dodsley's *Blind Beggar of Bethnal Green*, were given at the Crisps' benefit. Another Restoration tragedy, Lee's *Lucius Junius Brutus*, was performed at the Yarrows' benefit. Baker protected himself against the penalties of the Licensing Act, not only by sandwiching the play as a free entertainment between two parts of a concert, but by frequently advertising it as acted by people for their own diversion. He was careful to announce that 'the first

Part of the Concert will be over exactly at Half an Hour after Six' thus giving his patrons the cue as to when the play would start.

In the winter of 1746-7 the Theatre re-opened with the customary hospital benefit, the play chosen being Tate's happy ending version of *King Lear*, 'With Scenes, Machines and other Decorations proper for the Occasion.' For the Crisps' benefit Rowe's *The Ambitious Stepmother* and William Giffard's *Merlin; or The British Enchanter* were first presented at York. This latter was an ambitious effort 'With great variety of Scenes, Machines, Musick, Dances and other Decorations, all entirely new, and proper to the Entertainment. With the Statues of Queen Elizabeth, Minerva, British Druid, and Nurse, being the exact Representations of these admir'd Statues in Merlin's Cave, in Richmond Gardens.' 'No Expence,' it was announced 'has been wanting to make this the most grand and perfect Entertainment of the kind ever yet seen in the Country.' *Merlin* was given a second performance this season and was afterwards frequently revived. Among other new pieces were Sewell's tragedy *Sir Walter Raleigh* and Garrick's farce *Miss in her Teens* which had just been produced at Covent Garden and was to hold the stage for many years. *The Tricks of Harlequin; or The Dutchman Outwitted*[48] was a new pantomime. *Hamlet* was performed by a gentleman who had never before appeared for the benefit of a new actor, Jones. In 1747 and succeeding years the York Company held a regular summer season in Newcastle instead of Leeds, where they were replaced by Whiteley's company. When the company returned to York in 1748 the newcomers were Waker, who contributed to the singing and dancing between the acts, and the Wignells. We now first hear of a second charity benefit, which for many years followed that given for the hospital, and was for the two charity schools the blue-coat boys and the grey-coat girls. Mallet's *Mustapha* and Moore's *The Foundling* were new this year. The manager was careful to make the best of both worlds by assuring 'the Public that *The Foundling* is a Comedy where the Rules of Virtue and Decency are so strictly observed that the most scrupulous must approve it; and yet so diverting, and abounding in such a Variety of new Characters and pleasing Incidents that it must be equally agreeable; as well as instructive, to the gay Part of the World.' In this sentimental piece Mrs. Robertson acted the heroine Fidelia and Crofts the reforming villain Belmont. Revivals included Bullock's *Woman is a Riddle* after eight years, with 'a new beautiful fram'd Scene made on purpose for this Play', and Hill's *Alzira* after three years with the heroine newly dressed. Shakespeare was represented by *Macbeth* and *Hamlet*, with Wignell as the Prince of Denmark. The season closed on April 23 with a benefit for Norris, who excused himself from personal attendance as he was suffering from the gout. The Merchant Taylors' Hall was rented to rope dancers and tumblers who ended their performance with a pantomime *The Force of Magick; or The Birth of Harlequin*.

Baker announced that he had engaged some new actors from London for the 1748-9 season though, in fact, the only new name seems to be that of Conyers, who danced Harlequin in *Merlin* and played Loverule in *The*

Devil to Pay. At his benefit and that of his wife *The Pleasures of the Town; or Punch's Operatical Puppet Show* was revived with Wignell as the puppet master and Conyers himself as Signor Opera. It is advertised as 'the most extraordinary Piece that has for several Centuries been Perform'd by a Company of living Puppets – from the low Grimace of Punch to the elevating Sensation of the lulling Italian.' Originally given in a fair booth, it was evidently a skit on opera and puppet shows.

The pit subscription this season had been raised from 18s. to a guinea, the tickets being transferable. The proceeds of the hospital benefit were only £25, a considerable drop from the £55 of four years previously. Baker was now living in the house in Blake Street adjacent to the theatre which was to be for many years the manager's residence. The only new pieces of which we hear this season were John Cunningham's *Love in a Mist* which had been done in Dublin the previous winter and Garrick's farce *Lethe* which was to have a long theatrical history. Revivals included Otway's *Caius Marius* after ten years, Howard's *The Committee* after five and *The Tempest*, with entirely new scenery and machinery and the *Masque of Neptune and Amphitrite*. Baker besides being manager was also the scene painter though we do not know whether he was responsible for all the new scenery.

Otway's *Orphan* was the hospital benefit play for the 1749-50 season. Wignell, the company's leading tragedian, was Castalio, Mrs. Robertson Monimia, Miss Yarrow Serina and Davies, from Covent Garden, was Chamont. This last was Tom Davies, later the celebrated bookseller and author of the *Life of Garrick* and *Dramatic Miscellanies*, who was unsuccessful as an actor. He married Miss Yarrow in December 1749 or January 1750, and, after performing in Edinburgh in 1753, was engaged with his wife for a while at Drury Lane. Nichols[49] says that her 'beauty was not more remarkable than her private character was ever unsullied and ir-reproachable.'

The subscription this season was extended from twenty-five to thirty-three plays for which boxes were £1.13s. and pit £1.6s. The tomb scenes came in handy for Hill's version of Voltaire's *Merope*, brought out nine months previously at Drury Lane and graced in York with new dresses and decorations. Another new production was that of *Henry VIII* with the coronation of Anne Boleyn and the christening of Elizabeth. Lee's *Theodosius* had 'a new grand Altar Scene, representing the Cross that appear'd to Constantine the Great' and a new costume for Davies as Varanes. Davies also played Hamlet to the Ophelia of Mrs. Robertson, and the interpolated rôle of King Henry in *Richard III*, in which Adams played Richard and Mrs. Crisp Queen Elizabeth. *Tamerlane the Great* was revived with Davies as Bajazet, Wignell as Monoses and Mrs. Crisp as Arpasia. Robertson delivered Jo. Haines's celebrated epilogue riding on an ass and thereafter became popular as a speaker of prologues and epilogues.

Considerable additions to the troupe marked the 1750-1 season.[50] Sherriffe and Morgan made their débuts as Dorilas and Ismène in *Merope* for the benefit of the hospital on December 27, and the same evening Mrs.

Wheeler, a singing actress, made hers as Nell in *The Devil to Pay*. Maclellan, Pearce and Miss Pearce appeared as Mirabel, Sir Wilfred and Betty in *The Way of the World*. Mrs. Wheeler played Polly in *The Beggar's Opera* to the Macheath of Haughton. In *Macbeth* the principal rôles were thus cast: Macbeth = Crisp, Macduff = Sherriffe, Banquo = Achurch, Lady Macduff = Mrs. Crofts, Lady Macbeth = Mrs. Crisp. On March 2 for the benefit of Mrs. Crisp, *Romeo and Juliet* in Garrick's version was first performed in York following its successful revival at both the London theatres. The cast was: Romeo = Sherriffe, Capulet = Crisp, Montague = Yarrow, Mercutio = Achurch, Paris = Crofts, Tibalt = Morgan, Benvolio and Apothecary = Adams, Friar Lawrence = Oram, Nurse = Mrs. Crisp, Lady Capulet = Mrs. Achurch, Juliet = Mrs. Crofts. 'A new Tomb Scene and all other Decorations proper to the Play' were announced. The tragedy became henceforward a stock play. Another new tragedy was Whitehead's *Roman Father*; a new farce *The Cobler of Preston* made out of *The Taming of the Shrew*.

There were a number of alterations in the company in 1752. The Wignells had joined the Norwich company and Adams also had left, but newcomers were Mr. and Mrs. Dancer, Hopkins, Younger, Smith, Haddlesey, and last but certainly not least, Bridge Frodsham.

Frodsham was to become the idol of York and to be known as 'The York Garrick'. He was born in 1734 of an ancient Cheshire family which hailed from the town of Frodsham[51]. He was a scholar at Westminster School from which he twice ran away. The second time he attached himself to a troupe of players in Leicester and thus began his theatrical career[52]. He was only eighteen years of age when he joined the York Company, and he was to die in his thirty-fifth year at Hull on October 21, 1768[53]. Wilkinson tells us that he was by nature a great actor who possessed 'a quick genius, aided by a liberal education ... but his mind, his understanding, and superabundant good qualities were all warped and undermined by nocturnal habits' with the result that he became 'enfeebled, disordered, mad, dropsical.' The brandy bottle was 'his fatal and false friend'. As an actor he was awkward, merely from want of good training, and he never attained elegance, but he had strong feelings, a melodious voice and the capacity of tears at will. His Hamlet and Jaffeir, Wilkinson judges to have been surpassed only by those of Garrick and Barry. Unfortunately, 'The public were so infatuated (and indeed he was so superior) that he cast all others at a distance in his York situation; and the audience too blindly and too partially (for his good) approved all he did beyond comparison.' He had little opportunity for observation or improvement. Primarily a tragedian, Frodsham also acted the young sparks of comedy and made a 'decent Macheath', as he sang tolerably well. A deal of Frodsham's conceit and independent spirit is manifest in Wilkinson's anecdote[54] of how he visited Garrick during a fortnight's holiday in London. He left a card inscribed 'Mr. Frodsham of York' on the great man, who, struck by its simple title, decided to interview his caller. Garrick was surprised at the freedom with which Frodsham spoke, especially on the subject of Shakespeare. Frodsham did not hesitate to tell Garrick that he thought his Hamlet clever in parts but that he was unimpressed with his interpretation as a whole. Garrick, used to flattery, was amazed at his audacity, but gave him an order for the pit to see his Sir John Brute and an invitation to breakfast the following morning. After expressing delight at Garrick's rendering of Brute, Frodsham without fear or hesitation spoke, at Garrick's request, Hamlet's first soliloquy. Garrick offered him a London job and he was astonished to find that he had not come a-begging but merely because he adjudged his duty to wait on a brother genius. Robertson[55] in his satire on his fellow-actors has given us another picture of Frodsham's conceit and avidity for praise:

> Lo! Frodsham roars or whispers through the scene;
> He rants, he splits the tasteless groundling's ears,
> And Herod's self, out heroded appears,
>> Quaintly ridiculous his starts, his throes,
>> His attitude, his sing-song ahs! and ohs!
> Nor like a man pours he his plaintive strains,
> But blubbers, school-boy-like, his love-sick pains ...
> His robe with air affected he infolds,
> And like a bear his dulcinea holds ...
> Above mankind in his own mind he soars,
> Himself the idol he himself adores.
> Of coarse-spun flattery proud, we oft may view,
> Frodsham amid a low-liv'd servile crew;
> Creatures who, spaniel-like his footsteps tend,
> And to Sir Oracle with rev'rance bend;
> Among whom enthron'd he wields his critic rod,
> While gaping fools admire their wooden-god;
> Hence on the stage, spite of much grandeur's scene
> A taste indelicate, and manners mean;
> Those who with lepers herd, are seldom clean.

Frodsham gradually took over the leading parts from Crisp and attained a salary of a guinea a week. But Crisp was tenacious, and it was long before he would give up Hamlet to Frodsham and be relegated to the rôle of the Ghost. At first Crisp acted Richard III to Frodsham's Richmond and Sir John Brute to Frodsham's Col. Bully; later they took these parts alternately.

The first performance in which Frodsham can be traced is one of *King Lear* for the benefit of the Dancers on February 28 when he acted Edgar with Dancer as Lear, Achurch as Gloster, Oram as Kent, Younger as Edmund, Mrs. Achurch and Mrs. Morgan as Goneril and Regan, and Mrs. Dancer as Cordelia.

Mrs. Ann Dancer, afterwards Mrs. Spranger Barry and Mrs. Crawford, was to become one of the great actresses of her age. She was the daughter of a Bath apothecary named Street and was one of the belles of that gay city. After being jilted she met Dancer in the north, married him, and went on the stage. This scandalised her family and friends but, when her mother bequeathed her a small annuity on condition that she left the stage, she refused; she had the annuity in the end owing to the generosity of the man to whom it reverted on her refusal[56]. At the time she came to York Mrs. Dancer was only eighteen years old. According to Genest[57] 'she was graceful, genteel, spirited and feeling – she had a certain modest gaiety in her manner and address, – in her figure she was just above the middle size', of fair complexion with light auburn hair. She was well made and her features were regular. She is said to have played tragedy to please the town and comedy to please herself. She was the first of many great actresses to tread the York boards and in fullness of time she returned there as the great star Mrs. Crawford.

The Pleasures of the Town was revived with Robertson as Jack Pudding after which Master Morgan spoke an epilogue which was printed and delivered free of charge in the theatre at the end of the third act.

Owing to gaps in the newspaper files our information about 1753 is scanty. There was a new dancer in the person of Vandersluys who played Harlequin in a revised edition of *Merlin*. His wife was a singer and, together with Mrs. Wheeler, entertained with songs between the acts or between the play and the afterpiece.

By 1754 the Dancers had returned to Bath. Frodsham was now playing most of the leads. We find him as Jaffeir to the Pierre of his rival Crisp and the Belvidera of Mrs. Robertson; as Varanes in *Theodosius*, Osmyn which he chose for his benefit, in *The Mourning Bride*, Don Carlos in *Alzira*, Aribert in *The Royal Convert*, Tancred, Demetrius in *The Brothers*, Nerestan in *Zara*, and in the lighter rôles of Scapin and Macheath. In the new tragedies he played Southampton in Jones's *Earl of Essex*, which had first been seen at Covent Garden the previous year, and Dumnorix in Glover's *Boadicia* with Crisp as Ænobarbus, Mrs. Crisp as Boadicia and Mrs. Robertson as Venusia. He had married and his wife was an actress in the company. In the new pantomime *The Birth of Harlequin or the Burgomaster Trick'd*, Vandersluys danced Harlequin. Two other light pieces were Foote's *Englishman in Paris* and Mrs. Clive's *Rehearsal*. Baker himself, whose address this year is given as in Stonegate, sustained Perseus in Young's *Brothers* and Puff in Foote's *Taste* at his benefit. Master Morgan was used in entertainments between the acts and his younger brother James made a début in the favourite child's rôle of Tom Thumb.

Romeo and Juliet was chosen to open the season of 1754-5 with Frodsham as the new Romeo and Mrs. Robertson the new Juliet whilst Robertson now played the Apothecary, one of the several rôles in tragedies generally assigned to the low comedian. The funeral procession precluded admission behind the scenes which was still evidently allowed except on such special scenic occasions. *Romeo and Juliet* raised £26.17.5. for the hospital. The subscription was still for thirty-three plays. Mrs. Robertson and Mrs. Crisp had divided the women's tragedy leads for some time but now Mrs. Morgan and Mrs. Hopkins also took their share. Frodsham played in a variety of rôles in tragedy, comedy and musical entertainments. We thus find him not only as Dorilas in *Merope*, Ventidius in *All for Love* with Crisp as Anthony and Mrs. Morgan as Cleopatra, Orestes in *The Distress'd Mother*, Aboan in *Oroonoko* and Dumont in *Jane Shore*, but as Damon in *The Chaplet* for the first time, Campley in *The Funeral*, Moore in the burlesque opera *The Dragon of Wantley* and Courtwell in Bullock's comedy *Woman is a Riddle*. The Yarrows by now must have been growing old and their names seldom appear after 1751 though they were still accorded a benefit. Master Morgan continued to be a popular speaker of epilogues, one of which was written by a local man. He shared his benefit with Miss Achurch.

Several new pieces came out. Brown's *Barbarossa* was seen in York, six weeks after its production at Drury Lane, with Frodsham as Achmet, Mrs. Hopkins as Irene and Mrs. Crisp as Zaphira, all the chief characters being newly dressed. Mrs. Crisp played the title rôle in Whitehead's tragedy *Creusa* at her benefit with Frodsham as Ilyssus. In *Harlequin's Vagaries; or The Powers of Witchcraft* Frodsham appeared in the rôle of Harlequin and we remember that both Kemble and Kean also played the part in their early days. 'The Plan, Deceptions, Chorus's and other Decorations' were announced as 'entirely new' for this pantomime. Other pantomimes were *Harlequin Statue, or The Sheep-Shearers Joy* 'with Musick and Songs compos'd and set by the Society of the Temple of Apollo' with another new Harlequin in the person of Reed, *The Birth of Harlequin* with additional scenes and music from Woodward's *Queen Mab*; and Merlin's Cave with 'all the machinery etc. new painted'. New afterpieces were Foote's *The Knights*, called in York *The Cornish Knights*, Mrs. Centlivre's *Marplot in Lisbon*, and the *Press Gang*, a popular musical piece by Henry Carey the author of *Sally in our Alley*.

Barbarossa opened the 1755-6 season and obtained £20 for the hospital, *Henry V* given for the schools brought them £19.10.6. A number of Shakespeare plays and adaptations were put on this year. In *Hamlet* Frodsham succeeded to the title rôle to the Ophelia of Mrs. Robertson, the King of Achurch and Ghost of Crisp with Robertson and Morgan as the Gravediggers; Mrs. Hopkins and Mrs. Dancer both played Juliet. *The Merchant; or the Jew of Venice* was announced 'With a grand Buffet Scene, Caskets, Musick and all other Decorations proper to the Play'. Achurch was Shylock, Mrs. Morgan Portia, Frodsham Bassanio, Crisp Antonio, Robertson Gobbo, and Mrs. Dancer as Jessica had a new song in character.

The Dancers had returned after a two years' sojourn at Bath and Mrs. Dancer was seen in several tragic rôles, as Calista in *The Fair Penitent*, Elizabeth in *The Earl of Essex*, Cleopatra in *All for Love*, and Zara in *The Mourning Bride*. Frodsham repeated his performance of Harlequin in *Harlequin's Vagaries* with alterations and additions which had been received with applause at Hull.

Thomas Sheridan's *Brave Irishman* with Robertson as Capt. O'Blunder and Murphy's *Englishman Return'd from Paris* were new pieces. Dancer too presented 'the Ladies with A Dish of Mr. Foote's Tea', an entertainment which Foote had given at the Haymarket for forty-two successive mornings. Dancer repeated it two weeks later though Wilkinson in years to come was to have a failure with it.

Billy Leng, according to Wilkinson,[58] joined the company this year though I have not found his name in York before 1760. He was known as Beau Leng, and off the stage won all the hearts which the dirty and slovenly Frodsham only conquered on. Wilkinson writing of him in 1795, when he had become Good Old Leng, pictures him in his early days 'glaring in the noon-day sun, with a fierce gold laced hat, a flaming laced scarlet waistcoat – ever clean, regular and creditable to himself and his profession.' As an actor, though of no superior ability, he was conscientious and, when he had only to appear in the farce, he would be 'properly accoutred in character one hour at least before the first music is called.' He spent the rest of his career with the company and his name appears on cast lists as late as 1795.

The 1756-7 season opened with *King Lear*. A further gap in the newspapers up to 1760 leaves us without much information for succeeding years. Sometime during 1758, Baker paid a visit to London to find a successor to Mrs. Dancer, 'the York Heroine', who, with Dancer, had decamped to Barry's new Dublin Theatre[59]. He engaged 'the goblin Miss Roach, a horrid spectre.' According to Wilkinson she inveigled Baker into the belief that she was a great actress and a good woman, but York received her indifferently and she did not act three nights the whole season. However, she extorted a good benefit. 'She had much art, a cunning understanding, and a flow of spirits, yet affectation that would have been surfeiting in a beauty; but she flattered well.' Much more important than the engagement of Miss Roach was Baker's casual meeting with Wilkinson, which he was to remember and make use of five years later.

In December 1758 Foote's *Author* was stopped from performance in York as being libellous though it was given again in 1762. By 1760 there were many newcomers in the company including the Quins, the Grangers, Maguire and Bellamy. Mrs. Granger was both dancer and singer for she danced Columbine in the pantomimes and sang Polly in *The Beggar's Opera*. She played Shakespearian heroines such as Perdita and Rosalind, and remained in the company for three years.

Henry IV was revived for the benefit of the charity schools with Pearce as Falstaff, Frodsham as the Prince of Wales, Crisp as Hotspur and Achurch as the King. On the same occasion Frodsham undertook the additional scene of Lord Chalkstone in *Lethe*. The benefit only realised £13.3.9½d. Frodsham also sustained Richard III for the first time with Leng as Richmond, Mrs. Robertson as Lady Anne and Mrs. Frodsham as Prince Edward, a rôle often taken by an actress, though sometimes by a child. *Henry V* was still being played in Hill's version with Frodsham as the King,

Mrs. Granger as Hill's character of Harriet, and with a new patriotic prologue in honour of the British Militia spoken by Quin. *Cymbeline* was put on in Hawkins's adaptation which had been brought out the previous year at Covent Garden. Other old plays were Jonson's *Every Man in his Humour* and Lee's *Rival Queens*, revived with alterations and additions after fifteen years, with Frodsham as Alexander. His entry into Babylon was made the occasion for one of the processions which the age so revelled in, with a magnificent triumphal car drawn by four captive kings and a new choral ode composed for the occasion. A banquet scene adorned with several new dresses and a final scene representing the bower of Semiramis were additional attractions. A new satirical epilogue written by Frodsham was delivered by Robertson in the dress and character of the devil Ashmodeus.

New presentations were the Miller-Voltaire *Mahomet the Impostor*. 'With several new Dresses, new Scenes ... particularly a grand new Scene of a Pagan Altar, with Images and Idols', doubtless adapted from all the other altar scenes, and *The Rehearsal* with Frodsham as Bayes, and, 'In the 5th Act, a Dance of State and a Grand Battle: In which will be introduced an additional Reinforcement of Mr. Bayes' new-raised Regiment of Horse; as also a wonderful Eclipse of the Sun, Moon, and Earth.' New afterpieces were Townley's *High Life Below Stairs*; a pantomime called *The Novelty* with an additional scene, Harlequin – Venables, Columbine – Mrs. Granger; *Florizel and Perdita*, altered by Frodsham from *The Winter's Tale*,[60] with Frodsham and Mrs. Granger as hero and heroine; and *Harlequin Magician* in which Granger first appeared as Harlequin. Two entertainments were of special interest. The first was a 'Grand Masque – in Honour of the Brave General Wolfe. The Representation will be heightened by a beautiful new Scene painted purposely for this Use' in which Mrs. Robertson played Britannia, Mrs. Quin the Genius of Quebec and Frodsham the Genius of the Ocean. Wolfe had died before Quebec the previous September and this masque was the first of many attempts to bring contemporary events on the stage. Secondly on the same evening a mummer's play was presented by a company of sword dancers in which each performer on his appearance spoke verses expressing his character. A bespeak by several officers of the militia was given during the season.

At the opening of the 1761 season it was announced that care would be taken to have the house very well aired. In the empty months between the summer and winter seasons it probably got very damp and cold. *Cymbeline*, the opening play, obtained £25.9.4½ for the hospital. Fitzmaurice and his wife had joined the company. He had been at the Bath Theatre and had there married Miss Hippisley, daughter of John Hippisley, comedian and one time manager of the Bristol Theatre. Fitzmaurice's name disappears after 1769 but Mrs. Fitzmaurice remained with the York company until 1772 when she returned to Bath. He was the company's new Harlequin and his wife who had merit[61] undertook minor rôles such as Lady Capulet. Allan Ramsay's Scotch pastoral *The Gentle Shepherd* was first seen in York this year; so were two 17th century plays, Banks's *Albion Queens* and Shadwell's *Fair Quaker of Deal* in which Frodsham played respectively Norfolk and Beau Mizen. The new pantomimes were *Harlequin Salamander; or The Jealous Shepherd* and *Harlequin's Adventures; or, The Farmer's Sheep-Shearing* with new scenes, machines, music and dresses. The first of Colman the elder's pieces, the farce *Polly Honeycombe*, made its début this year in York with Miss Achurch in the title rôle. She also played Polly in *The Beggar's Opera*.

Home's *Douglas* was revived after three years with Frodsham as Douglas. In other revivals Frodsham acted Hengist in *The Royal Convert*, Witling in Cibber's *Refusal* and Artaxerxes in Rowe's *Ambitious Stepmother*. For their benefit the Frodshams chose *The Rival Queens*, Mrs. Frodsham playing Statira. For this Frodsham wrote the words and Camidge composed the music of a new choral ode for which a 'large Addition – both Vocal and Instrumental by some of the best Performers in the Town' was engaged; 'the Feast, Music and other Decorations' for the banquet scene were also new. Another grand chorus, that in Mendez's musical entertainment *The Chaplet*, was performed for the first time in York by the augmented band.

Shakespeare we find represented by *Othello* with Venables as the Moor; he wrote and spoke a new prologue and his wife delivered an epilogue. Garrick's *Catharine and Petruchio*, the only form in which *The Taming of the Shrew* was to be seen on the stage for many a long day, was given with Frodsham and Mrs. Maguire in the title rôles.

The old Theatre in the Thursday Market was once more in use on January 18 when a puppet show was given by Clark for the benefit of the bookseller Thomas Gent who had fallen on evil days. The poor old man spoke 'a long and pathetick Prologue' and 'a Benedictive Epilogue of Thanks To the Worthy and Charitable Beholders' who flocked to see this pitiful spectacle to such a degree that a second performance had to be given. Gent paid tribute to

> Theatric Glory, Master Keregan
> Dear Orator adorning each lov'd Place,
> With Cato's Virtues, and brave Caesar's Grace.

When Baker's company returned to York in 1762, there were three new-comers: Miss Oxnard, Owen and Buck. The last Wilkinson[62] characterises as 'a useful actor' and 'a worthy member of society'. He stayed with the troupe until 1779, when, owing to illness, he had to retire from the stage; he was accorded an annual benefit during the rest of his life by Wilkinson, who never forgot his old and tried actors. Robertson, Oram and Mrs. Crisp were able to enjoy independence in their old age as a result of their earnings; though their incomes were small they were steady, and careful saving enabled them to retire in security.

Whitehead's *School for Lovers*, with Frodsham as Dorilant, and Murphy's *The Old Maid* were new comedies. A new pantomime introduced scenes from the popular London ones; 'the Attitude Scene out of *Queen Mab*; the

Additional Scene of Action out of *Apollo and Daphne*, occasioned by Cock-lane Ghost – and the Taylor Scene out of *Queen Mab*.'

It was a good year for Shakespeare. *As You Like it* was revived after four years with Frodsham as Orlando, Achurch as Jaques, Robertson as Touchstone, Mrs. Granger as Rosalind and Mrs. Robertson as Celia. *Timon of Athens*, which had not been seen in York for twenty-six years, was given in Shadwell's version with Frodsham as Timon; in Hawkins's *Cymbeline* Frodsham sustained Palador with songs whilst his wife was Imogen. Miss Achurch was the new Juliet whilst Granger acted Mercutio; the tragedy was graced with a funeral procession, dirge and grand altar scene. Bryan the prompter chose *The Tempest* for his benefit in which Crisp played Prospero, Frodsham Ferdinand, Miss Achurch Ariel and Mrs. Frodsham the Dryden-Davenant character Hippolito.

At the benefit of a new actor, Swetnam, Mrs. Robertson essayed Roxana in *The Rival Queens* for the first time. On another night Frodsham and Miss Achurch acted Jack Stocks and Chloe in Fielding's *Lottery*, also for the first time. Leng seems to have succeeded Robertson as prologue speaker in chief and delivered a patriotic prologue suitable to the times before *Alzira*, and a prologue on that topical sensation the Cock-lane Ghost at a revival of *The Siege of Damascus*. A feature of the season was the introduction of comic interludes that had been performed at Drury Lane, such as *Hearts of Oak* and *The Farmer's Return from London*. These lengthened the programmes and later Wilkinson[63] was to root them out.

Frodsham was now at the height of his popularity and his salary was a guinea a week. His pre-eminence did him no good for he had no-one against whom to measure himself, and, since visiting actors were banned, no opportunity for observation. Nor were changes of character allowed since they were so often regarded by actors as infringements of their rights. Such rigid rules militated against a leading actor's improvement.

Frodsham was a keen Freemason and founded a lodge in February 1761, becoming principal of the Grand Royal Arch Chapter the following year.[64] In December 1762 he printed proposals for a course of lessons to be given by him in the art of reading and public speaking[65]. The scheme did not meet with success and Frodsham expressed his disappointment in an interesting letter to a fellow-actor.[66]

> Dear Aickin,[67]
> I am heartily sorry for your Loss – let that suffice – I have been rather tedious in remitting the Farce to you – but I reflected that if it came time enough for your Benefit the Purpose intended wou'd be answer'd.
> I have met with very ill Success here in regard to the Scheme I set about, owing chiefly to the damn'd Tribe of Levi – I gave a probationary Lecture to a numerous Audience – I read part of the Burial Service the 8th Cap.

of Matt. & the Ode upon St. Cecilia's Day by Dryden after which I desir'd any Gentlemen present to ask me any Questions concerning it – I was answer'd by a Clap of Applause – notwithstanding which their Pride is so very great that in short they will not submit to be taught by *Player* – tho' I have made a Shift to pocket fifty Pieces since I saw you by those Means – News, you know, is never stirring in this corner of the World – & for that very reason I cannot send you any – By the bye I have read the Discovery[68] – very elegant indeed – but as some of the Papers intimate it is rather upon the Richardsonian Stile – it is monstrously tedious, extremely affecting and I apprehend without good Acting in the *Country* will cut but an indifferent Figure.

For Heaven's Sake let me hear from you shortly if it is convenient to you – and believe me it is with Pleasure I subscribe myself

Yr sincere Friend

Bridge Frodsham

Here speaks the man who lectured Garrick about Shakespeare, and who was intensely interested in every branch of his profession. Though his lectures were a failure, he was so popular that on his benefit night, in 1763, when he appeared only in the afterpiece, he had to insert a notice in the newspaper, 'As Mr. Frodshams not appearing in the Tragedy may seem particular, he thinks it necessary to acquaint the Public, that it was absolutely impossible for him, in the Time, to make himself Master of both the Characters assigned to him in the Tragedy and Comedy; he therefore chose to give Preference to the latter', and he recited Dryden's *Ode on St. Cecilia's Day*, as a makeweight. The tragedy in which he did not appear but in which his two daughters took part was Mallet's new *Elvira*; the comedy was Murphy's *The Citizen*.

Many other new plays were presented in York this season. Among them were two Shakespeare adaptations, Garrick's version of *The Winter's Tale* cut down to three acts with Frodsham as Florizel, Crisp as Leontes, Achurch as Autolycus, Robertson as Clown, Miss Achurch as Perdita, Mrs. Fitzmaurice as Paulina and Mrs. Robertson as Hermione, and Victor's version of *Two Gentlemen of Verona*, so seldom revived, with Frodsham as Thurio, Leng as Valentine, Buck as Proteus, Robertson as Launce, Miss Achurch as Julia, and Miss Phillips as Silvia. Frances Sheridan's *The Discovery*, which Frodsham had criticised so adversely, was nevertheless brought out with him as Branville; and he also played Zamti in Murphy's *Orphan of China*. New afterpieces included the anonymous *Spirit of Contradiction*, Dell's *The Frenchified Lady Never in Paris* and Reed's *The Register Office*.

Frodsham in addition played Macbeth for the first time with Miss Phillips as Lady Macbeth, and Parolles in one of the rare revivals of *All's Well That Ends Well* with Miss Phillips as Helena and Mrs. Robertson as the Countess of Rousillon.

Miss Phillips was a newcomer who is said to have won great esteem from the genteel families of York.[69] She was an aunt of the famous Mrs. Jordan and was still alive when her niece entered the company in 1782. Besides the Shakespearian rôles already mentioned, she played Merope and Arpasia and spoke an epilogue on affectation. Another new actress was Miss Grainsby, an Irishwoman who gave little promise at first. But about 1765 she married Leng under whose training she became, according to Wilkinson, 'a very useful subject to my rural dominions' especially in old women's rôles.[70] She outlived both her husband and Wilkinson and was still making occasional appearances as late as 1805, after which her name disappears.

In addition to the Frodsham children, a Miss H. Achurch made her appearance as one of Alfred's children in Mallet's Masque *Alfred The Great* for which Arne wrote *Rule Britannia*.

The most important event of the year was the York début of Tate Wilkinson under whose management for thirty-six years the Theatre was to have its golden age. Wilkinson was at this time a young man of twenty-three. His father, the Rev. John Wilkinson, had been Chaplain to the Savoy until 1757 when he was transported to America for having solemnized marriages there against the law. Tate was educated at schools in Chelsea and Wandsworth and later at Harrow. With a passion for the stage he became a hanger-on at Covent Garden, and for a while he was a pupil of John Rich, who pronounced that he was incapable of becoming an actor. He proved, however, to be an excellent mimic, though this talent got him into trouble with Peg Woffington and he was banished from the green room. An intimacy with Ned Shuter led to his appearing at that comedian's benefit at Covent Garden in the unsuitable rôle of the Fine Gentleman in *Lethe* in which he was an utter failure. His next stage experience was as sharer in a scratch company got together by Wignell, whom we have seen as an actor at York, to play in Maidstone. In the meantime Wilkinson had obtained an introduction to Garrick who, impressed with his imitations, engaged him as a super at Drury Lane. Here he met Samuel Foote, who, also recognizing his talents as a mimic, took him on an expedition to Dublin where he made a hit in Foote's *Tea* and in imitations of his enemy Peg Woffington, and where he rose to acting Othello. He later sustained leading rôles at Bath and Portsmouth until Drury Lane reopened in 1758. There he appeared with Foote in *The Diversions of the Morning*. It was during this winter that he first met Baker at a dinner and perceived 'an oddity of humour and manner in this elderly gentleman, that demanded respect and esteem'.[71] The acquaintance ripened to an intimacy which was to determine the rest of Wilkinson's career, but before this happened he acted at Smock Alley, Dublin and Covent Garden, quarrelled with Foote, was reconciled and joined him at the Haymarket. In 1762 Baker, for the first time, decided to cover the York Spring Race Week. At that time stars were never invited to play in York but on this occasion Baker, casting round for someone to give a fillip to the last week of the season, remembered his young friend in London and against all previous custom engaged him for a few nights. Accounts differ as to Wilkinson's powers as an actor. Hitchcock says that 'independent of his powers of mimicry, he possessed capital abilities for the stage'[72] but Bernard[73] flatly pronounces that he was no actor. About his genius for mimicry there are no two opinions. Bernard thought him perhaps the greatest mimic on record, and he seems to have had the gift of being able to alter his face to resemble that of the person he was imitating, even if it were the beautiful Peg Woffington. Indeed his acting was mostly mimicry of other actors, and in tragic rôles, for which he was totally unsuited, he simply aped the manner of Garrick or Mossop.

Wilkinson first arrived in York about April 22 or 23, for he tells us that he saw bills plastered with the announcement of *Romeo and Juliet* and *The Frenchified Lady* for the benefit of Buck, a performance which took place on the latter date. He lodged with Baker, who had taken a great fancy to him, and made his début in Foote's *Minor*. He states that he was 'well received by a very genteel house'.[74] Indeed he was impressed with the quality and behaviour of the audience remarking how the ladies had 'a grace, a manner, a decorum not often met with outside London.' 'York,' he continues, 'certainly boasts a pre-eminence when the boxes on public weeks are crowded, that dazzles the eye of a stranger.' But the audience though dazzling to the view were lukewarm in applause when compared with those of any other established theatre.[75]

An advertisement for a repetition of Wilkinson's performance as Shift, Smirk and Mrs Cole in *The Minor* appears in the *York Courant* for May 3 to take place that day. It was announced as performed by him at the Theatre Royal in London; on this occasion no pit ticket was allowed to pass either 'into the boxes or on to the stage'. As Bayes in *The Rehearsal*, Wilkinson scored a triumph in a part in which Frodsham was esteemed capital. Wilkinson, however, considered that Frodsham was unsuited to the character and found in the applause he received in it an instance of the York public's undiscriminating worship. Wilkinson also played Cadwallader to the Mrs. Cadwallader of Miss Phillips in Foote's *Author* and on Wednesday, May 11, he attempted King Lear with Frodsham in his usual rôle of Edgar. 'My Lear', he tells us, 'was greatly received as it did not interfere with their darling Frodsham, and both being in the same play gave much satisfaction.' Frodsham was, in his opinion, the best actor he had seen in the mad scenes. On May 14 Wilkinson appeared as Horatio and Frodsham as Lothario in *The Fair Penitent*, after which *The Minor* was repeated. For his benefit on May 18[76] Wilkinson played Oakley in *The Jealous Wife*, Trappolin in *A Duke and No Duke*, and revived the entertainment of *Tea*. He found 'a crowded audience, both before and behind the curtain; for the stage was filled with gentlemen,' those frequenting the boxes being admitted behind the scenes. *Tea* was a failure, the satire and mimicry causing great disapproval, though, as we have seen, it had been played by Dancer without trouble.

In October the Theatre housed a visiting company of Italian singers who performed Rinaldo di Capua's *Fortune Teller*; Pergolesi's *The Maid the Mistress; The Amorous Robber*, and *Harlequin's Happiness in Love*. This, the first opera company to play in York, was received with approbation and honoured by a bespeak from the officers of the militia.

The season of 1764 opened with *All's Well* for the benefit of the hospital which, however, only brought £15.18.4d. Thomas Powell and his wife had joined the company. Powell was an inhabitant of York who, when acting at Wolverhampton in 1763, had eloped with and married Dolly Steward, a lady of fashion of a good Warwickshire family. Cast off by her mother she too took to the stage and the pair obtained an engagement at York. Powell, whose salary was 13/6, was found to be a useful actor and Wilkinson[77] says that he was 'a young man possessed of great industry, good behaviour and integrity – His person altogether was good tho' his voice not very pleasing either as a singer or speaker.' S. W. Ryley,[78] who met him after he had left the York company, confirms the judgment on his voice, speaking of him as 'an actor of good conception and sound judgment, but his voice was inconceivably disgusting, a kind of speaking counter tenor, capable of little modulation.' In spite of this he became 'a great favourite in Yorkshire.' Unhappily when Ryley knew him he was in a constant state of intoxication.

Mrs. Powell opened at York in Hermione but the part was beyond her capacity 'tho' she had been trained with a liberal education, and her person was good, tall and remarkably well-made'. Experience taught her that comedy was her forte and as Fanny in *The Maid of the Mill*, Lady Rusport and Lady Alton she gave good promise. 'Where natural hearty laughter was necessary for the character, she was in that point almost equal to the late and never to be forgotten Mrs. Clive. In the part of Nell, particularly where she tells Jobson, she is to keep a coach – which character, though excellently performed in the present day, yet Mrs. Clive, in that passage is not by any means surpassed or equalled.' Mrs. Powell later became corpulent and also took to drink. For some time she had to be confined and in the end fell into a stupor and died in November 1773. Powell remained with the company until May 1775.[79]

When Bickerstaffe's *Love in a Village* was given its first performance at York, Powell was the first Meadows and Frodsham the first Hawthorn. Many of the famous were in succeeding generations to sing and play in these rôles after them, for *Love in a Village* was to remain one of the most long-lived comic operas. Bickerstaffe's other new musical piece *Thomas and Sally* also made its début in York this year with Frodsham as Thomas. Altogether it was an enterprising season, other new productions being Mrs. Centlivre's *Man's Bewitch'd* with Frodsham as Num; King's ballad opera *Love at First Sight*; Brome's old comedy *The Jovial Crew*, probably in its ballad opera adaptation, with Frodsham as Hearty and Mrs. Mylteer as Anne; another old piece, Beaumont and Fletcher's *Philaster*, altered by Colman, in which Frodsham played the title rôle at his benefit; Murphy's *What We Must All Come To*; Whincop's *Scanderbeg* with Frodsham as hero; Colman's *Deuce is in Him*, and Foote's popular *Mayor of Garratt*.

Miss Phillips took a number of leads including Juliet, and Isabella in *Measure for Measure* with Frodsham as the Duke, Crisp as Angelo, Leng as Claudio, Robertson as Clown and Mrs. Frodsham as Mariana; in *As You Like It* she had only the small part of Audrey. Sometime this spring Mrs. Robertson died and Frodsham wrote a poem upon her demise[80]. In May Mahon, a dancer from Dublin, joined the company. Wilkinson returned for the last fortnight of the season. He appeared at the Powells' first benefit at which Powell acted Gratiano and Mrs. Powell Portia in *The Merchant of Venice*. He then made the great mistake of acting Othello on April 28. He was taken ill during the performance and the company was obliged to dismiss. Wilkinson was thereafter abused for his rash attempt to take over one of Frodsham's rôles, and rumours were maliciously circulated that he was either too afraid or too drunk to make further appearances. On his playing Major Sturgeon in *The Author* on May 1, he was greeted with hisses and oranges, and told that Achurch could do better; but on the following Saturday, when he acted Bajazet in *Tamerlane* together with Foote's *Orators* for the benefit of the actor Tenoe, he met with neither applause nor hissing. In Murphy's *Apprentice* he was considered shockingly bad as Dick in comparison with the beloved Frodsham, but was received once more into favour when he ceased to challenge the people's idol, and acted Kiteley in Ben Jonson's *Every Man in his Humour* and Cadwallader in *The Author*. Col. Thornton of the York militia bespoke his benefit and desired *The Mayor of Garratt*. That night Wilkinson performed Major Sturgeon and Matthew Mugg, Trim in *The Funeral* in which he introduced the Cries of London, and Crontes and Lindamira the Princess in Foote's *Tragedy à la Mode*[81] – a full programme. He was gratified to find 'great boxes and a very genteel house' which brought the large sum of £50 in receipts. This was the last year of the old Theatre which had had a life of twenty years. When the company returned in 1765 it was to a new building.

CHAPTER TWO

The First Theatre Royal and Tate Wilkinson's Management 1765–1779

ON January 22, 1761 the Corporation had granted Baker, in the name of Christopher Mitchell, the lease of a dwelling-house in Blake Street with garden and appurtenances as well as 'the tenement used as a playhouse near the same' from Christmas 1764 for twenty-one years at a rent of £20 a year, clear of all taxes, on condition that he covenanted to lay out £500 on the premises in lasting improvements within two years after the commencement of the term.[1] Already when Wilkinson came to York in April 1764 he found Baker 'busy with bricks and mortar, and in his high glory, giving directions to workmen, who were erecting part of a new theatre at York, at a great, and his sole expence.' 'It was intended' Wilkinson continues[2] 'to be (as it now actually is) in a much more capacious scale than the old one, though nearly on the same spot, as he was then finishing the tail of the new, while the players were employed in the head of the old.' The new theatre was completed during the summer and autumn and was ready for the company on their return to York for the winter season. It was opened on January 3, 1765 with a performance of *The Provok'd Husband* and *The Lying Valet* for the benefit of Baker. The prologue, which was written by John Cunningham and spoken by Frodsham, runs as follows:[3]

> Once on a Time, his earthly Rounds patrolling,
> (Your Heathen Gods were always fond of strolling)
> Jove rambled near the Cot of kind *Philemon*,
>   When Night, attended by a Tempest, came on;
>   And as the Rain fell patt'ring – helter skelter,
>   The Deity implor'd the Hind for Shelter.
>   *Philemon* plac'd his Godship close beside him
> (While Goody *Baucis* made the Fire that dry'd him)
> With more Benevolence than one that's richer,
> He spread the Board – he fill'd the friendly Pitcher,

And, fond to give his Guest a Meal of Pleasure,
Sung a rough Song in the wild Country Measure.
  Jove was so pleas'd with his good-natur'd Sallies
Philemon's House – he conjur'd – to a Palace.
  Taste, like great Jupiter, came here to try us,
(Oft from the Boxes I observ'd her spy us).
Whether she lik'd us and our warm Endeavours, –
Whether she found that we deserv'd her Favours, –
I know not – but 'tis certain she commanded
This humble Theatre should be expanded.
The Order she pronounc'd was scarcely ended,
  But, like *Philemon's* House, our Stage extended.
And thus the friendly Goddess bade me greet you,
This is the Circle where she means to meet you:
Pedants would fix her Residence with Heathens
But she prefers OLD YORK – to ROME or ATHENS.

The epilogue, which was written by Frodsham and spoken by Miss Phillips, anticipates the various comments of beau, coquette, peasant and Methodist and ends with a compliment to the audience as critic. The advertisement for the opening night declares that 'The Theatre is finished in an elegant Manner, and particular Care has been taken to have it well air'd.'

The following description was printed in the *York Courant* on January 8: 'This Theatre is by far the most spacious in Great Britain, Drury-lane and Covent Garden excepted, and for Convenience and Elegance it is thought to be equal, if not superior, to either of them – As the Drama has, by all polite Nations, been allowed to be the most rational and improving Entertainment, we beg leave to congratulate the Public on this accessional Ornament to the City.' These are large claims and we must remember that when Wilkinson took over the management two years later he found the theatre 'in a very declining state, even to the disgrace of the city: dirty scenes, dirty clothes, all dark and dismal.' We can form little idea of what the theatre looked like but we know that there was one more tier than in the previous theatre making in all three tiers above the pit: boxes, and first and upper galleries. The usual charges were: boxes 2/6, pit 2/-, first gallery 1/6, upper gallery 1/-. The subscription for thirty-three plays (or concerts as they still had to be called) had risen to two guineas for the boxes and £1.13.0. for the pit.

King Lear was played for the benefit of the County Hospital and *The Funeral* for the Charity Schools, the latter occasion bringing £24.6.3. to the Charity. On both benefit nights it was the custom for the musicians to give their services. Mrs Mahon was the chief addition to the company this year. Besides acting Juliet, Ophelia and other leading rôles she sang between the acts. Her husband, the dancer, undertook Harlequin for the first time when *The Novelty*, with alterations and additional scenes from entertainments of the Fair, was acted for their benefit. The heavier tragedy rôles were shared by Miss Phillips (Evandra in *Timon of Athens*, Almeria in *The Mourning Bride*, Lady Macbeth) and Mrs. Powell (Melissa in *Timon*, Zara in *The Mourning Bride*). Frodsham played several Shakespearian leads: Timon, Hamlet, Romeo and Macbeth. He wrote an epilogue to the ladies and gentlemen of York for *The Rival Queens*, and another, in the form of a dialogue between the characters of Jerry Sneak and Mrs Sneak from the *Mayor of Garratt*, that was delivered by Robertson and Miss Phillips after the latter had played Sigismunda for the first time.

Dryden and Lee's *Oedipus* was revived with alterations and additions and with new machinery, dresses and decorations; a grand incantation in the grove of furies to raise the ghost of Laius was said to be presented with all preparatory ceremonies after the manner of the ancients. We may perhaps see in this the beginning of an attempt at accuracy in spectacles. The Hon. Andrew Erskine's comedy *She's Not Him and He's Not Her,* which had been given in Edinburgh in 1764, was among the fresh pieces but does not seem to have caught on. The new Italian pantomime entertainment 'of a different Nature from any before perform'd here' was entitled *Magic; or Harlequin in the Shades* and was announced as having been performed in London for forty successive nights. A topical entertainment was a poetical and musical rhapsody, *A Briton the Son of a Briton,* on the birth of the Prince of Wales. The popular Foote was represented by his new comedy *The Patron.*

Wilkinson rejoined the company in Newcastle and acted in the new theatre for the first time when he came to York for Race Week. The relationship between Baker and Wilkinson was now like that of father and son and Tate could do no wrong in his elder's eyes.[4] Tate on his side declares that to serve so good a friend he would have performed during Race Week without emolument. Wilkinson relates an anecdote of this season which shows how much the unlicensed players were at the mercy of threats. He had determined to play Cadwallader in *The Author,* a rôle in which the York audience was partial to him. At the rehearsal he was called away to Baker's dining-room where a certain Apreece, after reminding Baker that his theatre was unlicensed, threatened that, if *The Author,* which he said was an impudent libel and had been forbidden further performance in 1758, was acted, he and his friends would not leave a scene or bench in the house. *The Mayor of Garratt* was silently substituted, since no excuse could be given, but when poor Wilkinson came on as the Mayor the bewildered and disappointed audience greeted him with hisses and continued their disapprobation throughout. The following night Wilkinson did well with *The Lyar* but unhappily again hit on a favourite part of Frodsham's – that of The Apprentice – for the afterpiece. He failed 'without a single hand to assist'; his imitations which were not known in Yorkshire, 'passed without the least effect'. On the Wednesday Wilkinson intended to act Sir John Brute with *The Upholsterer* but once again he was stopped from playing a favourite rôle. This time it was the ladies who sent a deputation objecting to so indecent a play as *The Provok'd Wife,* and declaring that they would not enter the theatre unless it was changed. This command from the boxes had to be obeyed and handbills were forthwith issued announcing the alteration to *Love in a Village.* As Razor in *The Upholsterer* Wilkinson imitated Woodward, but because his dress was contrary to Robertson's, his attempt was judged wrong and absurd and once again he was hissed. Such were the trials of a time when the drama's patrons interfered with its performances. Wilkinson thought to retrieve his fortunes with Macklin's *Love à la Mode* but, though the theatre was crowded, the first act met with frigid silence and the second was disapproved of because the part of Squire Gloom gave offence to the gentlemen of the turf on whom the receipts of this week depended. Many left the theatre, and Wilkinson, disgusted with his reception, did not act on the Friday but left Mrs Mahon in *The Maid of the Mill* and Robertson in *The Mock Doctor* to entertain a full house. Though *The Minor* was well received on Saturday, Wilkinson was not appeased and determined to quit the York stage for ever. Little did he dream at that indignant moment that he was to be associated with it for the rest of his life.

Four months later he was in York on his way to fulfil an engagement at Norwich when some gentlemen requested him to undertake the part of Sir Archy in *Love à la Mode* for the benefit of the County Hospital on December 31. He naturally demurred at first after the treatment he had previously suffered in this farce, but was persuaded by the argument that several leading York families would attend in the winter who had been out of town in the summer. This time the piece was received with 'a continued roar of approbation and laughter' and thus became the immediate cause of Wilkinson's long and happy connection with the York Theatre.[5] For so pleased with the performance were the leading patrons that the next day they called a meeting and urged one Tasker to propose to Baker that Wilkinson be asked to stay on as manager at York on terms which would make it worth his while to do so. Baker had run into debt through building the theatre at his own expense, was old, lazy and suffering from gout and rheumatism, so that the theatre was neglected. At first Baker resisted the idea, not wanting to yield up his power, and arguing that the theatre could not afford to pay Wilkinson sufficient to compensate him, but finally he came to see that he would be ruined unless he could borrow money from Wilkinson on the security of his property. Then Tasker, having tactfully brought Baker round, arranged the matter with Wilkinson in a half hour's walk in the Minster. Wilkinson immediately fell to the temptation of managing the company and a contract was drawn up and signed. Wilkinson lent Baker all his money, first £1,000 and subsequently at different times £400 more. Baker gave him interest on the loan, a salary as manager, benefits at York, Hull and Newcastle clear from all charges, had him to live with him in the house attached to the theatre, and left him all his playhouse property in his will.

The new manager immediately inaugurated improvements, which, at first, met with opposition from the ill-disciplined corps. Wilkinson, who had a great sense of the dignity of his profession, had been disgusted by the humiliating customs prevalent on the York stage. One, which required a man and his wife to return thanks at their benefit from the stage, Keregan had also objected to. Frodsham had once carried his wife on his back for this purpose. Another was that of actors and actresses, 'draggle-tailed Andromaches', delivering benefit bills from door to door, attending the Assembly Rooms to beg for support, and running after patrons in the street to solicit their purchase of box tickets. Wilkinson had been pained at the sight of 'Mr. Frodsham, bred as a gentleman with fine natural talents and esteemed in York as a Garrick, the Hamlet of the age, running after, or stopping a gentleman on horseback to deliver his benefit bill and beg a half a crown.'[6] In the teeth of the company's resentment Wilkinson abolished both practices.

Creswick was the only other new member in the company, 'a simpering, ogling, inoffensive character, a great admirer of himself.'[7] He had played small parts at Covent Garden and Wilkinson engaged him in Edinburgh. He had a bad memory, suffered from stage fright and was not a good speaker. Robertson wholeheartedly condemns him:

> On *Dulness'* form, begot by *Impudence,*
> Of both his parents the true quintescence,
> Creswick approaches; but alas, so dull,
> So *empty*, though of *self* so very *full*;
> So *flatly* pert, he tires our patience quite,
> We yawn, and wish the *creature* out of sight,
> Of vile Monotonists the very worst,
> On Lethe's bank with foggy opiates nurst.

He left the company in 1773 as a discarded actor and took to lecturing and speech training despite his poor pronunciation; he died in 1792.

The two benefit performances showed an improvement: that for the County Hospital at which *Measure for Measure* was given brought in £24.19.9, that for the Schools – *Love in a Village* and *The Deuce is in Him* – rose to £33.8.0. Besides *Measure for Measure* Shakespeare was represented by *King Lear* with Wilkinson as Lear, Leng as Edmund, Frodsham as Edgar and Mrs. Mahon as Cordelia; *Richard III* with Wilkinson playing the title rôle to Frodsham's Richmond, Leng's Buckingham, Miss Phillips's Queen Elizabeth, Mrs. Frodsham's Lady Anne, and Mrs Mahon's Prince Edward; *Romeo and Juliet* with Wilkinson as Mercutio; *Henry IV,* revived after 7 years, in which Wilkinson appeared for the first time as Falstaff with King = Crisp, Prince of Wales = Leng, Hotspur = Frodsham, Lady Percy = Miss Phillips.

At his benefit Frodsham spoke a eulogium on Shakespeare in which a representation of his tomb [sic] in Westminster Abbey was exhibited.

Among the new plays was Thomson's *Coriolanus* in Thomas Sheridan's adaptation with Wilkinson as Coriolanus, Powell as Cominius, Miss Phillips as Veturia, Mrs. Powell as Volumnia and a Roman triumph with decorations; Bickerstaffe's *Daphne and Amintor;* Foote's *Commissary* in which Wilkinson played Zac Fungus; Kane O'Hara's burletta *Midas*, as performed in London and Dublin after the manner of the Italians, with Wilkinson in the title rôle; Hawkesworth's *Edgar and Emmeline* prefaced by an address on the usefulness of the stage written and spoken by Miss Phillips; Dalton's stage version of *Comus* with Arne's music and Frodsham as Comus, Miss Phillips as the Lady, Mrs. Powell as the interpolated character Euphrosyne and Mrs. Mahon as Sabrina; Colman and Garrick's *Clandestine Marriage* with Wilkinson as Lord Ogleby and Miss Phillips as Mrs. Heidelberg; Richard Bentley's *The Wishes;* Gentleman's *Sultan,* under its sub-title *Love and Fame,* with a triumphal entry of the Sultan into Constantinople and new dresses; and, last, but by no means least, an ambitious attempt to stage Arne's opera *Artaxerxes*. This was given at Wilkinson's benefit and was advertised as exactly on the plan of the Italian opera at the King's Haymarket[8]; in spite of being contracted into two acts, the principal songs were retained. Though the attempt was difficult, and even dangerous, owing to the high standard of music required, Wilkinson was encouraged to make it owing to Mrs. Mahon's improved powers of singing.

There was evidently some difficulty in keeping the house warm and German stoves were employed for this.

Wilkinson says that he got rid of the lesser actors, the Tenoes, Swetnam and the Owens, but, though by 1767 the first two had departed, the Owen brothers were in the company another two years. The newcomers were Mr. and Mrs. Robson and Mr. and Mrs. James Shaftoe Robertson who, presumably to avoid confusion with James Robertson, called themselves Shaftoe. Robson was a native of Hull and originally a peruke maker with whom Wilkinson had played in Edinburgh.[9] He had a good person, an excellent memory and was of great service as a singer, but was hampered by his provincial dialect. He played only small parts such as that of Philario in *Cymbeline* and soon left the company, eventually to become manager of the Margate Theatre.

Shaftoe Robertson was a native of Ludlow who had absconded from grammar school to become an actor[10], but, though he had the advantages of a good education and understanding, he was ungraceful and 'walked like a crab.' He stayed with the company until 1772 when he left to superintend the Lincoln circuit under Whiteley. He afterwards purchased Whiteley's share and became manager of the Lincoln and Sheffield Theatres. Wilkinson says that he died in poverty but this is denied by Winston. His wife made her first appearance on any stage as Biddy Bellair in *Miss in her Teens* at York on April 25. Their chief claim to fame is that they founded a famous theatrical family, being the grandparents of Tom Robertson the dramatist and the ancestors of Madge Kendal.[11]

The 1767 season opened on January 1 with the customary benefit for the County Hospital which raised only £19.8.0.; but that for the Charity Schools brought in the large sum of £61.10.10^{1}/2d. The attraction was an Ode called *Charity* adapted for the stage and set to music by William Jackson of Exeter in which performers from the concerts and the cathedral, as well as the band of the Royal Horse Guards the Blues, assisted.

The presence of Mrs. Mahon in the company enabled Wilkinson to present several operas and comic operas. New to York were Gay's *Achilles* with Mrs. Mahon as Deidamia, Mendez's *Shepherd's Lottery* with music by Boyce, Mrs. Mahon as Phyllis; Charles Burney's *The Cunning Man*, taken from Rousseau's *Devin du Village* and adapted to his original music, Mrs. Mahon as Phoebe; and for her benefit Toms's *The Accomplished Maid* taken from Goldoni's *La Buona Figliuola* with music by Piccinni, Mrs. Mahon as Lady Lucy and Wilkinson as Kriegsman.

Other new pieces this season were Francklin's *Earl of Warwick* which Wilkinson chose for his benefit; Garrick's farce *Neck or Nothing*; Hull's comedy *The Perplexities*; Colman's *English Merchant* with Frodsham as Lord Falbridge, Mrs. Powell as Lady Alton and Mrs. Mahon as Amelia; a burlesque tragedy *The Death of Bucephalus* by George Wallis,[12] a local doctor, in which Robertson acted Alexander and Wilkinson the tragedy queen Statira; Gentleman's dramatic satire *The Mentalist* already given in Manchester; and Hill's *Athelwold* into which parts of Mason's *Elfrida* were introduced with Wilkinson in the title rôle and Miss Phillips as Ethelinda. William Mason, the friend of Gray and Horace Walpole, was at the time a canon residentiary and precentor of the Minster. *Elfrida*, his first tragedy written on ancient Greek models, had been printed in 1752, but was not brought out at Covent Garden until 1772. Later it was given full length presentation at York. *Cymbeline* was first acted in Garrick's version with Wilkinson as Posthumous, Leng as Iachimo, Robertson as Cloten – a rôle usually allotted to the low comedian, and Mrs Powell as Imogen. *Henry VIII* was revived after twenty years with Wilkinson as Wolsey, Crisp as King Henry, Fitzmaurice as Cromwell, Robertson as Gardiner, another low comedian rôle, Frodsham as Buckingham, Mrs. Frodsham as Anne Bullen and Miss Phillips as Queen Katharine. *Fly Soft Ideas* was sung in the first act by Mrs. Mahon. *Henry VIII* became a stock play probably owing to its capabilities for procession and display. Not so *Julius Caesar* which had also had a twenty years' absence from the stage, but evidently failed to take. The cast was Julius Caesar = Crisp, Brutus = Frodsham, Cassius = Creswick, Mark Anthony = Wilkinson, Calphurnia = Mrs Frodsham, Portia = Miss Phillips. A local enthusiast seeing Frodsham and Wilkinson as Hamlet and the Ghost was inspired to the following couplet:

'Tis well, thought I, let David charm the Town
Since York has now two Garricks of her own.[13]

Creswick obtained the patronage of the officers of the Horse Guards for his benefit. The garrison troops at York were consistent patrons of the theatre and many performances were given by their desire. Frequently too they allowed their band to augment the evening's entertainment by playing military music. Wilkinson's kindness to old players is reflected in the benefit given to Jacky Pearce who played minor rôles. We read that when he appeared to give thanks a burst of applause greeted the old man. The season closed with a benefit for the prompter Floor on May 27.

Once again playbills[14] announced that patrons would not be allowed on the stage or behind the scenes. Wilkinson appears to have been more successful than his predecessor in banishing this pernicious custom. For his benefit Wilkinson requested the ladies who sent servants to take places to be particular in the number they wished to reserve. He pleaded too for the favour of patronage since the business of the theatre required his utmost attention. An undated bill for Race Week, which must refer to this year according to the cast, records a performance of *Every Man in His Humour* with Wilkinson as Kiteley and Creswick as the fiery coward Bobadil.

In October the Leeds Company of Comedians opened at a Little Theatre in Jubbergate and stayed until the beginning of December. Nothing is known of this theatre, though it advertised boxes at 2/6, pit 2/-, gallery 1/-, nor do the company seem to have repeated their visit.

There were few changes in the York troupe when it reopened on December 31, 1768 with a benefit for the County Hospital which raised £21.4.8$^{1}/_{2}$d. That for the Charity Schools, though the Ode was repeated, only brought in £27.13.0. this year. Crisp died in February and the Robsons and the Tenoes appear to have departed.

Goldsmith's *Good Natur'd Man* was given its first performance in York on March 12 but, unlike its successor *She Stoops to Conquer*, it failed to become a stock play. The cast was: Honeywood = Frodsham, Croaker = Robertson, Sir William Honeywood = Leng, Leontine = Creswick, Jarvis = Buck, Lofty = Powell, Mrs. Croaker = Mrs Powell, Olivia = Mrs Frodsham, Garnet = Mrs. Leng, Miss Richland = Miss Phillips.

At Wilkinson's benefit Kelly's *False Delicacy* with Wilkinson as Col. Rivers, Miss Phillips as Mrs. Harley, and Mrs. Mahon as Miss Marchmont was given for the first time and followed by *A Peep Behind the Curtain or York Theatre, 1768*. This farce of Garrick's had been successful at Drury Lane chiefly owing to its interest for frequenters of that theatre, but Wilkinson by altering the characters and transferring the scene to the York playhouse, gave it the necessary local touch.

A Yorkshire play was given for Oram's benefit. It was *The Plotting Wives*, a poor comedy by Richard Linnecar of Wakefield which came out under the title of *The Double Marriage; or the Husbands Reform'd* on February 6.[15] Linnecar says that Powell, Robertson, Miss Phillips and Mrs. Fitzmaurice did justice to their parts: 'the other Performers were so imperfect, that they did not speak one Line as the Author wrote it. It was not damn'd; but the

Author was in Purgatory all the Time of the Performance.' Reading the play one readily forgives the actors. Wilkinson spoke the prologue excellently; these lines are worth quoting for their local appeal:

> Shall York, for learning and for poets fam'd;
> A town polite any as Europe boasts,
> Be still serv'd up with plays departed ghosts?
> Will no bright genius bring us something new?
> O Mason we have long look'd up to you.

Other new plays were Kendrick's comedy *The Widow'd Wife;* Hartson's tragedy *The Countess of Salisbury*; Murphy's tragedy *Zenobia* with Wilkinson as Rhadamistus and Miss Phillips as Zenobia; Colman's farce *The Musical Lady*; Bickerstaffe's farce *The Absent Man*, shown in York just a month after its presentation at Drury Lane; Beaumont and Fletcher's *Royal Merchant*, probably in Hall's comic opera version, with Mrs. Mahon as Jaculin and Wilkinson as Vandunk; Cumberland's opera *The Summer's Tale*, the first of his pieces to be given in York, in which Mrs. Mahon took the lead and sang the songs which were highly approved; and *King Henry V*, no longer in Hill's version, with the following cast: Henry V = Wilkinson, Exeter = Creswick, Archbishop of Canterbury = Oram, Fluellen = Robertson, Pistol = Powell, King of France and Chorus = Frodsham, Dauphin = Leng, Burgundy = Buck, Queen of France = Mrs. Powell, Hostess = Mrs. Fitzmaurice, Princess Katherine = Mrs. Mahon.

Other Shakespeare plays this season were: *As You Like It* with Frodsham as Orlando, Achurch as Jaques and Mrs. Powell as Rosalind, *Romeo and Juliet*, and *The Merchant of Venice* with Wilkinson as Shylock, Frodsham as Bassanio and Mrs. Powell as Portia. Farquhar's *Constant Couple* was revived after twelve years with Mrs. Powell in the 'breeches' part of Sir Harry Wildair and on May 23, the last night, Carey's burlesque opera *The Dragon of Wantley* was seen after fourteen years' absence. Frodsham must have given his last performance in York during Race Week since he died at Hull on October 21. Wilkinson had to endure aspersions that it was his ill-usage as manager that killed him whereas in fact he drank himself into an early grave.[16] The company thus lost their leading actor. Floor the prompter left the company when they were in Newcastle and was replaced by Bryan.[17] In October Wilkinson married Jane Doughty.

Kniveton,[18] who came with a strong recommendation from Manchester, was engaged to replace Frodsham but though he 'played several characters with merit and deserved success' he did not please in the lovers and returned to Manchester at the end of the summer season at Newcastle in 1769. He was to become part owner of the Liverpool theatre and died in the prime of life in that city. He first appeared in York as Tancred on February 4, 1769 and during the season played Hastings, Jaffeir and Lord Townly. Mrs. Mahon had left for Bath[19] – 'an irreparable loss' – and was replaced by Miss Garvey, a singer, who was to become Mrs Raworth in 1771. Another addition on the actresses' side was Mrs Baker[20] who came from Edinburgh and joined the company in Newcastle in August, 1768. She played Queen Elizabeth in *Richard III*, Belvidera, Lady Randolph and Roxana. Wilkinson says she 'was a woman of strong understanding, aided by a good and highly finished education, wonderful natural abilities, and an actress of great capacity ... Her features were very good, but her figure was short, clumsy, and against her in many parts.' Somehow or other she created a prejudice against her and offended the old stagers. Miss Phillips left during the spring of 1769, Mrs. Powell got annoyed, and Mrs. Crisp was jealous because Mrs. Baker took over her rôle of Lady Townly. Before she left in the summer she had surmounted the ill-feeling. She returned to Edinburgh where she died in 1778.[21] Such 'endless animosities, jars and discontents' must have rendered Wilkinson's life at times an unenviable one.

This season of 1769 is one of the most important in the whole history of the York stage for during it Wilkinson obtained the royal patent for his theatres at York and Hull. It was the third patent to be granted to provincial theatres, the preceding two having been conferred on Bath and Norwich. An Act of Parliament[22] was necessitated which repealed the application of the Licensing Act to York and made it lawful for the King to grant the patent. After this it was no longer necessary to resort to the subterfuge of advertising concerts; nor was there fear any more that the theatre might be shut down and the players be prosecuted as a result of action by an informer. The theatre became a Theatre Royal and was 'entitled to all the Privileges, and subjected to all the Regulations to which any Theatre or Playhouse in Great Britain is entitled and subjected.' The granting of the patents, which cost nearly £500,[23] was a public acknowledgement that Wilkinson 's two theatres were leading ones in the provinces.

This memorable season opened as usual with a benefit for the County Hospital on January 3 at which Miss Garvey made her first appearance singing between the acts. £23.19.4. was raised. The opening night as a Theatre Royal was on April 8; it was devoted to a benefit for Mrs. Baker, and Home's new tragedy *The Fatal Discovery* was presented with Mrs. Baker as Rivine, Wilkinson as Orellan and Kniveton as Ronan. This was followed by Wilkinson in Foote's *Tea* and by Bickerstaffe's comic opera *The Padlock* with a fresh scene. Wilkinson says that it was 'produced ... with uncommon effect; ... I was esteemed a very good Mungo.'[24] The prologue on this great occasion was written by Robertson and spoken by Wilkinson:[25]

> Too long the Thespian Muse, an alien deem'd,
> By stealth alone on York her influence beam'd;
> Her wings curtail'd – by Law forbade to roam,
> And proud Augusta doom'd her partial home;
> Scorning restraint, yet driven to submit,
> And forc'd, alas! to smuggle sense and wit;

But still the Muse was lawless and disguis'd,
Hated by fools, – or worse – by fools despis'd;
York's ancient Genius griev'd the sight to view,
His pride, his honour rous'd, like lightning flew,
Indignant flew, and kneeling at the Throne,
To Britain's Sov'reign made his sorrows known:
Ebor's complaint our Sovereign soon redrest;
Our Sov'reign reigns, to make his subjects blest: –
The Muse exulting clapp'd her magic wings,
And, after bending to the best of Kings,
Swell'd her prophetic raptures, while around,
Ebor's exulting vales re-echo'd the glad sound.
'On these bright plains, belov'd by every Muse,
Which Phoebus daily blesses as he views,
The sister Muses patroniz'd by Laws,
Shall pour their magic in fair Virtue's cause;
Their Mirror and their Lash aloft shall rear,
While Vice and Folly cringe with dastard fear;
And York, as second in Britannia's isle,
Shall with Augusta share the genial smile.
Nor shall the grateful Muse forget what's due
To King, to Laws, to Country, and – to You.
Henceforth each circling year, on this glad day,
Cytherean groves shall swell the festive lay,
And every flow'r and [sic] sweet Parnassus yields,
The Muse shall plant in Ebor's smiling fields,
Garlands of which, compos'd from Taste's rich bed,
She'll weave in wreaths to grace each patron's head.'
Long have I wish'd for, what with joy I see,
The Muse once more restor'd to liberty:
My little All I ventur'd in her cause,
And the reward I wish is – your applause;
On your known candour cheerfully depend,
And hope a sanction from each generous friend.

This is the first season for which we have an almost complete set of playbills, in the Minster Library. Tuesday, Thursday and Saturday were the regular days of playing, Tuesday and Thursday being devoted to the subscription and Saturday to the benefits. The last subscription night was on April 27 but the season continued with a series of benefits until the last night on May 31 which was for the prompter Bryan. No performances, of course, were allowed during Passion Week but this year oratorios[26] were given in the theatre for three nights, including *Judas Maccabaeus* and *The Messiah*. Morris of Oxford, Paxton of Durham, Pinto the conductor of the bands at Vauxhall and Drury Lane, and his wife, formerly Miss Brent, were engaged. The oratorios were well attended and Baker and his two fellow adventurers shared to good advantage. During public weeks, that is during the Assizes or the Races, prices were raised from 2/6 to 3/- for the boxes, from 2/- to 2/6 for the pit and from 1/6 to 2/- for the first gallery.

In addition to those already noticed, a number of new plays made their début in York. There were two other tragedies, Delap's *Hecuba* in which Wilkinson played Eriphilus to Mrs. Baker's Hecuba, and Hoole's *Cyrus* which was presented for Wilkinson's benefit in which he played Cambyses to the Arpasia of Mrs. Orde, whose first appearance in York it was. Baker obliged Wilkinson by painting a new scene for the occasion, perhaps the last that he ever did. Three of Bickerstaffe's pieces were brought out this year, his comic opera *Lionel and Clarissa* with Oldboy = Wilkinson, Lionel = Powell, Clarissa = Miss Garvey, his comedy *The Hypocrite* with Kniveton as Dr. Cantwell, and in August *Dr Lust in his Chariot*. Mrs. Griffith's comedy *The School for Rakes*, King's farce *Wit's Last Stake*, a new pantomime *Harlequin from the Moon; or The Devil among the Taylors*, with new music and decorations, Owen as Harlequin, Mrs. Shaftoe as Columbine, and, on the last night, Reed's comic opera *Tom Jones* with Powell in the name part, Kniveton as Squire Western and Mrs. Leng as Sophia, complete the number of new presentations. Most of these had been given at the London theatres earlier in the year or in 1768. It was often only a matter of weeks before York saw the pieces that had been acclaimed at Drury Lane or Covent Garden.

Among revivals were Moore's *Gamester* after 11 years, in which Wilkinson and Mrs. Baker acted Beverley and Mrs. Beverley, Brown's *Barbarossa* after seven years with Kniveton as Achmet and Miss Phillips as Irene, and Foote's *Knights*. It is an interesting concession to taste that the *The Mayor of Garratt* was given without the mob scene which, it was announced, had been omitted for some time by desire.

The season was particularly rich in Shakespeare, no fewer than eight of his plays being presented. In *Much Ado About Nothing*, Wilkinson played Benedick, Robertson Dogberry and Mrs. Baker Beatrice. Mrs. Baker was now Queen Elizabeth and Kniveton Richmond in *Richard III*, and in *Macbeth* they played Lady Macbeth and Macduff to Wilkinson's Macbeth. This was of course the Davenant version with singing in addition to speaking witches. Wilkinson acted Hamlet for the first time on March 29 with Mrs. Powell as Ophelia and Mrs. Baker as the Queen. In *The Merchant of Venice* he was replaced by Kniveton as Shylock. Kniveton was Cromwell in *Henry VIII* with Leng as the King, Mrs. Baker as Queen Katharine, Powell as Buckingham; whilst in *As You Like It* Kniveton took over Frodsham's part of Orlando and Robertson was Touchstone.

At Mrs. Frodsham's benefit her daughter Miss Sarah Frodsham, then a child, made her first appearance on any stage to speak an address to the ladies. A Ms. note on the playbill gives £77.8.0. as the amount taken this night – a very satisfactory sum for the widow.

When the company returned in August for the Race Week Sarah Ibbot from Norwich had taken the place of Mrs. Baker. Wilkinson[27] says of her 'She possessed great merit, good voice, education and understanding – not equal in expression to Mrs. Baker; her manner far from accomplished: however, if size was necessary, though Mrs. Baker was not a skeleton, yet Ibbot made more than treble amends as to quantity. She acted Queen Elizabeth, take it altogether, better than any person I have seen (Mrs. Pope excepted). Mrs. Ibbot played various parts with infinite ability, and would have been more successful on the Dublin and London stages, had her features been alluring.' Hitchcock[28] confirms that 'though far from being a good figure,' she was 'an excellent actress and a remarkably good speaker'; she played many characters in tragedy much above mediocrity but he admired her most in comedy. Our only record of her performances in York is as Queen Elizabeth in a revival of the *Earl of Essex*.[29] She left the company at Hull in the winter in dudgeon because Mrs. Powell, who was getting corpulent, but who with her husband was of great utility in a number of plays, took over some of her parts. Mrs. Ibbot returned to Norwich but retired from the stage on being left a fortune in 1787. With Mrs. Ibbot came Miss Willoughby,[30] a girl of good family with an elegant figure and sweet-toned voice. She played several leading characters in York and rapidly became popular but the study and hard work proved too much for her, and after she left the company she 'fell into a deep and rapid decline.' Though not 18 years old she was a credit to the theatre in her conduct. During the Race Week season she played Amelia in *The English Merchant* being advertised as a young gentleman 'whose Youth and Genius seem to promise a valuable Acquisition to the Theatre.' Summing up these years, Wilkinson says that the performers were 'a decent regular set; no blazing comets: The company was in general well rewarded, and, what was more extraordinary, the audiences were satisfied, though the troop was but la, la, and the wardrobe and scenery very indifferent, compared to the modern fashion of either; but the remains of Mr. Baker's scenery bore strong marks of the artist's hand, they had been done by that gentleman in his younger days'.[31]

When the York Theatre reopened on January 2, 1770 with the usual benefit for the County Hospital, it was announced that 'The House is entirely new painted and ornamented, and, to compleat it, Mr. Baker has contracted with a proper Person to assist in painting the Scenery &c., with all imaginable Dispatch. He has likewise engaged a young Lady, whose Person and Accomplishments seem to promise Satisfaction to the Public.' This young lady was Miss Mingay who made her first appearance on any stage as Monimia in *The Orphan* on January 27. She was the daughter of the Comptroller of Hull[32] and, having dissipated a small fortune, she 'packed up her tatters' and with her mother's consent followed the company to York. It was not unusual in those days to put a person of no experience on the stage straight into one of the leading tragic rôles, but it is not surprising that Wilkinson had to admit that she was quite unequal to the task. We hear of no further appearances and she soon after married a fortune-hunter who parted from her as soon as he discovered he had been cheated. Miss Willoughby was taking leading rôles such as Juliet, Perdita and Desdemona; her sister Miss C. Willoughby, who, Wilkinson says, was destitute of every requisite for the stage and a bad hat into the bargain, was also in the company. Mrs. Ibbot must have returned for a while for she was playing Constance in *King John*, Emilia in *Othello* and Roxana in *The Rival Queens*. On the male side there were two new names: that of Gay who stayed with the company for four years and who played such leading rôles as Castalio and Florizel, and Raworth, a singer who had been recommended by Moody. Wilkinson[33] says of him that when he first came 'he was a handsome young man, made more than common promise as a singer, was rather corpulent, but to my great surprise fell into a consumption, and soon after his leaving York died at Chester.' He was with the company for two seasons and, as we have seen, married Miss Garvey. Another acquisition was Master Rochford, a boy dancer, who sustained Harlequin in *Harlequin Salamander.* Bryan had died in 1769 and was succeeded as prompter by William Flower, aged sixteen, who was the son of the owner of the Star Inn in Stonegate, a favourite resort of the players. He was prompter until 1775 when he left the stage for the church.[34]

Wilkinson's energy did not stop at securing the patent and having the Theatre repainted. On January 4, after the play was finished, he set out for London to see the new productions. He wanted to present these at York at the height of the season and not wait until the spring.[35] He was also probably responsible for the farce of *The Fabulist*[36] abridged from Vanbrugh's *Aesop* which was presented on January 14 for the benefit of the Charity Schools. The performance raised £28.17.7.

What plays Wilkinson brought back from London we do not know but among those new to York this season were Colman's farce *The Oxonian in Town*; Bickerstaffe's comic opera *Love in the City* with music by himself and Charles Dibdin, in which Miss Leng made her first appearance speaking the epilogue; Whitehead's farce *A Trip to Scotland*; Cumberland's comedy *The Brothers*; Hoole's tragedy *Timanthes* with Powell in the title rôle, a procession and a scene of sacrifice for which an additional chorus was engaged; Garrick's *Jubilee* produced at Wilkinson's benefit; Hull's musical entertainment *The Spanish Lady*, and Garrick's *Cymon* on May 29, the last night, with a set of scenery painted by Williams from London and new dresses and decorations. This scenery 'for the last change in *Cymon*' cost no less than fifty guineas, 'heavy sum for a country Theatre'.[37] Williams, whom Wilkinson designates an excellent scene painter, had furnished the scenery for Dance's new theatre in Richmond Green. Wilkinson ordered from him £500 worth of scenery, 'which created good bills for canvas, colours, timber, &c.' At the same time he improved the wardrobe which he considered 'vulgar'.

Joseph Baker died on Easter Sunday, April 15, leaving everything, except for three legacies, one of which was £100 to Samuel Crisp, to Wilkinson and John Tasker, silk mercer, with the responsibility of paying his debts which amounted to £3000.[38] Wilkinson, whose own money had been sunk in the Theatre, evidently took it over as his share and since his credit was good, eventually came through his difficulties successfully. Among Baker's more immediate debts was a loss of £40 on the second season of oratorios given at the theatre during Passion Week. This year *Samson, Israel in Babylon* and *The Messiah* were chosen. The great male soprano Tenducci was engaged from the Opera House and was supported by Mrs. Hudson of York, Norris and Mathews. Places could be taken only for the boxes and the pit and for all the three nights at a cost of 7/6 a night. The charge for the first gallery was 5/-, for the upper gallery 2/6. The previous year there had been an inconvenient crush in the boxes and pit to remedy which the number of places in a row was reduced from 21 to 18.[39] The oratorios having lost money were not given again. It was from a party at Tenducci's lodgings that Wilkinson was hastily sent for to Baker's death-bed.

Mrs. Hudson who had sung in the oratorios, and Haxby, accompanied by a band of the principal performers in York, were called in to supplement the company's resources when Garrick's *Ode* upon dedicating the building and erecting the statue to Shakespeare at Stratford from the *Jubilee* with music by Arne was given.

Of Shakespeare's actual plays *The Merchant of Venice* is the only one which we know to have been repeated from the previous year. *King John* was presented with K. John = Wilkinson, Prince Arthur = Miss Willoughby, Hubert = Achurch, Bastard = Powell, Blanch = Mrs. Frodsham, Constance = Mrs. Ibbot. In *Henry IV* Powell played Hotspur for the first time to the Falstaff of Wilkinson, King Henry of Leng, Prince of Wales of Orde, and Lady Percy of Miss Willoughby. A note to the advertisement for *Othello* states that part of the first scene of Act V, where Othello appears on the balcony, would be revived 'by which, and some very little Alteration in the Performance of the following Scene, it is expected a Passage, which has hitherto appeared obscure, will be explained.' Since Cibber's days *Othello* had appeared on the stage in a version with large cuts,[40] which included Othello's appearance in the fight scene between Roderigo and Cassio. Wilkinson seems to have restored this passage earlier than the London theatres since Bell's acting version of 1773 and Wenman's of 1777 both omit it. It is a pity that we do not know of what the alteration in the last scene consisted. Wilkinson played Othello to the Iago of Achurch.

When Wilkinson moved on to Newcastle he found that he would not be able to renew the lease of the theatre there after that season; he therefore determined to replace it in the circuit by Leeds and forthwith purchased some ground and started building a theatre there.

Of the York race season in 1770 we know nothing. Wilkinson merely says that it was unremarkable: 'London Peers or their ladies had not at that time honoured our humble boards.' An interesting comment on the influence that an important patron could wield at that time is to be found in his reference to a gentleman of fortune named Cornelius Swan, who had had managerial experience at the Aungier Street Theatre in Dublin. He was,

Wilkinson says, 'at once a friend and an enemy. When his directions and teachings were obeyed, he was the prince of flatterers, and would eagerly stray from house to house to praise or abuse me, just as his mandates at the Theatre were adhered to or neglected.'[41]

Wilkinson continued to spend money on the embellishment of the theatre and when he reopened on January 5, 1771, it was 'with new Scenes and new Wings to change occasionally, new Cloaths, and the Boxes to be illuminated all round (both Inside and out) with Wax Candles: There will be *New Arms* over the Front of the Boxes, elegantly finished by Messrs. Fisher; and in order to make the House more warm the Stage is enclosed from the *Curtain to the Roof.*'[42] The new arms were the King's arms which the patent had given Wilkinson a right to use. The more expensive but less smelly wax candles replaced the tallow ones in part at any rate of the auditorium. Sylas Neville[43] who saw the playhouse on November 10, 1772 commented that it seemed 'a neat one by day-light & must look much better by candle-light.'

In order to meet expenses for the improvement Wilkinson raised the box prices from 2/6 to 3/-, which was the normal price at Bristol, Norwich, Edinburgh and Bath. He humbly hoped that his patrons would not be offended when they reflected on the considerable costs involved, and he further expressed his determination 'to render the Theatre-Royal at *York* worthy the public Encouragement, and to have it as *compleatly* finished as any in the three kingdoms, *London excepted.*' The box subscription was raised to £2.5.0. and the pit to £1.10.0. The theatre's patrons responded and the manager tells us 'I was high in public favour, and do not remember any season from that period to this when the theatre was so regularly and fashionably attended: There was a remarkable number of genteel families that year at York ... I do not recollect so numerous a resort of leading families since that year.'[44] It became the custom during Assize week for the High Sheriff and Grand Jury to bespeak a play. The Sheriff for 1771, Sir Griffith Boynton, bought £40 worth of tickets for his night and the following year Sir William St. Quintin spent £35 on tickets. Thereafter it was decided that this large expense was unnecessary, since the Sheriff's night was anyway always fashionably attended, and it was agreed that the Sheriff should in future send only five guineas to the manager for his ticket and have no more trouble or expense. Shaftoe who chose the Saturday before the Assizes for his benefit reaped a house of £71.

Dibble Davis from Covent Garden was a newcomer in the company. 'He was useful,' says Wilkinson,[45] 'and did not want merit on the stage; was the original Mr. Loader in *The Minor,* and played it very well'. With him he brought an actress who 'was handsome and sprightly' and who went by the name of Mrs. Davis though Wilkinson believed her real name to be Ogilvie. They only stayed one season, and later Davis, who led a wild life, lost all his looks and sank into premature old age. He played Portius in *Cato* and Orsino in *Twelfth Night* whilst Mrs. Davis undertook Viola and Charlotte in *The West Indian.* Another newcomer was Charles Wood a native of York, who made his first appearance as Lord Aimworth on January 22,[46] and his second as Cromwell in *Henry VIII*. As a boy he had been in the cathedral choir and later became a druggist's apprentice. His apprenticeship finished, he gave up his career and joined Whiteley's troupe. After a year with them he presented himself to Wilkinson, was tried out, and was 'so well received, that he was immediately engaged.' He stayed with the company until 1775 when he rejoined Whiteley but later he was again a member of the York troupe and remained so at intervals until his death. Wilkinson gives him an excellent character for honesty, fidelity, good nature, generosity and intense patriotism. He had musical talents but his memory was not good, though he always knew the other performers' parts and could prompt them without help of a book.

Another stage-struck native made several appearances on the York boards this season as an amateur. His name was Barker and he was well educated and heir to a good fortune. Hag-ridden for the stage he at last obtained his father's consent to appear locally and made his début at Powell's benefit, as Aribert in Rowe's *Royal Convert* on February 25. The receipts that night were £115.6.6. a sum seldom exceeded at common prices even when the theatre could hold more auditors.[47] Barker's friends received him with repeated plaudits and fulsome verses appeared eulogising him as combining Frodsham's form with Garrick's powers.[48] Shaftoe then induced him to appear for his benefit as Juba in *Cato*. Wilkinson says of him: 'His person and manner were pleasing: His voice was equally so; but not sufficiently powerful. Whenever he appeared he drew audiences, and was always favourably received.' In addition to his passion for the stage he conceived one for Miss Willoughby and in his love scenes with her in *The Royal Convert* was at his best. However the fires died out and Barker purchased a commission in a troop of horse, later to relinquish it in favour of the church.

Two of the great comedians of their day, Tom Weston and Henry Woodward, made starring visits in the spring. Both had been acting under Wilkinson's old master Foote in Edinburgh. Weston came first making his début as Scrub and Jerry Sneak, a part written for him by Foote, on April 4. On April 9 he played Sir Harry Sycamore in *The Maid of the Mill* and Jerry Blackacre in *The Plain Dealer*, and on April 20 for Raworth's benefit, he acted Abel Drugger and gave recitations.[49] Davies considered that he almost excelled Garrick as Abel Drugger, and Garrick himself declared it was one of the finest pieces of acting he had ever witnessed,[50] 'yet such was the partiality of the people of that city [York] to a low Comedian of the York company, that on a comparison of his playing Scrub with Weston's performance of that part, they said they could not perceive greater excellence in our hero, than Mr. Robertson.'[51] Henry Woodward, who gave Wilkinson a low opinion of Weston's private character, wrote to him concerning this benefit 'he must be meaner then [sic] I think him if he plays at York for *five guineas*; and especially after your absolute injunction to Raworth to assure Weston, that he will *deceive himself* if he thinks of

GETTING MORE. Let the transaction proceed upon that ground, and I think it will be for the advantage of *all parties*.'[52]

Henry Woodward himself followed. He had written to Wilkinson on March 26: 'You know my *forcible* characters as well as I do; – you know the taste of the public where you preside, and therefore make choice of plays and characters that seem most advantageous in your own judgment. I am told your catalogue of plays far exceeds any of our theatres royal, and if that be true, when we meet we shall not be at a loss to choose.' Woodward's first appearance was on April 17 as Marplot and The Citizen; his second as Bobadil and The Apprentice; his third as Captain Ironsides in *The Brothers*, and Buck in *The Englishman in Paris*; and his last, for his benefit, on April 27 as Ranger in *The Suspicious Husband*, Razor in *The Upholsterer* and the Fine Gentleman in *Lethe*.[53] The benefit was bespoken by Dr. Wallis, who was then Lord Mayor of York. He was 'justly admired' and indeed was the best Bobadil of this or perhaps any other day; it has been said that the part died with him. He had a good figure adapted rather to the rôles of fine gentlemen than the coxcombs, fops and scamps in which he excelled; 'but he was no sooner before the footlights than a ripple of funny emotion seemed to roll over his face; and this, with the tones of a capital stage voice, never failed to arouse a laughter which was inextinguishable.'[54]

For the first time York audiences saw two stars at the height of their fame. Wilkinson himself had been the first star on the York stage but we hear of no other such engagements until these two. At least eleven new pieces made their first bow in York this season. When Kelly's comedy *A Word to the Wise* was brought out on January 19 for Robertson's benefit a note was appended to the advertisement to say that it had not been permitted a hearing on the London stage because Kelly was supposed to be a party writer, but that the objection did not apply to York and that the piece had been received with applause in Hull where it had been allowed to be free from party tendentiousness. Though damned in London it was a success in York and was frequently revived. As it was only printed by subscription at 5/- a copy, it was not so universally known as it merited.[55] The afterpiece on this occasion was Moore's *Gil Blas*, with Robertson in the title rôle, which had been seen at Drury Lane twenty years previously. Bickerstaffe's comedy *'Tis Well It's No Worse*, Carey's interlude *Three Old Women Weather Wise*, Colman's *Portrait* with music by Arnold were among the lighter pieces. The new pantomime was *Harlequin Dr Faustus; or, Queen Mab's Frolic* with new music by Arnold and new machinery, habits and decorations. It was played by children: Master Rochford was the Harlequin, Miss Frodsham a Fairy and Miss S. Frodsham Queen Mab. The words of the trio could be had gratis from W. Powell the office keeper.[56] A new comedy by G. A. Stevens entitled *The True-Born Englishman; or The English Sailors in Falkland's Island* is otherwise unknown under this title but is probably his Bartholomew Fair droll *The French Flogged, or, British Sailors in America*. Cumberland was represented by his celebrated comedy *The West Indian* which was first presented at Wilkinson's benefit on April 13, with Wilkinson as Major

O'Flaherty, Powell as the West Indian, Mrs. Davis as Charlotte and Miss Willoughby as Louisa. Two new tragedies made their appearance, neither of which seems to have been accepted into the repertory; they were Mrs. Celisia's *Almida* taken from Voltaire's *Tancrède*, and Kelly's *Clementina* with Miss Willoughby in the title rôle and Barker as Granville. Lastly a new version of *Richard II*[57] was given with Richard = Wilkinson, Duke of York = Oram, John of Gaunt = Leng, Bolingbroke = Davis, Queen = Miss Willoughby. It was indeed an adventurous season for Shakespeare for, in addition to the stock plays of *As You Like It*, in which Wilkinson acted Jaques for the first time by desire of the High Sheriff on whose night it was given, and *Romeo and Juliet* with Barker as Romeo and Miss Willoughby as Juliet, *Twelfth Night* was revived after an absence of 30 years, the Dryden and Davenant operatic *Tempest* after 10 and an operatic version of *A Midsummer Night's Dream* was brought out at Wilkinson's benefit. *Twelfth Night*, rather curiously, never became one of the stock plays and its revivals were few and far between. The principal rôles were as follows: Orsino = Davis, Belch = Oram, Aguecheek = Robertson, Malvolio = Creswick, Clown = Shaftoe, Olivia = Miss Willoughby, Viola = Mrs. Davis, Maria = Mrs. Powell. In *The Tempest* which had more frequent revivals: Ferdinand = Creswick, Caliban = Orde, Prospero = Shaftoe, Ventoso = Robertson, Trinculo = Achurch, Miranda = Miss Willoughby, Hippolito = Mrs. Frodsham, Ariel = Mrs. Raworth. The operatic version of *A Midsummer Night's Dream*, performed as an afterpiece, was set to music by J. C. Smith, conductor of the oratorios in London and had several new and elegant scenes painted by Williams.[58] This may have been Garrick's adaptation *The Fairies*, given at Drury Lane in 1755, but more likely it was the later one brought out in 1763 by Colman entitled *A Fairy Tale*. Williams of Stonegate, who may have been the scene painter, drew and etched a portrait of Frodsham as Hamlet.[59]

Now that Wilkinson had exchanged Newcastle for Leeds as a summer circuit town, his proximity to York enabled him to accept Sir Griffith Boynton's invitation to open the theatre at the Summer Assizes. The visit in this and subsequent years caused Wilkinson a great deal of expense and it failed to be productive unless he engaged a star of Siddonian magnitude or unless it fell near enough to the Race Week to run one season into the other. In the first place the company had to be paid double salaries 'for', as Wilkinson says, 'if I move the company, for my emolument, out of their usual rout and where they are not to derive any advantages, but have to pull the oar in hot weather every evening, it is but reasonable to reward them with double salaries: if I did not, revolt might be the consequence'. Secondly, a star was usually engaged for that season, and lastly the expense of baggage waggons and carriages for so short a stay was heavy. The season opened on July 13 with *Love in a Village* in which Mrs. Hitchcock played Rosetta and Vincent Young Meadows. 'She was not then,' says Wilkinson[60] 'or since capital as a proficient in singing, but had a neat figure, was easy in carriage, and very lively.' Her husband Robert Hitchcock is known as the author of *The Historical View of the Irish Stage* and is praised by Wilkinson as a valuable friend and an honest man.[61] They came from Norwich and were on and off in the York company for many years, 'sometimes from interested motives, sometimes from caprice; sometimes in good humour; sometimes in bad; sometimes in hopes of meeting again, at another time vowing quite the contrary.'

Vincent had come from Edinburgh and Mr. and Mrs. King, who had acted in the company at Hull in 1769, had been re-engaged. King was a good actor of fops and his wife took the lead in capital rôles in tragedy and comedy. Hitchcock tells us that 'Nature had bestowed on her a tall, commanding, elegant figure, with a face capable of exhibiting every discrimination of the various passions of the drama; to these she added all the polished grace of action which a mind well informed could suggest. Her voice and manner were in a great measure accordant to her figure, strong and forcible, but devoid of those delicate touches of nature.' Tate says her voice was neither powerful nor musical but she had the great advantage of being 'always perfect, well dressed, and of good private behaviour.' She daily gained in public opinion and became one of the great favourites at York where she was esteemed equal to any actress on the stage. Her first appearance was on July 15 as Lady Townly, King's as Lord Foppington in *The Careless Husband* on July 18.[62]

But the great event of the week was the production of Dryden's masque *King Arthur* which was got up at an expense far exceeding any performance out of London for scenery, dresses, and decorations. The 'most splendid and good scenery, and all the changes as at Drury-Lane' were painted by Williams.[63] A hitch occurred at one point which may be related in the manager's own words: 'the change where the bridge and the enchanted tree break, instead of the sword of valour, wielded by its noble King, its magic lost its force, as the tree, in particular, entirely failed; which provoked one so highly, after all the pains taken, and the enormous expense, that two or three blundering carpenters should destroy the labour of a year – that thus perplexed I advanced forward, and requested the audience would honour me with a few minutes for preparation, and permit the act to begin again; this being granted, all that had been so fatally unhinged was hinged again, and to the agreeable surprise of the audience, and no less pleasing satisfaction of myself, not one blunder occurred, but all was smooth as the gentle waves where the Mermaids were lolling on the waters of tin and canvas to allure the love-sick Arthur.'

The company returned to York for a successful Race Week in mid-August even though no star supported it.[64] On August 30 Thomas Achurch, who had been with the company over 30 years, was found dead in bed in his lodgings at Leeds.[65] After seasons in their new theatres at Leeds and at Hull the company reopened at York on January 4, 1772 with *The Careless Husband* and *The Summer's Tale* which brought in £29.4.6. for the County Hospital. The subscription nights, on the advice of patrons, were reduced to 26, the charges being £1.19.0. for the boxes and £1.6.0. for the pit. As complaints had repeatedly been made of the interruptions caused by disorderly behaviour in the servants' gallery, Wilkinson made regulations to remedy the abuse as far as he could. No servants, henceforward, were to be admitted but those whose masters or mistresses were in the boxes; these had to apply to Powell for tickets without which there was no admittance to the gallery; any servant who made a disturbance would not be allowed in again.[66] Whether this had the desired effect of increasing the decorum we do not know, but it is evidence of the manager's sincere efforts to improve the behaviour in his theatre. He also set himself against late hours, considering that it was a disgrace to have servants out at a playhouse until past midnight as happened in many theatres. In order to avoid this he refused to have interludes between the acts thus keeping the programme to a reasonable length for the voracious appetites of these days.[67]

The company was now blessed with the presence of a comic genius for Master Dicky Suett aged 17 had joined them in Hull in November, where he had been well received. Previously he had sung at Marylebone Gardens and Ranelagh in 1769 and had been engaged by Foote the following May for juvenile rôles at the Haymarket. 'My pupil' Wilkinson calls him and indeed he was the first of a long series of famous players who trained in the York company. He was with them until 1780 by which time he had become of real importance to them. We only know of his first season that as Master Suett he sang *Soldier Tir'd of Wars Alarms* in the first act of *Timon* and played Bolgolam in Garrick's *Lilliput*. Wilkinson's kind heart dictated the engagement of 'the remains of an actress' known as Mrs. Bland, Hamilton or Sweeny after a succession of husbands. In her prime she had played as rival queen to Peg Woffington at Covent Garden but, since her dismissal from that theatre, had known penury, and was reduced to a minor strolling company where Wilkinson saw her. The York company was for her a haven of security. She appeared as Queen Elizabeth and Lady Brumpton but unhappily, whilst playing the latter rôle, her false teeth broke and she had to mumble her way through the remainder of the comedy. This lost her the indulgence of the audience who turned against her. Another generous manager Whitlock sent her another set, but, unfortunately, they did not fit. On Wilkinson's benefit night, when she was to play Mrs. Bridgemore in *The Fashionable Lover*, she found herself pursued by bailiffs; though corpulent, worn and tired she succeeded in eluding them by taking the staircase to Wilkinson's dwelling-house instead of that to the playhouse passage. 'Breathless, pale and full of tragedy horror' she entered his apartment and fell prostrate at his feet. He smuggled her into the theatre, secured the doors and had her safely conveyed to her lodgings where she was able to prove that the bailiff had no right to arrest her. This poor, unfortunate woman made her last appearance as Mrs. Heidelberg in *The Clandestine Marriage* on April 11 and departed from the city with an empty purse after a poorly attended benefit. After receiving help from her erstwhile comrades at Covent Garden, she ended her life on a pittance as wardrobe-keeper at Richmond, Surrey.[68] Her story shows the humanity of Wilkinson and the hardness of the audience when once displeased.

Young from Edinburgh made his first appearance in York on April 21 as Jaffeir and also played Young Meadows in *Love in a Village,* Macheath and Plume. He was of good education and family and started life as a painter but was won from that art to the stage. Wilkinson made use of his abilities and, when the speaking scenes from *The Jubilee* were given, Young contributed a transparent painting of the temple of Shakespeare with Roubiliac's statue in the garden of Garrick's house at Hampton.[69] From Edinburgh also came the child dancers Master and Miss West the offspring of one West of Drury Lane and pupils of Giuseppe Grimaldi, the great Joey's father. Wilkinson says 'They had merit and assiduity to recommend them to the audience, and continued with me some seasons. Master West was remarkable for making what we call a good bill, and has drawn extraordinary crowds of all denominations on his benefit nights.' In the course of time Miss West married Suett in York and retired from the stage.

Mrs. King, the company's tragedy queen, was growing restive under the flattery and applause which she was receiving.[70] Persons of distinction were saying that she would become one of London's leading actresses though she would be wise to stay a season or two longer at York in order to be ripe for a metropolitan appearance. Sir William Anderson and several other gentlemen waited on Tate at his house in York to thank him for what he had done for the theatre in the city, and offered to present Mrs. King with 50 guineas a year for three years and support her benefit every season if she would continue, as they thought advisable in her own interests as well as theirs, with the company. They further asked Wilkinson to grant her an extra benefit. He agreed to this, though he was paying the Kings his top salary and double for the three public Race Weeks, because he was anxious to keep such dependable players, and because Mrs. King was playing all the leads in comedy as well as tragedy. Contrary to his expectations the offer made her more discontented since she then complained that she was wasting her prime of life. She accepted the extra benefit but, hearing that the Barrys had left Dublin, for Drury Lane, she set her heart on replacing them. Tate gave up the struggle and, in his usual generous manner, negotiated an engagement for her when he went to Dublin for a few nights in the spring, and thither she and her husband departed in October.

Wilkinson must have spent a good deal on scenery and dresses this season. There were at least two new pantomimes, *The Elopement; or The Cheats of Harlequin* with new scenery, machinery and decorations, in which Colby played Harlequin for the first time and Mrs. Orde was Columbine, and *The Power of Love; or Harlequin in York,* in which every decoration was new and the scenery included views taken from different parts of York.[71] For a third pantomime, *The Miraculous Miller,* there was a view of a magical mill with the operation of grinding people who entered the hopper old and emerged young. All the characters were 'new dressed' for Garrick's *Lilliput*[72] in which the children of the company, the Misses Frodsham and S. Frodsham, Miss Hitchcock and Master William Powell had their chance; the principal characters were also newly costumed for *All for Love* in which King acted Mark Anthony, Wilkinson Ventidius and Mrs. Hitchcock Octavia for the first time, whilst the Cleopatra was the inevitable Mrs King; *Harlequin Salamander* had a newly painted scene and, when *Comus* was revived with alterations, the new palace scene from *Cymon* was used to render the performance as complete as possible. *Comus*, which had been performed at Covent Garden, may have been Colman's version;[73] in York Powell played Comus, Mrs. King the Lady, Mrs. Hitchcock the Pastoral Nymph and Mrs. Powell Euphrosyne. In addition to the pantomime already mentioned the new plays were Morgan's tragedy *Philoclea* taken from Sidney's *Arcadia*, in which once again the principals were newly dressed, Murphy's tragedy *The Grecian Daughter* with Wilkinson as Evander and Mrs. King as Euphrasia, Cumberland's comedy *The Fashionable Lover* with Wilkinson as Colin MacLeod and Mrs. King as Miss Aubrey and Cumberland's alteration of *Timon of Athens* in which Timon = Wilkinson, Apemantus = Oram, Alcibiades = King, Evanthe = Mrs. King. Other Shakespeare adaptations were Garrick's *Cymbeline* with King as Posthumous and Mrs. King as Imogen and Garrick's *Catharine and Petruchio* in which the Kings played the hero and heroine. When *Romeo and Juliet* was given a gentleman of the city played Romeo to the Juliet of Mrs. King. The custom of allowing amateurs to take leading rôles was an accepted one in London and the provinces; it could never have been satisfactory, even in days when there was no production of a piece as we know it and when every actor was a law unto himself; but the amateur often paid well for the privilege and in addition probably filled the house with his friends.

The theatre closed in mid-May and reopened for the summer Assize Week on July 30 with *Hamlet*. Wilkinson opened for the Race Week again on August 22, the Saturday previous to the races as many visitors arrived that day. He again put on *All for Love* which had been very well received and revived Garrick's *Country Girl* with Mrs. Saunders, late Miss Reynolds of Drury Lane, in the name part. Garrick had made the alterations for her and had tutored her himself. Unfortunately she was too fond of the bottle and went rapidly downhill though she stayed with the company until 1774. This was the last week of the Kings' engagement; Mrs King was replaced by Mrs M'George. She made little impression at first 'but by the help of a well-formed figure, in the prime of life, she by degrees got into very good esteem.' Though her features were good and her memory excellent she had been spoiled in Whiteley's company in which she had played the heroine for several years, and had become vain, obstinate and affected.[74] She first played in York in the 1773 season when she took such varied parts as Mrs. Sullen, Cleopatra in *All for Love* and Mandane in *Cyrus*. The Ordes for some unknown reason had changed their name to Eyles[75] under which cognomen they remained with the company until 1777.

In April Younger sent from Liverpool a young man who had applied to him for an engagement but for whom he had no vacancy, for a trial of his skill. His real name was Charles Murray[76] and he was the son of Sir John Murray, Bt. of Broughton who had been secretary to the Pretender in the

1745 rebellion. His father had been arraigned but pardoned, and Charles, after a classical education and a sojourn in France, was sent to study medicine and became a surgeon's mate at sea. But having performed with applause at a private theatre in Liverpool he determined to go on the stage. For family reasons he adopted the name of Raymur, a transposition of his own. At first it seemed as if there would be no part for him in the series of benefits then being held, but Gay wanted *The Fop's Fortune* for his on April 21 and had been unable to find a Carlos. It was a considerable part and difficult of study, but Raymur seized his chance, accepted it, performed it literally word perfect and was received as a good actor from that night on. Being quick and retentive he soon became a useful member of the company and in a few months was playing some leads both in plays and farces.[77] Another actor who appeared with the company this season was Fleetwood who met with a good reception on his début as Zaphna in *Mahomet* on May 1. He was the son of Charles Fleetwood, who had been patentee and manager of Drury Lane before Garrick and Lacy. For some years he had been an officer in the army where he dissipated a small fortune and so came to embrace the stage 'as a pleasing and certain resource'. He had acted at the Haymarket, Smock Alley in Dublin, Liverpool and for two years had played leading business in Edinburgh. He came to be much esteemed in York and Hull and had he lived might have become an excellent actor.[78] Wilkinson was in negotiation with Macklin about a visit at Whitsun. The manager had offended him by acting his farce *Love à la Mode* without permission but Macklin wrote[79] that he might be induced to come if Wilkinson would state a sum which he could insure his getting; at the same time he forbade him to act *Love à la Mode* before his arrival. To this Tate replied in forthright manner:[80]

> If y^r time for a few Days can be spar'd and be made Conducive to Health and Sitisfie [*sic*] y^r Curiosity the Jaunt may be taken this Whitsuntide, but if you mean to look at it in a Lucrative View the Project must Immediatly drop- Mr. Woodward can acquaint you with the Plan of this Theatre his Chance was better than y^{rs} because the Season of the Year was more in Favor, and York was in his *Road Home*; You on the Contrary have a Journey to come and go – After your Friendly Declaration it wou'd be Infamous in me to give an Idea of Profit equal to your Merit, The Town will be thin as to Company at that Season, but the Success of the Week must depend upon whether the Sportsmen of this county will support the Meeting for it is a New Affair entirely, the Houses may reach 30L, or 40L, or *More* or *less* I cannot even Guess.

> It will be supported by Charles Turner & Wentworth
> Esq. and several Gentlemen – Therefore can Only say the
> Sat. in that Week for y^r Benefit clear of any Charge, You
> Play 3 nights Tues., Wed. & Thur., and if the Sat. does *not*
> amount to any other it shall be made equal to the best
> Nights Reciept (*sic*) in the Week ... The House will hold
> 116L before the Curtain, but I say 30L because I am as
> much a Stranger to the Nature of the Week as you can be.

In a postscript Macklin is requested to name his plays and farces, 'that I
may be Prepar'd for y^r Reception at the Theatre and *at Home*'. But Macklin
never went.

At least eight new pieces were given during the winter season of 1773.
Two of them were by local dramatists. The more important, Mason's *Elfrida*,
was put on at full length for Wilkinson's benefit on March 27 and was
received with approbation. Mason's object was to reunite the form of Greek
tragedy, with its adherence to the unities and its chorus, with a modern
spirit 'in which the tender rather than the noble passions were pre-
dominant' and in which the characters were as private as would be con-
sonant with the dignity of tragedy.[81] Though poetically uninspired, and far
indeed from the nobility of its Greek model, whose sense of doom it
altogether lacks, it is not without dramatic merit. It had a local interest as it
was set at Harewood. One or two revivals were given in succeeding years
but it seems to have been rather a succès d'estime.

The other was Hitchcock's comedy *The Macaroni* which he brought out
for his benefit in March. It was the first piece to be licensed by the Lord
Chamberlain for the use of a Theatre Royal outside London since the
Licensing Act of 1737,[82] for it was unusual for provincial theatres to
produce dramatists of their own. The comedy met with success in the
provinces and was given at the Haymarket in September of that year. The
prologue was written and spoken by Creswick and the epilogue also spoken
by him was written by a friend. Creswick took the rôle of Epicene, the
Macaroni, to whom everything foreign was good. One plot deals with a joke
played on this coward, another with the villainous intrigue of Lord Promise
(Powell) to seduce the virtuous Maria (Mrs. Hitchcock), daughter of a
Yorkshire landowner. Though using many of the hackneyed situations and
types, the comedy has a certain liveliness, along with a fashionable serious
and moral strain. Other new pieces were Garrick's comedy *The Irish Widow*,
O'Brien's farce *Cross Purposes*, Garrick's *The Gamesters* altered from Shirley's
comedy of *The Gamester*, Mrs Griffith's comedy *A Wife in the Right*,
Bickerstaffe's 'comic serenata' *The Ephesian Matron* with music by Charles
Dibdin, which has been successfully revived in our own day, and last but not
least an expensive pantomime *Harlequin Fortunatus*. Concerning this last, it
is stated in the advertisement[83] that 'The expence exceeds anything of the
kind attempted here, as the plan alone, exclusive of the scenery, &c., has

been obtained at a very considerable charge, from the Theatre Royal, Drury Lane.' This plan of the scenery and tricks was sent to Wilkinson by the machinist Messink.[84] The overture was by Arne and there was a variety of new scenery, dresses, dances and other decorations. No half price was allowed. Luckily the pantomime pleased, otherwise Tate would have lost on it, as with a limited audience, pieces soon palled and could only be given a few nights each season. Tate thought it a better pantomime than its successor *Harlequin Sorcerer,* and it kept its place on the boards for over 20 years with a few alterations at every revival.

Wilkinson wished to present Garrick's alteration of *Hamlet* from which the Grave Diggers had been omitted, but, finding Garrick unwilling to oblige, set to and produced his own version. This he gives in *The Wandering Patentee.*[85] It makes a complete hash of the 5th Act, not only omitting the Grave Diggers but running the scene in which they should have appeared into the end one, which is entirely rewritten. The King and Hamlet fight, Hamlet kills the King while the Queen escapes shrieking. Then Laertes attacks Hamlet, Horatio rushes between them but Hamlet receives two wounds and falls into his arms. The curtain descends on the last words of a sorrow-struck Laertes, trumpets, a dead march and a tolling bell. It is a shocking farrago but luckily did not hold the stage. *Richard III* was revived after a two years' absence with Wilkinson as Richard, Powell as Richmond, the Misses Frodsham as the Princes and Mrs. M'George as Queen Elizabeth.

One or two points of interest may be added about the season. No play was given on Saturday, January 30, the anniversary of King Charles's martyrdom and the benefit due then was postponed until the Thursday.[86] When the Eyles's had their benefit the public was desired not to purchase box tickets 12-47 which had been dropped one night; to prevent imposition Eyles signed all the rest.[87] In addition to the two customary opening benefits, Wilkinson gave one on May 12 for the lunatic hospital at which Fleetwood played Sir George Airy in *The Busy Body.*[88] The season ended on May 19, but the company was back for a few days on June 8, again in July for the Assizes, and in August for the races. A Mr. and Mrs. Payne from Norwich had joined the company and remained with them until 1776. The stars for Race Week were Ned Shuter, one of the greatest of low comedians and Lee Lewes, a famous harlequin who played in all Woodward's parts at Covent Garden. Wilkinson had intended that Shuter should perform on his way back from Edinburgh, but some mistake in the time of his returning prevented his stopping in York.[89] Wilkinson then met him in London and prevailed on him to return with him. He opened on August 14 as The Miser 'which character he sustained with great comic humour; ... he pleased in the extreme, for he really was a rich comedian, though not so in pocket.' Other parts that the York audience saw him in were those of Don Choleric, Falstaff, Touchstone, Fribble (when he was drunk), Justice Woodcock, Don Manuel and Sir Francis Gripe.[90] Lee Lewes performed Clodio, Marplot and Harlequin.

Another visitor was Mrs. Weston or Wilson from Edinburgh 'who really threw excellent talents away, and died a martyr to her own folly.'[91] She played Lucy in *The Beggar's Opera* to Fleetwood's Macheath and Miss Notable in Cibber's *Lady's Last Stake*.

The Kings rejoined the company in October since Mrs. King had not succeeded as she had hoped in Dublin. But now she had a rival in the York Company in Mrs. M'George who had played most of the principal characters in her absence. The York public received their erstwhile favourite rather coldly after her desertion, especially as she did not come back to them in triumph. Between the rival queens 'therefore a natural spirit of resentment, jealousy, envy, disdain and even hatred – took root with every opportunity for discord.'[92] Wilkinson goes on to tell us of an amusing episode that occurred during the first night of Murphy's *Alzuma* in 1774. Mrs. M'George as Orazia had to enter some time before Mrs. King as Orellana and had twice prostrated herself at full length on the stage in tragic woe, a piece of business that always appealed to the gallery. Mrs. Hitchcock, who enjoyed a joke, came running to Mrs. King to tell her to make haste since Mrs. M'George had received great applause by her double fall; whereupon Mrs. King 'pulled up her train, and as fast as her pompous dress and paraphernalia would admit, got to the wing and rushed on the stage, where being arrived, she lost no time, but violently presented her full figure in the centre, to her own satisfaction, and that of the applauding gods, who saluted her with thunder', a counterblast to her enemy's success. On the male side Creswick and Fleetwood had both left the company.

During the spring season of 1774, there were two temporary engagements: Mons. and Madame Wanschor who were dancers, and the John Jacksons who came from Edinburgh to replace Wilkinson when he accepted an invitation to play for a few nights in Glasgow. The subscription was further reduced to 21 plays at £1.11.6. for the boxes and £1.1.0. for the pit. At least twelve new pieces were presented, the most important of these being *She Stoops to Conquer* which was first given for Robertson's benefit on January 12 with Tony Lumpkin = Wilkinson, Hardcastle = Robertson, Miss Neville = Mrs. Hitchcock, Miss Hardcastle = Mrs. King. It was followed by the first performance of G. A. Stevens's operatic farce *A Trip to Portsmouth*. Two other new musical pieces were Charles Dibdin's *The Deserter* and Garrick's *A Christmas Tale*. The scenery and machinery for this latter piece were prepared by Colby and included 'an elegant Transparent Scene' the first of its kind to be seen in York. The Songs and Choruses as performed in York consisting of 22 airs were printed and sold for 2d.[93] Though it was not usual to give the first night of such an expensive production for a benefit, Wilkinson made an exception 'in consideration of Mr. Colby's extraordinary trouble and assiduity in the Pantomimes' and brought out *A Christmas Tale* for his night.[94] Another piece for which elaborate preparations were made was the new pantomime of *Harlequin Sorcerer* which was produced during Spring Assize Week 'With a variety of New Scenery and Machinery, particularly two Scenes, being exact Representations of Mount Vesuvius. To conclude with a New Curtain Scene, painted by Mr. Dall (first Scene Painter at the Theatre Royal, Covent Garden)', and a new overture by Dibdin.[95] In employing Nicholas Dall, Wilkinson was enlisting the services of one of the leading scene painters of the day. He had, however, many connections with Yorkshire having been employed by the Duke of Bolton, Lord Harewood and others in the decorations of their houses.[96]

The opening night was patronised by the Assize judges and a note states: 'If the Judge comes in early, the play will begin at half past six; if otherwise to begin precisely at seven, to prevent the performance ending too late in the evening.' New comedies were Colman's *Man of Business,* Kelly's *School for Wives* and Cumberland's *Note of Hand* but there were no less than four new tragedies. We have already noted Murphy's *Alzuma* which included one of the favourite processions, this time of virgins to the Temple of the Sun; it was followed by Alexander Dow's *Sethona,* Hull's *Henry II* and *Eldred* by John Jackson who was, as we have seen, a temporary member of the company. This last had already been given at Dublin and Edinburgh but its performances in London did not take place until 1775. When *Henry II* was performed half price to the upper gallery was not taken until after Act IV so as not to interfere with half price to the other parts of the house after Act III. Half price to the upper gallery was not taken at all during Race Week.

All these new plays must have meant heavy work for the company which already had a large repertoire; indeed Wilkinson claims that he played a greater variety than any other theatre, as plays would not bear so many repetitions in York as they did in Bath, Norwich and other towns.[97] Among interesting revivals this year were *The Way of the World,* after an absence of eight years, with Mrs. King as Millamant and Payne as Mirabel, and Barry's alteration of *The Rival Queens* in which Mrs. M'George played Roxana for the first time.[98] Shakespeare was being a little crowded out and we only hear of *As You Like It* in which Mrs. King played Rosalind for the first time; *Cymbeline* with Wilkinson as Posthumous, Raymur as Iachimo and Mrs. Collins as the Queen; and *Hamlet* with the Jacksons as Hamlet and Ophelia and Mrs. M'George as the Queen.

John Moody from Drury Lane was the Assize Week star. He was the best stage Irishman of his day, and played his most famous part, that of Major O'Flaherty in *The West Indian,* at York. He also played another stage Irishman Teague, as well as Colin MacLeod in *The Fashionable Lover,* O'Clabber, Henry VIII and Ironsides.[99] Dodd and Mrs. Bulkley, who happened to be in York, starred as the Citizen and Maria for Moody's benefit. Moody and Dodd had a violent row but calmed down later. That autumn Wilkinson exchanged Beverley for Wakefield where he subsequently built a theatre.

When he reopened at York in January 1775, there had been several changes in the company. Mrs. M'George had deserted leaving Mrs. King in undisturbed possession of the female leads, Fleetwood had returned. A Miss Waudby of Hull, whom Wilkinson characterises as a pretty young woman who wanted power and talents for the stage and whose beauty captivated the prompter,[100] was a new acquisition. Mr. and Mrs. Cornelys from Norwich and Dublin were with the company for one season. They both possessed much merit, Cornelys in low comedy characters, such as Abel Drugger, and Peter in *Romeo and Juliet*; Mrs. Cornelys in Lydia Languish, Hypolita in *She Wou'd and She Wou'd Not* and as the tragic Andromache in *The Distress'd Mother*. Another new leading lady was Mrs. Woods from Edinburgh who first appeared as Belinda in *All in the Wrong* on January 7, the opening night. Wilkinson had seen William Woods[101] in Glasgow and engaged him; he was a 'gentleman of talents as an actor, and respected by everybody as a man of honour and strict integrity off the stage, also of good education and a poet.' Though an Englishman by birth, he pined for Scotland and only stayed with Wilkinson a year before returning to Edinburgh where he remained until his retirement in 1802. He played a wide range of leads in tragedy and comedy during the season such as Lord Hardy in *The Funeral*, King Arthur, Sir Callaghan O'Brallaghan, Mirabel, Achmet in *Barbarossa* and Pyrrhus in *The Distress'd Mother*.

In May[102] there were several changes as Mr. and Mrs. King, Thomas Powell[103] and Charles Wood left at the end of the season, Powell and Mrs. King taking their farewell on May 20th as Mark Anthony and Cleopatra in *All for Love*. Miss Waudby was offended at being asked to play one of the ladies of pleasure in *The Beggar's Opera* – always a bone of contention. She married the prompter Flower who retired to take up his clerical career. Mrs. King accepted an offer from Garrick and appeared at Drury Lane as Rosalind in the autumn but was not retained after the end of the season there. Her place in York was supplied by Mrs. Hudson from Exeter, who possessed a handsome face but had not a very good figure. She played Jane Shore and Maria in *The Busy Body*, was not greatly approved of at first, but, as she was persevering and perfect in her parts, grew into a good favourite in the circuit. On the male side, her husband made his first appearance as Aimwell in *The Stratagem* and Owenson and Death were also engaged. Owenson was Irish and played Irishmen well, eventually succeeding Moody at Drury Lane; he was tall and handsome and useful in the operas; he played Macheath, Tom Tug in *The Waterman*, Sir John Loverule and Sir Lucius O'Trigger. Thomas Death, whose cast was 'the Smarts and Footmen', came from Edinburgh and played Scrub and Marplot. His flattering reception induced him to stay two seasons after which he went to Covent Garden. He returned to play with the company for a short while in 1780. He bore some resemblance to Garrick, was of cheerful aspect, mild manners and convivial temperament.[104] After two years in the company Suett had attained adult status and was allocated quite good parts, supporting a few leads in comedy whilst filling in, as so many comedians in country companies had to do, with minor rôles in tragedy.[105]

Wilkinson extended his engagements this year at an expense exceeding that of any season in the hopes of rendering the Theatre a fashionable entertainment.[106] During the winter season there were twenty-three actors and the prompter, thirteen actresses and three children taking part in the performances. The previous year we have the names of only 15 regular actors, 8 actresses and 2 children. The company opened on January 7 with the customary benefit for the County Hospital which brought a profit of £29.5.8. Among the new pieces presented were two by local authors. Hitchcock followed up his *Macaroni* with another comedy *The Ladies' Stratagem* which was brought out at his benefit on March 3 but was never published. The prologue was spoken by Powell. Then on April 22 at Raymur's benefit George Wallis's *Mercantile Lovers* was given with a prologue spoken by Raymur and an epilogue spoken by Powell. This satirical comedy was specially written by Wallis to serve his friend Raymur who played Sarcasm. Even before it appeared there were rumours that the satire had a personal application, and, when it was printed, the scenes that were condemned as offensive were altered. As it stands it is a poor and uninteresting comedy which makes it hard to believe that its production lost the author his professional practice as a doctor,[107] and forced him to quit York.

The most important new play was, however, *The Rivals*, first acted on the York boards on April 8 for the benefit of Mr. and Mrs. Cornelys with the following cast: Capt. Absolute = Powell, Faulkner = Raymur, Acres = Cornelys, Sir Anthony Absolute = Eyles, Julia = Mrs. Hitchcock, Mrs. Malaprop = Mrs. Collins, Lydia Languish = Mrs. Cornelys.[108] York thus saw Sheridan's immortal first comedy only three months after its appearance at Covent Garden. More ephemeral comedies were Murphy's *No One's Enemy But His Own,* Cumberland's *The Choleric Man,* and Kelly's *Romance of an Hour*; new comic or ballad operas were Burgoyne's *Maid of the Oaks* 'with new dresses, scenery, illuminations, and decorations', Bate's *Rival Candidates* and Dibdin's long popular *Waterman.* The new pantomime was entitled *The Revels, or Harlequin's Jacket* in which Colby was the Harlequin. Two new tragedies were Francklin's *Mathilda* and Hull's alteration of Thomson's *Edward and Eleonora.* Among the revivals was a version of *Love for Love* altered by Digges, who claimed that he had cleared the comedy of indelicacy so that 'there is not a single word at which the nicest Ear can possibly take Offence.' Wilkinson had seen this alteration in Scotland and brought it out in York with the following cast: Ben = Wilkinson, Valentine = Powell, Mrs. Frail = Mrs. Cornelys, Mrs. Foresight = Mrs. Collins, Miss Prue = Mrs. Hitchcock, Angelica = Mrs. Woods, Foresight = Robertson. For *A Christmas Tale* the new scenery is particularised as 'the Seraglio, Nigromant's Palace, the Clouds descending, and a New Moonlight Scene'; also included were a dance of the furies by West and a procession of good and evil Spirits, attended by Tycho on a Rhinoceros.[109]

Two or three years previously[110] Wilkinson had got into trouble with Macklin for acting his *Love à la Mode* without permission with the result that the author had then refused permission to have his farce acted on any occasion whatever. This year he must have relented for it was given for one night by the author's permission, which, however, was accompanied by a peremptory prohibition of any further performance in York.[111] Wilkinson was again in communication with Macklin in July about coming to York for Race Week.[112] He frankly told the star that he could give him no certainty of applause or even of being followed with attention. He offered him £50 for five nights or the whole should the Saturday before the races or the Monday following them bring in more than £50. He assured Macklin that 'niether Myself, nor any other Person material on the Spot ever take a Benefit but on a Sat. Mr. Woodward had a Sat. it is the same at Bath & Edin^r. Sat in general the best Night'. As for plays he considered one tragedy, possibly *Macbeth* which Macklin had been the first to dress in Scottish costume, sufficient for Race Week and suggested *Richard* or *Othello* or *The Refusal* for the Monday. Wilkinson proposed that he should come early the previous week 'As the Troops will be Unemploy'd from Sat 5th of Aug^t, till Sat the 12th therefore may be Prepar'd for Bussiness and Drill'd as you wou'd wish to Dispose them, They are Us'd to Service as they have not One Holliday Passion Week excepted during the Year, Which Week we are *not* to doubt but is Properly Employed – As I only send from here [Leeds] such part of the Wardrobe as I want for Par^r. Plays, Cannot appoint these plays till I have y^r. *Positive Determination.*' Evidently the determination was in the negative for Macklin never came.

Shakespeare was well represented with seven plays. *King John* with Fleetwood as the Bastard and Mrs. King as Constance; *Henry VIII* with Wilkinson as Wolsey, Powell as Buckingham, Wood as Cromwell and Mrs. King as Queen Katharine; *Hamlet* with the gravediggers back and Woods as Hamlet, Mrs Hitchcock as Ophelia; *Romeo and Juliet* with Powell and Mrs. King in the title rôles; *King Lear* with Wilkinson as Lear, Powell as Edgar and Mrs. King as Cordelia; *As You Like It* with Wilkinson and Robertson in their old parts of Jaques and Touchstone and Powell as Orlando; lastly *The Winter's Tale* after 14 years in Garrick's version with Powell as Florizel, Mrs. Hitchcock as Perdita and Mrs. King as Hermione. The summer season ran from July 31 to August 23. The star was William Lewes from Covent Garden, a genteel comedian, graceful, airy, energetic, of whom Leigh Hunt said that 'he played on the top of his profession like a plume.' His first appearance was on August 12 as Ranger; he also played the West Indian, the part in which he had made his name, the Apprentice, Lord Duke in *High Life Below Stairs*, Archer in *The Beaux' Stratagem*, Gratiano, Hamlet, Lord Townly, Beverley in *All in the Wrong*, the Lyar, and Romeo. York did not see him as Mercutio or the Copper Captain, his greatest parts, but received him well. Mrs. Lewes played Portia and Lady Townly under the guise of a gentlewoman.[113] *She Stoops to Conquer* was put on for the Sheriff and Grand Jury's night, Death now playing Tony Lumpkin and Mrs. Hudson, Miss Hardcastle.

This autumn Wilkinson obtained the lease of a new theatre being built by the Corporation at Doncaster, which was now added to the circuit. At Wakefield Wilkinson took on Mrs. Montague[114] thus creating another rival queens' situation between her and Mrs. Hudson. Mrs. Montague was a wild and uncontrollable spirit, though after her outbursts she was for a time contrite and good-humoured. Wilkinson found that she gave promise of genius: 'Her person was good; she wore the small clothes with a grace; her powers and voice were uncommonly excellent; her dialect very erroneous and her ear not very exact, nor her mind equal to the patience of much teaching.' She was so well received in Hull and York that Wilkinson feared that a London manager would claw her from him, but she stayed with the company two years and returned to it again later. Whilst Wilkinson was in Hull he was pressed by two or three of the proprietors of the theatres for their money and in annoyance he advertised all his theatres for sale in the London papers;[115] but owing to the beginning of the American war there were no adequate offers. Wilkinson then obtained thirty subscribers who put up 100 guineas each in return for which they obtained interest, as well as a transferable ticket of admission to all the theatres in the circuit. They thus became part proprietors of the theatres, Wilkinson retaining his right to sell his share of the property, a point on which negotiations with a previous set of subscribers had failed. Wilkinson considered that he was to have a free hand as manager but, as we shall see, the proprietors thought otherwise and the agreement broke down after two years. In the meantime everything seemed plain sailing and one Buck was appointed as treasurer for both parties.[116]

Under this new regime the York theatre opened on January 4, 1776. An announcement in the *York Courant* of January 2 requested the Gentlemen Proprietors 'to pay their respective Sums to Mr. Wilkinson, at his House, on Monday or Tuesday, January 8 and 9 or on Wednesday, January 10 at the York Tavern – where their Company is requested at Six o'clock in the Evening, there finally to settle all Agreements. – Those Gentlemen who either from Distance of Situation or Business, cannot attend, are requested to depute. There are seven Shares in the Theatre still to be disposed of, as at present there are only 23 Subscribers to Mr. Wilkinson's Proposal for Property in the said Theatre.

The Theatre is newly painted, and the Boxes new hung, &c., &c. The Boxes are hung at Mr. Wilkinson's Expence.'

The subscription was again for 21 plays and a subscription during the Assize Week was promised when the proprietors would also be admitted.

There was a tightening up in the payment of bills, tradesmen being promised that if they were sent in at the beginning of the season they would be discharged as soon as possible. On the playbill for January 16, bills were desired to be sent in in future on the Friday of each week to be regularly discharged the following day when the actors too were paid. The *York Courant* of the same date announced that 'The new Regulation of the Boxes, with their proper Divisions and Distinctions, will commence on Mr.

Robertson's night'; what these were we have now no means of knowing, but obviously Wilkinson was doing his best to improve the organisation of the theatre in various ways.

In January Mary Davies from Bath was recommended by Yates and Mr. Maude of York to Tate Wilkinson. She was accompanied by her mother. 'On our arrival', she says, 'we were both much disappointed to find that a Miss Frodgham [sic] daughter of a favourite actor of that place, had been already engaged. But, from the respectability of our introductions, the manager engaged me for three nights, and allowed me on the third to send in tickets, which turned out much to our advantage ... Here, I first learned dancing, from Miss West, afterwards Mrs. Suet, who kindly taught me gratuitously: she was then the principal dancer in the theatre, and taught in the city.' She opened in the rôle of Cupid in *A Trip to Scotland* on January 11 and subsequently played Miss Biddy in *Miss in her Teens* and Cherry in the *Stratagem*. She was then only 14 but in the fullness of time was to become famous for her imitations as Mrs. Wells.[117]

Mrs. Montague made her first appearance as Margaret of Anjou in the *Earl of Warwick* on January 13; it was the part in which she had tried out and created so deep an impression at Wakefield.

In February Fleetwood suddenly fell into a decline and as little hopes were entertained of his recovery, Wilkinson engaged Beynon whom he had seen in Glasgow. He was of great service in the emergency although he had too high an opinion of himself. It was announced on February 20 that Fleetwood had recovered but the playbill for March 7 states that he had fallen from his horse and that this necessitated a postponement of *The Distressed Mother* with new dresses: 'The Audience having already this Season, more than once, shown their Indulgence by admitting the Reading of Parts, Changing of Plays, &c., in order to avoid more Repetitions of the kind, the Theatre will not be opened this Evening, nor will till *Saturday* next.' Eventually Owenson took Fleetwood's rôle of Pyrrhus whilst Beynon played Orestes. Poor Fleetwood made one last appearance for his benefit on March 23 playing Drummond in Mrs. Cowley's new comedy *The Runaway*; he died in Leeds.

During April Thomas Powell and Charles Wood returned to play for a few weeks during the vacation at Manchester. For Powell's benefit on May 13 *Edward the Black Prince* was revived and Younger, his co-manager at Manchester, offered his services to play Ribemont. He was a Falstaffian figure and as the warrior Ribemont lay dying, the audience was shaken with laughter at the sight of a mountain of flesh, behind which the head was completely lost to view; indeed every attempt to finish the play proved abortive though 'the curtain never dropped with more applause.'[118] Mrs. Montague had been difficult at the beginning of the evening and would have withdrawn from her part of Princess Mariana had not prudence dictated to her not to offend Younger. The trouble had arisen at Earby's benefit[119] on May 7; Earby, who was the new prompter, in the hurry of business, unintentionally gave orders too soon for changing the scenery and so cut out a scene in *The Rivals* in which Mrs. Montague and others were to play. She only mentioned the matter after the scenery had been changed and the next scene was proceeding when it would have made confusion worse confounded to have done anything about it. The company entreated her to take no notice but their request only added fuel to the flames and she refused to go on. The enraged audience called for Wilkinson and insisted on Mrs. Montague's making an apology but she took her chair home consigning audience, manager and players to the devil. Earby published a statement giving the facts of the case. The thwarted audience determined to show its power and authority and when the curtain rose at Powell's benefit shouted for an apology from the tragedy queen. The curtain had to be let down again and in Wilkinson's words, 'I led the princess on the stage, taking fast hold of her trembling lily white hand, and her white hand-kerchief, displayed with dignity as a flag of truce; but with all the courtesies, weeping and bowing, it was for some time a scene of confusion:– "Off, off!" "Go on!" "Pardon, pardon," &c. At length silence was obtained, she confessed her errors, sued for a pardon, and obtained it, was well received in the play and I do not believe she contradicted me, or called me *the devil* for a month.' Such riotous scenes in the theatre were not unusual; for the Georgian audience took a violent and passionate interest in stage affairs.

Shortly after Wilkinson had to cope with more jealous outbreaks, this time on the part of Mrs. Hitchcock. It so happened that Mrs Thomson,[120] a singer from Covent Garden, had been engaged and made her first appearance at Wilkinson's benefit as Diana in the pantomime of *The Genii* in which she had gained great applause in a song. With her came her niece Miss Poitier who 'had an elegant form, an enchanting pipe, and was truly, a charming singer.' She acted Leonora, Venus in *The Golden Pippin* and the Maid of the Mill to excellent houses. They were only engaged for a short stay as they were due to perform at Manchester at Whitsun. Mrs. Hitchcock was to leave for Bath at the end of May but even so she could not brook a rival in her singing parts and flew into a passion with the poor manager for having engaged Miss Poitier. She accused him of inflicting cruel injuries on her, told him he had no merit as an actor and swore she would never act under him at York again. However he seems to have taken the outburst philosophically and the fury's threats 'only served to make us more cordial at our after meetings.'

Owenson[121] was the next on Wilkinson's list of troubles. He was to leave in June for Dublin at the expiration of his articles. The opera *Artaxerxes* was revived for Mrs. Thomson's benefit and Wilkinson allotted the title rôle to Wood when Owenson expected it. The offended actor even challenged the manager to a duel for which Wood provided powder and ball and charged the pistols. Owenson cooled down, however, and the only sequel was that two years later, pistols being called for in a hurry for *The Beggar's Opera*, these were brought out and Wilkinson had a few bad moments when he remembered that they were loaded.

Two new tragedies came out – Jephson's *Braganza* and Hiffernan's *Heroine of the Cave*; the latter included 'The Triumphal Entry of Alberti and Constantia, with a Procession and Chorus of Virgins. The Music entirely new, composed for the Occasion.' Hitchcock produced a third comedy *The Coquette* which was brought out at York at the Hitchcocks' benefit on February 10. It was later published by subscription, among the subscribers being many present and former members of the company. The subject from Mrs. Hayward's novel *Betsy Thoughtless* had been suggested to Hitchcock by Wilkinson, who, however, did not consider the result as entertaining as it could have been.[122] Other new comedies were Mrs. Cowley's *Runaway* and Charlotte Lennox's *Old City Manners* in which the highlight was a ballet by 25 children of the city 'all in new Dresses for that Purpose'. Other light pieces were O'Hara's burlettas *The Two Misers* and *The Golden Pippin*, the latter being the first musical entertainment to be performed at York with recitatives and accompaniment; Garrick's *Bon Ton* and musical prelude *The Theatrical Candidates*, and a farce *The Alarm*, attributed in the playbill to Goldsmith. The new pantomime was *The Genii*, an Arabian Night's entertainment in two parts from Drury Lane. When this had been given at Hull, the painter had not had time to finish the palace scene and wings. The leading dancing master of the town recommended a young man named Julius who was a sign-writer and who did well for a first attempt in a very short time. As a result of this experience he got tired of his humdrum existence and went to London, where, after a struggle, he made his way and obtained prizes at the Royal Academy. His grand palace along with a new bacchanalian grove concluded the entertainment which cost Wilkinson nearly double any other pantomime performed in York.[123] *The Genii* was repeated several times during the season, always at full price.

At Wilkinson's benefit his own version of *The Duenna* was performed under the title of *The Mistakes; or The Double Discovery*.[124] Harris of Covent Garden refused to allow Wilkinson the use of Sheridan's comic opera and so, as he had seen it several times, he wrote his own version from memory, the published book of songs, reports in magazines plus the help of a collection of old Spanish plays. The hotch potch came to be known as Wilkinson's *Duenna*, and it was such a success that Harris used to tell applicants for a copy of the original piece that they could play Wilkinson's.

Nine of Shakespeare's plays were given. *Cymbeline* opened the season with Fleetwood as Posthumous, Raymur as Iachimo, Mrs. Hudson as Imogen and Suett in the minor part of Cadwall. *Measure for Measure*, never a popular play, was revived after twelve years with the following cast: Duke = Wilkinson, Angelo = Leng, Barnardine = Suett, Clown = Robertson, Claudio = Raymur, Isabella = Mrs Hudson. *Richard III*, after an absence of three years, was given two performances Wilkinson playing Richard, Raymur Buckingham, Owenson Richmond, Mrs. Hitchcock Lady Anne and Mrs. Hudson Queen Elizabeth. Another revival was *Much Ado* which had not been seen for 5 years with Wilkinson as Benedick and Mrs

Hudson for the first time as Beatrice. Mrs Hudson also played Portia in *The Merchant of Venice,* and Queen Katharine in *Henry VIII,* her husband taking Cromwell. In *Henry IV* Wilkinson played Hotspur, Eyles the Prince of Wales and Leng Falstaff. Raymur undertook Romeo for the first time. *All's Well* was revived for the last subscription night with Parolles = Death, Clown = Robertson, Bertram = Raymur, Countess of Rousillon = Mrs Collins, Helena = Mrs Gray who acted one or two rôles this season, Diana = Mrs. Hitchcock. The theatre had a famous visitor on May 18 in James Boswell, who saw Robertson play and afterwards sat with him at a coffee house; Boswell found him a modest man, with little knowledge or vivacity in conversation.[125]

When the company returned in August for the Race Week Mr. and Mrs, Miell[126] had joined it from Norwich. She was a singer with a powerful voice and a bad temper; he was an actor of 'good understanding, education and observation' who later became manager of the Worcester circuit. She played Leonora in *The Padlock* and Nell in *The Devil To Pay* whilst her husband was cast for Edward in *Edward and Eleonora* and Jessamy in *Lionel and Clarissa.*

The stars were Mr. and Mrs. Mattocks[127] from Covent Garden. Mrs Mattocks excelled in a broad comedy line and was at her best in abigails, citizens' wives and vulgar women. She opened on August 17 as Charlotte in *The Hypocrite* and *The Musical Lady,* and subsequently played Polly, Maria in *The Citizen,* Rosalind, the Grecian Daughter, Clarissa and Eleonora. Her husband, who was a good singer, took Macheath, Amiens and Lionel. Owing to the expense of engaging these performers at a capital sum, Wilkinson raised the prices of the boxes sixpence during the Race Week, carefully pointing out that, whereas this brought the box price to 3/6, at Bath and other places, the normal charge was 4/-.

Tate Wilkinson's account books for this and the two succeeding years have been preserved[128] and are of great interest. They record the net profits clear of all deductions and expenses of every night in the season throughout the circuit. Total net receipts for the year 1776 were:

19 weeks York	£2033	11	3
9 weeks Leeds	619	2	0
4 weeks Halifax	187	19	6
1 week Leeds 2nd Season	72	8	6
10 days York (Race Week)	550	0	0
2 weeks Wakefield	349	14	6
3 weeks Doncaster	445	12	9
13 weeks Hull	1181	15	6
	5440	4	0

It will be seen by this that York was the most important and remunerative town in the circuit, Hull being second. The subscription for the winter season at York brought in £250.8.6. The following nights brought in the most money:

1) Wilkinson's benefit	*Mistakes, Genii.*	£88 17 6	
2) High Sheriff's night	*Suspicious Husband*		
	Love à la Mode	73 13 0	
3) Oram's benefit, desire Masons	*Refusal*		
	Alarm	70 0 6	
4) Robertson's benefit	*Maid of the Oaks*		
	Revels	61 10 0	
5) West's benefit	*Old City Manners*		
	Tobacconist	60 17 6	
6) Buck's benefit, desire Mrs. Earle	*West Indian*		
	Bon Ton	59 10 6	
7) Assize Week Thursday	*Provok'd Husband*		
	Genii	57 15 3	
8) Mrs. Montague's benefit	*Zara, Irish Widow*	54 15 6	
9) Fleetwood's benefit	*Runaway*		
	Marriage à la Mode	54 11 0	
10) Suett's benefit	*Love in a Village*		
	Apprentice	54 1 0	
11) Hudsons' benefit	*Heroine of the Cave*		
	Bon Ton	51 13 0	
12) Hitchcocks' benefit	*Coquette, Roger and Patie*	50 16 0	
13) Miss Poitier's benefit	*Maid of the Mill, Midas*	50 7 6	

These figures are an indication of the popularity of the actors rather than of the plays. The importance of bespeaks is evident: Oram, for example, though a small part actor, always did well as he had the support of the Masons. In addition to the big amount brought in by the Sheriff's patronage, there was the 5 guineas that he himself gave for his box as arranged.

The poorest nights were the following:

1) 12th subscription	*Hypocrite, Man of Quality*	£3 14 6	
2) 8th ,,	*She Stoops to Conquer, Devil to Pay*	4 0 0	
3) 14th ,,	*Miser, Mayor of Garratt*	5 6 6	
4) 16th ,,	*Mahomet, Two Misers*	5 12 6	
5) 11th ,,	*Love Makes a Man, Commissary*	6 16 0	
6) 7th ,,	*Countess of Salisbury, Revels*	6 16 6	

It must, however, be remembered that the subscription tickets on these nights are not included. The Shakespeare play that brought in the greatest receipts was *Much Ado* at which £44.13.3. was taken, but then it was given on Assize Tuesday and at augmented prices. The same applies to *Romeo and*

Juliet given on Assize Friday which brought £32.16.0. and *Richard III,* Assize Wednesday, £28.6.9. *Cymbeline* for the benefit of the Hospital took £29.14.0. *The Merchant of Venice* was the least successful of Shakespeare's pieces bringing only £7.10.6. at the 10th subscription.

The Race Week receipts at augmented prices show a considerable average increase over those of the winter season. That week York was packed with visitors and their presence is reflected in the following figures:

Mon. Aug. 19	*Beggar's Opera* with the Mattocks.	£73	8 0
Tues. ,, 20	*As You Like It* ,, ,, ,,	70	18 6
Wed. ,, 21	*Runaway, Mayor of Garratt*	46	12 0
Th. ,, 22	*Brothers, Bon Ton*	87	17 0
Fri. ,, 23	*Grecian Daughter, Devil to Pay*		
	with Mrs. Mattocks	106	8 0
Sat. ,, 24	*Lionel and Clarissa, Genii*		
	with the Mattocks	87	3 0

After the Race Week Wilkinson opened his new theatre at Doncaster and another at Wakefield. A riot against Raymur at the latter lost him that actor's services,[129] though he played at least twice again in York in 1777 as Faulkland, and as Laertes for his benefit by the desire of Mrs. Hudson.

Robertson, 'the Yorkshire Edwin', was growing old and handed over a number of his characters to Suett, who was rapidly improving and gaining public favour.

Of the newcomers at the beginning of the season of 1777, the most important was Alexander Cummins who was to spend the rest of his career as the company's tragedian. Wilkinson says of him that he had 'an excellent and powerful voice, an expressive, handsome, manly countenance, with a good person, retentive memory, and great stage merit.'[130] Bernard[131] calls him 'that northern star of the dramatic hemisphere' who long maintained in the opinion of the York audiences a pre-eminence over his tragic contemporaries. At the time of his début with the company, Bernard tells us 'he was an actor – of marked originality in characters like Hotspur, Alexander and Chamont and possessed a genius for the bold, the rugged, and romantic, which one would have thought had been inhaled from the woods and rocks he had been born and bred among.' His voice was his great natural asset: 'this was indeed "a most miraculous organ". Barry's had more sweetness and flexibility, but Cummins's the greater compass and strength.' His power seduced him into a ranting habit, which, however, the public liked, so that Kemble was once outspokenly told by the gallery that he 'cud na shoot oot laik Coomins.'[132] As a man, he was a good husband, father and friend, strict in his payments, attached to Wilkinson's interests, popular with everyone. He made his bow in York on January 14, 1777 as Pierre to the Belvidera of Mrs. Montague and the Jaffeir of Miell. During the season he played Chamont in *The Orphan*, Alexander in *The Rival*

Queens, Anthony in *All for Love*, Iago, Edmund, Hamlet, Prospero, Selim in *Edward and Eleonora* and Caractacus. Wilkinson has particular commendation for his Lord Davenant: 'his pronouncing "I hope so too", is truly meritorious, and would not disgrace the first actor on any stage.' Mrs Cummins was a personable actress, a prudent and sensible woman and a good wife and mother.

Another newcomer, Wheeler, who was both actor and singer, only stayed a season with the company and then went on to be manager at Portsmouth.

Miss Simpson,[133] daughter of Simpson of Drury Lane, made a first appearance as The Comic Muse in *The Rival Candidates*. She too only stayed a season and though she showed promise, it was never fulfilled and she sank into obscurity.

Later on a Miss Holmes[134] was sent by Mrs. Hull to make trial of her talents. She was about 18 and made her début as Miss Aubrey with the epilogue in *The Fashionable Lover*. Though she, too, proved promising, she might have been still better. She stayed two years with the company but returned later to triumph as Mrs. Kennedy. A third actress, Miss Glassington, was also given a trial and appeared as Jane Shore and Juliet but was overshadowed by the visit of Mrs. Siddons. Mrs. (formerly Miss) Phillips returned after eight years as Mrs Malaprop in May. As Powell and Wood had done previously Mrs. Siddons and her husband came over from Manchester to play during the vacation there which lasted from Easter to Whitsun.

At that time the great actress was only 22; she had failed under Garrick at Drury Lane but she had been acclaimed in Manchester where she had been acting since November. Her genius indeed had not yet been fully recognised when she appeared for the first time in York as the Grecian Daughter on April 17, a memorable date in the history of the theatre. She was in poor health and Wilkinson[135] had doubts of her being able to sustain so fatiguing a rôle. She was opposed too by the friends of Mrs. Hudson, who saw in her another potential rival, and by others who had against her only the fact that she had failed in London. To the honour of the critical Swan let it be said that he took the lead in acclaiming her, and by the time she had performed Rosalind, Mathilda, Alicia, Lady Townly, and Lady Alton – a wide variety indeed – 'all bowed to her shrine.' Other parts played by her in these few weeks were Indiana in *The Conscious Lovers*, The Irish Widow, Arpasia, Horatia in *The Roman Father*, and Semiramis and Sir Harry Wildair for her benefit on May 17 the last night of the season. Her benefit only brought in £36.13.6.[136] though Wilkinson says that he never remembers so great a favourite as Mrs. Siddons became in that short period. He writes of her Arpasia: 'I recollect her fall and figure after the dying scene was noticed, as most elegant; nor indeed do I recognise such a mode of disposing the body in so picturesque and striking a manner as Mrs. Siddons does on such prostrate occasions.' Wilkinson was naturally eager to retain her as a permanent member of the company but his attempt to bribe her by a better wardrobe than Younger could provide in Manchester proved vain. For the part of Lady Alton, he decked her 'in a most elegant full sack, with a large hoop, (as then worn, and I am partial to for the stage) and that sack was really elegantly adorned with silver trimmings, &c. This struck her fancy so much that she declared herself delighted, and laughingly used to repeat, she wished she could convey it with her to Manchester, it made her feel so happy.' To Manchester she returned and the following year went to Bath whence she graduated to her final triumph in London.

There were other visitors of less note that season. Wilkinson went to perform in Edinburgh and engaged David Ross[137] to replace him for nine nights. Ross had been on the stage since 1749; he had acted both at Drury Lane and Covent Garden and had been manager at Edinburgh. Though he had ability, he was indolent and his chief claim to fame is that as George Barnwell his playing moved a would-be felon to repent, who in gratitude sent him a handsome annual pension. In York he did not please and the theatre was deserted when he acted. He opened as Essex on February 22 and played during his stay Lord Townly, Jaffeir, Lusignan, Othello, Oakley, Sir Charles Easy, Horatio in *The Fair Penitent* and his highly approved King Lear for his benefit. This last was not appreciated by the York audience and only brought £24.10.0;[138] as Wilkinson had to pay him £55.10.0. to cover the deficiency, the engagement proved an expensive one.

During Wilkinson's stay in Scotland he engaged Signor Ferzi and his company from Sadler's Wells. Ferzi was the first of a series of rope dancers. With him was another celebrated equilibrist, Richer, whose daughter, aged 9, performed 'on the Rope several curious Tricks without touching it with her Feet,'[139] and walked the wire in a large hoop. Their efforts were appreciated but though Wilkinson[140] says that Ferzi had a great night at his benefit in Assize Week, it only brought a profit of £33.10.6. Another entertainer who came at the same time was Signor Rossignol, who imitated birds and performed with his throat 'an entire new Symphonia' accompanied by the orchestra.[141]

New scenery was introduced in several revivals though we do not know who was the artist. Fielding's *Lottery* had a representation of the drawing of the state lottery in the Guildhall; *Harlequin Fortunatus* concluded with a new grand palace. The *Jubilee,* with alterations and additions, had as its grand finale a new transparency of Shakespeare attended by the tragic and comic muses, and at the Siddons's benefit a masquerade was staged illuminated with upwards of 500 lights.[142]

Places for the boxes on subscription nights were to be taken at the theatre; those for benefit nights were to be had of the actor whose benefit it was until the night preceding the benefit, after which they were to be had at the theatre. At the beginning of the season the sharers were summoned to a meeting at the York Tavern to receive their yearly dividend.

The second of Mason's tragedies on a Greek model – *Caractacus*[143] – was staged on April 8 for Suett's benefit. It had been played in Dublin in 1764 and at Covent Garden in 1776. Cummins enacted the hero, and Mrs. Hudson Evelina. The music had not been published but Suett with the assistance of Shaw, the first violinist, selected the airs and choruses from celebrated composers and supplemented them by original music and an overture of Shaw's composition. Thrackray played the violincello and Camidge jun. the harpsichord. The latter must have been Matthew Camidge, a young man of great musical ability, who was assistant organist to his father at York Minster. Wilkinson himself as Death performed the *Ode* at least to his own satisfaction. Mason himself was present either on the first night or on April 22 when the tragedy was repeated, and approved of the performance. It has a rather more heroic tone than the sentimental *Elfrida* but it peters out badly at the end. Both dramas are closet works and must have been somewhat dreary on the stage.

Two older tragedies were first given in York that season, *Sir Thomas Overbury* by the unhappy Richard Savage and *Lady Jane Grey* by Rowe. As for lighter fare Farquhar's *Sir Harry Wildair* made its début in York on May 17 with Mrs. Siddons in the breeches part of the hero, and Mrs. Butler, whose first appearance at York it was, as Angelica; new farces were Colman's *Spleen*. Foote's *Bankrupt*, Jackman's *All the World's a Stage*, Vaughan's *Hotel*, with Suett as Trimwell, and Dance's *Ladies' Frolick*. Colman's prelude *New Brooms* and a pantomime interlude called *York Races*, which included a pony race by two young gentlemen, were also new. Wilkinson had seen Shakespeare's *Tempest* in its original form, shorn of the ridiculous alterations of Dryden and Davenant, at Drury Lane and brought it to York for the first time on April 12 'with every Advantage of NEW DRESSES, variety of SCENERY and MUSIC, and in order to render it still more Entertaining, has taken the liberty to introduce a variety of pleasing SONGS, DUETS &C. from SHAKESPEARE'S Works, as set to Music by Dr. SMITH, and receiv'd with great Applause when the TEMPEST was perform'd as an OPERA.' The cast was Prospero = Cummins, Ferdinand = Wood, Caliban = Wilkinson, Ariel = Miss Simpson, Miranda = Miss Holmes, Attendant Spirits with duets = Baker, Mrs. Hudson.

As You Like It, The Merchant of Venice, and *Henry VIII* were also given this season. *Hamlet* had two performances in which Cummins played Hamlet, Raymur Laertes, Wilkinson the Ghost, and Miss Simpson Ophelia; in *Othello* Ross played the Moor to the Iago of Cummins, the Desdemona of Mrs. Hudson, the Emilia of Mrs. Montague, and when he played Lear, Cummins was Edmund, Wheeler Edgar, Mrs Hudson Cordelia. Butler made his first appearance as Romeo to the Juliet of Miss Glassington, with Siddons as Paris, Miell as Mercutio and that old stalwart Mrs Crisp as the Nurse.

Wilkinson's accounts for this season show a decrease in receipts as against the previous year. His total at York amounted to £1970.0.6. for 59 nights, whereas in 1776 it had been £2033.11.3. for 56 nights. The subscriptions brought in £207.7.6, a drop of £43.1.0.

The nights which attained over £50 were:

1) Suett's bft.	*Caractacus, Love à la Mode*	£83	3	0
2) Richer's bft.	*Henry VIII*, Entertainment by Richers etc.	81	18	6
3) Mrs. Montague's bft.	*Sir Thomas Overbury, Male Coquette*	80	4	0
4) Oram's bft.	*All for Love, Bon Ton*	76	13	0
5) Wilkinson's bft.	*Mistakes, Harlequin's Invasion*	75	3	6
6) Leng's bft.	*Funeral, Lottery*	60	1	6
7) High Sheriff's Night	*Clandestine Marriage, Two Misers*	59	6	6
8) Beynon's bft.	*Zara, Harlequin Salamander*	52	17	0
9) Robertson's bft.	*Love for Love, Wedding Ring*	52	5	6
10) Assize Tuesday	*Careless Husband, Mayor of Garratt*	51	10	0
11) Raymur's bft.	Desire Mrs Hudson, *Hamlet*	50	5	0
12) Hudson's bft.	*Rival Queens, Maid of the Oaks*	50	1	6

The poorest nights were:

1) 3rd subscription	*Word to the Wise, Devil to Pay*	4	10	6
2) 13th ,,	*Rivals, Cross Purposes*	4	10	6
3) 1st ,,	*Theatrical Candidates, School for Wives, Two Misers*	5	1	6
4) 16th ,,	*Fair Penitent, Catharine and Petruchio*	5	8	0
5) 18th ,,	*West Indian, Daphne and Amintor*	5	16	6
6) 5th ,,	*Maid of the Mill, Trip to Scotland*	6	1	0

The highest amount netted for a subscription night (exclusive of the actual subscription money) was on Assize Wednesday when £30.15.6. was reached for *The Merchant of Venice* followed by Ferzi's entertainments; the next was for the 4th subscription when £25.16.6. was brought in by *The Busy Body* and *Harlequin Fortunatus*.

Dodd and Mrs Bulkley reappeared as the stars of Race Week. They opened on August 16 as Sir Harry Wildair and Lady Lurewell and afterwards played Benedick and Beatrice, Ranger and Clarinda in *The Suspicious Husband*, the Copper Captain and Estifania in *Rule a Wife*, Lord Ogleby and Fanny in *The Clandestine Marriage*, and Aguecheek and Viola. In addition Dodd played Kecksey in *The Irish Widow*.[144] Dodd has been immortalised by Lamb as Aguecheek and Bernard, who acted with him in York, calls him 'the royal last one of the Fops whose dynasty commenced with Colly Cibber'.[145] Bernard[146] and his wife were engaged during the vacation of the Bath and Bristol company. He made his first appearance as Claudio in *Much Ado* and his wife played the Irish Widow, Queen Elizabeth in *Richard III* and Olivia. Bernard[147] has left us a picture of Wilkinson, who was already crusting into an eccentric, and his family at this time: 'Tate had a chatty and rather personable woman for a wife, and a son, John [aged 8] who had been tolerably educated, and was used to enunciate criticisms in the Green-room for the instruction of the actors. "Mr Cummings", said he one day at dinner, "reads Shakespeare better than any man in England!" – "The present company excepted, Jacky," responded Tate, with a mixture of personal pique and paternal fondness. Wilkinson is certainly one of the most well-known characters which the dramatic world in the past century produced, partly because he was the pupil and associate of Foote, partly on account of his talents and eccentricities, and partly in regard to his managerial importance.' Wilkinson, Dodd and Bernard dined daily together and 'When the bottle had mellowed the eccentric into good humour and memory, he would one day give us Shakespeare's "Seven Ages", distinguishing each age with the respective peculiarity of seven popular actors who played Jaques; at another time he would invent a game of whist between Macklin, Mrs. Clive, Shuter and Mrs. Pritchard; again he would fix on a particular person, Garrick for instance, and describe a scene between him and a sexagenarian washerwoman who had brought home Mrs. Garrick's things instead of his, and was reading the bill to him. But the most amusing matter of his table-talk was his personal anecdotes.'

Bernard also records one of the many instances of Tate's generosity towards his actors. The Bernards' engagement was for 60 guineas for 6 weeks, the manager to receive their benefits. Whilst they were in Wakefield, the Exeter manager sent for them to come a fortnight earlier than they expected, after they had played only five weeks and still had a benefit to come. Wilkinson, though it upset his plans, not only packed them off at once with a smile, but at their departure hurriedly pressed a packet into Bernard's hand which he later found to contain the full sixty guineas though he was only due to receive two-thirds of the sum.[148]

The fact that the visitors Mrs. Bulkley and Mrs Bernard had the leading parts during Race Week enraged the touchy Mrs. Hudson. Allotted the part of Berinthia in *A Trip to Scarborough* over a week in advance, she refused to play it the day before it was billed, and literally threw it in the poor manager's face. However, Mrs. Bernard read it at the performance with great credit and Mrs. Hudson, whose engagement was anyway at an end, departed under a cloud.

The Race Week receipts were again high:

Monday, Aug. 18.			*Much Ado, Tobacconist*	£56	8	6
Tues	,,	19		61	17	0
Wed	,,	20	*Suspicious Husband, Author*	62	19	6
Thur	,,	21	*Rule a Wife, Irish Widow*	100	6	0
Fri	,,	22	*Richard III, All the World's a Stage*	76	6	0
Sat	,,	23	*Clandestine Marriage,*			
			Harlequin Fortunatus	71	16	0

Dodd's benefit, however, only brought in £28.7.0, and for an additional half benefit the total sank to £14.0.0. The ten nights brought £521.9.6. to the coffers in comparison with £550.0.0. the previous year.

On the company's return to York in 1778, there were several new faces. The most interesting of these was that of Elizabeth Inchbald, who had been engaged by Wilkinson at Canterbury and had first performed with the company in Hull. 'My well-beloved, my beautiful Mrs. Inchbald,' he calls her.[149] Bernard, less rapturous, writes of her as 'a pretty but not clever woman with an impediment in her speech which stage-fright always took away.' She was only twenty-five at the time and was later to make a career for herself as a writer both of novels and plays. Her first appearance in York was on January 6 as Horatia in *The Roman Father*. Her other rôles included Lady Medway in *The Discovery*, Athenais in *Theodosius*, Eudocia in *The Siege of Damascus*, Calista, Mrs. Belville in *The School for Wives*, Lucia in *Cato*, Lady Brute, Oriana in *The Inconstant*, Lady Randolph, Violetta in *The Brothers*, Queen of Scots in *The Albion Queens*, Countess of Somerset in *Sir Thomas Overbury*, Arpasia, Alcmena in *Amphitryon*, Edwina in *The Battle of Hastings*, Rosamond in *Henry II*, Queen in *King Charles I*, Lady Macbeth, the Queen in *Hamlet*, Lady Sneerwell, Lady Restless in *All in the Wrong*. This list gives some idea of the variety in tragedy and comedy that was expected of a leading lady in a five months' season.

Of her husband, Joseph Inchbald, Tate says 'For the time he was engaged with me, I never experienced more ingenuousness, honour and integrity, nor did I ever know an actor of such universal worth, who confessed at least weekly (if not daily) the comforts he felt in his Yorkshire situation.' He opened as Hardcastle in *She Stoops to Conquer* and soon became a favourite in comic old gentlemen such as Sir Anthony Absolute. Inchbald was also an artist and used his talents as a scene-painter; his picture scene in *The School for Scandal* received particular approbation.[150]

Another newcomer was Mrs. Taplin from Dublin, the daughter of a Covent Garden actor named Dyer. Her mother had gone to the bad and her father had died when she was a child; she herself 'was ensnared into folly and dissipation, and her profession as an actress was a labour. Her figure was good, and she acted some parts with a degree of credit, as proved, (with pains and attention to character), she might have been a useful actress; but indolence and mind turned topsy-turvy, possessed her leisure.'[151] She played Lady Percy, Hypolita, Lady Townly and Queen Elizabeth in *The Albion Queens* and was commended by Wilkinson for her Mrs. Candour; but he did not keep her more than a year. Miss Mucklow[152] from Richmond, Surrey had joined the company in Doncaster and later married Charles Wood. She was cast for rôles as different as Julia in *The Rivals* and Monimia.

On the male side in addition to Inchbald there were two new actors: Tom Kennedy[153] who made his first appearance as Marplot and acted the fops and Harlequin, and Waddy[154] from Ireland of whom Wilkinson, with characteristic grammar, says that he was 'of the greatest utility of any actor I almost know.' He studied the difficult part of Mosca in *Volpone* in little more than a week and acted it well and intelligently. These actors left after this season. Kennedy eventually married Miss Holmes, whose acting had much improved, and returned with her to the company in 1788. The Hitchcocks and their children had rejoined the circuit after two years' absence, and remained until 1781, Hitchcock succeeding W. Powell as the company's treasurer.

In May two actresses paid short visits. One was Mrs. Webb[155] who acted Mrs. Heidelberg, Midas, and Dorcas in *Thomas and Sally* on her way from Edinburgh, where she was leading actress, to a summer engagement at the Haymarket; but judging from her benefit which only made £7.17.6. she could not have been a success. The other was Mrs. Massey from the Haymarket, whom Tate characterised as 'very so, so, though not destitute of some degree of merit', and who played Imogen, Jane Shore, Fanny in *The Clandestine Marriage* and Zara for her benefit. This benefit, owing to an unexpected accident, had to be postponed and when it finally took place Mrs Massey appealed for patronage as she had been put to great expense for her journey from London to perform in York in expectation of a good one. However, her total only came to £16.0.6. which could hardly have remunerated her.

Wilkinson this winter gave a few performances at Covent Garden and engaged West Digges for four nights to take his place. Digges, who had acted much in Scotland but had only the previous year made his début in London undertook Richard, Cato, Falstaff, Sir John Brute, Sir John Restless in *All in the Wrong* and the Drunken Colonel in *The Intriguing Chambermaid* in February, but failed to please[156] though his benefit reached £32.6.0.

Wilkinson's jaunt got him into severe trouble with the audience and the proprietors. They resented his month's absence which was taken without the permission of the proprietors who looked upon themselves as his masters, whilst Wilkinson considered that he himself was sole director. On February 17 there appeared in the *York Courant* an announcement from London as follows: 'Mr WILKINSON'S Respects to the Public, begs Leave to assure them (whatever Misconception or Misunderstanding may have unhappily subsisted between him and the Gentlemen Proprietors of that Theatre) whether he has the Honour to continue as Manager or retain his Property (on an equitable Footing) or not, he never shall lose Sight of that Gratitude for the Favours already received ... Mr. Wilkinson hopes to be at York immediately, and doubts not but Matters will be so adjusted between him and the Proprietors, as to render any future Dispute impracticable.' But the uneasy arrangement could not be continued. Wilkinson was annoyed because though his agreement allowed him only half receipts for his benefits, the proprietors insisted on deducting in addition the usual charges of the house from his share.[157] The truth was that Tate could not brook the control, which the proprietors on their side exercised in an overbearing manner. He convened a meeting, protested against their treatment of him, supporting his contentions with a legal opinion, and offered to pay them back the 3000 guineas in six months. This they agreed to, some because they did not believe that he could raise the money, others because they were not sure of their bargain since, owing to the fall in the receipts, their interest had diminished in the second year.

They parted on friendly terms and Wilkinson was jubilant: 'I am sure I was truly happy, and never regretted my repurchase from that hour to this, and firmly believe no theatre can be conducted with either pleasure, content, or profit, where so many heads must puzzle and confound each other.' At first it looked as though Tate would be unsuccessful in raising the sum by January 1779. As late as December 15, 1778, the following advertisement appeared in the *York Courant*: 'To be disposed of between this and the 1st of June, 1779, One Third, One Half, or the entire Whole of the Leases, Wardrobes, Scenery, &c. of the Theatres – Royal in York and Hull; with the Lease of the Theatres in Wakefield and Doncaster, and the Freehold Property of the Theatres in Leeds –.' A further note on December 22 adds untruly that the theatre had never been in a more flourishing state as regards receipts. In the end Wilkinson paid off the 3000 guineas by obtaining a set of new subscribers at York and Hull. They paid 100 guineas each; in return they obtained interest and a free transferable ticket, but this time Tate retained an option to pay them off when it suited him. There seem to have been no irksome conditions attached to this agreement and Wilkinson rejoiced to be 'free from the galling chains of thirty proprietors.'[158]

To return to the season of 1778. The historic event was the début of *The School for Scandal* at Wilkinson's benefit on April 21. The advertisement, after referring to its unprecedented success in London, Dublin and Bath, continues: 'It cannot, however, on any Consideration, be acted after this Night. The Public may depend upon *Mr. Wilkinson's* strict Attention in regard to the Representation; and that not any Expense or Care will be wanting to render it worthy the Approbation of the Audience, and no way injurious to the Credit of the ingenious Author.'[159] Every attention was paid to the manners of the performers and the entrances, exits and situations of the London production were exactly copied. The cast, all of whom excelled, was as follows: Sir Peter Teazle – Wilkinson, Sir Oliver Surface – Inchbald, Joseph Surface – Waddy, Sir Benjamin Backbite – Kennedy, Crabtree – Suett, Moses – Buck, Snake – Leng, Careless – Butler, Sir Toby – Wood, Trip – Beynon, Rowley – Oram, Charles Surface – Cummins, Mrs. Candour – Mrs. Taplin, Lady Sneerwell – Mrs. Inchbald, Maria – Miss Mucklow, Lady Teazle – Miss Holmes. There was a rush for places and Wilkinson cleared £88.6.0. Despite the advertisement the comedy was performed again on May 9. Another play of Sheridan's – *The Scheming Lieutenant* – was brought out on March 20. Curiously enough Sir George Collier's *Selima and Azor,* also presented this season, was attributed on the playbill to Sheridan – perhaps to increase its popularity. At its second representation Wilkinson announced that it would be more correctly performed as he had received all the orchestral parts from the Bath Theatre. Other new light pieces included *Wit Without Money* (presumably Beaumont and Fletcher's comedy), Colman's alteration of *Polly* and his *Spanish Barber*, which York damned,[160] Dibdin's comic opera *The Quaker* and a pantomimic farce *The Wizard of the Silver Rocks* "With a Variety of new Scenery and Machinery; particularly the Grocer's Shop, the Hotel, Silver Rocks, Cascade &c."[161] The reference to the shop foreshadows the later developments of the harlequinade. Three new tragedies came out. Havard's *King Charles I*, revised and altered by Younger, had been acted in other provincial theatres, and included a representation of the High Court of Justice in Westminster Hall at the King's Trial.[162] Cumberland's *Battle of Hastings*[163] was succeeded by a scene of the institution of the Order of the Garter in which 'The Genius of England will descend in a Chariot encircled with four transparent Paintings: 1st, Britannia presenting the Magna Carta; 2d, The Star and Garter; 3d, The Emblematical Silver Anchor; 4th, The George and Dragon supported by Cherubims [sic] in the Clouds.' Lastly Hannah More's *Percy* was given with Cummins in the title rôle. During a performance of *Hob in the Well* horse racing was exhibited for a saddle, and cudgel playing, in which Patrick Byrne of York was the first player, for a gold laced hat.[164]

Shakespeare was represented by *Cymbeline, Henry IV, Hamlet, Macbeth, The Merchant of Venice* and the operatic *Tempest*.

In March new arrangements for entering the theatre were made, and on the playbill:[165] 'Ladies are requested to observe, that the Mint-Yard Door will not be open'd in future; so the only Road for Carriages will be Blakestreet, where next Winter it will be commodiously cover'd into the Street. If the Ladies desire it, (by giving Notice) Carriages may take them *from the Theatre* in the Mint-Yard.'

The account books this year show a further drop in receipts from £1970.0.6. for 59 nights to £1801.13.5. for 55 nights. The subscriptions fell from £207.7.6. to £174.16.6.[166] The most profitable nights were:

1) Wilkinson's bft.	*School for Scandal, Summers Tale*	£88	6	0
2) Cummins's bft.	*Percy, Minor*	80	11	6
3) Oram's bft.	*Theodosius, Irish Widow*	77	5	0
4) Hitchcock's bft.		70	12	6
5) Assize Thurs.	*Duenna, Spanish Barber*	67	9	6
6) Sheriff's play		64	16	0
7) Leng's bft.	*King Charles I, Polly*	64	12	0
8) Eyles's bft.	*Discovery, Harlequin Pygmalion*	63	5	6
9) May 9	*School for Scandal, Selima & Azor*	62	1	0
10) Robertson's bft.	*Amphitryon, Æsop in the Shades, Harlequin Fortunatus*	59	4	6
11) Suett's bft.	*Every Man in His Humour, Cozeners*	54	17	0

The poorest nights were:

1) 11th subscription		3	9 0
2) 18th subscription	*Douglas, Midas*	3	10 6
3) 17th subscription	*Clandestine Marriage, Commissary*	4	4 6
4) 7th subscription	*School for Wives, Bon Ton*	4	6 6
5) 3rd subscription	*Love in a Village, Polly Honeycomb*	6	0 0

For Race Week Wilkinson brought with him from Leeds Miss Jarratt from Drury Lane, a beautiful girl with a good voice who starred in singing and comedy rôles including Ophelia, which by reason of its songs was usually cast to singing actresses. Thomas Jefferson also played that week as Don Juan in *The Chances* and Hamlet. He was a Yorkshireman, had played on and off at Drury Lane from 1750 to 1776, and was at this time manager of the Plymouth Theatre. From him in time descended the celebrated family of American actors. Yet another visitor was James Cawdell, manager of the Scarborough Theatre, who acted Young Philpot though suited rather to parts of a drier and more eccentric type.[167] Two new pieces were brought out: *The Volunteers; or Britons Strike Home*, a farce by William Woods of the Edinburgh Theatre, specially licensed by the Lord Chamberlain for the York circuit, and Murphy's *Know Your Own Mind* with Mrs. Inchbald as Miss Neville and Cummins as Millamour.

Receipts for the nine nights totalled £451.6.6. a drop of £70 on the previous year. Amounts taken during Race Week were:

Monday, Aug. 24		*Love in a Village, Scheming Lieutenant*	35	3 0
Tues	,, 25	*Chances, Volunteers*	48	14 0
Wed	,, 26	*School for Scandal, Lyar*	84	8 0
Thur	,, 27	*Duenna, Citizen*	72	11 6
Fri	,, 28	*School for Scandal, Quaker*	84	19 6
Sat	,, 29	*Know Your Own Mind,*		
		Harlequin Salamander	78	5 6

The popularity of *The School for Scandal* is evident from these figures.

The Inchbalds had made friends with John Philip Kemble in Manchester and Liverpool with the result that Kemble now applied to join the York company. He sent Wilkinson a list of parts he had performed asking him to mark those intended for him and to add any others to the list which he desired him to play.[168] Kemble opened in Hull on October 30. The greatest actor of his time was to spend three years in the York circuit preparing for his future triumphs. He was a young man of just on 22 when he first trod the York stage as Orestes in *The Distress'd Mother* on January 20, 1779, a part in which Boaden tells us that 'the scene where his imagination suggests to him the persecution of the Furies, was at all times one of his greatest efforts.'[169] At the rehearsal a quarrel broke out between him and Mrs. King, who was playing Hermione, as to whether his entrance in the 5th act should be on the P.S. or O.P. side. Wilkinson was called in to arbitrate and gave Kemble his way. Kemble's advent was a challenge to the supremacy of Cummins. The two had already been rivals in Wolverhampton, where Kemble had played second fiddle to the older actor in Chamberlain's Company.[170] During this season Kemble shared the tragic rôles with Cummins and Wilkinson and also sustained a fair proportion of comedy leads, even as Lord Mirror appearing in pantomime.[171] In addition he recited Sheridan's *Monody on the Death of Garrick* and Collins's *Ode on the Passions*. On April 15 a famous incident[172] took place which illuminates the proud character of the young Kemble. That night *Zenobia* was acted in order to introduce a Mrs. Mason from Northern Ireland, who incidentally turned out to be 'destitute of voice, variety and powers'; inexpressive, dull featured, crack voiced. A certain lady in the stage box took an antipathy to Mrs. King as the heroine and openly showed her contempt, which culminated in loud laughter and chatter during the death agonies of the last act. Kemble, who was playing Teribazus, at first merely looked disdainfully at the interrupter, but since this had no effect, he stopped dead and when the audience called for him to go on, bowed to the stage box and declared that he would proceed when the occupant had finished her conversation. The audience thereupon hissed her and several cries of "Out, out" were heard. She, in a rage, summoned the officers of the North-Riding Militia who were in the theatre, and at her behest they went to Wilkinson's house and demanded to see Kemble. He came cool and determined, in contrast to the officers who were warm and peremptory, but finally it was agreed that he should give an explanation. Meanwhile the less expensive parts of the house had decided that the lady was a disturber and that the officers wanted to degrade Kemble, so that when he appeared the pit and galleries called for no apology while the boxes insisted on his being heard. Kemble proceeded to give a dignified statement about the difficult position of an actor under the circumstances and continued with an extempore defence of the stage, whereupon the dissatisfied patrons of the boxes demanded an instant apology: 'Mr. Kemble, with face erect, voice distinct, pride manifestly hurt, and with expression equal to his best line in *Coriolanus* full of disdain, firmly said – "Pardon! – No, Sirs – *Never*" and left the stage with bursts of approbation from the audience.' It must have been a magnificent exit. The enraged and disappointed lady left the theatre in dudgeon. The next Saturday Kemble appeared as Douglas and the violent storm broke again. The quality resented an actor who was not subservient, the rest of the audience considered the quality too overbearing. A party in the boxes called again for an apology but were drowned by applause for Kemble from his supporters all over the theatre, applause which in reiterated bursts accompanied his performance to the end. Yet on April 20 when he played the Master in *The Toyshop* he was once more called upon to humble himself. He claimed a hearing for his case volunteering to make reparation if, after that, he should be deemed to have acted unworthily. He then expatiated so reasonably and diffidently that he was acquitted with three cheers and the incident was at an end. Kemble's behaviour increased his fame and popularity, for he had worthily upheld the dignity of his calling against insult.

Miss Leng, daughter of the old stagers, made her first appearance as Edwina in *The Battle of Hastings*. The Kings returned once more after a four years' absence and Mrs. King shared the leading rôles with Mrs. Inchbald. Among parts taken by the former were Lady Teazle, Calista, Lady Macbeth and Mandane (*Cyrus*) and by the latter Elfrida, Andromache, Jacintha (*Suspicious Husband*), Cordelia, Selima (*Tamerlane*), Julia (*Rivals*) and Fidelia (*Plain Dealer*). Mrs. King had expected to be received as usual but the capricious audience had deserted their erstwhile favourite and not even common justice was done to her performances.[173] Mrs. Inchbald had gained the hearts of both public and manager, with the result that Mrs. King threw in the sponge and retired with her husband in October to the Lincoln company; finally she set up a successful school for girls in King's Lynn and so ended her stage career.

A Mrs. Hunter was brought on the York boards for a few nights to oblige her friend General St. Leger; she had played with the company before and had since acted that winter in London but had actually fallen off in figure, stage manners and voice, and was not a success.[174] Richer returned with his Sadler's Wells company to York for a few nights in March, but curiously enough without approbation. His daughter Kitty danced on the rope at the tender age of three. On January 16, 1779 old James Robertson made his final bow on the stage as Scrub in *The Beaux' Stratagem*. A note on the playbill[175] says: 'Convinced by Age, and its usual Attendants, that it is high Time to quit the Bustle of a Theatre, Mr. Robertson humbly hopes that, upon this Occasion, his Last Benefit, (with which Mr. Wilkinson has kindly befriended him) he shall be honoured with the same Indulgence he has so often experienced from the Gentlemen and Ladies of York, to whom he shall ever be proud of owning himself under the highest Obligations.' He spoke a farewell epilogue and retired into private life after a career of over 20 years in the York theatre. He died on August 16, 1795 aged 82 and is buried in St. Olave's Church.

This season the subscription was reduced from 21 to 16 plays, box tickets £1.4.0., pit 16/-. The reduction was due to the failure of the subscriptions the previous year.[176] Subscribers tickets henceforward gave admittance to Hull and Leeds subscription nights, but were transferable only at York. Holders were requested to show their tickets and obtain a check from Hitchcock in order to facilitate the accounts.[177] Half price to the upper gallery was allowed after the 4th act except during public weeks. The number of benefit nights was also reduced so that the season, instead of lasting into mid-May, finished on May 1. An extra charity benefit for the Lunatic Asylum was held on April 29 under the patronage of Dr. Hunter at whose desire Kemble wrote a prologue to *The Foundling*.[178]

In addition to the usual bespeaks by the Masons and the High Sheriff, there were others by the Officers of the North-Riding Militia, by the Officers of the King's Dragoons, by Earl Percy and by the Sheriff's Lady. Military bespeaks were to become a regular feature henceforth of the York stage. Suett chose to have his benefit on March 6 the night of the Judges' arrival in York since it was sometimes fashionable to attend that night and in the past Shaftoe and West had been rewarded for their choice of it with crowded houses.[179]

At least seventeen new pieces were got up this season – a considerable increase over the usual number. The tragedies were Glover's *Medea*, as altered for Mrs. Yates's benefit, with Mrs. King as Medea; Jephson's *Law of Lombardy* put on six weeks after its début at Drury Lane; Colman's alteration of *Bonduca* in which Wilkinson's nine year old son John made a second and successful appearance in the child's rôle of Hengo;[180] and Kemble's *Belisarius* which that actor brought out at his own benefit on March 27 and which was well received. Herschel Baker gives a resumé of the plot and condemns the tragedy as intolerably dull and pompous. Kemble also produced a farce, *The Female Officers*, at Mrs. Hunter's benefit, the plot of which is narrated by Baker who designates it as a trivial but lively piece.[181] The evening was bespoke by the King's Dragoons, and Kemble had applied to use some soldiers in the procession. When this was refused on the score that the soldiers had better employment for their time, he approached Lord Percy and was granted permission.[182] Other farces were Pilon's privateer *Invasion: A Trip to Brighthelmstone* and his *Liverpool Prize;* O'Keeffe's *Tony Lumpkin in Town* with the new picture scene by Inchbald; and Charles Dibdin's burletta *Poor Vulcan*. New comedies were Colman's *Suicide* and Fielding's recently discovered comedy *The Fathers*. New comic operas were Sheridan's *Camp* with a 'Perspective View of the Grand Camp, painted by Mr. Inchbald, With a Grand Chorus, and a regular Review of the Battalions'; Bate's *Flitch of Bacon* with a representation of the ancient ceremony at Dunmow Priory; and M. P. Andrews's *Belphegor* 'with all Accompanyments which Mr. Wilkinson has been favoured with from the Theatre Royal, Bath.' An interlude entitled *The School for Scandal Scandalis'd* was given its first performance in any theatre on March 1 being subsequently presented at Covent Garden in 1780. The Larpent Ms. of it bears no indication of authorship but Collier attributes it, on the evidence of handwriting, to Kemble, a verdict with which Baker disagrees.[183] Dibdin's operatic pantomime *The Touchstone of Truth* came out as the afterpiece at Wilkinson's benefit and required 'so much Attendance in every Department of Stage Business' that he could not put on a new play as well. He had applied to Harris of Covent Garden for the Ms. and had been immediately favoured with it. We may compare Hitchcock's statement, with regard to the new pieces at his benefit, that he had obtained permission of the authors to perform them on that occasion only.[184] If permission were refused, the piece, as in the case of *The Duenna*, was likely to be given in a pirated version. One of the new pieces at Hitchcock's benefit was *The Fairy Tale: Nature will Prevail* acted by Master and Miss Hitchcock and other children of the company. In addition to these novelties *The Genii* was revived with new machinery and scenery which included a representation of York Minster and of St. James's Park by the York engraver Halfpenny.[185] Shakespeare productions included *Hamlet* with Cummins as Hamlet, Mrs. Hitchcock as Ophelia; *Lear* with Wilkinson as Lear, Cummins as Edmund, Kemble as Edgar and Mrs. Inchbald as Cordelia; *Macbeth* with Wilkinson as Macbeth, Cummins as Macduff, Mrs. King as Lady Macbeth; and the rarely played *Henry V* with Wilkinson as the King, Kemble as Exeter, Cummins as the King of France, Suett as Pistol and Mrs. Hitchcock as Katherine. For this last an additional spectacular scene with a grand coronation anthem and the ceremony of the champion in Westminster Hall on the accession of Katherine was included, as it had been at Covent Garden.

Whilst the company was in Leeds Joseph Inchbald died suddenly on June 6. He is buried there and the inscription on his gravestone is by John Kemble who was at this time in love with Mrs. Inchbald. At the request of the widow her stepson George Inchbald was engaged in July and stayed with the company until 1786.[186] He proved to be a serviceable actor, though not always attentive. Wilkinson, who had a very soft spot for Mrs. Inchbald, despite his difficulties with her, did all he could to retain her services. A holograph letter from her to Wilkinson in the York Public Library must belong to this time:

> S^r,
>
> I shall be very glad to accept your engagement with these small terms on my side –
>
> Giving up Miss Valance in the Fathers and never having a second part of such a stamp as that, and Miss Neville in she stoops to conquer sent me, with the permission of Playing Juliet my second, third, fourth or fifth part *as it may suit* on a subscription in Hull – the last request is what Mr. Inchbald himself told me he shou'd ask you, a few days before he died, and the other, considering how many bad *first* parts I am in possession of, such as the Queen in Hamlet, Lady Percy and a Song &c &c, I think no very unreasonable Demand, and you may depend upon it shou'd you think proper to engage me on these terms I shall do everything in my power to merit my Salary as a *Useful* Performer where there is no Glaring distinction between two womens parts in the same Play –
>
> I beg your answer as soon as possible as shou'd I quit you it will be most convenient at the End of this town and I shou'd wish to know of it as soon as tomorrow.

Other negotiations must have followed for Boaden[187] says 'The Manager's attention to her was unfailing. George Inchbald's salary was raised at her desire; but she was not contented, and disputed with him as to some character that he wished her to act: he promised an increase of her *own* salary but the day following she had a fresh dispute, and honest Tate, in explanation, said many very flattering things as to her talents, and, not the least flattering, as it went beyond words, absolutely offered, if she staid another year, to make her salary one guinea and a half per week.' And stay she did for one more season.

In July the company paid their first visit to Pontefract after the Leeds season had concluded. It was a success and led to the building of a theatre there. The Hitchcocks and Wood having departed for a while to London, Wilkinson re-engaged Mrs. Raworth and took on another actor named Tyler. The latter stayed until 1782, was useful both in operas and plays but was of a discontented disposition and suffered from what we should now call persecution mania.[188]

Mackle Emery and his wife, parents of the great John, were also members of the company during this season. The star was again Lewes who played Petruchio, Orestes (*Distress'd Mother*), Touchstone, Antipholus of Syracuse in *The Comedy of Errors*, The Apprentice, Lord Foppington to the Sir Charles Easy of Kemble (*Careless Husband*) and surprisingly enough, by particular desire, Hamlet. Mrs. Cowley's popular *Who's the Dupe?* made its first appearance on August 27 with Doiley – Wilkinson, Granger – Cummins, Gradus – Suett, Charlotte – Mrs. Inchbald. Another new piece was Pilon's interlude *Illumination*. *The Comedy of Errors* was given on August 30, cast as follows: Antipholus of Syracuse – Lewes, Dromio of Ephesus – Suett, Dromio of Syracuse – King, Duke of Ephesus – Leng, Ægeon – Emery, Angelo – Inchbald, Dr. Pinch – Oram, Antipholus of Ephesus – Cummins, Abbess – Mrs. Inchbald, Luciana – Mrs. Emery, Hermia – Mrs. Raworth, Adriana – Mrs. King. This was the version by Hull revised by Kemble who 'contrived to puzzle the house as well as the stage'[189] by making the two Dromios into black servants. In *As You Like It* Kemble played Orlando, Suett William, Mrs. King Rosalind, whilst in *Hamlet* Lewes was supported by Emery as the King, Inchbald as Horatio, Mrs. Raworth as Ophelia, Mrs. Inchbald as the Queen, with Suett doubling the rôles of Guildenstern and a Gravedigger.

During this short season Wilkinson made an agreement with David Ross to take over the Edinburgh Theatre for a year and thus found himself in need of recruiting a new company to serve up there. He opened in Edinburgh on December 18 leaving his Yorkshire theatres under the management of Cummins. The York patrons complained that the best performers had gone to Edinburgh, and the result was bad houses in both cities.[190] Tate was a sensible man and in the end decided not to neglect the substance for the shadow, as he puts it: 'if York did not receive such sums as Edinburgh, I reflected that York was not attended with near the expense:

My friends in Yorkshire were valuable and constant, my circuit honourable, and afforded a real gentlemanlike income, the other precarious; therefore a very little consideration, for once in my life, got the better of inconstancy and wish for change.' The experiment of 1779-80 was never repeated.

CHAPTER THREE

Tate Wilkinson's Management
1780–1792

INDEED the times, though golden in comparison with those 40 or 50 years later, were not auspicious. Tate blames the American war, and the lack of money and winter visitors for his thin houses. In addition the theatre's patrons were annoyed with him for his Edinburgh venture, though he meant, by having the two theatres, to command the best talents. Certainly the York audience did not realise that in their company were two of the greatest actors of their day – Kemble and Suett.[1] Among the new actors who appeared in 1780 at York was Johnson,[2] a comedian of merit who later enlisted under Jackson in Edinburgh and rose to high esteem. Miss Emmerson made her first appearance in Calista, which was only her second on any stage, and after that played a few leading tragic rôles. Mrs. Thornton, who had been well received in Vauxhall, was articled as a singer and made her first appearance as Rosetta in *Love in a Village*, subsequently playing Polly, Ophelia and Jessica. The Hudsons had returned and Mrs. Hudson made her first appearance as Mrs. Sullen after three years' absence. She divided the leads with Mrs. Inchbald, and together they played the rival Queens Statira and Roxana. Among Mrs. Inchbald's rôles were Juliet, Queen Elizabeth (*Richard III*), Hamlet, Portia, Mathilda, Almeria, Euphrasia (*Philaster*), Imogen, Constance, Mrs. Racket and Louisa (*Times*).

In April there was an influx of players from Edinburgh, including that firebrand Mrs. Montague who re-appeared as Margaret of Anjou and afterwards played Merope and Mrs. Oakley. Among the newcomers to York were Mr. and Mrs. Smith from Dublin who stayed with the company until 1785. Mrs. Smith, who made her début as Violante and subsequently acquitted herself well as Beatrice, became a great favourite.[3] Wilkinson preferred her to Mrs. Inchbald.[4] James Chalmers, from Edinburgh, who opened as Lissardo, was with the company until 1783. He then went to Covent Garden and Dublin, returned to York in 1790, and went to America in 1793 where he stayed until 1805. He died in Worcester in 1810. He was a particularly fine harlequin and one of his leaps was through a stage door seven feet high. After seeing Lewes perform that summer he imitated his style in genteel comedy. Wilkinson says that he had 'not his features at command, like his limbs, but he has spirit, utility, neatness, and merit in several particular characters.' He was reliable but short tempered, and he was prone to an inordinate 'love of lace, spangles and satin.' When actors were largely responsible for their own costumes, the attraction of finery frequently betrayed them into decking out a character most unsuitably in bright and glittering array.[5] Another new actor was Lane; he played gentlemen's rôles such as Sir John Melville, was sober, attentive and blessedly untemperamental, with a handsome, expressive face and a good figure. After a year he left for Dublin, whither Hitchcock enticed not a few of Wilkinson's troupe, and there he 'formed a fatal attachment, fell into a decline and died.'[6] Miss Mills, 'a charming little actress,' who came down from Scotland, was good in the young girls, eventually married Chalmers and also died young in May 1792. Death returned after three years for the season and played Tony Lumpkin, Mercutio and Cloten. Cautherley gave a few performances opening as the West Indian. He was reputed to be a son of Garrick, and had been instructed by him. He acted at Drury Lane in 1765 and in about 1778 was the hero of the Dublin stage.[7] As for dancers, when the season opened Aldridge, first dancer from Covent Garden, came from Edinburgh for a month and was succeeded by York's old friends West and Miss West. The company also had a new treasurer named Swalwell to succeed Hitchcock. For many years he was of immense value to Wilkinson as he kept the books so correctly that the theatre had claims to be the best regulated of any; he was steady, punctual and had the gift of obtaining everyone's good will.[8]

Old stagers were not forgotten by Wilkinson. Buck, who, owing to a long illness, was unable to act, was given a benefit on Assize Week Monday, a popular night, and thereafter had a benefit every year until his death. Mrs. Phillips, too, was obliged to quit the stage and was given a benefit in May.

A number of players this season lodged with the Tylers. They included Mrs. Inchbald who paid 12/- a week for her board and lodging; as she was receiving double salary she did not do so badly. Mrs. Inchbald's diary records details of her work in York this season, as for example:

March 8. "Was at rehearsal then sorted my things, etc. Play'd Bellario in Philaster – Farce Widow or no Widow. Was well pleased with my dress and performance."

Here is a typical week's work:

March 13: Rehearsal.
   ,,   14: Rehearsal. Played in School for Wives, Flitch of Bacon.
   ,,   15: Rehearsal of Fatal Falsehood until afternoon. Sorted things for Imogen. After tea at parts.

„   16: Rehearsal. Played Imogen & in All the World's a Stage.
„   17: Rehearsal. After dinner sorted things, working at them until
        supper. Played Fatal Falsehood and saw Deaf Lover.

Rehearsals were usually at 11 a.m. but were not always daily. A great deal
of time was taken up in sorting dresses and properties, presumably from
the stock box. Mrs. Inchbald often watched performances or afterpieces
from back stage or the auditorium.[9]

Kemble again produced a new piece this year for his benefit on February
26, a comedy entitled *Oh! It's Impossible.* Boaden identified this with his
alteration of the *Comedy of Errors,* but it was evidently an altogether different
piece as the adaptation had already been given the previous season.

There was also a contribution by Hitchcock, otherwise unknown, but
probably only an interlude, called *The Ladies' Wish; or The Freemason's Secret,*
which was brought out on May 6. Sheridan's *Critic* made its bow on April 29
with Wilkinson as Puff, Mrs. Smith as Tilburina, Smith as Sneer and Lane
as Don Whiskerandos. Other new farces were Jodrell's *Widow and No
Widow* and Pilon's *Deaf Lover.* New comedies were Mrs. Griffith's *The Times,*
Colman's *Separate Maintenance,* and Mrs Cowley's *Belle's Stratagem*, presented on the last night with Cummins as Doricourt, Mrs. Hitchcock as
Letitia Hardy and Suett as Hardy. This comedy was to become one of the
most popular in the repertoire, and York was to witness a series of famous
actresses in the rôle of Letitia Hardy. Another piece which made its début
this year and was long to hold the stage was O'Keeffe's comic opera *The Son-
in-Law* in which Wilkinson played Arionelli. Other new musical pieces were
Charles Dibdin's *Wives Revenged*; and Andrews and Miles's *Summer Amusement*, with a new overture and music selected from Scotch ballads or composed by Arnold, with all the original accompaniments to the songs; and
The Sultan which is attributed in the *York Courant*[10] to Mrs. Abington, but
must have been Bickerstaffe's comic opera. There were only two new tragedies, Hodson's *Zoraida* and Hannah More's *Fatal Falsehood.* A new pantomime *The Runaway; or Harlequin's Animation* was prepared and conducted by
West for his benefit. In it Miss West appeared in Harlequin's dress and leapt
through a hat box 6 feet high. It concluded 'with a very grand and exact
Representation of the Seafight off Scarborough, between Paul Jones in the
Bon Homme Richard, and Capt. Pierson in the Serapis.'[11] There was also
a representation of a gun battery on the Barbary coast with a perspective
view of Rodney's fleet under sail but, in order not to frighten the ladies, the
firing of the guns was omitted. Naval spectacles were the fashion this year
and were the heralds of the later nautical melodramas; thus in addition to
the two mentioned *The Summer Amusement* was supplied with a transparent
scene painted by a Drury Lane artist (presumably De Loutherbourg)
representing a naval review at Portsmouth. Another transparent painting
was of Sir Charles Hardy and Prince Henry for the *Illumination.*[12]

Wilkinson, as we have seen, had always set himself against interludes
which tended to drag out performances to inordinate length; but driven

perhaps by demand, he this year supplied at least three, *The Grenadier* from Sadler's Wells, Bate's *The Nut Brown Maid* and *The Ghost*. From these slight beginnings the pernicious habit of presenting three or even four pieces a night grew. Kemble acted in most of the Shakespeare plays this season as Orlando, Petruchio, Romeo, Henry VI, Richard III, Cromwell, Benedick, Shylock and Posthumous. *Hamlet* and *King John* were given in which latter John Wilkinson played Prince Arthur. At a second performance of *Hamlet* Mrs. Inchbald performed the prince 'and delivered many passages with great merit.' Tate did not really approve of the ridiculous innovation but occasionally gave warrant for such experiments.[13] Alas, Mrs. Inchbald was in years to come to be followed by many other actresses on the York boards.

Lewes once again starred with the company in Race Week playing Doricourt (*Belle's Stratagem*), Millamour (*Know Your Own Mind*), the Copper Captain, Ranger, Archer, Clodio (*Love Makes a Man*), Alwin (*Countess of Salisbury*), and Sir Charles Racket (*Marriage à la Mode*). York indeed was almost a second home to him. Bailey (whose real name was O'Reilly) had made a great success in Scotland, but his opening performance as The Mock Doctor in York was but coolly received. He wished himself back in Scotland but in six months he became the 'idol comedian of the county,'[14] universally beloved. As an actor 'his Jobson, Don Choleric, Mock Doctor, Scrub and many characters were sterling.'

Dicky Suett had received an offer from Sheridan at Drury Lane. He had risen to be Wilkinson's first comedian, was popular and successful and was under article. But the shrewd manager realised that he would never be content after the offer had been made, and luckily Bailey was at hand to help to replace him. So he generously wrote to Sheridan offering to give up Suett if Sheridan for his part would offer him an engagement for three years at an increasing salary. By experience Wilkinson knew that if Suett failed in London and returned to York he would get but a cold reception there from his former friends. Sheridan accepted the conditions and Suett took his leave of the York stage on August 28 as Scrub at a benefit liberally accorded him by the manager.[15] At Drury Lane Suett succeeded William Parsons in a variety of characters but his most brilliant successes were in old men, eccentrics and clownish servants. He was finely praised by Lamb who said that 'Shakespeare foresaw him, when he framed his fools and jesters' and that 'Care, that troubles all the world, was forgotten in his composition'; whilst for Leigh Hunt he was 'the very personification of weak whimsicality, with a laugh like a peal of giggles.' He was the first of a series of great comedians for whom experience on the York boards was a stepping stone to London triumphs.

Soon after Race Week Wilkinson also lost his beloved Mrs. Inchbald. He says that it was Lewes, backed by Harris, the manager of Covent Garden, that seduced her to London, but she had already been flirting with the idea and had spoken of an offer in April. In a holograph letter to Wilkinson dated April 3, 1780, she states that she must write to Harris by the next post with her answer and asks him to reply immediately as to whether he will accept her terms for staying: 'if I resign my London offer it can only be for your first Salary, the Liberty of giving up the following parts, the promise of Miss Younge's part in the Belle's Stratagem, the choice of my York Benefit next after Mr. Cummins and Mr. Kemble, and if I go to Hull (which I have not the smallest inclination to do) the Last Night. – Now I hope S^r you will not think any of these conditions extravagant as they are only absolute necessaries to rendering services in the way you now regard them of consequence, the salary you have before promised – as to my catalogue of parts I have omitted *fifty* most disagreeable ones; but as they go under the title of *first* parts am content with them – the part in the Belle's Stratagem is to repay me for Lady Sneerwell in the school for scandal – my permitting *two* Gentlemen to take choice before me in our York Benefits proper Humiliation, and my desire of the last night in Hull *of no consequence* as I had rather article only from X: Mas, and know a place I shall do much better in for that time – but if you shou'd have *real occasion* for me there I think I shall deserve that night as well as any other Lady nor can afford (knowing my Weak interest) to go without it – Now S^r, as I profess these proposals are made with a consciousness that (shou'd you refuse them) I shall be reduced in a year to accept of terms much inferior I hope you will not call me impertinent; yet I will not give up my London offer (fatal as I make no doubt it will be to me) for anything less and consider as a favourable circumstance I am not situated (like almost all my Sister Heroines) to extort a *double* Salary; moreover consider how Peaceable I am – how Good-natured – how *tall* – and how *Pretty*. –

Eliz. Inchbald

Bad Parts	Jacintha
Queen in Hamlet	Silvia in the R: officer
Hero	Mirander [sic. Busy Body]
part in the times	[?] Leonora
part in the Camp	and the part in Who's
Mrs. Candour	the Dupe if you please
Foible	
Lady Percy	
Millwood	
part in the Fathers	
part in its well its no worse –	
Lady Minikin	
Selema	
Lady Eliz. Grey –	
Mrs. Simony	
Miss Grantham'	

Evidently they came to terms for Wilkinson expressly states that she was under article from August 1780 until May, 1781,[16] but on the combined cajolements of Lewes and Harris he let her go. She quit York on September 19, but she always said that her training there 'had afforded her that moderate but steady encouragement which had placed her somewhat beforehand with the world.'[17]

Two very old timers left the company before it returned to York in 1781. One was Oram[18] who had his farewell benefit at Hull on October 31. Wilkinson was relieved to get rid of him as he was bad tempered and troublesome. From his salary and his benefits, which had for many years been supported by the Freemasons, he had managed to save £600 or £700; and Wilkinson gave him an annual benefit until his death in 1791. The other retirement was that of Buck[19] (whose real name was Bucknall), who was seized with a delirium on the stage when performing the Serjeant in *The Scheming Lieutenant,* and who never acted after December 1. He also was accorded benefits at Hull and York for many succeeding years. His salary as a small part actor had been only 16/- a week and he had mediocre benefits at York, Hull and Leeds, the receipts from which would have been contemptible to London actors, yet he was able to live independently for the rest of his days on the income from his savings. These two instances are proof that a country actor in a steady job in a good circuit with due economy, could expect to have a reasonably comfortable old age.

Mrs. Smith who had, on Mrs. Inchbald's departure, become leading lady, brought her sister Miss Scrace[20] (later Mrs. Bates of Covent Garden) to join the company. She was from the Dublin theatre and was an actress of 'great sensibility and merit.' Ryley[21] says she was 'a young lady of first rate abilities; she was extremely elegant in the woman of fashion, and very fascinating when habited in cavalier.' Like so many others in the profession she was doomed to die young of a lingering decline. She made her first appearance as Calista and during the season played Athenais, Julia, the Queen in *Hamlet*, Marcia in *Cato*, Emilia, Cordelia, Roxana and other parts.

Miss Leng was now old enough to be seen as Desdemona, Hero and Phoebe in *As You Like It.*

John Wilkinson graduated to his first big part as Tom Thumb. Kemble played Hamlet at his benefit on March 31 for that night only, but the audience, jealous for their favourite Cummins in the rôle, did not altogether approve. Wilkinson[22] tells the story of how one of his servants refused to go to the theatre with the remark 'I am sure I could not abide to see Mr. Kemble play Hamlet; you know, Sir, it is Mr. Cummins's part?' The audience, so fickle in some respects, were mistakenly loyal and conservative in others. Kemble's other Shakespearian rôles were Othello, Florizel and the Prince of Wales in *Henry IV.* He took the lead in several new and stock pieces, took part in the *Theatrical Fête*, recited the Ode on Shakespeare from *The Jubilee,* and gave a lecture on public speaking, divided into two parts, one on sacred and the other on stage oratory, ending with Portia's mercy speech and a recital of Sterne's story of Maria.[23] Percy Fitzgerald[24] quotes a passage from the *York Register* of about this time which he surmises was written by Cornelius Swan and which shows the impact that Kemble made: 'With all his faults we cannot but consider Mr. Kemble as a phenomenon in the theatrical world. His Hamlet is on the whole a most masterly performance. After this, his best characters *indubitably are* the Roman Actor, Bireno, and Demetrius. *They are unexceptionally inimitable.* In delivering odes, Sterne's stories, &c., he is happier than any person in our recollection'.

The *Theatrical Fête*[25] was a new experiment, the idea for which was given to Wilkinson by a man who was intending to stage an entertainment at one of the London theatres, consisting of scenes from various famous plays of Shakespeare. Wilkinson felt that it would be an injury to the stock plays to make excerpts from them, but would be a valuable thing to take from the lesser known plays of Shakespeare and others scenes whose great beauties would otherwise be lost to the stage. With this end in view he devised his entertainment from the following: I. *Julius Caesar*,[26] Act III, speeches of Brutus and Mark Anthony. II. Massinger's *Roman Actor* chosen because the part of Paris with his defence of the stage was so suited to Kemble. III. *Henry IV,* Act IV, with Wilkinson as the King. In this instance a stock play was selected. IV. Three acts from Young's *Brothers* with Cummins as Perseus. Kemble was particularly impressive as Paris and Cummins had great merit in his rôle. The whole hotch-potch received great applause.[27]

New tragedies this season were Mrs. Brooke's *Siege of Sinope* and Delap's *Royal Suppliants*; comedies were O'Beirne's *Generous Imposter*, Elizabeth Richardson's *Double Deception*, M. P. Andrews's *Dissipation* and Sophia Lee's *Chapter of Accidents*; musical entertainments were Andrews's *Fire and Water,* Burgoyne's *Lord of the Manor* and Lloyd's *Romp* which was in the repertory for years. Pilon's farce *Humours of an Election* was acted under the title *The Close of the Poll* with a representation of the candidates' hustings; and the one new pantomime was *Harlequin's Animation or the Fair Polonese* which opened with an exact replica of a fall of snow, embraced the dying scene from *Dr. Faustus* and concluded with Harlequin's front leap through a hogshead of fire.[28] Chalmers had met with an accident and Lane was the Harlequin to his wife's Columbine when *Harlequin's Invasion* was revived. For *Harlequin Fortunatus* the scenery included a perspective view of Greenwich Hospital;[29] *The Touchstone* had a grand illumined grove, and *Harlequin Dr. Faustus*, got up by West, new music and an overture by Arne. Rodney had captured the island of St. Eustatius in February, and a representation of this event with an emblematic transparent painting of Rodney was shown in March. Shakespeare was represented by Garrick's alteration of *The Winter's Tale*, with Kemble as Florizel; *Henry IV; Henry VIII; Hamlet,* once with Kemble and once with Cummins, Mrs. Chalmers as Ophelia; *Othello* with Kemble as the Moor; *King Lear; As You Like It* with Bailey as Touchstone and Mrs. Smith as Rosalind; *Much Ado* with Mrs. Smith as Beatrice, and *The Merchant of Venice.*

Among the benefits this year were those for the doorkeepers and the musicians of whom French was now leader, and a ticket night for the wardrobekeepers Lundy and Mrs. E. Frude who shared it with Mrs. Phillips now retired and keeping a school.[30]

The theatre had again been newly painted and care was taken to have it well aired. Another announcement states that 'At the request of several Families, the Pit Galleries will be formed into Green Boxes, Price 2s. 6d. where servants will be allowed to keep Places. – Half price the same as to the lower Boxes. – It having been made a Subject of great Complaints Servants going into the Pit in Liveries, they are requested to observe, not any Person in Livery can be admitted there in future.'[31]

This meant that the sides of the first gallery were partitioned off into green boxes for which the price was raised and which thus formed a second set of boxes above the lower tier. Servants were henceforth confined to the upper gallery.

Though the subscription was kept at the reduced one of sixteen nights the receipts were still falling off. The sums taken for the two charity per-formances were so poor that they would not be published, and Wilkinson decided that two nights were more than the great expenses of the Theatre would admit of. Thenceforward the first night receipts were shared between them without any deduction for expenses which Wilkinson himself bore. He pointed out that these amounted to more than twenty guineas every night the Theatre was open and that the charges laid on charitable benefits were a hundred guineas in London, sixty in Dublin and thirty-five in Edinburgh.[32]

From Wilkinson's account book we discover the drop in receipts that had taken place since 1778. The figures for the winter season are:

	£.	s.	d.
'York to Cash received from Jany 9th to May 5th	1590	8	6
York Races to Do Do from Augt 20 to Augt 31st	348	19	6
York To Cash paid	1583	0	9¼
Races to Do Do	420	6	8

Allowing that the winter season lasted a fortnight less since the cut in the number of subscription nights, the drop of £211 cannot be thus wholly accounted for. The profits are negligible. There was a loss of £68 on the formerly remunerative Race Week, the receipts being £70 less than in 1778. On the whole circuit the total receipts were £5454.5.8. and the total expenditure £5031.15.2¼ from which it is evident that Wilkinson was not making a fortune. It may be of interest to give the dates of the circuit this year:

York January 9 - May 5; Leeds May 7 - July 13; Sheffield July 13-22; Edinburgh July 23 - August 6; Newcastle August 13-18; York Races, August 20-31; Wakefield September 3-22; Doncaster September 24 - October 6; Hull October 23 - January 7.

The only real holiday the hard worked company got was a fortnight in October. By the time that they returned to York for Race Week, Hitchcock had quit to serve under Daly in Dublin. He induced Kemble and Lane to join him there in the Autumn so that this was York's last season of Kemble.[33] He acted Sir Giles Overreach in *A New Way to Pay Old Debts* which had its début at York. That he was conscientious in his study of a new part and not yet sure of himself as an interpreter is revealed in a letter that he wrote to Mrs. Inchbald after he had undertaken the rôle. 'Mr. Wilkinson obliges me to play it – Mr. Henderson's Performance is in everybody's Mouth, and the People hereabouts are inclined to do me the Honour of expecting I shall make a Figure in it ... and as I don't wish to lose in my very exit the little Credit I may have gained in the long time I have played with them, I would learn every mark of character in the Body and Mind of this Villain that I may bring him off as successfully as I possibly can.' He goes on to ask for details of Henderson's get up in the character down to whether he wore embroidered clocks on his stockings and adds: 'Moroseness and Cruelty seem to me the Ground of this monstrous Figure but I am at a loss to know whether in copying it I should draw the lines that express his Courtesy to Lord Lovell with an exaggerated or mere natural Strength – Will you take pains to inform me in what particular Points Mr. Henderson chiefly excelled, and in what manner he executed them.'[34]

Kemble took his leave of the York stage as Jaffeir; on which occasion Miss Scrace also made her farewell appearance as Belvidera.

A Mrs. Silverthorne, who had a wonderfully fine voice, played Eliza Greville in *The Flitch of Bacon* and Clara in *The Duenna*, and Wordsworth from Covent Garden appeared as Greville in the former play. Suett returned from Drury Lane to star playing Tipple (*Flitch of Bacon*), Bowkitt (*Son-in-Law*), Uniform (*Dissipation*), Squire Richard (*Provok'd Husband*), Petulant (*Way of the World*) and Diggory (*All the World's a Stage*).

Kemble's sister Fanny was engaged from Bath at this time and made her début as Lady Townly followed by Mrs. Dogeril in *The Register Office*. Wilkinson[35] says 'She had a strong understanding, and a fine informed mind; but was not so happy in her force on the audience.' She left the stage on becoming Mrs. Twiss.

The *Theatrical Fête* was repeated with the omission of the scene from *Julius Caesar* and another fête on the model of one at Drury Lane was brought out with scenes of a churchyard by moonlight and a view of the sea.[36]

When the company reopened the Theatre on January 8, 1782, John Philip Kemble had been replaced by his brother Stephen who had only recently started his career on the stage.[37] He did not compete with his brother in many rôles and on the whole his line was cast in comedy rather than tragedy.

Among the parts sustained by his sister Fanny were those of Lady Brumpton (*Funeral*), Mrs. Lovemore (*Way to Keep Him*), Lady Haughty (*Silent Woman*), and Mrs. Beverley (*Gamester*).

Mrs. Simpson – 'the pretty Mrs. Simpson' Wilkinson calls her – was taking the tragic leads. In April the company was strengthened on the women's side by the accession of Margaret Farren who had been strongly recommended by her more famous sister Elizabeth of Drury Lane.[38] When she first appeared as 'a young lady' in the singing rôle of Leonora in *The Padlock* on April 30, the playbill announced that her connections in London wished her to try out in York prior to any engagement there: 'they have preferred the York Audience as the first Judges in the Musical Line; and have solicited Mr. Wilkinson for that purpose.'[39]

On January 31 Wilkinson brought out the new pantomime of *Robinson Crusoe* already seen in Hull. The scenery included a new perspective view of Castle Howard by Halfpenny and new views of Crusoe's cave and bower, a ship under way for Europe and the quay of Cadiz. A Lilliputian family was also introduced.[40] Chalmers was the Harlequin and Bailey an excellent Friday. This pantomime, which Wilkinson had seen at Drury Lane, was got up as nearly in the manner of London as possible,[41] at considerable cost. Wilkinson points out that such entertainments did not survive long owing to the wear and tear of conveying the scenery from theatre to theatre, which was necessitated because its production at one would not pay, and because audiences became jealous if a spectacle shown at one town in the circuit was not also shown at all the others. Stock scenery was kept at each theatre for the usual repertoire but could not altogether serve new pieces. Another pantomime, got up by Chalmers, called *Mother Shipton* did not cost £10 yet drew more money than the elaborate *Robinson Crusoe*. It included a view of the Market Place, Hull, in which Chalmers took a flying leap over the statue of King William.[42] Yet a third pantomime, *Harlequin Freemason*, was played 6 times. Its chief attraction was a procession of principal Grand Masters from the creation to the present century in which the manager, the whole company and a number of supers took part. During the procession there were introduced views of the Tower of Babel, the Pantheon, the Temple on fire, the Tower of London, Windsor Castle, the Banqueting Hall, the Monument, St. Paul's, a grand royal arch and Solomon's Temple.[43] It was announced as the most expensive and splendid piece yet produced and very hazardous considering the great losses at the theatre that season. The reception of the *Theatrical Fête* the previous year was such as to encourage Wilkinson to give another. The plan was similar and little known pieces were again chosen. First came Randolph's *Muses' Looking Glass*, written in 1615 but altered and adapted to the age, with Cummins as Roscius; secondly, Acts IV and V of *Henry V* with Wilkinson as the King and Stephen Kemble as Chorus; thirdly Foote's *Piety in Pattens*; and lastly Mitchell's forgotten one act tragedy *The Fatal Extravagance* which dated from 1720.[44]

Other new pieces were: comedies: R. Griffith's *Variety*, Holcroft's *Duplicity*; tragedies: Jephson's *Count of Narbonne*, Pratt's *Fair Circassian*; musical pieces: Garrick's *May Day*, Jackman's *Divorce*, M. P. Andrews's *Dutch Baron*, Tickell's *Gentle Shepherd* and O'Keeffe's *Agreeable Surprise*. This last, in which Bailey played Lingo, Mrs. Chalmers Cowslip and Miss Leng Mrs. Cheshire, was long a popular favourite. Such had been its success at Covent Garden that Wilkinson arranged to keep the theatre open in order to present it; it was not published but Wilkinson had succeeded in obtaining a copy of the words and music.[45] *The Beggar's Opera Revers'd* was also put on with the men in women's parts and vice versa, Mrs. Hasker playing Macheath, Tyler Polly and Wilkinson Lucy. *Oroonoko* was revived with Hawkesworth's alterations in which the comic scenes were rejected as a disgrace to the stage though the tragic scenes were changed as little as possible.[46]

The Merchant of Venice was treated to two new scenes: Portia's Palace painted by an eminent artist from Drury Lane, and a scene in Act V by Browne of York; several characters were freshly dressed. In *The Tempest* Cummins played Prospero, Wilkinson Caliban, Miss Kemble Miranda, and Master Wilkinson Ariel. Stephen Kemble played Hamlet to the Ophelia of Mrs. Simpson and the Queen of Miss Kemble; Romeo and Juliet were sustained by Pollett and Mrs. Simpson, and Pollett played Orlando with Cummins as Jaques. *Richard III* and *King John* were also given. At Mrs. Phillips's benefit Grist from Dublin, on a journey which led him through York, offered his services as Othello, Mrs. Simpson playing Desdemona and Miss Kemble Emilia. Bespeaks were given by the ladies and gentlemen of the card assembly and by the officers of the 10th regiment of dragoons.

A second volume of Wilkinson's account books gives a full record of the expenses and takings this year. We find that Wilkinson had to renew the patents at York and Hull after thirteen years at a cost of £200. His debt of £3000 to the subscribers had been reduced to £26 but he now had to borrow another £150 towards obtaining the patents. A list of the company is given with their salaries as follows:

Men	Women	£.	s.	d.
Wilkinson		1	11	6
Cummins	Mrs. Cummins	2	11	6
Smith	Mrs. Smith	2	12	6
Simpson	Mrs. Simpson	2	12	6
Chalmers	Mrs. Chalmers	2	10	0
Bailey	Mrs. Bailey	2	1	0
Leng	Mrs. Leng ⎱ Miss Leng ⎰	2	6	0
Hasker	Mrs. Hasker	2	0	0
Pollet		1	5	0
Kemble		1	5	0
	Miss Kemble	1	3	0
Tyler		1	5	0
Colby			16	0
Hodgkinson			12	0
Inchbald		1	0	0
		26	12	0

Men *Continued*

	Brought forward	26	12	0
Earby [prompter]			15	0
Swalwell [treasurer]		1	0	0
French [leader of band]		1	1	0
Thompson			15	0
Matthew			15	0
Lundie [wardrobe keeper]			16	0
Betty			12	0
Large			10	0
Harry			10	0
Call Boy			2	0
		33	8	0

Quite what part all these last played we do not know but scene shifters, carpenters and candle snuffers have to be accounted for. Eleven door-keepers and Mr. Wright were paid 13/- every night and the cost of the music varied slightly. Mrs. Tyler and Master Wilkinson were paid 2/6d per performance and Master F. Wilkinson made appearances at 5/- and 1/-. There are frequent items for supers, as for example: 1 trumpet 1/-, 2 drums 2/-, 6 guards 3/-, 2 men in the cow 1/-, 6 savages 6/-, 6 children 6/-, 10 men 5/-, (these last three for *Robinson Crusoe*), 10 men and 10 women with banners 10/- (for *Harlequin Freemason*), 3 senators 1/6, 1 executor 1/- (*Venice Preserv'd*). A note was made whenever a new actor joined the company, giving his salary, and whenever an actor was absent for a week his salary then being deducted. Thus we find under May 11 'Miss Farren 2 wk 2-2-0. Simpson absent.' On January 15 Mrs. Bailey forfeited a week's salary for refusing to dance in *Love in a Village*. Definite forfeits were laid down in all companies for refusing parts or for being late at or missing rehearsals.

Many interesting items appear on the expenses side. There was carriage and porterage, as for instance: carriage of boxes from Hull by diligence 5/-, porterage of boxes 6d; carriage of scenes from Hull £2.17.6., carriage and porterage of same from London 10/6. There was extra billing such as three days billing town 3/-, five days 5/-, billing Miss Phillips's benefit 4/- paid Chalmers half extra billing 3/-. Special hairdressing cost 1/6 and was used for Huncamunca and Polly. Thomas Malton was paid £8 for a scene. This must have been Portia's Palace in *The Merchant of Venice* by an artist from Drury Lane where Malton was scene painter. Property items include the loan of two pairs of pistols 1/-, a pair of harlequin shoes 9/6 and another pair 6/-, half year's lamps 16/3. Mrs. Williamson paid Mr. Hudson of Hull 7/6 for a song. Coals cost £7.8.6. There are payments to land tax at £1.6.5½ a quarter and for 'Poors Sess' £2.4.0. for six months which was presumably some tax levied for the poor of the city. Rent was £20 a year, and £1.0.0. was paid for insurance of the Theatre. Interest, probably on the residue of the subscribers' loan, was £2.12.6. Every week the expenses were totalled. Wilkinson had a very humane method with benefits: he deducted £5 from the total receipts of the night and then shared the remainder. This was much better for the actor than the usual practice of making a heavy charge for the house which the receipts did not always cover. Here are a few examples:

Takings.					Actor's Share.		
Chalmers	£59	7	6		£27	4	0
Miss Kemble	39	14	0		17	7	0
Miss Leng	27	3	6		11	2	0
Wilkinson	68	7	6	(no deduction)	34	4	0
Kemble	24	7	6		9	19	0
French	27	4	6		11	2	6
Cummins	56	4	6		25	12	6
Earby	38	8	0		16	14	0

There was the alternative system of ticket nights by which the beneficiaries were allowed half profits on the tickets they could sell. Thus the musicians' benefit brought £50.11.6. out of which their half of the tickets amounted to £22.15.9; this had to be divided among 9 musicians. On the doorkeepers' night £84.5.6. was the total receipt, the doorkeepers' half tickets amounting to £40.14.9. which had to be divided between 15 men. Another evening tickets from Mrs. Frude and Lundie, the wardrobe keepers, and John Dalton of Clifton were accepted. Out of a total of £26.1.6. Mrs. Frude's share came to £2.17.6., Lundie's to £1.7.6. and Dalton's to £4.0.0.

From the receipts side of the accounts we learn that the subscriptions amounted to £119.12.0. consisting of 47 box subscriptions at £56.8.0. and 79 pit subscriptions at £63.4.0. The gross takings at every performance were entered, and at the end of the week the total takings, together with the amount received by Wilkinson as manager, (that is with the Saturday benefit money deducted) were recorded. One or two specimen weeks may show more clearly how the system worked.

Week.	Total Receipts.			As Manager.			Benefit.			Payments.		
	£	s	d	£	s	d	£	s	d	£	s	d
2nd	79	10	0	51	1	6	28	3	6	82	11	5
4th	77	11	0	77	11	0				70	3	2
6th	80	5	0	51	1	0	29	4	0	73	9	4
11th	145	4	0	89	4	6	55	19	6	197	9	4 1/2

At first sight it looks as though the expenses exceeded every week what the manager had in hand to pay them with, but it must be remembered that they included the money handed over for benefits so that the total expenses have to be balanced, not against the manager's share but against the total receipts. Even so the outgoings frequently exceeded the intakings on the week, though the manager had in hand as well the subscription money. That Wilkinson after paying himself a weekly salary and taking half a benefit did make money out of the York season is proved by the totals.

	Receipts	Payments
Jan 8 - May 18	£1843 5 9	£1708 1 11½
Aug 17-30	£ 468 5 0	£ 371 18 10
Total per circuit	£5395 8 9	£4818 2 11

This shows a profit of £577 on the whole circuit. We find that Wilkinson collected £2.17.0. for 57 nights or a 1/- a night from the fruit woman for the privilege of plying her wares in the theatre, and he received from Coultate, one of the doorkeepers, £2.18.0. for 174 lbs. of candle ends at 4d per lb. Only once was the house dismissed and that was at Miss Kemble's benefit on March 5; she was given another one two weeks later. Some rival kind of entertainment was given by Mr. Hamilton on the Green in May but arrangements were made for him to have two non-acting nights Monday and Friday.[47]

Old Mrs. Crisp died this year and Bailey left the company at the end of the season; he was a severe loss as he supported all the favourite comic rôles. Wilkinson, looking round to seduce someone from another theatre to replace him, succeeded in engaging Dancer from Norwich 'who had held the palm of great pre-eminence in that city.'[48] Mr. and Mrs. Powell came from Bath and appeared during Race Week, he as Lord Falbridge in *The English Merchant* and she as Cecilia in *The Son-in-Law*. Powell was well received and his wife 'was a good figure, sung very prettily, and was of great utility.'[49] They stayed with the company until 1787. Mr. and Mrs. Marshall from Edinburgh were introduced as singers. Wilkinson says of them[50] 'She had a good voice, was very handsome and shewed to view a brilliant pair of eyes with a remarkable set of fine teeth, which she did not neglect to keep in full view. Mr. Marshall was a very genteel figure, sung very pleasingly, and promised well as an actor.' They appeared together as Rosetta and Young Meadows in *Love in a Village* and stayed with the company a year. A better known newcomer was Thomas Knight from Edinburgh. Though originally intended for the bar, he studied elocution under Macklin and adopted the stage as his profession. He had failed in Richmond; he failed again as Lothario in Leeds. But tragedy was not for him and he soon became a great favourite in comedy, his particular forte being in drunken rôles such as that of Charles in *The Jealous Wife* and Spatterdash in the *Young Quaker*. He rose to the leads in his five years' stay with the company, after which he emigrated to Bath as low comedian. Eventually he became joint manager with Lewis of the Liverpool Theatre. He is said to have had an elegant figure and a melodious voice.[51]

But a much more important engagement than any of these was made at this time – that of Dorothy Jordan.[52] Her mother had acted with Wilkinson in Dublin in 1758 and her aunt Miss Phillips, then at death's door, had been a member of the York company on and off for some years. In July Mrs. Phillips arrived at Leeds from Dublin with her daughter, Dorothy, and two other children, Master and Miss Frances, in a destitute condition. She pleaded her daughter's talents so fulsomely that Wilkinson very nearly refused to take her in. Dorothy showed no vestige then of comic powers but was on the contrary 'dejected, melancholy, tears in the eyes and a languor, that pleaded wonderfully for assistance.' When Tate asked for her line tragedy, comedy, opera, she laconically replied 'All.' He was suitably astonished but agreed to give her a trial as Calista, and on his prevailing on her to repeat a few lines of that rôle was surprised and delighted at her good articulation and plaintive tones. She made a success on her appearance as Miss Frances in that part followed by a song in Leeds. When she came on with the company to the York Races she adopted the pseudonym of Mrs. Jordan[53] a name she was to make one of the most famous on the 18th century stage. A week after her arrival in York her aunt Miss Phillips died. Wilkinson was so pleased with Mrs. Jordan that he articled her on the highest terms[54] with an extraordinary benefit after Race Week. This was fortunate because otherwise Smith from Drury Lane, who was so struck with her performance as the Countess of Rutland and the Romp that he visited the theatre every night, might have enticed her away.

She opened as Calista followed by a song on August 17, 1782, and also played Macheath, and at her benefit Hermione in *The Distress'd Mother* and a scene from *The Son-in-Law* in the dress and manner of serious Italian opera. As Arionelli in the latter she was much admired whereupon Tyler, whose part it was, indignantly departed to Scarborough. Indeed Mrs. Jordan's sudden success and the grant to her of so early a benefit caused a deal of trouble and made her much hated. Mrs. Smith[55] 'swelled with indignation, and the constant Green-Room phrase, was, "Pray when, Ma'am is your benefit? and when is yours, for I see Mrs. Jordan begins with one on Wednesday." ' Wilkinson, aware, however, of how many mouths she had to feed, gave her every support and introduced her to Swan, who gave her lessons, instructing her particularly in Hill's *Zara* which he persuaded the manager to revive for her. She was so quick that after three lessons he pronounced her equal to Mrs. Cibber in the part. He declared that he had adopted her as his child (she was then 20 years of age) but he never left her a penny.

Mrs. Hopkins of Drury Lane, the mother of Mrs. John Kemble, was in York on a visit and was engaged for two or three nights. She played Mrs. Malaprop, Mrs. Peacham and Mrs. Heidelberg at her benefit. As Miss Barton she had made her first essay at the York Theatre and had now risen to succeeding Mrs. Clive.[56] Wilkinson, always ready to help someone in distress, gave a benefit for Lady Leake from Norwich, whose husband was in the King's Bench prison and who had been left destitute. She was to be given ⅓ of the profits but her share only amounted to £4.5.8.

During the actual Race Week there were some good houses:[57]

			£	s	d
Aug.	19	*Love in a Village, Romp*	45	9	6
,,	20	*E. of Essex, Two Misers*	57	2	6
,,	21	*English Merchant, Poor Vulcan*	81	9	6
,,	22	*School for Scandal, Son-in-Law*	61	7	0
,,	23	*Fair American, Irish Man of the World*	62	12	0
,,	24	*Rivals, Agreeable Surprise*	66	9	0

But after that Mrs. Jordan's benefit only brought £32.16.6. and Mrs. Hopkins's £28.2.6.

Salaries for the newcomers were as follows:

			£	s	d
Dancer	Mrs.	Dancer	1	17	0
Marshall	,,	Marshall	2	0	0
Powell	,,	Powell	1	17	0
	,,	Jordan	1	11	6
	,,	Farren	1	5	0
Knight			1	5	0

The Smiths had been raised 4/- to £2.16.6, the total salary list being now £36.1.0.

On the expenses side five guineas went in interest, 16/- to Wright for oil (for the lamps no doubt), 4/- to Browne for colours for scene painting, 1/- for a sedan chair, 6d to chairmen for bringing a piano, and 5 guineas as a contribution to the races.

About this time Wilkinson tried to inveigle back his favourite Mrs. Inchbald.[58] Her terms were as before with £40 for her benefits at York and Hull whether she cleared it or not. 'As to Cloaths' she continues, 'I say nothing about – Dress me as bad as you please, I am sure to look *better* than any other Person – but remember this – I buy no Decorations for your Cloaths, such as they are given to me, such I wear them – neither my *time* or *Income* will admit of my Dressing any more than my *Head* & feet.' She was not particular about parts and did not even object to a thief in *The Beggar's Opera*, 'but remember and the only reason why I quit Covent Garden Theatre I will not Play the Whore.' Tate, however, would only offer her 15/- a week which was less than she had before and this she indignantly refused, pointing out that there was a dearth of good actresses.

The company reopened at York on January 21, 1783. The box and pit seats were re-covered a few days afterwards.[59] There were one or two alterations in personnel. Barrett[60] played comic characters and excelled particularly as the Jew in *The Young Quaker* and Crazy in *Peeping Tom* and was also cast for old men such as Verges and Foresight. Stephen and Fanny Kemble had left but in March Elizabeth Kemble, later Mrs. Whitlock, made her first appearance as Elwina in *Percy*.[61] 'She was then,' says Wilkinson, 'possessed of great marks of merit, though wild as a colt untamed'; she had already appeared as Portia at Drury Lane that winter. In York she played Queen Katharine (*Henry VIII*), Violetta (*Brothers*), Jacintha (*Suspicious Husband*), Jane Shore and Selima (*Tamerlane*); she left again in June and was later to become leading lady at Newcastle. In May Lamash from Edinburgh joined the company and played Dick in *The Apprentice* and Macheath but did not stay out his year's engagement. Knight and Dancer had both improved, and, apart from the usual petty jealousies among the actresses, all went well. Mrs. Jordan, who, since her appearance in August, had given birth to an illegitimate child by Daly the Dublin manager, was well received. During the season she played both in tragedy and comedy, as well as in farce and comic opera.[62] Her forte for breeches parts led to her being cast as William, one of her best rôles, when Mrs. Brooke's comic opera *Rosina* was first brought out for Wilkinson's benefit on Easter Tuesday April 22. Mrs. Brooke's husband had been curate to Wilkinson's father at the Savoy, so the manager must have had a very personal interest in the production of this piece which was to prove one of the most popular in the repertory. Another well known comic opera first seen this season was O'Keeffe's *Castle of Andalusia*. Two new farces by O'Keeffe *The Dead Alive* and *The Positive Man* also came out; other new farces were Pilon's *Siege of Gibraltar,* in which was exhibited a view of the Rock with Spanish gunboats sinking in the bay, and his *Thelyphthora or the Blessings of Two Wives at Once,* Dent's *Too Civil By Half,* Macnally's *Retaliation,* and Hodson's *Adventures of a Night.* The only new comedy was Cooke's *Capricious Lady,* an adaptation of Beaumont and Fletcher's *Scornful Lady,* the only new tragedy Cumberland's *Mysterious Husband.* But there were three pantomimes: *The Power of Magic or Harlequin Turn'd Turk* which concluded with a new garland dance, *Harlequin Traveller or Agreeable Companion in the Post Chaise* in which Harlequin was attempted by Marshall, and *The Stockwell Wonder,* based on the antics of the celebrated poltergeist which had caused a sensation in 1772, and for which a new transparent arch had been calculated and designed by Dancer.[63] For *Robinson Crusoe* Browne painted a new perspective view of the Manor Shore.[64] Shakespeare was represented by *Much Ado* with Chalmers as Benedick; *The Merchant of Venice; As You Like It; Hamlet; Cymbeline; Richard III;* and *Henry VIII.*

In January George Saville Carey gave his lecture on mimicry.[65] The son of Henry Carey, he had failed as an actor, turned writer and devised a series of one man entertainments which he gave at Covent Garden and elsewhere, and of which this was one.

On the Sheriff and Grand Jury's night during the Assizes the demand for places was so great that 3 rows of the pit were railed into the boxes and servants were admitted there also to keep places.[66] The season closed on May 12 but on May 24 the company, for the first time, came back for a week from Leeds to entertain the gentlemen at the Spring Race Meeting, fortified with Ward, later manager of the Manchester Theatre, and Mrs. Baddeley both from Edinburgh.[67] Ward, who had a good person and a great share of spirits and vivacity, played Sir Charles Racket, Lord Foppington, Posthumous, La Brush in *The Register Office* and Lissardo. Mrs. Baddeley took several singing rôles such as Clarissa, Polly, Rosetta, Sylvia (*Cymon*) and Narcissa (*Rival Candidates*) as well as Imogen and Violante. Sophia Baddeley was then about 38 years of age and had first appeared at Drury Lane in 1765. Her line was genteel comedy but she was best known as a singer. At York she was much admired until on her last night she forfeited esteem, owing to an excessive dose of laudunum which almost prevented her from finishing the performance. Tate says indeed 'that the quantity of laudanum she indulged herself with was incredible: and though very little food approached her lips, her complexion retained its beauty to the last.' She was unsatisfactory to any manager because 'what with illness, laziness and inebriety you could not rely on her from one night to another.' She was also recklessly extravagant and though she received good payment from Wilkinson, she returned without a shilling to Edinburgh, where she died three years later 'a prey to disease and poverty.'

The accounts for this year take us only to the end of the first season on May 12. The salaries started with a total of £30.12.0. but the following were added: March 10 Miss E. Kemble £1.5.0., April 24 Miss Usher £1.11.6., May 1 Watts £1.0.0. Mrs. Powell's salary was advanced 3/- from February 8. Among weekly expenses varying amounts were nearly always paid to Benson, Jackson, Blanchard (printer), Daniel and Dalton. A wrestler was engaged for *As You Like It* for 1/- and G. S. Carey was paid a third of the total takings for his lectures on mimicry. Payments to Mrs. French, Miss Dancer and Masters Wilkinson and Frances were made for occasional appearances. Carriage expenses included a scene from Leeds 9/- and a payment to Benson for scenes from Hull £3.10.0. This season there are items for cleaning: Harry, cleaning theatre £1.0.2.; washing stage 1/6, room 1/-; washing rooms, stage, pit and boxes 6/6; cleaning candlesticks 2/6; cleaning a gown and petticoat 8/-. There are also items for copying: Barrett for writing 18/-; writing *Castle of Andalusia* 7/6; writing *Adventures of a Night* 2/-; Barrett for writing 13/2. £2.5.6. was paid for *Too Civil By Half* and a song though whether for the transcription or right to play is not clear. Butler was paid £8.16.0. for red baize, a spangled silk waistcoat cost 18/-, a serjeant's coat 10/- and a tailor's services for a day and a quarter was only 2/6d. Wright and Prest were paid £2.2.9. for oil and later four gallons of oil cost £1.4.0. At the end of the season 19 stone 10 lbs of candle-ends were sold at 4/8 a stone. Insurance had risen to £2.6.3. and interest was itemised three times: £2.12.6., £5.5.0., and £1.3.3. taken out of stock to make up the amount. The most successful nights were:

		£	s	d
1) Doorkeepers bft.	*Double Gallant, Rosina*	93	9	6
2) Sheriff's night	*Tamerlane, Son-in-Law*	88	13	6
3) Wilkinson's bft	*Which is the Man?, Puppets, Rosina*	82	12	6
4) Assize Thurs.	*Careless Husband, Agreeable Surprise*	75	0	0
5) Cummins's bft.	*Mysterious Husband, Arcadian Festival, Robinson Crusoe*	73	3	6
6) Oram's bft.	*Love's Last Shift, Gentle Shepherd*	60	4	6
7) Chalmers's bft.	*Much Ado, Power of Magic*	60	1	6
8) Smiths' bft.	*Capricious Lady, Fine Lady's Frolic*	55	19	0
9) Mrs. Jordan's bft.	*Zara, Arcadian Festival, Three Weeks After Marriage, Romp*	52	17	6
10) Assize Tues.	*Belle's Stratagem, Romp*	52	17	0
11) Inchbald's bft.	*Fair American, Touchstone*	52	15	6

The subscriptions totalled £131.12.0. comprising 53 box subscriptions at £63.12.0. and 85 pit at £68.0.0. This was an improvement of £12 on the previous year. The total takings for 49 nights was £1739.6.8. compared with expenses of £1565.14.4.

Wilkinson's generosity to his actors is exemplified by his treatment of Knight; as his benefit totalled only £22.7.0., his share being £8.13.6., Wilkinson gave him a second chance and on the proceeds of this, which amounted to 10/- more than before, paid him an additional 5/-. For Race Week Moss of Edinburgh was engaged; he played The Miser, Hardcastle and Lingo and recited Lingo's *Itinerary or, his Journey through York* describing New Walk, York Tavern, Assembly, Mansion House, Bishop Hill, Stonegate, York Races and the Theatre Royal. Samuel Butler, manager of the Richmond (Yorks) company, obliged by acting Sir Peter Teazle, and G. S. Carey returned with his *Lectures on Mimicry*. Mrs. Jordan added to her rôles those of Letitia Hardy and Lady Restless in *All in the Wrong*. Poor Dancer,[68] who had been seized with madness in Leeds was in the York Asylum, and Wilkinson arranged a benefit after Race Week for his wife and daughter who were left destitute. He fondly says that 'no place is more to be noted for the annals of good and benevolent acts, in the time of poverty and misfortune, than the ancient City of York.' Dancer recovered temporarily in 1784, but in May of that year was accorded another benefit as he was unable to continue on the stage; Wilkinson hoped thereby to fix Mrs. Dancer in a shop so that she could support herself and family.[69]

Another example of Wilkinson's generosity is to be found during the winter season of 1784. It had been an uncommonly severe winter and in order to relieve the consequent suffering Wilkinson advertised a benefit performance[70] for the poor of the city on the same footing as the players' benefits, the emoluments to be disposed of by a committee. The date fixed was March 6, the Saturday of the Judges' entrance into the city. It could not be arranged sooner as other Saturdays were already booked for actors' benefits; nor would it have been fair to have it mid-week because it would then have injured the following Saturday benefit and so have harmed the actor 'whose chief Dependence, for his or her Trouble and Expence during the Season, must arise from a Benefit.' *Lionel and Clarissa* was the play chosen in which Mrs. Jordan appeared, by desire, as Lionel for the first time to the Clarissa of Mrs. Ward. An epilogue by Cawdell in the character of a delegate for the poor of York was spoken by Cummins; the entertainments were *The Touchstone* with the temporarily revived Dancer as Harlequin and Mrs. Ward as Columbine. Wilkinson was able to hand over to the relief fund £31.6.0 of which £25.7.6 was profit from the evening, £2.12.6 his own subscription, £2.12.6 that of the players, and 1 guinea from R. Langley for a ticket.

Among new players in 1784 was Mrs. Ward[71] from Bath, a niece of Mrs. Sweeny – cum Bland – cum Hamilton's. She was well made but not handsome and her great desire was 'to sport her legs in small clothes against the Jordan' whom she bitterly hated. The rivals descended after the manner of their kind to childish tricks to put each other out of countenance. Mrs. Ward who was also a singer, sustained Serpilla in *La Serva Padrona,* Clara in *The Duenna,* Polly, Mrs. Sullen and Queen Dollilolly. Mr. and Mrs. Mills[72] came from Edinburgh. Mrs. Mills had appeared at Drury Lane and possessed the advantages of being ever ready to oblige both manager and fellow actors and of rapid study. She played Cleopatra in *All for Love,* Lady Macbeth, Roxana and the Countess of Salisbury. Her husband on the other hand was hot tempered and had failed at Covent Garden owing to inebriety; he appeared in comic parts and as Scrub and Polonius. Other additions to the company were Butler from Dublin, and, in April, the Strettons, dancers who played Harlequin and Columbine. Wilkinson made repeated endeavours to engage Mrs. Siddons on her way to Scotland in May. For a stay of 2 or 3 nights he offered her half the receipts of the theatre without deduction for expenses. These terms she refused so he tried to tempt her with £50 a night certain, a sum which he claims was equal to that which any theatre in the three kingdoms would give her, but she excused herself on the grounds of ill health and scantiness of time.[73]

Mrs. Jordan kept her ground this season.[74] She still sometimes appeared in tragedy, and the other leading lady Mrs. Smith, though retaining the estimation in which she was held, was wildly jealous of her rival's success. She had indeed gone to the length of seriously laming herself by taking the journey from Doncaster to Sheffield too soon after a confinement, for fear that Mrs. Jordan would continue to appear in her parts.[75]

Not a single new tragedy was presented this year but there were a number of new comedies: Andrews's *Reparation,* Mrs. Cowley's *More Ways Than One,* O'Bryen's *A Friend in Need is a Friend Indeed,* and Macnally's *Tristram Shandy.* There were two new comic operas by O'Keeffe *The Young Quaker* and *The Poor Soldier* the latter of which had brought crowded houses to Covent Garden, Newcastle, Norwich, and Dublin. O'Keeffe's adaptation of *La Serva Padrona or The Servant Mistress* with the original songs and music by Pergolesi, altered by Arnold, and Bate's *Magic Picture* with music by Shield for which assistant voices from the Minster were engaged, were new this season, as were a musical interlude *Tit for Tat or the Humorous Courtship*, and *The Country Madcap* which was Fielding's *Miss Lucy in Town* under an alternative title. In two of the three new pantomimes the recent invention of the balloon, in which the Montgolfier brothers had first ascended in 1783, was exploited. In *Harlequin Philosopher* an air balloon was sent off from the stage to float over the pit; another mock balloon after the manner of Charles's and Robert's at Paris was introduced into *Harlequin Junior.* The latter piece also included the view of Gibraltar, this time showing the heating of the red hot cannon balls which were conveyed in carriages to the batteries.[76] *May Day; or Harlequin's Whim* concluded with a transparent scene of the Temple of Hymen. Yet another pantomime, *Prometheus; or Harlequin Everywhere*, had first been seen in Race Week the previous year. The only new farce was Dent's *Receipt Tax*. A title of local interest otherwise unknown is the *Acomb Wife; or York Friar Turn'd Conjuror. The Revenge* was revived with new dresses, after two postponements owing to Wilkinson being ill. In the altar scene in *Theodosius*, Arne's songs and choruses from *Elfrida* were introduced and once again assistant voices were brought in from the Minster for *Hear Angels, Hear. The Merry Wives* was revived after 14 years with Ford = Cummins, Page = Smith, Falstaff = Mills, Mrs. Ford = Mrs. Jordan, Mrs. Quickly = Mrs. Leng, Shallow = Barrett, Master Slender = Knight. Other Shakespeare plays were *As You Like It, King Lear* (Cordelia = Mrs. Mills), *Macbeth* (Lady Macbeth = Mrs. Mills), *Othello* (Othello = Wilkinson, Iago = Cummins, Desdemona = Mrs. Mills), *Henry VIII* (Cromwell = Powell, Queen Katharine = Mrs. Mills) and *Much Ado* (Benedick = Knight).

Wilkinson's accounts for this season show that the salaries of Mrs. Ward and Butler were 25/-, that Mr. and Mrs. Mills were paid at the highest rate of £2.16.6. and that Kayne, an under actor who formerly received 18/-, was now married and that he and his wife were paid £1.14.0. The Powells had been raised another 4/-, receiving £2.4.0. The total week's salaries at the beginning of the season were £33.8.6. When the Strettons joined the company in April their salary was £2.10.0, the total thus being increased to £35.18.6. Occasional payments were again made to Masters Wilkinson and Frances and Misses Dancer and Swalwell, the children in the company. The singing boys, evidently those from the Minster, were paid 6/-. Bearpark the carpenter had a ticket night this season.

A number of payments were again made for writing: Barrett writing £3.1.4, French writing music 16/6, Kayne writing 3/6, 3 lengths[77] Amintor 3d, 5 lengths Daphne 5d, Barrett writing £1.6.5 and again 9/5, Swalwell writing 2/6, writing 45 lengths 3/9, Ward writing music 2/6, French ditto £1.17.6, Barrett writing 7/9. Ward was also paid £1.14.9 for advertisements. A copy of *The Duenna* cost 1 guinea, of *More Ways Than One* 5 guineas. Cleaning the house etc. cost £1.11.0. and 11/6, dyeing a dress and petticoat

16/6, making a regimental coat 7/- and Mrs. Ward was paid 15/8 for a dress. Rope for the 'front Green' [curtain] cost 1/6. £3 was paid in April for scenery and a few days later £1.14.0 to Helmes for scenery whilst the carriage of scenes to the waterside in May cost 4/- and from York to Leeds 5/6; the fire balls used in the pantomime cost 4/8. This season oil is put down as a weekly expense at 3/9; Parkes was paid £9.2.0. for coals. Insurance was £1.15.0. and there is no item for interest so presumably Wilkinson's loan had been paid off. Land tax and window tax cost £1.7.2½ and £1.6.9½ respectively. Wilkinson gave the poor 10/6 one night and the performers £1.11.6 another, and he lent Inchbald £2.2.0. The best night's takings were:

		£	s	d
1) Doorkeepers bft.	*Jane Shore, Scheming Lieutenant, May Day*	117	2	6
2) Smith's bft.	*Magic Picture, Acomb Wife, Catharine and Petruchio, Harlequin Shepherd*[78] *and air balloon*	93	18	6
3) Wilkinson's bft	*Bold Stroke for a Husband, Henry IV Pt. II (4th act), Harlequin Fortunatus*	89	0	0
4) Sheriff's night.	*All in the Wrong, Romp, Prometheus*	74	9	6
5) Cummins's bft.	*Reparation, Lady of the Manor, Harlequin's Whim*	66	11	0
6) Assize Thurs.	*Which Is the Man?, Rosina*	58	5	6
7) Oram's bft.	*As You Like It, Love à la Mode*	57	7	0
8) Bft. for poor	*Lionel and Clarissa, Young Actress, Touchstone*	55	15	0
9) Mrs. Jordan's bft.	*Theodosius, Daphne and Amintor, Old Maid*	54	17	6
10) Musician's bft.	*Venice Preserv'd, Recruiting Serjeant, Miller of Mansfield.*	52	11	0
11) Assize Tues.	*Young Quaker, Minor.*	51	3	0
12) Kaynes' bft.	*Cato, Gentle Shepherd* (des. Ld Galway, R. Milnes)	50	11	0

It will be noticed that on the five most popular nights pantomimes were performed.

The winter season and spring meeting together brought in £2003.18.6. and the expenses were £1672.14.6. – a profit of £321 odd compared with £173 odd the previous year.

The Browns[79] from Bath were newcomers when the company reopened for Race Week on August 21. Brown played Harlequin in *Harlequin's Invasion*; later he became a harlequin at Covent Garden. Mrs. Brown was a failure at Covent Garden but Wilkinson says she possessed great merit in particular characters such as Wowski, Old Kecksey and Old Dorcas in

Cymon but she varied very much in her performances even of the same character. The Browns's salary was £2.10.0.

The season started inauspiciously. Brown was to make his first appearance as Sir John Loverule but sprained his ankle and could not move from Leeds. The performers who were not appearing on the opening Saturday night did not leave Leeds until the Sunday. The great John Henderson was in the audience and saw the piece played without one of its chief characters. Henderson was so disgusted that he would not play during Race Week, but as he had asked an exorbitant fee and the houses were well filled without him, Wilkinson was the gainer by his refusal. The only visitors were a troupe from Sadler's Wells which included The Little Devil, and Thomiae, a clown from Brussels.[80] They performed feats and gave a new pantomime, *Harlequin called Foundling*, in which The Little Devil played Harlequin. Their emolument for two nights' performances was half a benefit which, however, brought them £22.15.0. During Race Week there were some good houses:

		£	s	d
M. Aug 23	*Young Quaker, Rosina*	46	4	6
T. „ 24	*Maid of the Mill, All the World's a Stage*	32	7	6
W. „ 25	*Mathilda, Poor Soldier*	100	10	0
Th. „ 26	*Jealous Wife, Harlequin's Invasion*	72	10	6
F. „ 27	*Merchant of Venice, Poor Soldier.* (Des. Ld. Galway, R. S. Milner).	82	17	0

Double salaries were paid except to the Strettons and Lloyd bringing the salary list for the week up to £70.15.0. Yet the manager made a good profit, the receipts being £509.1.6. and the expenses £396.14.4.

The account books close with an interesting inventory of scenery with notes as to its disposal. This must be cited in full as it shows the company's resources and how they were disposed of on the circuit, though it is doubtful whether it represents all available scenery.[81]

Old Hull Chamber Go for Use to Leeds.
Cornfield to go for Rosina and be Repaired.
Portsmouth Scene forward.
Camp Scene both Sides Good for Camp Scenes.
Y. Manor Scene
Julius's Pallace Go to Leeds to be Refreshed.
Leeds Painters Chamber to Leeds for him to Repair.
Garden Scene to be Refreshed.
Inchbalds Picture Scene stay at York.
Leeds M. Scene to Leeds him to Repair.
Genii Julius Garden – Stay at York to be Refreshed.
Crusoes [illegible] Scene to Leeds for Alterations.

Old Pallace to Leeds to be Refreshed.
Cymon Pallace and Wings. Go to Hull after Y. Races.
Sherwood Forest to Leeds, Hull, &c.
Old Inn Dover for a Street Scene Leeds Hull to be alter'd.
Old Inn Scene wants Imediate Alteration.
Prison Scene Wanted. Wings at Leeds.
Mason's Yard Go as a Street Scene.
Greenwich Hospital.

Cave Scene	Prison Paper Scene & a Black Ground to
Jobson's House	Padlock Scene to serve as Prison
Best Chamber	Rock of Gibraltar Go.
Front Chamber	
Back Scene, York Minster	
Front Chamber	
Pallace	
Cave Scene	Left at Leeds
Garden	
Dover Scene	Old Chamber at Leeds
Masons Yard and Street	
Mount Vesuvius	left at Leeds
Cut Grove	go to York
Prison	
Picture Scene	go to Hull
Moonlight Scene	left at Leeds
Genii Pallace	
Garden	left at Leeds
Mount Vesuvius	left at Leeds for a Cut Cave
Genii Garden Arch'd	go to Hull
Pallace, Mr. Colby's	left at Leeds to be refresh'd
Street	
St. Ustatia	
Moonlight Garden	Left at Leeds
Greenwich Hospital	
Cyprus Grove	
Camp Scene at York	
Fort Omai York	
Library at York	

It will be noted that the second list repeats the first in part but adds other scenes. They were probably made out at different times of the year. Old scenes for plays or pantomimes that were not likely to be revived were cut up or adapted to other uses. Alterations and refreshments were made to a considerable number of scenes, nearly all at Leeds. The company did not yet have a regular scene painter. Scenes were done by outsiders like

Williams, Halfpenny, Browne, Julius, or sometimes by a talented member of the troupe like Inchbald.

During November[82] of this year 1784 the Theatre was let, for the first time we know of, for astronomical lectures. Walker junior exhibited his Eidouranion or large transparent orrery, described as a splendid machine of 15 ft square which had been exhibited at the Lyceum in London, and other cities. The scenes showed the earth's movements, the moon's phases and all the planets and their satellites. A comet descended from the top of the theatre, revolved and re-ascended. A platform was laid over the pit which, instead of being sunk below, was then on a level with the boxes. The tickets were 2/6, 1st gallery 1/6, upper gallery 1/-. The Theatre was later frequently let for similar lectures. When the company returned in January 1785 it was to a Theatre newly decorated.[83] We know nothing of the embellishments except that they must have included new stage boxes for on a playbill of April 7[84] an announcement is included: 'The new Stage Boxes will be altered and rendered commodious and elegant before the Winter season.'

At Hull the manager, though he did not need another singer, had been so impressed by two performances which a Miss Wilkinson had given at benefits, that he engaged her, much to the annoyance of Mrs. Powell.[85] She was then about 15[86] but later was to become the famous vocalist Mrs. Mountain. Her parents, brothers and sister were circus performers and she herself had already made a success at the Royal Circus. She made her début in York on January 20 as Patty in the *Maid of the Mill* and her second appearance a week afterwards as Sylvia in *Cymon*, continuing in a succession of singing rôles.[87] She also gave G. A. Stevens's famous *Lecture on Heads* of which Tate says that 'in point of speaking, deportment, singing, humour not devoid of discrimination, I do honestly confess and profess, that I have seldom witnessed such a performance at so early an age.' She was very petite and well made even for breeches parts but too small for characters where consequence and elegance were required. With her and Mrs. Jordan the company was certainly strong on the women's side. The latter, however, was growing careless and inattentive[88] and was often ill, or malingering. Owing to a cold she would not perform in *Rosina* and Mrs. Brown had to study the part at a day's notice. There was a scene at Mills's benefit when she was to sing at the end of Act III of *Cymbeline* and to sustain the Poor Soldier. Though ready to play in the farce she refused to give the song. The audience clamoured until she finally appeared, dressed as the Poor Soldier, looking very pale, pleading illness and even fainting against the frontis-piece. Though obstinate she was forced to yield and finally obliged with 'In the prattling hours of youth' from the *Summer Amusement* for which she was quite unsuitably attired. Wilkinson remarks on the fact that during her stay in York, with the exception of the *Romp*, she rarely acted the roguish girls' parts in which she afterwards became famous. She sustained rather 'sentimental and gay ladies, chambermaids, opera parts, several breeches characters;' he himself did not think it possible that she would attain such fame as she was seen to do in girls' characters on the London boards. However, this season Mrs. Brown made a hit in Garrick's *The Country Girl,* an obsolete piece which had escaped Mrs. Jordan's attention; and it was seeing Mrs. Brown in this and similar rôles that determined her to try them when she went to Drury Lane. *The Country Girl* thus became one of her favourite parts and the consequence was that when poor Mrs. Brown appeared at Covent Garden critics accused her of imitating Mrs. Jordan.[89]

The great tragedienne Mrs. Mary Yates acted for one night on April 26, on her way from Edinburgh, in her favourite rôle of Margaret of Anjou in *The Earl of Warwick*. Wilkinson[90] tells us that 'she played as well that night as any time I had ever seen her – the audience were all gratified in the highest degree: The epilogue was equal to her assumed majesty; and she was as well pleased with her reception, as the audience were with her excellent acting.' It was the only time she appeared at York and was also her penultimate appearance on any stage as she fell ill and died in 1787. The prices were augmented to London level on this great occasion: boxes and green boxes 5/-, pit 3/-, 1st gallery 2/-, upper gallery 1/-. There was no half price to the upper gallery and no servant was admitted free. Mrs. Siddons was the only other actress of the day for whom Wilkinson could think of charging these prices, but he estimated that he would have a certain expense of £60 from this one night's visit. Mrs. Yates thanked for the kindness and patronage accorded her and, according to the *York Courant,* 'Her *Exit* after the Epilogue was as respectful as it was elegant, and as elegant as respectful. The Boxes were brilliant to a high Degree, and gave every Testimony of Good-Humour, Satisfaction and Applause.'

Another visitor was Mrs. O'Keeffe from Dublin who came all the way from London to act Belvidera, Julia and Hermione (*Distress'd Mother*) for the profits of a benefit night which was bespoken by the Officers of the Inniskilling Dragoons.[91]

Occasional performers of a very different order were Scaglioni's Dancing Dogs from Sadler's Wells who were engaged for 5 nights at the expense of £100. Nothing under full price was taken on their nights. Their feats included the storming of a fort with a dog scaling the walls and the ascent of a bull dog in a balloon which contained fireworks and stayed in the air three times as long as any previous one.[92] This curious entertainment drew packed houses and was very successful financially.

One alteration[93] was made this year at the request of several families who complained of the repetition of tedious interludes. In order to remedy this Wilkinson arranged not to put on any single scenes or little pieces until after the farce, when those who wished to could leave.

On the last night of the season, May 21, Mrs. Brown was to take her leave as Bridget in *The Chapter of Accidents* but was taken ill and her place supplied by Mrs. Smith. *Rosina* had to be substituted for *Peeping Tom* which was not too easy as the wardrobe was already packed and loaded on the wagons for Leeds.[94]

O'Keeffe's *Peeping Tom* was one of the new comic operas presented this season. His *Fontainbleau* with music by Shield, Stuart's *Gretna Green*, Colman junior's first piece *Two to One*, and Macnally's *Robin Hood* were others. *The Spanish Barber* which had previously been such a failure, was presented from a correct copy with the original music and got up with great care as a prelude to the début of Holcroft's *Follies of a Day*.[95] Holcroft's comedy was likewise a failure though it had been more successful in London than any piece since *The School for Scandal*. Wilkinson points out that pieces received with approbation in London were sometimes never called for a second time in York, yet he felt it his duty to let York pass judgment on any piece that had run 10-20 nights in the Metropolis.

Mrs. Inchbald's first piece *A Mogul Tale* was also brought out, the authoress being advertised as formerly of the theatre. Cumberland was represented by his tragedy *The Carmelite* and his comedy *The Natural Son*. The new pantomime was *Neck or Nothing: or Harlequin's Flight to the Gods* for which new scenery, machinery and transparencies were provided. The great attraction was Brown's flight from the stage over the pit to the upper gallery, and his return head foremost to the back of the stage. As a proof that there was no deception, he took off his hat and threw it into the pit as he ascended. The feat was performed by the aid of a wheel above.[96] There was a transformation from a Cook's shop into 'an exact Representation of the Draw-Bridge at Hull, with Part of the Dock'. Brown leaped over the bridge when it was drawn up and also into a cottage window 7 ft high. *Macbeth* was advertised as being dressed as well as in London; and *Richard III* had new dresses too. *Hamlet, As You Like It, The Merchant of Venice, Cymbeline, Henry IV* and *Romeo and Juliet* with Mrs. Jordan as the heroine, were also performed. *Measure for Measure* was revived after 10 years with Duke = Cummins, Claudio = Powell, Lucio = Knight, Angelo = Smith, Isabella = Mrs. Jordan.

The Browns departed at the end of the season. Mrs. Jordan had an offer from Drury Lane and was due to leave in September. Her last appearance on the York stage as a member of the company was as Miss Marchmont in *False Delicacy* on September 2. She had been with them three years and was to return as a star. This buoyant and ebullient creature was 'comedy incarnate' and by far the greatest actress trained in York.

Miss Valois[97] came from Norwich, who though a good dancer, failed to please and only stayed until the close of the winter season of 1786. Moody recommended Charles Dignum[98] for Race Week who was well received. He appeared in the singing rôles of Young Meadows, Don Antonio in *The Duenna*, Edwin in *Robin Hood* and Dermot in *The Poor Soldier*. He had first appeared at Drury Lane the previous year. He was a somewhat unwieldy actor but had a clear, full toned voice and was a good musician. Mrs. Farren came from Dublin during Race Week as Euphrasia and Isabella. Though once handsome her figure had grown corpulent and her acting coarse and heavy. She was insolent and commanding and soon broke her engagement much to the manager's relief.[99]

Wilkinson had again tried to secure Mrs. Siddons for Race Week but without success. This time she did not object to his terms but said she would not leave Scotland in time.[100] However, she visited the Theatre on August 27 and saw Mrs. Jordan in *The Poor Soldier,* giving it as her opinion that she was better where she was than on the London boards. Curiously enough Mrs. Yates had also given an adverse judgment on her merits pronouncing her 'merely a piece of theatrical mediocrity.'[101] Both were to be confounded by the event.

Miss Wilkinson's brother, the rope dancer from Sadler's Wells and Astley's, appeared for a few nights with his entertainment on the slack wire and his double set of musical glasses. This is the first time we hear of this latter form of entertainment which became very popular in Victorian times. Several new pieces were given: Knapp's *Hunt the Slipper,* O'Keeffe's *Beggar on Horseback,* Macnally's *Fashionable Levities,* Cobb's *Humourist,* for the copy of which the author received a considerable sum, and a pantomime, *Frolic or Harlequin in the Village* in which Miss Valois played Columbine and Bates, Harlequin.

On Mrs. Jordan's departure Wilkinson articled Mrs. Robinson[102] in her place. She was neat and had a good breeches' figure: 'her powers', Wilkinson pronounces, 'are good – voice not musical, and at times runs sharp to a degree – her judgment is good but sometimes hid and clouded' by affectation. She preferred to act in tragedy but was much more fitted to genteel comedy and was especially good as the Irish Widow. As we have seen by the paucity of new tragedies produced, and as Wilkinson himself declared, tragedy was yearly decreasing in public favour. Yet in York in 1786 Mrs. Robinson played at least fifteen tragic rôles as well as Rosalind. The treasurer's daughter Miss Swalwell, who had made her first appearance at her father's benefit in 1785, was now old enough to take parts in the musical pieces. Wilkinson[103] sums her up: 'Her person very good, an uncommon well made figure in the breeches characters, very attentive, a pleasing actress, understands a little music, has a sweet warbling pipe though not powerful.'

Matthew Browne[104] was engaged temporarily. He was the son of a Mrs. Browne of the Rooms at Scarborough, and, after abandoning the law for the stage, had been well received in many country theatres. He played Hamlet, Benedick, Glenalvon, Hastings, Jaques, Don John (*Chances*), Florizel, Master of the Toy Shop and, by special request, Richard III; though he was popular the audiences were very poor for the first month except at his benefit.

Later in the season there were several newcomers. Betterton from Edinburgh made his first appearance as Jaffeir on March 30. Originally a dancing master he was elegant and moved with grace. 'His voice' says Wilkinson[105] 'is good, but he wants ear to give modulation and variety; by reason of which many persons are apt to pronounce his voice bad, which is by no means the case.' He was quick of study but was conceited, and extravagant (he had already squandered a fortune in Ireland), and wanted to manage the manager. He was with the company until 1790 and later was engaged at Liverpool. His greatest claim to fame is that he was the father of the actress Mrs. Glover. Among his rôles this season were Archer, the West Indian and Capt. Absolute.

Southgate,[106] a promising young actor, had been with the company at Sheffield but made his first appearance at York on April 4 as Billy Bristle in *Hunt the Slipper* for the benefit of Swalwell. He had gifts enough to make him a first rate low comedian but was careless and indolent. He had the advantages of a neat person, humour and good articulation but he lacked smoothness and would sacrifice truth to character in order to gain a laugh. Irresistibly comic in some rôles he marred others by his lack of restraint. Later he married Miss Swalwell and improved under the influence of his wife and father-in-law. He performed with the company until his death but he never seems to have fulfiled his possibilities.

In May the Nunns[107] came from Bath. It was the rule for a newcomer to choose the part in which he or she first appeared and Mrs. Nunns, much against Wilkinson's advice and judgment, selected that of Letitia Hardy. Nunns's first appearance was as Old Doiley, 'a part he sustained with a good share of whim and pleasant humour.'

The end of the season saw the defection of many valued players. There were first the Smiths. At their last benefit Mrs. Smith[108] dropped her usual rôle of Mrs. Sullen to play Scrub as Mrs. Abington had done in London. Her last appearance was as Lady Flippant Savage in *The Fashionable Levities* on May 27.

The Powells left on account of jealousy of Miss Wilkinson, although the latter had procured an engagement at Liverpool for the summer and at Covent Garden for the winter and so herself departed at the end of the season.[109] She was an irreparable loss. During 1786 she acted Fanny in *The Clandestine Marriage*, a type of character in which she was much admired, and at her benefit she made a hit with *The Country Girl*. Her last appearance was on May 27 as William in *Rosina*. Mrs. Robinson too left shortly after the end of the York season. The loss of Mrs. Jordan, Mrs. Smith, Miss Wilkinson and Mrs. Robinson was a severe blow, but Wilkinson took it philosophically, realising that London would always snap up in the end any actor or actress who showed much promise.

G. S. Carey was engaged at considerable expense by the Kaynes for their benefit and gave his *Lecture on Mimicry* preceded by a performance of Oroonoko to the Imoinda of Mrs. Kayne. But the great event of the season was the appearance of Mrs. Crawford for two nights, on May 20 as the Grecian Daughter and on May 22 as Lady Randolph.[110] In her younger days she had been, as Mrs. Dancer, the heroine of the York stage.[111] Later she married Spranger Barry and as Mrs. Barry made her triumphs at Covent Garden. After his death she married Crawford whom she also survived. She was a great actress both in tragedy and comedy and as Lady

Randolph is said to have excelled even Mrs. Siddons. As a woman she was of variable temper, unreliable and money loving, a contrast to Mrs. Siddons who would rise from a sick bed, if she could, rather than disappoint her audience. Mrs. Crawford, of course, demanded a considerable sum and would not play on any less terms than Mrs. Yates or Mrs. Siddons[112] so that London prices were again charged. Wilkinson in defending this points out that when the York Theatre was full at common prices, the receipts did not at all equal those at Edinburgh, Bath, Dublin or Liverpool.[113]

Mrs. Crawford introduced Mr. and Mrs. Iliff, the latter of whom was to undertake the singing parts in succession to Miss Wilkinson. She made her first appearance on May 23, and was pronounced a capital singer; her husband played Douglas to Mrs. Crawford's Lady Randolph 'in which part his figure, youth, and sense of his author, with the aid of his able instructress, made him appear to very great advantage'.[114] At this time, too, Stephen Kemble returned with his wife (formerly Miss Satchell); she appeared as Miss Melville in *More Ways Than One* on May 26 but owing to her illness, Kemble himself was unable to undertake Othello the next night.[115]

The subscription was raised this year, as it had been at Hull, to boxes £1.12.0., pit £1.4.0. for 16 nights. Wilkinson[116] enters a long defence of this increase. He points to the very great expenses of the Theatre and cites the fact that salaries had risen £500 in the previous 6 years and £1000 since Baker's death. Up to the time when the new Theatre was built box subscriptions worked out at 1/3 a night, pit 7½d; after the opening of the new Theatre the raising of the pit subscription brought it up to 1/- a night; then after Baker's death the expenses grew to such an extent that the box prices were raised to 3/- and box subscriptions worked out at 1/6. Boxes at Newcastle, Bath and even at such a small theatre as Windsor were 4/-, and the lowness of the subscription rates with free admission of servants, Wilkinson claims, were unknown outside his circuit. The subscription receipts averaged out at about £12 to £15 per night but gradually the principal families withdrew theirs and patronised only individual plays. Then tradesmen and others bought blocks of subscription tickets and sold them for a profit for single performances. On weak or wet nights these tickets were hawked in the streets and thus the manager was deprived of the cash taken at the doors. Often when the house looked tolerably full it did not pay. We do not know whether the new prices, which raised subscriptions to boxes to 2/- and pit to 1/6, were judged exorbitant in York as they had been in Hull. There was evidently some trouble with the boys in the gallery for a playbill of February 28 announces that to prevent disturbances, none would be allowed there for 6d until after Act IV.

This year the Theatre was again newly painted and ornamented.[117] A York Guide of 1787 describes it as an 'elegant and spacious Building, on a Plan similar to those in London.' Miss Frude the wardrobekeeper had become Mrs. Bearpark and Kirk was now carpenter.

There were fewer new plays than usual; two of them were by Mrs. Inchbald, her farce *Appearance is Against Them* and her comedy *I'll Tell You What*. Perhaps the most important presentation was that of Macklin's *Man of the World* in which Mrs. Smith played Lady Rodolpha Lumbercourt and Mills the celebrated rôle of Sir Pertinax MacSycophant. He obtained great credit in this part[118] and, as he had been a country manager in various parts of Scotland besides playing for several seasons in Edinburgh, he spoke the dialect easily and naturally. At Wilkinson's benefit Burgoyne's *Heiress* and O'Keeffe's *Patrick in Prussia* were brought out. This latter had been produced at considerable trouble and expense, was adorned with new scenery and dresses and had a good London run to its credit, yet was a lamentable failure, and the poor manager was sternly rebuked for allowing 'such stuff' to be presented to a York audience.[119] The new pantomime, *The Birth and Adventures of Harlequin*, introduced the ascent of the dancing dog amid a display of fireworks, also an exact representation of the Lord Mayor's Show on the water as at Covent Garden in *The Flight from Lapland*. The pantomime was got up by Bates at his own expense, who selected the business and machinery from various London pantomimes and himself danced Harlequin. He had allowed Inchbald to have it for his benefit for a fee of five guineas, but thereafter reserved it, in spite of requests for its repetition, for his own night.[120] On March 15 'An Entire New Street Scene and New Wings' were displayed between play and farce.[121]

As You Like It was performed twice and *Hamlet, Much Ado, Richard III, King John, Catharine and Petruchio* and *Florizel and Perdita* once.

This summer, at last, Wilkinson secured the services of Mrs. Siddons who had not been seen on the York stage since her Manchester days. The prices were, of course, augmented, no money was returned after the curtain was drawn up, no servants were admitted free or allowed to keep places after the first act. Servants were to be at the Theatre by 5.30 to keep places as the doors opened at 6 and patrons were asked to bring silver to avoid delay.[122] July 29 was a great night for the York Theatre for on it Mrs. Siddons opened as Isabella while her Count Baldwin was the future famous tragedian G. F. Cooke whose début in York it was. On July 31 Mrs. Siddons played Jane Shore to the Hastings of Betterton and the Shore of her brother Stephen Kemble; on August 1 Lady Randolph; on August 2 Lady Macbeth to the Macbeth of Wilkinson; on August 3, by desire of the Sheriff and Grand Jury, Belvidera to the Jaffeir of Cummins and the Pierre of Wilkinson; on August 5 Mrs. Beverley and the Fine Lady in *Lethe,* and on August 8 Zara for Wilkinson's sole emolument. The season then closed and Mrs. Siddons accompanied Wilkinson to Hull but returned to play four nights during Race Week; on August 22 Euphrasia in *The Grecian Daughter*; on August 24 Elwina in *Percy* to the Douglas of Stephen Kemble; on August 26 Calista, and on August 28 Margaret of Anjou. For her eleven nights she received nearly £1100 without counting particular presents at her benefits.

The receipts were as follows:[123]

	£	s.	d.	
Isabella	44	8	0	
Jane Shore	129	5	0	
Lady Randolph	154	6	0	
Lady Macbeth	167	17	6	
Belvidera	192	9	6	
Mrs Beverley & Fine Lady	171	0	0	
Zara	103	9	6	Wilkinson's benefit
Euphrasia	140	1	0	
Elwina	169	9	0	
Calista	142	12	6	
Margaret of Anjou	71	7	6	Kemble's benefit at common prices
Total	1885	0	0	

The sum of £192.9.6. when she enacted Belvidera, was the greatest ever taken in any theatre outside London. Wilkinson's profits were not so large owing to the expenses of moving to Hull and back. The press to see the finest of all our actresses was as great as in London and her Isabella was received with the utmost astonishment and unbounded bursts of applause.[124] When she played Calista, however, the gallery was so turbulent that not a line could be heard throughout, though the offenders listened with attention to the after piece.[125] Wilkinson pays tribute to Mrs. Siddons's affability: 'As a proof – she has not known until she arrived at York, what play she was first to appear in, or what characters she was to act during a course of six plays. If a dress has not arrived in time by the carriers, she sometimes has asked what was to play such a night; never saying such a play will do better than another, or such a part would be too fatiguing, but is always ready to oblige.' A great treat she must have been after Mrs. Jordan and Mrs. Crawford.

The Stephen Kembles, as we have seen, played at the same time; in addition to the parts already mentioned Kemble acted Comus, Sir George Touchwood (*Belle's Stratagem*), Sealand (*Conscious Lovers*), and the Earl of Warwick; and Mrs. Kemble Polly, Indiana, Rosina, Lady Alton (*Heiress*), Mrs. Belville (*School for Wives*), Norah (*Poor Soldier*), Lady Grey (*Earl of Warwick*) and Cowslip (*Agreeable Surprise*). Mrs. Kemble was supported in singing rôles by Margaret Farren who had returned from Dublin and who performed among other parts Gillian (*Quaker*), the Poor Soldier, William (*Rosina*) and Laura (*Agreeable Surprise*).

As for George Frederick Cooke, then aged 31, he had played a few times at the Haymarket without attracting much attention, but had created a furore in lovers' rôles in Manchester and Newcastle where he had become a great favourite.[126] He left the York company for a while but rejoined it at Hull and played in York in 1787 until he took his farewell on May 12.

Unfortunately no playbills or newspapers for that year have come to light so we do not know what parts he played; nor can we tell whether he had yet fallen into the habit of drink which was to ruin his career. Oxberry[127] says that he acted Richard III and that little Julia Betterton, later Mrs. Glover, was the Duke of York. As the giant queen Glumdalca in *Tom Thumb* at his benefit he actually took up the child, who was playing Tom Thumb, and placed her in the palm of his hand, but the story is probably apocryphal as a playbill advertises her first appearance two years later.

To return to Race Week 1786, Fielding Wallis also then made his first appearance as the Irishman in *Rosina* and he remained with the company during 1787. As a lad he had run away from Ireland and joined the Richmond (Yorks) company but after his wife's death there he would never play in Richmond again. He was the father of Jane Wallis, better known as Miss Wallis of Bath, who was later also to appear on the York stage.[128]

The year 1786 had been a memorable one in the annals of the York Theatre since it had seen the reappearance both of Mrs. Crawford and Mrs. Siddons, the début of Cooke, and performances by lesser luminaries such as the Stephen Kembles. In 1787 there were several newcomers. One was Miss Eccles[129] later to be, as Miss Edmead, a well known actress at Norwich. She came of a good family and though a novice showed promise. She was well proportioned but not handsome and unfortunately delighted in playing male rôles. Her Leonora brought her greatest credit. She only stayed a season; so did another newcomer Mrs. Belfille.[130] who, though furnished with elegant and fashionable dresses by Davis of London, lacked animation and humour and therefore pleased but moderately.

Another Irishman who was in the company this season was James Field Stanfield.[131] He had been educated in France for the Roman Catholic priesthood, but instead of taking orders he went to sea in a ship engaged in the slave trade, and afterwards became an actor. He was very ugly but extremely quick in study and of good understanding. Later he became one of the principal actors in Scarborough and was the father of Clarkson Stanfield the landscape painter. He wrote a comic opera called *The Fishermen* which may have been acted during the season.

Darcy made his first appearance as Millamour[132] and played leading rôles with the company for two seasons. He was the nephew of Sir Ashton Lever of Museum fame, and had many assets as a player: 'his person was and is handsome, and well proportioned; and his face aided by marking features: He was one of the first Harlequins I ever saw; he leaped in a superior degree, not only as to height but neatness, aided by great agility. He sung pleasingly, and understood music'; in addition he was a masterly player on the German flute and a good draughtsman. His forte was comedy: 'he was a decent Archer, and an excellent Aimwell; he would act Plume or Brazen, and was able to sustain a first singing character in a manner greatly to his own credit and the satisfaction of the audience', and he grew into high favour. But he was quick tempered and easily took offence and in such moments would treat the manager like a stagekeeper.

At the beginning of the season Wilkinson brought to York a company of tumblers who called themselves the Italian Company. Their clown was Bologna senior who had arrived in this country in 1786 with his wife, two sons and a daughter, and was the founder of the famous family of harlequins. Wilkinson thought Bologna the best clown for doing wonders he had ever seen: 'he really did more than a man, for he went through performances incredible and masterly. I never saw any of them drunk, though the clown did not fear drinking a bottle of brandy, glass for glass as easily and with as much composure as I could wine.' Tate indeed was impressed by the company: 'They were well-behaved honest people; they had much merit, and their entertainment, on the whole, was the best conceived and the most worthy attention of anything of the kind I ever beheld.'[133] It was by Wilkinson's recommendation that they were engaged at Sadler's Wells where Bologna's son John was to be harlequin to Grimaldi's clown. They brought good houses but their quality spoilt the field for The Little Devil, Signora Spagniola and others from Sadler's Wells who arrived in February.[134]

Towards the end of the season Cumberland recommended John Fawcett[135] to Wilkinson thus introducing to the company another great comedian. He was then 19 and only a year previously had run away to become an actor at Margate. He opened on May 24 in a tragic rôle, that of Douglas, for he was engaged for the young heroes and melting lovers. Naturally he did not answer expectations and seemed mouthing in his manner. However, on the departure of Knight soon after he is said to have made a stipulation that he should never again be asked to play tragedy leads.[136]

On a visit to London Wilkinson had several times seen his old friend Mrs. Inchbald's new comedy *Such Things Are*.[137] He determined to bring it out in York at his benefit, managed to procure a copy and, from seeing it so often, was able to settle the business and dress the play properly. But Mrs.Belfille, having secured a copy from the Norwich manager to whom it had been sent by Harris, wanted it for her benefit. After much wrangling Wilkinson referred the matter to Mrs. Inchbald in the confident expectation that she would decide in his favour; but she, no doubt remembering how Tate had dealt with *The Duenna*, thought his version would be a jumble of his own, whereas she knew Mrs. Belfille's to be genuine. Despite her denunciations Wilkinson insisted on having it on his night when it was very successful; but the consequent quarrel with the authoress was not made up for four years. The production of this comedy also led to trouble with Knight who was shortly due to leave with Miss Farren (later to become his wife) for Bath. Knight objected to his name in the rôle of Twineall being put third in the bills. Wilkinson procured from Bath a playbill printed in the same order of characters but Knight would not be satisfied and the part had to be given to Betterton. Knight's friends intended to make a disturbance but thought better of it, and in the end the manager parted friends with the actor.

In addition to Knight, Cooke, the Kaynes, Stanfield, and Miss Eccles left at the end of the season.[138] During Assize Week in July Elizabeth Farren[139] acted in York as Lady Paragon, Lady Townly, Maria (*Citizen*), Mrs. Oakley, Widow Belmour, Charlotte (*Hypocrite*), Miss Tittup (*Bon Ton*), Lady Teazle and Emmeline (*King Arthur*). She drew great houses and was much esteemed and liked. Lady Townly was one of her best parts, indeed Colman thought that no-one could compete with her in the elegant levities of the rôle. Elizabeth Farren was then acting at the Haymarket and at Drury Lane where she had succeeded to Mrs. Abington's fine lady rôles, and she was to remain at both theatres until her marriage with the Earl of Derby in 1797.

During this season Wilkinson's son John,[140] now 18 years of age, made his début as an adult actor as Charles in *The Hypocrite* on July 26, the proud father playing Dr. Cantwell. He was favourably received. Though he was not a good actor, being diffident and nervous, at least he never spoiled the sense of his author. He himself was keen on the stage though his father would have preferred some other career for him.

The stars for Race Week were the singers, Mrs. Crouch and Michael Kelly.[141] She made her début as Rosetta on August 22 and also played the Maid of the Mill, Sylvia (*Cymon*), Clarissa, Gillian, Viola (*Strangers at Home*), Polly, Rosina, Leonora and Clara (*Duenna*) for her benefit which brought a great house. In *Comus* she and Kelly gave their new-fangled whimsical duet from the Italian '*O thou wert born to please me*'. 'The English nightingale', 'the beautiful and siren songstress', as Wilkinson calls her, was all the week afflicted with a fever and sore throat, but she never once disappointed her audience from whom her sweetness of voice and attractive manners won golden opinions. Kelly was Young Meadows, Lionel, Macheath, Don Carlos and Leander. He has described in his *Reminiscences*[142] his first meeting with the eccentric Tate, who, he says, 'was a great epicure, very fond of French cookery, and small dishes; large joints he never allowed to come to his table, and above all had the most sovereign contempt for a round of beef.' He played a joke on the manager by presenting himself got up in strange fashion; whereupon Tate made no bones about what he thought of him. '"What, that figure!" said Tate – "what, that my Lord Aimworth, – my Lionel – my Young Meadows – Ugh! send him away, Ma'am! send him back to Drury Lane! send him to Vienna! I can never produce such a thing as that, to a York audience, Ma'am."' However, on Kelly's returning properly dressed, Tate enjoyed the joke against himself.

Mills died of a decline and dropsy at Hull and his widow not long afterwards married Fawcett.[143] Three former members of the company had returned when the York Theatre reopened in 1788. One was Miss Hitchcock from Dublin 'now grown a handsome young woman, an improved actress, and could put her hand to anything, such as ladies, chambermaids, girls, singing, first and second characters'[144] and even ventured on Desdemona and Ophelia. The others were Mrs. Kennedy (formerly Miss Holmes) and her husband. Newcomers were Michell who played old men, had an excellent voice in Bannister's line and became the company's scene painter; Warren from Portsmouth, a useful and willing actor who was with the company until 1797, and Fotteral from Dublin.

We know more about this season than any other owing to the publication of the *Theatrical Register*[145] which contains detailed criticism of every performance. The volume is dedicated to Wilkinson to whom it pays tribute, firstly as a manager for rendering the Theatre a rational and polite amusement and producing as much novelty as any manager in Great Britain; secondly as an actor whose Zanga was equal to anything seen on the York stage. The standard of criticism in this publication is remarkably high and gives an excellent idea of the talents and failings of the company and of the faults and merits of the various productions. It will be convenient to consider some general strictures on the conduct of the performances, then pass to more detailed remarks about the actors and actresses in different parts, and about one or two special plays.

One of the critic's most frequent complaints was of inattention both in the conduct of the performance and on the part of the actors. The prompter was adjured to keep as much regularity behind the scenes as possible. A letter addressed to the *Theatrical Register* averred that the inattention at performances the previous year had been shameful and called for reform. The prompter ought to have weight in his official capacity to prevent this but, either from good nature or want of knowledge, he allowed frequent mistakes to occur. In *Such Things Are* a noise behind prevented Darcy going through his scene, and a green room joke interfered with Miss Hitchcock's giving one of the best of hers. People stuck in clusters in the wings were visible from the pit and occasionally an unwarranted intrusion was even made onto the stage. There were scenic hitches. In the *Castle of Andalusia* negligence on the part of the stagekeepers caused the opening scene of the thunderstorm to be played with the front lamps displaying their full brilliancy. The shifting of the scenery from a private apartment to a street was sometimes effected after the the delivery of two or three speeches, and the temporary doors hung so badly and loosely that the stagekeepers had to take them down or put them up in the middle of a scene. The prompter was asked to banish such absurdities. It was his fault too that the minutiae of the scene were sometimes neglected. A couple of old chairs, which needed re-covering, did service both in a lady's apartment, and in a gaol in the pantomime; even when they were re-covered they failed to match the crimson window curtains. It was a glaring absurdity that the prompter should allow Malcolm to sit in the banquet scene in *Macbeth*; and here again the singing witches were not provided with anything to throw into the cauldron. As for the actual business of prompting, Earby was once or twice criticised for being heard all over the house or in the centre of the pit and in the green boxes, though he should have learnt to whisper in every key which the performers spoke in.

Individual players were frequently censured for inattention and for laughing on the stage. This latter seems to have become a habit with some of them, particularly Southgate. One form of inattention was being imperfect. Draycott, a small part actor, was a constant offender to the embarrassment of those on the stage with him. In *As You Like It* actors in lesser rôles even forced the leads to cut their speeches and the critic was constantly insisting that small part actors should not be negligent. In *Venice Preserv'd* the conspirators were inattentive and had evidently disregarded rehearsals; one even came on without a sword. Wilkinson himself did not know his part of Sir Luke Tremor in *Such Things Are*. Sometimes it was a case of insufficient rehearsal, such as for example, spoiled the first two performances of *The Midnight Hour* and that of *The Confederacy* in which the short speeches called for extra rehearsals.

Unsuitable dressing was a point the critic had a keen eye for. Thus Southgate was got up to look like a monkey in *Such Things Are*. Fawcett as Renault in *Venice Preserv'd* had a wig which excited laughter: Misses Farren and Hitchcock in *The Wonder* were dressed more suitably for mistresses than maids; Mrs. Mills played Elizabeth without a ruff, and Molly Maybush in *The Farmer*, though she confesses poverty, appeared in satin shoes with elaborately coiffeured hair. In *Macbeth* the singing witches were ridiculously arrayed in engaging attire and might have passed for women of beauty; Bailey, as a speaking witch, on the contrary adopted an extravagant disguise and it would have been better had the others made up their faces to match; Ross and Banquo appeared as two fine powdered beaux with silk stockings on the barren heath; and Macduff should not have used powder in his hair. The new dresses for this production had been made in Lincoln[146] but though adjudged elegant, were none of them exactly right. In *As You Like It* the dresses were pretty near to character and Mrs. Kennedy was praised for her introduction of boots in the rôle of Rosalind, but the critic advised the abolition of the use of powder. *Henry VIII*[147] was got up this season in splendid style for Wilkinson's benefit, and the whole company in new dresses from London took part in the coronation scene procession whilst added voices swelled the coronation anthem. Wilkinson proclaimed it the best dressed play ever seen out of London, and the critic declared that the banqueting scene was superior to anything of the kind known in York. The manager had not spared expense to provide superb costumes, and the performers vied with each other for pre-eminence in splendour. The critic estimated that the dresses for this brilliant representation must have cost upwards of £1000. Most were enriched with gold and silver lace and embroidery. Only Miss Hitchcock's train should have been supported by someone nearer her own height. Vickers was principally concerned in the decorations, and Walmsley had supplied a new landscape scene, which at first disappointed because of its strong similarity to his curtain scene, but afterwards was seen to be as good as any he had done for this theatre. Who Walmsley was or how long he had been employed as scene painter we do not know. The critic also approved of the old English dresses which had now been provided for *Peeping Tom*. Michell is commended for a castle scene in *Richard Coeur de Lion* as well as for his scenery in the new pantomime of *The Enchanted Castle*. This latter, which cost £40 and more, consisted of a magic cavern through which was seen a shipwreck, an enchanted castle, an elegant bower of roses, a hermit's cell, the launching of a ship with a transformation to a baker's shop and a concluding scene of The Temple of Flora. Probably those scenes were not all new and we may conjecture that the Temple of Hymen also served the cause of Flora. The critic suggested that a few tricks in lieu of songs would have given more time for the changes. In the other pantomime *Queen Mab*,[148] a haystack changed to the York mail coach, and the Guildhall was transformed to a blacksmith's and barber's shop. On the other hand *Rosina* needed new scenery and lacked the representation of the setting and rising sun; the business of the stage in it was badly conducted as it had been even in the time of Mrs. Jordan and Chalmers.

A practice that our critic much objected to was that of a player's advancing to the front for a song when his supposed audience was on the stage. Darcy was guilty of this as Amiens and Miss Hitchcock in *High Life below Stairs*, whilst Mrs. Mills in *Love Makes a Man* approached so near the lamps as to have the person she was addressing behind her. Wilkinson as Jaques was rightly severely censured for handing over the last scene of his part to another actor. The year previously the comedy had been presented without an Adam. Indeed the critic frequently protested about cuts. *The Castle of Andalusia* was mutilated, *Fontainbleau* shorn down to an afterpiece and *The Maid of the Oaks* murdered as well as suffering the inappropriate introduction of Kelly's duet in the first act. The comedians too were apt to put in more than was set down for them. Southgate as Solomon in *The Quaker* added to the proverbs of the text, and Wilkinson[149] tells us how Darcy and Fawcett in the park scene of *The Farmer* introduced an impromptu dialogue about the latter's new born son only to be applauded for it by the audience.

One department of the theatre the *Theatrical Register* praised unreservedly and that was the music under French. Few theatres, the critic asserted, had so respectable a leader or so good a band, indeed it was the best out of London. French composed a new overture for *The Farmer* and parts for the various instruments for this comic opera, and he selected and composed the music for *The Fate of Sparta*. As for the attendance at the theatre this seems to have varied considerably. A correspondent stated that he could not recollect any period when it was less frequented; and the critic agreed that it was neglected, the pit and gallery being seldom half filled. The first night of Mrs. Hook's new comic opera *The Double Disguise* was played to empty boxes, though at a subsequent performance it brought in £20 at after price; *Hamlet* had but a thin house and *Much Ado* one of the worst; *The Careless Husband* drew only a score or two of spectators. During Race Week there were empty benches at the second performance of Mrs. Cowley's new tragedy *The Fate of Sparta* owing to the late hour of the race, and people were continually entering during the 4th and 5th acts. On the other hand Burgoyne's melodrama *Richard Coeur de Lion*, with music by Grétry, drew splendid houses and at its third performance the front boxes made an elegant appearance, whilst the afterpiece brought in not less than £18-20. When Miss Farren took her farewell as Wowski in *Inkle and Yarico*, prior to following Knight to Bath, there was a brilliant audience despite the fact that a fine concert was also held that evening.

On the whole, though, one's impression is rather one of decline. Loud conversations were often carried on by the occupants of the boxes during the performance, a habit that many actors naturally resented. During *The Merchant of Venice* some bucks made a disturbance in the pit, one leapt onto the stage and another discharged a volley of oranges from the green boxes. Because the trollops' scene was omitted from *The Beggar's Opera* the audience indulged in an uproar.

We next come to the criticism of individual performers of whom the most interesting was Fawcett. He was now fortunately removed from the miscast tragic rôles with which he had started. The forty characters[150] he sustained this season were varied enough. The two main criticisms levelled at him were in respect of his voice and his make up. As Saville he was throaty and apt to lisp, as Tinsel he bellowed so loudly that he was incapable of singing, though he redeemed himself in the second act by raising much laughter. As the season progressed he improved as far as the bellowing went and in *The Sultan* he had almost abolished it. As Peeping Tom his asides were too loud and as Dr. Druid he was not happy, dancing about and repeating 'look ye' forty times. As Pedrillo, his first part of the season, he might have passed for an actor of some experience but was too much of the rustic for the servant of a well travelled man and was made up with too [illegible] visage. His headdress in *The Romp* was also absurd and more like that of an idiot than a London shopman. He could not play the gentleman; as Horatio he was execrable, as Oliver in *As You Like It* he mouthed and turned the part to burlesque, whilst as Renault he was advised to reserve his 'comedy phiz' for more suitable rôles. In *Inkle and Yarico* he made the best of a trifling part, and he supported Rohlf in *The Disbanded Officer* with great credit endowing him with downright, honest colouring. But it was in the low comedy characters that he triumphed. He was so good as Launcelot Gobbo that he was advised to study this cast. As Clodpole he was well dressed, as Moses he was excellent throughout, and as Simkin he had more strokes of real merit than all the grimace and buffoonery too frequently adopted for this line. His David showed that he was benefiting from the instructions he was receiving from the best judges in the theatre and would reach the top; his Bullock added another to the many conceptions of the rôle; but his greatest success was as Jemmy Jumps in *The Farmer* a part with which he was long to be associated and in which he founded the reputation that eventually carried him to fame on the London stage. The piece was very successful in York and was even performed five nights one week, an unprecedented run. Wilkinson[151] says that Fawcett's song ' "Short legg'd ladies, thick legg'd ladies" was and is sung better by him than by any performer I have ever seen in the character, but I do not vouch the same for every other part of that character.' As for his Tinsel it was 'acted with such spirit that he was encored and received great applause. In short, after being thought but slightly of at the August meeting, he was an established favourite in three weeks after the York Theatre opened in the winter following. I was much pleased at his great industry, and the dependence I could place on his assiduity and his word, two great points on and off the stage; besides he was strict in his payments, and regular in his living.'

Of Cummins, the company's leading tragedian, the critic usually had nothing but good to say. His Zamti in *The Orphan of China* was dressed and played with judgment and showed that when he relinquished the young heroes he would be equally capable of the weightier tragic rôles. He was never seen to more advantage than as Macduff especially in the scene when he hears of the murder of his family, but his fault was too much violence both in this part and as Cleombrotus in *The Fate of Sparta* where he was inclined to address the pit. In *The Rival Queens*, though his voice was good in several modulations and of extensive range, he tore it to pieces and produced hoarseness. His Jaffeir was a less just conception than his Pierre, and he did not dress the character, as was customary, as a poor man. He was very happy as Percy and portrayed amazement in every feature when Elwina tells him of her marriage. To comedy he was less well suited and even tended, when he could not rant, to be inarticulate. Yet his Doricourt was all life and spirit, his Clifford in *The Heiress* gave great satisfaction in the delivery of several speeches, his Plume was easy and natural, his Haswell in *Such Things Are* was just, sensible and pathetic, and as Petruchio he was very animated.

Betterton too generally obtained commendation. His Minikin in *Bon Ton* was gracefully executed though he needed to introduce a few cadences in his speech and modulate the higher tones of his voice. In the difficult part of Felix in *The Wonder* he showed merit in the various transitions and dressed suitably; as Brass in *The Confederacy* he managed the wheedling insinuations well, and as Sir Harry's servant in *High Life Below Stairs* he presented a finished picture of the servant Ofton. He always looked a gentleman as his actions were natural, his deportment easy and his dresses in good taste.

Darcy varied a good deal. As Tivy in *Bon Ton* he was indifferent and forgot his rank in the army when conversing with Sir John Trotley. He had a want of dignity in his figure as Holberg in *The Disbanded Officer* but depicted that character's embarrassments very naturally. He was accused of inattention in *The Double Disguise* in which he made Lord Hartwell merely a walking figure and he dressed Sir Benjamin in *The School for Scandal* deficiently. On the other hand as Lord Duke in *High Life* he made the French dialect laughable, and as Henry in *The Deserter* he dressed, looked and acquitted himself better than in any other rôle. He had not a powerful voice but used it with discrimination. His Sebastian in *The Midnight Hour* showed him capable of low comedy; as a harlequin his leaps were sometimes disappointing, at others he equalled Chalmers.

Fotteral had few rivals as Sir John Trotley though the critic suggested the use of a cane as his hands were apt to drop into his pockets; as the knave Amphares in *The Fate of Sparta* he sensibly refrained from the custom of looking a villain. He divested the rôle of Sir Peter Teazle of extravagance, acting in a natural, easy style and marking his surprise at the throwing down of the screen in every feature. He discovered in Stockwell in *The West Indian* beauties that had been neglected by his predecessors and in the very different rôle of Henry VIII he combined passion with dignity. He was good in serious and elderly parts but was miscast in the fine gentleman.

Wilkinson himself did not act much this year as on March 27, whilst returning from an evening at the Mansion House, he fell down and broke his leg.[152] As Macbeth, the critic found him far above mediocrity, excellent in some passages in others disappointing. He made his return as Col. Downright in *I'll Tell You What* on May 3. As for his son John his Hamet in *The Orphan of China* showed his good figure to advantage and he delivered some of the speeches in a judicious style, but his gesture was defective and he was recommended to practise in front of a looking glass or an impartial friend. He lacked confidence and was not always perfect but as the season advanced he improved, becoming easier and more graceful.

Michell proved a useful actor and was the best Fitzroy in *The Poor Soldier* seen in York, his songs being particularly excellent. His forte was old men as his playing and dressing of Russet in the *Deserter* and his Old Philpot proved. He was recommended to use his arms more gracefully and assume more consequence. His Player King in *Hamlet* was said to be an insult to the audience.

Barrett, the Manager of the Norwich company, with whom Wilkinson had played a few nights the previous season, came to return the compliment in *Hamlet* and genteel comedy rôles. The critic thought little of him. His Ranger was sometimes sententious, sometimes a buffoon, 'sometimes, he was sliding about the stage as if he had been on ice, and at other times his legs were preposterously extended.' As Hamlet he was 'passable', but as Lingo he left his voice behind the scenes.

Charles Wood returned after 7 years for a few nights at the end of April. He had gained judgment, improved in looks and deportment and sang with taste and feeling, and the critic hoped Wilkinson would article him again. This he did not do but gave him a benefit of the full amount of the house as compensation for the trouble and expense of his journey.

Other visitors were G. S. Carey and Moses Kean who gave their imitations.

To turn to the women of the company. The critic waxed enthusiastic about Mrs. Kennedy who could do no wrong in his eyes. He praised her unreservedly in every rôle she undertook. In the *Country Girl* she changed her countenance with her dress when adopting boys' clothes; in *The Wonder* she was particularly good when endeavouring to work a reconciliation with Felix surrendering her hand with an exquisite look; she could play the assumed and the real lady equally well as her Clarissa in *The Confederacy* showed, and she could also play the coquette, witness her Clarinda in *The Suspicious Husband*. She enacted Rosalind to perfection, was capable of sustaining the softer line of tragedy as in *The Female Captive,* and in *The Rival Queens* worked up jealousy well. At the end of the season she appeared as Wowski, a singing part, for the first time, and shook with stage fright. As Portia she astonished by the pathetic beauty of her mercy speech and as Beatrice she excelled in flexibility of countenance. Her wardrobe, like her deportment, was always a perfect pattern of ease and elegance and the dresses she wore in *Seduction* were obviously expensive and her own purchase.

Miss Farren as Victoria in *The Castle of Andalusia* did not seem quite at home, was not perfect and her voice had some disagreeable tones. She was an excellent Lady Alton, a good breeches figure as Jacintha and specially happy as Wowski.

Miss Hitchcock had a voice above mediocrity and an engaging figure but was advised to exchange the Sestini style of singing for the English, and to be more deliberate in her pronunciation. She was several times blamed for inaudibility, and seems sometimes to have been lethargic, whilst certain parts, such as that of Lady Easy in *The Careless Husband,* were too much for her. Her Ophelia is commended, especially in the songs where her pathos drew tears.

Mrs. Mills, who became Mrs. Fawcett in May, played a wide range of parts with varying success. Her figure wanted consequence for tragedy and her voice too was inclined to be dissonant. In Mrs. Siddons's rôle of Chelonice in *The Fate of Sparta* she fell far short but she played Lady Macbeth in the old style and surpassed expectation. As Miss Alscrip in *The Heiress* she presented a finished picture of a new made lady, and she was sprightly, cheerful and easy as Lisetta in *The Disbanded Officer,* a rôle which suited her, but Flippanta in *The Confederacy* was her chef d'oeuvre. In other characters she was not so good: she lacked importance as Lady Strickland in *The Suspicious Husband,* misconceived Cowslip as arch instead of simple, and had not a good enough breeches figure for Sylvia in *The Recruiting Officer.* Mrs. Southgate had improved since her marriage, had an agreeable soft voice but needed a dancing master to correct her deportment. She was recommended to try the chambermaid cast to help her in this respect. Her best character was Louisa in *The Deserter.*

The critic has ever a kind word to say of old Mrs. Leng who was somewhat neglected. She took the old women, and Mrs. Malaprop was one of her best parts. Her good ground knowledge of a part like that of Mrs. Amlet in *The Confederacy* made her presentation unusually striking, and as Mrs. Heidelberg she was the only good performer in a bad production of *The Clandestine Marriage.* Miss Cummins appeared a few times this season, and, though still very young, was highly commended as Julie in *Richard Coeur de Lion.*

In May, Wilkinson gave a helping hand to Mr. and Mrs. Strickland from Edinburgh and their three children. Strickland had been afflicted with the dropsy for 9 months and his wife was in a precarious state of health. She played two nights, once as Letitia Hardy and the Poor Soldier, secondly as Elwina in *Percy* and proved incompetent though she did her best in the tragedy.

It is clear that the company was much stronger on the comic than on the tragic side. Cummins was the only tragedian of any stature and there was no actress who really had the authority for the heavier tragic rôles. The critic of the *Theatrical Register* went so far as to say that few companies could compare with the York one in the comic line and that some of the actors had abilities to bring them to the top of their profession. The presentation of the pieces varied a good deal. Thus Pilon's new farce *Barataria* was completely ruined; *Hunt the Slipper* had a poor and imperfect performance; Cobb's new comic opera *Love in the East* dragged in the representation and had evidently been got up with insufficient preparation; on the other hand for *Richard Coeur de Lion* the manager had spared no expense, and whereas the cost of supers usually meant that the battles were absurd in country companies, this one was waged with great vigour and brought applause from everyone, whilst the acting was excellent from highest to lowest. Jephson's new tragedy *Julia*,[153] though a poor play in which the trial scene only excited laughter, was well dressed and all means were employed to promote its success; the other new tragedy, Mrs. Cowley's *Fate of Sparta*, was also superbly dressed with two exceptions. Indeed it seems that sometimes great pains were taken with the presentation, at others none at all.

Many more bespeaks by private individuals were obtained this year; Lady Frankland, Lady Milner, Lady Winifred Maxwell Constable, Mrs. Saltmarsh and Mrs. Fawkes being among them. The subscription nights were reduced from sixteen to fourteen for which boxes were £1.8.0. and pit £1.1.0.

The contemporary agitation against slavery led by Wilberforce was then at its height and was reflected in the Theatre in an Epilogue on the African Slave Trade spoken by Cummins in February.

When the company returned to York for Race Week Mr. and Mrs. Lassells had also been engaged as dancers.[154] Lassells was an excellent clown, a clever harlequin and an industrious man. John Philip Kemble made his first appearance in York as a star since he had left the company in 1781, and attained fame at Drury Lane. He opened on August 18 as Hamlet to the Ophelia of Miss Hitchcock. On August 19 he played Shylock to the Portia of Mrs. Fawcett, on August 20 and 27 Othello with Cummins as Iago, Mrs. Fawcett as Emilia and Miss Hitchcock as Desdemona, on August 21 Benedick to Miss Hitchcock's Beatrice, on August 22 the Count of Narbonne, on August 23 Richard III to the Richmond of Cummins and Lady Anne of Miss Hitchcock; on August 25 for his benefit Macbeth to the Lady Macbeth of Mrs. Fawcett, after which he read the story of Le Fevre from Sterne as he had done when he was a member of the company. He wished to have *The Toy Shop* as an interlude this night but Wilkinson had made a firm regulation once more against them even as afterludes.[155] He had a second benefit on September 1 when he repeated Hamlet.

There was one new afterpiece – Macready's *Village Lawyer.*

Mention must here be made of the fact that in 1788 an Act was passed legalising dramatic performances in the provinces on the grant of licences by justices. York which was operating under a Royal patent was not directly affected but some of Wilkinson's other theatres could henceforward have a legal standing.

The company was opening at York rather later for the winter season and in 1789 did not start until January 31. The Iliffs[156] had returned. Her voice was powerful and melodious but had been strained in attempts to copy Mrs. Billington's execution. Fawcett was now well established and his reputation had increased in the circuit.[157] Mrs. Kennedy, besides acting comedy rôles such as Lydia Languish and Mrs. Sullen, was also cast as Imogen and Monimia. Wilkinson[158] himself did not act as he was still lame and in poor health from late hours and lack of exercise. Indeed he was never the same after his accident and henceforth made only occasional appearances. His son continued to act and performed Squire Richard, George Barnwell and Paris. According to the playbill of February 16, little Julia Betterton made her first appearance as the page in *The Orphan.*

Three celebrated visitors appeared on the York boards this season. The first was the singing actress Miss George[159] who played four nights in April as Rosetta and the Romp, Diana in *Lionel and Clarissa,* Rosina, Clara and for her benefit Wowski, a rôle she had created at the Haymarket. Though various troubles caused play and afterpiece to be changed on nearly every night of her stay, she met with a good reception, her nights were fashionably attended and she finished with a crowded house. She later became Mrs. Oldmixon and went to America about 1795.

Tom King,[160] unhappily, was not such a success though he had been manager at Drury Lane and his Lord Ogleby was renowned. On May 5 he played it to a house so empty that he wished the next day not to appear again, suggesting to Wilkinson that he would not be able to afford his fees. The manager expressed regret that he had not also acted in the farce, but King was simply astounded that playing in his first established character with his name and novelty he had not drawn a crowded house on his first night. The York audience was indeed unpredictable. In the end he promised, though he had never experienced such disgrace, to go through with his engagement, and he played Marplot with Sir John Trotley and the original prologue to *Bon Ton* on May 7, Sir Peter Teazle and Cadwallader on May 9, the Copper Captain and Puff for his own benefit, which was not crowded, on May 12, and Touchstone and Puff for Wilkinson's benefit on May 14. King had a beautiful delivery and it has been said that no one could speak the dialogue of Ogleby and Sir Peter Teazle with greater point. Lamb declared that 'his acting left a taste on the palate sharp and sweet like a quince.'[161] Lastly on May 23, Mrs. Siddons[162] returned, acting Isabella on her opening night, Belvidera on May 25, Jane Shore on the 26th, the Grecian Daughter on the 27th, Dianora in Greatheed's *Regent* – a part which was so exhausting that the run of the play had had to be stopped at Drury Lane – on the 28th, Mary Queen of Scots, with *Britannia's Ode* as spoken by her at Brooks's in London, for her benefit on the 30th. The prices were only the usual public week ones of boxes 3/6, green boxes 3/-, pit 2/6, 1st gallery 2/- and upper gallery 1/- but the receipts for the six nights amounted to £453. Though the crowds did not equal those of 1786 yet the houses were satisfying to her.

The Regent was the only new tragedy given this year. Mrs. Inchbald's drama *The Child of Nature* was brought out with Cummins as Alumanza and Miss Hitchcock as Amanthis, and her farce *Animal Magnetism* also made its début. Another farce by a former member of the company was Kemble's *Pannel*. O'Keeffe's *Prisoner at Large* and his comic opera *The Highland Reel* both provided good parts for Fawcett. The new musical piece *Marian* by Mrs. Brooke, authoress of the popular *Rosina*, with music by Shield was provided with new scenery, designed and painted by Michell, but failed to repeat its predecessor's success. The new pantomime was *The Vision of an Hour*[163] with scenery by Michell and music by French. It opened with the tomb of Harlequin which changed to a garland of flowers and concluded with the rising of Harlequin's temple and an apotheosis of William III. Darcy was the Harlequin and Mrs. Lassells Columbine. Lassells produced a new dance at his benefit[164] called *The Fairies' Festival* in which 12 children of the city presented a Grand Garland Dance with new dresses and garlands in the scene of the Temple of Flora. Hill's version of *Henry V* was revived after ten years with Cummins as the King and Mrs. Kennedy as Harriet. Other Shakespeare plays and adaptations were *Cymbeline* with Betterton as Posthumous and Mrs. Kennedy as Imogen; *The Merchant of Venice* with Iliff as Shylock; *As You Like It* with Betterton as Orlando; *The Tempest; Romeo and Juliet* with Betterton as Romeo and Miss Hitchcock as Juliet; *Hamlet* and *Richard III*.

It was the year of George III's recovery from his first mental breakdown and this was celebrated at the Theatre on March 16 when *God Save The King* was sung with two additional verses.

Bespeaks were given by Lady Smith, Mrs. Henry Goodricke, Mrs. Fawkes, Mrs. Saltmarsh, R. S. Milner, the Officers of the Queen's Bays and the Officers of the 1st Dragoons. The staircase was renewed this year and a notice appears on the playbill of August 14[165]: 'As the Ladies in general have complained of the Stair-Case being inconvenient and disagreeable, one entirely new and more commodious, will be finished against Tuesday Evening.'

Elizabeth Farren returned as the Race Week star 'and was in high esteem, not only as an elegant and beautiful woman, but as a charming actress, who received not only plaudits on the stage, but applause more lasting by a discerning list of persons of the first rank of both sexes, who daily paid their respects at the shrine.'[166] She played Beatrice, Lady Paragon in *The Natural Son,* Maria in *The Citizen,* Millamant, Violante, Emmeline in *Arthur and Emmeline* ('an exquisite and complete performance indeed'), Widow Belmour and Susan in *The Follies of a Day.*

Grist from Manchester, who had performed as a visitor in 1782, made his first appearance as a member of the company as Major O'Flaherty[167] in *The Natural Son* and also acted Mirabel and Lovemore. He was a well known actor in the provinces, popular socially among the fashionable families, entertaining, and master not servant of the bottle. Fennel, victim of a conspiracy against him on the Edinburgh stage,[168] played Othello to the Desdemona of Mrs. Coates also from Edinburgh, Alexander to her Statira and Petruchio.

The great event of the season was the visit of the Prince of Wales, later George IV, to the Theatre on August 27. A playbill for the occasion specially printed in red is in the Minster Library Collection. The pieces were *The Way of the World* and *The Citizen* with Miss Farren, and the performance, by command, did not begin until 8.30. Tate was most deeply impressed by the Prince's affable patronage,[169] from which he benefited to the tune of a house holding £197.10.0. as well as by a personal gift sent through Col. St. Leger. The prices every night during Race Week were raised to boxes 5/-, green boxes 4/-, pit 3/-, 1st gallery 2/-, upper gallery 1/-. On the opening night when Kemble's new farce *The Farm House* was given, the house was again illuminated with wax.

In the Autumn, at Doncaster, Darcy[170] who was articled until June 1790, eloped with a wealthy girl – Miss Murgatroyd of York – and quit the stage. This was a great blow for Darcy was fine gentleman, tragedy lover, fop and first singer and on him depended nearly every play, farce, pantomime and opera. It was a mistake, as Tate realised, to have given him nearly all the leading business as his unexpected departure involved manager and company in difficulty. Tate was so angry that he insisted on Darcy's paying the penalty of £50 for breaking his articles. This sum was chosen as a forfeit because it would not stand in the way of an actor with a chance of a London career, nor be too much for a country actor to afford. Betterton had also left the company and Grist was in 1790 sharing the principal rôles with Cummins. In addition to Shakespearian leads he was cast for Pierre, Sir Lucius O'Trigger and Zanga. John Wilkinson was assigned Malcolm, Charles (*Jealous Wife*), Lord de Courcy (*Haunted Tower*) and Faulkland. Chalmers had returned to the company after 6 years, reopening as Marplot. Newcomers were the Pensons and the Townsends. Penson[171] became a great favourite in comic characters and was better at study than many of his superiors. He and his wife stayed with the company until 1799. He opened as Sir Luke Tremor in *Such Things Are,* Mrs. Penson as Melissa in *The Lying Valet.* Townsend[172] was a promising singer, with an excellent voice though defective ear, but his person was good for many parts and he later attained to the London boards. He came from Norwich and opened as Charles in *The Busy Body.* Miss Hughes[173] from Dublin took several leads in the 3 weeks she stayed at York, from Belvidera to Lady Bab Lardoon. Wilkinson says, 'She was always well dressed, as her wardrobe was a very good one; she had some suits made at much expense, and with great taste.'

In April the company lost Miss Hitchcock who returned to Ireland to become Mrs. Green. Before leaving she gave an allegorical address to the ladies and gentlemen of York on her intention of quitting the stage.[174]

On May 11 Mrs. Jarman[175] made her first appearance in Juliet as a young gentlewoman who had never appeared on any stage. All the experience she had had was a few private rehearsals yet in her first and exacting rôle she 'brought forth notes not only pleasing and plaintive, but rather uncommon for a young beginner; added to this, her figure was and is excellent, and gave promise, with being familiarised to the stage, she would acquire elegance. And though she has not arrived at that, yet her form being truly a good one, will bear scrutinizing, when in small clothes, before that of many actresses who value themselves on their symmetry.' She was well received, was always pleasing and stayed with the company until her death in 1800. Her daughter, who was brought up in the circuit, became the celebrated actress Mrs. Ternan.

Poor John Wimperis Dancer[176] died in May in the York Lunatic Asylum. His widow, who now had a business, was given a final benefit in 1791 to help her purchase the freedom of the city which cost about £25.

In spite of his bad reception at York the previous year King[177] played again on his return from Edinburgh to London as Ogleby and Puff. This time he had a brilliant audience and was warmly applauded, with the result that he never acted better.

Another visitor from Edinburgh was Mrs. Esten, daughter of the novelist Mrs. Bennett who had given her theatrical instruction. Deserted by her husband she had gone on the stage and won popularity at Bath and Bristol, whence she had migrated to Dublin and Edinburgh. She is said[178] to have depended for her effects on her dresses and a languishing manner. She opened as Monimia and Wilkinson relates[179] that her 'peculiar neatness and elegance prepossessed the audience in her favour; and she had not finished her first scene before they, with one consent, adopted "the orphan", and wished to secure her as their own.' The following night she acted Rosalind 'with additional credit and violent applause' and then as a striking contrast, recited Collins' *Ode on the Passions* which added to her reputation. She was solicited to repeat it the next evening after Letitia Hardy[180] and again on her last night after Belvidera 'which', as Tate remarks, 'was very improper after a dismal tragedy, to be trembling and staring in a long recitation of blank verse immediately after Belvidera's sighings, screamings, starings and ravings.' However, it brought good houses.

Two benefits are of interest as showing once again Wilkinson's consideration for his own actors and generosity to others. Warren,[181] a small part actor, whose conduct and assiduity the manager labels as indefatigable, had not secured good benefits for the three seasons he had been at York; the sum he received, including the £3.17.0. that season, did not exceed £15. Such poor emoluments were not encouraging to a player rising in merit to give of his best, and therefore Wilkinson, in view of his utility and good deportment, appointed a second benefit. The other occasion was a benefit for Saville[182] who had been engaged from the Reading Theatre, but who, upon arrival at York, was arrested by Thornton, the Reading manager for a debt of £14 before he had had the chance of discharging it from the profits of his engagement. Wilkinson not only allowed him a weekly stipend of 10/6 whilst in prison but gave him a benefit in the hopes that the public would exert themselves to free him from his confinement. The tickets for the performance were to be had from him at Meggison's, Ousebridge Gaol. The prompter Earby, whom the *Theatrical Register* had so criticised, slipped up this year in neglecting to advise Chalmers in time when he was due to perform Beauchamp in *Which Is The Man?* with the result that the comedy had to be changed to *The Stratagem* and a note appended to the playbill in explanation.[183] This season we first hear of a new wardrobekeeper Johnny Winter who for many years was a character in the company and of whom we shall have more to say later.

At the Assizes that spring one William Roberts was sentenced to seven years' penal servitude for stealing a pair of red morocco buskins, a pair of linen ruffles and other articles belonging to Warren from the Theatre.[184]

Mrs. Inchbald's comedy *The Married Man* and Reynolds's popular *The Dramatist*, with Chalmers as Vapid and Mrs. Kennedy as Louisa Courtney, came out this year, as did Morris's farce *The Adventurers*. New musical pieces were Colman junior's *Battle of Hexham* with a new moonlight scene painted by Michell, Cobb's comic opera *The Haunted Tower,* which had been a great attraction at Drury Lane the previous winter, and the Hon. John St. John's *Iron Mask*, usually known as *The Island of St. Marguerite*. In this last the French Revolution found distant echo in the York Theatre, for its scenery by Michell included views, taken from drawings made on the spot, of the Bastille and of that prison, which had been razed to the ground the previous summer, in ruins. It concluded with the rising of the Temple and Genius of Liberty.[185] The new pantomime, the *Death of Captain Cook,*[186] also dealt with a contemporary theme and had had a long run at Covent Garden. Its scenery included a view of the sea and the ship *Resolution,* a morai or burial ground and, after the hero's funeral procession, a burning mountain. Books were to be had at the Theatre for 3d. For Chalmers's benefit *Harlequin's Animation; or Fancy Triumphant*[187] was presented in which he, as Harlequin, leapt through a transparency of George III and a brilliant sun of variegated fire. Yet another topical spectacle was brought out at Wilkinson's benefit, the 'Royal Procession to St. Paul's Cathedral. Exactly represented by Moving Figures in order of passing between Temple-Bar and Ludgate Hill, on the 23rd of April.'[188] On this occasion too Wilkinson made his return, after two years' absence from the stage, as Shylock before a crowded and brilliant house. Shakespeare tragedies were *Macbeth* and *Othello* with Grist in the title rôles, *Hamlet* with Mrs. Southgate as Ophelia

140

for the first time, and *Romeo and Juliet* with Grist as Romeo and Mrs. Jarman as Juliet. The comedies were *The Merchant of Venice* and *As You Like It,* and the histories *Richard III* with Grist as Richard and Chalmers as Richmond, and *Henry IV* with Grist as Falstaff and Chalmers as the Prince of Wales.

After visiting Leeds and Pontefract the company reopened for York Race Week on August 23. They had been joined by Archer[189] from Edinburgh, who had a good person, was always very clean and neat on the stage, even too fine sometimes for the character he was representing. He opened as Mercutio. He was only with the company a year. On the actresses' side there was Miss Reynolds who was timid and inexperienced as Rosina, but as Margaretta in *No Song No Supper* sang delightfully.[190] She was a niece of Mrs. Kennedy's but Mrs. Kennedy herself had once more departed. Mrs. Esten returned as star playing Juliet, Rosalind, Indiana, Roxalana, Beatrice, Mrs. Oakley, Isabella and Lady Bab Lardoon. This year her Rosalind, though attractive and received with attention, failed to win as much applause as expected. She 'was allowed, fashionable, clever, perspicuous, &c. yet from the inflammable air of our York balloon, or rather the York prints, the performance did not seem to elevate and surprise sufficiently.'[191] Acting opposite Mrs. Eston was Dimond[192] the manager of the Bath Theatre. Since many York families visited Bath in the summer he was no stranger to them and was known as 'a man of integrity, great good manners, and a gentleman', so that he had a crowded house for his Romeo. He also played Young Bevil in *The Conscious Lovers,* Benedick, Charles in *The Jealous Wife,* Lord Townly and Almanza for his benefit. His Charles, though not a leading character, gained him much credit. When it came to Mrs. Esten's benefit, the Monday after Race Week, he offered his services in play or farce or both, and Wilkinson hoped that in return she would offer hers for his benefit on the Wednesday. But she, offended by some conduct of his when he was her manager at Bristol, refused disdainfully, exulting in her rejection. She relied on the flatteries of her York friends, but Dimond obtained instead the services of Jane Wallis who was in the Bath company, but was then acting under Butler at Harrogate. She was a native of Richmond, Yorks, daughter of Fielding Wallis who had been for some months in the York circuit[193] and she had already played with the company for a few nights in Leeds. This was her first appearance at York and she played Lady Townly and Amanthis. 'The instant it was known,' says Wilkinson, 'public curiosity was on the tip-toe to see Miss Wallis.' The result was that Mrs. Esten's benefit was deserted, and half the thin house came in only after the curtain had fallen on the play. All sorts of excuses were made such as that people thought that the Theatre would be suffocatingly hot from overcrowding, that Isabella was a shocking rôle, that the manager had contracted to pay Mrs. Esten £60 anyway so she would not lose by it, that Monday after the Races was a bad night as patrons were tired with the amusements of the week, and the like, all of which Wilkinson is at pains to show did not apply when the audience was attracted. However it was, stay away they did; Wilkinson was the chief loser financially, but Mrs. Esten, disappointed and indignant, declared she would not play at York again. Soon after she procured an engagement in London.

Miss Wallis, who was a charming rather than a brilliant actress, was accorded a hearty reception in a packed theatre. In the stage box sat Miss Farren with Lady Milner. Dimond was happy and left York in high good humour, but Mrs. Esten was led by Wilkinson 'with solemn steps and haughty mien to her chaise.'[194]

Two new pieces had been brought out during Race Week. One was O'Keeffe's comedy *The Toy*, with Fawcett as Metheglin; the complications of which defied even Wilkinson's 'ingenuity at theatrical slaughter' and proved intractable to attempts to reduce it to a three-act afterpiece. The other was Hoare's *No Song, No Supper* with Fawcett as Robin, which became one of the most popular afterpieces in the repertory for many decades.

The subscription in 1791 returned again to sixteen nights. That year the company that came to York was a particularly good one, the pieces were well conducted, the band excellent and yet on no evening outside the benefits and Assize Week, did they succeed in producing an audience of £20. Wilkinson[195] attributes this failure to the bad influence of London stars. Since 'the Siddonian fever' the audience had been spoiled for the stock nights of the ordinary company and only fashionable bespeaks, particular benefits, or the visits of stars would bring good houses. Tate thought a visit to London necessary every year in order to see and purchase new plays and refresh himself; but this year he was away in the capital or the provinces longer than usual from February 16 to March 28. Just before he returned his *Memoirs* came out, in which he told, in his inimitable rambling fashion, the story of his life until he succeeded to the management of the York Theatre. The four little volumes are a mine of information about the theatrical history of the day as well as being full of amusing anecdotes, for Tate was a born raconteur in his own disconnected way. On his return to York he played Capt. Ironsides in *The Brothers* and Cadwallader at his benefit.

Miss Reynolds was sustaining leading singing rôles such as Sabrina, Clarissa and Polly. Two new actresses had been acquired. One was Miss Cleland[196] from Bath who had a good person and understanding but was too ambitious and wanted to captivate the audience by playing 'the amiable, the gentle, the tender, or the great' for all of which she was unsuited. She performed Imoinda, Imogen, Violante and Julia. The other was Miss Richards who was handsome and strong featured though rather short. She played a wide variety of characters with success and was particularly good in Mrs. Jordan's line as she was only 18 and had youth and spirits. She made her first appearance as Miss Hoyden in *A Trip to Scarborough* on February 8 and subsequently played such varied rôles as Polly Honeycombe, Lady Teazle, Ophelia, the Country Girl, Little Pickle, Letitia Hardy and Lydia Languish. She 'was justly admired in the girls, and in her various cast of parts got a strong hold on the public esteem.'[197] She professed to love Tate as a father and assured him she would never leave him, but she soon did. In the middle of the season she was released to act at Lord Barrymore's private theatre at Wargrave, and there she stayed longer than expected thus placing Miss Reynolds, who was depending on her for her benefit, in a predicament. When finally she did return, she was coolly received and this injured her own benefit with the result that she quarrelled and departed on August 5, shortly afterwards marrying the comedian John Edwin junior.

Among newcomers on the male side was Sandford[198] who had a good figure and a fullness of speech which promised well, together with the advantage of quick study. He played Hamlet, Roderigo and Dashwood (*Know Your Own Mind*). Another new actor was the singer Duffey,[199] recommended by Mrs. Esten, who had been a favourite at Dublin, performed at Covent Garden, and had a good and powerful voice, but left after April 16 for an engagement at Vauxhall.

Grist this season added Hastings, Posthumous and Macdermot (*School for Arrogance*) to his rôles and Mrs. Jarman those of Desdemona, Lydia (*School for Arrogance*) and Jane Shore.

Two comedies first seen in York in 1791 were *The School for Arrogance* and *The German Hotel*. There was one tragedy: Miss Starke's *Widow of Malabar* with new music and scenery and a procession representing the ceremonies attending the Indian rite of suttee.[200] New farces were Jephson's *Two Strings to Your Bow*, O'Keeffe's *Modern Antiques (or the Merry Mourners)* and Bickerstaffe's *Spoil'd Child*; the two latter were long retained in the repertory. Wilkinson presented at his benefit Bate's new comic opera *The Woodman* of which he had obtained a correct copy at great pains and expense. Michell executed scenery on a plan similar to that which Wilkinson had seen in London, and French's able conduct of the band insured the piece's success. Cross's interlude *Divertisement* was also new to York. The pantomime was *Harlequin Foundling; or The Fairies' Favourite* in which Southgate played Harlequin and Masters H. and C. Cummins young harlequins. The fairies, led by the Misses Cummins and Ward, also included children from the town. The storm and shipwreck scene from *Don Juan* was put on in which were displayed a small vessel riding at anchor, a boat seen conveying passengers on board, the hoisting of the sails and the ship proceeding under a gentle breeze, driven back in distress by a thunderstorm, struck by forked lightning, wrecked and swallowed up by the waves.[201] This was an elaborate spectacle but the details of how the effects were obtained are unfortunately unknown. The winter season at York was gradually being pushed forward from its original time at the beginning of January. Now it did not start until the beginning of February, and from 1795 not until mid-February. The first night benefit for the charities had been dropped and the season opened on February 5 with Oram's benefit, as usual by desire of the Freemasons, the play being *The Merchant of Venice*. Grist was particularly eager to act Shylock though the play was not, Wilkinson[202] tells us, usually an attractive one unless there was a Shylock of repute. Miss Cleland was Portia and Southgate had taken over Fawcett's rôle of Launcelot Gobbo. Other Shakespeare plays were *Hamlet, Othello, Macbeth* with Purcell's music, and *Cymbeline.*

An announcement on the playbill of February 8 stated that 'As several disturbances have frequently happened, attended with great inconvenience to Ladies and Gentlemen in the Boxes; to prevent such behaviour for the future, not any half-price to the Upper Gallery.' There was a bad riot in the theatre on May 12 on the occasion of the doorkeepers' benefit.[203] The galleries were crowded, a rare sight, and during the performance of *Venice Preserv'd* they were turbulent. The new and popular farce *No Song No Supper* followed and the gods roared applause, absurdly encoring a song by Miss Reynolds in the last act in which she sang of a cake, a leg of lamb, and a lawyer in a sack, all of which were promptly produced. Realising the absurdity of reproducing these for an encore she retired from the stage, the performers, amidst an uproar, proceeded quickly to the finale, and Wilkinson ordered the curtain to be dropped. This incensed the audience who were encouraged by some intoxicated occupants of the boxes. They demanded the return of the band who had left the theatre, and when Wilkinson appeared to defend himself he was saluted by the throwing of candlesticks, branches and flaming candles at his head and cries of "Knock the insolent fellow down." Enraged at the band's not returning to its place immediately, they began breaking the seats and one sprig from the boxes attempted to set the frontispiece on fire with a lighted candle.

At last some members of the band re-appeared and Miss Reynolds repeated her song amidst grease and broken brass arms. Then the boxes insisted on French, as leader of the band, asking pardon for quitting the theatre, to be followed by all the performers concerned in the finale including Fawcett. Fawcett somehow contrived to get out of it by declaring that it was the manager who had ordered the curtain to be dropped, whereupon Wilkinson was again forced to appear, and called upon to apologise abjectly. It was a bitter pill to one who by unremitting labour had raised the theatre in 25 years to be one of the most important in the provinces. This he urged, and that the theatre, the scenery and the wardrobe in many plays was equal to those of the metropolis, whilst more first London performers were seen there than in any other country theatre. He further pleaded that an error of judgment should not be taken as an affront, and in the end he was greeted with applause. But it was long before he forgot the ingratitude of his patrons.

Tate's troubles this year were by no means ended. Mrs. Jordan[204] had not played in York since she had left the company and risen to fame, but in 1791 Tate engaged her for the summer Assize Week on the same terms as he had done Mrs. Siddons and Miss Farren in previous years; that is she was to act on shares and have a clear benefit on the Saturday night; in return she was to give her services for the manager's benefit on any night he chose to appoint the following week, which happened to be the week of the Music Festival. Wilkinson advertised her in advance to open in *The Country Girl* and Nell in the *Devil to Pay,* but on arrival she positively refused Nell on grounds of ill health. *The Country Girl*, though popular in London, was not equally so in York where it was deemed crude and vulgar, so that Wilkinson knew that the audience would be disappointed. He knew too that the obstinate actress was not to be moved and so had the farce altered to *The Mock Doctor* with Fawcett as Gregory. The consequence was that the house was poor on that August 8 and there was no half price. Wilkinson succeeded in prevailing on his temperamental visitor to sing a song for which she was greatly applauded, yet afterwards she fell into the sulks again and acted but poorly in the play. The following night she played Miss Hoyden and Nell, was greatly received and was in good spirits. On Wednesday 9th her Letitia Hardy and Little Pickle brought only a shameful house, the ladies of York being little prone to follow London's worship of Mrs. Jordan in the fine lady's part. The actress was enraged and did not attempt to give of her best until habited in jacket and trousers as a young sailor in the afterpiece when 'from the lady in disguise Mrs. Jordan became herself again.' On Thursday she acted Rosalind, a part in which she was famous in London and which brought a good attendance at the theatre, but in which she did not receive the applause she expected. Indeed the audience was offended that on the previous nights she had expressed her contempt of them by indifferent acting. Jealous of Mrs. Esten's reception in the same rôle, 'when the applause sunk into more and more languor, she fell into a feeble vapour, and merely got through the part, very little better than would an actress of less renown.' In *The Sultan* she, by her own choice, played Roxalana, 'that self-important, conceited character,' whose popularity among actresses Wilkinson could never understand; at the end of the evening the audience was as tired as the actress. Mrs. Jordan's mortification resulted in a determination to continue to offend. She said that not only the audience but the company was stupid and that there was neither comprehension nor idea behind or in front of the curtain. Such sentiments rendered her unpopular with the comedians and by Friday the air was agog with rumours of what she had said of her York friends and 'a spirit of discontent and ill humour prevailed against her.' Her performance of Sylvia in *The Recruiting Officer* and Lucy in *The Virgin Unmasked* made obvious her wilful neglect; indeed in the play she announced in a voice which all could hear that she intended only to walk through the part, and so she did. There was only £25.1.0. in the house. But the audience took its revenge on her benefit night on Saturday when she played Hypolita in *She Would and She Would Not* and Miss Hoyden in *The Man of Quality*, for the boxes, though genteel were not great, and the rest of the house was scattered; she was disappointed as to presents too, receiving only five guineas from one lady. She was greeted with applause but not rapture and, instead of making her customary bow, turned her back. She was careful not to let herself go, though in spite of ill humour, she once or twice struck a spark. Wilkinson had already had the bills printed for her performance for the ensuing Monday and intended to give out her name, at the end of the play. She sent him word during the second act that she would not play on the York stage again and during the

farce she attacked the much harassed manager 'as to the beggarly engagement she had entered into, and the dullness and lack of generosity in
the York audience.' An altercation ensued in which Wilkinson pointed out
that the sum of £160 for a week was worth the acceptance of any actress,
though she had spoken of it in scorn. On Saturday Wilkinson received a
note from her protector that, though willing to act for him as arranged on
the Wednesday following, she did not wish to appear on other nights. At his
wits' end for a substitute Wilkinson rushed round to the Mansion House
where John Kemble was on a visit to Wilson, the Lord Mayor. It was finally
arranged that Kemble should take Mrs. Jordan's place at York in return for
her substituting for him at Newcastle. As Wednesday was the best night, he
arranged to take Mrs. Jordan's place then for 30 guineas. Tate agreed
though Mrs. Jordan had only wanted £30. Tate then wrote to Mrs. Jordan
asking her to pay £30 for her benefit in lieu of giving him her services on
the Wednesday as agreed, and this she did. The Theatre had to remain shut
on Monday night, a great loss since the city was full of visitors for the Music
Festival, but on Tuesday Kemble arranged to play Othello. On Monday he
and his wife dined with Wilkinson when he peremptorily declared that he
had decided that he would not play on the terms agreed to but only on
those of sharing the house. In spite of the poor manager's protestations
Kemble stuck to his point claiming that it was not worth his trouble to play
for under £160 for 5 nights. Wilkinson hoped he would be reasonable, for
the bills were printed, but Kemble did not attend the rehearsal, and
Wilkinson was ready to explain to the public and substitute another play
when the Lord Mayor intervened. Kemble was persuaded to abate part of
his demands and come to the rehearsal. He was greatly received as Othello,
doubtless to the chagrin of Mrs. Jordan who watched the performance. On
her arrival in Newcastle she found that the company, uncertain of what was
happening, had stayed in Lancaster and so she was left high and dry,
threatening to sue for damages. In the meantime Kemble appeared on the
much fought over Wednesday as Hamlet to a house of £109.19.6. Wilkinson
says[205] he never saw a more masterly piece of acting and Kemble himself
believed that he never had played the part so well. Mrs. Southgate was his
Ophelia. On August 18 he played Macbeth to the Lady Macbeth of Mrs.
Fawcett, and the Master of the Toyshop, and on the 19th Lord Hastings and
Petruchio with Collins's *Ode on the Passions* to a very poor house of £28.14.6.
because it was the principal night of the Festival at the Assembly Rooms. In
spite of the fact that he boasted that a thin house did not affect his acting,
he was not up to his usual standard. But on his last night he acted Zanga to
a brilliant house, and his receipt for the week bordered on £150.

The Race Week followed on immediately and though Wilkinson feared
poor houses after the Music Festival he was agreeably surprised. Kelly and
Mrs. Crouch[206] came on their way to the Newcastle Music Festival and
opened on August 22 as *Lionel and Clarissa*. On the 23rd they played *Inkle
and Yarico* both with additional songs, followed by Harry and Louisa in *The
Deserter,* and on their way back from Newcastle, took their benefit on the

last night, September 1, as Lord William and Lady Eleanor in *The Haunted Tower* followed by Richard I and Mathilda. In spite of the drain of two public weeks they played to crowded houses. Kelly[207] speaks of Wilkinson as 'certainly one of the most eccentric men I ever met with.' He tells us how the manager would hide chocolates and sweets in the holes and corners of his house for the pleasure of finding them again, and how, after a few glasses of Madiera [sic] he would mix his conversation about theatricals and eatables together. So many people have left us records of his curious, rambling talk that we can hear his very accents. Take this from Kelly: 'Then there's that Miss Reynolds; why she, Sir, fancies herself a singer, but she is quite a squalini, Sir! a nuisance, Sir! Going about my house the whole of the day, roaring out "The Soldier tired of War's alarms," ah! she has tired me, and alarmed the whole neighbourhood.'

Wilkinson had prevailed on Mrs. Esten to return to the York boards and she appeared on August 22 as Lady Townly and Emmeline in *Arthur and Emmeline*, to a brilliant house. Her Rosalind[208] to which the York audience was very partial was bespoke by no less a person than Charles James Fox and brought a receipt of £109. She also acted Lady Bell in *Know Your Own Mind*, Amanthis, and Monimia, this last to a veritable babel in the crowded galleries which was only stilled by Fawcett's Jemmy Jumps in the afterpiece.

Unfortunately her benefit, when she acted Indiana and Roxalana and recited Collins's *Ode on the Passions*, was an even worse failure than that of the previous year, the receipts amounting only to £37.18.6. Once more she declared she would never act in York again. The ladies had wanted her when annoyed with Mrs Jordan, 'she was so delightful, so genteel, so pretty, Mrs. Jordan's characters and acting were low and vulgar', and yet when Tate overrode her objection to coming they failed to support her.

It had been a harassing season for the manager but the citizens of York, within a month, had had the opportunity of seeing five of the most eminent stars of the day, besides another great actor in embryo. Fielding Wallis had recommended to Wilkinson as a second Garrick a young man of seventeen named Robert Elliston[209] who was then acting in Bath as Tressel in *Richard III*. Though it was inconvenient to engage him as late in the season as the end of May, Wilkinson did so instantly after hearing him rehearse. He made his first appearance at York on August 8 as Belville in *The Country Girl* and at Kemble's benefit played Don Carlos in *The Revenge*. Kelly,[210] who was in the Theatre that night tells us that he acted 'with great judgment and feeling, considering his youth, and considering, moreover that Kemble was the Zanga. He was particularly impressive in the speech of

> 'Hope thou has told me lies from day to day
> For more than twenty years.'

Tate describes his person as very good, 'his features and voice very pleasing, but his powers not extensive'; he had the advantage of not ranting but was inclined to lack quickness and variety. He soon improved and became of great service to the company, until he left it in 1793 to make a success at Bath. Later he was to become, not only a famous actor of wide range, but the 'great lessee' of Drury Lane.

Mr. and Mrs. Brown[211] returned to the company after a six years' absence in Norwich, London and Dublin. Wilkinson wanted Mrs. Brown to make her re-appearance as Wowski but she elected to make it in *The Romp* in which she had to measure up against Mrs. Jordan. Her husband appeared as Young Cockney; he had the power but wanted the will to render himself useful in a country theatre.

Fawcett took his leave of the company in Race Week making his last appearance as Edward in *The Haunted Tower* and Florestan in *Richard Coeur de Lion*. Both he and his wife were a great loss, but he went to make his name at Covent Garden. They were replaced by the Cherrys from Dublin.

Andrew Cherry, though not as great a comedian as Fawcett was nevertheless a very good one. Wilkinson[212] says he possessed great merit in such rôles as Shelty, Lazarillo, Darby and that, when he performed a part not suited to his abilities, he was not just himself but conceived his character well and used his art to distinguish it from others. Cherry was the third in the line of renowned comic actors to be a member of the company, but unlike Suett and Fawcett he was not a beginner with little experience when he came to it. Already 29 years old, he had been on the stage for twelve years, first in strolling companies in Ireland and then at Smock Alley, Dublin, where he had gained a high reputation. In York he became a favourite and his benefit, which was bespoken by Lady Frankland, wife of the High Sheriff for that year, brought £110 in receipts.[213] His début was on the second night of the 1792 season – February 9 – when he played Shelty in *The Highland Reel* and Lazarillo in *Two Strings to your Bow,* and during the following 3½ months we hear of him in 35 parts. Elliston was not used to anything like the extent of Cherry and we only have record of him in 13 rôles.[214]

Elliston used to tell how Wilkinson, if a member of the company refused to listen to his advice, would mount into the gallery on a night when he was playing and hiss him. On one occasion, so doing, he was ejected from his own gallery.[215] Stephens was a newcomer, 'a very useful actor, with a study bordering on the marvellous, when he pleases – in person he is above the common standard – he claims a right to encouragement, by approbation in many parts, and is of great utility in the theatre.'[216] Mrs. Taylor was a new actress and singer from the Haymarket who possessed the assets of a pleasing person and a powerful voice and was far better than many leading singers.[217]

As for John Wilkinson he was now playing such leads as Cromwell, Cymon and Orloff in *A Day in Turkey.*

There were four visitors during the season. Bowden came for four nights in February and played Macheath, Hawthorne, Don Ferdinand in *The Duenna* with additional songs, Robin Hood and Comus. Though his singing was much admired he was not sufficiently supported to reward his trouble.[218]

On March 22 Matthew Browne reappeared from Dublin for one night, after an absence of 6 years, and spoke a Monody written by Pratt entitled *The Shadows of Shakespeare or Shakespeare's Characters doing homage to Garrick.*[219] He was followed in April by Frederick, a novice whose only experience had been in *Oroonoko* in Edinburgh, and for whom Wilkinson had no room in the company. He was a young man of means and good education, gave his performance of Oroonoko without emolument and was puffed in the newspaper as one 'who bids fair to gain a seat among the first Actors of the age.' Tate says, in fact, that he showed great promise 'his action was unembarrassed and good; his voice remarkably pleasing, but *not* powerful; and his figure, though particularly neat, was deficient in height.' Tate recommended him to Yates of Birmingham by whom he was engaged for several first characters. He lost all his belongings in the fire at that theatre and subsequently went to Richmond, Surrey, and Norwich.[220]

Lastly, Elizabeth Kemble, now Mrs. Whitlock, came to perform a few characters including Zara (*Mourning Bride*), Lady Townly, Jane Shore, Isabella and Julia in the tragedy of that name to her husband's Manoa. Wilkinson[221] whilst according her sterling merit which rendered her 'a great treasure for a country theatre', opined that she was apt to fall into mediocrity and recommended her to pay more regard to uniformity of acting and character.

The subscription which had been on the decline for some years, was now finally abandoned.

Colman the younger's musical play (not yet known as a melodrama), *The Surrender of Calais*, was brought out with new scenery by Michell, Cobb's comic opera *The Siege of Belgrade* was presented 'in a very superb manner, both as to scenery and dresses. A London critic would have been surprised to have seen a play in a provincial theatre so accoutred.'[222] Michell's new scenery included views of the village of Servia, the Turkish and Austrian camps and grand Turkish tent, and of Belgrade and its castle. At Hull too much gunpowder and smoke had half stifled the audience, but, after this, the bombardment scene was done in another way as invented by the machinist at Drury Lane: lights were attached to the ends of two wires and whirled round to give the effect, which, however, proved less good in a small theatre than in London.[223] Cummins was Col. Cohenburg and Miss Reynolds, Catherine. Mrs. Cowley's comic opera *A Day in Turkey* and Cobb's musical farce *The Doctor and the Apothecary* also made their début this year. Delpini's *Don John*[224] which had been seen in London, Dublin, and at Lord Barrymore's private theatre, was now presented at full length as all the instrumental parts had been sent from the Haymarket. The pantomime concluded with a view of Pluto's dominions. It did not go down well, being adjudged 'horrid' or what we should today call horrific. It was followed by *Blue Beard*[225] which contained among its scenery and tricks: 'A View of the Sea, and Blue Beard's Domain; Blue Beard flying from the Clouds on a Fiery Dragon; a Monument and Trick Chair, which changes to an Arbour: A Hedge and Gate which changes to a Bridge: – Several Leaps, particularly

Harlequin will jump down Blue Beard's Throat.' Another spectacular piece was *The Soldier's Festival* concluding with the Siege of Quebec and Death of Wolfe brought out at Wilkinson's benefit.[226] *General Wolfe*, as done in London, was too short, for Wilkinson would have no interludes on his stage; and he therefore bethought him of resurrecting the ill-fated *Patrick in Prussia*, transferring the scene from Ireland to America and then tagging on the spectacle at the end. This revamp he entitled *Darby in America* and with Cherry uncommonly happy in the rôle of Darby, the piece proved an immense success exceeded only by those of *The Poor Soldier* and *The Farmer.* Luckily no-one recognised the piece that had failed so dismally six years before. The military spectacle was shortly followed by a naval one entitled *Neptune's Levee*, in which there was a naval procession of British Admirals and Seamen from the time of the Armada, concluding with 'a brilliant Transparent representation of Neptune resigning the Reins of his Chariot to Britannia, amidst Tritons, Naiads, Mermaids, etc.'[227] Thus both military and naval patriotic sentiment was catered for.

Colman the younger's *Ways and Means,* O'Keeffe's popular *Wild Oats* and Holcroft's famous *Road to Ruin* were new comedies this season. The last named was first given on March 27 with Cherry as Dornton, Southgate as Goldfinch and Elliston as Harry Dornton. Wilkinson now began to announce his well known characters for the last time. Thus at his benefit he was to make his last appearance as Wolsey with Mrs. Jarman as Queen Katharine; the receipts at common prices amounted that night to £116.12.6., a fine house for York.[228] The procession again enabled Tate to ride his hobby horse by introducing into it a profusion of rich dresses.

The star of the Race Week this year was Mrs. Elizabeth Pope, who as Miss Younge had learnt to act under Garrick. Though inferior to Mrs. Siddons in tragedy and Miss Farren in comedy, she was a great actress with a wider range than either.[229] She opened on August 20 as Portia with Wilkinson playing his favourite rôle of Shylock, also announced for the last time.[230] He had acted it so often that he was weary of it. He had a great reception throughout and Mrs. Pope a very gracious one. Though rain descended in torrents the Theatre was patronised by the first rank and fashion of the city and receipts neared £100. On the 21st Mrs. Pope played Zara whilst Wilkinson appeared as her father Lusignan for the last time, and Cummins played Osman exceedingly well. 'Nor', Tate boasts, 'was I wanting in decorating the Sultan most superbly, to let Mrs. Pope see they had *not all* the good dresses in London.' For her third appearance on the 24th Mrs. Pope played Lady Rodolpha in *The Man of the World* and played it incomparably; it was followed by *The Author* with Wilkinson and Mrs. Pope as Mr. and Mrs. Cadwallader. Wilkinson, who had acted three times that week, found himself taken dizzy in the second act and was evidently now unable to support such exertion. On the 25th Mrs. Pope sustained Queen Elizabeth in the *Earl of Essex* to the Essex of Cummins 'bedecked in her London regalia, and in one of the richest characteristic dresses I ever saw.' But the Saturday night gallery audience resembled that of a bear garden, and was not to be quieted until *The Soldier's Festival* came on. So often they were attentive only at the afterpiece indulging in rowdyism throughout the play. The week was most successful and had brought in £518.10.6. Mrs. Pope took her benefit on the Monday as Imogen with her husband as Posthumous to a crowded and enthusiastic house. A criticism was made that Pope as Posthumous did not don his own dress after Cloten's death, but at rehearsal he had refused to put it on pointing out that Cloten was not wearing the garb in which Posthumous had appeared, but one given him by Pisanio which the audience had not yet seen. The incident shows the care with which such a matter was considered by some actors, whilst others gave no thought to appropriateness of costume at all. In *High Life Below Stairs* Mrs. Pope played Lady Kitty.

An actor named Hamerton had joined the company from Ireland. He was exuberant, of a handsome, manly appearance, and had studied Lewis's manner. In Reynolds's new comedy *Notoriety* he played Nominal to the O'Whack of Cherry and the Miss Sophia Strangeways of Mrs. Brown.

At this point Wilkinson has an interesting paragraph[231] about his scenery, in explanation of the difficulties of fulfilling the complete scene plot of an elaborate spectacle designed for the large London theatres in the more confined space of a provincial one. As illustrating the capacities of the York Theatre for scenic effects at this time it is worth quoting in full: 'As to scenery being adapted in every theatre-royal out of London, it is impossible. I can venture to affirm that I have treble the quantity of most theatres, and a great deal of excellent changes, but the size of the stage, the flats being chiefly on rollers, and many other circumstances, without mentioning it as an enormous expense, which no theatre out of London can bear: yet it is impossible to have performed some particular pieces, and a long various Pantomime with scenery all exactly proper, for they are so fixed, and the preparation behind wanting time and room, occasions it an absolute and unavoidable necessity to drop a handsome apartment down occasionally to cover in, which should with propriety very likely be a farmer's house. But many plays and entertainments are strictly right as to dresses, scenery, and decorations; and that is saying a great deal, all things considered.' Further on Wilkinson prints a letter[232] in which the scenic arrangements in Hull come under fire. The correspondent cites the indiscriminate use of the same scene for St. James's Park and the wilds of America, and the employment of an interior through the windows of which a street could be seen for the inside of a lonely cottage. Wilkinson in his reply admits to the impeachment but points out that there was already more scenery than could be worked, as also that in the second instance the fault lay with the carpenter who thought one chamber as good as another. After promising to rectify both inconsistencies he elaborates on his previous thesis: 'I do aver I have treble the scenery of any manager in England, Scotland or Ireland, out of London; but my stages are too confined, and not having room for many sliding scenes, the drop ones can only be let down from their fixtures and those fixtures unavoidably often contradict the work of the play, and also the farce, and from the size of the stage cannot be altered. Palace-wings to prisons and plain chambers are no doubt a great and glaring absurdity but not to be prevented, as in a full piece there is not room to stir.' He excepts York, however, among his theatres from the charge of being intolerably confined in every part. This same correspondent also comments on the disturbances caused by the calling for *God Save the King* from the gallery. From Tate's reply we learn that he tried at York to have it at the end, after the farce, but this simply made worse disturbances. Jacobin patrons who supported the French Revolution, objected to being obliged to listen to it, Royalist patrons sang it all the more. It was a time of high political passions and Tate wisely counselled patience believing that the obstreperous element would in time weary.

Wilkinson[233] also enters into some financial considerations, making it clear that without his three annual benefits he could not have kept the company together. The expenses were great and the manager's nights before the benefits rarely good. Making up the deficit on the poor benefits, when the expenses were not covered by his share, lost all the profits he made on the good ones. His only other source of income was from autumn seasons at York, Wakefield and Doncaster when there were no benefits, and which therefore, except for the extra expense of the double salaries at the public weeks, were pure gain to the manager. The main York winter season no longer paid its expenses as it had done ten years previously in the Theatre's best days.

CHAPTER FOUR

Tate Wilkinson's Management
The Last Decade 1793–1803

THE 1793 season opened on February 7, but the houses were poor for many nights.[1] However, the losses incurred were made up by a more than usually productive Assize Week for which 'uncommon Patronage' Wilkinson printed his thanks.[2] Some adjustment was made in the prices of the Green Boxes and the following announcement appeared in *The York Chronicle*:[3] 'The Price to the Green Boxes being made the same as the Balconies, that is raised to the lower box prices, Mr. Wilkinson respectfully informs the Public is not done as a subterfuge for gain, for he believes, that, in taking the Season throughout, it may be more injurious than profitable, but as he has observed both at York and Hull, the nightly inconvenience of persons who, having only paid Green Box price, waiting for opportunities, and getting into the Balconies without paying the regular admission, and by such methods rendering the audience liable to frequent disturbances and disputes with the door-keepers; Mr. Wilkinson has judged it expedient to throw the Green Boxes and Balconies together, which alteration can only affect the first part of the night, as the half price was the same as to the other Boxes; and it is universally known that in London, Bath and Edinburgh *All* the Boxes are of one price.' The boxes were 'newly furnished with an elegant fashionable paper, and the seats will be fresh covered in a few days'.

The company was practically the same as in 1792 except for the addition of Mrs. Simpson,[4] who returned after eleven years. She had in the meantime become a great favourite at Bath; she was a 'pleasing elegant actress, both in tragedy and comedy, but not powerful or great as the commanding breath of kings'. She played such parts as Mrs. Beverley, Lady Teazle, Queen Elizabeth in *Richard III* and Mrs. Sullen.

Elliston, whose last season it was with the company, had been promoted from juvenile leads to a few full ones. Oxberry[5] says, nevertheless, that he left in disgust because he had no opportunity of playing leading characters, gave up the stage for a while, but eventually returned to it to make his

153

name in Bath. Wilkinson himself played at least twice this year as Captain Ironsides and Cato.

Mrs. Mountain[6] came back on a visit for a few nights and played Sophia in *The Road to Ruin,* Don Carlos in *The Duenna, The Maid of the Mill* and Patrick in *The Poor Soldier.* Unfortunately she fell from a horse and broke her arm two days before her benefit on May 14 and her place as Lady Alton and Rosetta had to be taken by Miss Reynolds, though she sang the song of *Sweet Echo* behind the scenes as her contribution; but, of course, her receipt was not what it should have been.

Mrs. Inchbald's comedy *Every One Has His Fault* was acted better than any play that year and was a success for many to come. Richardson's *Fugitive* was the other new comedy, a piece that Wilkinson considered flagged and lacked fire and variety.[7]

There were again no tragedies but the first drama by Thomas Morton, *Columbus,* with Cummins in the title rôle was produced. The big effect was the destruction of the Temple of the Sun by a hurricane and the discovery of a volcano in eruption. The usual crop of new musical pieces included Merry's *Magician No Conjuror,* Pearce's *Hartford Bridge* and Hurlstone's *Just in Time.* Two new farces appeared, Macready's *Irishman in London* and O'Keeffe's *Little Hunchback.*

Cherry's first effort at dramatic composition was the pantomime *Harlequin in the Stocks* which was brought out at York on April 16 with incidental scenery by Michell, many entertaining transformations and every necessary decoration.[8] *Neck or Nothing or Harlequin Everywhere*[9] had a 'Cascade, which changes to a Transparency Exhibiting an exact Representation of the different Punishments inflicted on the … Heathen Heroes … Hedge and Gate which change to a Bridge [used in *Blue Beard*] – A pleasing Deception with a Forte Piano – A Country House which changes to several Huts belonging to Gypsies, &c.' Wilkinson[10] says that a good pantomime, got up as it should be, never repaid its cost in a country theatre.

We only know of three Shakespeare performances this season: *Richard III, Hamlet* and *Twelfth Night* with Malvolio = Hamerton, Orsino = Stephens, Sir Toby = Penson, Sir Andrew = Cherry, Clown = Southgate, Olivia = Mrs. Cherry, Viola = Mrs. Jarman.

The season ended on May 18 with a benefit for the prospective widows and children of seamen and soldiers who might be killed in the war just declared on the French. Wilkinson himself contributed £2.2.0. but the profits from the evening only amounted to £11.13.3.[11] out of a total receipt of £27.17.6. The Race Week season opened on August 19 and was successful without the aid of any star.[12] Instead there were several new pieces: Rose's melodrama *The Prisoner* with new scenery; Reynolds's comedy *How to Grow Rich* followed by *The Surrender of Valenciennes*; and on the last night Morris's *False Colours* followed by Hoare's musical farce of *The Prize.* The new bombardment contraption of whirling lights served again in *The Surrender of Valenciennes.* The critic at Hull picks the production and situation in this entertainment to pieces, finding that the Austrian army officers were unrecognisably nondescript, that the Duke of York hobnobbed in a chorus with a corporal, and that the great attack seemed rather to resemble a preliminary skirmish in which not a single soldier of the allied army was killed and only one wounded.

Earl Fitzwilliam bespoke one night and Wilkinson said that he had seldom known the theatre better supported than it was that week. York people grumbled at having to pay 4/- to the boxes though there was no London star, but as the manager points out, the tax fell mostly on visitors, since the local people rarely came more than once in the week. The new pieces were put on at a considerable extra cost and Wilkinson depended, anyway, on profits from the Assize and Race Weeks to pay his winter season's bills.[13] Many patrons urged him to give up half price during the public weeks, which he would willingly have done as, owing to the lateness of the dining hour then, all the best seats usually remained unoccupied until half price at the third act; but he would not make the innovation unless openly requested for fear of being thought avaricious.

For the first time we hear of a circus which competed as an attraction in August with twice daily performances outside Micklegate Bar.[14]

There were no changes in the company when they re-opened in York on February 8, 1794. Indeed for three years from 1792-4 the personnel was remarkably stable. John Wilkinson had married Miss Reynolds, but she continued on the stage.[15] A fracas which had started in Hull between the Cherrys and the Pensons, on the usual score of possession of rôles, had split the company into two factions, both of which were rebellious against the manager who, in exasperation threatened to disband the whole troupe from June to August. The rumour having circulated that the entire company, good and bad alike, were to be discharged and a new one recruited brought nothing but blame from everyone on Wilkinson's head. He did not, however, carry out his threat and finally fractious tempers cooled.

Cherry's new pantomime, *Harlequin Shipwreck'd or The Grateful Savage* was taken from Smollett's *Ferdinand, Count Fathom* and concluded with the Indian ambuscade scene from *Nootka Sound*, another pantomime.[16] Cherry left soon after the termination of the York season at a few days notice and returned to Dublin,[17] because Fawcett had taken a few of his parts on a visit to Leeds.

Wilkinson announced on his benefit bill that this was to be the last season but one in which he would perform, and he appeared for the last time as Vandunk in a revival of *The Royal Merchant* with alterations. This was followed by *Robinson Crusoe* in which the second part, not performed for several years, was revived ending with a view of the seat of Sir Francis Dashwood.[18]

The first visitor was Wewitzer from Drury Lane who appeared for one night on his way to Edinburgh as Shadrach in *The Young Quaker* and Bagatelle in *The Poor Soldier*. He specialised in Jews and Frenchmen, but Wilkinson thought that his naturalness was on the tame side and should have been heightened in colouring and accent.[19]

Next came Hannah Brand on March 20 on the recommendation of Woodfall. Poetess, actress and would-be blue-stocking, she amused Wilkinson[20] by her pompous mode of expression, her mispronunciations, her general pretentiousness and her old fashioned and extraordinary attire. Her first appearance as Lady Townly in the formal style 'met with rude remarks of disgustful behaviour'. On the last night of the season May 21 her tragedy *Agmunda* was acted. She would not allow the prompter to have her MS lest he should steal it, but wrote out a copy without a line of her own part. At the end of the act she demanded that an altar table should be more advanced otherwise 'If the theatre were to fall in one momentous crush she would not begin'. At the end of the fourth act 'with the most dignified solemnity' she told Earby 'that she would not proceed in her business unless he first assured her she might depend upon TWO FLOURISHES previous to her entrance'. No wonder the tragedy ended as a comedy. According to another anecdote related by Wilkinson at the rehearsal, after a long pause, she turned profoundly round, and in blank verse tone said 'Observe, Mr. Warren, I have stopped thus long, that you may remember at night, all this length of time *I shall be Weeping*'. Indeed for all her grand pretensions she seems to have been a figure of fun.

In April Collins gave two performances of his famous entertainment *The Evening Brush* which he had exhibited for 264 nights at the Lyceum and patent theatres. It consisted of sketches, anecdotes, ballads and an 'allusion to the abuses of the drama' and was well received.[21]

A large number of new pieces was brought out this season: Jerningham's tragedy *The Siege of Berwick*, Colman's popular *The Mountaineers* with new scenery by Michell, Cummins as Octavian and Mrs. Simpson as Zorayda; no less than three pieces by O'Keeffe, his two comedies *World in a Village* and *The London Hermit* and his comic opera *Sprigs of Laurel*; Morton's musical piece, long to hold the stage, *Children in the Wood* with Miss Cherry making her first appearance as the Girl, and Master H. Brown his second as the Boy; Hoare's musical farce *My Grandmother* which was well approved; Waldron's comedy *Heigho! for a Husband*; Holcroft's *Love's Frailties* which was badly received; and Cumberland's *Box-Lobby Challenge*.

The company paid two visits to York in August from the 4th to the 11th for Race Week and from the 16th to the 25th for Assize Week. Mr. and Mrs. Kelly[22] from Portsmouth had joined. Mrs. Kelly was the daughter of Collins, the Portsmouth manager, and though her vocal powers were not extensive she was pleasing and tasteful and possessed that rare quality – artless simplicity. She was particularly cut out for such parts as Rose in *The Recruiting Officer* and Amanthis; in the latter she pleased Wilkinson more than performers of much higher reputation because she was so natural. The Browns and Hamerton had quit the company. The famous tenor Incledon was the star. He opened on August 4 in Young Meadows to the Rosetta of Mrs. John Wilkinson and subsequently played Macheath, Lionel, Arionelli, in which he introduced a song in the manner of a celebrated

Italian singer, Don Carlos in *The Duenna*, Captain Fieldair in *Hartford Bridge*, Dalton in Bate Dudley's new comic opera *The Travellers in Switzerland*, Lubin, Edwin in *Robin Hood*, Belville in *Rosina* and Cymon to the Sylvia of Mrs. J. Wilkinson. He also sang the last night of the race season *Black Ey'd Susan, Sally in our Alley*, and *The Storm*. He was the finest ballad singer of the day and Wilkinson says 'his reception was such as he merited; and surely to no performer was I ever more indebted, for not only his success, but for his unremitted and I may add very laborious endeavours to please'.[23] He received for the week at York £114.12.0., high terms, though in Liverpool he had £138.[24] He was re-engaged four nights for Assize Week, which brought a different set of visitors and added to his rôles Capt. Greville in *The Flitch of Bacon*, Welford in the *Woodman* and Tom Tug, besides the songs of *Hearts of Oak* and *Rule Britannia*.

For this season too Mrs. Johnson[25] came from Bath, with high recommendations from the dramatic connoisseurs Meyler and Knight. She turned out to be the wife of a Johnson, who had been with the company in 1787 and had abandoned his engagement hurriedly on account of some trouble about scenery, after which Wilkinson had engaged with him in epistolary altercation. However, all was forgiven to the extent that the manager over-puffed the lady, stating in the advertisement[26] that in Meyler's opinion she bid fair to stand foremost in the list of theatrical candidates for fame and that her figure was deemed equal to that of any actress. Actually she had this last qualification, dressed to great advantage, and had a good portion of merit in comedy and tragedy. She played Lady Teazle and Alicia.

By 1795 there had been several changes in the company. Poor Leng, who had long been ill, was forced at last to retire. Henry Mills[27] from Edinburgh, who was barely 18, was one of the newcomers. He was the son of Mills, who had been in the company from 1784 to 1786, and whose widow had married Fawcett. Another was Sandford, from Bath, who played juvenile leads until 1798. Cherry was succeeded as low comedian by John Edwin junior, son of a more famous father. He had married Miss Richards, who had been with the company in 1791, and she returned with him. He played Jacob Gawky, David in *The Rivals*, Lenitive, Nipperkin, Gingham in *The Rage* and Edgar in *Edgar and Emmeline*, whilst his wife sustained Bridget in *The Chapter of Accidents*, Rosalind and Emmeline. Mrs. Edwin had considerably improved since last she had been with the company, was particularly good in the burletta scene in *The Prize* and was able to play Mrs. Jordan's type of youthful characters better than anyone but Mrs. Jordan herself. Her husband had not been long on the stage, but Wilkinson considered his Tag in *The Spoil'd Child* the best he had ever seen, and he dressed his characters better than any actor he recollected on the York stage, better even than Cherry, who also gave this point great attention. Between them they played so extensive a range that when their benefit failed, Wilkinson gave them another to induce them to continue their engagement, which they did for another two years.[28] In the end, Edwin who had learnt dissipation from Lord Barrymore, drank himself to death in 1805.

Miss Stretton,[29] whose experience was limited to two nights at Cheltenham, was engaged by Wilkinson on the strength of a puffing paragraph from Meyler at Bath, but she proved but a mediocre actress. Some of the leads this season were taken by Mrs. Yates,[30] who had been recommended by Hull from Covent Garden. She opened as Euphrasia, and also played Mandane, Countess of Rutland, Constance, Lady Eleanor Irwin, Mrs. Belville and several other parts. She possessed a powerful voice, but needed experience to give it modulation and variety. She was already in the prime of life, and very conceited of her abilities, so that Tate opined that she had hardly started young enough for she needed 'great study, *diffidence,* and labour' to bring them to fruition.

Lee Lewes came for two nights, during Assize Week, performing Goldfinch and Dashwou'd followed by comic sketches written by himself and G. A. Stevens.[31]

Unfortunately the second week of the Assizes fell in Passion Week when the theatre had to be shut; also the judge did not arrive as usual on the Saturday but on Tuesday. As Wednesday was the Assembly and Friday the Concert this only left Wilkinson the Thursday and Saturday in which to recuperate the losses of a season of playing to houses of £7.10.0 and £12 a night.[32] It was not wholly owing to the war that the theatre was so badly attended, since other theatres, including Hull, did not suffer; but it seemed that it was no longer considered a place for fashionable amusement, and, though the city had a better sprinkling of genteel visitors than usual that winter, they did not come to the Theatre.

Mrs. Cowley's last comedy *The Town Before You* was brought out as well as Reynolds's *Rage* and Cumberland's *The Jew,* with Wilkinson in the title rôle and his *Wheel of Fortune* with Cummins as Penruddock. New musical pieces were Pearce's *Netley Abbey,* Arnold's *Auld Robin Gray* and Andrews's *Mysteries of the Castle* with Mrs. Yates as Julia and Edwin as Hilario. Hurlstone's *Crotchet Lodge* was the only new farce and Edwin's medley *Valentine and Orson* the only new pantomime. Lastly there was a 'serious ballet' *La Forêt Noire or The Natural Son* which was said to be a domestic tale founded on fact. It had been given at the Théâtre de l'Ambigu in Paris and at Covent Garden; Mrs. Yates was Madame Duval and a child of the city, whose first appearance it was on the stage, was the Natural Son.[33] It was followed at its second representation by the spectacle, painted and designed by Yates, of the grand naval engagement between English and French frigates in which Capt. Robert Faulkner lost his life. Yet another patriotic spectacle was a transparent historical picture representing the King in his coronation robes attended by allegorical figures, particularly Neptune holding a medallion of Lord Howe, in celebration of his victory over the French fleet on the glorious first of June, 1794.[34] Thus the Theatre once again brought to its audience a presentation of the events of the day.

Wilkinson closed the Theatre on May 9 and reopened for four nights on May 18 for the spring race meeting. Two of these were occupied by Collins with a revised version of his *Evening Brush,* and two with another *Theatrical Fête* selected the first evening from *As You Like It,* Cibber's *Oracle, The Minor* and *Thomas and Sally,* and the second from *The Register Office, Damon and Phillida, Piety in Pattens, The Diversions of the Morning, The Case of a Cow,* and *The Chaplet.* Elizabeth Farren was once again the star for the summer Assize Week which she opened as Lady Bell in *Know Your Own Mind* and during which she played Lady Paragon (*Natural Son*), Violante, Julia, Maria (*Citizen*), Clarinda (*Suspicious Husband*), and Beatrice with Sandford as Benedick, Edwin as Dogberry and J. Wilkinson as Claudio.

John Palmer, owner of the Royalty Theatre and a good all round actor, starred during Race Week. He opened on August 24 as Don John in *The Chances* and the Mock Doctor, and on subsequent nights played Penruddock, Puff, Tobeni, Joseph Surface, and Petruchio. He was the original Joseph Surface and is said to have had no competitors in the part to which he was suited by temperament. Holcroft's comedy *The Deserted Daughter* was brought out on August 26.

In December Prince William of Orange paid a visit to York and expressed a wish to see some plays. Wilkinson was requested to bring his company from Hull for four nights. The company was convened and the majority consented though all urged the great expense, the hurry, the fatigue and the disbursements which even treble salaries could not cover. Hull was appeased by being given a week longer at the end of the season, and Wilkinson, assured of the patronage of the Prince and the support of the principal families, opened on December 19 with *The Provok'd Husband* and *The Midnight Hour.*[35] In the company were two players who were to become famous. One of them was Mrs. Spencer (formerly Miss Campion, later the second Mrs. Pope) who played Julia in *The Rivals* on the last night; the other was John Emery who was to become the greatest of stage Yorkshiremen. Though born out of the county in Sunderland, he had been educated in the West Riding; both his parents were strolling players who had been in the York company for a short while in 1779.[36] Though only 18 he had already performed at Brighton and on August 23rd he appeared for the first time in York as Jabal in *The Jew.* He was the fourth in the line of great comedians attached to the York company. Whether Prince William attended all the four performances we cannot be sure. [Wilkinson's *Wandering Patentee* was published in April this year and his account of his adventures in the York circuit had closed with the Winter season. Hereafter we have to depend on playbills and newspapers and occasional biographies for our information, which necessarily becomes less full and intimate.]

The company which opened on February 17, 1796 was strong on the comedy side. Southgate, Emery and Edwin divided the comic business.[37] Mrs. Spencer succeeded Mrs. Yates in the leads which she shared with Mrs. Jarman. She played Alicia, Lady Eleanor Irwin, Monimia, Euphrasia,

Juliet and Perdita. Something of the care with which Wilkinson coached and criticised his players is revealed in a letter he wrote to her:[38]

> Dear Madam, – Without comp[t] I think that your Balcony Scene in many Passages, has more simplicity than that of any Actress of y[e] many I have seen from y[e] year 1752. But here and there you want Quickness and Variety; as, for instance, "Romeo, Juliet, all slain," &c., which sh[d] run to a sudden climax; and you sh[d] say *Pha e ton*, not Phaeton. You sh[d] also be discovered on y[e] bed, exactly y[e] same as when left after y[e] Draught. In y[e] Soliloquy, you sh[d] plead to Tibalt, in your Frenzy, on one side, & on y[e] other, as to Romeo. I can give you a better mode of waking in y[e] Tomb; and where you stab y[r]self, I will shew you Mrs. Cibber's method. When you have to say, "There rest and let me die", y[e] dagger sh[d] remain, and not be thrown away, as that is a contradiction to y[e] Words. Favor me with a call by half p[t] 12 on Thursday, after I have seen y[r] Monimia, and every Hint in my Power you may command for y[e] mutual Interest of

> Yourself and yours
> Tate Wilkinson.

Tate's vast experience, his shrewd common sense and the infinite pains he took with the teachable were of untold value to the young players in his company. Unfortunately Mrs. Spencer was taken suddenly ill in mid-season and never returned, leaving a gap that it was no easy task for Wilkinson to fill.[39] Miss Barnet from Edinburgh took some singing rôles, remained two years with the company and returned to it in 1807.

Richer, the rope dancer, gave several performances in February and March. He performed on shares and nothing under full price was taken on his nights. His performances included a pantomime ballet, *William Tell,* in which he danced the Swiss hero. According to the *York Herald*[40] his dancing had the elegance of Vestris and his amazing manoeuvres on the tight rope were executed with an ease and neatness that established his superiority over all other European rope dancers. In his leaps he suspended himself in air but did 'not give the most delicate feelings the least occasion for alarm'.

The war is reflected in a bespeak by the York Volunteers at which their band performed military music, and in the presentation of a number of patriotic and historical pieces. On St. George's Day an historical play Watson's *England Preserv'd; or Magna Carta Renewed* was followed by Cross's new musical drama *British Fortitude and Hibernian Friendship, or An Escape from France.* Another historical play was Cumberland's *Days of Yore* whilst other new musical dramas were Cross's *Apparition* and Birch's *Adopted Child.* Though not yet known by the name of melodrama, this species of entertainment was growing in popularity. The only other new musical piece was Cobb's comic opera *Cherokee* with music by Storace. The usual writers contributed their almost annual new comedies: Reynolds's *Speculation*, with Mrs. Spencer as Emmeline, and Edwin as Jack Arable; Cumberland's *First Love*, Edwin as Sir Miles Mowbray, Mrs. Spencer as Sabina Rosny; Morton's *The Way to Get Married*, Wilkinson as Capt. Faulkner, Edwin as Dashall and Mrs. Spencer as Julia Faulkner; and Holcroft's *Man of Ten Thousand*, with a new scene by Michell of a picturesque cottage and landscape containing a view of the seat of the Earl of Harcourt.

Shakespeare plays were *Romeo and Juliet* with Sandford as Romeo, *Florizel and Perdita*, *Henry VIII* in which Wilkinson once again played Wolsey and *Henry IV* with Edwin as Falstaff for the first time.

Mrs. Siddons came for the summer Assize Week, opening on July 9 as Mrs. Beverley in *The Gamester* to the Beverley of Cummins and the Stukely of Grist who reappeared after 4 years. On August 11 she played Zara in *The Mourning Bride*, on the 12th Almeyda in Miss Lee's new tragedy of that name, the 13th Isabella, the 14th Hermione at the Sheriff's bespeak, the 15th Belvidera and on her last night Jane Shore and Catharine in *Catharine and Petruchio*.

By Race Week the Theatre had 'received many Alterations and Embellishments: Also a New Scene with a set of Wings: All finished under the direction of Mr. Pickering of Leeds.'[41] A *York Guide* of 1796 states that 'The Scenery and Dresses are equally superb with any in the Kingdom.' Incledon was again the star, adding to the rôles already played in York those of Welford in *The Woodman*, Chearley in *Lock and Key*, Greville in *The Flitch of Bacon*, Lubin in *The Quaker* and Henry in *The Deserter*.

In October, after twelve years, the Theatre again housed the Eidouranian or transparent orrery with an astronomical lecture.

When the company returned on February 16, 1797 they opened with *Hamlet* for the benefit of the Doorkeepers. Other Shakespeare plays given were *Richard III; Henry IV;* and *Othello* in which the Moor was played by Smith of York who made his first appearance on this stage. The Edwins had departed and Emery[42] had all the main comic business. When he played Frank Oatland, Wilkinson who was watching from the gallery, thinking the audience unappreciative, called out 'Clap him! Clap him! Ugh! you don't deserve good acting'. The critic of the *Monthly Mirror*[43] foretold, that if he would pay more attention to himself, he would make a considerable figure on the London boards in a year or two.

Mrs. John Wilkinson did not appear this year and Miss Keys from Dublin, sister to Mrs. Lee of Covent Garden, was engaged to replace her and Mrs. Edwin in singing and comedy rôles. She also gave great satisfaction as a dancer,[44] appearing in a dance entitled *The Caledonian Lovers* which was so fatiguing that it had to be given after the farce as she was too exhausted to play afterwards. In May she married young Mills. On March 14 the Duncan family from Dublin made their début in *The Road to Ruin*, Dornton = Duncan, Mrs. Warren = Mrs. Duncan, Sophia = Miss Duncan.

161

Maria Duncan was then only eighteen. Tate was so delighted with her performance that he soon raised her salary and gave her the leads in light comedy. She was of middle height with raven black hair and masculine but expressive features, and she had the advantages of a melodious voice and a fine ear. She had been on the stage since a child but this seems to have been her first regular engagement. She was with the company until 1800 when she went to Edinburgh, finally attaining fame at Drury Lane in light and sentimental comedy as Mrs. Davison. She excelled in the same line of characters as Mrs. Jordan and was, after her, the most famous actress to obtain her training under Wilkinson.[45]

Instead of acting this year at his benefit Wilkinson delivered a comic olio written by Garrick as an introduction to Stevens's paraphrase on the seven ages of man. Charles Wood was lucky in obtaining the patronage of the York Volunteers at his benefit which was therefore attended with an elegant and numerous assembly.[46] Two new comedies came out this season, Reynolds's *Fortune's Fool* and Morton's *Cure for the Heartache;* there were also two melodramas, Birch's *Smugglers* and Morton's *Zorinski*,[47] and four musical entertainments, Brewer's *Bannian-Day,* Holman's *Abroad and at Home,* G. N. Reynolds's *Bantry Bay,* and *The Poor Sailor.* The new pantomime was *Harlequin at Amsterdam; or, The Devil among the Dutch*[48] in which the concluding scene by Michell, was of The Cape of Good Hope from Table Bay. Michell was Harlequin, Emery Pantaloon and Mrs. Southgate Columbine. Cross's little entertainment *The Way to Get Unmarried* also made its début. Tate[49] wrote an affectionate letter to his old friend Mrs. Inchbald asking whether her new comedy, *Wives as They Were,* was to be published and when.

Except for the fashionable nights, the season, which closed on May 27, was an indifferent one.

Miss Betterton (later Mrs. Glover), who had appeared as a child on the York stage 8 years previously, came with her father from Bath to star during summer Assize Week in the place of Miss Wallis who was unable to fulfil her engagement owing to her marriage and retirement from the stage. Julia Betterton was still only 17 but was due in October to make her début at Covent Garden at a salary of £15.19. a week. The announcement of her forthcoming appearance in the *York Herald* was cited by the *Monthly Mirror*[50] as an example of 'the Grand Puff preparatory'. She opened on July 31 as Elwina in *Percy,* her father playing Douglas, and she subsequently performed Joanna in *The Deserted Daughter,* Margaret of Anjou, Letitia Hardy, Lady Eleanor Irwin and Amanthis.

Once again no star appeared during Race Week though Mrs. Coates from Dublin played Violante for one night. On the last evening of the season Arnold's new comic opera *The Shipwreck* was brought out.

Though there were few changes in the company during the winter season there were to be many of importance before the year 1798 was out. Many parts old and new fell to Emery and he also gave a *Whimsical Description of The Tower of London.* Miss Duncan now played most of the young heroines and some singing rôles, but only one tragic part, that of Jane Shore.[51]

Earby, who had been prompter to the company for 23 years, retired owing to ill health and was given a final benefit. He was succeeded by John Jarman.[52]

There were several visitors. Lee Lewes played Sir Peter Teazle and gave his sketches on *Folly and Fashion* on April 19. With Miss Duncan as Lady Teazle and Emery as Crabtree this must have been a notable performance of Sheridan's comedy.

Mrs. Hindmarsh from Edinburgh played some singing characters. In May another star from Edinburgh – Miss Gough – played a round of tragic and comedy rôles: Alicia, Calista, and Lady Priory in *The Count of Narbonne*. The *York Herald*[53] quotes from the *Monthly Mirror* of 1795 a criticism which says that in Alicia her eye seemed the very mirror of madness, and she appeared to be attracted by a supernatural agency. She did not spoil the part by making it that of a fury as others did. Her otherwise graceful deportment had one fault, in that she had a strange inclination of her arms forming an angle from her elbow; her taste in dress was elegant except for the oriental folds about her head.

The season is remarkable for the number of famous plays which were first brought out in it – plays which were to remain stock ones for many a year. There were two pieces by Colman the younger: *The Iron Chest* taken from Godwin's novel *Caleb Williams:* Sir Edward Mortimer = Cummins, Wilford = Emery, Barbara = Miss Duncan, and his comedy *The Heir at Law:* Dick Dowlas = Sandford, Pangloss = Michell, Zekiel Homespun = Emery, Caroline Dormer = Miss Duncan. An even more famous melodrama was Monk Lewis's *The Castle Spectre* presented at Wilkinson's benefit on April 10 with new scenery and machinery including portraits, armoury, sliding panels, an oratory, subterraneous dungeon and transparencies, a romantic paraphernalia. The piece as printed was too lengthy and the acting version used at Drury Lane was adopted; Cummins played Osmond, Emery Motley and Miss Duncan Angela. It was received in York, as it had been in London, with applause by a crowded audience, and on its repetition so full a house was expected that no printed orders were allowed entrance. One other lesser known melodrama, Boaden's *Italian Monk*, also made its début. Morton's *Secrets Worth Knowing* was another comedy that had a long life; it appeared on March 14 with Emery as Nicholas Rue and Miss Duncan as Mrs. Greville. Two popular comedies by Reynolds *The Will* and *Cheap Living* as well as Cumberland's *False Impressions* were also new, as were a farce entitled *Honest Thieves* by Thomas Knight, formerly a member of the company, and a pantomime *Mirth and Magic; or Harlequin's Frolicks.* There were two ballets. One was the famous serious *Raymond and Agnes* with new dresses and decorations by Michell, including a woodman's cottage, the breaking down of Raymond's chaise, inside of a hovel, vanishing of the spectre of a bleeding nun and a cavern. The taste for the mysterious and romantic was in the ascendant. The other ballet was *Fanny's Love; or The Scotch Ghost* for which Wilkinson had obtained all the parts of the music for the band.

On May 23 a representation of the Royal Procession to St. Paul's at the national thanksgiving for three naval victories was exhibited. The pasteboard figures had been conveyed by Elliston from Bath to Edinburgh for his benefit, and he asked Wilkinson to show them in York before the season closed. Another echo of the war was a benefit towards a voluntary fund at the Bank for the 'Defence of Old England' at which all performers, musicians and doorkeepers gave their services, and £93.2.0. was raised.[54]

John Bannister junior starred at summer Assize Week for seven nights opening as Col. Feignwell with Emery as Periwinkle in *A Bold Stroke for a Wife*, followed by Harry Hawser in *The Shipwreck* with Miss Duncan as Fanny. He played a comedy and farce each night, sustaining Young Rapid, Peeping Tom, Marplot, Sylvester Daggerwood (in this piece's début at York), Coupee, Sheva, Lenitive, in which he sang Dibdin's *Capt. Wattle and Miss Roe*, Howard in *The Will*, Will Steady, Spunge, Dick, Rostram, Bowkitt, Scout, Jonas in Holcroft's new comedy *Knave or Not* and Young Philpot. A first rate low comedian, his sailors were unrivalled, and he was accorded a hearty welcome.[55]

When the company returned for Race Week there had been some important additions to it. By far the most valuable of these was Charles Mathews who was to succeed Emery as the fifth great comedian to train at York. Mathews, who was then 22, had performed as musician, dancer and mimic under Daly in Dublin and in a round of comic characters for two years in Wales. Hearing that Emery was to leave for London he had applied to Wilkinson for his place in January.[56] Tate replied that he would be mad to engage a young man of whom he knew nothing with a company already loaded, nor would it be practicable for Mathews to come so far on trial. Mathews persisted and sent Wilkinson his cast of characters which provoked the manager to remark 'Your Cast is a Good One, but how you can Perform that cast is a material question – For if You come here and are not equal to the Task why it will be a mutual Disappointment'. Nevertheless he decided to give him a chance at 18/- a week from the first Saturday of June until the end of October with double salary at York Assizes and Races: 'And then I shall be Able to Judge whether you can sustain such an Undertaking. If you Can it will be a fine Opportunity. It is a natural Surmise if Clever, How you can be so lost in the Mountains'. In a further letter in February Wilkinson refused the requests of the 'Man in the Mountains' for certain business: 'I shall want a Comedian that can Strike the Audience well as to say, this will do, and *then* advance Y^r Situation – And as to coming in to a first Situation, and the Bussiness You wrote for, No such thing can be complied with – Mr. Emery is in full Possession of fame and Characters, so suit y^r convenience as to Staying away … Mr. Emery will not quit Me until the London Theatre Opens, therefore You can Only Play Occasionally but You will have full Scope, untill the end of Octr and then I can judge of Continuance or raising of terms according to y^r Desert and Success. For a good comedian only will do if I can get him'. Mathews received another characteristic letter from Wilkinson in March advising him to postpone arriving until Race Week or later so that he could immediately enter into a full field of business. He continues: 'I have two Ladies on My hands now I wish at Camarthen, Yet the One not destitute of Merit, a Mrs. Howard daughter of a Mr. Maxwell, a good Education Good Person Good Wardrobe Good Voice and an Income. She has Played Mrs. Sullen, and neither with or without approbation – She is in a few Nights to Play Calista, but I have 13 Ladies and in that upper Department most Superior – the other Lady came down as a Lady of Quality, but has not produced the Certificate it seems lost on the Road – As to her Abilities I know not but she is to try in Laetitia Hardy'. Whether Tate got rid of his two troubles on the Welsh manager, whom he had heard 'well spoken of as a gentleman, a happy and Unusual Praise to a Manager', we do not know. He ends 'I am a great Invalid have been Ill with New Dislocations Strains, Gout &c., and am Realy Poor Old Tate Wilkinson'. Then Penson, with whom Wilkinson was on bad terms, decided to leave in August and the manager was able to offer Mathews £1 a week and a year's engagement.

Mathews was elated at being accepted by a company which was considered second only to Bath as a nursery for metropolitan performers. He arrived at Pontefract with a scanty wardrobe consisting of 8 or 10 comical wigs, and has described in his *Memoirs* his first meeting with the eccentric manager. His greeting was not particularly encouraging: 'What a maypole! Sir, You're too *tall* for low comedy', and then 'You're too *thin*, sir, for anything but the Apothecary in Romeo and Juliet; and you would want stuffing for that'. Then, muddling the poor actor's name in his usual fashion, Tate asked him whether he was quick of study, and after a few cutting remarks advised him to go back to trade. After an unhappy start in Pontefract Mathews opened in York as Silky in *The Road to Ruin* followed by Lingo in *The Agreeable Surprise*. Here 'his efforts were more noticed and more successful than at Pontefract; his manner was more assured, and altogether his reception was very creditable'. Emery, though he had lent Mathews his part of Lingo for the night, resumed it when the piece was repeated, and though kind, was not encouraging, rather attempting to persuade him to give up acting, or at least to return to strolling in Wales. Mathews had a rival in another new actor, Rock from Edinburgh, who was announced to appear on the second night in the first comedian's part of Sir Benjamin Dove in *The Brothers*. Though Rock was not very successful he temporarily robbed Mathews of the hope of succeeding to Emery's cast of old men. He is said to have been idle and seldom perfect, and to have stood like a statue when silent[57] yet he was chosen for the favourite part of Old Duberley in *The Heir at Law*. He left, however, after this season. A new actor, Denman from Drury Lane and Edinburgh, was also engaged for old men's rôles and took over Kenrick in *The Castle Spectre* which Mathews had played at Pontefract but to which Denman was more fitted, and poor Mathews 'sighed when he beheld himself in green and gold, again figuring away in the odious ballet' *Raymond and Agnes*. He was also relegated to the chorus of *The Castle Spectre*, played Rundy in *The Farmer* and The Governor in *The Chapter of Accidents* and *The Critic*. Another important newcomer was Melvin, also from Edinburgh, who opened as Harry Dornton in *The Road to Ruin* and also played Belfield in *The Brothers*, Dick Dowlas and Sir George Versatile in Holcroft's new comedy *He's Much to Blame*. Melvin stayed with the company until 1806 when he went to Covent Garden. Though he never rose to be a first rate actor, he was said to be 'an agile, locomotive little fellow, who understands all the finesse of the stage, and has as much vivacity as any of our actors, except Mr. Lewis'; he spoke articulately and with good sense and his deportment was never awkward.[58]

The star was the old York stager Thomas Knight. He had remained in Bath after he had left Wilkinson for 8 years and in 1795 had made his début at Covent Garden. He appeared as Puff, Nipperkin and Farmer Harrow. Thus in the space of one week York saw in Mathews a beginner who was to become famous, in Emery a comedian who was leaving after 3 years to make his name in London by replacing Thomas Knight, and in Thomas Knight himself a former member of the company who had become a metropolitan star.

Emery's last night was on August 25 when he played Motley in *The Castle Spectre* and Jemmy Jumps. York gave him a splendid send off for the receipts that night were £120.12.0.[59] Emery's forte was country men; Zekiel Homespun in *The Heir at Law*, which he had created that year at York, being one of his best characters.

Mathews proved a disappointment at first, and suffered discomfiture and setbacks during the seasons at Hull and Wakefield. So dubious was Wilkinson of his ability to fill Emery's place that he sent for one Hatton from Windsor as a reinforcement on the low comedy side. According to the *Monthly Mirror*[60] Hatton turned out to be full of conceit and audacity, florid and boisterous in his style of acting, but negligent and careless; nor was his private life such as to render him welcome in a company in which 'character was as much noticed off as on the stage'. After a while he fell into disfavour whilst Mathews soon gained ground by his assiduity, quickness of study and dependability and at the same time his powers became more evident. His comic singing was particularly admired for the oddity and quaintness of its style. The season of 1799 saw him finally become established as the principal comedian. He wrote from York in April: 'I think I am still gaining ground with audience and manager. We have had a very good and pleasant season here; and close on the 12th of May … I have been more comfortable since the critics have been quiet'. By October he pronounced that he had every reason to be satisfied though he would not like to pass all his life in a country company. He adds that the audience in York was used to good acting so that their approbation and that of the manager meant something: 'If I could take three or four inches from my height, I should fear nothing'. Wilkinson told him that after the line of feeble old men he should succeed in Suett's parts and as Silky, Kecksey, and Crazy in *Peeping Tom*. He did play several old men during the season including Sir Anthony Absolute; he also supported several leading comic rôles, played clowns in the pantomimes and undertook some of the low comedy rôles of Southgate who had recently died. Of him Mathews says: 'he had been a careless, slovenly person in his profession, and unstudied in it further than to make the unskilful laugh. His *hits* were at the galleries; his life was dissipated, and he took the least possible time in selecting his dresses and putting them on.' Mathews, who was particular about his wardrobe, rejected the stock smock which had been used for all countrymen, and thereby disgusted Johnny Winter the wardrobekeeper, dresser and tailor. Winter hated newcomers, new demands and change of habits, but most of all he hated spectacles and Shakespeare because they gave him so much trouble. His pet abomination was *Henry VIII*, and all such historical plays that required numbers to be dressed he attributed to the abhorred name of Shakespeare. As for supernumeraries he dubbed them superneedlesses and resented having to look out dresses for them. Bishop Gardiner in *Henry VIII* was always played by the low comedian and so was assigned to Mathews; when he applied to Winter early for a dress, the wardrobekeeper who was an anti-episcopalian, merely threw at him an ordinary soldier's coat saying it was good enough for any bishop. This eccentric character was in fact spoiled by manager and actors alike.

Mathews says of Tate that he was 'one of the most generous men and *certainly* the most generous *manager* in the world'. At the end of an unusually prosperous season he would give the actors presents. In Mathews's *Memoirs* we catch a glimpse of him at his daily levee at which Swalwell the treasurer, Winter, French the leader of the band, and Mrs. Bearpark the ladies' wardrobekeeper were each granted half an hour's audience. Mathews tells us one or two amusing anecdotes.[61] The part of the Lord Mayor in *Richard III* was assigned to Mathews before Hatton arrived, for Wilkinson always gave it to the low comedian. Some wags told the inexperienced Mathews that he was expected to get a laugh by shaking powder from his periwig as he acknowledged Buckingham's remark 'Pity that the Lord Mayor should lose his title with his office'. Mathews, glad of a comic point, piled $1/_2$ lb. of hair powder on the top of his wig which, as he bowed, descended with a thud on the stage and covered the amazed Buckingham in a white cloud, whereupon the laughter was such that not a word more of the scene could be heard. Tate who was watching from his customary perch in the gallery, called for hissing in vain, then descended in high dudgeon to flay the offender. Mathews eluded him but expected his discharge. Nothing further, however, was heard of the matter until Saturday settling time when Swalwell presented him with a bill of 5/- for flour.

On another occasion when *Richard III* was given Mrs. Jarman, who was cast for the Queen, was taken ill at the last moment whilst Tate was having his afternoon nap. Her husband the prompter did not dare disturb the dormant manager and Mrs. Wood, who had retired some years ago, volunteered to take her place. When Wilkinson woke up he found the Queen 'arrayed as she was in faded finery, and pumping out her wrongs in the true tragedy tone of her day'. Tate drew Jarman from the prompting seat to the first entrance to the stage, and pointing to the resuscitated actress, demanded an explanation. So furious was he when this was given, that he threw off his hat and wig and cast them at the Queen's feet, 'who for a moment lost sight of her maternal sorrow in order to investigate the cause of such a windfall'; he then trotted across the back of the scene, as if for a wager, to his room in a passage near the side scene, and banged and locked his door. The hat and wig were borne from the stage by a green coat man in herald's dress, and hung outside Tate's door for the rest of the evening.

When *Pizarro* was played Wilkinson took his station in the back row of the gallery and at the end of the performance descended to the green room in ill humour, full of criticisms. He proceeded to mimic the actors in their varied pronunciation of the name Rolla. Mathews himself was the greatest of all mimics and gave samples of his talent twice during the season by imitating John Kemble, Holman, Munden, Incledon and Suett.

A newcomer in 1799, who was to be the company's leading man, was Toms from Liverpool who opened as George Barnwell. He was pronounced a most promising young actor and his performance a masterpiece. In a company which bordered on the elderly the modern style of a young man showed to advantage. He had a sound judgment, was perfectly accurate, and careful about his dress and appearance.[62] With a graceful figure and finely marked and expressive countenance he was somewhat effeminate and better adapted to sentimental comedy than to tragedy. His feelings in *Macbeth* so overpowered him and his utterance was so rapid that he destroyed the effect of correct enunciation. Indeed his voice, though agreeable, was not powerful. He played Faulkland, Almaviva, Don Felix, Benedick, Florizel, Prospero, Posthumous and Othello. It was probably owing to his presence in the company that more Shakespeare was given this year than for some time.

The *Monthly Mirror*[63] critic thought that with diligence and study Melvin would make a good actor; his figure was agreeable for genteel comedy, his voice sonorous, soft and musical though not extensive. He played Harlequin, Figaro, Acres, Vapid, Sheva and Abednego during the season.

Miss Duncan was the leading lady and played in a wide variety of parts. Mrs. Mills had left and was replaced by Miss Cornelys who was a failure and who together with Hatton was discharged at the end of the season. She was insipid and affected with a disagreeable monotony in her voice.[64] The only visitor during the winter season was Saxoni the rope dancer.

The Kotzebue craze was at his height and York saw four adaptations of his dramas during 1799; Mrs. Inchbald's *Lovers' Vows* with Miss Cornelys as Amelia Wildenhaim, Thompson's[65] *The Stranger* with Miss Duncan as Mrs. Haller, Thomas Dibdin's farce *The Horse and the Widow,* and Sheridan's *Pizarro*. Colman's melodrama *Blue Beard* had new scenery by Michell and the effects included an oriental procession with a grand elephant, an enchanted blue chamber, a view of Bluebeard's Castle, and the magic sepulchre which changed to a brilliant garden.[66] This piece had brought nearly £300 for 3 nights in Hull and was got up in liberal style, the painter having produced a spectacle almost unbelievable on a provincial stage.[67] It was given seven times during the season. New comedies were Thomas Dibdin's *Five Thousand a Year*, O'Keeffe's *Lie of the Day*, Morris's *Secret*, Reynolds's *Laugh When You Can* and Holman's *Votary of Wealth;* farces were Thomas Dibdin's *Jew and the Doctor* and Colman's *Blue Devils*. Dibdin's musical entertainment *The Mouth of the Nile* and an otherwise unknown musical piece *Rival Loyalists; or Sheelah's Choice* also made their début.

The new pantomime was *The Prodigal Son or Harlequin in Spain* in which Hatton as Harlequin leaped through a circle of fixed bayonets. *Harlequin Salamander* was revived after 15 years with the original scenes and tricks and Harlequin flew, by means of a parachute, from the stage to the back of the theatre. Lastly Kemble's version of *The Tempest* appeared with Toms as Prospero, Michell as Caliban, Mrs. Jarman as Hippolito, Miss Duncan as Miranda and Mrs. Southgate as Ariel.

There were not less than 6 military bespeaks which must have been a help to the company's finances.

John Kemble returned for seven nights at the Summer Assizes playing The Stranger, Hamlet to the Ophelia of Miss Duncan, Rolla in the first performance of *Pizarro* on July 9 with Miss Duncan as Cora and Mrs. Jarman as Elvira, Penruddock, Octavian in *The Mountaineers* and Macbeth. *Pizarro* was got up in two or three days with only two rehearsals yet was perfect as a stock play, 'so much may be done by a respectable company, under good management, when the actors are disposed to exert themselves.'[68] The new scenery and dresses were good, the former including Pizarro's tent, the Temple of the Sun, a falling bridge, mountainous country, a dungeon and a cascade. This drama did well, bringing £130 in August when it was done with the stock company with Cummins as Rolla.

W. Burton, who had played a season at Covent Garden, and his wife were newcomers. She opened as Charlotte in *The Stranger* and he as a Grave-digger.

Mrs. Siddons followed her brother in August. The following receipts were taken during Race Week.[69]

			£	s	d
M.	Aug. 19	*Castle of Montval* by Whalley, Countess of Montval – Mrs. Siddons	111	3	6
T.	Aug. 20	*Laugh When You Can, Bluebeard*	39	4	0
W.	Aug. 21	Isabella – Mrs. Siddons, *Prisoner at Large*	160	8	6
Th.	Aug 22	*Pizarro, No Song No Supper*	127	1	6
F.	Aug 23	*Venice Preserv'd*, Belvidera – Mrs. Siddons	106	0	6
S.	Aug 24	*Castle Spectre, Blue Beard*	97	4	6
M.	Aug 26	*Mourning Bride*, Zara – Mrs Siddons	72	2	0
T.	Aug 27	*Henry VIII; Catharine and Petruchio,* Queen Catharine and Catharine – Mrs. Siddons.	99	17	6

To Mathews, though he was out of most of her plays, it was a feast: 'I think,' he writes 'she looks more beautiful than ever, and never could have played better. I never saw her to such advantage as now, as the London theatres are too large for her powers'.

When the company returned in 1800 there was a new actress for the singing parts – Miss Jackson. A pupil of Kelly's she opened as Amanthis and played Leonora, Rosina and Patty. Mathews had undisputed title to all the principal comic rôles. He again gave his imitations including those of Kemble as Rolla and Lewis as Young Rapid. His benefit though was a failure and Wilkinson gave him and Williams a chance night for a second one.

Miss Duncan, whose last year it was with the company, played many new leads and at her benefit performed Cordelia and Miss Hoyden in *The Man of Quality* and gave an address to the town in the character of a York Cavalry volunteer concluding with a Hungarian broad sword exercise.[70] She had become an extraordinary favourite and was long remembered as one of the great dramatic geniuses that York had given London. Mrs. Stanley who had formerly been the Hon. Mrs. Twisleton made three appearances as Lady Teazle, Elvira and Mrs. Dorville in *What Is She?* with Susan in *The Follies of a Day*. She had eloped with the Hon. Thomas Twisleton with whom she had performed in private theatricals and had subsequently gone on the professional stage. She was quite well known in the provinces, though better perhaps for the scandals attached to her marriage and its annulment than for her powers as an actress.

On March 11 Mrs. Jarman died after performing Elvira the preceding evening. She is said to have been an actress of considerable merit whose loss was severely felt by the manager.[71] About this time too old Leng, long bedridden, died. Adaptations from Kotzebue were again prominent among the new plays; such were Dibdin's *Birthday*, Mrs. Inchbald's *Wise Man of the East*, and Miss Plumptre's *Count of Burgundy*. Reynolds's comedy *Management*, Moultrie's *False and True*, Charlotte Smith's *What Is She?*, Franklin's farce *The Wandering Jew*, and Dibdin's musical entertainment *The Naval Pillar* were also presented. In this last the pillar, decorated with emblematical and marine devices, expanded to form itself into a representation of Britannia on her throne. There were two pantomime ballets: *Alonzo and Imogene*[72] taken from a Spanish ballad in *The Monk*, with new scenery by Michell and a procession of knights embarking for Palestine with their ensigns and banners, and *The Scotch Wedding* for which the music had been compiled and adapted by Miss Duncan. There were also new pantomimes, *Hurly Burly; or Harlequin's Frolics* with Melvin as Harlequin and Mrs. Burton as Columbine, and *Tippoo Saib or the Plains of Hindustan* with scenery, dresses and decorations specially executed in Indian style. This last was given for Wilkinson's benefit and he wrote to Emery:[73] 'I had £123.14s.6d – and Got through with Vigour, [as Shylock after 8 years] Perfect and with Discrimination – Saw the Entertainment Afterwards before which I had some Good Grog and after part of a Bottle of Madiera. Gout seems to threaten earnestly last Night and to Day. Tippoo was I assure you very Splendid but cost a Great deal too much Money. Toms in Tippoo had nearly lost his Hand by a Cut with the Broad Sword, if under his Wrist, it must have been Fatal. It was Oblig'd to be Sew'd up.' Later he says that £80 went on expenses for *Tippoo*, the supers falling very heavy. In this same letter we find the manager eagerly enquiring after new talent: 'Don't forget the Sketch for the Plough scene and the Fire Works ... Is Mr. *John* Whitmore a Good Scene Painter and a useful actor – As to Irishmen *Denman* has claw'd most of them. I shall not think of a Painter until Nov^r,' and again 'Give Me Your serious Opinion as to the Abilities &c. of Miss de Camp Sister, as I understand She Acted at Brighton the last Summer, Her Engag^t with Me must depend on Y^r Secret Serious Opinion to Me', and 'There is a Mrs. [torn] from Windsor now Playing at Nottingham, What is said of her?'

It was another good season for Shakespeare. *Romeo and Juliet,* with Toms as Romeo and Miss Duncan as Juliet was followed on the same evening by *Florizel and Perdita* in which Mathews played Autolycus. *Henry V* was revived with Toms as the King, Mathews as Fluellen and Mrs. Burton as Katherine. Two performances of *Hamlet* were given with Toms as Hamlet, Mathews as Polonius and Miss Duncan as Ophelia; *Macbeth* with Toms as Macbeth and Miss Duncan as Lady Macbeth; *King Lear* with Toms as Lear, Miss Duncan as Cordelia; *Richard III; As You Like It* with Melvin as Touchstone, Toms as Orlando, Miss Duncan as Rosalind; and *The Merchant of Venice* in which Wilkinson reappeared as Shylock after 8 years with Miss Duncan as Portia and Miss Jackson as Jessica. There was no star at the Summer Assizes but a new actress, Mrs. Johnson, made her début in York, and three new pieces, Dibdin's *St. David's Day*, Cobb's *Ramah Droog* and Morton's celebrated comedy *Speed the Plough* with Mathews as Farmer Ashfield, were brought out.

For the first time since he had been a member of the company Elliston returned to play as star during Race Week. He opened as Rolla in *Pizarro* with Mrs. Johnson as Elvira and afterwards performed Sylvester Daggerwood. He also played Dr. Pangloss, the Lyar, the West Indian, Vapour in *My Grandmother,* Hamlet, Frederick in *Lovers' Vows* and Jemmy Jumps, a selection which displayed his vast range from tragedy to farce.

Benjamin Wrench[74] had joined the company from Windsor and played Henry in *Speed the Plough* on August 27. He was in time to become a well known, though not a first rank, comedian at Drury Lane. At this time he was twenty-three years of age and his previous experience had been under Mrs. Robinson,[75] a former member of the York company, in the Nottingham circuit. Later he became the third husband of this actress who was much older than he was. Wrench was short and ill-proportioned with high shoulders and flat features, but despite this had a pleasing personality on the stage. Oxberry says he was the worst level speaker he knew and uttered everything in a kind of chant. An imitator of Elliston, he could boast little originality; in comedy he was dull or vulgarly vivacious but was good as a bustling farce actor. The first night that he played in York Wilkinson[76] hobbled into the dressing room at the conclusion of the play and said to him 'I am come, sir, to tell you that you have a great deal of roast beef about you', implying thereby a passport to fame if he would use it. The *Monthly Mirror*[77] pronounced him promising though added that he needed instruction from dancing and fencing masters. He left the company in 1801 as his rapid progress and improvement led to an engagement at Edinburgh.

According to the *Monthly Mirror* the company which came to York in 1801 was inferior to that of the preceding year. Miss Duncan was an irreparable loss. She and her parents had gone to Edinburgh where her father died at the beginning of the year.[78] Michell the scene painter was also dead[79] and his widow was accorded a benefit. Mrs. Southgate had married Williams. On February 19, the opening night, three newcomers made their appearance: Miss Errington, who soon was to become the second Mrs. Jarman, as Albina, Mrs. Ward from Liverpool as Mrs. Rigid in *The Will*, and Lewis as Sandy in *The Highland Reel*.

Miss Adelaide de Camp made her début as Amelia Wildenhaim. She was the sister of Marie Therese de Camp of Drury Lane, later to become Mrs. Charles Kemble, and she played the same type of rôle. According to the *Monthly Mirror* Melvin was inattentive and needed to study more; but Miss Jackson had improved and displayed vocal powers.[80] She had become a favourite and came to sustain all the principal operatic characters as well as the heroines of sentimental comedy 'for which the delicacy of her form, her youth, and a pleasing style of delivery particularly qualified her'. We are told too that her figure was 'symmetrically proportioned, her features, interesting and expressive, and her deportment easy and graceful'. Wilkinson took a paternal interest in her and gave her much advice, whilst she received 'most signal marks of attention and regard from the natives of Yorkshire whom she never mentions without expressing the most lively and grateful sense of their kindnesses.'

Mathews was going from strength to strength; he wrote 'from the reception I constantly meet with, the cast of parts I am entrusted with, and from the veteran Tate's Opinion of me I do not think it unlikely that in time I may meet with an offer from London'.[81] Tate who had at first sworn that the praise of all the *Monthly Mirrors* would not make him into a first rate actor nor his principal low comedian, now confessed that he was a good comedian. After watching him play Frederic in *Of Age To-morrow* the manager appeared on the stage and, in front of all the performers, recanted his unjust opinion of him and raised his salary to the highest sum given. Mathews's benefit the previous year had only brought £25, but by 1801 he had become a great favourite. The care he took is illustrated by his enquiring about the dresses worn in London by Fawcett as Caleb Quotem and Gabriel Lackbrain in *Life*, two parts he created in York and which were among his first original ones. It was his custom too to attend the Assize trials as he derived therefrom a useful stock of observation of life and character.

Burton's *A Pasquinade on the Performers of the York Company* was printed at Leeds this year and, though far from being a pasquinade, it describes his fellow actors and actresses. Toms, who, he states in a note, is rumoured to have been a son of the Earl of Sandwich, is the only one about whom he is satirical: he was effeminate and scorned his fellow players yet 'As an actor he's perfect, always clean and correct'. Miss Duncan he hopes will win even fresh laurels in Scotland.

> Your acting of Nell, I have at my will,
> For every line discovered your skill;
> Your steps as a Hoyden, I can't e'en direct,
> For none with such ease, can produce such effect,
> Your Peggy I'll mention, it deserves a good fate,
> And say great was not your song in the new Turnpike Gate.

He praises Denman's[82] Hawthorn, a rôle to which he was very suited:

> When round the huge oak, he stands forward to sing,
> With attention I listen, and feel my heart ring.

Poor Halpin, a new actor, refined and gentlemanly, was the butt of insults from a lady of York notorious for such behaviour though 'His Kitely discovered his skill as an actor'. Burton remarks, as others had done, that the audience often talked louder than the actors and he appeals to the young beaux, though intoxicated, to refrain from treating the performers like dirt. Of Mrs. Johnson, who had failed in her benefit, he writes:

> Characteristic in dress, she always plays well
> And her graceful deportment none can excel.

Her forte was the fashionable, fine ladies, and he commends her Lady Townly for pathos and finds her Dorillion the best he had seen. His passage on Mathews is as follows:

> His genius so strong, that it seldom walks lame ...
> What ails his Miser, at short notice study'd,
> How did you like him, where Lovegold was flurry'd,
> No scrape – all could appear more seemingly cross'd
> Than he did, when he *found* his money was lost;
> If a shilling you'd give to wipe away sorrow,
> Then come and see him, when he's 'Of Age to-morrow'.
> With his powder and comb, you'll find him so funny,
> 'Twill be well worth your while, you'll not grudge your money.
> In his 'feeble old Men' he can give you a kick,
> He's not a bad actor, though they call him a stick.

an allusion, of course, to his thinness.

Williams he pronounces a fair actor, of noble figure, well acquainted with his author who at the end of a performance would announce the play for the next night 'with the grace of John Palmer'. Of Miss de Camp he says,

> All the words which she utters, she sensibly feels;
> In the last modern play, not a word in her part
> > [Julio in *Deaf and Dumb*]
> Yet in *spite* of yourselves, she draws tears from your heart.

and of Miss Errington,

> Her Bridget is *good,* and equal to any,
> In ladies quite pert, she's useful as many.

Dunn had a comic appearance and was a charming singer in the plaintive style but is advised not to say more than is put down for him. Charles Wood, the other male singer, was growing old. Cummins, also no longer young, is commended for his Del'Epée in *Deaf and Dumb*. Wrench was coming forward fast, being especially good as Frederick. Of Wilkinson as critic and manager he had nothing but praise:

> If he wishes you well, and your foibles to halt,
> He'll frequently address you, and frequent find fault;
> When he thinks you are lost, and the good of you gone,
> You may go your own way, for he'll let you alone;
> His rebukes may sound harsh to a fair stranger's ear,
> But under his protection you've nothing to fear;
> His liberality's great ...
> A Theatrical Monarch, he's justly esteem'd,
> By himself the father of his people he's deem'd:
> He studies their welfare, to their comfort he'll add,
> And when he can serve them, appears the most glad.

Mrs. John Wilkinson was beautiful and

> When she sings in the Stranger, of *her* silent grief,
> I would *steal* all her woe, though I pass for a thief:
> When as Gilpin I stand in O'Keef's Highland Reel,
> Her first song in Jenny, I most pleasingly feel;
> None can doubt my account of this musical bird,
> Who can remember when first Miss Reynolds they heard.

He then considers the non-acting members, commencing with the Treasurer Swalwell who greeted you with a smile when he distributed the salaries on Saturday morning. He mentions the privilege, accorded to York tradesmen, of examining the books containing the weekly income of the performers whilst the money owed them was being counted out. Of that character Winter he writes:

> Here comes 'Wha calls?' with his hair neatly curl'd,
> And wishing no Bishops there were in the world;
> In a full busy piece his assistance he'll lend,
> And still will be found a supernumerary's friend.
> With his advice ever ready to buskin and sock,
> And his trouble to save, recommends the smock-frock.

The reference to the super is of course ironical and his antipathy to them is mentioned in a footnote. Of Ellis the stagekeeper he says:

> His science sufficient for the post of stage-keeping,
> Tho' from Chesterfield's manners, he's never been reaping.

George Wilson, who had been attacked as a critic by Burton, replied in *The Retort Courteous* dedicated to Wilkinson. He writes of his pleasure in former members of the company, Inchbald, Bailey, Mills and Jack Southgate. Of Wilkinson's acting he says:

> I've seen him in *Ironsides, Sheva,* and *Lear,*
> *O'Flaherty, Evander,* and Otway's bold *Pierre.*
> Did always regret when he'd finished his part
> For his acting ne'er failed to enliven my heart.

He is praised too for the way he trained Kemble, Mrs. Jordan and others who had attained greatness.

> In short, to amuse you, he spares no expence,
> In scen'ry, in actors, or anything else.

Wilson requests him, though, to introduce forfeits for gagging.

John Wilkinson appears to have given up acting about this time. Mathews[83] tells us that, though he had a passion for the stage, and possessed judgment in theatrical matters, he was destitute of histrionic talent. His mother, in over-weening fondness, often urged her husband to put him in characters above his powers such as Rolla but Tate, who realised his son was a bad actor and had murdered many a hero, would have no more of him even in the lesser rôle of Pizarro.

The tight rope dancer Richer reappeared for a few nights this season and was rewarded by a benefit of £96. The house on his last night, at advanced prices during Assize Week, was £143 – 'So much,' Mathews remarks, 'for heels'.[84] Richer brought out Fawcett's pantomime *Obi* with music, scenery, dresses and decorations as in London. Arnold had composed the overture and most of the music, the rest being adapted from eminent masters to suit the action which was founded on an incident that occurred in Jamaica in 1780.[85] For Wrench's benefit his former manager Mrs. Robinson, now Mrs. Taylor, performed Euphrasia and Lady Bab Lardoon.

The prolific Dibdin had three new pieces in York this season: his comedy *Liberal Opinion*, his comic opera *Il Bondocani* and his musical farce *Of Age To-morrow*. Two other new musical pieces were Holman's *What a Blunder,* and Ryley's *Civilian*. Other new comedies were Reynolds's *Life* and Macready's *Bank Note*. Charles Kemble's *Point of Honour* was a new drama, and Holcroft's *Deaf and Dumb*, founded on Kotzebue, a new melodrama. Miss de Camp from Drury Lane had helped by her instructions with this last production, and, as she only wanted to be dumb one night during her Race Week engagement in York, Wilkinson out of gratitude for her assistance gave the second night to her sister for her benefit.[86] Besides *Obi* there were several new pantomimes and spectacles. *The Cave of Acheron* had a night scene with a shower and snow, and Miss de Camp as Columbine. In *The Witches of the Rock; or Harlequin Wood Cutter,* Dunning was Harlequin. In *Harlequin's Descent from the Clouds* Weston took a flight across the stage into a chamber window 10 feet high. In addition Cross's spectacle *Black Beard* and a dance, *Peggy's Love or the Highland Wedding*, were brought out. In the revival of *The Deserter of Naples* a patriotic note was introduced by soldiery appearing in the procession and going through military evolutions. After the season had closed the theatre was rented for four nights to Lloyd for astronomical lectures with his orrery in which forty changes of classical scenery were employed.

Bannister was engaged for the Summer Assizes. Parts in which he was seen for the first time were Acres, Gregory Gubbins, Gabriel Lackbrain, Sir David Dunder, Tony Lumpkin, Frederick in *Of Age To-morrow,* Pangloss & Walter in *Children in the Wood*. Dwyer from Norwich made his bow as Capt. Absolute which he followed by Dick Dowglas and Young Marlow. The *York Herald*[87] pronounced him a valuable acquisition, of good person and deportment who gave the text correctly though his voice was occasionally deficient. Another newcomer, Bennett, was a useful actor though his Ezekiel Homespun was as nothing after Emery's. This is the first occasion on which a York newspaper contains dramatic criticism.

Maria de Camp made her first appearance at Race Week. She opened on August 24 as Letitia Hardy and Patrick in *The Poor Soldier,* and subsequently played Albina in *The Will*, Caroline in *The Prize,* Lady Teazle to the Sir Peter of Mathews, Phoebe Whitehorn in *The Wags of Windsor,* Irene in *Blue Beard,* Julio with the epilogue in *Deaf and Dumb,* Hypolita in *She Wou'd and She Wou'd Not* and for her benefit Arionelli, Maria in *The Citizen* and Caroline. She chose three short pieces rather than a 5 act play since many were desirous of seeing her in characters in which she was famous. A Viennese by birth she had, as a child, been brought up in the ballet and the circus ring, but graduated to the Haymarket in her early teens. She was a good but not powerful vocalist; she excelled in chambermaids and the sprightly parts of genteel comedy and also in melodramas such as *Deaf and Dumb* where a good deal of miming was involved.

During the season of 1802 Mathews was at the height of his popularity in York. The *Monthly Mirror* pronounced him one of the best low comedians out of London and pointed out that his performances were seldom charged with buffoonery.[88] It was one of the instances in which Wilkinson with all his experience had been wrong. He now acknowledged to Mrs. Chapman, a new actress, that Mathews 'was the most promising young man he ever remembered to have had – the most perfect and attentive to dress, and the greatest favourite he had had for many years, particularly in York'. Even Fawcett had never been so popular nor had Emery achieved so good a benefit as Mathews did this season. The 'plain bill' of *Beaux' Stratagem* and *The Lying Valet* had been the fare, yet the night brought in £96.15.0, a figure which was exceeded only by Wilkinson's who had the advantage of Dibdin's new comic opera *The Cabinet* plus a new pantomime. And at this time £50 was reckoned a great house.[89] No wonder that the comedian wrote: 'I assure you I am most comfortably situated, and never expected to be so fortunate in the profession. I have the first business – first salary – first benefits – first acquaintance; and never had an unpleasant word with the manager in the course of my engagement.' At Wilkinson's desire he studied Falstaff and played it twice. The manager was so delighted with his performance that he told Stephen Kemble, who thought much of his own Falstaff, that Mathews played it better and with more humour. On May 25 Mathews's wife Eliza died from consumption at the age of 27 and was buried in St. Mary's, Castlegate. Though not an actress she had appeared at least once at her husband's benefit in 1801 as Sophia in *The Road to Ruin*. The new pieces *The Cabinet* and Cobb's melodrama *Paul and Virginia* could not be played without Mathews. At the manager's request he agreed to act Dominique in the latter on May 29.[90] He also gave this season imitations of ventriloquism. Melvin was praised in the *Monthly Mirror*[91] as a fine performer who never fell below mediocrity; his rendering of Jews, sailors and many of Lewes's characters such as Abednego, Jack Junk, and Young Rapid placed him in the first rank as a general actor; the tough old tar and the gay young rake came equally naturally. Dwyer, on the other hand, is advised to content himself with second-rate characters and not to attempt Macbeth since his powers as an actor fell below his appearance; his voice, though musical, was weak and ill managed, his action contracted and bad. Before the season had ended he went to London. Mathews who wrote to enquire after his reception there, stated that in York his benefit had only brought £26.

Stephen Kemble came to play for four nights, and Chalmers, a former member of the company who had since been to America, acted Hamlet to the Ophelia of Mrs. Williams. J. C. Collins returned after several years in retirement with an entertainment entitled *Care sent to Coventry*.[92]

The new pantomime *The Magic Oak; or Harlequin Triumphant* was composed, designed and painted by Bennett and was pronounced as good as these spectacles usually were in the country. The new scenes included[93]

'The Cave of Merlin, with the Magic Oak withered – A beautiful Grotto of Shell Work – A Wonderful Deception with a Magical Chest – A Wind Mill – The Magic Oak in full Leaf – Superb Golden Equestrian Statue of Marcus Aurelius in the Capitol at Rome, as large as life – A ludicrous Metamorphose from the change of a Table – a Prison – and a beautiful Bower, with Garlands of Roses in the Centre, a Golden Fountain in Motion, with Figures spouting Water etc.' Bennett himself was the Harlequin.

The great comedian Munden made his début in York as the summer Assize Week star. He played Capt. Bertram in *The Birthday,* Sir Abel Handy, Dornton, Old Rapid, Peter Post Obit in *Folly As It Flies,* Jemmy Jumps, Sir Robert Bramble in *The Poor Gentleman,* and Darby.

For Race Week Miss de Camp returned for two nights on her way to Scarborough, her new rôle being Lucy in *The Beggar's Opera* with Incledon as Macheath. Incledon, who came for 6 nights, also played Paul to the Virginia of Mrs. J. Wilkinson and the Dominique of Blanchard, Lorenzo in *The Cabinet* to the Whimsiculo of Blanchard, and Tom Tug. The appearance of the native William Blanchard[94] must have been quite an occasion. Born in 1769 in Nessgate, where his father was a staymaker and hosier, he had been brought up by his uncle, the proprietor of the *York Chronicle.* After working for three years in the newspaper office he had resolved to become an actor and had joined Welsh's company at Buxton. Later he became manager of a Northumbrian circuit, and from there comedian in the Norwich circuit. He made his début at Covent Garden in 1800 and by some was preferred to Fawcett. He is said to have been the best drunken man on the stage and was perhaps the greatest of York born actors; this seems to have been his first appearance on the boards of his native town.

In September Mathews[95] received an offer from Colman to act at the Haymarket from May 1803, and succeeded in obtaining his demand for £10 a week. He claimed to have performed the entire range of principal low comedy at York and to be well studied. In February, 1803 he advised Colman that he was going to marry Miss Jackson who had supported the first line of singing at York and was young and well favoured, and solicited an engagement for her as well. The next month Colman with his son George Colman arrived at York to see his new acquisition. He was impressed with the comedian's talents, and as for Miss Jackson, he engaged her as soon as he had seen her play Harriet in *The Guardian.* Though Wilkinson knew Colman had come to rob him of his trump card, with his customary hospitality, he requested him to dine with him every day. Mathews related that on his first visit Cummins was also present. Colman, with a view to discovering more new talent, asked what the play was to be, and on being informed it was *The School for Scandal* enquired who was cast as Charles as he needed a dashing actor for such parts. Cummins, 'a respectable gentleman … who had mumbled his dinner, and whose well-powdered head had a cauliflower appearance, and his face the visible impress of sixty winters', was indicated, whereupon he bowed with the precision of the old school. Colman started in astonishment and resorted to his snuffbox. He then enquired after the actresses and who was to play Virginia. Again his attention was directed to Mrs. John Wilkinson 'a bulky matron who certainly had once been young, and still was handsome', at which juncture he whispered in despair to Mathews '"Fore gad, Mathews, yours is a superannuated company".' In the end he bore off Mrs. Ward and Denman; Wilkinson though far from pleased took it philosophically as the fate of a country manager. Whilst in York Colman read his *John Bull* to the company, as they were getting it up, and 'his perfect representation of every character' was a delight.

On March 28 Mathews was married to Miss Jackson at St. Helen's Church. He took his farewell at York on May 7, 1803 as Proteus in *Family Quarrels* and Ralph in *Lock and Key*. On May 16 Tate wrote[96] to congratulate him on his successful début at the Haymarket calling it 'a Feather in the Cap of the York Company'. More than one actor was required to fill his place. Edward Knight, known as Little Knight, was one. He had opened as Frank Oatland on February 17 but, though his début had been successful, he was only allowed scope for his talents after Mathews had left. Knight,[97] who was born in Birmingham in 1774, had run off the stage in fright when he first appeared on it at Newcastle-under-Lyme. Subsequently he had had experience in Staffordshire and North Wales. Though only 5ft. 2in. in height he had a good figure, made up well, and had a voice not unmusical. He is said to have applied to join the company a year previously armed with an introduction from one Philips. Tate protested he knew none such except a Quaker who would never have recommended an actor to the theatre, and ended, 'I don't want you'. Knight replied in Tate's own coin: 'I should as soon think of applying to a methodist parson to preach for my benefit, as to a quaker to recommend me to Mr. Wilkinson. I Don't want to come'. Wilkinson remembered the letter and when the time came wrote to Knight: 'Mr. Methodist Parson, I have a living, that produces twenty-five shillings per week, Will you hold forth?'

On September 20th 1802 Wilkinson wrote to Knight[98] from Wakefield stating that Mathews, who was subject to fits, had had a bad one. 'He is a Great Favorite – I know your Cast Perfectly well, You shall Play Any two Parts You Like, but it is Impossible to Ascertain a Cast. If Mr. Bennett goes there will be Plenty, If Mr. Mathews Relapses I shall want two Comedians. Necessity will Oblige Me to keep You As I wish You Fame and Not to lose it, I will get up Any Two Plays or two Farces *not* in the *Catalogue* – An Opportunity may occur in the Spring for Mrs. Knight. Your Opening shall be Appointed as you wish'. After giving dates and distances of the circuit towns he adds a proud postscript: 'From York is Certainly in Fav^r at London so many have done Greatly'. Then Mathews accepted the Haymarket offer and Wilkinson wrote again to Knight: 'Mr. Fawcett, Cherry, Knight, Emery and Myself are Good Friends for when they left they did it for the best. I am likely to lose Melvin, which will be a Great Loss, Do You Act Sailors? He is not only Excellent in those but in Lewis's Cast of Rapid, &c. – I Congratulate you on Mr. Mathews quitting Me for the Hay Market

10^L Per *Week* and Benefit. – I will make a Great Open indeed – And may lead You to the same Good Fortune'.

Knight, when finally he arrived in York, enquired which were Mathews's worst parts and being told Frank Oatland and Old Bromley[99] in *The Jew and the Doctor* he prudently chose to open in them. 'Egad, my boy', remarked Tate, 'you've chosen my two *rough* ones'; 'I shall get on the more smoothly in them' replied the ready comedian. As was his wont Tate demanded to see him every night when dressed for his character, but never gave him a word of encouragement. Knight was even contemplating quitting the company when one night he was called in to be looked over as Davy in *Bon Ton*. This time Wilkinson smiled at him, and, opening his bureau, presented him with a chest containing a complete actor's wardrobe, saying that he had long looked for someone who would value it. Knight became unequalled in pert servants, old men and rustics. 'Those,' said the *York Herald*[100] at his death, 'who have witnessed his Sim, Hawbuck and Jerry Blossom, must ever retain a recollection of his exquisite genius; intense affection, developing itself with the innocency of a child, characterized his free rustic, the rover of fields and barns; he was the simple, unpolluted work of nature … he looked a part of the rustic landscape'.

But an even greater than Knight was engaged by Tate for some of Mathews's parts – the grave faced comedian John Liston. Wilkinson[101] wrote to him on March 24 'Here is a Great Opportunity for You and Me if you Can Enter On the Comic Singing *Irish* Characters Also Dennis Bulgrudery &c. All Vacant With the Unexpected Departure of Mr. Denman. Now I should suppose a very little Attention You would soon attain a Good Brogue, In short Lump is a Line of Acting much in that Road. Therefore Wish You can be here all last Week in April, Act Lump before Mathews's Departure, … I am in the same bad Way, & indeed One Third of the Company in dreadful Colds'. In a further letter Tate made the position clear: 'Mr. Mathews Plays Full Casts of Comedy. I take it Granted in very full Plays, You will Assist and Not Object to Pantomime Utility, Being a Lord Mayor, a Witch &c'. He proceeds to quote a long list of parts he expected Liston to undertake, ending with further references to his ill health: 'I am quite fatigued and truly Unable to Proceed or Write Again so Very Ill as I am – Therefore Write to My Son, or Expect his An^{sr} If you write to Me'. Liston opened as Lump to the Caleb Quotem of Mathews on April 26.[102] His humour was not yet matured and passed unrecognised by the York audience. Mrs. Mathews tells us that she could not raise a smile at his Lump. The *York Herald* expressed its disappointment, though it conceded that with care and industry he might rise above mediocrity. Liston had a disagreement with Tate about performing Denman's rôle in *A Tale of Mystery,* but though this was set to rights he did not remain with the company after this season. For once York audiences failed to encourage a comic genius.

There was a new leading lady this season in the person of Mrs. Aicken from Weymouth who made her first appearance as Rosalind. The *York*

Herald[103] proclaimed that she was the best for many years, had a correct conception of her part and was an excellent breeches figure. It praised her Milwood in *The Irish Widow* and her Lady Randolph. Like many actresses of her time she played Hamlet.

Sarah Smith,[104] more famous as Mrs. Bartley, came from Edinburgh. She had, after three years under Stephen Kemble, retired from the stage in disgust, but now returned to it. Wilkinson had written to her the previous autumn: 'I am Informed Your Figure is very good & Your Talents are very Good for the Delicate Sentimental, but not for Lady Townly, Lady Paragon & the Dashing Line of Miss Farren'. In York she was pronounced a delightful Maria in *The Citizen* and showed tragic powers as Young Norval. Indeed her genius was for the two extremes of tragedy and low comedy. She only stayed one season, as on Wilkinson's death she migrated to Birmingham and Bath, and in 1805 was engaged at Covent Garden. She eventually succeeded Mrs. Siddons as leading tragedienne until deposed by Miss O'Neill.

Another newcomer was Gattie from Exeter who became low comedian at the Lyceum in 1813 whence he graduated to Drury Lane. When he came to York he was a sufferer from stage fright but subsequently was well known as a player of old men and eccentrics, particularly those with a dialect or foreign accent.[105]

Colman's popular comedy *John Bull* came out at Wilkinson's benefit on April 12, with Peregrine = Cummins, Job Thornberry = Bennett, Dennis Brulgruddery = Denman, Caroline = Mrs. Jarman. Holcroft's equally famous melodrama *A Tale of Mystery* made its début on the same occasion as afterpiece. Other new comedies were Reynolds's *Delays and Blunders*, Holcroft's *Hear Both Sides* and Allingham's *Marriage Promise*. Another new melodrama was Boaden's *Voice of Nature*, and new musical pieces were Oulton's *Letter*, Dibdin's *Family Quarrels* and Cobb's *House to be Sold*. Dibdin's farce *The Mad Guardian* was also brought out. The pantomime was *Trick upon Trick; or Harlequin's Frolics* composed by Bennett who acted Harlequin with Miss de Camp as Columbine.[106] The new scenery included a calm sea with boats in motion, a romantic landscape with a view of a distant city, Harlequin's car drawn by reindeer, the transformation of Harlequin and Columbine into a giant, and a Temple of Cupid with a burning altar and a paraphernalia of doves, bows and arrows, flames, darts and wreaths of flowers.

Tate was failing but his wish was to live to see his favourite Fawcett perform again on the York stage. His wish was granted, for in Race Week Fawcett opened on August 22 as Job Thornberry and Gunnel; on the 23rd he played Goldfinch and Motley, the 24th Frank Oatland and Caleb Quotem, the 25th Ollapod and Lingo, the 26th Paul Postpone (*Delays and Blunders*) and the 29th for his benefit Vapid and Muns. Ms. notes on the playbills give the receipts for the 24th as £85.9.6. and for his benefit as £102.4.6. Whilst he played, the assiduous Knight stood in the wings and took notes of his points. Fawcett was so flattered and impressed that one day he feigned illness and gave up his part of Risk to the young man. Knight is said not to have lost by the comparison.[107]

Tate Wilkinson died on August 25 at the age of 63. His last thoughts were of his actors.[108] He had been agitated the previous day by hearing that Fawcett had not been paid for his services in Pontefract. That night he was anxious about the comedian's reception in *The Wags of Windsor* in which Mathews had scored a great success. He was delighted to hear it had gone off well but again fell into a passion when his youngest son William said that he preferred Mathews as Quotem. On Thursday he desired that the Theatre should not be shut if he died and at 4 o'clock he passed away. The company played that and succeeding nights according to his wishes though in general gloom. As G. C. Carr, one of the actors, wrote to Mathews, 'He was completely worn out, and though he did not expire till the taper of life had long blinked in the socket, his reason and the ruling spring of all his actions, his generosity and honesty, strongly evinced themselves even to his last moments'. The *York Herald*[109] spoke of his undeviating attention to his duties; of his kindness to the performers; his skill in instructing them; his correctness with regard to money matters which made them regard him as a father rather than a master; and of his friendly, and generous disposition and fund of anecdote.

He was buried at 7 o'clock in the morning at All Saints Pavement Church on August 28. There were only two coaches, one for his four trustees and the other for his three sons and Cummins. A mural tablet to his memory was placed in the north aisle of the church where it may still be seen. By his will[110] his theatres, scenes, dresses, and letters patent were bequeathed to four trustees, Thomas Wilson, George Suttell, merchant, John Wallis, apothecary, and John Brook, attorney. His son John was to have the management of the theatres with the duties of engaging and discharging performers and staff, fixing their salaries and appointing times of performing, for one year and afterwards until the theatres should be conveyed or sold to anyone else. The trustees were to receive the profits and to pay therefrom rents, salaries, repairs, new scenes and dresses, according to what was deemed necessary by the manager for the time being. John was to be paid £1.11.6. a week, and was entitled to an annual benefit at York, Hull and Leeds from which he was to receive, as his father had done, a full half of the receipts without deduction for the expenses of the house. The rest of the profits were divided into equal sixths for Tate's widow, his four sons and his daughter. John was not to be responsible for sums not actually received or for losses of scenes and dresses unless through carelessness. He was not to pay to his wife Sarah any greater salary than she then received nor to allow her a separate benefit. If he himself performed he was not entitled to an additional salary. Provisions were made for John's refusal of the management and for his resignation after the year's term. Tate's widow was to have the dwelling house rent free. The trustees had power to renew the leases of the theatres and letters patent as well as to rent the former. An annual benefit was stipulated for Alexander Cummins at York, Hull and Leeds whether or not he was with the company.

Tate had been both a great and a beloved manager. He was an autocrat who did not brook interference with his rule, 'But having proved that it could not with impunity be interfered with, he would become as gentle and as kind as his generous nature was capable of being'.[111] He had great pride in his profession and did all he could to raise the status and support the dignity of the actor: 'his manly independence with his audience was as remarkable as his generous feelings towards his performers when he found them illiberally used by the public'. He would let an actor have his head who pressed for an unsuitable part, as he believed that he would learn from the experience. His judgment was not infallible but he made generous amends when he discovered his mistakes. He did not suffer fools gladly and could be discouraging to the beginner, but where he spotted talent and perseverance he would take infinite pains and trouble to coach and counsel the possessor. He trained some of the greatest actors of his day and raised the status of the York Theatre to that of being second only to Bath in the provinces.

Testimonies to his generosity and excellence as a master and to the affection in which his lovable and eccentric nature was held, abound. Hitchcock[112] says he was 'universally beloved, and esteemed by those who have the happiness of his acquaintance'; Carr speaks of 'his integrity, generosity and solid virtues of heart', Cooke[113] of his honourable conduct and of the advantage which young performers reaped from his acquaintance with the London theatres and players of Garrick's days; Mathews of his poignant grief, on hearing of his death. We have seen many instance of his generosity, one further will suffice. Ryley[114] relates how a young man in the company with a salary of 16/- lived on 11/- and gave 5/- for his parent's support. Wilkinson, coming to hear of this, sent for him and enquired how his parent was maintained, then told him that he had been raised to 25/- two months ago. When the actor attempted to express his gratitude Tate pushed him out of the room. Ryley too gives us a vivid picture of him: 'the singularity of his appearance corresponded with the eccentricity of his character. The cape of his coat was turned back, so as to expose the neck and shoulders, his little brown wig cock'd up behind in a most laughable manner, and his hat, wrong side before: thus equipp'd, he shuffled about the stage, making observations on the performance of the preceding evening, in so ludicrous a manner, that though many laugh'd, to some, I could plainly perceive, it was wormwood.' Thus he told one performer that he did not like his method of tagging. 'I was in the gallery last night, and saw you come forward with "Even Scandal dies if you approve". I don't know whether *they* approved or not, but I'll be d–d if I did.'

Innumerable anecdotes are told of 'the wonderful spirit and vivacity with which he pursued his unconnected discourse'; of the stories which he never finished without forgetting his subject and piecing it out with another; of his delight in animadverting on and mimicking the old actors whose merit in his opinion was never equalled. He was 'considered as a sort of short-cut to the acquaintance of Garrick, Barry, Macklin, and a dozen more, of whom he gave imitations, both in and out of character so that you had the originals before you in the full strength of their visible distinctions'.[115]

We have spoken of his passion for the spangle and glitter of theatrical costume. He often bought rich court suits at extravagant prices without caring whether or no they were suitable; hung them all on a line in his room of audience; lit them up with wax candles, and paraded before them in pure enjoyment of their finery. Poor Cummins, as the elegant Doricourt, was once forced to wear a coat which did not fit him and was entirely unsuitable to his part because it had been worn by the Prince of Wales. On another occasion Tate purchased the dress and ornaments of an Indian Chief which he determined to use in *Paul and Virginia*. Mathews refused it, Adelaide de Camp preferred her own simple costume, and so it was foisted on to French who, as a mere super, outshone the principal performers in it.

Tate was one of the great eccentrics of the 18th century, yet all the quirks of his temperament and the peculiarities of his behaviour and manner made him but the more beloved. For he had a warm heart and he was essentially just and honest. When he died everyone in the company was convinced that they would not look upon his like again; and indeed with him the golden days of the Theatre Royal departed.

CHAPTER FIVE

John Wilkinson and His Successors 1804–1824

Henceforward the start of the winter season was advanced from mid-February to the beginning of March so that the Theatre re-opened under John Wilkinson's management on March 1, 1804. He and his wife took over Tate's Easter Tuesday benefit and, as was customary, presented two new pieces, Cobb's melodrama *Wife of Two Husbands* and Colman's musical farce *Love Laughs at Locksmiths*. The receipts were £111.15.0.[1] There were some other good houses during the season; that at Melvin's benefit, when he spoke in the uniform of a volunteer an address to their patriotism written by a gentleman of Hull and at which Franklin's new farce *The Counterfeit* was brought out, was £98.10.6., and that at the Knights's benefit bespoken by the Officers of the Leeds Volunteers at which Miss Lucretia McTab of Selby spoke an address as a female volunteer and went through the manual exercise £80.12.0. The bespeak by the Officers and Corps of the York Volunteers brought £63.12.6. and others were given by the Officers of the Ouse and Derwent Volunteers and of the Craven Legion. A benefit was given for the York Volunteers on March 6 at which Melvin spoke an *Address to the Patriotism of the English* in the character of a British Sailor written by Colman. Mrs. Aickin at her benefit spoke a patriotic address to the defenders of their country and followed it by the Hungarian broad sword exercise. The Napoleonic invasion scare was over but patriotic sentiment was given an outlet and stimulus in the theatre.

A new light comedian Carleton opened as Jack Meggott in *The Suspicious Husband* but was adversely criticised in the *York Herald*.[2] As Lord Trinket he dressed as a man of fashion in white pantaloons with stripes of red, black and yellow tape and a headdress that was only fit for Bartholomew Fair, whilst he acted and spoke like a clown in the pantomime. Megget, a new tragedian, opened in *Hamlet*; though he showed promise he overacted and indulged in excessive pauses in Kemble's style. Miss Mills[3] the daughter of a former actor in the company, made her début in Mrs. Jordan's rôle of Emma in *The Marriage Promise* and subsequently played Charlotte Rusport,

185

Ophelia and Columbine. Her figure was petite but good, her voice harmonious, her eye expressive, and her performance better than might have been expected from a girl of 18. Sarah Smith had left and was succeeded by her lesser known sister Susan from Liverpool, who made her début as Sigismunda and subsequently played Perdita and Mrs. Harlow in *The Old Maid*. She was beautiful and had an excellent voice but lacked animation in sentimental comedy. She was the company's leading lady until 1810 and became as much the rage in York as Miss O'Neill in London.

Besides the new pieces already mentioned Kenney's *Raising the Wind*, Allingham's *Mrs. Wiggins*, Hoare's *Paragraph*, Dibdin's *Will for the Deed* and Cherry's *Soldier's Daughter* came out in York in 1804. This last drew a brilliant audience and is said to have received the greatest applause ever heard in York. *Richard II* compressed into three acts was revived after 33 years with Richard = Cummins, Bolingbroke = Williams, Queen = Mrs. Jarman, but only brought in £33.2.6. On the other hand Bennett's new pantomime *The Fairy* raised £88.19.6. The Dominions of Pluto from *Don Juan* came in for this show, which also included a grand view of the City of London, a view of the Temple of Liberty in vertical motion, and another of the British Fleet, all designed and painted by Bennett.

Mathews revisited York for three nights playing *The Miser* as revised in 3 acts, and Frederick on April 26, Old Wiggins on 27th and Lord Ogleby and his popular Caleb Quotem on 28th. His second night brought a house of £137 and his benefit £102.17.6.

Mr. and Mrs. Henry Siddons, son and daughter-in-law of the great Sarah, came for Assize Week in July opening as Othello and Desdemona, and among other parts playing Don Felix and Violante in *The Wonder*. Siddons inherited nothing of his mother's genius and was cold and declamatory.

For Race Week in August Fawcett was the star. York gave their erstwhile favourite a great welcome and the house the second night held £94.8.0. He added to parts played in 1803 those of Jack Junk, Sheva, Pangloss, Falstaff, Risk in *Love Laughs at Locksmiths*, Motto in *The Will for the Deed*, and Abednego. The *Monthly Mirror* points out that, in the country, he liked to appear in rôles such as Vapid and Sheva which were out of his line in London.

When the theatre opened on March 2, 1805, it had been repainted and papered. By a new rule seats for benefits were no longer to be had of the actor whose night it was but at the theatre which was open for booking every week day from 11 to 2; no seats could be secured unless paid for at the time of taking them.

After two years absence Mrs. Ward had returned to the company and remained with it until 1813. Mrs. Barnard from Covent Garden appeared as Oriana in a revival of *The Inconstant* with Knight and Melvin as Old and Young Mirable. This comedy, which was performed with alterations from the Drury Lane prompt book, had not been seen on the York stage for 20 years.

Two pieces by members of the company were produced. G. C. Carr's drama *St. Margaret's Cave* on March 28 and Knight's musical farce *The Sailor and the Soldier* on April 30. The former[4] which was brought out at Carr's benefit was his first dramatic attempt and was founded on a novel by Mrs. Helme, the dialogue being in parts lifted straight from the original. Knight's farce was also given for his benefit after the first performance of Dibdin's comedy, *Guilty or Not Guilty*. Other new pieces were Kenny's musical entertainment *Matrimony*, Reynolds's operatic romance *Out of Place* and his comedy *Blind Bargain*, Mrs. Inchbald's last comedy *To Marry or Not To Marry*, Colman's *Gay Deceivers* and two long celebrated pieces Tobin's *Honeymoon* and Dimond's melodrama *The Hunter of the Alps*. Melvin altered the *Deserter* into a serious pantomime[5] as *Female Heroism; or Virtue Triumphant* for which he also supplied the music. At Bennett's benefit another panto-mime by a former member of the company was produced, Fawcett's *La Perouse*. Bennett was the company's scene painter and for this piece[6] his scenes and effects included a violent storm and shipwreck, a natural grotto with hanging icicles and a 'stupendous' arched bridge of rocks. The roman-tic movement was stirring the scenic world to an exploitation of the wild and grand.

Maria de Camp, though her sister had left the company after 1803, was the Assize Week star. She opened as Bizarre In *The Inconstant* and Yarico on July 29; and among other parts played Emma in the *Marriage Promise*, Nell in *The Devil to Pay* and the Widow Cheerly. She brought out her own interlude *Personation* in which she and Melvin sustained the only two parts. It was pronounced[7] to be the best and most neatly acted petite pièce that had been seen in York with rapid changes and well managed dénouement. In *She Wou'd and She Wou'd Not* Miss de Camp excelled in the final scene where Hypolita discloses herself to Don Philip, but Cibber's old comedy was considered objectionable and marks of disapprobation greeted Knight as Don Manuel in some passages. Maria de Camp was re-engaged for Race Week but was taken ill in Harrogate and, it was carefully announced, was forbidden to play by her doctor.[8] John Wilkinson dared what Tate never had, to abolish half price throughout the August meeting in order to avoid the confusion caused by latecomers from the races, but, on account of the star's illness, this new regulation was postponed until 1806.

Just before Race Week the great sensation of the day, the child prodigy Master Betty, who had swept London off its feet the previous December at Covent Garden, appeared for two nights. On August 16 he took his famous rôle of Young Norval with Mrs. Wrench (formerly Mrs. Robinson) as Lady Randolph and the following night he acted Frederick in *Lovers' Vows*. At the height of his ridiculous fame Betty was commanding enormous prices and the *York Herald* even saw fit to thank the manager for not increasing the charges more than for Mrs. Siddons, that is boxes 5/-, pit 3/-, gallery 2/-, upper gallery 1/- and no half price.

Wrench with his wife had returned for a few nights from Edinburgh and Bath and played Diddler in *Raising the Wind*, Edward in *The Irishman in*

London and Gossamer in *Laugh When You Can*. But after Master Betty Race Week must have been an anti-climax. The only notable event was the début of Colman's *Who Wants a Guinea; or The Irish Yorkshireman* with Knight as Jonathan Oldskirt. At least one patron was disgruntled with the fare offered. On July 11 Mrs. Harriet Green wrote to Sarah Smith, who was then at the Theatre Royal, Bristol, about the York stage: 'I never knew it so *ill stocked* since I knew York, & tho' Mr. G. & I have been in Town all the Season & had nothing but want of inducement to keep us from the Playhouse, we never went but Twice, once to Swalwell's benefit, & for the sake of a party, the other to compliment a Lady who bespoke the play – we were so little entertained, that we applauded our wisdom in keeping away.'[9] At the end of the season Miss Mills was engaged at Bath and Mrs. Williams, formerly Miss Swalwell and Mrs. Southgate, died at Hull on March 7, 1806.[10] In November the theatre was let for some nights to Moritz[11] and his Phantasmagoria from the Haymarket. This was an exhibition of optical illusions which included the ghost scene in *Hamlet*, Macbeth and the Witches, Lady Macbeth, and Monk Lewis's *Bleeding Nun*. Moritz claimed to disclose the artifices by which pretended magicians had imposed upon a credulous public.

Despite the fact that there were a number of new performers in the company and that more novelties than usual were presented, the 1806 season was not a successful one. As the *York Herald*[12] put it a cloud seemed to envelop the theatrical hemisphere; houses were frequently indifferent and sometimes miserable. Only the advent of Stephen Kemble for two nights in June cheered matters up. A fashionable audience welcomed him as Falstaff in *Henry IV* and the following night he played the same rôle in *The Merry Wives*. The *Herald* declared him to be the best fat knight they had seen, and his description of the 11 men in buckram to be a chef d'oeuvre. One of his claims to fame was that he could play the character without stuffing.

Of the newcomers the Sedleys were from Bath.[13] Sedley excelled in parts of a mild and gentlemanly type and his wife's forte was the pathetic; she made an excellent Mrs. Haller to her husband's Stranger. Lewis, the son of William Lewis of Covent Garden, who had been a favourite star on the York stage, succeeded to Carleton's parts and was a better actor; he possessed something of his father's eccentricity though not so good a figure. D'Arcy from Liverpool was the new first singer; he had an exceedingly powerful voice and was advised to avoid 'thunder-like crescendos'. Mrs. Bramwell from Newcastle had a pretty, little figure, an uncommonly clear voice and a tolerable share of sprightliness and ease. She sang in a style to which the York stage had been for many years unaccustomed, allowing her voice to have a natural effect and not destroying the melody by indulgence in frequent cadences and trills. She lacked consequence in such a rôle as Violante but was commended as the Widow Cheerly and as Clara in *Matrimony*. This strengthening of the company on the vocal side enabled Wilkinson to bring out Dibdin's *English Fleet* which the *Herald* said was the best performed opera seen in York for many years. Mrs. Wilkinson had a part that suited her and Melvin was excellent as the drunken old sailor. Melvin indeed was playing a wide variety of characters in this, his last, season, including Ranger, Marplot, Tony Lumpkin, Duke Aranza and Tristram in Allingham's new farce of *The Weathercock*. Other new musical pieces were Dimond's *Youth, Love and Folly*, Cherry's *Spanish Dollars*, Hook's *Invisible Girl in August*, and the melodramas of *The Venetian Outlaw* by Elliston, *The Hero of the North* by Dimond and *The Travellers* by Cherry. This last, mainly a vehicle for music and scenery, was magnificently staged; the first and the last scenes exceeded anything of the kind that had been seen before; the painter and the machinist were specially commended for the ship scene, and the dresses were splendid; nevertheless the theatre was poorly attended. Other new pieces were the comedies of *The Delinquent* by Reynolds and *The School for Friends* by Miss Chambers. Carr brought out his second drama *The Towers of Urbandine*, taken from a novel entitled *Ancient Records* and already given at Hull, on March 27 and it was received with approbation. Trafalgar found an echo in Cumberland's spectacle of *The Death and Victory of Lord Viscount Nelson*,[14] 'with a Transparency of his Lordship rising from the Ocean'. The new pantomime *Provocation; or Spanish Ingratitude* concluded with an engagement between four English and four Spanish frigates in which one of the latter was blown up.

Cummins chose *The Merchant of Venice* for his benefit[15] in order to bring out his daughter as Portia. She had previously played only small parts, and from the weakness of her voice and timidity of her deportment had given little promise. Though her voice still wanted strength and modulation her performance in the trial scene showed more effect and judgment than was expected. Cummins himself played Shylock for the first time while Sedley took over his usual rôle of Bassanio. Some members of the company were reproved for laughing in tragic scenes. *Henry VIII* was also put on this year with Mrs. Bramwell singing *No More I'll Heave the Tender Sigh* in the banquet scene.

The company had acquired a new scene painter named Brownlee in addition to Bennett. He was responsible for the scenery of *The English Fleet* and *The Travellers* and for fresh scenery for *The Castle Spectre* and *Pizarro*.

Master Betty was re-engaged for six nights at Assize Week during which prices were raised as before except that this time half price was admitted. Betty opened on July 21 as Achmet in *Barbarossa* which he followed by Selim, Hamlet, Romeo, Orestes and Rolla. The critic of the *York Herald* was by no means carried away.[16] He found that as Selim the prodigy excelled where he could give scope to his voice but lacked refinement and delicacy in the love scenes. Hamlet gave him no chance for the whirlwinds of passion in which he astonished; he had the bye play and trick of the scene but it looked like a trick; indeed the critic only too rightly concluded that Hamlet was 'too arduous a character for a youth to bustle with'. His youthful figure and elegant deportment better qualified him for Romeo but his voice was not musical and he naturally had no real idea of passion. He disappointed too as Orestes but was handicapped by a severe cold which was worse when

189

he played the even more unsuitable rôle of Rolla. The prison, pavilion and dying scenes were well done but his address to the soldiers was nothing out of the ordinary. One is glad to see that in spite of the pervading craze for this boy the York writer preserved his critical sense. Mr. and Mrs. Foster joined the company, he for old men's parts and his wife, who reminded of Miss de Camp, for comedy rôles such as Maria in *Of Age To-morrow*. Melvin[17] who had been engaged at Covent Garden, took his leave on August 25 as Michael in *The Adopted Child*, having played a round of his favourite characters during the week. He was greeted with such bursts of applause that he was greatly affected. He spoke an almost impromptu farewell address as a friend who had promised to write one was prevented from doing so. Some lines are worth quoting:

> Here, on this deck, in many a different scene,
> Thro' nine successive seasons have I been ...
> *Here*, I found a home
> From all my cares – and wish'd no more to roam ...
> For York had made the Actor feel himself the Man.

In October the Theatre was again let to Walker 'formerly of this city' for his astronomical lectures.

Two old stagers returned to the company in 1807. The more important was Wrench who, after two years in Bath, reopened as Walter; with him came his wife formerly Mrs. Robinson. The other was Miss Barnet, now Mrs. Phillips, who reappeared after 10 years as Catharine in *The Siege of Belgrade*. Knight, whose wife had died a year previously, had married Susan Smith in the teeth of a phalanx of rich and powerful rivals.[18] The Sedleys had returned to Bath. The Jarmans' little daughter Frances then about 4 or 5 and later to become celebrated as Mrs. Ternan, appeared as the Boy in *The Children in the Wood* and Julio di Rosalvi in *The Hunter of the Alps*.[19]

New plays given were Dibdin's comedy *Five Miles Off*, the dramas of *Adrian and Orrila* by Dimond and *The Curfew* by Tobin, Monk Lewis's *Alfonso*, Hook's melodrama *Tekeli* and his musical pieces *Catch Him Who Can* and *The Soldier's Return*, Kenney's comic opera *False Alarms* and a farce *The Man of Enterprise* which may have been the piece of that name by Shillito produced at Norwich in 1789. The pantomime was *Harlequin and Oberon*[20], the scenery and effects for which included a panoramic view of Hull with new Shambles, streets and the Humber, a balloon ascent by Foster as Clown, and a 'grand change', seed of the Victorian transformation scene, from a dark wood to Oberon's bower of fancy, in the centre of which was a golden statue surrounded with Dolphins spouting water, probably the same as that used in 1802 for *The Magic Oak*.[21] Lewis was Harlequin, Mrs. Foster Columbine and the machinist was Collison.

Mrs. Siddons came to take her 'farewell' during Assize Week opening on July 13 as Isabella which she followed by Margaret of Anjou, Zara in *The Mourning Bride*, Constance, Lady Macbeth and Belvidera for her benefit.[22]

She was succeeded in Race Week by her brother Charles Kemble now married to Maria de Camp. His first appearance in York was made on August 24 as Hamlet to his wife's Ophelia and he subsequently played Lovemore, Charles Surface, Benedick, St. Alme, Don Felix, Durimel in his own drama *Point of Honour*, Lovel in *High Life*, whilst his wife undertook Widow Belmour, Lady Teazle, Beatrice, Violante for the first time, Julio, Bertha in her husband's play with singing rôles in the afterpieces.

In 1808 a third sister, Miss S. de Camp, made her first appearance as Celestina in *The Fortress*. Wrench and Knight were dividing the comic business playing respectively Tristram Pickle and Briefwit in *The Weathercock*. We first hear this season of Vause as wardrobekeeper and dressmaker in succession to Winter.

In addition to Hook's melodrama *The Fortress*, Kenney's *Blind Boy* and *Ella Rosenberg* catered for the taste for melodramatic spectacle. Colman's operatic romance *The Forty Thieves* was also new and had scenery by Brownlee, machinery by Collison, and dresses by Vause and Mrs. Bearpark. Charles Kemble's drama *The Wanderer*, Morton's comedy *Town and Country*, Kenney's *The World*, Henry Siddons's *Time's a Tell Tale*, Thomas Dibdin's comedy *Errors Excepted* and his comic opera *Two Faces Under a Hood* make up the tale of new pieces.

On June 21 Mrs. Mountain, who had been in the company as Miss Wilkinson, and was now a famous singer rendered songs from Cherry's *Traveller*. On July 2 Bannister had the Theatre one night for his *Budget*, an entertainment of songs and recitations arranged and revised for his tour by Colman. Emery returned for Assize Week in a round of his favourite characters. York saw *Speed the Plough* with three excellent comedians in it, Emery as Farmer Ashfield, Knight as Sir Abel Handy and Wrench as Bob Handy. Emery was also seen in the Yorkshire rôles of Tyke and Lump, as Joey (*Modern Antiques*), Zekiel Homespun, Sam (*Raising the Wind*) Frank Oatland, The Miser, Sheepface, Stephen Harrowby, Captain Bertram and, on his last night, in Reynolds's new comedy *Begone Dull Care*.

Emery was succeeded by another star of a very different kind who had been a member of the company – G. F. Cooke. He played Richard III to the Richmond of Phillips; Iago to the Othello of Wrench and the Desdemona of Mrs. Knight; Sir Giles Overreach, Sir Archy MacSarcasor, and Sir Pertinax MacSycophant. Miss Duncan starred at Race Week performing her most famous rôle, that of Juliana in *The Honeymoon*, for the first time in York, and also appearing as Clara in *Matrimony*, Lady Townly and Maria in *The Citizen*. York must indeed have felt proud of its three pupils now grown to fame.

In November, by permission of the Lord Mayor, Hall of the Royal Circus, son of Charles Hall of York, returned after 7 years to his native city with an entertainment of comic songs written and selected by Dibdin entitled in the curious manner of the day *Whimsiphuscion*.[23]

For the first time in 1809 we may picture a little what the theatre looked like. From a guide book entitled *A Description of York*[24] we learn that 'It is

191

fitted up in a neat uniform style, capable of containing a numerous audience. There are two tiers of side boxes, one front box, two front galleries, and two side galleries. Over the front box are placed the royal arms with supporters, and the stage boxes are adorned with emblematic devices, musical and warlike trophies, &c. and edged with gilt mouldings. The length of the stage, from the lamps upwards, is 37 feet; in breadth from the opening of the curtain, 18 feet 6 inches, or from wall to wall 42 feet; and in height from the pit floor to the ceiling 34 feet.[25] In front of the entablature is the following motto, surrounded with ornamental painting,

Veluti in Speculum
Quicquid Agunt Homines.

The interior is coloured orange, green, and white, and the seats covered with crimson cloth. The scenery, dresses, &c., are various, and in general superb.'

This was the last year in which Knight and Wrench played with the company. Bannister had seen Knight the previous year when he had come to York with his *Budget*, and gave so favourable an account of him that he was offered a three years' engagement at Drury Lane. Knight modestly wrote that he professed nothing but country boys and old men but was nevertheless accepted. Unfortunately for him Drury Lane was burnt down as soon as he arrived in February 1809, and there was nothing for it but to return with his family to York. However he was recalled again in the autumn when the Drury Lane company had found a temporary home at the Lyceum. On October 14, 1809 he opened there as Timothy Quaint and Robin Roughhead, whilst on the same night Wrench and Mrs. Edwin also made their first appearance. That evening the Lane saw the début of three members of the York company who were to add lustre to its stage.[26] Wrench, who owed so much to the wife from whom he received his early training, subsequently deserted her and whilst he was earning 10-12 guineas a week, allowed her in her old age to pine in poverty.[27]

Two famous visitors graced the York boards in the spring season – Cooke returned and played Richard III on March 11, Macbeth, Overreach, Shylock, MacSycophant, Iago, and Falstaff in *Henry IV* on his last night, March 25. In May Wilkinson prevailed on Mrs. Siddons, who was travelling north, to appear once again for two nights as Mrs. Beverley on Whit Monday and Jane Shore the following night. It is noteworthy that the prices were raised only to the usual public week prices of boxes 4/-, pit 2/6. 1st gallery 2/-, upper gallery l/-. Master Betty had commanded more. Bannister returned with a second and entirely new *Budget*, written and revised by Colman, on July 8. A very old stager, Mrs. Leng, once more trod the stage as Mrs. Woodcock in *Love in a Village* at her benefit. Firth was now the Theatre's treasurer. New pieces were Monk Lewis's tragedy *Adelgitha*, Dibdin's melodrama *The Forest of Hermanstadt*, Reynolds's opera *The Exile*, Hoare's old operatic farce *The Three and the Deuce*, Allingham's musical farce

Who Wins?, Charles Kemble's farce *Plot and Counterplot*, Arnold's comedy *Man and Wife*, Tobin's *School for Authors* and a pantomime *Harlequin Gipsy; or The Black Tower* with music by the machinist Collison, which was under the direction of the Harlequin Benwell and concluded with a display of optical and mechanical fireworks.

Mrs. Edwin returned as the star for Assize Week, playing among other parts Letitia Hardy, Juliana, Lady Bell, Widow Cheerly, Beatrice, Widow Belmour and Ella Rosenberg. Emery also returned for six nights at Race Week, playing among his newer parts Giles Woodbine in *Blind Bargain*, Mat Mushroom in *Family Quarrels* and Hawbuck in *Town & Country*. On August 11 Corri and his pupils performed a Musical Mélange called *Harmonia* which consisted of duets, glees and trios interspersed with readings and recitations by Browne from Bath and Dublin. By special request the entertainment was repeated in October.

The season of 1810 was ushered in by no less an attraction than Mrs. Jordan, now no longer young. It started a month earlier than usual – she opened on January 29 as the Widow Cheerly, in which rôle York had never yet seen her. She then played Violante, Letitia Hardy, Helen Worrett in *Man and Wife* with Lady Hacket, and on her last night for her benefit the Widow Belmour with Nell. Public week prices were charged but half price was taken; houses were good.[28] There was a number of newcomers to the company. J. Russell replaced Knight in comedy leads playing Autolycus, Polonius and Muns; he was young but a powerful actor; he stayed with the company until 1813, and later became a comedian of repute at Covent Garden. Phillips[29] who had joined the circuit in 1808 was now its leading man. His Hamlet and Macbeth evinced judgment and force but he was a little addicted to whirligig motions of the head. Mrs. Johnson[30] known as 'the Siddons of America', who had been with the company 1800-2, now played the matronly line in tragedy. Her daughter undertook the dashing and beautiful belles and pathetic parts like the Blind Boy, but though a good actress she was not beautiful. The *Monthly Mirror*[31] opined that the female department was more numerous than valuable, though it had been improved by the retirement of Mrs. Wilkinson. John Wilkinson made one of his rare appearances this year as Kalig in *The Blind Boy* and was dubbed by the *Monthly Mirror* a Jack of all trades and master of none who inherited some of Tate's eccentricity but none of his talent.

Richer joined the company for a while and produced a series of pantomimes in which he played the chief rôles including *La Perouse, Oscar and Malvina*, and *The Deserter of Naples*. Arnold's musical entertainment *Britain's Jubilee* concluded with an illumination of the ship Britannia and a medallion of the King. Other new pieces were Dimond's popular melodrama *The Foundling of the Forest*, Sir James Burgess's drama *Riches*, Hook's operatic farce *Killing No Murder* and two farces by Griffiths, *The Budget of Blunders* and *Is He a Prince?* It is interesting to note that Lillo's *Fatal Curiosity*, which dated from 1736, was first performed in York this year. The season ended on April 27 and on May 1 Wilkinson opened his new theatre in Humber

Street, Hull. Three stars came in August: firstly Miss Duncan for three nights, during which she sustained Lady Bell, and Priscilla Tomboy; secondly Henry Johnston, an actor new to York, who opened on August 13 as Young Norval and Walter and subsequently performed Hamlet, Tancred, Rugantino in Lewis's new melodrama, a rôle he had created at Covent Garden, Frederick in *Lovers' Vows* and Felix in *Hunter of the Alps*, Octavian with Single in *Three and the Deuce*, Francisco in *A Tale of Mystery* and *The Stranger*; lastly on August 20 Mrs. Charles Kemble, who played Lady Restless to Johnston's Beverley in *All in the Wrong* and Catharine to his Petruchio. Johnston, hailed as a young man as the Scottish Roscius, was now about sixty though he still played his favourite juvenile rôle of Young Norval. Mrs. Kemble stayed on until the last night and enabled York play-goers to compare her Letitia Hardy with that of Mrs. Jordan a few months previously.

From another *Description of York* published in 1811 we learn that the seats were now covered with dark green cloth instead of red.

Lewis and D'Arcy had rejoined the company after an absence of three years when it reopened on March 7, 1811. Among the newcomers were the Evatts from Edinburgh who stayed two years and Mrs. McGibbon, formerly Miss Woodfall, who opened in Lady Macbeth and later played Cora, Roxana, and Amanthis. Jarman's two daughters Misses Frances and L. Jarman made several appearances in children's rôles. Frances's included the Page in *The Orphan*, in which so many children started their stage careers, Mamillius, Fleance, and a Child in *The Black Forest*, in addition to which she gave recitations.

York said farewell to a very old and tried stager when Mrs. Leng made her positively last appearance as an Old Lady in *Henry VIII* at her benefit.

The quality of the performances at this time may partly be gauged by a criticism of *Pizarro* in the *York Herald*.[32] The parts were said to be judiciously though not perfectly cast. Cummins had a just conception of Rolla and Phillips made the most of Pizarro. Robson as Alonzo was, however, careless in some of the most tender scenes, though in others he evinced more feeling than expected. Mrs. Barnes, who was pathetic as Cora, was reminiscent of Mrs. H. Siddons and continued to act even when she was not speaking. Two faults of diction were common to all but Cummins, a frequent omission to aspirate h's and a confusion of thee and thou. Poor Rolla tried his best to animate half a dozen supers as the Peruvian army 'who only showed that they were not statues, by moving off when the scene was concluded'.

On the second night of the season Miss Feron from the Nobility Concerts made her first appearance in York as Rosetta to the Hawthorn of D'Arcy, followed by Caroline in *The Prize*. On her two subsequent nights she sang Adela in *The Haunted Tower* with Margaretta in *No Song, No Supper*, and Floretta in *The Cabinet*.

In April Giroux and his three daughters, dancers from the King's Theatre, together with Giroux's pupil Flexmore were engaged. Flexmore was the father of the famous clown Dicky Flexmore. They appeared in a series of ballets composed and produced by Giroux. They opened on April 15 with *The Rival Rustics* and the next night, which was Wilkinson's benefit, appeared in a divertisement called *The Medley*. In addition to several ballets d'action they presented a comic pantomime *The White Witch; or Harlequin's Flight from the Moon* with new music by Ward, scenery by Brownlee, and machinery and tricks by Collison.

The rage for melodrama was growing and no fewer than four new ones were brought out. Dimond's *Peasant Boy*, Colman's *Africans*, Dibdin's *Valentine and Orson*, and *Twenty Years Ago*, the first effort in this line by Pocock later to become one of the chief purveyors of this form of entertainment. One of the first of the burlesques Rhodes's *Bombastes Furioso* made its appearance this season. Comedy was not neglected, and was represented by Masters's *Lost and Found*, Miss Chambers's *Ourselves*, Holman's *Gazette Extraordinary* and Eyre's *High Life in the City*. Dimond's drama *The Doubtful Son* and the operatic farces of *The Bee Hive* by Millingen and *Transformation* by Allingham were the rest of the new productions.

Shakespeare was better represented than for some time. *Othello*, *Henry VIII*, *Winter's Tale*, and *Macbeth* were played and Phillips appeared as Macbeth at his benefit at which he gave his farewell address to the York audience. Another farewell was that of Mrs. Jordan who had recently been abandoned by the Duke of Clarence. During the summer she played for six nights during Assize Week as The Country Girl, Lady Teazle, Widow Cheerly, Lady Racket, Widow Belmour, Belinda in *All in the Wrong*, Violante, and Beatrice, a part in *The Pannel* altered by Kemble especially for her. She returned for Race Week playing Letitia Hardy, Beatrice in *Much Ado* to Robson's Benedick, Bizarre, Helen Worrett, Roxalana and on August 26, for her benefit and farewell performance, Miss Hoyden in *A Trip to Scarborough* and Nell. In 1815 she went to France where she died two years later.

In September, by permission of the Lord Mayor, Incledon and Mathews combined to give a new entertainment called *The Travellers, or Hit and Miss*.[33] It brought a house of £106. Mathews wrote to his wife 'you know York is a bad town – and now it is empty – and more than usually poor – all croaking – but such a darling set – such a reception! I don't know when I have been so gratified – it really appears to me as if it is – was – my native Country – the sound of the dialect after my various visits was music to my ears – and I am now quite fixed in my opinion that the most friendly and truly hospitable people I have met, are the Yorkshire folks ... This has been a delightful day – I have been caressed by all ranks.' York was already then considered a poor town theatrically and later Mathews exclaims in surprised delight 'What a house for deserted York'. He returned again in December and in another letter to his wife dated December 29 once more expresses his affection for York and its audience: 'We had £80 again in York on Friday – notwithstanding it snowed all day – which I expected would have ruined us. I felt like a child returned to his parents and relations. Oh how they did applaud. I could not but remember they made me first – and we were mutually pleased with each other.' How many great actors must have felt that way when they revisited York as stars.

The most important newcomer to the company in 1812 was Robert Mansel from Manchester who had recently joined it at Doncaster. Six years later he was to become one of its most notable managers. His father was a clergyman, his uncle Bishop of Bristol and his brother-in-law Frederick Reynolds the dramatist. He started his career at sea, then relinquished it for the stage on which he performed for some years under the pseudonym of Montague. He had been in Penley's Windsor circuit for a time but had failed as Young Marlow at Covent Garden. He was then about 43, and his first appearance on the York stage was on March 7 as the Prince of Wales in *Henry IV* to the Falstaff of another newcomer, Hall.[34] This season he played such rôles as Mercutio, Leontes and Capt. Absolute. Frederick Brown[35] who had joined the company in May 1811, succeeded Phillips in the leads and Mrs. Sterling[36] from Liverpool took over the first singing line, whilst Miss Mathews from Bath played comedy leads. Mrs. M'Gibbon was the tragedienne playing the Elviras and Alicias though she also appeared for the first time as Miss Hardcastle. In May after many years absence Mrs. Kennedy, the former York heroine, once again returned to the company as the Nurse in *Romeo and Juliet*. This was the Jarmans' last season and at their benefit Frances Jarman played the Duke of York in *Richard III*. There was a new scene painter, Willis, who provided fresh scenery for a revival of *Obi*, including an extensive view of plantations, cave scenes, and a view of wild country; for *The Exile* he painted a view of the launching of the *Lord Anson* from a drawing taken on the spot.

From March 13-18 Mathews starred in York playing Dick Cypher in Pocock's new operatic farce *Hit or Miss*, Ollapod, Frederick, Croaker, Twineall, Mingle, and, for his benefit, in a three piece programme the dual rôles of Sir Fretful Plagiary and Puff, Johnny Atkins in *A Mogul Tale* and Buskin in *Killing No Murder*. This was the year in which Mrs. Siddons bade farewell to the stage and Wilkinson secured her for two nights on March 20, 21, when she played Lady Randolph and for her final leave-taking Isabella in *Measure for Measure* revived after 27 years in Kemble's version with Duke = Cummins, Angelo = Evatt, Claudio = Wilks, Lucio = Mansel, Pompey = Russell, Mrs. Overdone = Mrs. Ward, Mariana = Mrs. Evatt. Other Shakespeare plays this season were *Henry IV*, *Richard III*, *The Winter's Tale*, *Hamlet*, with Brown as Hamlet and Mrs. Sterling as Ophelia, and *Romeo and Juliet*, revived after 7 years, with Brown and Mrs. M'Gibbon in the title rôles.

Pantomime had a good innings. Goadby from Sadler's Wells directed and played Harlequin in *Harlequin Gladiator; or The Fairy of the Grotto* in which new tricks of his invention were introduced, and for which Willis painted the scenery and Collison devised the machinery. In a ballet *The Blood Red Knight; or The Spectre of the Cavern* the spectre rose surrounded by blue fire. Morton's *Knight of Snowdoun* founded on *The Lady of the Lake*, was the first of a long series of dramas taken from the works of Walter Scott. Dimond's melodrama *Royal Oak*, Reynolds's opera *Free Knights*, Pocock's operatic farce *Anything New*, Hook's farce *Trial by Jury* and Clarke's comedy *The Kiss* altered from Beaumont and Fletcher's *Spanish Curate*, were other new pieces. In July Sarah Smith, now established at Covent Garden, came back to star for 8 nights playing Isabella, Jane Shore to the Hastings of Mansel, Mrs. Oakley, Belvidera to the Jaffeir of Brown, Calista, Sigismunda and Isabella in *Measure for Measure* – she also recited Collins's *Ode on the Passions* and sang the national airs of foreign countries in Thomas Moore's melologue on music. The Misses Waldron and F. Waldron made their first appearances in York as Ninette in Dimond's new comic opera *The Young Hussar*, and Little Pickle respectively. On the last night Mrs. Lefanu's comedy *Sons of Erin* and Kenney's operatic farce *Turn Out* were presented for the first time.

William Dowton was the Race Week star making his first appearance at York on August 24 as Dr. Cantwell, one of his best parts, and Sir David Dunder. He also played Sheva, Major Sturgeon, Oddly in *Sons of Erin*, Doiley, Sir Francis Gripe, Restive in *Turn Out*, Sir Robert Bramble, Peeping Tom, Sir Anthony Absolute, and Lenitive. Dowton had a natural style of acting; stressed character, was a master of dialect and a fine representative of old men. During the first half of September the company acted with an equestrian troupe from Covent Garden under the direction of Messrs. Parker, Davis and Crossman. Two famous equestrian melodramas were produced: Monk Lewis's *Timour the Tartar* and Dibdin and Fawcett's *Secret Mine* in which a greater number of horses appeared than had ever been seen on this stage. The craze for spectacles of this kind was to grow by what it fed on and to prove disastrous to the more legitimate forms of drama.

When the company reopened in York on March 8, 1813 they had with them a new leading comedian John Pritt Harley who made his first appearance that night as Ludovico in *The Peasant Boy*. Harley, who was born in 1786, had had his first stage experience in amateur theatricals and had subsequently played in Kent, Sussex and Southend. He stayed with the company two years, after which he went to the Lyceum and finally succeeded John Bannister at Drury Lane. He rose to be an excellent comedian, had a correct ear, and a counter-tenor voice. Extremely thin like Mathews before him, he was playfully known as 'Fat Jack'. He played a large round of comedy parts in York[37] and as Somno in *The Sleep Walker* gave imitations of Kemble, Cooke, Mathews, Fawcett, Decamp and Blanchard. In his *At Home*, he imitated the notorious amateur of fashion 'Romeo' Coates as Romeo Rantall. Mrs. H. Cummins daughter-in-law of Cummins, formerly Mrs. Woodhouse, had joined the company from Bath, and Miss Mathews had married an actor in the troupe named Payne. Mansel was playing comedy leads such as Ranger and Charles Surface.

One tragedy was brought out this year – Coleridge's *Remorse* with Don Ardonio = F. Brown, Donna Teresa = Mrs. Payne, Alhadra = Mrs. M'Gibbon. Kemble's version of *Julius Caesar* made its début too with Brutus = Cummins, Cassius = Mansel, Portia = Mrs. M'Gibbon. There was the usual crop of melodramas including Kerr's *Wandering Boys*. Kemble's

21-year-old *Lodoiska* was given its first showing in York with scenery by Willis, which included the storming and burning of the castle of the Tartars. Among the effects for *Aladdin or The Wonderful Lamp* by Grosette were a necromantic cavern, flame-breathing serpents, a rock which changed to a brazen car drawn by flying dragons in which the necromancer and a red dwarf ascended, a procession of dwarfs, a brilliant cloud palace, vertical columns in motion, and the necromancer sinking in final flames. M. G. Lewis's new drama *Veroni*, Arnold's comic opera *The Maniac*, Beazley's operatic farce *The Boarding House*, Morton's comedy *Education*, Kenney's long popular farce *Love, Law and Physic* with Harley as Lubin Log, *How to Die for Love*, a farce adapted from Kotzebue, last echo of a bygone vogue, and Hook's farce *Darkness Visible* were other new pieces. The equestrian craze was catered for by the pantomime *Voorn the Tiger; or the Horse Banditti*. Willis's panoramic view of the storming of Badajoz by Wellington on April 16, 1812 was displayed at Collison's benefit.

Mathews returned for summer Assize Week together with the four Misses Adams, principal dancers from Covent Garden and Dublin. He added to his usual repertoire Goldfinch in *The Road to Ruin*, Buskin in *Killing No Murder*, Dick Cypher in *Hit or Miss*, Flexible in *Love, Law and Physic*, and Mingle in *The Bee Hive*. Miss F. Waldron had married R. Hall, an actor in the company since 1812; she played The Sleeping Beauty in the melodrama of that name. The elder Chippendale from Glasgow had joined the company and played Silky and Sir Peter Teazle to the Lady Teazle of Miss Adams, but left the next year for Edinburgh. Emery was the Race Week star, playing in the new characters of Broadcast in *Education*, Andrew in *Love, Law and Physic* and Ben in *Love for Love*, revived after 30 years with Mansel as Valentine, Chippendale as Foresight, Miss Adams as Angelica, Mrs. R. Hall as Miss Prue, Mrs. Eborall as Mrs. Foresight and Mrs. Leonard as Mrs. Frail. Betty, no longer Master but Mr., followed in September playing Achmet, Young Norval, Alexander, and Charles II in *Royal Oak*, but his brief glory had departed with his childhood.

When John Wilkinson opened the York Theatre in the spring of 1814 he was tottering towards bankruptcy. His new theatre at Hull had proved too costly a venture and already by November 1813 he was seeking to dispose of it.[38] He carried on until mid-May. Knight reappeared for one night on April 2 as Sim in *Wild Oats* after an absence of 5 years. The famous Juvenile Theatre melodrama *The Miller and his Men* made its bow at York, and *Henry V* was revived after 14 years.

Mansel published his *Free Thoughts Upon Methodists, Actors and the Influence of the Stage* at Hull in May. At his benefit night on May 16 Reynolds's comedy *Notoriety* was revived after 18 years and at the end of it was exhibited 'a highly finished Transparency by a Lady representing the Bust of the Duke of Wellington, Crowned by Victory, and Britannia offering a Coronet and other Honorary Badges.'[39] Then the crash came. The *York Herald* of May 28 announced that the Theatre would re-open on Whit Monday for two nights for the benefit of the whole company: 'By the unfortunate pressure of circumstances, (which terminated in an abrupt closing of the Theatres) the Performers have been deprived of their Situations, without receiving the customary Notice of Two Months. – Thus circumstanced they have ventured to throw themselves upon the liberality and generosity of the Public, with all the confidence which experience can give and every hope that remembrance of past favours can elicit. The peculiarity of the case altogether, would readily furnish materials towards working up a forcible appeal to the feelings of Individuals, and a strong Demand upon the attention of the Public at large; the Performers of the York Theatre will not avail themselves of such a measure – the truly liberal will know how to appreciate their silence.' The play chosen for May 30 was *The Poor Gentleman*, a title appropriate to the players' predicament. Anxious to make the night a success they engaged Signor Rivolta whose feat was to perform on six to eight instruments simultaneously. The players thanked their patrons for their liberal support and hoped for a continuation of favour on June 2 when the Amateur Concert Committee bespoke a performance of *The School for Scandal*, in which Chippendale played Sir Peter followed by *How to Die for Love* and Signor Rivolta.[40]

Silence then falls until July 23 when the *York Herald* announced that Fitzgerald had taken the lease of the York and Hull Theatres Royal and the Leeds, Doncaster ard Wakefield houses from the trustees of John Wilkinson. Robert J. Fitzgerald's real name was Gerald[41] and his father had been the manager of a small strolling company in Kent. He had been for a week or two in the York company under Tate Wilkinson but had been discharged for impertinence and incapacity. When he joined the Norwich company he clapped a Fitz onto his name and gained sympathy by posing as the descendant of the patriot Edward Fitzgerald. He seems to have been altogether an unpleasant person. The new lessee, soliciting the patronage of nobility, gentry and the public in general, promised 'an unremitting assiduity on his part to please his Patrons and Supporters, by producing such Dramatic Entertainments as may be considered worthy of their approbation, in a style and manner every way adequate to the encouragement he may be honoured with, and by a determination that no effort on his part shall be wanting to engage Performers of known respectability and diligence.'[42]

A lease of the Theatre[43] for 12 years had been granted on January 5, 1814, to Thomas Wilson, Wilkinson's trustee, at a rent of £20 a year payable in two instalments in January and July. It was a repairing lease and the lessee was required to do repairs if requested within 3 months. He was not allowed to sell or grant the Theatre to any other but a citizen of York. On October 4 the Corporation[44] granted Wilson permission to sublet to Fitzgerald for 7 years, for the benefit of John Wilkinson's creditors, the remainder of the term to be assigned to trustees for the same purpose.

So Wilkinson, except for his annual benefit, passes out of the story for some time. He retired to Acomb and appears to have taken no further active part in theatrical affairs until 1828.

Fitzgerald opened his season on Monday July 25 with *The School of Reform* and *No Song No Supper*. Places for the boxes were to be had of Hope at the box office between 11-2. A few members of the old company remained including Cummins, Foster, Mansel, Hall, Mr. and Mrs. R. Hall, Miss Waldron, Mrs. Eborall and the scene painter Willis. Among the new members were Remington from Dublin, Mr. and Mrs. Baily from Portsmouth, Mrs. Hammerton and Miss Rennell from Covent Garden, Miss Horribow from Drury Lane and Miss Greenfield from Norwich. Fitzgerald made his first appearance as Charles II in *The Royal Oak* on July 27 and subsequently played comedy rôles such as O'Trigger, Abednego, Denis Brulgruddery, Gradus, Sir Pertinax MacSycophant, and Sheva. The new machinist was French from Covent Garden. Miss Horribow was the first singing lady; Mrs. Hammerton took the heavier rôles such as Mrs. Haller and Charlotte Rusport and Mrs. R. Hall the lighter comedy ones such as Lydia Languish. In *Henry IV* Cummins played the King to the Prince of Wales of Mansel and the Hotspur of Fitzgerald. The season continued until the end of August. There was no star, but Sieur Sanches showed his antipodean powers for a few nights by walking on the ceiling over the stage head downwards, the first man we hear of to perform this trick in York. One new piece was brought out, Kerr's melodrama *The Wandering Boys*.

When the season opened in March 1815 Fitzgerald had reverted to the distinction between the lower and upper boxes, charging 4/- for the former, 3/- for the latter. Days of playing were Monday, Tuesday, Thursday and Saturday. Another change was the introduction of those interludes against which Tate Wilkinson had so firmly set his face. Many programmes henceforward consist of three pieces: a typical one is *The Miller and his Men*, followed by Poole's new interlude *Intrigue* and concluding with Arnold's melodrama *The Woodman's Hut*. This either lengthened the entertainment or involved the presentation of short pieces only. The five act drama and afterpiece were gradually crowded out by a succession of worthless farces and musical trifles. Indeed so many new pieces were introduced each season that space will no longer allow us to keep track of them, and only the more important will be mentioned.

At least four new melodramas appeared this year. Nautical melodramas were particularly popular and Reynolds's *The Renegade* featured an engagement between a Christian ship and a Barbary corsair concluding with the rising and bursting of a water spout. The popular Pocock was represented by *For England Ho!* and by his comic opera *John of Paris*, and the poet Thomas Moore by his comic opera *M.P.* Goadby, who had returned as Harlequin, devised a new pantomime *Harlequin Fisherman* with music by French and machinery by Sollitt. The *York Herald*[45] hailed it as surpassing any ever produced in York for its tricks and scenic business. 'The restoration of the Rose, and the metamorphosis of the Pie-crust into a Chandelier were quite bordering on the marvellous.' For Barrymore's canine melodrama *The Dog of Montargis* the machinery was by French and the original dog dragon from Covent Garden was produced. The new wardrobe keepers were Mr. and

Mrs. Nicolls. Fitzgerald acted the King in Kemble's version of *Henry V* with Mansel as Fluellen and Mrs. Hall as Katherine.

A curious display took place at the benefit of Mr. and Mrs. Dobbs. Dobbs, who had invented a new reaping machine, showed how it worked on the stage where wheat was planted, and cut and bound by the machine as in a field. An engraving of it appears on the playbill.[46] Fitzgerald gave benefits for the York Dispensary, the relief of widows and orphans of men who had fallen in the battles under the Duke of Wellington, and on July 21 towards the establishment of a Theatrical Fund. For this last a sum of £8.0.6 was raised.

Fitzgerald declared his intention of giving the profits of a benefit in each of the circuit towns towards the Fund and of resigning his title to two-thirds of all forfeits to the Fund, the remaining third to go to the prompter.[47] The performers on their part were to relinquish their salaries at the benefits or, if absent, pay 7/-. The Fund was formally instituted on July 22 and several members of the company immediately became subscribers at 1/- a week. Fitzgerald, who had been treasurer of a similar fund at Norwich, was made treasurer and a trustee with T. Brook and Joseph Wilson. A committee was elected of Mansel, Bailey, Foster, Remington and Hope with Parsons as secretary. Evidently a previous scheme had been mooted in 1813 since subscribers to it who had left the company were allowed to join the new one if they chose, and six performers took advantage of this. Contributors had to show seven years' regular payments before they could make a claim. Contributors in arrears forfeited their claims, but any who left the company after having contributed for at least one season could secure their claims by continuing payments. No actor was admitted a member until the second season of his engagement with the company and then had to be proposed by a member of the Committee and voted upon. Only the secretary for the time being was exempt from payments. Annuities of £50 a year were to be given to those who became incapacitated for work and who did not possess an income of more than £50 a year, otherwise annuities were lowered accordingly. The disbursements were not to exceed the annual receipts and should they do so were lowered to keep within them. The fund existed until 1881 when the balance of £1200 was merged into the Royal General Theatrical Fund.

For the Fund benefit Blanchard produced his spectacle of *Sydney and his Dog Faithful*. During his visit he also played the Miser, later Pantaloon, in a new pantomime *The Miser; or The Mysterious Purse of Gold* in which Miss Blanchard was Cupid. The pieces were such a success that he took the Theatre for three more nights with them.

The lighting of the Theatre at this time was by wax candles placed in glass chandeliers of a novel form, and brilliant appearance.[48] They prevented the wax lights from running and 'falling on the heads of the visitors in the pit – a nuisance which was formerly much complained of.' Not only the stage boxes, mentioned in 1809, but what are called the manager's boxes and the stage doors were now ornamented with plain gilt moulding.

When the company returned in 1816 a famous comedian was in its ranks. This was Joseph Leathley Cowell,[49] later to make a great reputation in America. His real name was Witchett and he was born in 1792. He was discharged from the navy after a romantic career and took to painting and the stage, first appearing at Plymouth and then playing a wide variety of comic and tragic parts at Richmond. He commenced scene painting at Woolwich and Covent Garden, and at Brighton was both actor and painter. Then whilst acting under Anderson and Faulkner in their northern circuit he received an offer from Fitzgerald which he accepted with alacrity, though he had to wait out the six weeks of his notice, and had it not been for the generosity of Lord Normanby, would not have found the money for the journey to Hull. Fitzgerald, as Cowell soon found, had offered him comedy leads with the highest salary under pressure from his powerful friends. The manager received him in a most unfriendly manner for he himself wished to push Bailey whose wife was his mistress. Cowell paints a very unpleasant picture of Fitzgerald who came both to fear and hate him. He accuses him of being a tyrant to those beneath, and a fawner on those above him; a rake whose wife had attempted a short while before to poison herself, and only survived with prostrated nerve and broken spirit. He had a dog who was the original dog in *The Forest of Bondy* whom he appeared to like, but simply because he made money for him. Cowell describes him as 'a tall, good-looking man when *made up*, but had a bad countenance; "his brow, like a pent-house hung over" his small, gray eyes, a fine Roman nose, and a mouth struggling to be handsome in defiance of a continual sensual expression'. His hair was red and his temper fiery. Cowell once thrashed him because Fitzgerald had called him a liar and refused to withdraw it. He thought his manager a vile actor though he had a superior knowledge of costume. Old Johnny Winter, who had left the theatre at Wilkinson's death, had a breeches maker's business and was employed by Fitzgerald to make a suite of dresses for *Macbeth*. The old man was then 70 though he retained in figure and manner of address 'all the flippancy of youth in an extra-ordinary degree'. Fitzgerald flew into one of his violent rages with Winter about these dresses, but Winter coolly replied 'Now, ye see, ye mun get someone else to finish t' job, or do 't yersen; ye see, I recollect ye when ye was a poor, ragged lad, an' war kick'd out o' theatre, Mistre *Gerald*.' Cowell speaks of the two doyens of the company, Cummins who suffered from heart disease and nearly always dressed at home, and Charles Wood, who had been a member longer even than Cummins and whom no manager dared discharge. Wood, now stone deaf, was cheerful and good-tempered and though his wife was in her dotage, and his large family had mostly turned out badly, went humming and whistling about the Theatre. Cowell says that Mrs. Humby[50] was the only member of the company who arrived at eminence. As Miss Ayre she had trained as a singer under Domenico Corri, and been engaged by Fitzgerald in 1815 when she appeared as Yarico and Katherine in *Henry V*. That same year she married the actor Humby who was so prudent in many matters, that he was known in the company as 'Young Calculation'. Cowell says that Mrs. Humby was 'excessively pretty, and in simple innocent characters, a charming actress. She was the best Cowslip I ever played with.' She also played Rosina, Lucy Bertram and Lydia Languish. She left the circuit in 1818 for Bath and a few years later made her reputation at the Haymarket and Drury Lane in the pert chambermaid line.

Cowell himself became very popular. He sustained a few of the stock comedy rôles but also appeared in melodramas and in a wide range of new pieces.[51] He tells us how he played Tiptoe's drunken scene in *Ways and Means* during Race Week when he was drunk, and a large section of the audience probably in the same condition. He avoided any effort at acting. Fitzgerald, because Cowell had some reputation in this part, was induced to watch him in the last act, and afterwards complained to him that he was bad and mistaken because he was rather a man who wanted to sleep off the effects of intoxication than one recently exhilarated by them. Winter, who was hanging around his old haunts, expressed surprise that Fitzgerald had the acumen to make so penetrating a distinction. Cowell made his last appearance on August 27 as Trot and Lubin Log. He tells us that he spent a pleasant and profitable year with the company which, however, since Tate's days 'had fallen from its high estate, though it still maintained a feeble superiority among its compeers from the recollection of what it had been'. He obtained better terms in the Lincoln circuit, and later was engaged by Elliston at Drury Lane and the Adelphi. In 1821 he went to America.

Another newcomer in 1816 was Carter who played Romeo; Macduff to the Macbeth of Fitzgerald and the Lady Macbeth of Miss Diddear; and St. Aldobrand in Maturin's celebrated new tragedy *Bertram* with Fitzgerald as Bertram and Miss Diddear as Imogene. Both Carter and Miss Diddear stayed for three years. Willis had done new scenery for *Macbeth*[52] which included a romantic heath with a bridge and waterfall, a Gothic gallery and hall, clouds and a car for the ascension of Hecate, and the witches' cavern with the transparent shades of the 8 kings. Mansel played Falstaff for the first time in *Henry IV* at the benefit of Emmerson the box check taker.

This year saw the ripening of the Scott craze. In *The Lady of the Lake* Fitzgerald was Roderick Dhu and Miss Diddear Lady Margaret and Willis's scenery included a romantic view on Loch Katrine, and a wild glen with the preparation of the fiery cross.[53] This was followed by *Guy Mannering*, Henry Bertram = Carter, Dominie Sampson = Cowell, Lucy Bertram = Mrs. Humby, Meg Merrilees = Miss Diddear. One of the most famous of melodramas, Pocock's *The Magpie or the Maid* also made its York début this year with Mrs. Bailey as the heroine Annette. Thomas Dibdin's extravaganza *Harlequin Hoax* displayed a Chinese Bridge and pagoda as represented in St. James's Park on the night of the grand illumination in honour of the allied sovereigns.

By 1817 Miss Green, a new dancer from the Opera House, had joined the company. She produced a divertisement called *St. Valentine's Day* and announced in the *York Chronicle*[54] that she would give dancing lessons and attend ladies at their own houses. It was very usual for a dancer to supplement his or her salary in this fashion. Cowell had been succeeded by Thomas Kilner, an excellent actor in hearty old men, who went to America in 1818 and later made a name for himself at Boston where he became manager.[55] The spring season was the last in which Cummins appeared in York. He dropped dead on the stage in Leeds on June 20, aged 62, when acting Dumont in *Jane Shore*.[56] His last words are said to have been:

> Be witness for me, ye celestial hosts!
> Such mercy and such pardon as my soul
> Accords to thee, and begs of Heav'n to show thee;
> May such befal me, at my latest hour.

But such stories of appropriate last lines uttered by actors who died on the stage are so frequent as to raise suspicions that they were usually legendary. Cummins was buried in St. John's Church, Leeds, and an immense concourse, including the whole of the theatrical corps, attended his funeral. He had been with the company 40 years and for all his ranting style was in his heyday a favourite without rival, and in his age was universally esteemed in his profession. So passed the last of the old time tragedians.

Fitzgerald continued the fare of melodramas and operatic spectacles, among them Morton's *The Slave* with its Yorkshire comic character Sam Sharpset, Dimond's *Broken Sword,* and, in August, Soane's *Innkeeper's Daughter* in which the hero is thrown from his boat on to the rocks in a storm and is rescued by a lifeboat. When *The Conquest of Algiers* by Reynolds and Dimond was brought out the scenery painted by Willis was from models by Grieve and Casson, once more from drawings taken on the spot. The grand finale consisted of the bombardment and destruction of Algiers, the pyrotechnics being prepared and arranged by the principal artist in the ordnance department at Woolwich. On March 20 York first saw *Illusion or The Trances of Nourjahad*, attributed in the playbill to Lord Byron,[57] with splendid gardens, apartments, bowers and fountains by Willis. At Mansel's benefit[58] the whole of the stage was formed into a Palm Tree Grove decorated with variegated lamps, terminating in a beautifully illuminated temple for a masquerade on the plan of the one given by Jones at Covent Garden. All the members of the company, as well as additional performers and amateurs, took part, and members of the audience, who wished to join the motley group on the stage, could be provided with dominoes, the tickets being 10/6, character tickets 7/-.

A benefit was given for the orphaned Miss Cummins in which Harley made his first reappearance at York since quitting the company. He played through July and August in a series of old and new parts. Among the latter were Paragon in Kenney's *Touchstone*, Phantom in Oulton's *Worried to Death*, Smart in *Incog*, Sam Dabbs in Poole's *Who's Who*, Dr. Pother in Charles

Dibdin's *Farmer's Wife* and Crockery in Jamieson's *Exit by Mistake*. He also gave his imitations.

A benefit for the Theatrical Fund[59] was postponed. The necessity for such a fund was brought home by the case of Cummins who after 42 years on the stage had been unable to ensure the independence of his daughter. Had there been one ten years previously the orphan might not have been thrown penniless on the world. Fitzgerald therefore appealed for donations to be paid into the York banks. In the meantime profits from the benefits for Miss Cummins in each of the circuit towns went to purchase an annuity for her.[60]

Many actors now came and went, the majority remaining two seasons at most. Unusually constant in these shifting times were Remington, who had come from Dublin in 1814 and stayed until 1826 and W. Remington who joined in 1816 and remained until 1831.

By 1818 the Wallacks from Norwich were in the company. Henry Wallack was the brother of the famous tragedian James Wallack. Like his brother he later went to America where he became well known as a stock actor.[61] He opened as Baron Montaldi in *The Peasant Boy* and later played Aboan in *Oroonoko*. He left the company at the end of the year but rejoined it in July, 1820 for a few months.

Mathews[62] presented his *Budget of Budgets* for one night only during his northern tour in May. It consisted of English, Irish and Scotch recitations with comic and serious songs followed by a mélange entitled *The Irishman in Naples*.

Some famous pieces were first put on this season. Most important to posterity was Mozart's *Don Giovanni* which was presented on April 7 with the following cast: Pedro = Young, Giovanni = Wallack, Leporello = Mallinson, Donna Elvira = Miss Diddear, Donna Leonora = Mrs. Wallack, Zerlina = Mrs. Humby, and a set of new scenes. It was repeated on April 13. It was a portent and a herald. The opera craze was to succeed the melodrama craze but was to have a much more far reaching effect since it was to be one of the chief causes of the overthrow of the stock companies. Singing actors and actresses would cope with English operas but the foreign operas needed voices of a kind which the ordinary circuit companies could not supply.

Meanwhile the melodramas flourished. The famous *Rob Roy*, most popular of all dramatisations of Scott, appeared in York on April 14 though we do not know in which of its many versions. The cast was Rashleigh Osbaldistone = Wallack, Francis Osbaldistone = Larkin, Rob Roy = Mansel, Bailie Nicol Jarvie = Mallinson, Diana Vernon = Mrs. Humby, Helen M'Gregor = Miss Diddear. Another famous melodrama Soane's *Falls of Clyde*, as well as Pocock's *The Ravens* and *Heir of Vironi*, also made their début. *Hamlet* was given with Mansel as the Prince, and Mrs. Humby as Ophelia. Miss Cummins was again accorded a benefit. The season was much shorter than usual and closed on April 18. On May 31 when the company was at Wakefield, Fitzgerald died in the 45th year of his age and was buried in St. John's church there. On his tombstone are the lines 'Monarchs, sages, peasants must Follow thee and come to dust'.[63] Mansel, who was intending to retire, was induced by his friendship for Fitzgerald to take over the management of the theatres for the remainder of the leases for his widow and daughter.[64] Fitzgerald, it appears, had embarked the whole of his property on the precarious profits of his seven years' lease. His initial expenditure had been considerable, and theatrical times were bad, but he looked to the last three years of his term for remuneration. The circuit at this time consisted of York, Leeds, Sheffield, Hull, Doncaster and Wakefield. The *York Herald*, which announced the new regime on June 13, said that Fitzgerald had brought to the theatre zeal, energy, perseverance and anxiety to deserve the favour of the public which he had communicated to the performers. Mansel, it pointed out, had the advantage of long experience, was respected for his talents as an actor, and his good qualities and manners as a man; he had fine taste, accurate discrimination and was eager to purge the drama of its impurities: 'We are sorry to say', it concluded, 'that occasionally, the conduct of some performers, as well as the character of some of the performances, tends to estrange persons of delicacy'.

The new regime was inaugurated in York on July 13 with the engagement of Mrs. Henry Siddons for a few nights. She opened as Rosalind to the Orlando of Carter, Jaques of Wallack and Touchstone of Mansel, and portrayed admirably that heroine's playful manner, easy gaiety and sweet disposition.[65] In *Much Ado* she was Beatrice to Mansel's Benedick and the following night she was Juliet to the Romeo of Carter. As Portia she made a deep impression by the soft and impressive style of delivery of the quality of mercy speech as well as by the modest meekness of her demeanour and her graceful action. As Imogine 'the eye glistening with tears, the voice trembling with emotion, she imparted a greater degree of interest than we ever recollect to have seen before – distraction and despair appeared in her countenance and the gradations of madness were faithfully delineated'. The versatility of her talent was further evinced by her performances of Amanthis and Julia. Mansel also brought Mrs. Garrick from Covent Garden, a pleasing actress and a 'sweet and scientific singer' who played Jessica, Diana Vernon, Lucy Bertram and Rosina, the last two for the Theatrical Fund benefit. She returned for the Race Week introducing into *Guy Mannering* several songs including *Ye Banks and Braes*.

Hargrove whose *History of the City of York*[66] appeared in 1818, describes the theatre as 'spacious, very handsomely fitted up, and brilliantly lighted with wax candles in splendid glass chandeliers. The scenery and dresses are valuable, elegant, and exhibit considerable variety.' He incidentally tells us that Keregan's old theatre in the Minster Yard had been pulled down.

By 1819 the Kilners, the Humbys, the Wallacks, Carter and Miss Diddear had left the company. Among the newcomers was Frederick Baltimore Calvert. He had been born in 1793 and was son to the steward of the Duke of Norfolk; like John Kemble he had been intended for the Roman Catholic priesthood but instead had gone on the stage. He is best known for his

Defence of the Drama, which he published in 1824. He opened as Don Carlos in *A Bold Stroke for a Husband* on March 10 and sustained among other parts during the season Edgar, Bruce, Rolla, and Saville in *The Belle's Stratagem*. Ralph Sherwin had also joined the company. According to Oxberry[67] he made his first appearance in York as Dandie Dinmont in July, 1818 under Fitzgerald, but Fitzgerald was then dead and, when the piece was played in August, Dandie Dinmont was taken by Robertson. Oxberry says that Sherwin played Scotchmen and sailors with success as well as some parts in Munden's line. Fanny Kelly particularly admired his Farmer Cropley in *The Touchstone*. He objected to being sent on in small rôles in tragedy and eventually Mansel offended him, whereupon he 'drew out his pencil instead of his pistol and caricatured the manager', in addition mimicking him to his fellow comedians. The result was dismissal. But Sherwin made good at Drury Lane in 1823 where he played Emery's line. He was stout, of a florid complexion with jet black hair and dark eyes.

Fanny Kelly from Drury Lane was the Assize Week star. She was the original of Lamb's Barbara S – and the niece of Michael Kelly under whom she had studied music and singing. As a singer she had filled Madame Storace's parts at the English Opera House, as an actress she was successful in Mrs. Jordan's cast of characters, in the pathetic, and most of all in domestic melodrama. York saw her in her original rôles of Mary, The Innkeeper's Daughter, Ellen Enfield in *The Falls of Clyde*, Dinah Cropley in *Touchstone*, Sophia in Ayton's new operetta *The Rendezvous* and Harriet in *Is He Jealous?* in which she accompanied herself on the piano, as well as in such old favourites as Letitia Hardy, Miss Peggy and Nell. On May 6 Charles Wood made his first appearance as Don Lopez in *The Wonder*; he had first played on the York stage 48 years previously. The three piece a night programme had come to stay and involved the constant production of new farcettas, interludes and other short pieces. The most significant of these was *Amoroso* the first burlesque by the prolific Planché, which was to start a vogue in this kind. A new pantomime *The House that Jack Built* was brought out on Easter Monday with Stanley as Harlequin, Miss Green as Columbine and an exhibition of the newly invented velocipede or 'Dandy's Hobby Horse', precursor of the bicycle. Pantomime was beginning to turn for its themes to the nursery rhyme and story. Tragedy was represented by Shiel's *Apostate*[68] with Calvert as Heymeya and Milman's *Fazio* with Calvert in the title rôle. Coburg melodramas included *Meg Murdoch* and *Robert the Bruce*, the latter introducing the new invention of red fire which was used for the conflagration of the mill. New pieces based on Scott were *Marmion* and T. J. Dibdin's *Heart of Midlothian* presented at Mrs. Fitzgerald's benefit. *Wallace*, directed and superintended by Montague, who adapted old Scotch melodies to the piece, had new scenery by Willis, machinery by French and dresses by Nicholls. The company again gamefully tackled full blown opera, and Rossini's *Barber of Seville*, arranged by Bishop, with Mansel as Almaviva, Chapman as Figaro and Miss Poole as Rosina, was so successful that Mansel chose it for his benefit along with Jones's new comedy *The Green Man*.

On May 17 there was a minor riot in the Theatre. During one of the intervals, a gentleman called out for *Rule Britannia* whilst others called for *God Save the King*. The band struck up the latter and some members of the audience remained seated, hissing and hooting 'with seditious audacity'. A cry for hats off resounded through the theatre and confusion reigned until a bold spirit stalked from the boxes and forcibly uncovered one of the offenders in the pit. An altercation, of course, ensued but was finally composed.'[69]

For summer Assize Week Mansel obtained the services of Edmund Kean for 6 nights. This was not the first time he had acted in York though it was his first appearance at the theatre. In 1811[70] after wandering from town to town in the north he had arrived in the city destitute, with his wife and children. The wife of a dancing master named Nokes heard of the family's plight, visited Mrs. Kean and pressed £5 into her hand, thus rescuing them from starvation. Nokes himself lent them the ballroom in Minster Yard where he received his pupils and there on October 10 Kean and his wife performed scenes from *The Honeymoon, The Waterman, The Castle Spectre* and *Sylvester Daggerwood*, and Kean gave his imitations. They raised £9, and were able to proceed to London. Three years afterwards Kean brought London to his feet by his performance as Shylock and he now returned to York as the greatest actor of his time. His terms were high but Mansel, relying on the largeness of the theatre and the liberality of the public, did not advance the prices though he cancelled the half price. Kean opened on July 19 as Richard III and was judged particularly admirable in the scene with Lady Anne (Mrs. Stanley) where he was required to exert his voice.[71] On the 20th he played Shylock to the Portia of Miss P. Hargrave but a wet evening prevented the house from being as well attended as expected; on 21st he acted Sir Giles Overreach in the closing scene of which the 'whole house resounded with loud and long continued acclamations'. On 22nd as Othello he volunteered his services to Mrs. Fitzgerald and the house was crowded; Mrs. Stanley was Desdemona and Neville Iago. On 23rd he played Macbeth with Miss P. Hargrave as Lady Macbeth; on 24th Hamlet to the Ophelia of Miss Poole and Queen of Miss P. Hargrave; on 26th Rolla for the first time in the country. Kean was followed by the rope dancer Wilson, fresh from successes on the Continent and advertised as 'the most elegant performer of the age'. The season ran right on into Race Week when Mathews was re-engaged. Among his parts this visit were Old Croaker in the *Good Natur'd Man*, Chip in Knight's *A Chip of the Old Block*, and the Actor of All Work in Colman's farce of that name; he also gave an entertainment called his *Mail Coach Adventures* which had been produced under the title *At Home* at the English Opera House and which consisted of songs, imitations, ventriloquism and recitations. He was suffering from a swollen tongue which the heat and acting six nights a week, did not improve. He enjoyed once more meeting old friends and finding that his wife's health was drunk.[72]

When the company re-opened on March 6, 1820, Lydia Kelly from Drury Lane and Dublin, sister of Fanny Kelly, was engaged for a few nights and stayed on for the rest of the season. She made her début in Belvidera and also played Juliet and singing parts. At her benefit on March 25 her more famous sister performed Lucy to her Polly and Yarnold's Macheath in *The Beggar's Opera*.[73] This was too tough for the times, and objectionable scenes had been omitted though all the original melodies were retained. Yarnold, a singer from Drury Lane, was also a newcomer. There was a new dancer too in the person of Bland from Dublin who made his first appearance in a ballet which he got up called *All in a Mist*. Dancing was becoming increasingly popular in the intervals between pieces and Mansel promised to present a variety of new ballets, quadrilles and waltzes. The quadrille had been introduced into England in 1816 and the waltz, after an unpopular start, had grown in to favour about the same time. Ballets as interludes were also a feature of the season. Mansel promised a list of 32 new pieces and revivals though we do not know whether he actually put them all on. Among the better known ones that were given were Shiel's tragedy *Evadne*, and Howard Payne's *Brutus* with Calvert in the title rôle, chosen for Mrs. Fitzgerald's annual benefit, and again for Willis's. Willis's new scenic effects included an equestrian statue of Tarquinius Superbus shattered by a thunderbolt and a conflagration of the Palace of Tarquin. Fires and wrecks were about equally popular dénouements to the melodramas of the time. W. T. Moncrieff's famous extravaganza *Giovanni in London* was brought out on April 18 with 'pleasing and beautiful views of the infernal regions'. The playbill is the first of a facetious type that was to become customary for extravaganzas. We are informed on it that 'There will also be exhibited a New Moon, which is expected to be FULL about Half-price, that the dresses are as good as the proprietor can possibly afford and that the properties are very little use to any but their own.'

Among Shakespeare plays were a revival of *Julius Caesar* after seven years with Mansel as Brutus; *Much Ado* with Mansel as Benedick and Mrs. Stanley as Beatrice; *Romeo and Juliet*; *Hamlet* with Calvert as the Prince and Lydia Kelly as Ophelia; *Macbeth* with Calvert and Miss Hargrave, and Kemble's alteration of *Coriolanus* with Calvert in the title rôle, Miss Hargrave as Volumnia. *The Tempest* was given new scenery by Willis including Prospero's cavern terminating in a triple vista and his study surrounded by instruments of magic.

In mid-season Mansel had a disagreement with Mrs. Fitzgerald and retired from the management.[74] He took his final benefit on April 15 at which he spoke a farewell to the York audience. The piece performed was appropriately *The Manager in Distress*, followed by *The Dramatist* with Mansel as Vapid, and Garrick's *Arthur and Emmeline* in which the apotheosis was heightened by a display of the novel red fire.[75] The playbill requested that all demands on the Theatre should immediately be sent in. Calvert succeeded Mansel as manager in May. After his performance of Coriolanus on May 27 the *York Herald*[76] pronounced him unquestionably the most promising performer in the company. On the last night, May 30, he took his benefit with that and Jones's new farce *Too Late for Dinner*. The house was unusually crowded and before the farce Calvert spoke an address. He referred to the 'declining interests of the drama' and stated that negotiations were pending for the return of some regretted favourites. He promised to retain all that was praiseworthy in the late order and to rectify on public demand whatever was faulty or defective. He ended by hoping that the house would no longer be the scene of party contentions. Apparently there were still violent scenes whenever the musicians were called upon to play *Wallace, God Save the King* and some other tunes. Indeed it had frequently been found necessary to bring offenders before the magistrates who had bound over some to the sessions, one of whom had been fined two guineas for knocking a young man's hat off.

Charles Edward Horn[77], composer of *Cherry Ripe* and the music of some comic operas, appeared during Assize Week, opening as Henry Bertram in *Guy Mannering*. He had an extraordinary range of voice which enabled him to sing baritone and tenor parts at will. Wallack, who had been acting in Philadelphia, returned after two years' absence and in August obtained the services of his famous brother James, who had also recently returned from an American tour and who appeared as Hamlet.

In September the Theatre was rented for three nights to a company of tumblers which included Mlle Seraphina Ferzi from Paris, Mlle Nina Ferzi from Vauxhall 'whose astonishing Evolutions have been the admirations of the British Empire' and the Young American from New York[78] who ascended a tight rope from the stage to the upper gallery and, on his return, was surrounded by a display of fireworks. It is of interest to note that 'clowns to the rope' were employed.

When the Theatre reopened on March 21, 1821 Calvert had ceased to be manager, for Mrs. Fitzgerald herself announced that it would open with Hook's new comedy *Exchange is No Robbery*. The most important newcomer in the company was Thomas Downe who was later himself to be manager. Melodrama was still the most popular form of entertainment and new ones included Dibdin's *Fate of Calas*, Planché's *Vampire* and Farley's *Battle of Bothwell Brigg*, taken from *Old Mortality*. A new version of *Aladdin* was brought out at Kelly's benefit. He had procured the ms. from Covent Garden at great trouble and expense and the elaborate scenic effects included a palace rising into the air at the waving of the magician's lamp and its later descent complete with some of the dramatis personae. But a new voice was this year heard on the York boards, whose dramas were to rival in popularity the more spectacular pieces; Sheridan Knowles's tragedy *Virginius* was the first of his plays to be seen in the city.

The Comedy of Errors was revived after ten years in three acts as at Covent Garden. This was Reynolds's comic opera version which was enlivened by songs, duets, glees, and choruses selected from the plays, poems and sonnets of Shakespeare, set to music by Arne, Sir J. Stevenson, Stevens, Mozart, and with new music by Bishop.

Fitzgerald's sub-lease was due to expire in the autumn. In March the Corporation[79] extended the head lease to Wilkinson's trustees by 2½ years from January 1, 1826 to July 21, 1828, at a rent of £200 a year. This leap from £20 in 1814 is an astonishing testimony to the increased value of the property. The extension enabled any new sub-lessee to procure a lease of 7 years. And the new lessee was Robert Mansel. The *York Courant* announced on May 1 that the theatres in the circuit had been let to him at a considerable advance.

No sooner had Mansel secured the lease than he petitioned the Corporation for help towards altering the entrances to the Theatre. The General Committee was empowered to lay out a sum of £150 on this and other improvements provided that Mansel contributed £100 and Wilkinson's trustees the same sum. Later it was found desirable to add a saloon at the cost of £100 and on August 20 the amount of the Corporation's contribution was raised to £200 provided that the two other parties raised theirs by £25 each.[80] On July 12 Mansel advertised[81] to builders that 'Such Persons as are willing to Contract for Improving the Avenues and Staircases to the Theatre-Royal, York, may see the Plans and Specification at the Office of Messrs. Atkinson and Sharpe, Architects, after the 16th instant. The Tenders, to be delivered, sealed up, at the Guildhall, on Friday, 27th July, before Eleven o'Clock in the Forenoon.'

On July 26 he announced a preliminary improvement: 'The covering for the seats of the boxes having become offensively dirty, the Manager has been induced to substitute canvas for the present; it will have the recommendation of being clean and will eventually be exchanged for Moreen or Broad Cloth.'

Mansel was unable to make the alterations in the Theatre before the Assizes and he therefore opened on August 4 without them. For this night he distributed 900 free admission tickets, stating that this was in lieu of what he would have done had the Theatre been open at the Coronation of George IV.[82] The pieces performed on this memorable occasion were *Guy Mannering* and *Raising the Wind*. The company consisted of eighteen actors, Messrs. Calvert, Wilders, Pritchard, Williams, Yarnold, Downe, Hammond, Rayner, Kelly, Andrews, Elston, Bland, Smith, Webster, Morelli, W. Remington, Bywater and Dumbleton, and eleven actresses Mesdames Weston, Darley, Rayner, Andrews, Webster, French and Misses Chester, Johnson, Hague, Scruton, Green. Of the actors, Downe and Pritchard were to become managers of the company. Pritchard appeared as Capt. Absolute, Cassio, Pythias in Banim's tragedy *Damon and Pythias*, the Vampire and Rashleigh Osbaldistone to the Rob Roy of Calvert. The Nicol Jarvie was Lionel Benjamin Rayner, the leading comedian and the company's most important acquisition as an actor. He already had connections with it, since in 1812 he had married Margaret Remington the daughter of the prompter. He was a Yorkshireman, born in Heckmondwike about 1788. Seeing Mathews act Farmer Ashfield in Leeds he realised that the rustic rôle was his future too, ran away and joined a company in Stafford. Later he was seen by Bannister playing in the Nottingham company and recommended by him to the Haymarket where he made his London début in 1814. Here

he acquired the friendship of Emery to whose parts he eventually succeeded. It was, however, not until after he left the York company in 1822 to
join Elliston at Drury Lane that he made his reputation on the London
boards. He was a stout man with an air of the rustic about him and he excelled in the Yorkshire rôle of Tyke as well as in Giles in *The Miller's Maid*
and in the Job Thornberry line, though his countrymen were not considered as good as Emery's. He opened in York as Dandie Dinmont and
during his stay enacted several yokel rôles.[83] Miss Chester was the leading
lady. Born in 1799 she had made occasional appearances at Drury Lane but
on the advice of her friends enlisted under Downe to get experience in
York in comedy. She was a voluptuous beauty but affected and inclined to
be vulgar. Poor Downe who escorted her from London was put to the blush
because at the inn she took up the fowl in her fingers and wiped the sauce
off it with a table cloth. There is a story that one night an actor observed her
sobbing and moaning and beating her breast behind the scenes and when
he in alarm begged her to retire to her room she exclaimed, 'Leave me, Mr.
H – I am working up my feelings for the next scene.'[84] This became a bye-
word in the circuit. She played mainly in sentimental comedy but occasionally in tragic rôles such as Desdemona. Her Lady Teazle was a failure, her
Mrs. Oakley one of her happiest rôles. She was a mannerist and given to
what Oxberry calls 'lackadaisyism.' But her beauty prevailed and when
Charles Kemble saw her in York in 1822 he soon carried her off to Covent
Garden where she was given parts to the exclusion of better actresses.

Willis remained as scene painter, Bailes was head carpenter, Ward and
Miss Bearpark dressmakers, Remington prompter, Jackson leader of the
band and Hope treasurer.

The first novelty presented under Mansel's regime was Howard Payne's
melodrama *Therese* during the course of which a pavilion was struck by
lightning and set on fire. Though the piece met with a flattering reception
Mansel refrained from puffing it. On August 27, the last night, *Othello* was
given with Calvert as Othello and Hammond as Iago. The *York Courant* congratulated Mansel on the talents of his company and he was presented with
a giant double handed sword inscribed 'R. Mansel, Esq. Theatre Royal,
York, 1821'. This sword Percy Hutchinson later unearthed at an antique
dealer's and bought it back for the Theatre where it hung for many years.[85]

The £450 that was to be spent on reconditioning the Theatre soon
proved insufficient, and the manager threw himself on the liberality of the
public. 'He observes with regret', ran the announcement,[86] 'that he has
only obtained half his wish; the approaches are now so superb that the
INTERIOR of the Theatre with all its inconveniences is a disgrace to the
Improvements. Anxious as Mr. Mansel is to make the York Theatre what it
should be, neither prudence nor circumstance will admit of his advancing
any more money: which will be readily credited when he affirms that the
alteration already made will cost him nearly Three Hundred Pounds.' From
the workmen's estimates it was ascertained that another £500 at least was

required to make the interior worthy of the approaches 'and when that is completed, York will have to boast as beautiful a Theatre as there is in the Kingdom.' A subscriber's fund had been formed at the meetings held at Etridge's Hotel on November 8 and 19. Lord Dundas was in the Chair and those present formed themselves into a committee for carrying into effect the improvements by public subscription. Lord Dundas gave £50, Messrs. Raper, Swann & Co. £30, Robert Chalmers £25 and a subscription list was opened at the office of Howlet in Lendal. By February 1822[87] the amount subscribed was still insufficient and a special appeal was made to the ladies to make a subscription purse in order that the work, which would particularly add to their comfort and convenience, might be completed. This new list was headed by the late Lady Mayoress Lady Dundas, the then Lady Mayoress, the Hon. Mrs. Chaloner and Lady Johnstone who each subscribed a guinea.

In the meantime the first occupant of the Theatre in 1822 was Mons. Alexandre who gave exhibitions of ventriloquism on February 14.[88] Mansel agreed with him to abstain from dramatic performances that night so that he should have the patronage of those who objected to plays but did not mind conjuring. The new entrances were in use and there was henceforward a division; that to the boxes and pit being in Little Blake Street, that to the gallery in Mint Yard. The entrance to the boxes and pit was very spacious and the former were approached by two flights of fire proof steps 15 to 18 feet wide.[89] On ascending those steps one found on the left a large saloon with a recess for the fruit sellers. The interior was entirely reconstructed and the shape of the auditorium was converted from square to semi-circular, resembling that of Smirke's Covent Garden built in 1808. The semicircular shape had been introduced from France at Bristol as far back as 1766, and a number of new theatre buildings in London and elsewhere had followed suit, so that York was rather behind the times. There were three tiers as before but two of them were now completely devoted to boxes with several doors of entrances and convenient lobbies. A plan exists of the first tier showing three centre and eight side boxes.[90] The third tier consisted of a front and side gallery. Below was a commodious pit. The lighting was by wax candles in handsome glass chandeliers. The house was calculated at the ordinary prices of boxes 4/-, pit 2/-, gallery 1/-, to hold £150.[91] The decorations were of course not completed when Mansel arranged the grand opening on Saturday, February 14 with *The School for Scandal* followed by Mons. Alexandre. The *York Courant*[92] saw in the choice of play a promise that the York stage would be redeemed from the false taste of the day for meaningless pageantry to its true function of depicting real life and satirising contemporary follies, for nursery stories and oriental romances had ousted Shakespeare, Otway and Sheridan from the scenes. These hopes were to be but partially fulfilled. The opening address which was written and recited by Calvert is on the same theme and is worth reprinting in full.[93]

To *you* her Stage the mourning Muse commends,
And turns for hope, where dwelt her earliest friends.
When barbarous, sunk, subdued, our country lay,
Here arts and empire held their sovereign sway;
Hallowed by memories of the great and brave,
The throne of Kings – the birth-place – and the grave, –
Time as it flowed, but added to her fame,
And genius wove his wreath for Ebor's name.

In you still burns the ardour of your sires,
Our drooping hearts that hope alone inspires,
There – whence our bright example we should draw,
Crushed is the Drama's pride – contemned her law.
Scared by the plaudits of the senseless throng,
Sickened with pageant and translated song,
Taste flies, despairing, her polluted fame,
And blushing genius seeks an humbler reign.

Hither forlorn the suppliant wanderers roam
And ask – 'tis yours to give – a happier home.
Ye, who have dared, in sense and feeling strong,
To quit the path where fashion frisked along,
Gave your rapt souls to Shakespeare's verse divine,
With Otway wept – and glowed at Brinsley's line –
Beneath whose cheering smiles our SIDDONS grew,
The grand reality her master drew;
Whose judgment pointed Kemble to the goal,
And traced with many a name Thalia's scroll,
Still as of old, with independent pride,
Judge for yourselves – and for yourselves decide.
Thus to your generous hands we trust our cause,
Our hope – our aim – our triumph – your applause.

Mansel did indeed attempt to revive the classics. In addition to *The School for Scandal* in which Downe played Sir Peter, Calvert Joseph, Mansel Charles and Miss Chester Lady Teazle, *She Stoops to Conquer* and *Jane Shore* were given. Among Shakespearian productions were *Macbeth* (Macbeth = Calvert, Macduff = Pritchard, Lady Macbeth = Mrs. Bunn); *Othello* in which Pritchard and Hammond reversed their former rôles, playing Iago and Cassio respectively; and *The Merchant of Venice* (Shylock = Downe, Portia = Miss Chester). On the other hand the three piece a night programme was much in evidence and the staple fare continued to be melodrama and farce. Mansel introduced 'fashionable nights' which were inducements to the gentry to patronise certain evenings. There were eight of them including April 27 the last night of the season; two were bespoken by Mrs. Bethell and the Officers of the 15th Hussars. At the Sheriff's bespeak the house was filled to overflowing, and on other nights the new Theatre proved sufficient attraction to procure numerous or respectable attendances.[94] On March 6 Mansel announced that the passage round the pit was opened and on March 11 that he was erecting an organ at considerable expense which would be inaugurated by a professional organist.

Another attraction in March was the visit of Mrs. Alfred Bunn[95] from Covent Garden on her way from Newcastle to Dublin. She played her favourite rôle of Bianca in *Fazio*, Elizabeth in an adaptation of Schiller's *Mary Stuart*, Lady Macbeth, and, in comedy, Lady Racket. She was of a commanding figure, which served her in bad stead with Kean whom she overtopped, and her forte was heavy tragedy.

The company had acquired a new scene painter, Montague Penley, who produced scenery for Faucit's melodrama *The Miller's Maid* and for one of the many versions of Scott's *Pirate* of which the pièce de résistance was the blowing up of a pirate ship. A new dancer, Doré, from the Opera House had joined the company and at his benefit a pantomime entitled *Bampfylde Moore Carew; or Harlequin King of the Beggars*, evidently based on the adventures of that strange itinerant, was brought out.[96]

Spectacle had much too great a hold to be banished from the stage and in May Mansel announced that he had, at unprecedented expense, engaged Lee, stage manager of the Adelphi, to produce a facsimile of the *Coronation of George IV* as given at Drury Lane.[97] The dresses, regalia and other decorations were entirely new and made from patterns and models of those used at Drury Lane by permission of the proprietor. Mrs. Lee and her assistants were responsible for the costumes, Morris of Drury Lane for the properties, and Goodbee of the Haymarket for the crown, coronets and imperial robes. A hundred assistants were engaged, an organ erected (presumably the same that was advertised in March), extra singers and a military band employed. A platform was thrown across the pit over which the King passed on his way to the Abbey. For this first scene an accurate view had been taken on the spot of the various galleries fitted up for the spectators of the procession with the towers of the Abbey in the distance. The second scene showed the interior of the Abbey with the altar, coronation chair, and regalia; the third scene, vehicle for dialogue and songs, was of Bird Cage Walk and the last of the interior of Westminster Hall prepared for the royal banquet. The ceremony of the King's champion was introduced, the champion in complete armour being mounted on a real and fully caparisoned charger. It was the most splendid spectacle yet seen on the York stage. Lee opened on May 13 without any dramatic adjunct in order to satisfy those who were prejudiced against plays, as well as children and servants. Five more performances were given in which an afterpiece followed the spectacle.

When the Theatre reopened for the summer Assizes on July 22 the box lobbies had been made all round the house, but the decorations were not yet completed. In order to finish them the Theatre was shut from August 10-19[98] on which latter date it reopened 'one of the most beautiful

Theatres in the Kingdom'. A variety of artists was employed, principal among them being Joseph Rhodes of Leeds. Rhodes,[99] who was later known as 'the Father of Art in Yorkshire', was the most prominent artist and art teacher in the county during the first half of the 19th century. In London he had been employed in japanning furniture and adding painted decorations to mansions. Owing to his contract he had had to refuse an offer from the managers of Drury Lane to be a scene painter, but on his return to Leeds he was the obvious local choice for the York Theatre. He executed a series of ornamental groups in basso relievo, from designs from the Parthenon taken from Stuart's *Album*, on the panels of the boxes and the gallery front, and he painted the pilasters of the proscenium in imitation of Siena marble.[100] The box seats were upholstered in scarlet cloth. Mansel claimed that he had spared neither trouble nor expense in making the Theatre worthy of the circuit and carefully advertised that he had declined, for fear of being thought intrusive, the suggestion that a special benefit should be given towards defraying the expenses.

J. Russell, who had been a member of the company under John Wilkinson from 1810-1812,[101] returned as star from Covent Garden playing a typical series of low comedy parts. Another visitor was Montague Corri, son of Domenico Corri the composer, who came with his wife. She played Juliette in Farrell's *Dumb Girl of Genoa*, the Ms. of which melodrama had been obtained from the Coburg at great expense; Corri produced the Coburg ballet *Philip Quarl*, and arranged from the writings of John Amhurst another melodrama, *Graham, the Regent of Scotland*. The scenery for this was by Penley, the properties by Yarnold, the machinery by Bailes and Collison and the dresses, comprising several suits of armour, were designed and executed by Ward and his assistants. Corri also collaborated with Doré in the comic scenes of a new pantomime, *The Magic Pipe, or Harlequin and Snowball*. He played Pantaloon, his wife Columbine, and Bland Harlequin. But of greater consequence than these spectacles was the first production in York of Mozart's *Marriage of Figaro* which took place on August 27, the last night of the season, with Hammond as Figaro, Crook as Almaviva, Mrs. Leonard as Marcellina and Miss Johnson as the Countess. Thus memorably closed one of the most important seasons in the Theatre's history.

The doors re-opened in November, firstly for a concert of instrumental and vocal music from the operas of Mozart and Rossini in which Spagnoletti from the King's Theatre led the band, and Giuseppe de Begnis and his wife, who had first performed in London this year, sang: and secondly, for a few nights for the Signore Ferzi in ballets in which they were supported by the Corris, Miss Vause, Doré, Parker and Morelli. Since their previous visit to York in 1820 they had performed at a gala given by Louis XVIII at the Tuileries.

In 1823 Mansel opened on March 17 and the houses that week were unusually crowded. Rosina Penley from Bath, daughter of the provincial manager under whom Mansel had acted in Windsor, had succeeded Miss Chester as leading lady and made her first appearance as Juliet.

During Passion Week, when no dramatic performances could be given, Lloyd, the 'Annual Lent Astronomical Lecturer' from the Haymarket, opened the Theatre with his course of astronomical lectures illustrated by a Dioastrodoxon. He proudly announced that this instrument had no connection 'with the Eidouranian or any other minor exhibition. Doré took his final benefit in April at which he produced a new pantomime, *Mother Hubbard and her Dog*; *or Harlequin Poacher*, himself selecting and composing the music and playing Harlequin for the first time. The pantomime was written by Yarnold around his dog Dragon.[102] Indeed pantomime and melodrama had by no means been banished, though the pantomime now purported to cater principally for children. *Kenilworth* came out on March 31 with scenery and decorations from the original designs of London artists, painted by Phillips from Covent Garden and Birmingham.[103] The interest of this production is that it is one of the first examples in York of the archaeological school of scene painting. Kemble had introduced increased realism, and now old plates were being consulted for the sake of accuracy. Thus the scene of the Arden front of Cumnor Manor House was from one such, whilst Robert Laneham's contemporary description of the entertainments was consulted for the castle scenes. A procession with the queen was followed by a pageant in which Cleopatra's galley sailed down the Cydnus with Cleopatra reposing under a Golden Canopy; it sailed into the centre of the stage, the motion subsided and the full musical strength of the company broke into a chorus.

The Tempest was adorned with scenes showing the King's galley in distress and her loss, a lake by moonlight, a mountain in a lake, the rising and vanishing of the banquet, the appearance of two furies, the bursting of a mountain into a volcano, the ascent of Ariel and in conclusion, the discovery of the King's galley riding in smooth water, decorated with flags.[104] In Act IV of *Twelfth Night* a grand masque was represented before the Duke in his own theatre, the proscenium of which was painted by Phillips. The masque was presumably that from *The Tempest* since it included a storm scene, a rainbow by Willis, the descent of Iris down the rainbow, Ceres in her car of cornucopias drawn by children preceded by others bearing emblems, Juno descending and ascending in a peacock car and Iris and Ceres borne up by the clouds. This was Reynolds's version, like his *Comedy of Errors* interspersed with songs and glees arranged by Bishop. Hammond was Malvolio, Downe Sir Toby, Miss Scruton Viola and Miss Johnson Olivia. For the new melodrama, *Cherry and Fair Star*, Phillips painted scenery which included a fairy abode with a variety of birds, the arrival of a splendid Greek galley at Cyprus, probably Cleopatra's, a fairy temple by moonlight and a burning forest; Willis contributed a sea and Yarnold prepared a superb car. The scenery for Dibdin's *Ninth Statue* included the favourite temple with revolving pillars illuminated with 'gerino fire'[105] painted by Penley.

One of the most famous pieces of the day, Moncrieff's *Tom and Jerry*, was first seen in York on March 18 with Crook as Tom and Hammond as Jerry. Five new scenes by Phillips were painted for this production. Henry

Bishop's best opera, *Maid Marian*, was brought out on April 19 and Mary Mitford's tragedy *Julian*, with Calvert in the title rôle, on May 10.

The child prodigy, Clara Fisher, then about twelve years old, was star of the Assize Week. She not only appeared in the suitable *Spoil'd Child*, but she took the male lead of Marplot, and showed off her paces in *Old and Young* and *The Actress of All Work* in which she assumed a variety of characters. This year Mansel opened the Theatre for the Musical Festival Week in September with no less an attraction than Macready. No half price was taken owing to the expenses of his salary. Mansel declared, however, that as the profits of the Musical Festival were given to charity, he would give 10 gns. to each of four institutions no matter what the outcome of the speculation.[106] As it happened Macready proved a great draw, the theatre was crowded to excess and numbers were turned away.[107] The receipts for the six nights were £110 for *Virginius*, £130 *Richard III*, £156 *Othello*, £158 *Macbeth*, £160 *Rob Roy*, £129 *Hamlet* and Delaval in *Matrimony* – a total for six nights of £843. The critic of the *York Herald* acclaimed Macready's performances: his powerful exertion and the strict command of his feelings rivetted attention; whilst his Macbeth surpassed anything the writer had seen.

In 1824 Mansel applied to the Corporation, through Wilkinson's trustees, for a grant to enable him to light the Theatre with gas.[108] The expense was computed at about £200 and Mansel considered that as the Corporation owned the Theatre the cost should be borne by them. It was finally agreed that Mansel should undertake the work at his own expense, but that if he did not renew his lease at the end of the term, the Corporation would pay him a fair valuation for his expenditure – the amount to be decided by referees nominated by Mansel and the Corporation. Gas had been introduced into the London theatres in 1817 and in a few provincial theatres very shortly after. Exactly when the work was completed in York we do not know. A valuation[109] of the fittings belonging to the trustees of the Theatre speaks of a 180 light gas meter, 12 rich cut glass chandeliers and 3 lamps to the entrance, the whole with fittings being valued at £147.10.0. Whether or not the stage was also lighted in the new fashion is uncertain.

The craze for scenic effects, and the increasing demand for instructional entertainment were catered for very successfully by Mons. Thiodon who displayed his *Theatre of Arts* in January and February at the Theatre. This seems from the description in the *York Herald*[110] to have been on the lines of De Loutherbourg's Eidophusicon: 'This Theatre is composed of beautiful Representations of Celebrated Cities, Landscapes, Sea and River Views, &c., enlivened by Figures of Persons, Shipping, Carriages, Horses and other Animals, with varying aspects of Light and Shade; all the Actions and Movements representing Nature in the most perfect and interesting manner ... The effects are produced neither by Transparencies, nor by flat Scene Painting, but by the most finished Models.' The views ranged from Tophania, arsenal of Constantinople, to Waterloo Bridge, and the effects included aquatic exhibitions at Florence, Bonaparte crossing the Alps, and

the death of a sportsman and his dogs in the Valley du Torrent. To ac-
commodate the spectacles alterations had to be made in the house and
places were fitted up into front seats 2/- and second seats 1/-. Thiodon
stayed much longer than he had at first anticipated and he gave a benefit
to the County Hospital. Experiments of this kind were later turned to use
for regular scenery.

Macready opened the spring season of 1824 as Virginius, subsequently
playing Wallace, Leontes, Rob Roy, Caius Gracchus in the début of
Sheridan Knowles's tragedy of that name, Aranza and, on his return from
Newcastle, for a further two nights, Cassius to the Brutus of Calvert and
King John, with Almaviva in *Follies of a Day*.

W. J. Hammond, later to be manager of the company, had joined it from
the Haymarket and made his first appearance as Sam Savoury in Lunn's
Fish Out of Water on March 23; he played singing rôles such as Ralph in *Lock
and Key* and Autolycus. Another newcomer was Montague Stanley[111] who
was to become a well known landscape painter. He remained with the company until 1827 and sometime during his stay some of his companions provoked a quarrel between him and a fellow actor in order to test his courage.
They met in a duel though, unknown to Stanley, the charges in the pistols
were blank. After the first and, of course, ineffective discharge the joke was
explained.

Frimbley from Exeter had replaced Doré as ballet master, to which he
added the title of melodramatic director. He wrote an otherwise unknown
melodrama called *The Ruffian Boy or The Castle of Waldemar*, founded on a
tale by Mrs. Opie, which he brought out on April 19. Other melodramas
were produced under his direction such as *The Anaconda*, dramatised from
a tale by Monk Lewis, in which a serpent made by Yarnold was managed on
the same principle as its London predecessor which, however, it exceeded
in size. Frimbley also wrote the new comic pantomime *Harlequin and Goody
Two Shoes* in which he played his original rôle of Will Dobbins. Phillips was
kept busy painting the new scenery for these productions. But Shakespeare
was not altogether neglected. Apart from the performances by Macready,
Much Ado with Mansel as Benedick, Miss Penley as Beatrice, Downe as
Dogberry and *Coriolanus* with Calvert in the title rôle and Mrs. Weston as
Volumnia were performed. Among the new pieces was Kenney's popular
comic opera *Sweethearts and Wives* with Downe as Admiral Franklin and
Mansel as Charles Franklin.

This year the circus was brought into the Theatre when Cooke[112] and his
equestrian troupe performed there for a few nights in May. Cooke's circus
had been founded about 1752, but Thomas Taplin Cooke, the second in the
line of this vast family, was at this time the proprietor. He is said to have had
19 children, and 40 members of his family were in the troupe. With profits
from performances in Portugal he had erected amphitheatres in many of
the northern cities and these soon became rivals of the theatres. At the
Theatre he produced Moncrieff's melodrama *The Cataract of the Ganges* with
scenery by Phillips and W. Remington, machinery by Seagrave, processions

directed by Frimbley. A troop of native cavalry and a car drawn by six horses took part in the bridal procession. For his benefit he gave Planché's equestrian melodrama *Cortez*.[113] In the company was Dicky Usher[114] who, with his wife and children, joined the stock company in August. Usher was the best clown that had ever appeared on the York stage. He had made his name at the Liverpool Amphitheatre in 1809 and afterwards became the great favourite at Astley's, being known as the John Kemble of his art. His jokes were full of originality and point and never coarse. He directed a new pantomime *The Poet's Last Shilling*, and his own *Pinder of Wakefield*; *or Harlequin in Yorkshire*, and *Love, Hope and Poverty* in all of which he played Clown. The scenery for the second was by Hilyard from Edinburgh and W. Remington, the final scene being described as a 'Fairy Palace – All Gay and Happy'. Usher gave whimsical imitations of Chinese and Indian jugglers, whilst his daughters, one of whom was a tightrope walker, represented Tyrolean peasants on stilts 6 feet high. His wife, a sister of James Wallack, performed in melodrama and pantomime.

Other visitors in August were Samuel Butler, the tragedian, who played Sir Edward Mortimer; Mrs. Bailey a former member of the company; Faulkner from Edinburgh, soon to be manager, who made his first appearance as Antonio in *The Merchant of Venice*; J. Russell and Miss Goward. Russell now fancied himself as a tragedian and chose to act, like many comedians before and since, in a series of characters including Shylock and Richard III for which he was utterly unsuited. More important was Mary Anne Goward later to become famous as Mrs. Keeley. Born in 1805 she was trained for seven years with Mrs. Smart and had made her first appearance on the stage the previous year in Dublin. She sang at the York concerts and had a soprano voice remarkable for its purity as well as for its range. As yet unknown, she sang Laura in *Sweethearts and Wives*, Lucy Bertram, Polly to the Macheath of Charles Bland, and for her benefit played Victoria at the opening of Croly's new comedy with songs *Pride Shall Have a Fall*, followed by Margaretta in *No Song No Supper*. She was as fine a comedy actress as a singer.

In October Mansel[115] was on his way to London to see *Der Freischütz* which he intended to bring out at his theatres. Riding on the outside of the coach on a cold day he felt ill and was obliged to quit the coach at Wansford. The next morning, October 16, he was found dying of an apoplectic fit at the Haycock Inn and the surgeon, who lived four miles away, arrived too late. He was buried at Wansford on October 19. He was about 49 years of age[116] and bore a high character as an affectionate husband, warm friend and kind master. The cause of the drama he had defended in pamphlets and had attempted to revive on the stage. As a manager he was active and spared neither pains nor expense to make the theatre worthy of patronage. His fault was that he was over confident in his own judgment. As an actor 'he was one of the best representatives of those characters in light, genteel comedy ... in the Doricourts, Gossamers, Tangents &c. of the drama, Mr. Mansel was excelled by very few performers of the present day; and his

Young Dornton was a fine performance characterized by good feeling, and admirably conceived. On and off the stage he was the perfect gentleman.' At York he had made the greatest improvements in the Theatre since Tate Wilkinson's day. He left the following lines scratched on the glass of the Green Room which may serve as his epitaph:

The rich man's name embellish'd stands on brass;[117]
The actor simply scribbles his on glass,
Appropriate emblem of his wayward fate,
A brittle, shining, evanescent state:
The rich man's *brass* consum'd, farewell his fame;
The poor man's glass consum'd, farewell his name.

Figure 1. Portrait of Tate Wilkinson.

Figure 2. John Langford Pritchard as Rob Roy.

Figure 3. John Wilkinson as Simkin.

Figure 4. Mrs. Inchbald as the Abbess in *The Comedy of Errors*.

Figure 5. Mrs. Jordan as Nell in *The Devil to Pay*.

Figure 6. Samuel Phelps as Macbeth.

Figure 7. Henry Compton as Launce in *The Two Gentlemen of Verona*.

Figure 8. (a) Exterior of the Theatre Royal, York, c.1870.

(b) Exterior of the Theatre Royal, York, 2000.

CHAPTER SIX

From Downe to Pritchard
1825–1850

MANSEL'S lease was not due to expire until July 1828. A Joseph Mallinson from Bath, who had York connections, wrote to the attorneys, Messrs. Brook and Bulmer, to inquire about the disposal of the circuit. He wished to know if the trustees to Wilkinson included all the theatres as well as the scenery, books, music and wardrobe.[1] He was unsuccessful since the remainder of the lease and the management of the circuit were taken over by two actors in the company, Thomas James Downe and Samuel Faulkner. This was the first time that the York Theatre had been run by a partnership, and a short lived and uneasy one it was to prove. Faulkner[2] had had previous managerial experience in a Sunderland circuit with Anderson. Unknown to Downe he had contracted considerable debts in connection with the Sunderland Theatre and he was also involved in a Chancery suit respecting a bond of his father's. He was a widower, his wife having died in Edinburgh a year previously, leaving two sons and three daughters, the youngest of whom was about 3 at this time. Faulkner had already had one mental breakdown and his father had died in an asylum at Gateshead. The new managers promised a strict adherence to the legitimate drama, the production in rapid succession of favourite new pieces (a contradiction in itself) and unremitting attention to the blending of morality and amusement.[3] They made a popular move by reducing the price of admission to the 2nd circle of boxes except in public weeks. The charges were now listed as dress boxes (the first time this term was used) 4/-, half price 2/-; 2nd circle 3/-, half price 1/6; pit 2/-, half price 1/-; gallery 1/-. During public weeks all boxes were 4/-, half price 2/6, and the pit was 2/6, half price 1/6. Since the pit had a separate entrance, a pit treasurer named Dixon had been appointed.

One alteration in the Theatre was made by the Corporation early in 1825: the old wardrobe was pulled down, the floor lowered, and a new wardrobe room constructed at a cost of £19.11.6.[4]

A number of fresh actors and actresses were engaged, including Butler and Miss Rock from Edinburgh, H. Knight, the son of Little Knight, who appeared as Sam Sharpset, and Miss H. Lacy a dancer. Parnell from Drury Lane was the new leader of the band and musical director and Hilyard continued as scene painter with the assistance of W. Remington. Miss Goward sang and acted with the company during the spring season taking such parts as Linda in *Der Freischütz*, Norah in *The Poor Soldier* and Little Pickle. Her benefit under the patronage of the 6th Inniskilling Dragoons attracted a numerous and elegant audience.

The new management opened on March 12 and on March 19 brought out *Der Freischütz* with augmented orchestra and chorus; London artists collaborated with Yarnold in devising the monsters and properties. The opera was given five performances during the season. Dimond and Bishop's opera *My Native Land* was also produced this year for Parnell's benefit on May 5. Tom Moore's *Lalla Rookh* had made a sensation in 1817 and at Faulkner's benefit, a melodrama *Hafed the Gheber* based on the Fire Worshippers in that poem was seen for the first time in York. The *York Herald*[5] pronounced that the dialogue fell miserably short of the original but that the piece was got up 'with as much splendour and effect as could be expected in the confined space allowed for machinery, &c. in our Theatres.' On the same occasion Lewis's comic opera *Rich and Poor* was brought out. Miss Rock's Zorayda was praised for its transitions from the lively to the tender and the pathetic, and as being free from 'constrained effort, whining cant, or the ravings which are calculated to disgust rather than to affect.' Faulkner as her father depicted the struggle between parental tenderness and the sternness of an insulted and wounded man with impressive dignity. Yet the theatre was far from full. Wilkinson, however, had what was now known as a bumper benefit bringing £108.15.0,[6] with Planché's version of Rowley's old comedy *A Woman Never Vext*. On March 22 Sheridan Knowles's tragedy *The Fatal Dowry* was first given. The new pantomime *Harlequin's Tomb; or The Golden Key* included a view of the new Ouse Bridge with the toll house, a good scenic effect, whilst the tricks with one trifling exception were cleverly managed. The newspapers, whilst praising the performers and the decorative effects during the season, direct the managers' attention to the bad behaviour of the gods who threw things on the audience below. *Macbeth* was given on May 18 with Calvert as Macbeth and Miss Davies as Lady Macbeth.

Mrs. Macnamara from Edinburgh joined the company in July opening as Mrs. Malaprop. She was particularly good in the old women and remained until 1834. Calvert returned after a year's absence in Dublin. He played Knowles's William Tell to the Emma of Miss Phillips, a newcomer from Norwich. The *York Herald*[7] commented on his ripened performance and on her sound acting. *The Bride of Lammermoor* was the new addition to the long roll of Scott adaptations. *Romeo and Juliet* was given with Calvert as Romeo and Mrs. Pindar, a newcomer, as Juliet. The managers opened the Theatre for the Music Festival in September but it was only thinly attended.

On October 22, the *York Herald* had a paragraph stating that widowed Mrs. Bailey, formerly of the Theatre, had received upwards of £20 from her friends in York.

Whilst in Hull Downe and Faulkner had a disagreement and by the time the company reached York in 1826, Faulkner, overburdened with financial worry, showed signs in conversation and conduct of a deranged intellect. He became rapidly worse and on March 31 attempted to hang himself. The following day his friends watched over him until the afternoon when they thought he was asleep, but later that night he drowned himself in the Ouse. The verdict was of temporary insanity and he was buried in St. Mary's Castlegate on April 5[8] in the 50th year of his age. Downe took his family under his care and promised to hand over to them their share of the emoluments. On April 18 he held a benefit for them for which the receipts were £108.14.6; the pieces played were the appropriate ones of *Every One Has His Fault* and *The Adopted Child*[9] and the playbill for the night was black bordered. On May 25 Downe gave a benefit for the distressed manufacturers.[10]

Once again several new engagements were made for the 1826 season. They included Miss Melvin from Bath who opened as Belvidera, Miss M. Nicol from Edinburgh, Miss Davies from Newcastle, Ivers a new leader of the band from Newcastle, and Jackson a ballet master. Under the direction of the last a series of ballets were put on, in one or two of which a new scene was used of the gardens of Tivoli brilliantly illuminated. Dearlove had replaced Hilyard as scene painter and Yarnold was now designated not only machinist but decorator and artist in fireworks. Perhaps the most elaborate production was that of Soane and Terry's romantic drama *Faustus* which came out on May 1 having been in preparation the whole of the season. The overture was by Weber, other music by Bishop, Horn and T. Cooke, the scenery by Dearlove and W. Remington. Weber was also responsible for the music of Dimond's comic opera *Abon Hassan*, brought out in July. Poole's *Paul Pry* came out at Wilkinson's benefit on April 4 and brought a receipt of £92.[11] Scott was represented by *The Talisman* as well as by revivals of *Ivanhoe* and *The Heart of Midlothian;* Shakespeare by *Romeo and Juliet* with Miss Davies as Juliet; *Macbeth* with Calvert as Macbeth and Miss Davies as Lady Macbeth; *Othello* with Calvert as the Moor and Miss Davies as Desdemona and *As You Like It*. On July 27 Frederick Yates, for one night only, gave his *Reminiscences* with all the original scenes, wonderful changes and apparatus as in London, Edinburgh, Glasgow and Newcastle, and was rewarded by a house in which the lower boxes were well occupied by 'some of the most respectable inhabitants of the city' and a full pit. Yates excelled in eccentric parts so that it was said of him 'Give Mr. Yates an excrescence of nature and he is at home.'[12] In August Rayner returned as star and at his benefit played Rolamo in Howard Payne's *Clari, The Maid of Milan* with music by Bishop. This melodrama has a claim to fame since in it was first heard the song *Home Sweet Home*.

On December 19 a link with the palmy days of the Theatre was snapped by the death of Jane Wilkinson, Tate's widow.

When the company returned in 1827 a young man of twenty-two, who had joined it at Wakefield the previous August, was playing minor rôles for 18/- a week.[13] He was Samuel Phelps whose first professional engagement it was. We do not know in what rôle he made his first appearance in York as the playbills for 1827 are not complete, and we first find him as Lothair in *The Miller and his Men* on May 18. Though he remained with the company until 1829 his genius passed unrecognised and he never rose beyond the status of an under actor. He, however, modelled his own Sir Anthony Absolute and Old Dornton on those of Downe who, he declared, was the best actor in old men he ever saw. Three stars were engaged by Downe during the spring season. First came Charles Kemble for three nights, playing Hamlet to the Ophelia of Mrs. T. Hill, Charles Surface, Octavian, Lord Townly and Charles II in Howard Payne's comedy. He was followed by Sapio the tenor from Covent Garden who had started as a concert and oratorio singer, but had commenced a dramatic career in 1824. He had a love for bravura and was a good rather than a great singer.[14] He sang Prince Orlando in *The Cabinet*, Seraskier in *The Siege of Belgrade*, Harry Bertram and the Grand Scena from Weber's new opera *Oberon*. Lastly charming Maria Foote, later to become Countess of Harrington, appeared in some of her best characters: Letitia Hardy, Rosalind, Variella, and, for her benefit, under the patronage of the officers of the Yorks Hussars, Violante and Maria Darlington.

The most elaborate production seems to have been that of Fitzball's *Flying Dutchman* in which Dearlove and Remington were assisted with the scenery by Morris of Drury Lane. Miss Mitford's tragedy *The Foscari* was given its first performance on May 11, and, at his benefit, Calvert played Oreste in a scene in French from Racine's *Andromaque* in imitation of Talma. A benefit was again given for Faulkner's orphans.

Downe provided several attractions for the public weeks' season and in spite of the rivalry of the puppet Théâtre du Petit Lazary, the Panorama, and the Circus, succeeded in obtaining better audiences than of late.[15] Two old timers made their appearance. Harley now at Drury Lane returned after an absence of 10 years on July 31 as Acres and as John Brown in the farce of that name, a part he had originally created. In many of the rôles he played he had not been seen in York. Among these were Barnaby Brilliant in *White Lies*, Popolino in *The Sleeping Draught*, Zabouc in *Abon Hassan*, Fogrum in *The Slave*, Dominie Sampson, Matty Marvellous in *The Miller's Maid*, and Gabriel in *My Uncle Gabriel*. Rayner joined him in August and sustained Sam Sharpset the Yorkshireman with the genuine bluntness of a native, as well as Giles in *The Miller's Maid*, one of the few characters in which he surpassed Emery, and Andrew in *Love, Law and Physic*.

When Downe re-opened at York in 1828 he brought five new actors and seven new actresses. The company was no longer the stable one it used to be and changes are bewilderingly frequent. The major provincial companies no longer held such important positions in the acting world and the minor theatres in London were rival absorbers of talent. Bill Anderton was a new leading man from Liverpool and Miss Burrell from Bath specialised in breeches parts and made a great hit in her original rôle as the hero of *Giovanni in London*. Phelps was used a great deal in minor parts and played nearly 40 different ones during 1828 in melodrama, comedy and comic opera. But Anderton had the leads and Phelps was only given one really good chance. This was when Downe was taken ill on the night of a members' bespeak for which a big house had assembled. Phelps was called in to take the rôle of Peter Simpson in *Simpson and Co.* at a moment's notice, without more rehearsal than running through his lines in the green room. Luckily he had seen Terry play it at Covent Garden and he astonished everyone by his performance, so that Anderton thereafter christened him Peter a nickname by which he became known in the company. Phelps told Coleman in later years that Downe gave him 'a lot of bitter bad parts. I kicked at them and got kicked out in consequence', and so did not go with the company to Leeds. This cannot be correct for Downe retired at the end of the season and Phelps was still in the company in 1829.

Emma Love from Covent Garden and Drury Lane was engaged for five nights in a number of singing characters including *Giovanni in London*, in which she introduced popular airs, and *The King of the Shamrock, the Thistle and the Rose* especially composed for her by Bishop, and Vespina which she had created and which showed all her powers and her faults. 'What an exquisite creature she appears, as she skims across the stage; for she neither walks nor runs.[16] What a lovely piece of vanity is she, as she gazes at her own pretty features in the glass' exclaims Oxberry of her in this rôle. Indeed she was one of the most delightful actresses on the stage.

Mrs. Glover returned in May. She was now nearing 50 but was still one of the great comic actresses of her time. She played Mrs. Simpson in Poole's *Simpson and Company*, one of her most successful parts, and Mrs. Dingle in Lacy's *Love and Reason* which was a comedy new to York this year and the first of a series of adaptations from the plays of the prolific Scribe to be seen there. She also appeared in old tried favourites such as Mrs. Oakley, Mrs. Malaprop, Elvira in *The Duenna* and Agatha in *Lovers' Vows*. She was supported by her daughter who had made her first appearance at Drury Lane four years previously. At their benefit on May 9 her eldest son Edmund made his début on any stage as Fred in *Lovers' Vows*. He developed into a sound actor, a talented pantomimist and artist, and was to become manager of the Glasgow Theatre.

Buckstone's melodrama *Luke the Labourer,* with Cooke as Luke, was the most celebrated novelty to be seen this season. The scenery, dresses and machinery for *Peter Wilkins* were under the direction of T. Grieve. Shakespeare was quite well represented with *As You Like It*, with Cooke as Orlando and Miss Love as Rosalind, *Lear* with Calvert as Lear and Miss Davies as Cordelia, and *Othello* with Anderton as Iago. Other items of interest were the presentation of a masquerade and fancy dress ball for which the stage was fitted up with oriental and Grecian lamps and ornamented with festoons of flowers to resemble Vauxhall on gala nights; and a benefit for the fund in aid of the sufferers at the ill-fated Brunswick Theatre which had collapsed three days after its opening in February.

In May William Leman Rede joined the company. He was then 26 and had already had one piece performed at the Coburg. He was later to write a long series of burlettas, burlesques and melodramas for the London minors. He opened on May 1 as Lord Trinket in *The Jealous Wife* and played such light comedy parts as Capt. Absolute, Ollapod and Sim in *Wild Oats*. He remained two years with the company at a time when his future collaborator at the Strand, W. J. Hammond, had quitted it temporarily. Downe's lease expired in July and in June he gave a short farewell season at which he engaged Miss Foote. She played Lady Teazle to his Sir Peter, Violante, Clari, Lady Julia in *Personation,* and Letitia Hardy and Maria Darlington to Downe's Hardy and Sir Mark Chase at his last appearance on June 27. His management of the circuit ended on June 30.

The head lease also expired, but in March John Wilkinson[17] had enquired the terms on which it might be renewed for 14 years. He pointed out that he had interests in the Hull, Leeds and Wakefield Theatres and wished to keep the circuit together. A committee appointed to consider his application finally granted a lease of 7 years at an annual rent of £200. A letter is extant from John Brook asking the Corporation to forego their condition for a security as under the circumstances Wilkinson would find it painful to apply to a friend. The terms of the lease laid down that the theatrical season was to commence on or before the first Monday in March and was to continue until the end of the last week in May, and that the theatre was also to be open during the midsummer Assizes and the August Race Week. Except that the Corporation was responsible for the roof, main walls and timber, the lease was a repairing one. An interesting list of scenery and properties belonging to the Theatre was probably made about this time.[18]

The circuit was let by the trustees for Wilkinson and his creditors to Charles Cummins. Cummins was a musician, not an actor, the first manager who did not himself perform. He opened in York with what was largely a new company on July 21. His unremitting efforts, according to the *York Chronicle,*[19] resulted in increased attraction to the Theatre. Expense was not limited to the production of new pieces but *The Turnpike* had a beautiful new opening scene and *The Siege of Belgrade* a new scene by Wilton from the King's Theatre and fresh dresses by Mr. and Mrs. King. The newspaper claimed that the operatic department was unrivalled in any other theatre in the kingdom and commended the regularity of performances, subdual of nuisances and the early hour of termination since the curtain fell before 11 p.m. We must, however, bear in mind that new managements were generally thus hailed and only when a fresh one came along was the old decried or, perhaps, the truth told about it. Such statements then can be taken with a grain of salt.

In November the Theatre was let for several nights to Philipsthal for his *Mechanical and Optical Museum.* This entertainment included views of places and events, a ballet, automata, rope dancers, hydraulic and hydrostatic experiments and fireworks, a mixture of the spectacular and the educational then coming into vogue.

Phelps had quit the company when it reopened in 1829 but W. L. Rede was still a member and wrote the Easter pantomime *Harlequin Harpooner; or The Demon of the North Pole* in which he played Clown. W. Remington and Dearlove painted new local and incidental scenery from drawings specially made for it; the tricks and properties were by Mr. and Mrs. T. King, the machinery by Bailes, dresses by Percival and his assistants, the overture by Ivers and the vocal and pantomime music selected and adapted by Cummins.

Cummins also provided new instrumental accompaniment for *The Padlock* and wrote and composed a vocal extravaganza for Baker which he sang for his benefit at the Theatre.

Baker, who had joined the company from Bristol when Cummins took over, was highly praised for his physical attributes, skill and versatility by the *York Chronicle*.[20] His Falstaff, Nicol Jarvie and Ogleby were particularly commended. Miss Cleaver from Sheffield , who opened as Penelope in *The Merchant's Wedding*, was a new leading lady and was said to be of handsome figure and prepossessing countenance. The management was acclaimed as improving the wardrobe and decorations, and getting up new pieces in splendour unprecedented. Certainly Cummins provided many novelties – at least 14 in the spring season alone of which 5 were melodramas, 3 comedies and 2 tragedies. The tragedies were Walker's *Caswallon* and Miss Mitford's *Rienzi*, the latter of which was rather spoilt because the performer of the hero was only 5 foot tall. Scott was represented by *Peveril of the Peak* and Murray's *Mary, Queen of Scots* founded on part of *The Abbot*. There were two pieces by Planché, *The Merchant's Wedding* and *The Green Eyed Monster*. Most popular of all was Morton's operatic farce *The Invincibles* with new scenery by Wilton which received an ovation and had no less than six performances.[21] It was a good season for Shakespeare. *The Merry Wives of Windsor* was revived at Wilkinson's benefit after 24 years, probably in Reynolds's version since it was interspersed with music. Baker was Falstaff, Rede Slender, Calvert Ford, Anderton Pistol, Miss Cleaver Mrs. Ford, Miss Angell Mrs. Page, Miss Burrell Ann Page and Mrs. Macnamara Mrs. Quickly. Other plays were *Othello* with Mrs. Baker as Desdemona; *Much Ado* with Benedick = Garton, Beatrice = Miss Cleaver, Dogberry = Baker; *The Merchant of Venice* with Shylock = Calvert, Portia = Mrs. Fisher; *The Tempest* with Prospero = Calvert, Ferdinand = Garton, Miranda = Mrs. Baker, and *Macbeth* twice. *Macbeth* was treated to new dresses by Percival, decorations by the Kings and new instrumental accompaniment to Locke's music by Cummins; a whole chorus of sopranos and basses rendered the music of the singing witches.

On May 12 Calvert took his farewell benefit after 10 years, almost the whole of his theatrical career, in the circuit. In his address[22] he told how he had started with no fixed engagement but was to stand or fall by the opinion of the public; how his crude and boyish efforts were well received and how 'by their deliberate fiat' he was eventually placed in his present situation. He paid a tribute to Mansel 'a worthy and noble minded individual' who had foretold that a leading position would reward his efforts. 'The whole circuit' he concluded 'has been to me only a species of more diffusive and extended home.' The piece he chose for his exit was *Virginius* and he was patronised by a brilliant box audience. He left to become a lecturer on the works of the poets. Stuart from Bath was engaged to take his place and made his début in York on July 28 as Cola de Rienzi. He was very correct in his text and gave unceasing attention to the business of the scene but he occasionally strained after effect by a contortion of his features.[23] The musical side was strengthened by another newcomer from Bath, G. Horncastle, a singer said to be the cleverest performer in his line. His voice was not of the first quality but had uncommon flexibility; he was a good musician and had a correct verbal and musical delivery.

Cummins made great efforts to attract by elaborate new productions. Rossini's *Barber of Seville,* with the original overture and additional music never yet performed on the English stage, was presented on July 27 with Almaviva = Maitland, Figaro = Horncastle, Marcellina = Miss Horncastle, Rosina = Mrs. Cummins, Bartolo = Baker. It had been a great success in Leeds and was acclaimed the most finished performance out of London. Horncastle received a unanimous encore for one song (we may guess that it was *Largo al Factotum*) and Baker's performance was pronounced masterly.[24] It was repeated three times. *John of Paris* was revived in a production more splendid than the original with the whole of Boieldieu's music which had not been heard before. Yet in spite of his efforts Cummins failed to draw audiences. The critics were unable to account for the apathy and fell back on the explanation of depressed conditions and the comfort that Manchester and Liverpool audiences were even thinner. The unrest and uncertainty induced by the beginnings of the industrial revolution were undoubtedly contributory causes to the theatre's decline all over the country. Many others have been cited, among them the poor quality of the drama produced; the rivalry of other spectacular entertainments such as circuses (Ducrow opened an amphitheatre at York in October); the expenses of the prevalent star system; the insatiable rage for melodrama and the growing one for opera, both costly, and the coming in of later dining hours. Whatever may have been the reason Cummins was unable to pay his rent, and in January, 1830, the trustees released him from his contract as tenant.[25] On December 17, 1829, the *York Chronicle* bore the following advertisement: 'The Yorkshire Circuit of Theatres, Comprising the Theatres-Royal of York and Hull, and the Theatres of Leeds, Wakefield and Doncaster, To be let, by Proposal, At the Kingston Hotel, in the Town of Kingston upon Hull, on Wednesday the 20th day of January next, at Twelve o'Clock at Noon, (Unless a Tenant shall be contracted with previous to the 13th of the same Month, in which case notice will be given). The Theatres Royal at York and Hull, and the Theatre at Leeds, from the First Day of March next, for Five years; the Theatre at Wakefield for the same period, if the Owner of it shall live so long; and the Theatre at Doncaster from Year to Year.' Proposals were to be sent to the solicitors, Messrs. Brook and Bulmer, who had printed particulars of terms.

No tenant was found.[26] Meanwhile in January, 1830, the child prodigy Master Joseph Burke, then about eleven, performed for a few nights, 'at the particular request' of friends, and patrons of the drama as well as musical amateurs were invited to witness and judge 'the extraordinary talents of this highly gifted child', whose fiddling was even better than his acting. He opened as Richard III in a selection of scenes from that play, sustained six characters in a farce called *The March of Intellect,* performed a concerto by de Bériot and led the orchestra in Bishop's overture to *Guy Mannering* 'thus displaying the united Talents of the Tragedian, Comedian, Dancer and Musician.' For this exhibition the house was pretty well attended and the prodigy drew repeated plaudits for his Richard. The York critics,[27] who had kept their reason about Master Betty, fell for this child whose acting they said was not the result of schooling but that of one who formed his own opinion of his parts from an acquaintance with the human mind far beyond his years. He was delightfully free from conceit and oblivious of applause. Other parts he essayed were Tristram Fickle, Sir Callaghan O'Brallaghan, Young Norval and Terry O'Rourke in *The Irish Tutor.* In this last 'his audacity and humour, his wig, his littleness, his laugh and his Irish accent, kept the audience in a roar of laughter.' Moncrieff had specially written for him a farce *Home for the Holidays* in which he again assumed a number of different characters. Where Cummins had failed he succeeded in drawing the town. Children and schools were admitted to the boxes and pit at half price. It was even rumoured that his father had taken the theatres in the circuit though he does not seem to have gone beyond an offer.[28]

It was Samuel Butler who reopened the Theatre on March 20 for a limited period. He had been manager of the Richmond circuit in succession to his father, but this had now broken up and he was managing the Sheffield Theatre. With him came Phelps and his wife, Butler's sister Mrs. Percy, a child Rosalind Telbin, sister of the great scene painter who later acted at the Haymarket and in the U.S.A., and a few of the old timers like W. Remington, Dearlove, Miss Angell and Mrs. Macnamara. Charles Cummins had been engaged as leader of the band at the Caledonian Theatre in Edinburgh and had taken with him Baker, Miss Horncastle and W. L. Rede as stage manager.[29]

Butler was 6 foot 4 inches in height which rather militated against his success in a small theatre. He was a tragedian of great fire who abandoned himself to passion and was gifted with a powerful voice.[30] Westland Marston was more carried away by him in Shylock than by any other actor and tells us that he would arouse masses to enthusiasm. As a man he was of unstable temper and his hauteur made him rather feared than loved. In York he played Shylock as well as Richard III and one of his other best parts Coriolanus, and he acted a series of leads in current melodramas such as Luke the Labourer, Will Watch, Wallace and Massaroni as well as Cato and

William Tell and in comedy Lord Townly. He also spoke a *Defence of the Acted Drama*. Phelps was now playing second leads such as Richmond and Bassanio as well as some chief rôles in melodrama; he again appeared in a wide variety of parts.[31] The company's talents were praised by the newspapers particularly those of Butler, Mrs. Percy and Miss Angell. Great attention was paid to the scenic department and more novelties than ever were presented; among them one must mention Jerrold's famous nautical melodrama *Black Ey'd Susan* with Butler as William and Phelps as Crostree. By arrangement with the trustees Butler carried on over the May Races for which he engaged Liston. He raised the upper boxes from 3/- to 4/ for this visit and the house was fairly well attended. Liston played Paul Fry and Neddy Bray, both admirable comic portraits. He was not as good in Bill Lackaday but his Lubin Log was a unique representation of a foolish, purse-proud cockney. Sometimes his voice failed him, for he had lost some of his teeth, but one forgot his occasional indistinctness in the richness of his humour which caused his audience to laugh both with and at him.[32] His features were more expressive of comic humour than any others and 'as care cannot sit in company with his laughter-moving countenance, we doubt not but the citizens of York will, for the time forget taxation and parish regulation bills.'[33] His other rôles were Mawworm, Adam Brock in *Charles XII*, Tony Lumpkin and Gillman in *The Happiest Day of My Life*. Village feasts in May were among the reasons given for empty benches. Butler closed his season on May 21 a serious loser. He was succeeded by William John Hammond who at first took the Theatre for the public weeks. He brought with him a new company including Miss Penley who had not acted in York for five years and Miss Mayoss from Norwich. He did not promise, as some of his predecessors, to revive the legitimate drama but frankly declared that he would endeavour to procure the latest and most popular novelties of the day. He opened on July 26 with an address as Paul Pry and one of the novelties in the shape of *The Englishman in India*. A new scene painter R. Donaldson from Drury Lane and Covent Garden painted scenery for Somerset's *Shakespeare's Early Days* which included a dioramic view of Stratford. This was the first time that we hear of a diorama or moving scene being employed at York though in the coming years they were to be plentiful enough. The machinery was by Breckell, the dresses by Miss Smith, the music selected and arranged by Aldridge from Liverpool. On July 30 the public was informed that the election militated so greatly against attendance at the theatre that the management was compelled to suspend performances until the conclusion of the contest. It reopened on August 2 and closed again on August 7 with a benefit for Hammond at which Jerrold's *Press Gang* was brought out. The music was composed and se-lected by Ivers and the last scene by Donaldson exhibited 'a View of the Larboard Quarter of H.M.S. Trident. With the appalling Preparations for the Punishment of the Pressed Man Through the Fleet'. Thus were the audience's jaded tastes titillated by a promise of horrors, as they have been down the ages.

A notable engagement at the end of August was that of Madame Vestris who trod the York stage for the first time on August 26 as Kate O'Brien in *Perfection* and Justine in *Rencontre.* Like so many singing actresses she introduced additional songs into most of the pieces in which she played for she had a lovely voice. She acted Phoebe in *Paul Pry,* Apollo in *Midas,* Laura in *Sweethearts and Wives,* and Elizabeth in a new farce *Sublime and Beautiful.*

In September, Frederick Yates, for some years co-manager of the Adelphi, paid his second visit to York in an entertainment of songs and imitations and a 'monopologue' entitled *Stop Thief.* He was followed in October by Andrew Ducrow of circus fame. He stopped for four nights on his way to Scotland, whither his equestrian company had preceded him, and presented, for the first time out of London, his *Poses Plastiques* which he brought from Paris and which had created a furore at Astley's. He called the entertainment a 'New Classical, Historical, and Mythological Entertainment Raphael's Dream', and it seems to have consisted of a procession of Greek and Italian statues posed by Ducrow and tableaux of pictures in a setting of dialogue by Somerset with a musical chorus of the arts by Callcott. It opened in Raphael's study with Johnston as Raphael.[34] The picture gallery scene and the dioramic views that accompanied the statues were by Danson and Phillips, scenic artists from the London theatres; they were illuminated on a new principle and had been conveyed from London at great cost. Ducrow delineated figures such as Mercury and Apollo, the athletic Hercules and Sampson, and the grotesque Pan: 'the astonishing precision with which Mr. Ducrow, at once took the attitude of the statue he illustrated, with the firmness and boldness with which it was preserved' was highly approved. The tableaux concluded with an equestrian group representing Ducrow surrounded by the attributes of his profession and supported by his faithful steed. Then after a gymnastic interlude by the posture master von Marchenburg, the entertainment ended with a harlequinade for juveniles by the three Ridgway brothers. This curious form of exhibition, which Ducrow thus inaugurated, drew crowded houses and continued to be popular in the theatre for many years.

A description of the Theatre Royal in 1830 tells us that it was lighted by gas and that 'The fronts of the Dress Boxes are panelled in pink draperies defined in gold braiding, and in the centre is a superb antique silver Rose the distinguishing badge of the "House of York." The seats are covered in crimson cloth. The galleries are also panelled in pink, with the antique silver Rose, and the Lotus on burnished gold, alternately.'[35]

Edmund Kean acted for three nights in January, 1831, playing Shylock, Richard III and Overreach. His powers were on the wane and, though he had the same expression of countenance and a just conception of character, his voice was not so strong as it had been on his previous visit. His first house was but thin, his other two tolerably well filled;[36] it was his last appearance in York.

When Hammond reopened on March 21 the Theatre had undergone a complete renovation and was elegantly painted and decorated by Donaldson the company's scenic artist.[37]

Samuel Butler was in the company; he played Rolla and Faulkland and, at his benefit, gave a selection of acts from *Hamlet*, *As You Like It*, *Lear*, *Macbeth* and *Coriolanus*. W. H. Oxberry, stepson of Leman Rede, had been engaged and opened as Cocklet in *The Bold Dragoons*. His first professional experience had been at the Olympic and for a while he had given up the stage and worked for Leigh Hunt on the *Examiner*. He was a small man but a lively actor and dancer in burlesque. His farce *The Actress of All Work* had already been seen in York and he was the author of several other burlettas and burlesques. He only stayed with the company a year. The dancers and pantomimists the Ridgway brothers were with Hammond this season and produced a series of ballets and pantomimes. In one of these, *Harlequin Pedlar*, a quadrille by six musical horses and a moving diorama of the Manchester-Liverpool railroad by Donaldson were introduced. The latter was painted on 3000 yards of canvas and comprised all the localities and prominent objects to be seen on the journey, taken from views by artists on the spot. The recent invention thus celebrated was to spell the doom of the stock company though this result was as yet undreamed of. Ironically the second great factor in its doom, the growth in popularity of opera, was also represented this season by the production of Auber's *Masaniello*. Charles Bland from Covent Garden and Hart from Edinburgh were specially engaged, for the company was not strong enough to sustain such a piece. Bland was Masaniello, Hart Pietro, Miss Penley Fenella and Miss Mayoss Elvira. Trophies, banners and censers were by artists from the metropolis and the final eruption of Mount Vesuvius was arranged on a novel principle which showed the various stages in the appearance of the mountain. The influence of the tableaux set a fashion for scenery taken from pictures. Thus three scenes in *Massaroni* were from mezzotints after Eastlake. Indeed Donaldson was kept busy in the scenic department with the assistance of Dearlove and Nelson, with Breckell as machinist.

Downe came to play for five nights. After him came the great nautical actor T. P. Cooke, who opened on April 18, for the first time in York, in his most famous part that of William in *Black Ey'd Susan* in which he had appeared for over 200 nights at the Surrey; in the afterpiece *Mons. Tonson* he played Mons. Morbleu. He then appeared in Peake's *The Fate of Franken-stein*, as Philip in *Luke the Labourer*, Jack Sykes in Fitzball's burletta *Nelson*, in which he introduced a rowing hornpipe and sang a long yarn of a sea serpent, Arthur Bright in *The Press Gang*, and Long Tom Coffin in *The Pilot*. At his benefit he presented *Lo Studio*, which had been written for him and in which he portrayed by recitation and action the living forms of antique sculpture. The diorama and the poses plastiques had come to stay.

During the July season Miss Byfield from Drury Lane, J. F. Williamson from the Haymarket and Reynoldson, musical director of the Edinburgh Theatre Royal, were engaged to sing in a series of operas and comic operas.

They opened in *The Barber of Seville* followed by *The Marriage of Figaro.* Though acclaimed as a treat for the admirers of music the houses were only thinly attended.[38] In August Miss Phillips from Drury Lane appeared in a series of comedy and tragedy rôles. She was particularly successful as Mrs. Haller and as Violante but her depth of feeling and fine intonation fitted her for tragedy rather than for comedy.

In November Mathews drew crowded audiences to his one man *At Home.* Many people were unable to obtain places and a second performance was given. This veteran was as vigorous as ever, kept the house in roars of laughter, and took his leave to thunders of applause.[39]

John Wilkinson applied for a reduction of his rent.[40] He pointed out that since Cummins's failure the trustees had been unable to continue the allowance of £150 a year which his creditors had agreed should be allowed him. Hammond had only taken the Theatre at a materially reduced rent and had made it a condition that Wilkinson should no longer have a benefit at Leeds. Recently Hammond had given notice that he would not continue as tenant unless a further considerable reduction of rent was made and this the trustees had been forced to accede to. Wilkinson further pleaded the depreciation of theatrical property in most parts of the country and, particularly in York, where alterations made in Assize and Race Week arrangements had diminished the receipts at the most financially rewarding seasons. A reduction to £150 and then to £160 was proposed but in both cases was turned down by the Commons.

The company that returned to York in 1832 was practically a new one. Mude was the leading man and Mrs. Cramer, formerly Miss M. C. Poole of Brighton, the leading lady. They played King Lear and Cordelia. Mr. and Mrs. Joseph Wood,[41] the vocalists, were engaged for 4 nights in May and filled the chief rôles in a series of popular melodramas and comic operas. Jerrold's famous drama *The Rent Day* was brought out at Hammond's benefit with new scenery by Donaldson, on April 10. It was one of the first plays with a social purpose and realised the subjects of popular engravings after Wilkie. Another famous drama, Buckstone's *Victorine,* made its début this season as did Moncrieff's *Eugene Aram* with Mude in the title rôle. The Theatre closed on June 1. Later in the month Yates paid his third visit to York, this time with his wife, formerly Elizabeth Brunton of Norwich. Their last performance was patronised by the officers of the Royal Horse Artillery and 8th Hussars. The long programme consisted of *The Wedding Day* with Yates as Lord Rakeland and Mrs. Yates as Lady Contest, *The Young Widow* with Yates as Splash and Mrs. Yates as Aurelia, and Yates's monopologue and imitations.

On August 28 Knowles's successful drama *The Hunchback* was first seen in York with the following cast; Master Walter = Mude, Clifford = Preston, Wilford = J. F. Williamson, Fathom = Hammond, Julie = Miss Hilton, Helen = Miss Rae. On September 7 Hammond took his farewell benefit as Lissardo in *The Wonder* followed by his monologue *Bachelor's Torments.* His management came to an end the next night with *The Hunchback* and *Eugene*

Aram in which Hammond played Peter Dealtry, under the patronage of S. A. Bayntun, M.P. Hammond became low comedian under Macready at Covent Garden and was later manager of the Strand Theatre where his Sam Weller and burlesque Othello took the town by storm. Finally he took over Drury Lane which landed him in the Bankruptcy Court. Coleman[42] says of him as an actor that 'he had wigs of all kinds and costumes of every description, but he was always Hammond in another wig and another coat.' As Paul Pry, Tristram Sappy in *Deaf as a Post* and Fixture in *A Roland for an Oliver* he was hard to beat and he was a passable vocalist.

On November 16 de Begnis, at the suggestion of several persons of distinction and musical taste, got up a performance of *Il Barbiere di Siviglia* in Italian for the first time. The decorations and wardrobe were produced from artists in London and Paris and a cast was assembled from the King's Theatre, de Begnis himself singing Figaro. The lower boxes were 7/6, upper boxes 4/-, pit 5/-, gallery 2/- and places in the boxes were to be had at Sotherans.

John Wilkinson now petitioned the Mayor and Commonalty to allow him to give up his lease and to appoint a committee to settle matters concerning it, the patent, scenery and props with his trustees. The General Committee, to whom the matter was referred, reported in favour of rescinding the lease, and relinquishing all claim to the arrears of rent upon possession of the premises, 'and all the Gas Apparatus Machinery, Scenery and other Articles therein being immediately delivered up to the Corporation' and an assignment of the patent being made to them.[43] Actually this was never done and Wilkinson's lease continued.

In 1833 O. E. Read brought an entirely new company to the York Theatre. Clifton was his stage manager and his leading man was Waldron. Mrs. Fawcett, later in the year to become Mrs. Higgie, was one of his leading ladies, and Miss Aldridge, a pupil of Alexander Lee who had sung at the Nobility Concerts, was a sweet and powerful vocalist who died the following May. Charles Wood's daughter now Mrs. Spiller appeared as Lady Contest. It is impossible to assess the relative merits of the managements that now swiftly succeeded one another. The papers occasionally criticise an actor or a piece of business, but on the whole superlatives reign, actors are un-rivalled, pieces got up with more splendour than ever before, and manage-ments are the most worthy of support that have been in York for years. Whether the manager himself contributed the notices or whether the news-papers wished to encourage the Theatre either from disinterested motives or on account of its advertisement value we cannot tell – only the monotony of the encomiums proves them untrustworthy. Read is praised, as Cummins before him, for his attention to costume, a department which had been fre-quently outraged.[44] He made a popular move by abolishing the augmented prices during the public weeks and he admitted children under twelve at half price from the start. He revived the fashionable nights, but he also had a bespeak by the merchants, innkeepers and tradesmen of York. For Whitsun he arranged for the appearance of the ventriloquist Flemmington as an 'economical treat' for children on holiday; and he presented several pieces of local interest and provided them with local scenery. Thus on May 17 he brought out *Waltheof or the Siege of York* for the first time on any stage. It was written by the Rev. T. Coomber, a descendant of the De Combre who was one of the dramatis personae, and it told a tale of the investment of York by William the Conqueror. It had been pruned by Waldron who played the Governor of York. Turner, the new scene painter from Vestris's Theatre, had done a splendid scene of the City Walls with Clifford's Tower and the spires of several churches in the background and another of Monk Bar in the olden time. The dresses by Mears and Sanderson were said to be correct and magnificent.[45] In August another piece *Mr. Tompkins or 47, Blake Street* had a view of York painted expressly for the occasion, representing St. Helen's Square with the Minster in the background.[46] *Richard Turpin, the Yorkshire Highwayman,* which the critic stigmatised as having neither plot, dialogue nor incident, was given on August 10 the last night. A piece that was of interest as being written by a former member of the company, W. L. Rede was *The Rake's Progress,* another example of a play founded on pictures, this time by Hogarth. One of the most elaborate spectacles was Knowles's *Vision of the Bard,* a masque in honour of Sir Walter Scott, who had died the previous year. The opening scene showed Dryburgh by moonlight with Waldron as the Bard delivering an address in honour of the dead author. There followed visionary tableaux grouped from the novels and admirably arranged. The finale was a gorgeous scenic effect in which all the characters were gathered together. The scenery was said to be admirably adapted, the costumes in perfect keeping with the times, and Clifton was commended for his ingenuity in producing panoramic successions. The masque had the advantage that at revivals the tableaux could be changed.

Another of Knowles's dramas was brought out, for the first time out of London, on May 13 less than a month after its first performance at Covent Garden. This was *The Wife* in which the hero Leonardo was played by Sherard, the heroine Mariana by Mrs. Fawcett, the reforming villain St. Pierre by Waldron and the unrepentant villain Ferrando Gonzago by Welsh from Edinburgh.

Read engaged a Russian Horn Band consisting of 22 musicians for 4 nights. Their precision was said to be astonishing and the audience was delighted with their performances of Rossini and their Cossack songs with vocal chorus.

The three piece programme was now the usual order of the day but Shakespeare was by no means neglected, *Lear, Romeo and Juliet, The Merchant of Venice, Macbeth* and *Richard III* being given during the year. Juliet was played by Mrs. G. Egerton, formerly Mrs. Percy who in July returned to the company after 4 years; Courtney was Romeo and Waldron Mercutio; Mrs. Egerton also played Portia to the Shylock of Waldron and the Bassanio of Clifton, and Lady Macbeth to Waldron's Macbeth.

At first Read did badly, though some nights drew audiences; thus Wilkinson's benefit brought nearly £90, which was considered a good house though the Theatre held £150.[47] As the season progressed Read appears to have done somewhat better, yet the *York Chronicle* on July 25 expressed its inability to account for the 'late declension of Theatrical interests; as far as York is concerned, the utmost attention is paid to the proper business of the Stage; everything of an immoral tendency is carefully excluded; and under the present management, the legitimate object of the Stage – "to hold the mirror up to nature" – is fully accomplished.' Read, however, came off better than some of his predecessors, and in taking his leave was able to tell his patrons that owing to the success of the season, he could pay his salaries and tradesmen.'[48] All the same he did not return the next year. On October 31 the *York Chronicle* reported that he had obtained a licence to act at Wakefield, one of the theatres up till then in the circuit, that Hammond had taken Sheffield and that Downe was recruiting a company in London for the York circuit to open in Hull.

In the meantime there had been some interesting visitors to the Theatre. In September James Wilkinson, who had acted with the company for a season in 1818 and had since fallen on evil days, had a benefit at which Downe, Rayner, Miss Aldridge and members of Smedley's Pontefract company performed.[49] On September 28 Benjamin Grossmith, a child of 6 years, performed 12 different characters in his *Adventures in the Reading Coach*: he was assisted by his older brother, William, aged 15. They acted in a 'little moveable Theatre, which was fixed in the middle of the ordinary stage, ... a very ingenious contrivance, the size of the proscenium bearing such proportion to the height of the juvenile actors as to make them appear much taller than they really are.' Benjamin subsequently became a missionary but a younger brother George was the father of Weedon, and grandfather of George Grossmith. On October 12 Paganini made his second appearance at York at the Theatre Royal. The concert was arranged by Watson, composer to the English Opera House and Covent Garden, and the prices charged were boxes 7/6, pit 5/-, gallery 2/6. The boxes were well filled but the other parts of the house were thin. Paganini played his *Preludio* and *Rondo Brillante,* his variations on the air *Nel Cor Piu* and on the *The Carnival of Venice,* and his *Sonata Militaire* on one string. The *York Chronicle* found the performance more surprising than pleasing.[50]

Theatrical managements, particularly those in the provinces, were affected by the Copyright Act of this year, by which the ownership of any unpublished dramatic piece was vested in the author, who alone could grant the right to represent it. Managers could no longer with impunity put on plays without a fee to the playwright. The Copyright of twenty eight years or the residue of the author's life was extended in 1842 to forty two years or seven years after his death. The Dramatic Authors' Society was formed to implement the Act.

Mathews returned once more in February 1834 in the fourth volume of his *Comic Annual for 1832,* and his *Sketch Book for 1831*. It was announced that the Chair would be taken at 7.30 (was this a forerunner of the music hall?) and carriages were to be ordered at 10.30.[51]

Downe, once again in the saddle, opened his season on March 10 with an almost entirely fresh company. In the usual fashion he gave out that he would endeavour to restore 'the York Circuit to that station in the Drama which it once so prominently occupied,' and pledged himself to produce both legitimate drama and every novelty of merit. By permission of the trustees he met the wishes of the residents of York by reducing the prices to boxes 3/-, half price 1/6, pit 2/-, half price 1/-, gallery 1/-; in the public weeks the boxes were raised to 4/-, half price 2/-. Downe had a bumper house at his own benefit and the receipts on the Sheriff's night were about £90 but for the most part attendances remained poor. Downe had stipulated that Wilkinson should no longer have his annual benefit on Easter Tuesday or in the public weeks, because they were popular nights. Waldron was still leading man but left for Liverpool in May and was replaced by Barton from New York who appeared in a round of Shakespeare tragedies, *Hamlet, Lear* and *Macbeth*. The *York Chronicle* found him deficient in voice and prosing and slow in articulation.[52] The leading lady was Miss Wyndham from Cheltenham. Montague Stanley had returned with his wife, though he now played a rather different line, excelling as the bustling, impudent valet. A native actor was W. H. Maddocks who made a successful début in *The Wedding Gown*. A well known comedian was engaged in the shape of William Chippendale whose father had been a member of the company in 1813 and who was himself to become a popular comedian in Edinburgh. Born in 1801 he took to the stage at the age of eighteen, led a strolling life for some years and first appeared in Edinburgh in 1823.[53] He specialised in old men and his Polonius was unequalled. From Lincoln came J. H. Chute to play second rôles such as Horatio, Edmund, and the Prince of Wales in *Henry IV.* He married Macready's daughter and many years later was one of the most successful managers of the Bath and Bristol Theatres.

Miss Burrell, now Mrs. Wilkins, made her return after five years' absence in *Giovanni in London*. One of the finest vocalists of the day Mrs. Edmunds, formerly Miss Cawse, from Covent Garden was engaged to sing in operas and comic operas for a few nights. She opened as Susanna in *The Marriage of Figaro* and among her other rôles were those of Polly to her husband's Macheath, Diana Vernon, Rosetta and Elvira in *Masaniello*. Dowton came in July and returned for Race Week during which seasons he played thirty-two rôles including Shylock, which was out of the usual comedy range, Sir Peter Teazle, Abednego, Dornton, Jobson, Rolamo and Falstaff which he had first performed in London in 1830 and in which he is said to have been unapproached since the days of Henderson.[54]

A local drama, *A Voyage to the North*, based on Capt. (later Sir) John Ross's recent adventures in search of a North West Passage, was brought out on April 14 with ten new scenes by Newnum, music by Ivers, dresses by Howell and assistants, properties by Mr. and Mrs. Seymour, and machinery by Bailes and Dibbs. *Gustavus of Sweden*, brought out on April 11, was expressly licensed for the York circuit and had been seen in Hull. Newnum was the company's new scene painter and he was to remain with them until 1838.

For the pantomime *Harlequin Red Riding Hood* he painted a diorama on 1000 feet of canvas with ten views illustrating the works of Byron; they were acknowledged to be splendid specimens. He also designed tableaux vivants, and one evening these and his diorama were exhibited with musical accompaniment only, for those who did not wish to witness plays. In August he produced a Cosmorama consisting of five curiously mixed scenes: Bolton Abbey, Kirkstall by moonlight, the Falls of the Tees at Rokeby, Joshua commanding the sun to stand still and Belshazzar's Feast, the last two being after the pictures by John Martin. Scenery for its own sake had taken hold of popular taste.

The new street, St. Leonard's Place, was now in the course of construction on the site of Mint Yard, and plans to bring the Theatre into line with it were in hand. On June 13 the General Committee was authorised to employ John Harper, an architect, to draw up the plans and direct the work of improving the front of the Theatre towards St. Leonard's Place.[55] Before this could be done, however, the gallery staircase and a building had to be pulled down.[56] It was then discovered that the main walls of the Theatre were dilapidated and insecure and would have to be strengthened. The survey was then extended to the interior where it was found that the old stage 'was so much decayed as to be actually dangerous to the Actors.' The Corporation also decided to install a hot water apparatus for warming the house since, whilst the other work was in progress, it could be put in at moderate expense, and it would be an advantage to the Theatre to have such an apparatus available at times when the company was absent. The authorities were the readier to embark on these additional expenses because the lease to Wilkinson was due to expire in July 1835 and they knew that unless they made repairs and improvements they would find it impossible to re-let the house. The total expenditure was about £800.[57] Alteration of the exterior consisted of the conversion of the awkward and unsightly gable opposite St. Leonard's Place into a pseudo-Elizabethan one, ornamented with pinnacles; the introduction of a mullioned window, and the erection of an arcade likewise surmounted with pinnacles. The front was stuccoed in imitation of stone to hide the heterogeneous materials of which the old work consisted. Up till then the lack of a separate entrance to the boxes had been highly prejudicial to attendances and this was remedied by making one under the arcade. The gallery was no longer approached from this side but a new staircase was built at the Little Blake Street entrance which now gave access to pit, as before, and gallery. This portion of the work cost about £500. A water colour, though painted many years later, shows the unaltered exterior.

As for the interior, it too was renovated and the box seats newly covered. A new stage was laid by Messrs. Munroe and Jordan, principal machinists from Newcastle, and was 'adapted by a novel and ingenious mechanical process, to all the purposes of illusion upon the principle of the first London Theatres.' The stage was made to descend if required in one mass to the extent of 20 x 14 feet; or a number of smaller traps could be used.

Such a piece of mechanism was first employed at the Adelphi in the re-presentation of an earthquake. Lastly during the Easter recess of 1835 Newnum repainted the proscenium and supplied a new act drop.[58] Of the former it was said: 'The drapery, crimson and gold, has a good effect, which is heightened by the City of York Arms, which are introduced in the centre, in bas relief.' The act drop was a Grecian composition: 'a ruined temple, on the left, rearing its columns on the margin of a beautiful lake. A bridge in the background, and trees, with all the other adjuncts of a landscape, – and three figures (Grecian) in colloquy, on the right.' The Temple was taken from a picture by Stansfield and was admirably painted, the drawing, the colouring and the chiaroscuro being judged equally beautiful.

Downe opened the Theatre on March 23, 1835 and it was stated by the *York Chronicle*[59] to be 'as handsome and compact a little theatre as any in the provinces'. It was open every night except Wednesday. The resources of the new stage machinery were first demonstrated at Downe's benefit on May 12 in a burlesque burletta *Orpheus and Eurydice,* in which the infernal deities descended to the realms of Pluto en masse on the sinking stage in a mag-nificent tableau. Owing to the magnitude of the spectacle the green curtain fell instead of the act drop.[60] The machinery was employed again for the concluding pictures of Tableaux Vivants which represented the last days of Pompeii in illustration of Lytton's novel. The care for archaeological detail was shown in the reconstruction of the Temple of Fortune before the eruption from Sir William Gill's description. Another spectacular piece was the Rum-Antic burletta *The Easter Card Party* in which the performers represented a pack of cards. Newnum painted a scene of the front of the Great Mogul with the motto 'Downe's patent playing cards' and devised a drop scene of a spade ace which occupied the whole front of the stage and was much applauded. The piece included a travesty of scenes from *Macbeth* and a parody of operatic songs.[61] Particular attention was given to the vocal side of the company. Miss Atkinson from Covent Garden, who was known in York from having performed at the Camidge concerts, was the singing actress. She had a clear and melodious voice and good articulation. On the male side there was T. F. Williams, who on July 27 brought out his domestic drama *Forgery Detected.*[62]

Then Mr. and Mrs. Joseph Wood were re-engaged prior to their de-parture to America, and sang with the company in April and May. As Mary Anne Paton she had been the original Agatha in the London production of *Der Freischütz.* Born in 1802, she had appeared at the Edinburgh concerts as a child and at the age of 20 first appeared on the stage at the Haymarket. At this time she was considered at the head of her profession both in the theatre and the concert room. After an unsuccessful marriage with Lord William Lennox she had married the tenor Joseph Wood about 1831, and in 1833 they took up their residence at Woolley Manor, Yorkshire. She had a pure soprano voice with the extensive compass of 18-19 notes and she could execute the most difficult passages with the utmost facility, being mistress of the florid style then in fashion. She opened on April 24 as Rosetta to the Hawthorn of her husband and subsequently sang Rosalind in *The Devil's Bridge* with many extra songs, Susanna in *The Marriage of Figaro* to Wood's Almaviva, Julia Mannering, Diana Vernon and Wilhelmina, to Wood's Henry Bertram, Francis Osbaldiston and Tom Tug. They graced the leading rôles in the first production in York of Auber's *Fra Diavolo* when the Band of the 6th Dragoons augmented the orchestra. In *Love in a Village* she generously played second to Miss Atkinson; the only time she had done so except to her model Madame Catalini.[63] Her acting in this was said to have been as admirable as her singing. In *The Quaker* she executed delicious runs and in closing a cadence fell two octaves perfectly in tune and without effort. Mrs. Wood complimented Ivers on his conducting and told him she had rarely been so well accompanied. A light on the perfunctory way in which operas were performed in stock companies is shed by the *York Chronicle*: in *The Barber of Seville* Chute as Figaro would not attempt the solos but joined in the concerted pieces, whilst none of the company had seen the music for *Fra Diavolo* until the Saturday before it was given.[64]

Another visitor was Fanny Wyndham who played a large round of comedy and melodramatic parts with vivacity and archness; she had a good figure and sang delightfully. Samuel Butler, who had in the meantime visited America, returned for three nights to play Hamlet, Virginius, Puff and two new parts David Duvigne in Jerrold's *Hazard of the Die* and Walder in Lovell's *Avenger*. His Hamlet was proclaimed a beautiful performance in which he neither raved nor ranted, but excelled especially in the scenes with Ophelia and his mother and in the fencing scene. He redeemed the sombre horrors of *The Avenger* by his fine acting.[65]

Henry Compton, to become the most famous Shakespearian clown of his day, was a member of the company this and the two succeeding years. His real name was Charles Mackenzie and he was the grandfather of Compton Mackenzie the novelist and of Fay Compton. Born in 1805 he had made his stage début at Lewes and, for three years previous to his joining the York company, had been in the Lincoln circuit where he had formed a firm friendship with J. H. Chute. On his first appearance as Mawworm he showed all the requisites of a good comic actor and his singing was humorous.[66] From his *Memoirs*[67] we learn that 'he at once hit the taste of his audience, and in one rival playhouse and another so mastered his art, that his name became celebrated in all that part of the country, while large houses were the result of his name being put up for a benefit, and enthusiastic and delighted audiences greeted him everywhere.' For the first two years he was in the circuit, 1835-36, it was not doing well: 'though we *worked hard, played hard, fought hard,* and had many *hard* engagements we brought home very little *hard* cash with us.' His last season in 1837 was more successful and in his parting speech at Leeds, he acknowledged the usefulness of his experience in the company. The actor's day was taken up by study and rehearsal in the morning, followed by a walk and dinner, then an hour or two was spent with his pipe and paper chatting with a friend about the profession and tea, then the theatre ending up at a tavern. His first season he played Osric and Peter in *Romeo and Juliet* as well as the clown in *Twelfth Night,* in which Chippendale was Sir Toby Belch, Newnum Sir Andrew Aguecheek, Chute Malvolio, Mrs. Edwards Olivia and Miss Atkinson Viola. He is commended for having studied the character and not merely learnt the words. Compton played Darby in *The Poor Soldier* as an Irishman and not, as was only too usual, as a Yorkshire clown.[68]

Whether the season was successful we do not know but the Sheriff's night brought to the boxes a galaxy of beauty and fashion such as had graced the theatre in the olden times but which it had despaired of ever seeing again.[69]

The company performed in September during the Musical Festival and were supported by two more child prodigies Master Brooke and Miss Allison, just over 4, who had the temerity to essay *Romeo and Juliet* for which they were heartily commended in the *York Chronicle*.[70] How absurd they must have looked o'er topped by the adult actors! On September 11 the performance was by command of the Duchess of Kent and Princess Victoria, so soon to become the Queen, but they did not attend.[71] The following night the great Jewish tenor Braham made his first appearance in York as Harry Bertram and Tom Tug.

Another lease was granted to Wilkinson for 7 years from October 1st at the same rent of £200. A schedule of properties belonging to the Corporation included all the machinery of the sinking stage; the heating apparatus; the shelves, and doors to them, on both sides of the wardrobe room; the fruiterer's box fitted up with a circular front in the saloon recess; the brass ornamented chandelier suspended from the ceiling, another new one with glass drops to the box entrance, 12 chandeliers with glass chains and drops suspended from the iron brackets in front of the boxes with a glass over each light, three other chandeliers with Argand burners; glass lanterns at the entrances and on the stairways; and lastly, all the gas fittings, ranges in rooms where there were fireplaces, and locks and bolts.

In January 1836 Downe gave York an expensive treat by bringing over from Leeds for four nights, Mr. and Mrs. Yates and Miss Betts from Drury Lane in two new operas, Balfe's *The Siege of Rochelle* and Halévy's *The Jewess.* The pieces were performed by sanction of Alfred Bunn, the Drury Lane manager, and Downe claimed that never before had such a combination of attractions been offered to an audience on the same evening. The expenses of the lavish productions were over £1000. In *The Jewess* the knights were mounted on fully caparisoned steeds and armed cap à pie whilst the bodyguard were in coats of mail manufactured purposely for this occasion. In order to give the full effect to the splendour of the costumes a platform was once more erected from the stage to the pit. Mrs. Yates played Rachael and in *The Siege of Rochelle* Miss Betts performed Clara. The event drew crowded houses but it was a bad precedent. The stock company was inadequate for these operatic pieces and was therefore relegated to supporting stars brought from London as principals.

When Downe opened his regular season it was to thin houses, partly owing to the rival attraction of Ducrow at the Amphitheatre. Buckstone's new drama *The Dream at Sea* was presented with exceedingly rich scenery, though the *York Gazette*[72] had little to say in favour of it as a piece. Compton gave a fine comic performance hitting off a character the simplicity and naiveté of which suited him. He also played Dogberry this year, a character in which he was quaintly dogmatic and self-satisfied; but it had a touch of superciliousness that was foreign to the part. Compton was a deliberate rather than an impulsive actor and excelled in rôles of the unconsciously eccentric, the conceited or the self-satisfied stolid types.[73]

This year witnessed the inauguration of the Easter pantomime which was to become a feature of the York stage for many decades. The pantomime had usually been brought out at Hull at Christmas. *The Sleeping Beauty or the Rival Columbines* included an Eidophusicon with six pictures by Newnum. De Loutherbourg had invented a miniature theatre of this name in which he had experimented with perspectives, lighting, sound effects and machinery some years previously[74] and this was evidently copied by Newnum. On the pantomime's last night it was put on as a first piece in order that the children might retire early. Indeed the pantomime was on the way to becoming a special show for children. Another version of *Turpin's Ride to York* entitled *Rookwood* was adapted from the romance expressly for the York stage. The Misses Hunt and Gillman put on a number of new ballets notably *The Troubador,* with music by an amateur named Crouch. The sinking stage made it possible to include the incantation scene in *Der Freischütz.* Yet Downe was still commended for his attempt to maintain the legitimate character of the York stage under discouraging circumstances.[75]

Laura Honey came as star in July. Her mother Mrs. Young had been an actress at Sadler's Wells and there she first appeared in juvenile rôles. She had since sung and acted at a number of the minor theatres. She played in several light pieces including Selby's *A Day in Paris* and the burletta of *The Mazourka* which had been specially written for her, and in which she gave imitations of Grisi, Malibran and Mrs. Yates. She had a rich mezzo soprano which could assume remarkable power and depth, and her enunciation was clear and forcible but she lacked finish and even refinement of style.[76] She was unable, however, to complete her engagement first because of a cold, when Downe printed the doctor's certificate on the playbill to prevent suspicions of malingering, and then because her husband, who had merely lived on her earnings, was found drowned in the Thames.

The famous pantomimists and dancers the Leclercqs paid the first of many visits to York in a series of ballets and melodramas in July. The family then consisted of Charles Leclercq and his wife, his daughter Fanny by a previous marriage, and the infant pantomimist Mlle M. Leclercq.[77] The parents played in *The Dumb Girl of Genoa* and *The Wild Boy of Bohemia,* the latter of which had been specially written for them by Walker. Among their ballets were *Bacchus and Ariadne*, a Tyrolean pas de deux as danced by Taglioni and Elssler, and a nautical pantomime *False Signals.* Leclercq in *The*

Engaged Musician gave an imitation of Paganini on the violin and played a serenade on four musical instruments. Downe opened the Theatre for five nights in October when the attraction was a new vocalist, Miss Paget from the Olympic. Hunt, the new ballet master, was praised for his suppleness and lightness in a Chinese dance.[78] Later in the month the theatre opened for one night under the patronage of the Royal Hussars for Master Phillipps an infant trumpeter.

The new season started on March 6, 1837 with Talfourd's classic tragedy *Ion* which drew but a thin house at its second representation. In the title rôle was a young actor from Exeter William Creswick who was leading man in the company for two years. His forte was tragedy and grave comedy though he occasionally played lighter rôles such as Benedick.[79] He married Miss Paget in 1839 and in later years he became manager of the Surrey and was known as the apostle of Shakespeare to transpontine London. Mrs. Brooks, Mrs. Lambert and Miss Paget were the principal actresses. The last had become a great favourite and we have a charming glimpse of her as Little Jockey 'with her top boots, inexpressibles, and green jacket, with pink and black cap.'[80] Chute, who played Dandini, Lord Allcash and Ferdinand in *The Tempest*, was also popular, and was presented during the season with a watch and appendages by his friends as a tribute to his private character and talent as an actor, at a dinner at the White Hart in Stonegate.[81] Compton took all the comic leads including Nicol Jarvie, Trinculo, Goldfinch and Paul Pry, until he made his last bow with the company on July 15.

It was again the operatic department on which Downe lavished money. Michael Rophino Lacy[82] was engaged to lead the orchestra and take charge of the operas. Lacy was born in Spain of an English father and Spanish mother and made his début as a violinist at Bilbao at the age of six. After studying under Kreutzer in Paris he came to England where he first appeared at the Hanover Square Rooms as 'the young Spaniard.' For ten years he abandoned music for the stage and performed genteel comedy rôles in Edinburgh. Later he directed the Liverpool concerts and the ballets at the Italian Opera. His knowledge of languages enabled him to adapt foreign libretti and he composed himself. In York he was in charge of an augmented orchestra. His version of Rossini's *Cenerentola* came out on March 7 with his young pupil, Miss Delcy, a native of York, as Cinderella. The machinery was by Morris the company's new machinist, the properties by Seymour. In his adaptation of *Fra Diavolo*, which was given with the whole of the music for the first time, Miss Delcy sang Zerlina, and Binge, a newcomer from Edinburgh, Fra Diavolo. Lacy's own comic opera *Love in Wrinkles* came out on April 24 with Miss Delcy as Countess de Sterloff. Miss Delcy, who was only 17, possessed a rich soprano voice of great flexibility and sweetness and she was an attractive and pleasing actress so that a great future was predicted for her, a prediction which appears to have been mistaken.[83] The operatic department was pronounced one of the best out of London, the stage management, scenery and machinery all that could be wished and the performers perfect in their parts.

Heavy expenses compelled Downe to close the season as early as April 20 and reopen for the Race Week nights only in May and June. By July the Theatre had been redecorated by Newnum. The ceiling was particularly elegant.[84] 'Instead of the old distorted representation of an open cupola, we have now a circular canopy as of green satin with a very effective ornament of serpents in the centre. The four corners of the square of the roof are occupied with classical medallions. A remarkably graceful frieze of the arabesque or grotesque character, runs along the top of the proscenium: the drapery beneath and the civic arms are newly and very richly painted. Above each stage door is a medallion portrait, on one side of Shakespeare, and on the other of Mrs. Siddons as the tragic muse: surrounded with enrichments of the same novel and variegated character as the front of the dress circle of the boxes presents. The upper circles are equally elegant, but less enriched. The Royal Arms are very handsomely painted: but unfortunately this part of the work was executed before the death of the king; and the appropriate change for a new reign does not appear. The whole effect of the new decorations is very elegant and pleasing; and the labour and artist-like taste of Mr. Newnum are well displayed in the renovation.' This is the first use of the term 'dress circle' then applied to the lower boxes. Queen Victoria had ascended the throne on June 20 and a new social era was ushered in.

Sheridan Knowles came for 5 nights in July to perform in a series of his own dramas; he acted Walter, St. Pierre, William Tell and Robert in his new piece *The Wrecker's Daughter,* as well as Petruchio. In August four Hungarian singers were engaged and performed popular airs and national melodies; they imitated instruments but were found more singular than beautiful by the critic of the *York Courant.*[85] Downe opened again for the Hussar week in October, and in November Benjamin Grossmith, now 9 years old, and his brother paid a farewell visit to York on their way to Edinburgh.[86] They gave a new entertainment in which he appeared in forty characters with forty changes of scenery and dress in his little theatre.

In January 1838 Gyngell, 'the emperor of cards'[87] from Vauxhall, exhibited his illusions and wonder working mechanisms. He played on the musical glasses, now become a favourite form of entertainment, and walked on a tight rope over the pit, a nerve racking experience for its occupants. On his last night he released a Montgolfier balloon from the pit door to which was attached a brilliant light which changed colour and from which a quantity of variegated stars shot out when it reached a considerable altitude.[88]

Miss Tyrer was now playing the leads such as Jane Shore, Juliet to Creswick's Romeo, and Lady Anne to his Richard III. Chute's farewell benefit took place on May 30 when *The Pickwickians* was first performed. This inaugurated the Dickens vogue which followed upon the Scott one. The famous characters were taken as follows: Pickwick = H. Mellon, Snodgrass = Houghton, Winkle = Binge, Jingle = Chute, Sam Weller = Suter. The receipt of £75 was now considered a good house. Newnum too took his farewell this season, making his last appearance at his benefit on May 15. An act from 5 of Shakespeare's plays was given and tableaux vivants, which included the nine muses paying adoration to the Bard. A respectable audience gathered in spite of the classical bill of fare. The Theatre had owed much to his talents as an artist and his industry, indeed a good deal of the stage management had devolved on him.[89] His last new scenery was for a revival of Kemble's *Lodoiska* for which a grand baronial hall had been designed by the celebrated artist and scene designer David Roberts.

The engagement of Elizabeth Martyn, her sister Miss B. Inverarity and her husband Charles Martyn, a bass singer, gave the company the opportunity of presenting a series of operas. Mrs. Martyn was a well known Scottish vocalist who had made her début at Covent Garden in 1830 as Cinderella. She is said to have been a fine looking woman but an indifferent singer and actress. The Martyns opened as Figaro and Rosina followed by Corporal Max and Lisette Geirstein in *Why Don't She Marry?* They subsequently sang among other parts Caspar and Agnes in *Der Freischütz*, and the Baron and Camilla with Miss B. Inverarity as Olivia in the first performance in York of *The Black Domino* with music by Auber. The next visitor was Morris Barnett, the greatest exponent of French characters of his time. Originally brought up to the profession of music he had passed his early life in Paris; then taking to the stage had appeared as a comedian in Brighton and Bath. His Mons. Jacques in his own burletta had created a furore at the St. James's the year previous to his appearance in York. He opened on April 26 in this rôle followed by John Thistle in *Love is Blind* and Mons. Millefleur in *The Station House*. He gave an exquisite performance as Mons. Jacques and the *York Gazette* declared that if such true delineation of character and refined acting were more frequently met with, the drama would not be stigmatised as insufficiently intellectual.[90] Barnett employed his musical talents in *Harmony Hall* in which he sang a Scena Buffa and introduced a violin solo à la Ole Bull the Norwegian violinist. Downe then engaged him as author, actor and stage manager for the rest of the season, and after a sojourn in London to settle his affairs, he reappeared on May 11 as Moses in *The School for Scandal*. Among his other parts were Rory O'More in Lever's stage adaptation of his novel, Dulcimer in his own *Royal Visit* and the leads in his *Yellow Kids, Double or Quits*[91] and *Ducks and Drakes*.

Yet another star was Louisa Nisbett. She was noted for her beauty which was enhanced by coils of dark hair. Like Mrs. Jordan she had abounding animal spirits and was one of the greatest comedy actresses of her time. Her best part was Constance in Knowles's *Love Chase* in which her wild spirits soared into poetry,[92] and this she performed on her opening night,[93] May 28, with Downe as Sir William Fondlove. She was the first to play the famous rôle of Pauline Deschappels in Lytton's *Lady of Lyons* when this made its début in York on May 31; Claude Melnotte was played by Creswick. Her other rôles were Mrs. Trictrac and Cornet Fitzhenry in *Lesson for Husbands*, Lady Teazle, in which she was whimsical, brilliant, tantalising, charming, but unrepentant, Ellen Marsden in *Match in the Dark*,

Mrs. Simpson, Widow Cheerly and Louisa Lovetrick in *The Dead Shot*. She returned again for Race Week in August adding her famous representation of Caroline Gayton in *Catching an Heiress* as well as those of Mrs. Turtle in *Hunting a Turtle* and Lady Contest in *The Wedding Day*. Jim Crow Rice had created a furore in 1836 and this is reflected in *Jim Crow's Trip from New York to Old York* recited by Herbert, the low comedian, at his benefit. This season was summed up as brilliant in point of talent, but unremarkable for pageant and spectacle (for which the stage was anyway too circumscribed). Nor was the operatic department so strong as it had been under Lacy the previous year. The successes had rather been in melodrama and in a revival of the legitimate drama with something of the old zest. The whole set of stock scenes needed repainting. In one instance an old complaint was renewed that candles had been placed on the table for a night scene whilst the faded drop showed an interior with sunshine streaming through the Gothic windows.[94]

Hooper, later to be manager, was in the company in July playing comedy rôles such as Frederick Bramble, Tristram Fickle and Jeremy Diddler. In *The Rivals*, officers played Capt. Absolute and Sir Lucius O'Trigger and 'bore themselves in their novel situation, as British officers will anywhere, like gentlemen.'[95] *The Coronation, or The Launch of the Victoria* was staged on July 10. Hervio Nano, the celebrated manfly who walked on the ceiling, appeared in *The Gnomefly* for 7 successive nights, and in *La Mouche à Miel* flew from the top of the ceiling across the gallery, pit, orchestra and stage and alighted on a village spire. Mr. and Mrs. Yates returned with Collins and Mrs. Hooper and brought out Coyne's spectacle of *Valsha or The Slave Queen* with scenery by Muir and dresses, banners and properties from the Adelphi. They received enough encouragement to prolong their stay by two nights when Yates gave his *At Home* with imitations.

September saw the first appearance in York of Charles Kean who opened as Hamlet, subsequently playing Othello, Richard III, Macbeth and Claude Melnotte. The critic of the *Yorkshire Gazette*[96] thought his Hamlet a noble impersonation though slightly disappointing in some parts. As Macbeth he looked the part and 'the struggle between conscience and a bad ambition, prompted by his wife's haughty spirit, seemed to grow with the truth of nature out of a mind at first unconscious of the evil within; then came the terrible remorse, and last the hardened, but wretched heart.' In the banquet scene 'the stricken and affrighted soul of *Macbeth* was depicted fearfully, in the action and voice, and in the expression of the countenance.' In the fight with Macduff Kean narrowly missed disarming his opponent, a demonstration of his skill as a swordsman but misjudgment as an actor. Mrs. Brooks was Lady Macbeth and Mrs. Garner Ophelia and Desdemona.

Certainly Downe had not stinted this year on stars which were now essential to attract audiences.

During the winter of 1838-9 the Corporation's surveyor found the roof of the Theatre in a very 'dilapidated and shattered' condition, and a recommendation for its repair at the cost of about £100 was agreed to.[97]

When the company reopened in 1839 the new leading man was Woolgar who had come from Nottingham with his daughter aged 14. She was later to become the well known actress Mrs. Alfred Mellon. She opened on March 11 as Little Pickle but her great success was as Smike in *Nicholas Nickleby* which was presented on March 18. 'Boz's' 'cockney notions' of Yorkshire and Yorkshiremen were not altogether acceptable. Henry Holl who played Nicholas was a visitor from Covent Garden.[98] During his stay he brought out his nautical melodrama *Wapping Old Stairs* in which he himself played Tom Garland. Another interesting member of the company this year was George Coppin who succeeded to Compton's low comedy rôles at 30/- a week; he went to Australia in 1842 and became manager of the theatres in Melbourne and Adelaide.[99] At the end of April the now inevitable operatic stars appeared. This year they were Frederic Shrivall, from Bristol, G. Beresford from Brighton and Miss Cooper from the nobility concerts. In *Rob Roy* their singing was much applauded especially Miss Cooper's *John Anderson my Jo*, and Shrivall's *Auld Lang Syne*.[100] Morris Barnett took his farewell benefit on April 12 playing Lapoche in *Fontainbleau*, Monsieur Jacques and Mantalini in *Nicholas Nickleby*. Three days later a masonic lodge with the attractive name of the Antient Free Gardeners bespoke the benefit for Holmes the Treasurer. The Theatre was decorated with the banners of the different lodges and the city brass band under Walker attended. At Downe's benefit Knowles's drama *The Maid of Mariendorpt* made its début in York.

For the Assizes, Henry Hall, portrayer of rustic and Irish characters and master of burlesque, was engaged from the Strand and St. James's Theatres. On the first night he appeared as Iago in the burlesque of *Othello* and gave an imitation of Macready, catching his attitude and countenance to the life. The travesty was a pretended adaptation for the minor theatres at which no word could be spoken.[101] As Sam Slap he was the accomplished cockney bravo, racy and amusing but realistically repellent. He also played Gerald Pepper in Samuel Lover's *White Horse of the Peppers,* Newman Noggs, the Irish Tutor, and Larry O'Gig in the *Robber's Wife* in which two last his native brogue was dashed with delicacy. Compton returned for a few nights, after having scored a success at Drury Lane and other theatres. His new creations were Jerry Chance in Mark Lemon's *M.P. for the Rotten Borough,* Chaff in *My Man Tom* and Tobias Shortcut in *The Spitfire;* Liston himself had not greater gusto in his personation of the snuffling half fool, whole knave, Mawworm.[102] Elizabeth Lee, daughter of the Taunton manager Henry Lee and later wife of Leigh Murray, was among the newcomers.

The railways[103] enabled parties from London to make visits more easily to the north and again in August three stars came to support an opera season. The most notable of these was Priscilla Horton from Covent Garden, afterwards Mrs. German Reed. She was then twenty-one and had been playing as Macready's leading lady since 1837. She had great musical ability as well as being a gifted actress and mimic, and her range of parts was large. In York she sang Amina in *La Sonnambula*, Annette in *The Maid of Palaiseau* (adapted by Bishop from Rossini's *La Gazza Ladra*) and Eolia in *The Mountain Sylph* by John Barnett, the last two of which were new to the city.

This year the Theatre was open from October 9-23 first for Race and Cavalry Weeks and then for the annual visit of the Yorks Hussars. Lysander S. Thompson, a comedian from Sheffield had joined the circuit and opened as Johnny Atkins in *The Descent of a Balloon*. This was Downe's final season after a management of 7 years' duration. His farewell benefit was on August 22, but the following night he gave his services as Simpson for a clear benefit for the performers. On this occasion the band was augmented in order to give effect to some Strauss waltzes.

The poor condition of the stock scenery was still a cause for complaint, and behaviour was sometimes rowdy. One night Herbert was pelted with missiles by people concealed in the slips, and declining to submit to such treatment, retired from the scene to the applause of the rest of the audience.[104] Downe was evidently not encouraged to renew his lease and the management passed to Edward Hooper from Drury Lane, the Olympic and St. James's Theatres who had acted in York for a few days two years previously.[105] Hooper disapproved of the star system 'as bad and unprofitable' though there might be exceptions as, for example, Taglioni. He proposed to work the circuit with 'an effective and sufficient stock company' and to exclude all stars for one year at least.[106] The company, once again practically a fresh one, opened March 6, 1840 and Hooper advertised that 'during the Recess, the Theatre has been thoroughly cleaned. The Boxes, both Upper and Dress have been newly papered. The Seats and Rests newly covered. Fires are constantly kept, and the Warming Apparatus employed, and no Expence has been spared to ensure the Comfort of the Audience.' The curtain rose to the singing of *God Save the Queen* by the whole company followed by an address by Mrs. Hooper.

This time there was no promise to support the legitimate drama and three short pieces were the fare the first night, including a novelty, Mrs. Planché's burletta, *The Handsome Husband*, with Hooper as Henry Fitzherbert and Mrs. Hooper as Laura. Mude returned from Drury Lane after seven years as stage manager and shared leads with Hooper. The newcomers were mainly drawn from the minor theatres. Among them was Robert Roxby who had acted under Hooper at the St. James's. He came of a well known theatrical family; his father William Roxby adopted the stage name of Beverley from the Yorkshire town; his brother Henry was later for a few weeks lessee of the York circuit, and another brother was William Beverley the great scene painter. Robert himself became manager of the Manchester Theatre and stage manager at Drury Lane for 11 years. He played light comedy and made his début in York as Wyndham in *The Handsome Husband* but only remained with the company one season. H. T. Craven, later author of many domestic dramas and farces, made his first appearance on any stage but also only remained one season. A greater actor than either of these was Henry Leigh Murray. He was announced as from the Olympic[107] when he made his début on the opening night as Stephen in *The Handsome Husband*. He took small parts including Tom in *The Jealous Wife*, Trip in *The School for Scandal*, Fag in *The Rivals*, Macaire in *Victorine*, Desmolins in *The Lady of Lyons*, Lord Tinsel in *The Hunchback* and Grantley in *Rent Day*. He only stayed a few months and went to the Adelphi, Edinburgh in September. The new scene painter was Nicholls, the machinist Goodall; the properties were in charge of Seymour and the dresses in charge of Mrs. Seymour and Mrs. Russell, whilst Giles was leader of the band. Though the *Yorkshire Gazette* commended the selection of simple pieces rather than pomp and pageantry, and eulogised the stage arrangements and Mrs. Hooper's talents, houses remained empty. Leman Rede's extravaganza *Hero and Leander* had a run of four nights and brought better patronage. But hopes that had been placed on a version of Harrison Ainsworth's *Jack Sheppard*, specially written for York, were doomed to failure. The piece was found to be made up of claptrap incidents, devoid of humour, long, gross and stupid. The audience was blamed for not supporting the approved authors and the talented acting of Mude and Mrs. Hooper in stock pieces. Mrs. Hooper was pleasing in whatever rôle she undertook evincing not only grace and vivacity but feeling and pathos as Lady Teazle, and making a vivid Mrs. Haller, and a spirited Julia in *The Hunchback*. In Lytton's new drama *The Sea Captain*, brought out on March 19, Mude's acting as Norman bordered on rant.[108]

Hooper did not provide any foreign operas or operatic stars, but in July he engaged 'the prince of clowns', Tom Matthews, with Mathew Howell and two dancers, Mlles Juliette and Eloise, from Her Majesty's. They all appeared on July 13 in the ballet of *Daughter of the Danube*, Howell dancing his original rôle of Rodolph. In *Harlequin Ploughboy* Matthews was Clown to Howell's Harlequin and Mlle Juliette's Columbine and on other nights he sang the famous *Tippitiwitchet* and *Hot Codlins* and danced the Cachucha in imitation of Mlle Duvernay in which he had created a sensation at Drury Lane for 150 nights. A pupil of Grimaldi he had become his successor in clowndom. The audiences improved. Hooper ventured on two Shakespeare plays, *The Merchant of Venice* with Mude as Shylock and Mrs. Hooper as Portia, and *Romeo and Juliet*, with Higgie and Mrs. Hooper in the title rôles and Hooper himself as Mercutio. In September for Cavalry and Race Weeks, J. Russell returned in a round of comic parts and in November the manager engaged Carter, the American Lion King, with his troop of animals. In a new French melodrama, *The Lion of the Desert*, Carter regaled the audience by a combat with a tiger and by driving a lion in harness.

If opera was neglected in 1840 it was paramount in 1841. No less than three groups of vocalists were engaged. In March came Mr. & Mrs. Alban Croft and F. Shrivall. Members of the choral society were engaged for the choruses. Not only the foreign operas of *La Sonnambula*, *Fra Diavolo* and *Cinderella* were given but the English ones of *Rosina*, *The Quaker* and *The Beggar's Opera*. The last was one night played straight with Mrs. Alban Croft as Polly and her husband as Macheath, and another night with the rôles reversed and Shrivall as Lucy. Miss Delcy, now at Drury Lane, returned in May, supported by Templeton and G. Horncastle. Her Zerlina and Amina were declared enchanting and Templeton was a fine and bold Tom Tug. Rophino Lacy also returned to conduct.[109] No sooner had they left than they were succeeded by the Misses Smith, vocalists from the St. James's, and R. Shrivall from the Royal Academy of Music. With them came Sam Cowell from Edinburgh. His father, Joseph Cowell, had been a member of the York company. Sam was known as 'the young American Roscius' and had acted in all the chief theatres of the U.S.A. (Ten years later he was to embark on his great career in the music hall.) They played in lighter pieces, Cowell sustaining Allcash and Peter Spyke in *The Loan of a Lover.* Cathcart from Covent Garden played a round of Shakespearian and other characters. He was a good actor, but had unfortunately a celestial nose and a huge torso 'which protruded before and behind and was supported by a pair of clumsy wooden legs.'[110]

Yates brought a party from the Adelphi in July consisting of Mrs. Yates, George Wieland, Edward Wright, Lyon and Paul Bedford. Wieland was a pantomimist of whom Edmund Kean declared, 'That boy could convey by gesture alone the significance of every line of Hamlet;'[111] like Tom Matthews he danced a burlesque cachucha and he also brought out his entertainment entitled *Flip Flap Footman*[112] and his burletta *Deeds of Dreadful Note.* Wright was the Adelphi's first comedian but Bedford, the second comedian, was a greater figure in stage history. On their last night[113] he played his famous rôle of Joe Blueskin in *Jack Sheppard* with Yates as Mendez, and Lyon as Jonathan Wild. On this night too they gave *Robespierre* with Yates in the title rôle, Bedford as Cato Boze, Wright as Herault Sachelles and Mrs. Yates as Honoré de Beaupré. Other Adelphi melo-dramas they presented were *Victorine* with Bedford as Bonassus and *Agnes St. Aubin* which was new to York. Bedford relates an amusing incident about the former which necessitated the use of a lifesize dummy known as 'the Victim'. This dummy was taken in the train in a potato bag from which its head hung out with the result that whilst the actors were dining the police came to arrest them as body snatchers.[114]

Charles Kean was engaged in October and added to rôles already played in York those of Shylock, Beverley in *The Gamester* and Duke Aranza in *The Honeymoon.* He received £96.15.0. for four performances which was half the receipts and gave one night free.[115] The year had seen the opening of the De Grey Rooms as a further place of entertainment. On the other hand the population of York had increased from 8000 in 1823 to 28,842, though the Theatre did not seem to benefit by it.

During 1842 Hooper brought to York a long list of stars. But before we deal with them we must notice two new members of the company. One was Alfred Ormond, who opened on the first night as Clarmont in G. A'Beckett's farce *The Artist's Wife,* and subsequently played in a series of melodramas; the other was John Langford Pritchard who was to succeed Hooper as manager. Pritchard[116] had been born at sea in 1799 and had started life as a midshipman. By way of amateur theatricals he abandoned the sea for the stage and in 1821, as we have seen, he was for a short time a member of the York company. Since then he had played leading business for eleven years in Edinburgh and had made his first appearance at Covent Garden under Macready in 1835. Macready was accused of keeping him back but in fact, though a sound, he was never a first-rate actor. Now he returned to York to play the leads and as stage manager. Among his rôles were those of Rob Roy, in which he particularly excelled, Rolla, Hastings, Faulkland and Sir Harry Vivid in Bell's comedy *Marriage*.

The first star was Charles Kean who now came with his newly wedded wife – formerly Ellen Tree – to play the Stranger and Mrs. Haller on Easter Monday. For this and the following night at Leeds they received £98.2.9.[117] In April, James Wallack made his second appearance in York playing Hamlet, Othello to the Iago of Pritchard and Desdemona of Mrs. Hooper, Richard III to the Richmond of Pritchard, and on his last night, Shylock and Benedick with Mrs. Hooper as Portia and Beatrice – a rather full programme.

Close on Wallack's heels came the comedian William Farren, now in his fifties, and the best actor of old men of his day. In York he played what was probably his greatest part, that of Lord Ogleby, as well as Sir Peter Teazle, Uncle Foozle, Nicholas Flam, Sir Anthony Absolute, Hectic in *Petticoat Government* and Uncle John. In mid-May the Woods returned for two nights supported by Horncastle in *Fra Diavolo*, *La Sonnambula*, *The Quaker* and *The Waterman*. Mrs. Waylett accompanied by her husband Alexander Lee and by Bedford and Wright, made her first appearance in July. Known as the Queen of the English Ballad she rivalled Madame Vestris in popularity as a singer and excelled in soubrette rôles, breeches characters and in the now popular extravaganza. She had married Lee the previous year and he composed many of her songs for her and accompanied her at the piano. Once a page to the notorious Lord Barrymore he had in turn become musical director at the Haymarket, Drury Lane and the Strand, and had composed music for several pieces. With Wright, Mrs. Waylett sang a sketch of a *Lady and Gentleman in a Peculiarly Perplexing Predicament*, and some duets with Bedford, and in *The Loan of a Lover* she played Gertrude to Wright's Peter Spyke.

The Boleno family of pantomimists appeared in August in ballets, panto-mimes and tableaux vivants. They consisted of Signor Boleno, presumably the popular clown Harry (whose real name was Mason) then at the start of his career, M. Mason and M. Sidini Boleno. In the pantomime *Ride a Cock Horse* Signor Boleno was the clown, Mason Boleno Pantaloon, Sidini Boleno Harlequin and Miss Hunt Columbine; the scenery was painted by Easling. Their tableaux included *L'Atelier de Canova* in which they personated statues on revolving pedestals, and the *Olympic Athletes or Struggles of the Gladiators* in which feats of strength were exhibited. In the Raphael tableaux coloured fires were employed to illuminate the pictures. On September 2 the greatest dancer York had yet seen made her appearance – this was Mlle Cerrito.

She danced *La Gitana* and the *Pas de Deux* from *Alma* and *La Varsovienne* with Miss O'Bryan from Her Majesty's Theatre. On her fourth and last night, in order to give everyone the chance of seeing her, she performed at half price at 9.30 in *La Cachucha* and a Polish dance *La Liluana*. Dining hours were later so that the Theatre was apt to be empty until half price.

Two other items of interest may be noted: a curious performance of *Romeo and Juliet* in which Mrs. Hooper played Romeo to the Juliet of Miss Waverley, and the début of another play from Dickens, *Barnaby Rudge*. Hooper took his farewell benefit on October 16 as Sparkish to his wife's Miss Peggy in *The Country Girl*, followed by Charles Paragon to her Kate O'Brien in *Perfection*. Years afterwards Coleman[118] met him as manager at Ipswich and found him a 'a very genial old gentleman … the very image of Turveydrop,' who was in and out of prison for debt. The next day it was announced that Pritchard, then playing in Dumfries, was the new lessee,[119] his circuit consisting of York, Hull, Leeds and Dumfries. The lease to Wilkinson expired on August 1 and he was granted a year to year tenancy at the reduced rent of £150.[120] Nothing could more clearly testify to the declining state of the Theatre in York.

On October 17 the Keans returned for one night as Felix and Violante preceded by *The Iron Chest* with Kean as Mortimer. Towards the end of the month Herr Louis Dobler the Magician from the St. James's rented the Theatre for some nights, among other wonders lighting 200 candles which instantaneously illuminated the whole stage, by one pistol shot.

Pritchard was one of the outstanding managers of the York circuit. Like others before him he aimed to re-establish the legitimate drama and revive plays of merit; unlike some of them he stuck to his guns and actually put on a large number of such plays, almost entirely eschewing in his first season the 3 and 4 piece programme. He opened on March 6, 1843 with *Othello*: Othello = Thomas Holmes, Iago = Bruce Norton, Desdemona = Miss A. Orelia, all newcomers. He followed this up by presenting more Shakespeare than had been seen in York for many a long day except when some star had performed. *Much Ado* with himself as Benedick, Miss Waverley Scott as Beatrice; *As You Like It*; *The Comedy of Errors* with songs; *Romeo and Juliet* with himself and Miss Scott in the title rôles; *Richard II*; *Macbeth* with Holmes as Macbeth; *Lear* with Norton as the king; *The Merry Wives* with Reynolds as Falstaff; *Catharine and Petruchio*; and *The Merchant of Venice* in which Pritchard played Shylock. In this last the 5th act was not omitted as had been customary and the manager announced that the only omissions in old plays would be the verbal ones necessitated by morality and good taste. Yet he allowed the 3rd act of *Hamlet* to be played on its own with Miss Saunders as Hamlet. Shakespeare was not the only standard dramatist to be revived. Among plays given were the evergreen trio *The School for Scandal*, *The Rivals* and *She Stoops to Conquer*, as well as *The Provok'd Husband*, *The Wonder*, *Pizarro*, *Venice Preserv'd* and *The Jealous Wife*. *Ivanhoe* was resuscitated after many years with costumes from the exact period of the 12th century including robes of the Knights Templar. According to the *Yorkshireman*[121] 'for gorgeousness of scenery, richness of costumes and ingenious machinery, a long period of time has indeed elapsed since the theatre royal of this city exhibited a counterpart.' Pritchard took the rôle of Wilfred which he had created at Covent Garden. Of the new plays perhaps the best known was G. Dibdin Pitt's *Susan Hopley; or The Vicissitudes of a Servant Girl,* a domestic drama with a double murder and a ghost which played in York for 5 successive nights and had a long vogue.

As for the company it had as usual been selected from many parts of the country though not, as much as others, from the London minors. Pritchard and Thomas Holmes were the leading men, with William Gourlay as low comedian. Miss Waverley Scott was leading lady, Miss Woulds from Bath the principal songstress. A. E. Reynolds who had been born in Norwich in 1788, undertook comic old men and was a member of the company for many years,[122] and in E. W. Gomersal, Pritchard acquired a young man who later became a well known low comedian. J. Halford was recommended as a first singer by Mackay of Edinburgh and engaged for a year. In May he published a protest[123] against the way he had been treated, alleging that Pritchard, a novice in management and ignorant of the technicalities of opera, had then engaged a first tenor not realising that they were the same line. Halford was convinced that Pritchard was withholding him from public notice except when he thought the audiences would be thin, forcing him into unsuitable parts, and assigning his business to another. Halford disliked Pritchard's levelling system by which an actor who played a lead in one piece might have to take a subordinate rôle in the next, and argued that it rendered the company dissatisfied, degraded the players before the audiences, and was at variance with the standing of the Theatre 'which has ever been characterised as the finishing school for dramatic talent.' The disgruntled actor also stated that Pritchard rarely attended rehearsals unless he were the hero, and that no stage manager was appointed whose business it was to ensure punctuality. Pritchard came, if at all, an hour after the rehearsal had been called 'preferring bed to business.' He alleged that fines for unpunctuality were unfair; that he himself had been stopped 1/6 for being $^1/_4$ hour late though an actor who was an hour late, because someone detained a book, was not docked at all; unpunctuality had spread to the performances and the audience had twice in one month been kept waiting $^1/_2$ and $^3/_4$ hour because Pritchard did not arrive at the Theatre until 7.30 though needed at the onset. Against these allegations we have to set a letter to the *York Courant*[124] from a citizen of Old Ebor, commending Pritchard for producing a succession of fine dramas in correct costume with appropriate and beautiful scenery and an excellent orchestra. Pritchard, he affirmed, had gained the esteem of York citizens for his talents as an actor and for his exertions in preserving from decay 'the fine old dramatic nursery of York.' Newspaper comments, for what they are worth, were unanimously favourable, and the manager's considerateness and his cheerfulness in taking subordinate parts were remarked upon.[125] The truth probably was that Halford was not a success (he received an adverse criticism for his Robin Hood) and was consequently relegated to the background. One of his complaints was remedied later in the season when Bruce Norton became stage manager.

The leader of the band and director of music was Hope, and the band itself consisted of repetiteur Gleadow, 2nd violin R. Saynor, Tenor A. Reynolds, Violincello Stanley from Drury Lane, Contra Basso Brown, Flute Waylandt, Clarionet George, Drums Blythe. Easling, who had been with Hooper, remained as scenic artist. Campbell, from Ducrow's Royal Amphitheatre, was machinist, Bath master carpenter, H. Saunders ballet master, Saunders superintendent of wardrobe with Weems as wardrobe-keeper, James Dewar property man, John Holmes treasurer and box book-keeper, John Coates secretary, bill deliverer, pit checktaker, W. Partrick box keeper and Andrews librarian. This list gives an idea of how the non-acting staff of the theatre had grown.

The box plan was now available at the box office from 11-3 when John Holmes was in attendance to allot tickets and places. The manager requested innkeepers, proprietors of lodging houses and shopkeepers to display bills in their windows and those wishing to have bills regularly delivered at their houses were asked to send in their address to the box office. Pritchard also introduced a system of numbering the season and night on the playbills which had become much longer and fuller, sometimes running to more than a page.

The manager's brave attempt to revive the drama, and to depend on his stock company – for but one star appeared this season – did not meet with encouragement and support. No wonder that the *Yorkshireman* alluded to his policy as a 'desperate experiment.'[126] The *Courant* declared that the drama in the previous 10-12 years had fallen very low indeed and that Pritchard had practically achieved a reformation and had, in addition, purified it from every cause of offence. In an address at the end of his first season the manager compared himself with a mariner who had made an unsuccessful voyage but who determined 'neither to complain of the past, nor to despond for the future,' since he trusted in York's taste on which he had risked a fortune.[127]

W. J. Hammond, now lessee of Liverpool, was the only star. Among his rôles were his famous Sam Weller and burlesque Othello which he had created at the Strand.

When the company returned in July James Elsegood from the English Opera House had become the ballet master. He also arranged tableaux of the *Labours of Hercules* and brought out *The Dumb Boy of Brussels*, a domestic drama which had been written for him. This season saw a new form of entertainment introduced in York – the minstrel show. Concerts were given by the South American Minstrels Wolcott, Robbins, Parker and King. They showed the sports and pastimes of the Negroes accompanied by Negro ditties as sung by slaves at their merrymakings. The entertainment was advertised as being free from objectionable features in word, look and action. During August the Lion King Carter returned, this time in Boyle

Bernard's melodrama *Mungo Park* for which music was specially composed by James Gleadow. The audience was also regaled with the sight of the animals being fed.

The October playbills in the Minster Library have the receipts written in on them from which we learn that the best house, under the patronage of the N.C.O.'s and privates of the Yorks Hussars, only brought £32.4.0., the second best under the Officers £24.6.6. and the lowest on the opening night £7.2.5. These figures were much worse than those of Wilkinson's day though the rent of the theatre had soared since then and the company and staff were considerably larger.

The year 1843 saw the passing of the important Act for Regulating the Theatres which finally abolished the monopoly of the patent houses. Licences to present plays of all kinds could be issued to any theatre outside London and the royal residences by the local justices in session, and thus the minors were no longer restricted to musical pieces. This had little effect in York where there was no minor theatre; nor did it encourage any attempt to start one. Indirectly it probably had its influence on the re-cruiting of the already impoverished stock company, since the London minors could now offer more attractive openings for beginners and pro-vincial theatres were no longer the only stepping stones to the metropolis where a full repertoire could be played. Although York was a theatre under royal patent it seems henceforward to have come under the jurisdiction of the justices from whom an annual licence had to be procured.[128] Another provision in the Act was that playbills must bear the name and address of the lessee and these duly appear from this time on.

Pritchard reopened on March 11, 1844 with a company strengthened in nearly every department. Several former members came back for a few nights. The native-born Hield, who had since visited America, was the first. Rayner, who had succeeded Emery in Yorkshire rôles, gave his famous impersonation of Tyke and at his benefit performed Lubin Greenwell in *Love's Frailties*, a drama expressly written to display his talent in both strong passion and subdued feeling. Another native, W. H. Maddocks, now principal tragedian at Plymouth returned after ten years in Richard III, Othello, Bertram, Lear and Frederick Bramble. Charles Bland, who had been a popular singer in the circuit in 1831 sang Tom Tug and Rodolpho, his original rôle in *Der Freischütz*.

Two famous plays came out this year: Knowles's *Love* on March 25 with Hield as Huon and Boucicault's *London Assurance* with Dazzle = Hield, Sir Harcourt Courtly = A. E. Reynolds, Max Harkaway = Bruce Norton, Charles Courtly = Sydney Davies (a newcomer), Spanker = Gourlay, Mark Middle = Smythson, Lady Gay Spanker = Miss Mathilda Ross, Grace Harkaway = Miss Villars, Pert = Mrs. Gourlay. Dickens was represented by *A Christmas Carol* with Norton as Scrooge, for the production of which Pritchard engaged the author Edward Stirling; and in October by *Martin Chuzzlewit* by the same adapter. Shakespeare burlesque was represented by J. S. Coyne's *Richard ye Third* a sample of the synopsis of which read 'The

Queen raveth – the Kinge trembleth – the Duke of York up bloweth – the Queen away goeth.' Once again a local drama made its début in any theatre on these boards. This was *The Jew's Revenge* by John Duncan, editor of the *Yorkshireman*, which came out on May 20. The author offered his tragedy to Pritchard because he saw him struggling to resuscitate the drama to empty boxes, and he felt that an inferior tragedy from a local hand might provide the novelty which stock tragedies often enacted could not. Pritchard played Levi and Miss Scott his daughter Judith. The songs were set to music by Hope, the scenery was by Gilbert and Dalby, the costumes of the 13th century were made by Weems and his assistants under the direction of Pritchard and the author, the machinery was by Bath and the properties by Dewar and Reeves. The piece was played 6 times during the year. Another piece of local interest was a petite comedy *York Wives* brought out at Pritchard's benefit on May 23 and repeated several times. Downe's idea of bringing the Hull Christmas pantomime to York on Easter Monday was revived. This season it was *Harlequin and the Ocean Queen* written by Elsegood and produced under his direction. The 16 scenes were painted by Gilbert and Dalby, who had succeeded Easling as the company's scene painters, and included an extensive mechanical change of waters dispersing to discover the boudoir of Amphitrite and the now established transformation. The Ruby Castle and the Silver Lake were pronounced to be extremely beautiful and well painted. Elsegood, who was to be the Clown, sprained his ankle at rehearsal[129] and his part was taken by Gourlay. In May a benefit was given for Woodcock who had been an actor in the provincial theatres for 27 years but had gone blind and was unable to provide for himself; his night brought him £26. *God Save the Queen* was played on the last night of the season as it coincided with the Queen's birthday. At least 8 Shakespeare plays were given and *As You Like It* was announced as from the text, though *The Tempest* was still in the Dryden Davenant version and *Lear* in Tate's. The summer and autumn seasons saw a return to the 3-piece a night regime but then the public weeks had always been provided with lighter fare. On July 10 the polka was danced on the York stage for the first time, so it was claimed, in a country theatre, by Elsegood and Miss Clara Harcourt to Pergni's music. The dance had swept the capitals of Europe and was now the rage in the saloons and theatres of London. At the end of the month the Leclercqs, with Miss Leclercq and Miss Louise Leclercq, now the infant pantomimist, returned with some new ballets. Mark Lemon's drama *The Turf* was given a local flavour by a new scene representing the Knavesmire race course. The company now adopted the title of Her Majesty Queen Victoria's servants. The British Association met in York in September and the Theatre opened for the occasion. Among the pieces was a petite comedy *The Benefit Night* written by a member of the B.A. for which Pritchard had received a licence, and which made its first appearance on any stage on September 28.

Mons. D'Augvigney's puppets from the Théâtre du Petit Lazary visited the Theatre in November staying three weeks. Their exhibition had been given in York 14 years previously but not in the Theatre. The charges were boxes 2/-, upper boxes 1/6, gallery 6d, and the ladies were advised that they need not fear taking cold from the damp as the patent warming apparatus was constantly in use.

Repairs and improvements were made this year to the gas installations and Brook applied to the Corporation on behalf of the Trustees for a payment towards the cost of £46. They agreed to pay £10 since the Gas Company made an allowance for the old fittings.[130]

Pritchard came to York in 1845 after a successful season in Hull. Though there were often thin houses he did well enough to thank his patrons at the end of the July season for enabling him to restore the circuit to its pristine health. Pritchard brought with him Mrs. Ternan who as Miss Jarman had formerly appeared in the York Company when a child. She had been to America for three years and was then engaged for Drury Lane. She played many leading rôles in York from Lady Teazle to Lady Macbeth. In the sleepwalking scene she obtained an almost deathlike silence and 'her form seemed to dilate during the workings of her fierce determination.' She had a worthy Macbeth in Holmes who electrified the house by his delivery of 'She should have died hereafter.' The critic thought that the banquet scene would be more effective if Banquo's ghost did not appear.[131] Mrs. Ternan took many other Shakespearean heroines, Rosalind, Juliet, Ophelia, Cordelia, Desdemona and Catharine. With her were her three daughters Fanny aged 7, Maria and Ellen. Fanny joined the ranks of infant prodigies and like others before her appeared in sketches specially written to show off her paces in different personations; the copyright of *The Pet of the Admiral* and the *Little Tiger* were purchased by Pritchard for this purpose. Maria appeared as Tom Thumb and danced the polka with her sister, and Ellen was one of the children in the wood.

Rayner reappeared for a few nights, and officers of the garrison of Leeds, York and Sheffield performed twice. Gomersal rejoined the company in August and remained for two years. Frederick Corby Fisher from Manchester was the company's new scene painter, Hutchings the director of vocal music; Miss Thomassin had succeeded Elsegood in the direction of the ballet; Kemp from the Marylebone was assisting Bath as machinist; Kimber was responsible for the properties, and H. Montague was prompter and deputy stage manager.

Two famous pieces were brought out in 1845, one was the drama *Don Caesar de Bazan* on April 1, the other Balfe's *Bohemian Girl* on May 9. Duncan's second tragedy *The Spy of Venice* saw the light on May 7 with Pritchard as Bernardo, Holmes as Antonio and Mrs. Ternan as Bianca. A considerable portion of the profits of the first night went to the author towards the purchase of the copyright but the piece did not have the success of its predecessor. A version of Dickens's *The Chimes* attributed to Broadfoot[132] was performed. The pantomime was *Baron Munchhausen* which came out a month after Easter with Miss Thomassin as Columbine. On the same night the York Union Society of Change Ringers introduced some new and beautifully toned handbells on which they played popular airs. In April the playbills advertised for 40 young ladies of good figure, prepossessing features and taking manners for the new burlesque *Open Sesame*. They would be given free instruction and furnished with 'boots, spurs, sabres, moustachios, jackets, unmentionables.' *The Merry Wives* was revived in July with Reynolds as Falstaff.

An interesting announcement for the revival of Morton's *A School for Grown Children* states that 'A new Set Drawing Room Scene after the French Fashion' had been painted by Corby Fisher. This was probably a box set, a type which had first been introduced at Drury Lane in 1834. A great attraction in October was the Danseuses Viennoises who had made a sensation at the Opera House and had appeared before Queen Victoria, the Queen Dowager and a good many of the crowned heads of Europe. They consisted of 36 juvenile dancers under the direction of Madame Josephine Weiss. Rates of admission were as usual but the complimentary list, except for the press, was suspended.

John Wilkinson died at Acomb on January 20, 1846 at the age of 76 and was buried in Acomb church.[133] By his will[134] his interest in the Theatres of Hull, Leeds and York was left, subject to the trust deed of 1815, to his daughters Sarah, Jane and Ann Wilkinson and Martha Groom. Ann was bequeathed a ^{2}/5ths share in order that she might supply his son Tate with board, lodging, wearing apparel and other necessaries during his lifetime. The annual benefit granted to him now passed to Tate the younger.

Following an innovation in the London theatres Pritchard introduced the practice, at the request of patrons, of turning down the gas lights in the auditorium during the performance and restoring them in the intervals. Up till then the lights had been full on all the time, and this innovation increased the brilliancy of the stage and reduced the heat and glare. Nevertheless, it was adversely received by the *York Gazette*[135] whose reporter did not like being in the dark: 'The new arrangement may, perhaps, render the stage more striking, but it casts a strange grim reflection upon the house.' It was tried for a few nights as an experiment only but was probably continued. The manager had also to ban bonnets from the dress circle. An interesting bespeak was that of the Licensed Victuallers Society. Tradesmen as well as the law, the military, the masons, hunts and the gentry were now patronising the theatre. Attendances were improving with the exception of some nights. Yet in May the *York Gazette*[136] stated that support was lacking and that if it were not forthcoming the manager would be compelled to revert to light and frivolous spectacles. Many condemned him for his unwearying search of novelty though he risked his capital in the process; yet if he presented the higher drama he was told his company was not equal to it. The *Gazette* rather agreed. 'For pageantry, grouping, and decorative effect, the present company is as complete as could be wished for in a provincial theatre; but, with regard to the standard representations, it is, not altogether, but for the most part, insufficient.' Pritchard was urged to make every effort to rescue the stage from pollution and, more practically, to have a less numerous but more talented company.

The manager did bring out a great many new plays in 1846. Among them were Boucicault's *Old Heads and Young Hearts,* Buckstone's famous melodrama *Green Bushes,* Archer's *Georgette, Daughter of the Regiment* adapted from Donizetti, Thomas Abbott's version of *The Cricket on the Hearth*[137] and Somerset's military drama *War with the Sikhs.* For this last and *The War in Afghanistan,* 50 supers were engaged. Pritchard even purchased the acting rights of Somerset's American drama *The Maid of Oregon* thus enabling him to forestall the London production. Local interest was encouraged. A drama by a gentleman of Leeds called *Nick of the Woods* was written expressly for the circuit, and Mrs. Green, a lady of Leeds, wrote a sketch for Fanny Ternan when she returned in July, entitled *Young France.* The titles of pieces were adapted to local circumstances: Thomas Morton junior's Adelphi farce *Seeing Wright* being brought out as *Seeing Gomersal,* and Coyne's *Did You Ever Send Your Wife to Camberwell?* was translated to Bishopthorpe. For the pantomime, *Whittington and his Cat,* the English costumes were taken from the illuminations to Froissart, the African from Horace Vernet. Dresses were now in charge of Harry, Mrs. Gibbs and Mrs. Updell, properties the charge of Gibbs and Metcalfe, and Bath was assisted in machinery by Emmett and Isaacs. The pantomime was given again in May for the fair and holiday folks of Clifton and Fulford. Pritchard had also arranged with the celebrated composer Jullien for a regular succession of his popular quadrilles, waltzes, polkas and galops for the orchestra. Shakespeare was by no means neglected, at least six of his plays being seen this year. Miss Land, a niece of Liston, was engaged for a short time from Covent Garden to sing the Rosettas and Rosinas, and introduced into the rôle of Jessica *O Bid Me Discourse* and *Lo! hear Beautiful Venice.* The singing witches in *Macbeth* had reached a regular chorus of 23. The Danseuses Viennoises and Mrs. Ternan and Fanny returned in July, and in October two pupils of Mrs. Glover, the Misses Fitzpatrick and Acosta, were brought out as Lydia Languish and Julia. They both captivated their audience. Miss Acosta was acclaimed for the genuine heart storm of her love scene with Faulkland.[138] She subsequently played Juliet, Hero, and Juliana in *The Honeymoon* and remained with the company for three years. Of Miss Fitzpatrick Westland Marston says that in her acting 'humour and lively characterization were combined with rare good taste and refinement';[139] her rôles included Beatrice, Catharine, and Helen in *The Hunchback.* They were still the leading ladies when the company returned in 1847 but many of the 24 actors and 14 actresses who composed it were newcomers – a matter of regret – since the old faces with all their imperfections were popular in York.[140] Holmes returned, however, in May playing Othello to Norton's Iago, and Miss Acosta's Desdemona, and Hamlet to the Ophelia of Miss Thompson. Pritchard himself was seen for the first time as Sir Giles Overreach, and acted his favourite rôle of Rob Roy which he had performed more than 900 times in 14 years including once in Edinburgh before Sir Walter Scott.

For one night the American actress Charlotte Cushman and her sister Susan appeared on their way north. Pritchard congratulated himself that when theatres were vying for her services York was among the first to obtain them. She had come to England in 1845 and created a sensation as Romeo, the part she chose for her York appearance. Her deep voice and mannish bearing led her into undertaking masculine rôles and caused her to be dubbed Charley de Boots. She drew a brilliant house but disappointed the critic of the *York Gazette* who came to the conclusion that the part should be played by the correct sex. She had pathos and passion, grace and ability, but also unpleasant mannerisms, and she was best in the scene of delirium with Friar Laurence. Coleman praises her at the death of Tybalt and in the banishment scene but sums up her performance as 'the effort of a monstrously clever woman – but it was not Romeo.' Coleman found her sister's Juliet 'about as puerile an effort as I have ever seen. Its most conspicuous feature was its costume and its corsetage.' The *York Gazette* critic was kinder and adjudged it a pretty piece of acting, tame in the balcony scene, but faultless in the last scene with Romeo, that is if it had not been marred by the blundering of scene shifters.[141]

Bayntun Rolt, the brother of Capt. Bayntun who had been M.P. for York, appeared as Macbeth and Richard III. *Macbeth* was said to be played from the text and the scenes with Lady Macduff and her children, long banished, were restored, though the chorus of witches and spirits remained. The tendency was towards getting back to the real Shakespeare though *The Comedy of Errors* was, on the other hand, given in a three act version with omissions of objectionable passages, as concocted by Woods of Edinburgh. In July *Twelfth Night* was presented for the first time under Pritchard with Orsino = Holmes, Belch = Bower, Aguecheeck = Gomersal, Malvolio = W. Artaud, Clown = Reynolds, Olivia = Miss Acosta, Viola = Miss Thompson.

The Misses Le Batt and Georgina Le Batt were engaged for a few nights for comic operas and melodramas but failed to draw. More successful were the Ethiopean Serenaders, a blackface minstrel troupe from the Surrey, who performed in Stirling's *The Buffalo Girls*, a sketch of Negro life and melody.

Ballet was not neglected and Shaw and Miss Vaughan were engaged and danced among other pieces the pas de deux from *Giselle*. Marsingale was now leader of the orchestra in which there were 9 players, and Tannett from Dublin was the scene painter.

In June Madame Vestris and her husband Charles J. Mathews made a farewell appearance before their retirement from the stage. As Nanette in *A Speaking Likeness* she displayed all the gaiety and buoyancy of her early days; whilst Mathews in *Patter v Clatter* transformed the outer man and by his wonderful volubility kept the audience in peals of laughter.[142] For their second night he played Sir Charles Coldstream in *Used Up*, Hans Moritz to his wife's Minnie in Planché's *Somebody Else* and Motley in *He Would Be an*

Actor. Mathews was seen in York again several times. Creswick, who had been the tragedian in York 1837-38, returned for a few nights in August. He had been in America for four years, had played at Sadler's Wells under Phelps, and was now at the Princess's Theatre. With him came Emmeline Montague who later married Henry Compton, and together they played Romeo and Juliet, Master Walter and Julia, Claude Melnotte and Pauline, Jaques and Rosalind. More vocalists and dancers were engaged for opera at the end of September when *Lucia di Lammermoor* was brought out with Donald King as Edgar, M'Mahon as Raymond, Weiss as Henry Ashton, Mrs. King as Lucia, and an augmented orchestra. Audiences were, however, not numerous.[143]

Limelight was first used on the York stage in November when diagrams and views in a scientific entertainment from the Royal Institution were illuminated by the new invention.[144]

The Corporation agreed to slate the roof at a cost of about £80 as the pantiles let in the water every time there was a heavy rain storm.[145] When the Theatre reopened on March 13, 1848 it had been repainted and decorated by the former scene painter Newnum and his pupils. Early in the season Pritchard obtained leave of the trustees to reduce the prices except for special occasions. The dress boxes which had been 3/-, 2nd price 2/- were henceforward 3/-, 2nd price 1/6; upper boxes which had been 2/6, 2nd price 1/6 were reduced to 2/- and 1/-; pit from 2/-, 2nd price 1/- to 1/- and gallery from 1/- to 6d. Arrangements were also made with Sotherans of Coney Street that box tickets and places could be secured there after the theatre box office shut at 3 o'clock. The decreased prices brought better audiences to the pit and gallery but the boxes remained empty. This was attributed by the *York Gazette*[146] to the puerilities and monstrosities that were presented which caused many sensible people to hold the Theatre in contempt. Archer's *Bottle*, a dramatisation of Cruikshank's illustrations 'fraught with Moral and Salutary Lessons', which ran for six nights, was classed among these representations. The right of acting this drama in the circuit had been purchased of the author, and a gentleman of Leeds had been so impressed by its moral value that he had bought 150 copies to distribute to his workpeople. Knowles's *Wrecker's Daughter* came out on May 26. Another complaint was that performances were frequently changed after they were advertised which particularly incommoded suburban patrons.

A previous practice of cutting Shakespeare plays to the size of afterpieces was introduced this year, the operation being performed on *The Merchant of Venice, Romeo and Juliet* and *Henry VIII* which were replaced as the main offering by the despised *Bottle*.

Gomersal had left the company. He had sued Pritchard in Hull because the manager had deducted a guinea from his salary of 30/- on his refusal to play Robin in *No Song No Supper*. He claimed he was not a low comedian but the verdict was in Pritchard's favour.[147]

The most important addition to the company was Isabella Glynn, who had been recommended by Charles Kemble whose pupil she was. She was one of the last actresses of the Siddons School, of commanding stature, large gestures, powerful voice and strong and expressive features. At that time she was 25 years old, had first appeared in Manchester the previous year and had made her London début at the Olympic. Her opening part in York was Juliana in *The Honeymoon* and she also played Mrs. Oakley, Portia, Rosalind, Beatrice, Juliet, Catharine in *Catharine and Petruchio*, Queen Katharine, Lady Macbeth and Lady Townly at her final appearance on April 5. Later in life she was to become famous for her Shakespearian readings.

A famous theatrical name this year graces the York company – that of Terry, for among the newcomers was the Irish actor Benjamin Terry and his wife, formerly Sarah Ballard, 'a rather willowy but handsome woman',[148] parents of Kate and Ellen. Kate herself, aged 5, acted Macduff's son and sang between the acts. Ellen had only been born the year before. Terry played *The Wandering Jew* in an adaptation of Sue's drama; singing rôles such as Amiens and Borachio; Escalus, Rosencrantz and Clown in the comic pantomime *Davy Jones's Locker;* his wife was Lady Capulet, Lady Macduff, Queen Gertrude and Alicia in *Jane Shore.*

Lewis Hall was another newcomer and opened in E. L. Blanchard's *York Railway Station.* He remained with the company two years and later was to be the low comedian under Phelps at Sadler's Wells. He played Launcelot Gobbo, Touchstone, Dogberry, Cromwell and Harlequin in *Davy Jones's Locker.* Adeline Lonsdale was the new dancer and Columbine, and the Misses Le Batt were re-engaged for a short season. A novelty was the first appearance of a troupe of Bedouin Arabs in national costume who, attended by Marabouts (priests), performed feats of strength and agility for five nights.

The season is remarkable for the succession of stars that were brought to York. Miss Cushman returned this time in the feminine rôles of Queen Katharine, Mrs. Haller, Juliana, Mrs. Simpson and in her celebrated Meg Merrilees. She was called for by the audience who were reminded of the palmy days of the Theatre.[149] On May 1 the Charles Keans played Walter and Evelyn Amyott in Lovell's Haymarket success *The Wife's Secret.* Macready played Hamlet on May 15 and Richelieu, one of his greatest parts, the following night with Miss Acosta as Julie di Mortemar. His leading lady, Helen Faucit, made her début in York as Juliet on May 31 with I. Faucit Saville as Mercutio. Subsequently she played Pauline, one of her original creations, Rosalind, one of her best rôles, and Mrs. Beverley; in the poetic drama she held unchallenged pre-eminence and many contemporaries bear witness to the radiance she shed in Shakespeare's heroines.

The Theatre opened in July for the Royal Agricultural Meeting when a legitimate comedy was presented every night. Hunt had been re-engaged as ballet master and brought out the first romantic ballet *La Sylphide* as well as two melodramatic ballets by T. G. Blake, *Daughter of the Danube* and *Spring-Heel Jack; or The Clifton Ghost.* The orchestra was now led by Zink from Bath and Bristol. Lysander Thompson acted a round of comedy characters, mostly rustics; he now specialised in Yorkshire rôles such as Tyke; his make-up was wonderful, an art that seemed nature, and he was successful too in scenes of pathos and tenderness. Creswick reappeared in August playing Quasimodo by his friends' request and Melantius in the first performance of Beaumont and Fletcher's *Maid's Tragedy*. September brought Mrs. Gustavus Brooke (formerly Miss M. A. Duret) in heroines such as Pauline, Violante, Constance and the Widow Cheerly, and George Butler Wentworth as Hamlet, Aranza, Huon, Evelyn in *Money*, and other characters. The popular song writer Henry Russell took the theatre in December for an entertainment of singing interspersed with anecdotes of Negro life and character. He was the composer of *Cheer Boys Cheer* and *Life on the Ocean Wave*, and the father of Sir Landon Ronald. In the same month the Theatre was opened for Assize and Great Horse Show Week by Van Ambergh with his collection of trained animals, including a black tiger hitherto classified as untameable, in *Mungo Park*. Van Ambergh was the greatest of all wild animal trainers and had appeared at Astley's ten years previously. At the end of the year the Theatre opened for the Bush People, 'wild and uncivilised travellers' they are designated, in a New Scenic Delineation, Miller's *Magical Entertainment for the Bosjosmans* together with a lecture.[150]

On January 29, 1849, Farren returned supported by the company for six nights; as well as repeating several rôles in which he had been seen previously, he appeared in two new ones, Peter Britton in *Peter and Paul* and Michael Perrin in *Secret Service*. In his famous part of Grandfather Whitehead he displayed the good-natured cunning, the nervous irritability and the physical prostration of old age. His elocution, however, was not good and he drew only poor houses.[151] He was followed by Madame Warton who engaged the theatre for a few nights to show her *Tableaux Vivants* and *Poses Plastiques* as exhibited at the Walhalla in Leicester Square. The tableaux were taken from the works of painters, ending with a night of Etty. Though an unfounded prejudice prevented the Theatre from being packed, it was reasonably well attended and sufficiently encouraging for Madame Warton to return in September.[152]

The Theatre possesses a bound volume of playbills, complete for the year, with a printed list of the company, and plays performed. The Theatre was open every night of the week, for 65 nights during the 11 weeks of the spring season. There were 24 actors and 19 actresses besides 12 visiting stars, exclusive of an opera company. The orchestra under Zink consisted of eight members. Chicheley was prompter and deputy stage manager, Veroni, who later was harlequin in the Drury Lane pantomimes, ballet master, Charles Fisher scene painter, Bath master carpenter with an assistant, Patterson librarian, Metcalfe property man, Chapman master tailor, Miss Batson housekeeper with a charwoman under her, J. Fallan flyman, John Holmes remained Treasurer to the Trustees and money taker with an assistant. In addition there were four checktakers for the four parts of the house and two box-keepers. Mrs. Metcalfe was the fruiterer.

For the first time we find stern prohibitions of smoking accompanied by a threat of ejection by the police. Carriages were to be ordered at 10.45, performances usually closing at 11, so that they lasted from $3^1/2$ to 4 hours.

Of the newcomers Mrs. Dyas was leading lady and F. B. Egan, for a short time to be manager, sustained genteel comedy rôles. The former had a negligent style of expression which was a relief from the 'monotonously sobbing, reaching intonation' popular with stage heroines of the day.[153] The latter had a prepossessing appearance, was firm without being stiff and did not pace the boards when he had nothing to say. Thomas Holmes returned in April after an indisposition, and Bruce Norton and Gomersal each came back to act for a night.

Charles Fisher had painted a new act drop, and the effects for Blake's *The Lonely Man of the Ocean* included a train dashing across the stage and a ship on fire. Trains were the subject too of the Easter pantomime *The Iron King, or the Origin of Railroads*. The last scene was of a palace of the Dolphins with a fairy star, crystal fountains and a brilliant display of coloured fires. Veroni was Harlequin, Mathewman Clown, Mlle Angelina Columbine and Fanny Holmes, who had danced in the company since 1840 and was a daughter of the faithful John, Harlequina. Ballets staged by Veroni included Act II of *Giselle* under the title of *The Night Dancers*; *Jeannette and Jeannot*, a military ballet supported by the entire strength of the company; and the drawing room scene from Blake's ballet of *Alma*.

George Owen, who had been a child prodigy, came to play some Shakespearean and other rôles. The *York Gazette*[154] pronounced that though they admired his attitude and expression, his voice was too rough for Romeo and he wanted pathos and light and shade. Mrs. Dyas, on the other hand, had a sweet and mellow voice as Juliet though she could not rise to the frenzy of despair or the tragic termination. A description of her pale face, streaming hair and flowing white garments, in harmony with the change of scene, enables us to envisage her. The critic suggested that if fencing could not be properly done it would be better if the vanquished were not to draw at all but be stabbed by surprise or treachery.

The merry joyous laugh of Mrs. Nesbitt once more rang through the theatre in her buoyant performance of Constance. This time she came with her sister Jane Mordaunt who was the Lydia but who had not learned to cast away conventions for natural enunciation.[155] Mrs. Nesbitt also played Lady Teazle and the Widow Cheerly. In May Butler Wentworth returned in Romeo, Othello, Claude Melnotte and other rôles. He was tall, commanding and well proportioned with an agreeable voice[156] but was more fitted for comedy than tragedy.

As a Whitsun attraction George Wild and Fanny Williams were engaged. Wild was a clever comedian who had been manager of the Olympic Theatre from 1841-4. They appeared in a round of Olympic farces and dramas such as Leman Rede's *Our Village* and *Jack in the Water* and Blanchard's *Artful Dodge* and *Pork Chops,* and were such a success that they paid a second visit in July. In this month Macready came as part of a provincial tour to take his farewell before final retirement. On July 19 he appeared as Richelieu and the following night as Othello to the Iago of Holmes and Desdemona of Mrs. Dyas. The house was crowded. An Italian opera company, under the direction of Signora Borsi-Deleurie a contralto from the Malibran, Venice, sang *Il Barbiere di Siviglia* and *L'Elisir d'Amore*. For their visit the dress boxes were raised to 4/-, the upper boxes to 3/-, pit to 2/- and gallery to 1/- but as this resulted in thin audiences they were reduced for the last night. Pritchard was now procuring from Murray at Edinburgh a series of vaude-villes and farces which he produced in rapid succession. Alfred Drummond returned for a few nights in October with his wife, formerly the leading lady Miss Waverley Scott; he acted Othello and she Susan Hopley. Yet another child prodigy followed in the person of Master Edmund Boothby aged 14. His parts ranged from Young Norval and Florian in *The Foundling of the Forest* to Oliver Twist and Frederick in *Lovers' Vows*; mercifully he avoided Shakespeare. The long season went right on until November 24.

Another Italian opera company, this time under Signora Montenegro, from the Scala and His Majesty's, were at the Theatre in January 1850 and they gave Bellini's *Norma* for the first time in York. This time only the dress boxes were raised to 3/6. Hermann Vezin started his stage career with the company, appearing in April in minor rôles.[157] He had been introduced to Pritchard by Charles Kean when he had arrived in England. A small man, only 5 feet 5 1/2 inches in height, he was to become one of the leading actors of his day, of the intellectual rather than emotional type. Pritchard was ill nearly all the season and appeared for the first time as Col. Tangent in Murray's *Unfit for Service* on May 10. By the summer season Holmes was acting manager. In June the police were called in to trace some jewellery and two dresses missing from an actress's dressing room. There was also a strike of subordinates which was, however, quelled without an appeal to the audience.[158]

Buckstone's celebrated melodrama *The Flowers of the Forest* was brought out this year and a piece of local interest, Roger Clarke's *Fayre Maid of Clifton*, made its bow on April 24 with new scenery taken on the spot by Fisher. On Easter Monday Scribe's *The Prophet* was produced with a panoply of banners, trophies and combats. It was followed by Blanchard's panto-mime *Lord Lovell and Nancy Bell*, partly founded on the ballad of *The Mistletoe Bough*, with transformations by Metcalfe and music composed and selected by Zink. *The Jewess*, too, which had been such a success in 1836 was revived and magnificent suits of real armour manufactured by Granger in Paris were hired by Pritchard. The emperor in gold armour, knights and nobles in plate or chain, cardinals in scarlet, and members of the royal family in dresses overlaid with costly metal moved across and round the stage, occupying every inch of it, performing intricate involutions with pre-cision; yet the splendid scenes were rendered ineffective by the incapacity of the stage for such an array.

As for ballets, T. Ridgway, celebrated clown and pantomimist from Covent Garden, produced his *Trois Tettes de Bois*. In June the Manchester

Ballet Company under W. H. Payne paid a visit to York.[159] Payne, a celebrated buffo-pantomimist who had appeared with Grimaldi, danced the poet and Mde Annie Payne Esmeralda in the ballet of that name.

As for the legitimate, George Owen returned in several Shakespeare rôles including that of Richard II, given for the first time under Pritchard's management, as well as in Miss Mitford's *Julian*. On May 15 the Charles Keans played Count Tristan and Iolanthe in *King René's Daughter* by the Hon. E. Phipps, the Recorder of Scarborough. Kean acted like a master whilst Mrs. Kean portrayed the blind heroine with tenderness and simplicity. *Much Ado* was relegated to an afterpiece with the Keans as Benedick and Beatrice. On Mrs. Kean's Beatrice the *York Gazette*[160] waxed eloquent: 'if she may be equalled in this character, we think surely she cannot be excelled. Her style of acting is so refined – so true – so full of detail – so broad in effect – so marked and yet so delicate. Nay further, her natural grace – her judicious and elegant use of ornament – her propriety of expression – her variety of dramatic colouring, all combine to render her conception of the character clear, full, and perfect.' For this and two succeeding nights at Leeds they netted £101.19.6, a clear half of the receipts.[161]

In July Young Hengler 'allowed to be the first rope dancer in the world' combined his feats with a performance of *Hamlet*. This was on August 2 the last night of Pritchard's management. After 8 years tenure he was compelled to retire owing to ill health and three days later he died of enlargement of the liver and dropsy at the age of 54.[162] On August 1 the trustees of the Hull, Leeds and York Theatres, which were all that remained of the circuit, assembled to choose his successor from among the numerous applicants, and their choice unanimously fell on John Caple, formerly manager of the Queen's Theatre in Hull.[163] His wife (formerly Miss Goddard) was a fine actress who had been a distinguished Hermione under Phelps at Sadler's Wells.[164] It was a tribute to Pritchard's management during a poor period for the drama, that this time there was keen competition for the lesseeship.

CHAPTER SEVEN

The Decline of the Stock Company
1850–1876

THE Theatre was directed to be painted on August 12.[1] Caple opened on August 19 with a company which retained some of the old faces. He engaged Alfred Bunn to appear in a monologue entertainment which was illustrated with a series of scenes, painted in London, depicting the genius and career of Shakespeare.[2] Bunn, notorious for his feuds, had been lessee of Drury Lane and Covent Garden and had only left the former in 1848. In September the most famous travelling opera company of the day, Harrison and Pyne's, visited York and performed Balfe's *Enchantress* there for the first time as well as *The Crown Jewels, The Bohemian Girl* and others. Louisa Pyne made her first and only appearance in *Maritana*. At a grand fashionable night in December Caple himself played Lt. Kingston in *Naval Engagements* whilst T. W. Paulo, C. Ridgway, Charles Reeves and Fanny Holmes appeared in a pantomime ballet called *Statue Blanche*.

The fortunes of the company may now be followed more briefly. Its personnel no longer matters greatly since it was forever shifting, and declining into being merely the support of fashionable visitors. Stars and opera companies recur with a wearisome monotony. Worthless farces, vaudevilles, extravaganzas and spectacular melodramas of little interest held the stage. Occasionally an actor of eminence or a piece of some interest appeared on the boards but for the most part manager succeeded manager to the same round of trivialities and the same hectic search for worthless novelties.

Thus the spring season of 1851 was chiefly remarkable for the performances of A. Abel and his dogs Hector and Wallace in a series of canine dramas including *York in 1747 'or, The Murder in the Forest of Galtres founded upon fact'*. Caple himself appeared as Belphegor an itinerant player, 'in his new rural locomotive Theatre Royal', a stage within a stage. The scenery was by E. Morris. In *Tricks and Trials* a view of the Crystal Palace in Hyde Park was shown. Lysander Thompson and the Leclercqs appeared during the season.

The Theatre was only open for a week in August and was then under the management of Henry Roxby Beverley a well known comedian, sometime manager of the Victoria Theatre and proprietor of the Durham circuit, who was the shortest lived of all managers. He engaged his brother the low comedian Samuel Roxby, at that time proprietor of the Sunderland and Durham circuit, for four nights, and presented a series of comedies including the Mortons' *All That Glitters Is Not Gold*. Beverley soon ended up in York Castle for debt. Henry Russell took the Theatre for four nights in October in a *New American Entertainment* in which his descriptions, anecdotes and songs were accompanied by a moving panorama. Of his compositions he sang *Cheer Boys Cheer, Life on the Ocean Wave* and *The Old Arm Chair*. His audiences were numerous; not so were those of the Italian Opera that visited York in November. The *York Gazette* lamented that 'far less attractive productions would have fetched bumper houses in the palmy days of play-going'.[3]

There had been no full summer and autumn season in 1851, there was no spring one in 1852. For the first time the Theatre remained empty except for Assize Week. In August Caple made an attempt to resuscitate its fortunes. He got together a stock company and opened for Race Week with French dancers as a fresh attraction.[4] The Pyne and Harrison company was engaged but, though plaudits showered down from above, the boxes remained obstinately empty. The *Yorkshireman* in December[5] characterised the Theatre, as 'one of the most contemptibly managed concerns out of London'. One of the managers (probably Beverley) had actually been arrested by bailiffs when announced to play. For the last year the productions had been wretched, a great deal of objectionable matter was to be heard whilst for the educated patron there was no rational amusement. According to Atkinson, the Corporation's architect, the building was in a tumble-down condition. Taste too had changed and the pseudo-Elizabethan exterior so admired in 1837 was now stigmatised as 'curious looking'.[6] No wonder then that the executors of Brook, the late trustee, gave notice of the termination of their tenancy from Lady Day 1853. Groom, the lawyer husband of Wilkinson's daughter Martha, started to negotiate for the lease on behalf of his wife and her three sisters the Misses Sarah, Jane and Anne Wilkinson, already proprietors of the Hull and Leeds Theatres.[7] On November 9 the Council was asked to ratify an agreement with Groom by which the Theatre and house were to be put into good and tenantable repair at a cost of £500 towards which the lessees were to contribute £300. The lessees were also to carry out interior decorations and fit chandeliers at a further cost of £100, the chandeliers to become the property of the Corporation at the end of the lease. The rent was to be reduced to £120 and the tenancy to be from April 6, 1853 for fourteen years, the lessee having the right to terminate it on six months' notice at the end of any year.

One alderman contended that the Theatre should have been let by public competition and not advertised. Another proposed that application should be made to the Lords of the Treasury for leave to sell it. This was supported by other Councillors and carried. The puritanical element had triumphed. Their consciences were sore at the thought that they owned what one of them denounced as 'Satan's Synagogue' and they wanted to be rid of it. There was an immediate outcry that this had been a plot sprung by surprise and pressed to an immediate vote. The decision was pronounced an 'audacious act of a tyrannical majority' and one Councillor even received a letter threatening his property and person.[8] Fuel was added to the flames by a rumour that the Roman Catholics, who had an adjoining chapel in Little Blake Street, wanted to build a cathedral on the site. Sarcastic advertisements appeared in the local press to the effect that Messrs. Mawworm Cant and Hypocrisy 'in consequence of the Corporation of the Ancient City of York having, through Embarrassed Circumstances resolved to sell the Theatre' were offering the Guildhall, Walls and mace for public competition. The Council had to bow to the weight of public opinion and a long and high-tempered meeting ensued in December at which the former resolution was rescinded by a large majority. The opponents of the sale pointed out that it was contrary to the feelings and opinions of the vast majority of the citizens; that a worse nuisance (half a dozen small buildings perhaps) might take its place; that visitors without public amusements would be confined to their inns whilst servants regaled themselves in gin palaces (a potent argument). It rose to being taken as an attack on the innocent amusements of the people. The debate became extremely heated and bitter words were flung. The question of economy was raised but it was pointed out that the City had been receiving £150 a year from the Theatre and had laid little or nothing out for some time past; that the Council would only have to pay £200 out of the £500 required, and that if, with a respectable tenant and a reasonable rent, there was still a small loss, the citizens had a fair claim on the Council to make it good. And the respectable tenant was forthcoming, no less than the Misses Wilkinson (Groom having died in the meantime) in whose family the theatre had been for 88 years. On December 28 their offer for a seven years' lease on the above terms was accepted.[9]

However low the Theatre had sunk, the violence of the controversy raised by the attempt of the Corporation to get rid of it, showed the affection that the York citizens had for it even in its nadir.

The alterations and repairs were proceeded with during 1853 and fell within the original estimate.[10] Unfortunately we do not know in what they consisted.

Caple continued as manager and put on plays of a standard character, drawing pretty good houses especially during the April Race Week. For the Easter pantomime, *Jack the Giant Killer*, the pit and gallery were tolerably full but the boxes not so well attended.[11] Henceforward there were no more benefits for the younger Tate Wilkinson.

In July the Manager brought MacKean Buchanan, the American tragedian, to York, and he played in two American prize dramas, perhaps the first American plays to be seen on that stage. The first was *Mohammed, the*

Arabian Prophet which had won Edwin Forrest's award of 1000 dollars for the best original tragedy; the second was *Caecinna, the Roman Consul* which had been specially written for Buchanan and was seen at York for the first time in England.

An Italian opera company brought out Donizetti's *Lucrezia Borgia* in October with Fanny Huddart, and for their stay private boxes for 4 could be had for £1.[12] They were followed by Hamilton's panorama of the Arctic regions and a moving Alpine diorama, painted by Alfred Adams who had decorated the York Banqueting Hall on the occasion of Prince Albert's visit. A representation of the ascent of Mont Blanc was achieved by a novel perpendicular movement invented especially for this entertainment.[13] The Pyne and Harrison opera company returned in November and on the 19th of that month there appeared at a concert Miss E. J. Greenfield known as the Black Swan. She was a negro vocalist who only 1½ years before had been a slave. Her mistress bequeathed her liberty and a fortune but the latter was held back by the heirs. She had come to England to perfect her singing and to raise popular esteem for her race and had already appeared in London. She had great compass and depth of voice and produced her sonorous lower notes with ease and strength. With only a limited training she had precision in executing intricate passages and a high degree of musicianship.[14]

The Theatre re-opened in January 1854 with yet another diorama, the mail route from Southampton to Calcutta, and more astronomical lectures. The Pyne and Harrison Company returned in February and William Harrison took his farewell in *The Bohemian Girl* prior to his departure to America. Coleman[15] tells us that he could hardly sing at all, and if he did it was through his nose, but his failing in this respect was partly compensated for by the splendour of his physique. The *York Gazette*[16] was 'glad to see our beautiful Theatre so much like itself again on so interesting an occasion.' The famous *I Dreamt I Dwelt in Marble Halls* was encored together with *When Other Lips and Other Hearts*. George Owen played a round of characters in March and during the Assizes Caple met with fair patronage. In the Easter pantomime M. Bologna as Harlequin showed 'an amount of agility truly surprising, performing several daring feats with promptitude and ease'. He must have been a descendant of the famous family of clowns and harlequins who had appeared on the York Stage so many years before. Stilt was the Clown. Caple then retired from the York circuit, taking his farewell on April 29. Two days later George Owen, who succeeded for a brief season, opened with an entirely new company. He declared that he would trust to the sterling abilities of a good stock company rather than to rewards from an occasional star with poor support.[17] Coleman says that Owen, though not brilliant, 'was a sensible and intelligent actor, the soul of humour and a gentleman in the truest sense of the word'.[18] As he was a tragedian several standard plays were put on, and among his rôles were those of Hamlet, Macbeth, Overreach and Zanga. Sheridan Smith was acting manager. Rebecca Isaacs, directress of the Strand theatre and a well known singing actress of her day, came for a few nights, played Ophelia and sang some songs especially composed for her. George Wild and Fanny Williams were the attractions for the July Assizes, and Race Week brought good houses.

Anderson, the Wizard of the North, paid a farewell visit after 13 years, in September, before his far from final retirement.[19] His programme was the same as that given before the Royal family at Balmoral and included an exposure of the delusions of spirit rapping. Anderson had commenced his career by making properties and fighting broadsword combats in a showman's van in Edinburgh. His ambition to be an actor was never fulfilled and his success as a conjuror never compensated him for this grievous disappointment. He originally learnt his sleight of hand from an old Italian property man in the Highlands, and performing with 'a glittering paraphernalia of gold and silver plate' he became both wealthy and famous. He was tall and handsome with fine features, a well balanced head and a profusion of fair hair, and he wore an elaborate evening dress with a wonderful embroidered shirt. He spoke a strange jumble of cockney and Glaswegian but 'although his grammar was of dubious quality, his legerdemain was never at fault'.[20]

The tragedian John Vandenhoff, then about to retire, paid his only visit to York on October 28 and succeeding nights, accompanied by his daughter. They appeared as Master Walter and Julia, Matthew and Margaret Elmore in Lovell's *Love's Sacrifice,* their original creations, and Richelieu and Julie in Lytton's *Richelieu.*

Sheridan Smith had taken over the management when the Theatre reopened in March 1855. The Charles Dillons were attached to the circuit for a short while and took the leading rôles in *Much Ado, Ingomar, Don Caesar de Bazan, Belphegor,* in which Dillon excelled, and other plays. Dillon had been manager at Sheffield and was the idol of the grinders. He was an unintellectual actor of rugged and even repulsive countenance who, though he lacked breeding, succeeded in making his passion so electrifying and his pathos so convincing that he stirred and melted his audience. Though at one time manager of the Lyceum, something of the provincial actor always clung to him and his celebrity was mainly in the country.[21]

The April pantomime with the curious title of *Goggle Eyed Greedy Gobble, or The Fairy Queen of the Gold Diggings* purported to be founded on a black letter book written in Richard I's reign and discovered whilst excavating the new Houses of Parliament. The comic scenes were written and produced by T. W. Paulo who was himself the Clown. The scenery was by R. Corri and assistants, machinery by Cox, properties by Kemp and dresses by Mrs. Flint. The ballet was invented and arranged by Kate Kirby who danced Columbine. The Fairy Palace and the last tableau were brilliantly illuminated by coloured fires. A juvenile night was arranged when the pantomime was given first place in the evening's entertainments, and at which Sheridan Smith distributed prizes to the audience.[22]

Reynolds, secretary to the proprietors, who had travelled the circuit for many years was accorded a benefit on May 5. Fanny Wallack, later Mrs.

Charles Moorhouse, an American actress, sister of James Wallack, starred for a few nights as Romeo, Miami in *Green Bushes* and Cassy in *Slavery,* an adaptation of *Uncle Tom's Cabin,* which she had originally played for fifty nights.

For Race Week the Theatre opened with yet another lessee – Edward Addison an actor from the Princess's Theatre. He brought with him a company from there and the Olympic which included George Vining and Charles, Arthur and Louise Leclercq. Addison arranged for the visit of a troupe of Italian opera singers and it is for this occasion that we first hear of stalls for which the charge was one guinea. They may have been reserved pit chairs or possibly single seats in the private boxes. Places for them and for the private boxes at 5 guineas were to be balloted for if necessary. The dress boxes were 10/-, upper boxes 7/-, pit 3/6, lower gallery 2/6, upper gallery 2/-, the highest prices that had yet been charged in the Theatre. In October Addison brought Charles Kean's company for the York Union Hunt Meeting and on October 20 he opened the Theatre for one night for Sims Reeves to sing Henry Bertram. The famous tenor was pronounced exquisite and Fanny Ternan as Julia had a charming voice but the chorus was deficient in strength.[23] Addison returned in mid-December for the Winter Assizes and put on *The Merry Wives of Windsor* with himself as Falstaff, and the celebrated drama *The Courier of Lyons,* better known by its later title of *The Lyons Mail.* Addison himself played Choppard, and Langton the dual rôles of Dubosc and Lesurques. The playbills made capital of the fact that one of the judges in open court had recommended every one connected with the administration of justice to see the piece.

Mr. and Mrs. Sims Reeves were re-engaged by Addison in February 1856 and sang Francis Osbaldistone and Diana Vernon, Tom Tug and Wilhelmina and Macheath and Polly. The next star attraction was Ira Aldridge, the African Roscius, who had first appeared on the London stage thirty years previously. Advertised as an African prince who had escaped from slavery he was less romantically rumoured to have been the son of a native minister of the gospel and James Wallack's dresser in New York.[24] Aldridge opened in his famous rôle of Othello on April 7 to the Iago of Horsman and the Desdemona of a new leading lady Elise de Courcy, and he subsequently played Rolla, and the coloured rôles of Ginger Blue in a farce *Virginian Mummy,* Fabian the Creole in *Lovers of Bourbon* and Gambia in *The Slave.* His acting was marked by energy and intelligence and he possessed a strong physique and powerful voice. In tragedy he was majestic and solemn yet in broad farce he could be comic and ludicrous. As Gambia he brought out the nobler human qualities, enlisting sympathy for his oppressed race.[25] His reception was flattering and he returned in July. After Aldridge's departure Addison sustained a series of favourite comedy characters and made a number of new engagements including the pantomimists the Leopold Brothers and Mr. and Mrs. Charles Horsman, who had been members of the company in 1845.[26] The stock company was followed in

June by the Drury Lane opera company with Miss Lanza as the leading soprano, R. Herberte as the tenor, Eugene Dussek as the baritone, and Henry Corri as the bass. Though the pit and gallery were tolerably well filled the box attendance was, as usual, thin. The operas given included *Fra Diavolo, Maritana, The Elixir of Love* and *The Daughter of the Regiment*.

Charles J. Mathews, advertised as England's greatest comedian, paid visits in June, July and September.

On July 26 Addison closed his brief career as manager of the York circuit to a thin house. In his farewell address he regretted his failure, for his year's tenure had proved extremely unprofitable. He stated that he had brought to York a company which could not be excelled in any provincial town but, owing to lack of support, he had been compelled to withdraw it and engage another at a cheaper rate. He had struggled on in vain, for York was apathetic as far as the drama was concerned, and so he had decided to retire to avoid further pecuniary liabilities.[27]

The new lessee who opened in August was Thomas Cooper Clifford (born 1819, died 1895) formerly of the Lyceum and Olympic companies and lately director of Coventry and other Midland theatres. He himself was a light comedian and his wife, formerly Agnes Kemble, granddaughter of Stephen Kemble, had a commanding voice, graceful figure and intelligent countenance.[28] Among the pieces they played in were Taylor's *Masks and Faces* and Taylor and Lang's Olympic drama *Plot and Passion*.

The great star of the 1857 season was Barry Sullivan who first played in York on January 18 with the stock company. He appeared in *Hamlet, The Stranger, The Lady of Lyons* and *Richelieu* but even he could not draw good houses.[29] In April he returned and added to his rôles those of Macbeth, Don Caesar, Evelyn in *Money* and Sir Giles Overreach. When he played on April 27 his Horatio was Henry Irving who had come from Edinburgh for a couple of weeks or so to play a few small rôles in the stock company. Irving was then an unknown young actor of 19 who had started his stage career six months previously in Sunderland and had migrated to the Scottish capital in February. During his brief stay in York he played the Marquis de Cevennes in *Plot and Passion*, Nouredin in *Cherry and Fair Star*, Jack Nightingale in *Jessy Vere*, Valere in *The Secret*, Gasper in *The Lady of Lyons*, Charles in *Lottery Trick* and Earnest Vane in *Peg Woffington*. George Clair was the leading man and Mrs. Clifford the leading lady in the stock company. They played Dred and Cora in the anti-slavery drama *Dred* founded on the novel by Harriet B. Stowe. The Easter pantomime was replaced by a revival of the melodrama *Cherry and Fair Star* with new scenery by Huggins, machinery and appointments by Cox and music arranged by Saynor the leader of the orchestra. G. Peel was stage manager and Clifton prompter. The National Opera Company paid two visits, bringing out *Il Trovatore* in February and *La Traviata* in April. Miss Escott was the soprano and Haigh the tenor and the former's Lucy Ashton in *Lucia di Lammermoor* created a furore. In *La Traviata* she sang Violetta in an English version especially adapted for the company. The opera had been assailed by the press for immorality with the usual result that it was a great success. The *York Gazette*, however, defended it.[30] The stock company was called in for the minor rôles. Yet even the opera company failed to bring good houses and the *Gazette* lamented that whereas two theatres were open in Hull, the one in York met with wretched encouragement.

Some great attraction was now required to bring a fashionable audience, but Mathews was such an attraction. His finished portrayal of Young Rapid in *A Cure For the Heartache* brought to the house one of its rare fashionable assemblies.

In June his imitator, Sir William Henry Don, Bart. played for four nights. Don was a romantic figure who, at the age of 20, had squandered a patrimony. Thrown on his own resources he turned to the stage where he had already performed as an amateur. He made a success in America and was now continuing his career in order to pay off his remaining debts. He was a talented mimic. His future wife, Emily Saunders, daughter of John Saunders of the Adelphi, played with him. He was followed in July by Dillon, now from the Lyceum and Drury Lane, who played Hamlet and Othello. In the former he was best in the pathetic scene with Ophelia, but hurried over the meditative passages, had no clear conception of the character's mental development and lacked dignity. In the latter he achieved only 'the chafe and fret of passion but without its volume, and underswell'.[31] Of his Richelieu the *York Gazette*[32] said, 'Old, weak and feeble in body, yet in spirit and mind fresh and vigorous as in his palmiest days, the Richelieu of Mr. Dillon is a masterpiece.'

August saw yet another lessee, John Bellair, who brought a company gathered from Drury Lane, Dublin and Edinburgh, which once again included members of the Leclercq family. He raised the prices to boxes 4/-, half price 2/6; upper boxes 3/- and 2/-; pit 2/- and 1/; gallery 1/- and 6d. He brought out Taylor's *Still Waters Run Deep* with J. L. Pritchard (probably a son of the former manager) as John Mildmay and Miss J. Bellair as Mrs. Mildmay. He gave a season in December which was better patronised than usual and in January 1858 he brought the Pyne and Harrison opera company back to York. Every seat in the dress circle was taken for the first performance of Balfe's *Rose of Castille* on the opening night but Louisa Pyne was detained in London by indisposition and *Fra Diavolo* had to be substituted. Some parties withdrew but the audience was still a good one. *The Rose of Castille* finally appeared on January 29. The company was considered superior to some of the others which had visited York and had been marred by wretched choruses and worse orchestras.[33] The merit of the Pyne and Harrison Company was that even the small parts were excellently given.

John Coleman, the tragedian and manager of the Lincoln Theatre, had joined the stock company and played the leads with Miss M. A. Bellair. Bellair advertised that he was licensed to perform pieces of the Dramatic Author's Society and T. H. Lacy's productions.

Sir William Don returned in April with his wife and played among other rôles The Kinchen in *Flowers of the Forest,* Nicol Jarvie and Toby Twinkle in *All That Glitters is not Gold.* After this Bellair faded out and was succeeded by J. L. Pritchard who was also a lessee of the Hull Theatre. He opened on November 29 with Miss Marriott as Evadne and followed this up with the usual opera company.[34]

On April 16, 1859, the *York Gazette* advertised that the York Theatrical Circuit consisting of the Theatres at Hull, York and Leeds would be sold by auction by Messrs. Hands & Sons on May 18 either in one or more lots. As far as York was concerned the lease was due to expire on April 6, 1860 and Pritchard's tenancy on August 6, 1859. The scenery was said to be in good order. The Theatres were duly offered for sale and amongst those present on the occasion were a representative of Knowles, lessee of Manchester Theatre Royal, John Coleman, Pritchard, and Reynolds, who was still secretary to the proprietors. The circuit was put up in one lot at a starting price of £12,000. This was subsequently reduced to £10,000, but the only bid was one for £1000, for Hull alone which was declined. The property remained on sale by private contract and Hands shortly after received three offers for it.[35]

In the meantime Pritchard carried on with a season in August but there was no confidence in his management. His Hull Theatre was burnt to the ground on October 19 with the consequence that in February 1860 he filed a petition for bankruptcy in the Hull Court. Some of the figures given are interesting. Pritchard had a capital of £200; his and his wife's joint wardrobe was valued at £400; their expenses for travelling and clothes were estimated at £400; the travelling expenses of the company at £80; the cost of the pantomime was £1000, of bills and printing £350, and the loss by fire amounted to £850.[36] Pritchard was granted an order in March 1860.[37] The destruction of the Hull Theatre, which was not rebuilt for six years, spelt a temporary end of the circuit.

At York the Theatre was taken by Frederick B. Egan (born 1818, died 1877) manager of the Queen's Theatre, Manchester, who commenced a season in December 1859. He was the ninth lessee in the decade since the elder Pritchard's death. No wonder that, where so many had failed, no one wanted now to venture. Egan's tenure was even briefer than those of his predecessors. In January 1860 he had the Theatre thoroughly cleaned and engaged the Charles Keans to play for three nights with the principals from his own company. They performed Sir Walter and Lady Amyat in *The Wife's Secret,* Louis XI and Mathé in *Louis XI* and Hamlet and Queen Gertrude. The charges were 2 guineas for the private boxes, 5/- for the dress boxes, 3/6 for the upper circle, 2/- for the pit and 1/- for the gallery.

The lease to Sarah Wilkinson and her sisters expired in April and the Theatre was offered for public competition. Among numerous applicants W. S. Thorne from the Princess's Theatre, Leeds, formerly owner of a portable theatre, had such eulogistic testimonials that a lease was granted to him from May.[38] In the interim the Theatre underwent a thorough renovation and redecoration and many improvements were carried out. When it re-opened on May 10 it was found[39] that a 'degree of comfort now pervades what formally had almost about it an air of desolation. The stage arrangements are greatly improved, an additional flood of gas light is thrown upon it, and the new scenery presents fine artistic effects.' Among the scenes was a new drop. Thorne announced that the renovations were not yet completed; that no immoral words or improper actions should defile the stage, and that arrangements had been made with the appropriate authorities to maintain the utmost order and decorum. Perhaps even more popular than these promises was the reduction in prices to dress circle 2/6,[40] half price 1/6; upper boxes 1/6, 1/-; pit 1/-; gallery 6d. The house was crowded on the opening night when *Money* was given with Evelyn Evans, who was stage manager, as Alfred Evelyn and the lessee's young daughter Marguerite Thorne as Clara Douglas. Though inexperienced, she had grace and vivacity and was to become a favourite with York audiences. Thorne made his début as Jaques in *The Honeymoon* on June 13 but rarely appeared afterwards. His son R. Thorne was the scene painter and the comedian was J. B. Watson. Attendances increased and the company seems to have been an improvement on its predecessors. Burlesques were all the rage and Thorne put on Brough's burlesque pantomime *Conrad and Medora*, and a travesty of *Macbeth* which drew upon him the condemnation of the *York Gazette* critic who considered travesties of Shakespeare's tragedies 'among the most despicable products of shallow and heartless writers'.[41]

Stars engaged were Walter Montgomery, the Shakespearean actor and reader, who appeared as Hamlet, Macbeth, Virginius and Duke Aranza, and Dillon who performed Mercutio and Reuben Holt in Marston's *Hard Struggle*. The inevitable opera company, this time from Covent Garden, put in an appearance in July and was duly followed in September and again in December by Hamilton Braham and Manley's operatic troupe.

When the Theatre re-opened for Race Week on August 20 the interior had been 'Painted, Renovated, and Improved by Mr. R. Thorne and Assistants, including entirely New Decorations to the fronts of the Dress Circle, Upper Boxes, and Gallery; the interior of the Boxes New Papered, the Seats Re-stuffed, and covered with Rich Utrecht Velvet and Crimson Cloth; the Ceiling New Painted, and altered so as to give Parties occupying the very Back Seat in the Gallery as good a view of the entire Stage as those seated in the Front Row, – an alteration and improvement long needed'.[42] The Theatre was pronounced 'remarkably clean, pretty, comfortable' and Thorne 'a liberal, enterprising and clever manager'.[43] In addition to the dramatic company, a corps de ballet with the Misses Gunniss was engaged from Her Majesty's Theatre, and a burlesque company, headed by George Lee and Miss Cuthbert, from the Strand Theatre presented a new burlesque of *Fra Diavolo*. The ballet was a great improvement on former troupes which in recent years had sacrificed grace to mere agility; the Misses Gunniss performed a rapid succession of steps, leaps, pirouettes and entrechats which recalled the days when Fanny Holmes delighted York with her powers as a dancer.[44]

In December the attractions were the child prodigy Lelia Ross, about whose five years the critic professed some scepticism, and the American tragedian Joseph Proctor who appeared as Wandering Nathan in *Nick of the Woods*.

Coleman was the first star in the 1861 season and his versions of *Ruy Blas*, *Katharine Howard* and *The Man in the Iron Mask* were among the novelties.

Dion Boucicault's famous Irish drama *The Colleen Bawn* was put on on April 20, for a run. The scenes, including the original Water Cave scene from the Adelphi, were painted by R. Thorne, and the mechanical effects were by Alexander M'Leod. Several special artistes were imported who claimed to have been coached by Boucicault himself. His rôle of Myles-na-Coppaleen was taken by Charles Verner who produced the piece, Father Tom was played by D. W. Leeson for whom the part was written and who had come from New York to play it whilst Miss Marguerite Thorne was the Colleen Bawn. It ran until May 10, except for a week's interval when the Keans came with a number of supporting actors and actresses to show in York something of the famous series of Shakespeare revivals that Kean had staged at the Princess's. They called on all the Theatre's resources in scenic display. Kean gave a masterly reading of Shylock and Mrs Keen was superb as Portia in the trial scene. In *Much Ado* her Beatrice tempered exuberant high spirits with womanly grace and elegance. As Hamlet Kean passed from severe tragedy to occasional flashes of comedy and the 'To be or not to be' soliloquy was rendered so thrilling and impressive that a breathless silence reigned in the house. Yet attendances were poor, possibly owing in part to the raising of prices to private boxes 2 guineas, dress circle 5/-, upper circle 3/-, pit 2/-, gallery 1/-.[45]

Walter Grisedale was engaged as the new leading man in May, and in June Henry Loraine played with the company as Othello, Overreach, Virginius, and other characters. On June 13 *Charicles or the Power of Friendship* by J. C. McClellan of Clementhorpe York was presented but does not seem to have caught on. At Watson's benefit *A Chapter of Accidents* by F. Scrimshaw of the city had witty local hits.[46] More popular were the burlesques – that of *Lalla Rookh,* for instance, brought crowded houses during Race Week. There were the indispensable opera companies in July and October. In September the burlesque actress Clara St. Casse delighted with her sweet voice and piquant manner.[47] Madame Celeste, who had made her name in melodramas at the minors, acted her great part of Miami in *Green Bushes*. She also played some of her breeches parts and was praised for her versatility, her genteel deportment and absence of boldness.[48] All the same she failed to attract. In December Thorne engaged G. V. Brooke who appeared as Overreach, and his wife Avonia Jones who had a high reputation in Australia. The audiences again were poor even for so great a star and the season must have been rather damped by the death of the Prince Consort. Master Percy Roselle, a dwarf known as the Little Wonder, was engaged for six nights. It is of interest to note that a few season tickets were available from the manager, and that arrangements were made for families, living at a distance from the city, to book seats by post.

Thorne was the most successful lessee the Theatre had had for years for he had caught the taste of the public.[49] He catered for their love of novelty and was continually engaging stars or other lesser known actors or actresses to play for a while. Sometimes parties came from London theatres. The stock company was rapidly being relegated to mere supports for the continued stream of visitors. Take as typical the year 1862. The season opened in March with Montgomery prior to his appearance at the Princess's, followed by Clara St. Casse, now Mrs. Graham, in burlesque and by Henry Vandenhoff and Miss Seaman from Sheffield. The theatre was then shut for a fortnight in preparation for Thorne's first York pantomime which came out on April 21 and ran until May 10. *Harlequin Little Red Riding Hood* contained a ballet of fairies drilled by Miss Thorne, a fuchsia grove and the final fairy realms of bliss. Jessy St. Clair was the Columbine, Oscar de Brough the Harlequin and A. Stilt the Clown. The machinery, we are told, worked tolerably well, the scenery by R. Thorne and Hart was excellent, but the music was execrable. The new act drop was the first one to contain advertisements each in its gold frame.[50]

Wybert Rousby and Gomersal were visitors in May, and in June the Pyne and Harrison opera company brought out Benedict's *Lily of Killarney,* founded on the *Colleen Bawn,* and Balfe's *Puritan's Daughter.* They were followed by the Female Christy Minstrels. For the Assizes Mlle Albina de Rhona, a danseuse, was engaged; for Agricultural Show Week Charles and Arthur Leclercq, Maria Stanley, a burlesque actress from the Royalty, and a detachment of London players. Next Master Percy Roselle reappeared in *Hamlet,* among other pieces, and Maria Stanley gave way to Maria Simpson in burlesque who appeared in Byron's *Miss Eily O'Connor* a burlesque of the *Colleen Bawn.* In September the stock company was called on to support a series of amateur performances succeeded by another batch of London performers in Falconer's famous sensation drama *Peep o' Day.* This was produced under the superintendence of F. B. Chatterton from the Lyceum 'on a scale of grandeur and completeness hitherto unattempted in this city', the scenery being painted by R. Thorne from the original models. It brought crowded houses so that as the *York Gazette*[51] has it, 'the old walls of the Theatre could scarcely contain themselves for very joy'. It ran well into October.

For the Assizes in December the American actress Helen Western appeared in *Our Female American Cousin,* and on Boxing Night Thorne staged the first Christmas pantomime to be given in York, *The Sleeping Beauty,* in which the children of York danced a fairy ballet.

It is impossible to mention all the visitors who came during the succeeding years and one can only choose the most prominent among them. Thus 1863 saw Coleman and Helen Western return; Boucicault's *Willow Copse* produced at Easter and his *Jessie Brown* for Gala Week with the help of Phillip and Webb's trained dogs; and one of the versions of *Lady Audley's Secret* came out at Whitsun. The Theatre was again renovated for the July Assizes during which Sothern made his York début in his famous rôle of the lisping, foolish Lord Dundreary in *Our American Cousin*. August Race Week was graced by the Lauri family (Septimus, Henry, Edward and Fanny) who were comic dancers and pantomimists. Their concluding tableau consisted of Professor Wheeler's dramatic fairy fountain with 'illuminated columns of real water'. Mr. and Mrs. Howard Paul in *Fra Diavolo* followed and she gave her famous imitation of Sims Reeves.[52] The Wizard of the North converted the theatre into a 'Psychomantheum' in October for three hours' magic and, during this month and November, performances by the 16th Lancers in aid of charity crammed the houses to suffocation. So did Smith's panorama with prize tickets. *Pepper's Ghost* was the chief attraction for the December Assizes. This famous device, invented by Henry Dircks, and exploited and improved by John Pepper, enabled phantoms to appear on the stage by means of a sheet of glass hidden from the spectators but reflecting the image of an actor on an understage along with the visible actors. The spectral drama in which it was employed was entitled *The Stricken Oak, or Dreams Without Faith* and was supposed to have been especially written for York by Charles Rice[53] later lessee of the Bradford Theatre who himself played the principal part. The Easter pantomime for 1864 was *The House That Jack Built*. The local company no longer provided the props and dresses, the former were from Drury Lane, the latter from London and even Thorne's scenery was supplemented by that of Bull & Co. from the metropolis. Marguerite Thorne was the principal boy and Morelli the Clown. Juvenile nights were given and special terms were arranged for schools. One night the children from the York workhouse were invited; they were met at the door by the manager who conducted them to reserved seats and presented each one with a bun and an orange.[54]

Among the new plays were a version of Miss Braddon's novel *The Outcast*, *Warp and Weft*, a tale of the Lancashire cotton famine, and Watts Phillips's drama *Camilla's Husband*.

The tercentenary of Shakespeare's birth on April 23 was celebrated by a performance of *Much Ado,* not by the company but by amateurs of the Leeds Artillery Volunteers and the Rifle Volunteers under the patronage of the Lord Mayor and City Sheriff. Amateurs of one kind or another were frequently in possession of the Theatre.

Burlesque still flourished exceedingly and Miss Cuthbert and George Lee regaled Whitsun holiday audiences with Byron's *Aladdin or The Wonderful Scamp.* Sothern reappeared in August in Byron's burlesque *Lord Dundreary Married and Done For* as well as in *David Garrick.* In the absence of the stock company the Lyceum Company revived *Peep o' Day* in October with scenery by Roberts; then came Sam Baylis's French Marionettes with afternoon and evening performances.

In November J. C. Chute, formerly lessee of the Birmingham Theatre, brought King's Improved Patent of Marvellous Ghost Illusion which he claimed was an advance on Pepper's in that it could be seen from all parts of the house.

The lease of the theatre was due to expire on April 6, 1865 and an advertisement was inserted in the *York Gazette* of December 17 announcing that it would be let for a period of 3 or 5 years by public tender, the sealed tenders to be in by January 13. That Thorne had raised the status of the Theatre is proved by the fact that the Finance Committee had to choose from a host of applicants. Their choice fell on John Coleman, already lessee of the Leeds, Oxford, Cambridge and Lincoln Theatres. Coleman, who was then 34, had been a member of the York stock company in 1858. The rent was £150 a year. The Corporation was to repair the house and hot water apparatus, to make the upper and lower boxes more comfortable, and to place chairs or 'stalls' in the latter.[55] The estimates for the work which was entrusted to Perfect and Dennison were for £229;[56] the plans and drawings were prepared by Thomas Pickersgill, Surveyor to the Lord Mayor. Actually the front row in the lower boxes was removed and chairs, elbowed and cushioned after the fashion of Drury Lane and Covent Garden were substituted, whilst the remainder of the seats in both tiers of boxes were newly cushioned. When the Theatre was re-opened by Coleman on May 15, 1865, there was found, in place of an Augean stable, with an accumulation of decay and filth that had served but to inspire melancholy reflections on its fallen greatness, 'a comfortable, clean, happy looking bijou of a theatre'. The decorations of the front of the house which had been entrusted to Perfect, were simple and unobtrusive in a scheme of gold, white, light yellow, salmon and crimson, and their drawing room character and quiet elegance were 'extremely well in harmony with the peculiar tastes and associations of the aristocracy of this large county'. The new gas fittings of the auditorium were carried out under the superintendence of Braddock, manager of the York Gas Company. The new gas lighting apparatus for the stage was designed and executed by Smith, gas superintendent of the new Prince of Wales's Theatre at Birmingham. The proscenium was partially reconstructed to enable gallery patrons to have an unobstructed view of the back of the stage. A new stock of scenery was supplied by John Johnson, Vining, Wood and Howard. The new act drop, painted by Johnson of Covent Garden after Linton, had as its subject the triumphal return of the Greek armament to Athens, and was commended as a specimen of purest classic, warm, chaste in colour, pleasing in perspective and scenery. The curtain did not rise on *Ruy Blas* until 8 o'clock. At the end of the play Coleman appeared in his character costume which he had not had time to change. He would make no large promises, preferring that his intentions should be judged by his actions. He appealed to the galleryites to help him keep up the character of the establishment, an appeal which doubtless made grateful hearing to the Lord Mayor and Corporation, who were present. The afterpiece was Brough's extravaganza *Turko the Terrible*.[57]

Coleman was ambitious and had in view the re-integration of the York Circuit. He bought the Leeds Theatre, which he pulled down and rebuilt, and in the end he achieved what was known as the Great Northern Circuit comprising York, Leeds, Hull, Doncaster, Liverpool, Lincoln, Glasgow and the Isle of Man.[58] For the first time York became part of a big business enterprise. The circuit company was the first provincial one to be accepted as a starring combination. On Whit Monday June 5 Coleman brought out Reade's *It's Never Too Late To Mend* which had been rejected by every manager in London but had been put on by Coleman at Leeds where it had run for 8 consecutive weeks. It was not seen in London until October. It was the first play in York to occupy the entire evening without an afterpiece. Reade himself had said that nowhere could the play be so well acted. The scenery was better painted than any seen at York for years and the mechanical effects were extraordinary, but the audiences stayed away, whether because of the prices, the fine weather or the rival entertainment of Newsome's Circus in St. George's Fields no one knew.[59]

The English Grand Opera Company gave the first performance of *Faust* in York on June 26 with Brookhouse Bowles, who had much dramatic fervour but a limited voice, as Faust, Rowland as Mephistopheles and Mde Haigh Dyer as Marguerite. The York Rifle Volunteers' Band joined in on the stage for the Soldiers' Chorus, but the chief attraction seems to have been the scenic effects in the garden scene dazzlingly lit by limelight.[60]

The renovations to the Theatre were complete by August and it was crowded during Race Week. W. H. Payne and sons Fred and Harry, (the latter of whom was to become a famous Drury Lane Clown) from Covent Garden appeared in ballets which included *Lass o' Gowrie* arranged by W. H. Payne, and a ballet pantomime *The Merry Millers.* For the Regatta Week in September Alfred Davis was engaged and he was followed on October 9 by Charles Wyndham for 6 nights. Among the parts Wyndham sustained were those of Howard Ormsby in *Her Ladyship's Guardian* and O'Callaghan in *His Last Legs.* Miss Lydia Thompson, who had begun her career as a ballet dancer but was now the idol of opera bouffe,[61] came to play Ixion in Burnard's burlesque which was mercifully free from the unpleasant use of the 'gag'. Then Loveday's opera returned but was not well attended, though the operas and oratorios in the Concert Rooms were packed.[62]

Coleman had the advantage of having the control of several theatres and companies and when he needed a pantomime for York at Easter 1866 he transported the Christmas pantomime company lock, stock and barrel from Liverpool in Byron's *King Kokolorum.* It would not have paid him to produce this for York alone with its limited population but he also produced it at Leeds. His productions were on a big scale and this was said to be 'one of the most brilliant, costly and artistic productions ever witnessed on the boards of a provincial theatre'. The scenery was admirably painted by Robinson, George Vining and Smithers and the transformation scene was a blaze of brightness and beauty, the costumes rich and elegant. Stanislaus Calhaem, a comedian who had made a success in London as Jockey in *It's Never Too Late To Mend,* kept the audience in a roar as King Kokolorum and Grace Leigh was the heroine Princess Springtime. The pantomimists (E. W. Royce as Harlequin, Gabriel Duvani as Clown) worked well together and their comic business was original and excluded the orthodox tricks. A new feature was a corps de ballet. The only poor part was the band and this remained one of the weak features, as it had been in Thorne's time. The boxes were filled night after night.[63]

During the summer, Coleman at his own expense, effected extensive alterations in the auditorium, the Corporation reserving the right to have the former shape restored if deemed desirable. The central gallery was removed to the improvement of the ventilation. The dress circle was divided into sections, the centre having reserved and numbered seats at 3/-, the other boxes being reduced to 1/6. The centre of the upper box tier was combined with the gallery into an amphitheatre capable of accommodating 800, double the capacity of the previous gallery, at the low price of 6d; the upper side boxes were 1/6. As we have seen the upper boxes and pit were frequently crowded and the dress circle empty. Tradesmen sought respectable and comfortable accommodation in vain since they declined, from delicacy or prudence, to patronise the dress circle, yet could not risk their wives and daughters among the rough crowds in other parts of the house. The side boxes in the dress circle were now destined for their use. No alteration was made in the 1/- pit.[64] During the summer the doors opened at 7.30, the overture was played at 7.50 and the curtain rose at 8. The box plan was in future to be kept at the box entrance in St. Leonard's Place where tickets and plans were to be had from Reynolds between 12-2. It was sternly announced that 'Persons who, either by smoking or by noisy and offensive conduct, in any way interfere with the Artists on the Stage or the audience in the front, will be immediately ejected and given in charge of the Police'. How Tate Wilkinson would have approved.

Mlle Beatrice an Italian from the Odéon and London, who was soon to become one of the pioneers of the touring dramatic company, appeared in August as Gabrilla in *Lady of Belle Isle* adapted from Dumas by Fanny Kemble. She had a commanding figure, a charming manner and a melodious voice to which her occasional foreign accent gave piquancy; light and buoyant in her happier scenes, her powerful expression of a broken spirit elicited three rounds of applause.[65] She was less well suited as Pauline in *The Lady of Lyons,* and as Desdemona she proved that blank verse was a sealed book to her. Coleman's Othello, however, was one of his best parts.

On August 27, York first saw Boucicault's famous *Octoroon* with Beatrice Shirley in the title rôle and Calhaem as Uncle Pete. The production was superintended by Delmon Grace who played Salem Scudder, in which rôle he had succeeded the author at the Adelphi. The scenery was by Frank Browning from sketches by Boucicault. The drama ran well into September.

Reynolds, the Treasurer, took his farewell benefit on September 21. He had been connected with the York circuit for over 20 years, having joined it in 1842 for the rôles of comic old men. He had an extensive knowledge of theatrical matters, was a man of strict integrity and good business habits and was well liked for his courtesy and kindness. 'What a host of recollections,' speculates a writer in the *York Gazette*,[66] 'must have crowded themselves on his memory when he recalled the fact that twenty years before he had played the same part [Sir Peter Teazle] with Bruce Norton, Tom Holmes, Pritchard, Smythson, and Miss Waverley Scott'. At the end of the play Coleman led the old man onto the stage and spoke a valedictory eulogy. Changes in organisation now rendered the office of treasurer and box office keeper a sinecure. Moore succeeded him as box office keeper.

Coleman who had just returned from the Isle of Man played a round of parts including Rob Roy, Macbeth and Hamlet. Alfred Davis was re-engaged in December and played Rip Van Winkle. It had been the most successful and prolonged season for many years.

Doncaster was added to the circuit in 1867 and the new theatre at Leeds erected. It was then claimed that Coleman had the best circuit in the provinces.[67] The Charles Keans appeared for one night in January in *The Merchant of Venice* on their return from a tour round the world. The Easter pantomime was *Jack the Giant Killer* by H. J. Byron for which the Leclercq ballet and burlesque company was engaged. Arthur Leclercq was a graceful Harlequin and his brother Charles won no less repute as Clown whilst Caroline Adams danced Columbine. The new scenery was by Wallace and the transformation was the ascent of Phoebus in the chariot of the sun. The Theatre was open for a week in June for the production of Watts Phillips's drama *Lost in London*. Even more significantly a special company was brought to York in December to stage Boucicault's racing drama *The Flying Scud*. This was the first time that a full company was brought to York for the run of a particular play, and was a foretaste of the touring system which so soon was to replace the stock company. The great 'sensation' of this piece was the staging of the Derby Day scene.[68]

During 1868 several different companies visited York. In January the Newcastle company brought back John Pritchard as tragedian in a series of dramas which drew less admirers than the sensation pieces.[69]

The American actress Kate Bateman, granddaughter of Joseph Cowell, played her famous rôle of Leah, in which she gave a blood curdling delivery of the curse, in Augustus Daly's drama of that name in February.

The York circuit company was responsible for the Easter pantomime *The Fair One with the Golden Locks*. John C. Chute was acting manager and Charles Horsman stage manager. The pantomime was original in that, instead of the opening being done in dumb show as usual, the goblins, fairies and eccentrics spoke racy dialogue full of jokes and puns, a legacy from the burlesques. The ballet led by Marian Inch was a fish one. The spectacle included a colossal face of Mammon with rolling eyes, a dragon in the Dripping Well who vomited sulphurous flames, and the customary fairy bowers with flying nymphs which glowed, perhaps for the first time, under light from electric rays. The scenic artists were Robinson and J. S. Lenox. Royce was again the Harlequin with Hilyard from the Princess's as Clown. This pantomime had a hitherto unprecedented run of three weeks. It served as an afterpiece when Henry Loraine came to act in Fitzball's biblical romance *Azael the Prodigal,* and when W. Sydney brought his north country drama *Light in the Dark,* but on this latter occasion the harlequinade was dropped.[70]

The German actor Bandmann and his future wife Milly Palmer, an experienced actress at the minors, were accompanied in May by the Leeds company. They played in *Narcisse,* a drama translated from the German. Bandmann was a graceful and easy actor with a commanding bearing and a profusion of black hair that reached to his shoulders.[71]

Another new company presented light comedy, broad farce and burlesque, and a series of melodramas during Race Week. In October Coleman himself reappeared as Richard III, and Sir Charles Coldstream. Brough's burlesque *The Field of the Cloth of Gold,* in which Calhaem took part, was given every evening and Boucicault's *After Dark* was also brought out and ran several nights.

The process of engaging visiting companies was continued in 1869 with the difference that most of them were not provincial troupes from Leeds and Newcastle but companies sent on tour from London. In February Capt. Disney Roebuck's United Services company came for 12 nights including in their programme *East Lynne.* Clouston Foster's comedy and burlesque company and troupe of champion knights, complete in silver-plated and jewelled armour, came in May, and Race Week was taken by Mrs. Swanborough's comedy and burlesque company from the Strand in which Edward Terry appeared. They were followed in October by Brough's burlesque company. When the great Fechter came with Carlotta Leclercq in the same month, with a London company, he played Maurice de Layrac in *Black and White* by himself and Wilkie Collins and Ruy Blas, but his genius only drew small houses. Phelps returned next for one night with a specially organised company, and 'the Great National Tragedian', who had once been an obscure member of the York company, played Sir Pertinax Mac-Sycophant in *The Man of the World* to the Lady Rodolpha of Beatrix Shirley now of Drury Lane. The changing expression of his features and his perfect elocution drew praises from the critic[72] but the dress circle and boxes were not well filled.

Meanwhile the stock company was used for the pantomime *Bluebeard,* for which the introductory burlesque had been suggested by Coleman, and to support a series of stars. In April it was Wilson Barrett and Miss Heath who played Archibald and Lady Isabella Carlyle in *East Lynne,* and Reuben and Azael in *Azael*; in May it was Kate Bateman in *Leah* and Charles J. Mathews in his usual repertoire. Lastly in December the Colemans came to act with them, the acting manager being E. Clinton Hall.

At least seven touring companies came to York in 1870. Of these the first was one travelling with a particular play, the Firefly dramatic company under Edith Sandford. Its special attractions, the trained horse Etna, and the fire scene in which the heroine rides up a precipice through flames, failed to bring other than meagre support.[73] The combined Manchester and Sheffield companies under Chute came in February and were followed by Loveday's English Opera Company and by an Italian Opera Company from Covent Garden with Mlle Titiens and Herr Formes and band, chorus and corps de ballet in *Don Giovanni*. The stage manager was Augustus Harris the elder. For this occasion the whole of the pit was converted and numbered. Though seats could not be booked for the side boxes and amphitheatre, tickets purchased in advance would admit by the box entrance in St. Leonard's Place an hour before the door was opened to the general public. This is the first instance of the practice to become regular as early doors. Private boxes were 5 guineas and £2.12.6, dress circle and pit stalls 10/6, upper boxes and amphitheatre 5/- and gallery 2/6.[74] The lovely Kate Saville came with Reginald Moore's company in May, and on the 20th she played Mrs. Broughton in the first production on any stage of Moore's comic drama *Better Luck Next Time*. She also performed Ruth in Moore's *Jewish Maiden*, Lady Isabel Carlyle in *East Lynne*, and Anne Carew in Taylor's *Sheep in Wolf's Clothing*. Another foreign opera company followed from the Porte St. Martin Theatre in Offenbach's *La Grande-Duchesse de Gérolstein*. Hortense Schneider took her original rôle and 60 artistes were imported from Paris. But though Schneider was sparkling and the ensemble excellent, houses were only half full and the audience was not enthusiastic.[75]

For Gala Week in June yet another burlesque company appeared in H. J. Byron's *Ivanhoe* and other pieces. They included Clara Tellett, later Mrs. Sam Emery and mother of Winifred Emery, whom Coleman[76] described as 'a perfect pocket Venus, and one of the brightest and most vivacious of soubrettes'. H. J. Byron in person performed in his pieces *The Prompter's Box, Not Such a Fool As He Looks, Cyril's Success* and *Blow for Blow* during Race Week. Kate Bateman returned in October in another of her famous rôles, that of Mary Warner in Tom Taylor's drama.

The stock company filled in in between, in a series of sensation dramas in March, in the pantomime of *Robinson Crusoe,* and with the Colemans in May. The pantomime was a great success as usual, and included in its scenery a street in Hull and the town and port of Hull in 1659, as well as the representation by dissolving views of a ship under different circumstances, with a finale of coloured lights and an abundance of gas grandiloquently entitled Realms of a Thousand Halos in the Refulgent and Glittering Shades of Perpetual Bliss. Calhaem was Friday, Miss B. Adams Robinson Crusoe principal boy, Caroline Adams Columbine, Romaine Harlequin and C. W. Barrett Clown.[77] A morning performance, the first of its kind, was given on Saturday May 7 from 2-5.

Coleman's lease expired on April 5 but was renewed for 5 years at the same rent of £150.[78] The stage was found on examination to be in a dangerous and dilapidated condition after its 50 years of service. Fechter, Mlle Titiens and Mlle Schneider all complained that it was insecure and the Italian Opera Company simply refused to go on until it was shored up.[79] The lack of requisite machinery hampered the pantomimes. The Corporation decided in favour of having a completely new stage, the lessee being asked to contribute in the shape of an increased rent of £10. A specification and plans were drawn up[80] by George Styan surveyor to the Corporation, and the work was given to William Dennison on his tender of £245. According to the *York Gazette* Dennison worked from a model prepared by Coleman's carpenter Jones. The slides for the bridges and traps were to be put together carefully and the bridges and traps themselves were to be constructed in the most approved manner. Two drums for raising the bridges were to be provided. The new stage which provided the Theatre with the latest mechanical improvements also involved some structural alterations. The pit was enlarged by the addition of two benches with back rails and risers to form steps. The wooden partition between the orchestra and the pit was replaced by a handsome screen of polished iron surmounted by a mahogany handrail. The Theatre lost some of its remaining Georgian character by the abolition of the proscenium doors, now obsolete, whose place was filled by statues of Melpomene and Thalia. The auditorium was redecorated by Coleman's artists; seats in the boxes were cushioned with American cloth and Utrecht velvet; the panelling was adorned with bas-reliefs and intaglios in white and gold in the style of Louis XIV; the ceiling was blue and gold.[81] The new stage was first in use on August 22 at the opening of the Race Week season.

The Franco-Prussian war entered the theatre in 1871 in the form of a diorama. This was followed by a touring company which was to make many appearances in York, called the Lost Em'ly company, which specialised in adaptations from Dickens. Dillon acted Othello and Lear in February. The pantomime this year was by Brough and was entitled *Kobo King of the Silver Mines*.[82] In the cast were Calhaem, George Leitch as King Hardup, Alice Finch and Johnny Mathewson the Clown.

J. L. Toole paid his first visit to York in July with a company from the Alexandra Theatre, Liverpool and played in *The Weaver's Steeplechase, Ici On Parle Français, Uncle Dick's Darling, Bardell v. Pickwick* as well as giving imitations. W. S. Gilbert's pieces *Randall's Thumb, The Palace of Truth* and *Creatures of Impulse* were brought by Marie Litton's Royal Court Theatre Company in Race Week and in October L. S. Sefton engaged the Theatre for the much loved Mrs. John Wood, directress of the St. James's Theatre, who sang her famous *His Heart was True to Poll* in Burnand's *Poll and her Partner Joe*.

A benefit for the sufferers by the Great Fire in Chicago took place in November; and the next month Mrs. Hermann Vezin, formerly Mrs. Charles Young, a fine actress, played Constance to Coleman's Falconbridge.

The year 1872 opened with Dillon now touring with his own company in *Louis XI* and *Hamlet*. Then Richard Younge's company first brought to York T. W. Robertson's famous comedies *School* and *Caste* in which Fanny Brough played Bella and Esther Eccles respectively. In the company was the author's brother Frederick Craven Robertson. When they returned in November they added *M.P.* to their productions. Even the new stage did not suffice for the pantomime *Aladdin and his Wonderful Lamp*. We read that

'In order that the scenic effects – The Joss House, The Flying Palace, and Brew's great transformation, The Birth of Venus – may be produced in their entirety, still further changes have been effected in the machinery. The whole of the flies have been pulled down, and re-constructed, in order that the magnificent scenery which excited such admiration for ten consecutive weeks at Leeds, may be exhibited in their completeness'.[83] Charles Brew was assisted by his brother William and by Robinson and Morris. Upwards of 100 artists appeared. Leitch was the Widow Mustapha and Edwin Saunders the Clown. At his benefit Leitch revived his favourite local songs from the previous year's pantomime. During the first fortnight, nearly 19,000 people, close on a third of the entire population of York, visited *Aladdin*.[84] At Coleman's benefit in May one of the numerous versions of *The Polish Jew,* made famous by Irving as *The Bells* the previous year, was brought out in York. Sefton's company visited in County Gala Week, this time with Gilbert's *Pygmalion and Galatea.*

Offenbach's opera bouffe *Geneviève de Brabant* had caused the town to flock to Islington the previous year, and was still running there. Now the Liverpool Prince of Wales's company brought it to York, but unfortunately an injunction was issued from the Court of Chancery owing, it was thought, to the make-up of the Prime Minister which too closely resembled a modern statesman, and a costume recital had to be substituted.[85] The Offenbach craze was at its height and Henry Leslie's company brought *The Princess of Trébizonde* to York in November, returning for Horse Fair Week in December. The big scale on which some touring companies operated is illustrated by the visit of Mr and Mrs Henry Vandenhoff with a company of 50 and corps de ballet of 100 in *Kenilworth*. Young ladies were impressed as soldiers and the York stage taxed to its limit to hold the production. It was claimed that the jewelled armour and paraphernalia cost upwards of £2000.[86] During the recess between August and November the lobbies and passages were fitted up with new doors and curtains to prevent draughts that had been the subject of complaints.[87] The year ended with the Christmas visit of Mr and Mrs Wybert Rousby in Tom Taylor's *'Twixt Axe and Crown,* a drama that attracted full boxes, dress circle and pit but from which the gallery patrons stayed away preferring lighter fare.[88]

The first extant programme dates from January 2, 1873 and is for Younge's company in *School*.[89] It consists of one page with an advertisement on the back and was printed for the tour, the name of the individual theatre being filled in by hand. Henceforward the programme replaced the playbill for use in the Theatre.

Dillon followed with his customary Shakespearean season with Fanny Huddart as his leading lady and in February Wilson Barrett brought Caroline Heath (his wife, and his senior by many years) and his London company to play in *London Assurance* and *East Lynne*. J. Eldred, whose company was to become an annual visitor to York and who was lessee and manager of the Sheffield Theatre, sent E. Romaine Callender's strike drama *True as Steel* which showed men at full operation in the iron works. The author himself acted in it.[90] The pantomime, curiously advertised as 'the only pantomime in England' was *Cinderella* and the scenery was the work of Johnson, Maltby and Robinson. Tessy Gunniss was the première danseuse and Tom Slater the Clown. As usual it was followed by a season in which Coleman appeared with the stock company.

Gilbert à Beckett and W. S. Gilbert's burlesque *The Happy Land*, which had been at first prohibited by the Lord Chancellor on account of its witticisms at the Government's expense, was brought by Miss Evelyn's company for Whit week, and Gilbert's fairy comedy *The Wicked World* appeared in June.

Then J. L. Toole returned adding to the rôles he had already played in York those of Michael Garner in Byron's *Dearer Than Life* which had been specially written for him; Billy Lackaday in *Sweethearts and Wives;* Harry Coke in Clement Scott's first comedy *Off the Line*, and Jack Strong in *Your Life's in Danger.*

The great Italian tragedienne Madame Ristori made a single appearance on July 23 in Schiller's *Marie Stuart* on which occasion the charge for the private boxes rose to 4 guineas. The *York Gazette*[91] critic found that her powers had not suffered with advancing years: 'the fine feeling, the strong and dignified declamation when aroused proclaim her the Queen, and her perfect intonation bids defiance to adverse criticism'.

The playwright Edmund Falconer acted in his own *Killarney* in August but the critic pronounced that his company did not understand Irish character or instincts.[92]

Charles J. Mathews gave his farewell performances in York in September playing his favourite rôles in *Used Up, Cool as a Cucumber, Game of Speculation* and *Patter v. Clatter.* He was followed by the original Geneviève de Brabant – Emily Soldene. The Wizard of the North had the Theatre for 12 nights in October, and in November the Prince of Wales's Minstrels made their first appearance since leaving London. There were 14 performers, some of whom had been with the original Christy's. Coleman and the York company made a 12 nights' visit in December but Coleman himself was unable to act owing to having met with an accident.[93] He advertised in the *Era Almanack* for Star companies and concert parties for his theatres; the theatres themselves were to be let at intervals on rent or sharing terms.

The York circuit company played a rather bigger part in the programme for 1874. It opened the season in January with John Chute as managing director, Charles Fox as scene painter and Alice Finch as leading lady. At least one new play was given, Watts Phillips's *Nobody's Child.* The auditorium of the Theatre was then cleansed and decorated and the Royal as it was now affectionately called, re-opened with the pantomime *Twinkle Twinkle Little Star* for which the opera singer Madam Haigh-Dyer was engaged. In the cast were George Thorne, brother of Thomas, manager of the Vaudeville Theatre, George Lewis as Clown, and Therese Bassano as Columbine. The comedy company of the circuit then brought out Boucicault's *Janet Pride* with Richard Younge as the star. Coleman himself later appeared as Hamlet and Macbeth to the Lady Macbeth of Mrs. Kirby Hudson and in a new version of *The Polish Jew* called *The Sleigh Bells*.

Lecocq's gay *Fille de Madame Angot* was brought to York at the end of May by Selina Dolaro and company. In July the Bandmanns returned in *Hamlet, Othello, Macbeth, Dead or Alive, Richard III* and *David Garrick*. Then in the wake of various touring companies Coleman came back in September in a series of stock plays. Helen Barry, the statuesque Amazon Queen of the ill-fated and ruinous *Babil and Bijou* at Covent Garden, appeared with David Nunn Fisher, a member of the famous Norwich circuit family and well known actor at the Princess's, Adelphi and Lyceum, and a selected company. The York circuit company returned once again in October first with Eliza Saville the tragedienne and then with Mr and Mrs John Billington as stars. The two last played in the latest Adelphi dramas *Rough and Ready* by Merritt and *Hand and Glove* by Merritt and Conquest. In his farewell address Billington, who was a Yorkshireman, declared that it had always been his ambition to sustain a York character before a York audience, who had been celebrated for years as judges of acting, and he had told Merritt that he wanted a Yorkshire drama with characters of real flesh and blood; Merritt had obliged with *Rough and Ready* and Billington had achieved his goal.[94] Kate Santley paid the first of many visits to York with her opera bouffe company in November and sang in Clay's *La Cattarina* 'with rare delicacy and compass, her voice being of a quality clear, melodious and penetrating'.[95] The York company returned for Horse Fair Week in December when a benefit was given for Robert Hawkins who for many years had superintended the Royal during Coleman's absence. He was a veteran actor and citizen of York.[96]

Coleman's lease was due to expire on April 6, 1875 and he wished to renew it for ten years, offering to redecorate the Theatre and to make alterations and improvements, in addition to restoring the upper boxes and galleries to their former condition, which by the existing lease he was bound to do if so required. The Corporation received another offer from William Alfred Waddington, a music seller in Stonegate, who for some years had been running the Festival Concert Room, and was also lessee of the Londesborough Theatre in Scarborough. He wanted a lease of 14 years and offered to spend £600 on altering and decorating the theatre according to plans to be submitted to the Corporation. Neither offered a specific rent. The Corporation adopted the terms mentioned by Waddington as the basis of a tender for the new lease. Coleman offered £200 and Waddington £210 with a stipulation that a reasonable time should be allowed for alterations when no rent should be paid. The Corporation considered that by inserting this clause he had reduced his offer to an indeterminate sum and had departed from the terms of the competition laid down by himself; they therefore accepted Coleman's offer.[97]

The pantomime of *Hop o' My Thumb* was on a more sumptuous scale than ever. Upwards of 200 artists and auxiliaries before and behind the curtain took part and the outlay was £2000. The Theatre could not adequately stage such a show and there were consequent hitches in the working of the machinery. A Watteau ballet and cascades of real water scintillating in tinted lights were among the effects. An interval of 10 minutes was introduced before the harlequinade in which Allnutt was Clown and Mlle Allnutt Columbine; additional clowns and columbines were added on the last night. The hero was taken by Master Coote a child of 7 or 8 from the U.S.A.[98]

Wybert Reeve came with Miss Adeline Stanhope during Whit week and played in Wilkie Collins's *Fosco or The Woman in White* as well as in *The Lady of Lyons, Perfection* and the balcony scene from *Romeo and Juliet*. George Walter Browne made his début in York this year as a young man of 19 as Sidney Daryl in *Society*. He became a playwright as well as actor and vocalist and his first pieces were given in York.

On May 28 a terrible blow fell. The Leeds Theatre, which had cost £50,000 but was only insured for half that amount, was completely destroyed by fire. The properties were a total loss and the damage estimated at £30,000 to £35,000. This proved to be the final death blow of the York circuit and the stock company.[99] A Testimonial Fund was started in York and a performance was organised to give public expression of sympathy to the Colemans. This took place under the patronage of the Lord Mayor, Lady Mayoress and James Lowther M.P. The piece appropriately chosen was *Money* in which Mrs. Coleman sustained Clara Douglas. Coleman, overcome by emotion, could only utter a few words.[100]

During Race Week the burlesque actress Nelly Power came in Frank Musgrave's company. Known as 'Merry Nelly' she was an excellent male impersonator and had a gift for putting over a song. Sothern, in spite of increased prices and a heavy downpour, drew a good audience in *David Garrick* and *Dundreary* in September, and the following month Kate Santley sang the Prince de Conti in Lecocq's *Prés St. Gervais*. On October 20 Bob Hawkins, who for 25 years had been connected with the York Theatre, died after a three days' illness. He was the last of the old stagers, as Coleman himself put it, 'a type of a class rapidly passing away and if not of the highest order, he was earnest and conscientious',[101] a loyal servant of a particular playhouse. Coleman promptly gave up to the benefit of his widow his special revival of *Macbeth* on October 23, at which Locke's music was rendered by 50 voices selected from the local choral societies.[102] Another benefit was given by the York Garrick Club in November.

After this the Theatre was shut for alterations on an extensive scale. The pit, generally the most paying part of the house, was far too small for its habitués, and its area was enlarged by carrying it underneath the box circle on either side. Thus the Theatre was brought partly into line with Victorian and modern practice and the Georgian conception of a pit enclosed by a semi-circle of boxes was done away with. The process was completed in 1888 when the rest of the space beneath the dress boxes was opened out. The old proscenium was removed and a new one 'a massive and stately structure of the Corinthian Doric style, elaborately decorated in gold, with fluted columns, cornices and architraves' now formed 'a perfect frame to the stage'. The proscenium opening was 21 feet, the stage measurements 30 feet deep and 50 feet wide.[103] The shades of the footlights were replaced by patent reflectors, the lights being so adjusted that the audience was shielded from the glare of gas and the full blaze was concentrated on the stage. Where the stage doors had stood (they had already been replaced by statues in 1870) 'two circular stage boxes' were built. Radiating from them on either side were 4 family boxes each accommodating 4 people. The rest of this circle, 'the dress circle', which formerly contained four rows of seats was reduced to three and consisted of 83 comfortably upholstered fauteuils.[104] An entirely new upper circle was constructed fitted up with commodious arm chairs, at the back of which a promenade capable of holding about 100 people was available on exceptional occasions. This was the restoration of what had been the upper boxes. The gallery was restored to its old form and though less spacious was more comfortable. A painting – sadly now lost – showing the interior of the Theatre at around this time probably dated from after the alterations. (A slide of the original painting, in the Evelyn Collection in the York Public Library, gives no information as to date.) There are some discrepancies with the description, the family boxes being two instead of four and there being no fauteuils in the circle. It may be that the other two family boxes were in the second tier and that the picture was painted before the chairs were installed. The picture shows, though not clearly, the excavation of the pit to extend under the two first tier boxes, and the new stage boxes and proscenium.

As for the decorations the panels of the boxes were of satin and gold upholstery raised and embossed in a sumptuous manner. Around each tier of the boxes, circle and gallery, were borders of Utrecht velvet and the private boxes had draperies to harmonise with their surroundings. Charges were stage boxes 2 guineas, family boxes 1 guinea or 6/- for a single ticket, dress circle 3/-, upper circle stalls 2/-, upper side boxes and promenade 1/6, pit 1/-, gallery 6d – half price to dress circle only 2/-.

Two other improvements were found to be badly needed. There had been complaints about the excessive coldness of the Theatre in winter and a new warming apparatus was necessary. An additional scene dock was required and Coleman proposed to enclose the passage at the west side of the Theatre, adjoining Swaine's Garden, for this purpose. He approached the Corporation on both these matters and arranged to erect a new warming apparatus at his own expense whilst the Council on their part agreed to provide the scene dock, Coleman to pay interest on the expenditure at the rate of 5 per cent per annum. Coleman immediately expended £100 on a new heating apparatus invented by William Walker, a York citizen, and it was installed at short notice.[105]

The inaugural performance took place on Boxing Night – the play given being Oxenford's *The Two Orphans*. The next night the Lord Mayor and Lady Mayoress, the Sheriff and the civic authorities attended.

The year 1876 opened with the *Christmas Carol*. The Theatre was crammed, the private boxes and dress circle being occupied by a fashionably attired audience; but in the gods there were altercations. Later in the season we read that the gallery patrons were so rowdy that the performance was rendered inaudible; there was continuous whistling and orange peel was thrown down into the pit.[106]

The stock company made a prolonged stay of 2½ months during which time they brought out Hatton's drama *Clytie* with Margaret Leighton in the title rôle, *The Bells* and on February 12 for six nights, Boucicault's Irish drama *The Shaughraun* with George Clarke as Conn, Shiel Barry as Harvey Duff and Miss Leighton as Claire Folliott. Of Margaret Leighton Coleman[107] says 'she was a beautiful and accomplished young woman, whose personal magnetism, high intelligence and magnificent contralto voice were eminently adapted to the classic garb'. The acting manager was Stephen Artaud. Performances still lasted for four hours, the overture being played at 6.50 and carriages being ordered for 10.50. There were complaints of excessive intervals lasting 15 minutes.[108]

The commander-in-chief, the Duke of Cambridge, when he was the guest of Lord Londesborough bespoke a performance of *The School for Scandal* but the party failed to turn up.[109] Wybert Rousby with his own company joined the stock company in February. Rousby played Shylock, the Man in the Iron Mask, Bertuccio in Taylor's *Fool's Revenge* and Etienne de Vignolles in the same author's *Joan of Arc* which was new to York. Margaret Leighton was the Joan and she also essayed Romeo. George Browne brought out his first piece on any stage, a one act comedy entitled *Hearts and Homes* on February 11. Though there was an occasional thin house the attendance was on the average better than it had been for 25 years, and indeed during this time the population of York had considerably increased.[110] A letter, however, appeared in the local press[111] stating that the Theatre had been gradually declining since Pritchard's day and was at a low ebb. When Coleman had made room five years previously for more cheap seats, Richard Younge had declared that he had travelled over half the globe and had nowhere seen such a disgraceful assembly. Coleman promptly published in answer to this a letter he had received signed by thirteen managers among whom were Phelps, Hollingshead, H. J. Byron, and Wybert Reeve condemning the attack as contemptible and expressing their appreciation and sympathy.

Wilson Barrett came with Miss Heath and company in March and produced W. G. Wills's *Jane Shore* in which Barrett played Henry Shore. He also acted Archibald Carlyle in *East Lynne*, Smaily in Gilbert's *Charity*, and Benedick.

The stock company returned in April with the 11th Easter pantomime – *Whittington and his Cat* which E. L. Blanchard had written for Drury Lane. The scenery was by Brew, the transformation of the Fairies' Wedding having been designed by him for the Crystal Palace pantomime. The Payne family from Covent Garden were the principals in the harlequinade, Harry being the Clown and Fred the Harlequin. In the last week of the four weeks' run they introduced into it a new comic scene. Since the Leeds Theatre was no more, all the expenses this year had to be borne by York.[112] On April 3 the Council of the Corporation[113] met and discussed the Theatre. We learn that Coleman had spent more than the sum stipulated on the improvements so that 'the City now possesses, a Theatre as beautiful and attractive as any in the Kingdom'. The estimated cost of the new scene dock according to the plans prepared by Styan was £621. It was then felt that the exterior of the Theatre needed big improvements to render it more of a credit to the city, more worthy of the admirable site which it occupied and more in harmony with the alterations which the Fine Arts and Industrial Exhibition was to make. Styan had been instructed to prepare a plan to include provision for a commodious cloakroom over the Piazza. The cost he estimated at £1420. Coleman had been interviewed and had expressed himself willing to pay an additional rent of £50 for the extra rooms. The alterations were agreed to. At a further meeting on June 5[114] the Council issued instructions that no sanction was to be given to the lessee or any sub-tenant to sell liquor on the premises 'in view of the moral evils' likely to result.

Meantime a series of touring companies had filled the weekly bill. Sefton's brought W. S. Gilbert's fairy drama *The Broken Heart*, in which Rose Leclercq played Lady Hilda and Florence Terry, sister of Ellen, Lady Vavir. Then followed Mlle Beatrice's company, now in its 7th year, in adaptations of meretricious French plays; W. Sydney, manager of the new Leeds Theatre, with his opera bouffe company in H. B. Farnie's burlesque opera *Loo;* and Chippendale's company, of which George Leitch was now a member, in standard old comedies. There was plenty of variety – what was lacking was the local interest that a stock company provided. The Theatre then closed for several weeks and reopened at the end of August for the last time with the stock company. The brief season started inauspiciously, a carpenter named Pinder dying as the result of injuries sustained from an explosion which occurred whilst he was preparing a vessel charged with chemicals and gas for the limelight apparatus.[115] In November Toole came for two nights and stayed a third to satisfy the demand for seats.[116] On Boxing Night W. Duck's company brought Byron's *Our Boys* to York with Fanny Brough, Mrs. F. B. Egan and T. H. Craven. This celebrated comedy had already run 600 nights at the Vaudeville and was to continue for over four years.

Coleman, after a disastrous season as the lessee of the Queen's Theatre, filed a petition of bankruptcy on October 19 and obtained his discharge in November. His renewed lease of the York Theatre had never been executed and his bankruptcy rendered it void. He still owed £300 of the £1200 he had spent in improvements and he owed the Corporation £215 in rent. On October 23 he was interviewed by the Finance Committee, who promised that, if his friends would help him pay the rent they would grant him a new lease on his discharge.[117] His assets of scenery and properties he declared would be of little value in a forced sale but might be worth £200-£300 if left on his hands.

Shortly after W. A. Waddington, who had competed for the lease with Coleman previously obtained promises from 7 members of the Corporation Finance Committee that a lease should be granted to him. Armed with this support he made an offer to Coleman's trustee Buffen for the assignment of the rest of Coleman's lease. Buffen and Waddington together visited one of the Committee of Inspection who gave his assent whereupon Buffen entered into a provisional agreement with Waddington to dispose to him of Coleman's interest in the lease, stipulating that he should have power to cancel it should it not be confirmed by the rest of the Committee of Inspection. Buffen also accepted £720 on deposit. A sum of £740 was then offered by a friend of Coleman on his behalf and this higher offer was accepted by the Committee of Inspection whereupon Buffen returned Waddington's deposit. Waddington, who considered his contract binding applied for the keys of the Theatre on December 2 and, on being refused, himself went and put padlocks on the box and pit entrances. Then he hired a gang of men to break into the Theatre with crowbars, took possession and opened it with a touring company. On December 28 Coleman issued a writ for recovery of possession and damages for forced entry, partial destruction, ejection of his servants and injury done by preventing him carrying on his business. Waddington was also summoned for keeping the Theatre open without a licence from the justices and was fined £1 per day for every day the Theatre had been open.[118] At the new year, 1877, both Coleman and Waddington applied for an annual licence. Waddington obtained one for a month without prejudice to Coleman's interests; it was subsequently renewed, and in May finally granted for the rest of the year on Waddington's undertaking that he would not sell refreshments or liquor and that he had already stopped the sale of oranges.[119] In February Waddington asked for an order in court on Buffen to carry out his contract. This was refused because only one member of the Committee of Inspection had given his assent to the agreement. At the same time Registrar Murray expressed his view that Waddington had reason to complain of the cavalier treatment of his contract and blamed the trustee for cancelling it without consulting Coleman's creditors. Waddington then appealed from the decision. The Court of Appeal held that the contract was binding after the assent of one member of the Committee of Inspection had been obtained, the documents handed to Waddington and his deposit accepted. The former decision was reversed and an order made that, on Waddington's returning the £720, the trustee must fulfil the contract and assign the lease to him. Coleman threatened to carry the case to the House of Lords but eventually acquiesced in the decision. The Corporation had been holding their hands until the issue was settled but in August, having received an intimation that the trustee was not intending to carry the matter further, the Council was recommended to grant a formal lease to Waddington on the same terms as the original agreement with Coleman.[120] A memorial from Coleman's creditors, who had been employed in work on the Theatre, requesting the Council's aid in recouping their losses was refused.

Whilst all this was going on the Theatre was being run by Waddington. His management, however, opens a new era in its history for it represents the end of the stock company and the complete triumph of the touring system.

CHAPTER EIGHT

Touring Companies 1877–1934

Except for a brief season in autumn and winter the Theatre was now given up entirely to touring companies who came for six or twelve nights or occasionally for two or three. Some of these presented a single production such as *The Shaughraun* or *The Flying Scud* but most had a repertoire of two or three pieces sometimes by the same, sometimes by different authors. In the next years we find the rapid decline of the afterpiece, its replacement in some cases by the curtain raiser, and the final shortening of the programme by its confinement to the main drama.

The pantomime for 1877 – Frank Green's *Jack and the Beanstalk* with the Walton family – was provided by Richard Younge's company. The touring companies brought their own stars so that in their first flush the provinces continued to see some of the finest actors and actresses of the day. Fanny Addison came in Pitt's company in June and in July the Dan'l Druce company performed Gilbert's play of that name with a cast which included David Fisher, Charles Vandenhoff and Florence Terry. But September was the great month for stars. They were led by Ada Cavendish who acted Pauline, Mercy Merrick in Wilkie Collins's *New Magdalen*, and Juliet. As the last she was fine in the balcony scene, her facial expression betokening intense emotion. The Mercutio was Edmund Willard, a well known actor of our own day.[1] Toole followed, adding to his well-known rôles that of Edward Titscrap in Albery's *Man in Possession*. The climax was on September 28 when Irving came with Isabel Bateman and the Lyceum Company in *Hamlet*. The house was crowded to see the actor who, a few years previously, had passed unnoticed in secondary rôles in the same theatre. The *York Gazette*[2] pointed out his tendency to staginess and found him in some passages inarticulate, but conceded him high dramatic instincts and a power of riveting the attention.

Waddington brought a stock company in October with T.H. Potter as stage manager. Helen Barry starred in it as Lady Gay Spanker, and Margaret Hayes in Taylor's *Arkwright's Wife*. On its return in December Miss

299

Wallis and Edward Compton, son of the old York stager Henry Compton, played Pauline and Melnotte, Rosalind and Orlando and Parthenia and Ingomar.

Smoke rooms were opened for box and pit patrons.[3]

In the meantime preparations were going forward for the reconstruction of the exterior of the theatre. Styan's amended plans to bring the upper portion of the front, as well as the lower, into line with the piazza and thus to provide a good deal more space were approved at an estimate of £2200. Waddington proposed that some portion of the additional rooms on the first floor should be available as a dwelling house and offered to pay an additional rent of £100 if his proposals were incorporated in the scheme. This was agreed to as it was felt it would increase the value of the property.[4] In November 1877 tenders for the work were accepted from Kilvington and Hughes carpenters, Lyons plumber, Croft plasterer, Hodgson white-smith, Carhill slater and Pearson painter.[5] In the same month Styan reported that the exits were inadequate for an emergency. His recommendations of an additional doorway at the N.E. end of the Theatre to relieve the exit from the pit, others from each of the corridors at the back of the dress circle and upper boxes, and from the gallery, all leading onto the staircase, were accepted. The exits from the different parts of the house were thus divided instead of being concentrated.[6] The vaults which had been used for storage purposes were vacated and the ancient crypt was opened to visitors. A proposal from one of the Councillors to sell the Theatre was this time turned down with only three votes in its favour.[7]

Among the well known actors who came with touring companies in 1878 were J. H. Clyndes, who played Conn the fiddler in *The Shaughraun* (acted without an after-piece), Hamlet, Othello, Richelieu and Richard III; George Leitch who once again sang some of the old favourites from his pantomime rôle of King Hardup; the singer Harry Liston who appeared in E. Byam Wyke's *Slander* as Jack Trafford; and 'the marvellous Girards' dancing grotesques from the Alhambra. The pantomime, which had done duty at Glasgow at Christmas and then at Manchester, was *Sinbad the Sailor*, put on by Sidney's company with G. Preston as Clown.

The Colemans had a farewell week in May and were assisted by Margaret Leighton and George Thorne who had recently returned from Calcutta. Coleman chose as his parts Denough in Taylor's *Clancarty*, Ethelwold in his own *Katharine Howard*, Robert Landry in *The Dead Heart*, Don Caesar de Bazan, Charles Surface, with Mrs. Coleman as Lady Teazle, and Shaun in *Arrah-na-Pogue*. In his farewell address he explained his monetary affairs and declared that the loss of the York Theatre had been the cruellest blow he had sustained.[8]

In November W. Sidney came in person and played Rip van Winkle, Uncle Tom in *Uncle Tom's Cabin*, Jonas Isaacs in *Conquest* and Pettitts' drama *Queen's Evidence*, as well as in his own adaptation of Mrs. Burnett's novel *That Lass o' Lowries*, and the Yorkshire drama *Aurora Floyd* adapted from Miss Braddon. The year ended with Miss Bateman and the Lyceum

company in Leah, Mary Warner and Queen Elizabeth. A heavy and prolonged frost in the winter of 1878-9 held up the work on the Theatre but it
was continued all through the latter year.[9]

The stock company henceforth ceased to exist and the Theatre was
entirely given over to touring companies. There was in 1879 plenty of variety. Of tragedians there came Osmond Tearle, who played the usual round
of Hamlet, Othello, Richard III, Beverley, the Stranger and Richelieu, and
John Dewhurst in *Macbeth* (which was still presented with singing witches),
Shylock and Ruy Gomez. At the other end of the scale there were the
Majiltons (Charles, Frank and Marie) a well known family of grotesques,
and the Vokes's of Drury Lane pantomime fame, irresistible in operatic burlesque and saltatorial extravaganzas. A troupe of freed slaves and jubilee
singers was followed by Irish comedians. The pantomime was an entirely
new one called *The Yellow Dwarf* adapted from Planché's fairy extravaganza
by the local playwright George W. Browne. The company was under the
management of George Thorne and no less than four scene painters, including Emden, were employed on this show.[10] Perhaps the most interesting event, however, was the first production of a Gilbert and Sullivan
opera in York when the D'Oyly Carte company brought *H.M.S. Pinafore* on
September 22. Mansfield as the First Lord had an amusing style of laconic
gravity, Hogarth, a powerful baritone, was Capt. Corcoran, Cadwalader, a
pleasing light tenor, Ralph Rackstraw, Miss Trevelyan Little Buttercup, and
Miss E. Pierson a slightly insipid Josephine. It played to crowded houses.[11]
Another famous piece first seen in York this year was *Diplomacy*, which the
Bancrofts had put on the previous year at the Prince of Wales's.

Kate Santley, now manageress of the Royalty Theatre, brought her
company and played Mrs Honeyton in S. Theyre Smith's *A Happy Pair*,
Claudine Baganelle in *A Black Business* written for her by A. Mattison,
Ernestine in Rummins's *Reception* with music by Offenbach, and four characters in Alfred Thompson's impersonation piece *Three Conspirators*; she also
sang a celebrated song of the day entitled *Awfully Awful*. On October 20 for
6 nights, the Great Macdermott sang a number of topical songs, including his famous '*We don't want to fight but by Jingo if we do*' written by Hunt
when the Russians threatened Constantinople and honoured by quotation
in Parliament. He also sang *Two Obadiahs* and *Says Aaron to Moses*, appeared
in a long drawn out piece *Through the Fire* and in Dallas's burlesque scena
Visions.[12]

By the opening of the year 1880 work on the exterior of the Theatre was
sufficiently advanced for a long description of it to appear in the local
press.[13] Visitors to the city, said the writer, had for too long exclaimed on
seeing the exterior, 'What, that your Theatre Royal'. The old piazza was in
such a shabby state that it looked almost as old as St. Mary's Abbey. This
was removed and set up in Fishergate where it may be seen to this day, and
a new open piazza of 5 arches took its place. On the floors above a suite
of rooms was provided. The new Victorian Gothic frontage, considered
'handsome' at the time, was much as we see it today. A new wing was added

on the north side which provided the additional exit from the pit and at the stage end housed the new scene dock. This was approached on the ground floor by a covered way rising to the dock, to facilitate the transit of animals. The dock itself, which was raked with the stage, was 34 ft. long, half that width and 26 ft. high from the centre. To crown all, the Town Clerk, J. Wilkinson, presented a statue of Shakespeare to occupy the ornamental stone canopy which surmounted the gable. Inside Waddington improved the upper auditorium so that seeing and hearing were easier than under Coleman, and a smoke room and refreshment bar was completed to the left of the dress circle entrance. A new drop scene was in use. The reconstruction neared completion only in November when the Council commended Styan on his work and flattered themselves that they had greatly added to the architectural adornment of the city.[14]

H. Beerbohm Tree, almost at the beginning of his career, appeared in Offenbach's *Madame Favart* as the amorous old Marquis de Pont Sable in H. B. Farnie's company early in 1880. The pantomime was T. F. Doyle's *Cinderella* from the Prince of Wales's Theatre, Liverpool given by Eldred's company. The Liberals and Conservatives each had a night of it when their candidates visited the Theatre; on the latter occasion Eldred gave his impersonation of Lord Beaconsfield.

Scenic effects were the chief attraction at Merritt and Rowe's *New Babylon* in which Clarence Holt played the American detective Flotsam. A collision in the Atlantic, views of Tattersalls, Cremorne Gardens illuminated, and Goodwood Races were painted by Henry Emden, the great scenic artist from Drury Lane, and Dugan.

Carmen was first brought to York in May with Emily Soldene as Carmen and Signor Leli as José; *Les Cloches de Corneville* was given in September. George Browne, in collaboration with Hugh Moss, wrote *Ripples*, a comedy which made its first appearance on any stage at York on November 19. The D'Oyly Carte company paid two visits, the second time with *The Sorcerer*. Charles Wyndham appeared for three nights in *Brighton* and Dillon added to former rôles the heroes of Wills's *Bolivar* and Knowles's *Bridal* compressed into 3 acts by W. C. Day. With the Chippendale comedy company came the unknown Fred Terry in minor parts such as Trip in *The School for Scandal*.

Now there was no stock company, Waddington engaged and organised a special one for the presentation of *The Streets of London*.

Waddington's lease expired on April 6, 1882 and was renewed for 14 years at the greatly increased rental of £300.[15] Waddington by his new lease was not to use the Theatre for gaming or other unlawful purposes, was not to sublet for more than three months nor make structural alterations without the consent of the Corporation. He was to maintain and retain the Theatre in full repair except for reasonable wear and tear or damage by fire or tempest. The schedule of fixtures belonging to the Corporation was much the same as that of 1835[16] but it now included all the gas fittings, except those connected with the stage which belonged to Waddington.

There was now a large star light over the pit and 16 brackets in the boxes of one light each. Another inventory, dated December 9, 1881, mentions footlights and guards and a gas bracket and wire guard for the prompter. According to this inventory there were now four dressing rooms, one large and one small for actors, one for actresses and one for a star. In the paint room there was a painting frame and machine for hoisting it, and an apparatus for lime light.

A few stars came with the touring companies in 1881. George Rignold, who has been described as 'a robust actor somewhat in the style of a modern and modified Charles Dillon'[17] paid his first visit to York as Henry V which he had played at Drury Lane, and on a second visit played Amos Clark in Watts Phillips's drama of that name as well as the sailor rôle of William in the old favourite *Black Ey'd Susan*. Rose Leclercq appeared as Joan Lowrie in *Joan* a drama of Lancashire life written specially for her by Charles Reade, as well as in *Galathea*, Mrs. Harriet Routhe in Taylor's *Black Sheep*, *Lady Audley's Secret* in G. C. Murray's version, Princess Zeolide in *The Palace of Truth* and Lady Isabella Carlyle. Miss Wallis appeared in September as Rosalind, Beatrice and Ninon in Wills's melodrama.

The pantomime in April was *Little Red Riding Rood and Bo-Peep* and special late trains were put on for the benefit of country visitors during its run.[18] On August 15 the D'Oyly Carte brought *Patience* with George Thorne as Bunthorne, Arthur Rousby as Archibald Grosvenor, Miss McAlpine as Patience and Elsie Cameron as Lady Angela. Probably the first of Pinero's plays to be seen in York was his comedy *The Money Spinner* which was brought by Duck's company. G.R. Sims's *Member for Slocum* was seen at York four months after its production at the Royalty. Amateur performances were given in aid of the Royal School for Officers' Daughters in November.

The following year, 1882, saw the first pantomime under the direction of Victor Stevens who was to be responsible for many succeeding ones. This was George Capel's *Robinson Crusoe* for which scenery had been especially painted by Harry Mapleson. It ran for over 5 weeks and ended with a benefit for the author.

Capel's drama *Above Suspicion* was first acted on any stage at York on May 19. Noteworthy visitors were Edward Compton and his wife Virginia Bateman. He played Malvolio, Tony Lumpkin, Jack Rover in *Wild Oats* and Acres. With them Lewis Ball, formerly a member of the stock company, played Belch, Hardcastle and Sir Anthony Absolute. Kate Santley sang Betina in Audran's *La Mascotte*, and Offenbach's *La Fille du Tambour Major* was brought by Richard South's company. The famous American actor Edwin Booth came for one night on September 18 as Richelieu with the Adelphi Company and Bella Pateman as Julie. Among the plays seen this year were Dion Boucicault's *Forbidden Fruit*, and Hamilton's *Moths*, taken from Ouida's novel and acted by the company from the Olympic under Marie Litton. A completely new domestic drama, *Woodleigh or On and Off the Stage*, made its bow in York on February 9, 1883.

Stevens's pantomime that year was Capel's *Dick Whittington* with scenery by Mapleson. The transformation was a Harvest of Wild Flowers and in the harlequinade Hal Forde was the Clown. Waddington invited the workhouse children one evening, an offer at first rejected on the grounds that the theatre was a bad influence, but finally accepted. The year held little of interest except for the début of *Iolanthe* with Frank Thornton as the Chancellor, and the first visit of Ben Greet's company in July with Minnie Palmer as leading lady. Greet himself played Austin in F. W. Broughton's *Runaways* and Dudley Harcourt in F. G. Maeder's *My Sweetheart*. As the touring system became organised and more companies took the field, less stars were seen in the provinces. The London theatres sent out second companies, not the original ones, with their successes to the country theatres.

By October 1885 Waddington had taken his three sons, W. H., Alfred and Walter Waddington into partnership in his enterprises at York and Scarborough. Harry Mapleson and J. H. Hemingway were the scenic artists, G. Wilson the master carpenter and T. Barnes jun. the gas engineer.[19] Edward Compton and Virginia Bateman (now Mrs. Compton) returned in 1884 with *The Comedy of Errors* and *The School for Scandal*. Wilson Barrett's No.1 company brought out two famous melodramas, Sims's *Lights o' London* and Henry Arthur Jones's *Silver King*. At the end of the year the D'Oyly Carte company presented *Princess Ida* for nine nights. Stevens's pantomime was *The Babes in the Wood* by Capel in which there were scenes of Bootham Bar and Stonegate by Hemingway and Egerton. During Race Week the Theatre was occupied by the Lila Clay Company of Ladies, which consisted of over 40 members with a ladies' orchestra and ballet. On September 22 York first saw the beautiful Lily Langtry who was supported by Charles Coghlan. Mrs. Langtry played Lady Ormond in *Peril*, Lady Teazle and Miss Hardcastle. Familiar stars were Kate Santley, who sang Princess Mackinshoff in Hervé's comic opera *La Cosaque*; Sothern who reappeared after his American tour, and Toole who sustained Barnaby Doublechick in Byron's *Upper Crust*, Benjamin Guffin in *Mr. Guffin's Elopement* and Tittums in *The Steeplechase*. Charles Macdona, later to be widely known for his Shaw travelling company, appeared as Sir Percival Glyde in *The Woman in White*. By this time the Free Trade Music Hall and Roe's Palace of Varieties in Tower Street were rival places of entertainment.

Among famous pieces first seen in York in 1885 were Charles Hawtrey's *Private Secretary* and *The Mikado*. In the latter, Ko Ko = David Fisher junior, Nanki-Poo = Charles Rowan, Poo-Bah = Furneaux Cook, Yum-Yum = Ethel Pierson, Katisha = Fanny Edwards. The pantomime, once again by Capel, under the direction of Stevens was *Aladdin* in which Stevens himself, who was one of the best of Dames, played the Widow Twanky and Clown. The scenery was by E. Egerton and Clarke and the transformation represented the Nereides Home in the Coral Haunt of the Mermaids.

Interesting visitors were Lottie Venne who played Mrs. Dick Chetwyn in B. Howard's *Young Mrs. Wintrop*, Mary Moore who played Lady Dorothy Osterley in Justin McCarthy's *The Candidate*, Edward Terry and his company who had the Royal during Cricket Week, the Vokes family, and the handsome Lewis Waller who came with Florence West and her Haymarket company in December. He played Dr. Basil North to the Phillipa Lafarge of Florence West and the Sir Mervyn Ferrand of Charles Macdona in Comyns Carr and Hugh Conway's *Dark Days*. Morning performances were given by some companies especially for country visitors.

The year 1886 was uneventful. Edward Terry returned and played Capt. Ginger in *The Weak Woman*, Darby in *Darby and Joan*, Paul Pry and two of his happiest rôles Montagu Jolliffe in *In Chancery* and Chevalier Walkinshaw in *The Rocket* both by the rising young dramatist Pinero. The run of pantomimes directed by Victor Stevens was broken and this year's *Goody Two Shoes* was directed as well as written by Lloyd Clarance. Two morning performances were given for children.

Toole came to York on a northern tour in September and has left some amusing anecdotes of his visit. He tells us how he paid entrance for some newsboys congregated in the locality of the Theatre and how he pretended to the porter that he took the ecclesiastical looking building for a chapel.[20]

The afterpiece, and even the curtain raiser, were gradually being dropped and an increasing number of pieces were put on without either. Some old favourites reappeared in 1887: Kate Santley as Indiana in Audran's opera, Kate Bateman who added to her rôles that of Margaret Field in H. A. Jones's *His Wife* and Toole in his new part of David Trot in *The Butler* with Violet Vanbrugh as Lady Anne Babicombe.

Among newcomers was Benson's famous Shakespeare and Old English Comedy Company in which Thalberg played Iago, Laertes and Bassanio, and Henry Vibart appeared as the Ghost, Antonio, Cassio and Crabtree. Geneviève Ward and W. H. Vernon visited York on their first tour of Great Britain, Miss Ward appearing as Stephanie in *Forget-Me-Not* and as the Duchess of Marlborough in Grundy's *Queen's Favourite*. The pantomime *Little Red Riding Hood* came from Manchester, and among the five scene painters was no less a one than William Telbin, who did two glade scenes in autumn and winter. *Ruddigore* was the new Gilbert and Sullivan and in it Henry Lytton appeared as Robin Oakapple. The officers' regimental uniforms were exact reproductions of those worn in 1812, from designs supplied by the military fine art gallery, and the heavy changes of scenery necessitated an interval of twenty minutes.

In October the Corporation sent a sub-committee with the City Surveyor to inspect the Theatre with a view to the provision of more exits, and plans for these were then drawn up and passed. The exit from the pit which led towards the proscenium was abandoned in favour of two new exits at the back of the pit, one on each side of the house. These were provided by opening out and adding to the pit the whole of the enclosed space beneath the dress circle which now became a balcony and lost its last vestige of Georgian construction. The new portion of the front wing, which up till then had been let for theatrical lodgings, was now converted to contain two staircases one for the dress circle and upper boxes, the other direct from the street to the gallery. The entrance to the former was through the centre of the Piazza. The old dangerous gallery staircase was abandoned and in its stead, the former dress circle and upper boxes staircase was continued up to the gallery. Access both to this and the new staircase was available from the dress circle by emergency doors. For the previous nine months Waddington had limited admissions to the gallery to 250 for the sake of safety. Other improvements were a new stair direct from the P.S. stage to the passage in Duncombe Place, another O.P. to the back staircase in the scene dock, iron ladders from the flies on each side of the stage, an exit from the dressing rooms direct to the St. Leonard's entrance lobby, the rendering the walls fireproof, and the installation of a safety curtain. Before the work was carried out the Council asked for a statement of their receipts and expenditure on the Theatre for the past twenty years; this showed that they had spent £5177.2.7d and received only £4155.10.10.[21] The Theatre now held 1400 people.[22]

Pinero's *Magistrate* and *Dandy Dick* were first given in March by the Royal Court Theatre company. Lloyd Clarance's pantomime was *Sinbad the Sailor* and in it Miss Clara St. Clair was principal boy, Ada and Addie Blanche were Sinbad and his sweetheart Tootsie, Fred Cairns was Ally Sloper, J. G. Laurien Harlequin and Louis Martini Clown. During the months that the Royal was shut performances took place at the Assembly Rooms and the Festival Concert Rooms. By October the Theatre had reopened its doors and among the new pieces presented by companies this autumn were the Sims-Pettitt drama *Harbour Lights* and the Merritt-Harris Drury Lane melodrama *Pleasure*. In November Professor Crocker's 15 educated horses performed their evolutions and children were able to ride round the stage on ponies and donkeys.

The alterations to the Theatre were finally reported to be finished in February 1889 but in June it was agreed to re-cover the cushioned seats and re-paint the walls of the dress circle which had suffered damage. Waddington offered £50 to complete the repairs.[23]

Two famous Victorian novels were put on the York stages in 1889. The first was *The Mystery of a Hansom Cab* by Fergus Hume and Arthur Law, the second *Little Lord Fauntleroy* for which Horace Lingard's company had been selected and engaged by the authoress Mrs Hodgson Burnett. On the musical side *The Yeomen of the Guard* was first given with George Thorne as Jack Point, and the operetta *Dorothy* with Fred Emney as Lurcher. The pantomime of *Blue Beard* was once again written and produced specially for the York Theatre by Victor Stevens with scenery by Egerton. The stars who visited York this year were all actresses. There was Isabella Bateman who played Jane Shore in Wills's drama, Mary Warner and Pauline Deschappells; there was Mrs. Bandmann-Palmer as Pauline, Lady Teazle and Margaret Gyde in *Tares*; there was Mrs. Langtry as Rosalind, Esther Sandraz in the play by Sydney Grundy, and La Marquise de Pompadour in Osborne's *After the Rehearsal*; and lastly there was a newcomer Kate Vaughan who had been one of the best English dancers of her time at the

Gaiety but had, for reasons of health, exchanged dancing for comedy, and who was seen as Raymonde de Montaiglin in *Love and Honour* adapted by Campbell Clarke from Dumas *fils*, Peggy in *The Country Girl*, and Viscount de Letorieres in Hermann Vezin's *Little Viscount*. Among those who were to become well known at a later period were Henrietta Watson who represented Mrs. Hummingtop in Grundy's *Arabian Nights*, and E. Lyall Swete, who was the Joseph Surface and Beauséant in Mrs. Bandmann-Palmer's company.

The Carl Rosa Light Opera Company made a first appearance in York in January 1890 in Planquette's *Paul Jones*, and in December for one night in Gounod's *Romeo and Juliet*. In December too, Benson returned in the *Merry Wives* in which he played Caius and his wife Mistress Ford, in *Richard II* which was advertised as being Shakespeare's text, and in *The Merchant of Venice, Hamlet, Much Ado, The Taming of the Shrew* and *Julius Caesar* in which Benson was Mark Antony. Two of Mark Melford's pieces had their first performances on any stage at York: the comedietta *A Clever Capture* on March 7 and the farce *The Rope Merchant* the following night. The pantomime of 1890, produced by Milton Rays, was Percy Milton's *Beauty and the Beast* in which Ada Blanche played the principal boy introducing *Where did You get that Hat?* and *That's how He carries on*. Ada Blanche returned later in the year with Auguste van Biene's Gaiety burlesque company in *Ruy Blas* and the *Blasé Roué*. Haidée Wright appeared as Ethel Arden in Pettitt and Grundy's *Union Jack* and in June the Vokes family returned, followed by William Terriss and Miss Millward who gave a dramatic costume recital of the balcony scene in *Romeo and Juliet* and scenes from *The Taming of the Shrew* and *The Hunchback*.

During 1891 York had the first presentation of three new pieces: *Trooper Hugh*, a dramatic sketch on May 8; *A Double Event*, a comedietta on August 7, both by Alfred Wilkinson; and a one act piece *For Valour* by W. Fawcett on October 16.

This year also saw the début in York of Pinero's *Sweet Lavender* with T. W. Robertson as Dick Phenyl, *The Gondoliers* with George Thorne as the Duke of Plaza-Toro, and *A Pair of Spectacles*. In Percy Milton's pantomime of *Aladdin*, Kitty Loftus played the principal boy, Percy Milton the Widow Twanky, and Nellie Wallace Chee-Kee. The new scenery was by T. Pilbeam of Brighton but H. Caprani was responsible for local scenes. O'Connor and Brady's company provided a week of variety which was followed by H. Crozier and P. Milton's *Fair Play* with mechanical effects of a landslide.

As for stars W. S. Penley played Sir John Pye in Arthur Law's *The Judge*; Mrs Langtry added Lady Clancarty to her previous rôles; Isabel Bateman those of Julia in *The Hunchback* and Clarissa Harlowe; and Louis Calvert paid his first visit to York as Admiral Kingston in *Naval Engagements*, in *The Corsican Brothers* and as Shylock with Haidée Wright as his leading lady.

The usual prices were private boxes 2 guineas, one pound ten shillings and one guinea; dress circle 3/-; pit stalls reserved 2/6; pit stalls 2/-; upper boxes 2/-; side boxes 1/6; pit 1/-; gallery 6d. Performances generally began at 7.30. According to the *Dramatic and Musical Directory* of 1892 the measurements for the proscenium opening were 21 ft. and from footlights to back of stage 33 ft. Caprani was the scenic artist and Barton musical director.

Afterpieces were almost a thing of the past and among the programmes of 1892 only one is recorded. In the programmes of this year too we first come across the term matinée used by the Benson company. 'Morning performance' was still preferred by Milton Rays's pantomime company which came with Percy Milton's *Robinson Crusoe* with scenery by John and Joseph Clark. *Lady Windermere's Fan* was brought to York in September by J. Pitt Hardacre with Angela Fenton as Mrs. Erlynne, George Harker as Lord Windermere, G. P. Polson as Lord Darlington and Maggie Hunt as Lady Windermere. Oscar Wilde witnessed the performance on September 23 from a stage box and received an enthusiastic call to the footlights whence be bowed his acknowledgements.[24] The Rousby operatic company, during their annual visit in November, introduced *Cavalleria Rusticana* to York. The D'Oyly Carte Company varied Gilbert and Sullivan with Grundy and Solomon's *Vicar of Bray*, and Eille Norwood gave the first performance anywhere of his farce *The Noble Art* in which he played with Kitty Loftus. Kitty Loftus reappeared later in the Gaiety burlesque *Cinder-ellen Up Too Late*. Other stars who appeared were Minnie Palmer, the American actress, who doubled the rôles of the girl and boy in *My Brother's Sister*; Kate Vaughan who added to her characters that of Lady Alice Harborough in Harvy's *John Jasper's Wife*; Sir Charles Wyndham and Mary Moore who appeared in *David Garrick* and in their new Criterion play *The Fringe Of Society;* Louis Calvert who acted Lagardere in *The Duke's Motto*, William in *Black Ey'd Susan*, Noel Mistral in Louis N. Parker's *Love Knot* and the dual rôles in *The Lyons Mail*. Two spectacular railway accidents were staged in 1893: a tableau of the smash up in *The Swiss Express* with the scenery, dresses and effects from the Princess's, and a collision on the line in *The Pointsman* advertised as 'the most Realistic Scene ever produced on the stage'. Pieces were now often on tour for an inordinate length of time, witness Victor Stevens's burlesque company's *Bonnie Boy Blue* which was in its second year when it came to York. The pantomime of 1893 was *Mother Goose* by William Wade which came from the Comedy Theatre, Manchester. The term musical comedy is first found as a description of *In Town* which George Edwardes's Gaiety Theatre company brought for Race Week; in it George Honey appeared as the Duke of Duffshire. With the D'Oyly Carte company came Kate Kavanagh who played Dorcas in Grundy and Sullivan's *Haddon Hall* and Lady Angela in *Patience*. Calvert returned in *The Corsican Brothers* and as Pierre Lorance in *Proof*. In A. E. Drinkwater's *Two Christmas Eves* Miss Lillah McCarthy took the part of Naomi the gipsy.

The name of Percy Hutchison, later lessee of the Royal, is first found as stage manager for his mother Emma Hutchison and her Criterion Comedy company in February 1894; he played Harry Greenlanes in *Pink Dominos* and Fred Carter in *Brighton*. In March Tree's company brought *A Woman of*

No Importance with H. B. Conway as Lord Illingworth and Miss Lingard as Mrs Arbuthnot. In September the company returned in Grundy's *A Bunch of Violets*. The pantomime was *Red Riding Hood*. In April Violet Loraine played Lopez in *Little Christopher Columbus* with W. Greet's company and in May, the last and least successful of the Gilbert and Sullivan operas, *Utopia Ltd.* was first seen in York. A drama of local interest Wilton Jones's *A Yorkshire Lass* with F. J. Nettlefold as Jack Selwyn came in June and a much more famous piece, the perennial *Charley's Aunt* was brought by W. S. Penley's company in September.

Frank Boyce was the Royal's acting manager in 1895 and in July of that year a benefit was given for him under the patronage of the Lord Mayor at which Ada Blanche sang. An extension of lease was granted to Waddington and his sons for five years.

A number of celebrated pieces were first seen in York that year. There was Barrett's dramatisation of Hall Caine's *The Manxman* with Henry Vibart as Phillip Christian and Haidée Wright as Kate Cregan; Wills's *Royal Divorce* with J.H. Clyndes as Napoleon; *The Notorious Mrs Ebbsmith* with George Arliss as the Duke of St. Olpherts and H.A. Saintsbury as Lucas Cleeve; Sardou's *Fédora*; H.A. Jones's *The Masqueraders* and Jerome and Eden Phillpotts's *The Prude's Progress* with Leon Quartermaine as Jack Medbury. Percy Milton was once again the author of the pantomime, *The Forty Thieves*.

Percy Hutchison returned as Sir Philander Rose in Meilhac and Halévy's *Hot Water* and Richard Melville in Shannon's *The Covent Garden Ball,* but the most notable visitors were in Ben Greet's company which included H. B. Irving, Granville Barker and Lillah McCarthy. In *Romeo and Juliet* Irving played Romeo, Lillah McCarthy Juliet, Ben Greet Friar Lawrence and Granville Barker Paris. Irving also played Leontes in *The Winter's Tale* with Granville Barker as Clown and Lillah McCarthy as Paulina; Sir Charles Pomander in *Masks and Faces* with Lillah McCarthy as Peg Woffington; Armand D'Arcy in Grundy's *Village Priest* with Lillah McCarthy as Marguerite; Benedick in *Much Ado* with Edyth Olive as Beatrice, Lillah McCarthy as Hero, Ben Greet as Dogberry and Granville Barker as Don John; and Claude Melnotte.

H. B. Irving returned the following year, 1896, in William Greet's company as Marcus Superbus in *The Sign of the Cross* advertised as "The greatest Production now travelling in the Provinces", with Lillah McCarthy as Mercia and a company of 60. Lawrence Irving too came as Svengali in *Trilby*. *The Second Mrs. Tanqueray* arrived in March with Dawson Milward as Aubrey and Cecil Cromwell as Paula. On the musical side there was *Hansel and Gretel* by the Carl Rosa company, *The Grand Duke* with Kate Kavanagh by the D'Oyly Carte and *The Geisha*. In Percy Milton's pantomime *Bo-Peep or Little Miss Muffet* Marie Dainton was the principal girl.

The season of 1897 was uneventful. Milton Bode's company was responsible for the pantomime of *Jack the Giant Killer* by Stanley Rogers with local hits by Harry Yorke. H. A. Jones's *Saints and Sinners* came to York in

August and in November the Royal was the scene of amateur performances in aid of charities.

Stanley Rogers and Harry York again combined to write *Cinderella*, the pantomime for 1898. This year is notable for the visit to York of Mr. and Mrs. Kendal in March. They played Andrew Quick and Dorothy Blossom in *The Elder Miss Blossom*, in which they found full scope for their 'peculiar excellence in presenting embarrassing situations of ordinary life, with intervening strains of comedy and pathos',[25] Sir John Molyneux and Kate Desmond in Grundy's *A White Lie* and Mr. and Mrs. Armitage in the same author's *The Greatest of These*. Houses were not full perhaps because prices were raised to dress circle 5/-, pit stalls 3/-, upper circle 2/-. Celebrated plays that year were Sardou's *Madame Sans-Gêne*, *The Sorrows of Satan*, in which C. W. Somerset played Prince Lucin Ahriman, and Barrie's *Little Minister*. This was the first of Barrie's comedies to be seen in York, and in it Fred Emery played the Earl of Rintoul, Hilda Trevelyan her famous Lady Babbie and Oswald Yorke Gavin Dishart. From Barrie to Wagner is a far cry, but the first Wagner opera we hear of at the Theatre was *Tannhäuser* brought this year by Rousby's company. By 1899 the curtain raisers had become few and far between. The names of the touring companies are rarely mentioned on the programmes, but nearly all stayed the full week, so that the Theatre was open every night. This militated against the visits of stars who generally could only perform for a night or two between other engagements, and henceforward they came but seldom. The chief interest lies rather in the appearance of well known pieces. Thus in 1899 York saw Audran's *La Poupée*, *The Gay Lord Quex*, *The Belle of New York*, H.A. Jones's *The Liars* directed by Percy Hutchison, and the military drama *Tommy Atkins*. G. Calvert Dent was the Royal's acting manager.

Waddington's lease was due to expire on October 11, 1901 and public tenders for a fourteen year lease were invited in the press. Sixteen were received varying from £800 to £200 per annum. Waddington and Sons offered £800, Milton Bode of the Reading Theatre £810, and both were prepared to spend £1000 on redecorating. The offer of William Henry Waddington, who had succeeded his father, was accepted and he became the new lessee.[26]

The Boer War had brought in its train a spate of military dramas and during 1900 there came to York pieces with such titles as *Death or Glory Boys*, *The Victoria Cross*, *Bootle's Baby A Story of the Scarlet Lancers*, and *Soldiers of the Queen*. In *The Victoria Cross* Tyrone Power appeared as Azimullah, and he also played Myles-na-Coppaleen. It was the era too of musical comedy "girls" several of which York saw this year, including Sydney Jones's *A Gaiety Girl* and *The Telephone Girl* in which Ada Blanche sang. Sydney Jones's *San Toy* was also given, but perhaps the most celebrated piece of the year was *Magda* with Muriel Wylford as the heroine. The pantomime, once again written by Stanley Rogers, was *Aladdin*.

In 1901 the Carl Rosa Opera Company produced *Lohengrin* and Lily Hall Caine played Gloria Quayle in *The Christian*. On February 2 the

Theatre was shut for the funeral of Queen Victoria. Milton Rays's Easter pantomime *Beauty and the Beast* was written by Percy Milton, produced by Arthur Milton with Sydney Milton as Clown.

From May 1901 until February 1902 the Royal was closed for its last great reconstruction. The Corporation, afraid that its property might suffer depreciation owing to the erection by a syndicate of the new Grand Opera House[27] (now the Empire) to hold 1800 people, proposed to re-build the interior of the Theatre and supply a new roof, leaving only the outer walls and façade intact. Frank Tugwell, A.R.I.B.A., an architect from Scarborough, was asked to submit a report. In this he stated that the auditorium was out of date since theatre planning had undergone con-siderable development in the past 10 years. The Theatre was unsatisfactory for actors and spectators alike; the three tiers were crowded with un-necessary columns which interfered with the view; their centre was so far back from the stage that only those spectators in the side of the front row could see properly, and since none of them was raked those at the back could not see over the heads of those in front. The pit was 10 feet above the level of the street. The stage roof was so low that proper staging and working of machinery was impossible. The timbers of the roof over the auditorium were worm eaten and dangerous and some of them had been dried to powder by the heat of the sun plus lack of proper ventilation. A fall of snow might easily cause the roof to collapse. Tugwell proposed to replace both roofs and to carry them by columns and iron girders; and to overhaul the sanitary arrangements, lighting and decorations. He planned to throw into the auditorium an additional width of 17 feet in the N.W. which would allow for reconstruction according to modern ideas and for a stage of adequate size. The pit was to be levelled to the ground floor, thereby easing the entrance difficulties. The dressing rooms were to be left but to have a new mode of access. Refreshment bars were not provided. The decorations were to be in fibrous plaster with a simple and artistic, but not gorgeous, finish. The estimated expenditure was £5292. Waddington was to pay £1000, the Council £1000 and the balance was to be raised by borrowing, on which Waddington was to pay interest at 7½% per annum during the term of his new lease.[28] Actually the cost came to nearly a £1000 more.

The new Royal had a grand opening on February 24, 1902 before a brilliant audience, though the finishing touches were not yet complete. The D'Oyly Carte Company inaugurated the proceedings by singing the National Anthem in their *Iolanthe* costumes. Then Waddington led on the Lord Mayor (Alderman L. Foster) who, in performing the opening ceremony, recalled the stock company days of Thorne and his daughter Marguerite and of the Colemans, and mentioned the Waddingtons' 25 years' connection with the Theatre. It was still sometimes said, he con-tinued, that the Corporation had no right to be landlords of a playhouse but, having inherited the obligation, they had to make the best of it.[29] The *Gazette* describes the Theatre in detail. Extra outlets were provided all over the building. The old pit entrance now served the new dress circle and

311

stalls. By doing away with a west wall about 14 feet had been added to the gallery. The decorations throughout were of pure white, gold, and a brilliant emerald green. The dome in the ceiling was stencilled in greys and dull reds, and in the gallery the stencilling was grey and emerald green. The dress and upper circles were in fibrous plaster enriched with gold and emerald with a dash of vermilion under the lights. 'The proscenium front is formed of a huge moulding, the boldest parts of which are gilded solid. In the centre are the City Arms cast in fibrous plaster in bold proportions, and decorated in appropriate colours, enriched with gold. Above the proscenium opening is a large cove, also richly decorated with gold and emerald green. The three tiers of boxes on each side of the stage are also treated in a similar fashion ... The proscenium curtain is of emerald green plush. The walls behind the galleries, dress circle etc., are covered with a hanging of rich red, with a grey pattern.' The vestibule to the dress circle was ornamented with a raised design in gold and sealing wax red forming a panelled dado, whilst the upper portion was a broad frieze in purple and the woodwork was enamelled white. The dressing rooms were in the end reconstructed and additional ones were built. 'The stage is very lofty, and one of the largest we have seen, being capable of accommodating any of the great London attractions which hitherto have not visited the city, on account of lack of space for scenery and mounting.' A portion of the old wall of St. Leonard's was laid bare on the left of the stage and was preserved intact whilst the ancient crypt was opened out. Electric light was being installed and the lighting of the auditorium was carried out on the same plan as in Mrs. Langtry's new Imperial Theatre. The seating, except in the pit and gallery, consisted of red velvet tip-up chairs.

Shakespeare made but infrequent appearances on the York stage but in 1902 Esmonde Bramley's company brought *Othello* and *Macbeth*. Percy Hutchison directed *Mrs. Dane's Defence*, and the last work of Sullivan, *The Emerald Isle*, was presented by William Greet's Savoy Company. A number of well-known actors of our day came with various tours: Sydney Farebrother in *Little Jim*, Ralph Lynn in *Sporting Life*, Leon Lion in *The Messenger Boy* and Louise Hampton in Walter Melville's *The Worst Woman in London*.

There was a Christmas as well as an Easter pantomime. This was James Kiddie's production *Little Cinderella* written by Joseph Barry. For the next five years York was to boast two pantomimes. Thus in 1903 the Easter one was Milton Rays's *Robinson Crusoe*, the Boxing Night one *Little Red Riding Hood* from His Majesty's, Aberdeen. In 1903 too, came *Florodora* with Amy Augarde, Hall Caine's *The Eternal City*, and *The Light That Failed*. Mrs. Brown-Potter gave a matinée of recitations and J. Robert Hale appeared as Samuel Twankson in *The Silver Slipper*. The red letter night of 1904 was July 16 when Sarah Bernhardt appeared for one night only in *La Dame aux Camélias*. On this occasion boxes were £3.13.6d, dress circle 10/6d, pit stalls 7/6d, upper circle 5/-, pit 3/-, gallery 2/-. Notwithstanding these prices she drew a large audience on whom she made a profound impression.[30]

Mrs. Patrick Campbell gave matinée recitations in August, Martin Harvey brought his famous *Only Way* with Leon Lion as the Public Prosecutor as well as *A Cigarette Maker's Romance* in which Milton Rosmer, son of Arthur Milton of the Milton Rays company, was Schmidt. Wilde's *Ideal Husband* was presented by the Marquis of Anglesey's company, whose scenery, properties and effects were brought from Anglesey Castle; only the Earl himself was replaced as Lord Goring by Cecil Newton. Other productions of interest were *Alice in Wonderland*, *Old Heidelberg*, *The Rogues of the Turf* (with four real racehorses), *The Marriage of Kitty*, *The Duchess of Dantzic* and Barrie's *Little Mary*. The last of the Easter pantomimes was Milton Rays's *Little Bo-Peep*, the Christmas one was A. E. Smith's *Aladdin*.

The vogue for blackface minstrels had not yet died out and *In Dahomey* was an entertainment by octoroons, creoles and mulattos from the Shaftesbury Theatre. At their second visit they introduced the cake walk, then the rage. But business was bad and Waddington applied to the Corporation to transfer the interest in his lease to Frank MacNaughton of Sadler's Wells. In an interview he said 'That in consequence of the altered terms and conditions since his firm took the Theatre, and in view of the opposition which they have had to meet since the commencement of this Lease, they have not been able to run the Theatre at a profit, and in fact for some time have suffered a considerable loss.' The opposition was, of course, the Opera House. A rumour that the Theatre was to be converted into a music hall led a group of prominent citizens to present a protest. They pointed out that the inhabitants would be deprived of their only opportunity of witnessing legitimate drama and opera, and stigmatised as 'deplorable' the prospect that 'this historic house, with its worthy past, should pass into a "twice nightly" variety place.' The Council was urged to safeguard the interests of the citizens 'who look to a well conducted Theatre as a potent educational force.'[31] York people were backward in patronising their Theatre but when it came to their losing it their pride in it was awakened, as it had been before when there had been question of the Corporation selling out. It may be that the protest had its influence in the Council's decision to come to terms with Waddington by foregoing the 7½% interest on the outlay for improvements, thus reducing his rent by £351.

The year 1905 was inaugurated by two pantomimes A. E. Smith's *Babes in the Wood*, and at the end of January, instead of at Easter, Milton Rays's *Beauty and the Beast*. Sarah Bernhardt and Mrs. Patrick Campbell acted together on July 24 as Pelléas and Mélisande with the company from Bernhardt's Paris Theatre. The *Herald*[32] said that nothing could exceed the beauty and poetry of the scene at the window and that the love and dying scenes were full of tender melancholy. The audience was not large but recalled again and again these powerful emotional actresses. Another foreign company was Shing-Yengazika's Tokio Theatre Company which presented a Japanese drama *The Geisha's Revenge* in their native tongue. The principal characters appeared in beautifully embroidered national costumes. Unhappily they did so badly that a fortnight later they returned to York stranded and had to appeal to friends for relief.[33] The Moody Manners company with 70 performers and a chorus of 35 appeared in a series of popular operas. *The Earl and the Girl* was brought by W. Greet's company; Messager's *Véronique* and Sutro's *The Walls of Jericho* were other well known pieces this year. Norman V. Norman came with his company in *Under the Red Robe*, *Nell Gwyn* and *David Garrick*, and Ada Reeve, star of many a musical comedy and pantomime, in *Winnie Brooke, Widow*. The Christmas pantomime was Stanley Rogers's *Dick Whittington*.

Some weeks were given up to variety in 1906 and, for the first time, a twice nightly programme at 7 and 9 was instituted. Charles Macdona's chief company brought *Are You a Mason?* from the Shaftesbury and Lionel Rignold made his first appearance in York with Ada Blanche in *What the Butler Saw*. The two pantomimes were Little and Darcy's *Forty Thieves* in January and Charles Chard's *Goody Two Shoes* in December. This latter was followed in January 1907 by Kiddie's *Dick Whittington*. The rivalry of the cinema was about to cast its shadow on the Theatre but at the beginning the Theatre accepted the film, as it previously accepted the music hall, as part of its own entertainment. On July 1, 1907, the London Bioscope Company presented 'animated pictures' at the Theatre at prices ranging from 3d to 1/-. The titles of the films were a foretaste of the dramas, comics and documentaries to come, for among them were *Foiled by a Woman*, *The Policeman's Little Run* and *The Wonders of Canada*. As for plays, Knoblock's play of Boer farm life, *The Shulamite*, was seen this year, as was *Raffles* with Leonard Boyne as the attractive crook. Madame Albani sang with a concert party at a matinée. The general manager of the Royal was H. J. Dacre. Prices were dress circle 3/-, pit stalls 2/-, upper circle 1/6, pit 1/-, gallery 6d. The early door system enabled patrons to enter at 7 by paying 6d extra to the pit and upper circle and 3d to the gallery.

Dramatically, 1908 was of great interest in York since Shaw and Ibsen were then first seen on the Theatre's boards, Shaw preceding Ibsen. Miss Horniman had recently completed the first season of the first of English repertory companies at the Midland Theatre, Manchester. The company under Iden Payne then went on tour and at York brought out *Widowers' Houses* on January 13 with Lewis Casson as Dr. Harry Trench, Basil Dean as the Waiter, Penelope Wheeler as Blanche and Iden Payne himself as Lickcheese. This was followed by *Candida* on the 17th with Mary Price Owen as Candida, Henry Austin as Morell and Iden Payne as Marchbanks. Ibsen waited until June when Leigh Lovel brought *A Doll's House*, *The Master Builder*, *Rosmersholm* and *Hedda Gabler* in all of which he played leads opposite Olive Kenmore. Then on October 8 for three nights and a matinée Ellen Terry and James Carew played Lady Cicely Waynflete and Brassbound in *Captain Brassbound's Conversion*. The aging actress who still retained her power to charm was acclaimed by a crowded house.[34] This by no means exhausts the interest of this season which includes the visit of Fred Karno's troupe of pantomimists with over 10 tons of scenery; and of

Ian Maclaren and his company in *Hamlet*, *David Garrick* and *She Stoops To Conquer*; the début in York of *The Hypocrites* by H. A. Jones, *The Mollusc* by H. H. Davies and *The Merry Widow* with Clara Evelyn in the title rôle. The bioscope was used to represent the race in the 2nd act of *The Little Jockey*. Twice nightly variety stole the place of the Christmas pantomime.

The pantomime was given instead in February, 1909, and was *Mother Goose* from the Crown Theatre, Peckham. Some well-known pieces came to York that year including Rubens's musical comedy success *Miss Hook of Holland*, Stevenson and Henley's *Admiral Guinea*, Shaw's *You Never Can Tell*, Pinero's *His House in Order*, and *When Knights Were Bold* with James Welch and the company, scenery and production from Wyndham's. Mrs. Brown-Potter returned for a concert party matinée, Lauri de Frece appeared as Yarker in the Apollo success *Butterflies*, and Benson enacted a round of Shakespeare rôles. On December 23rd the Royal was the scene of the International Wrestling Match for the middleweight championship of the world – a novel rôle for the house.

In 1910 the pantomime, *Babes in the Wood*, again hailed from the suburbs, this time from the Elephant and Castle Theatre. It was followed by *Aladdin* in February. The Carl Rosa Company brought the first production on the English opera stage of Verdi's *La Forza del Destino*. Two celebrated musical pieces *The Arcadians* and Leo Fall's *Dollar Princess* also came this year. *The Passing of the Third Floor Back* with Ian Robertson as the Passer By, and *Brewster's Millions* with Percy Hutchison and the company and production from Wyndham's were other novelties. Pélissier paid a flying visit with his *Follies* on July 30 and earlier that month the Theatre had housed a concert of vocal and instrumental music in commemoration of the centenary of Schumann's birth. Among well known visitors were Zena Dare in the *Little Duke* and Marie Dainton in *The Mountaineers*. The Christmas pantomime returned in the shape of Fred Little's production of Frank Ayrton's *Sinbad the Sailor*. The first Sunday opening of the Theatre took place in February 1910 when Waddington was granted special permission by the Council to hold a concert in aid of York children's holiday camp.[35]

During the summer the lessees applied for a modification of the lease which would enable them to let the Theatre during part of the year for other than theatrical purposes. They said they had been driven to this by the changed tastes of the public which rendered it impracticable to confine the house to dramatic production. They had suffered considerable losses and as an alternative offered to surrender the remainder of their lease. The Council asked the Estates Committee to consider these propositions, after an amendment that the Theatre should be run as a municipal one had been lost. On September 22 the Council agreed to the recommendation of the Estates Committee that Messrs. Waddington and Sons should be released from their lease from January 1, 1911 and that tenders for a seven years' lease should be invited. From the nine tenders received that of Percy Hutchison was accepted for a rent of £650 with an option to renew at £700 for another seven years.³⁶ Performances were to be given for not less than thirty weeks in the year, the character of the performances to be at the discretion of the lessee subject to the approval of the Council.

Thus ended the Waddington family's thirty-five years' tenure of the Theatre.

Percy Hutchison, as we have seen, was no newcomer to York, for he had both produced plays and acted in them at the Royal. Born in 1875 he had first appeared with his mother's touring company in 1888 and for some years had been stage manager for his uncle, Sir Charles Wyndham. Unlike the Waddingtons, then, he was a man of the theatre, as Coleman and most of his predecessors had been. Like Coleman too he had wider interests than the York Theatre and was for the most part away on tour in the Dominions or running theatres in London, returning to York only at intervals with one of his companies or plays. This necessitated the appointment of a resident business manager, a post held for the first three years by E. W. Silverthorne.

The Royal opened under Hutchison's regime on January 16, 1911 with *Arsène Lupin* which was the 50th play to be produced by him and in which he played the Duc de Chamerace. The scenery was the work of Walter Hann and Sons who were the scene painters at Drury Lane. The pantomime *Robinson Crusoe* followed, written by F. Leslie Moreton. The music hall was having its effect on this traditional entertainment and for the first time we find a feature of speciality turns which spelt the introduction of a variety element. Prices were slightly altered. The dress circle was divided into three rows at 3/- and two back rows at 2/6; stalls remained at 2/- but were 2/6 if booked in advance; upper circle was reduced to 1/- and pit and gallery remained at 1/- and 6d. The starting times were 7.45, Fridays 8, and early doors were available at 7.15. Among the plays given during the year were the celebrated Edwardian musical comedy *Our Miss Gibbs*, W. G. Wills's *Royal Divorce*, Somerset Maugham's *Smith*, Pinero's *Preserving Mr. Panmure*, Conan Doyle's *Speckled Band*, *The Chocolate Soldier*, the Drury Lane sporting drama *The Whip*, and *A Butterfly on the Wheel*. Among the more unusual offerings in opera were the Carl Rosa's *Queen of Sheba* by Goldmark and the Italian Grand Opera Company's *André Chénier*.

The most famous visitor was Ellen Terry who, on a special matinée in October, gave her lecture on Shakespeare's heroines with illustrative acting to a large audience. The *York Gazette*³⁷ said that she had lost none of her powers of expression or depth of interpretation: 'Her versatility is perhaps the most remarkable of her gifts, and each of Shakespeare's heroines whom she portrayed was represented to the life, with all the magnetic charm of gesture and richness of elocution that have made Miss Terry famous.'

That same month Edward Terry appeared as Posket in *The Magistrate* and Dick Phenyl in *Sweet Lavender*. Other notable visitors were Maud Allan, of *Salome* fame, in a matinée of her classical dances, Evelyn Millard in her original rôle in Anthony Hope's *Adventure of Lady Ursula* with Herbert Waring as Sir George Sylvester, and George Tully in *Inconstant George*. Hutchison himself played in *Brewster's Millions* in July when the Theatre was visited by Prince Arthur of Connaught, and in November took his farewell, prior to a South African tour, in *Arsène Lupin* and *Peter's Mother* with his wife Lilias Earle as his leading lady.

Alterations were made to the Theatre in July when it remained shut for a month. A portion of the garden of the recently purchased De Grey house was taken in to provide a new side entrance which would offer additional exits, at a cost of £356. Inside the house was re-decorated by Messrs. Hunter and Smallpage. Improvements were made in the orchestra and pit stalls and new cloakroom accommodation was provided on the stalls level. The new colour scheme was white, gold and crimson.[38]

Every year since their inception in 1903 the Yorkshire Amateur Operatic and Dramatic Society had produced a musical piece for a week's run but this year they launched out into a local production entitled *Killibegs*, the book and lyrics of which were by K.E.T. Wilkinson, the music by T. Tertius Noble, the Minster organist. The Boxing Day pantomime was J. F. Elliston's production of *Puss in Boots*.

There is a certain monotony about the touring companies that weekly came and went. Pieces frequently returned for second and third visits; the Carl Rosa and D'Oyly Carte companies made almost annual appearances and Hutchison himself usually brought one of his plays before or after a tour. Martin Harvey and Benson were frequent visitors, and now and again there came stars less known in the provinces, or players, later to be well known, who were getting what training they could on tour. One can but record the most outstanding.

Among the plays of 1912 were Lehár's *Count of Luxembourg*, Graham Moffat's Scottish comedy *Bunty Pulls the Strings*, *Milestones*, and the No.1 company of *The Miracle* with J. H. Clyndes as the Father and Betty Stannard as The Madonna. Frank Cellier played Malvolio and Macbeth in the Glossop Harris (later the Glossop Cellier) Shakespeare company. Benson brought Dorothy Green as his leading lady and Baliol Holloway and Dennis Neilson Terry in minor rôles. Martin Harvey acted *The Breed of the Treshams*, *Hamlet* and *The Only Way* with Franklin Dyall as a member of his company. Russian ballet made its appearance with the 'World Famous Russian Classical Dancers' who, however, do not seem to have impressed their names on posterity. There were still patrons for melodrama, who were catered for by *An Arabian Vengeance* and Wilson Barrett's *Sledge Hammer*.

The spectacular *Ben Hur* came early in 1913. In a list of bookings this year there are 17 straight and 12 musical plays. The straight included *Bella Donna*, *Kismet*, *Hindle Wakes* advertised as 'the most discussed play of the century', *The Great Adventure*, with Ion Swinley as Ilam Carve and Sara Allgood as Janet Cannot, *Man and Superman* brought by Iden Payne's company and *Milestones* with Lynn Fontanne as Gertrude Rhead. Musicals included Oscar Straus's *Waltz Dream*, Lehár's *Gipsy Love* and Paul Rubens's *Sunshine Girl*. The January pantomime was *Little Red Riding Hood* by George Slater which had as a speciality the Gaby Glide Rag Time Rage and the Turkey Trot.

Julia Neilson acted in *Sweet Nell of Old Drury*; C. Aubrey Smith and Lilian Braithwaite starred in *Margery Marries* and *Instinct*; Violet Vanbrugh came on a flying visit with scenes from *The Hunchback* and *Her Wedding Night* in which she was supported by Roland Pertwee. On this last occasion York also saw the great ballet dancer Stanilaus Idzikowski who, with Katrina Blakowska as partner, danced to Weber's *Invitation to the Waltz*, a Chopin waltz and an adagio by Rubinstein. Percy Hutchison's offering was *Officer 666* in which he had appeared before the King and Queen of Spain. His uncle, Sir Charles Wyndham, also came on a flying visit with Mary Moore in *David Garrick*. There were now two cinema houses in York but films found their way into the Theatre twice, firstly in Paul Rainey's *British East African Expedition* and secondly in Charles Urban's *Kinema-colour* in which the colour was exploited by such themes as the Durbar, flowers and butterflies, sunset in Egypt and the review of troops by the King and the Kaiser.

Holland and Dean's *Aladdin* from Southport, written by William Holland and with a cast of 100, opened the 1914 season for a fortnight and was followed in February by H. Flockton Foster's *Dick Whittington*. The late Wilson Barrett's *Claudian* had an elaborate production including an earthquake spectacle with scenery by Edward Hann and W. Hull, the archaeology of the costumes being in the hands of F. Goodwin F.A.S. Mary Moore returned for a flying matinée with the Criterion company in H.H. Davies's *Mrs. Gorringe's Necklace*, and Fred Terry acted in *The Scarlet Pimpernel* opposite Violet Farebrother. Maskelyne and Devant's touring company started the school holidays and, when war broke out, Walter Howard's *Story of the Rosary* was occupying the York boards. The war immediately made its impress on the Theatre. *Sealed Orders* was advertised in August as a naval and patriotic play. In October prices were reduced to dress circle 2/-, or 2/6 early doors or reserved; orchestra stalls 1/6 or 2/-; upper circle and pit 9d or 1/-; gallery 6d or 9d. Private soldiers in uniform were admitted at even cheaper prices. A series of performances in aid of war charities was inaugurated with *The Blue Mouse* in which Hutchison himself played for the Soldiers' and Sailors' Families' Association and a Theatrical Charity. Later, *Officer 666* was given in aid of local Belgian refugees. In November Horace Hodges came in *Grumpy*, which was a great favourite at York, and the kinemacolour this winter showed the fighting forces of Europe.

Dick Whittington was again the pantomime in 1915. Among the plays shown this year were *Potash and Perlmutter*, the Royalty spy drama *The Man Who Stayed at Home* by the York dramatist J. Harold Terry, with George Tully, *The Three Musketeers* with Lewis Waller as D'Artagnan, *Peg o' My Heart*, *Quinneys*, *The Land of Promise* and *Peter Pan* with Stephanie Stephens in the title rôle. An important event was the first repertory company to be seen in York. This was one brought by Muriel Platt in Clyde Fitch's *The Truth* produced by W. Bridges Adams who himself played Tom Warden; *Candida* with Adams as Marchbanks; *Helen with the High Hand* from Arnold Bennett's novel; Maugham's *Penelope* and Masefield's *Nan*. After June plays were given twice nightly for a while but the Bank Holiday attraction, Eva Moore and H.V. Esmond in *When We Were Twenty One*, reverted to once nightly. Changes took place in the management: William Patrick succeeded Silverthorne as business manager in April and was himself succeeded in July by Wallace Stranack. Percy Hutchison came in October with *Stop Thief*, an American success, in which he was supported by Marie Illington and Hayden Coffin. Seymour Hicks and Isobel Elsom brought *Broadway Jones* in November, and in December the Moody Manners Opera Company staged *Samson and Delilah* for the first time in York as well as the rarely performed *Eugene Onegin*. J.F. Elliston's *Goose With The Golden Eggs* was the 1916 pantomime. Light fare was popular: *A Little Bit of Fluff* was followed by the Theatre's first revue, C.B. Cochran's *More*, and in the autumn an all French Entente Cordiale revue was presented. Martin Harvey aptly revived Stephen Phillips's *Armageddon*, and a domestic drama in July was topically entitled *Brave Women Who Wait or the Munition Girl's Love Story*. At Easter Oscar Asche and Lily Brayton came in *The Spanish Main* and *The Taming of the Shrew*, in September Arthur Sinclair's late Abbey Theatre Players put on *The Lover's Arms*, and in October Violet Farebrother was the first of many Madame Cavallinis in *Romance*. Pleydell's *The Ware Case*, Maugham's *Caroline*, Vachell's *Mrs. Pomeroy's Reputation*, in which Violet Vanbrugh acted, and Brighouse's *Hobson's Choice* were other well-known plays. To the Theatre too came that tremendous film spectacle, D.W. Griffiths's *The Birth of a Nation*.

The crypt had been opened in March as a smoking room and lounge where refreshments were served. From May 15 the entertainment tax raised the 3d-6d seats by 1d, the 6d-1/9d by 2d and the boxes by 1/-.

Hutchison put on his first and only pantomime in 1917. This was *Cinderella* by A.M. Thompson and Robert Courtneidge. The production was by Wallace Stranack whose daughter Elsie played the heroine. After this Pavlova's film *The Dumb Girl of Portici* was shown and in February the popular *Bing-Boys Are Here* came to York, followed by Maltby's *The Rotters*. On the morning of March 7 the Theatre was discovered to be on fire, the first and only fire it ever suffered, an unusual record. Though the fire was overcome in less than an hour it had done extensive damage to the tune of £2000.[39] Starting in the upper circle it spread to the gallery and most of the auditorium was affected. The stage with its heavy fireproof curtain was untouched. The Theatre was closed until April 16 when it re-opened with Harold Terry's *General Post*. The author, a native of York, himself appeared and Stranack read a telegram from Hutchison who was playing in Edinburgh.[40] Hutchison himself came later in the month with *A Kiss for Cinderella* with Hilda Trevelyan as Miss Thing. Octavia Kenmore, who had been touring for 12 years with Ibsen's plays, brought *Ghosts*, and Albert Chevalier played Eccles in *Caste*, now advertised as 'the Great Victorian War Play'. Geneviève Ward performed her original rôle of the Duchess of Autweille in Louis Parker's *The Aristocrat*, and C.V. France was the Doctor in Brieux's much discussed *Damaged Goods*. Lighter fare included *Daddy Long-Legs* and *The Maid of the Mountains*. In September Henry C. Alty replaced Stranack as acting manager. Hutchison had added to his commitments the lesseeship of the Queen's and St. James's Theatres; two years later he had the Garrick.

There was no pantomime in 1918 until the end of the year, when J. Bannister Howard's *Jack and the Beanstalk* was given with, for the first time, a flying ballet. For the first time too, we find the Theatre being used as a try-out ground prior to London production; this was for Walter Ellis's *A Week End* in which Dennis Neilson Terry, Ernest Thesiger, Yvonne Arnaud and Kate Cutler appeared. Other plays were Elinor Glyn's *Three Weeks*, *The Better 'Ole* with Martin Adeson as Old Bill, and Barrie's *The Professor's Love Story*. Matheson Lang acted in *Under Cover*, Marie Blanche (niece of Ada) in *Phyl*, Seymour Hicks and Isobel Elsom in *Sleeping Partners*, and Allan Jeayes in *Pigeon Post*. Griffiths's next film *Intolerance* was shown. Neither the Carl Rosa nor the D'Oyly Carte came but opera was provided by the Allington Charsley and the O'Mara companies.

Carl Rosa and D'Oyly Carte returned in 1919 and the O'Mara company sang Verdi's *Un Ballo in Maschera* for the first time in York. Martin Harvey presented *Rosemary* and Maeterlinck's war play *The Burgomaster of Stilemonde*; Marie Löhr acted in *Nurse Benson*, Julia Neilson and Fred Terry in *Henry of Navarre*, Hilda Trevelyan in *Double Event* and Irene Vanbrugh made her first appearance in York on a flying visit in Barrie's one act *Rosalind*. Barrie's *Dear Brutus* also made its début this year with Frank Forbes-Robertson as Dearth. Percy Hutchison brought *The Luck of the Navy* with its sensational submarine scene. On the musical side there was *The Lilac Domino* and Cochran's *As You Were*. During the summer, which was generally a dead season, a new experiment was tried, which was to be continued in succeeding years, of running a series of so-called 'high class dramas' at cheap prices.

Bannister Howard's third pantomime *Cinderella* opened in January, 1920. In February Follett Pennell succeeded Alty as acting manager. Hutchison, who was on tour in Canada, did not appear in York until December, when be acted in the farce *A Pair of Sixes*. Ethel Irving played *La Tosca* and the Birmingham Repertory Company brought Drinkwater's *Abraham Lincoln* with Herbert Lomas in the title rôle.

Charles Doran's Shakespeare company paid its first visit in September. In the company was a student, who owing to the illness of a member of the company, was called upon to take a series of minor parts. Thus Donald Wolfit made his first appearance on the stage in York. The record-breaking *Chu-Chin-Chow* was presented in November, and a *Pageant of Children Through the Ages* was organised by the various churches in aid of the Waifs and Strays Society in December. Two military command nights took place during the year.

Hutchison made use of programmes for publicity and kept in touch with his audience by reports of his activities and successes in other parts of the globe. A photograph of himself or of a scene from a play in which he was acting was usually included. In this way he attempted to focus local interest on his personality and thus to some small extent to replace what had been lost when the stock company disappeared. The programmes also ran a series of historical notes about the Theatre.

Bannister Howard's pantomime in 1921 was *The Babes in the Wood* in which May Murray performed an electrical dance act which was 'a blaze of revolving light'. Hutchison paid a two-day visit to York to interview the Estates Committee about re-seating part of the auditorium. As a result the Council agreed to put in tip-up seats in the pit and in the first three rows of the gallery, the seats to become the property of the Corporation on the termination of the lease.[41] After the plush upholstered seats had been installed in the pit, it was said to be the most comfortable pit in the north of England. In order to avoid queues, in October the upper circle became bookable for 2/4, two hours before the performance.

Among the plays that came this year were *Mary Rose, The Young Person in Pink, The Charm School*, in which Owen Nares, Sydney Farebrother, Joyce Carey and Keneth Kent appeared, *The Blue Lagoon* and, for the first time on any stage, Harold Terry and Rafael Sabatini's *Rattlesnake*, the scenery for which was built in York and sent to London to be painted by Terraine. Franklin Dyall, Fisher White, Cathleen Nesbitt and Milton Rosmer were in the cast. Renée Kelly, who was henceforward a frequent visitor to York, acted in *The Heart of a Child* and Percy Hutchison himself in *Nightie Night*. The 'high class drama' in the summer consisted of melodramas the titles of which are indicative: *Unmarried Mother*, *Other Man's Child*, *Ignorance*, *Married to a Rotter* and *Soiled*.

Shakespeare was given both by Benson, who himself played Shylock, Petruchio, Hamlet, Malvolio, Jaques and Macbeth, and by Doran's company. In this latter, Donald Wolfit was now playing comedy parts such as Trinculo, Launcelot Gobbo, Aguecheek, Nym and Snout, as well as taking the first Witch and doubling the 2nd Player and 2nd Gravedigger in *Hamlet*, and Ralph Richardson was acting in minor rôles such as Lorenzo, Curio in *Twelfth Night*, Gower in *Henry V* and Guildenstern, whilst Neil Porter and Abraham Sofaer were also members of the troupe.

The York Amateur Operatic and Dramatic Society produced *Merrie England* in aid of the County Hospital, and, in July, a pageant play, *The Heart of Yorkshire* by Lady Bell, was put on in aid of the Minster Windows' Fund. George R. Foss produced it and Edith Craig and Tom Heslewood were responsible for the costumes. The three scenes dealt with the story of the Five Sisters in the 13th century, the Siege of York in the 17th, and an air raid in 1916. *Cinderella*, a Bannister Howard and Percy Hutchison pantomime, came out on Boxing Day.

Hutchison brought his new play *In Nelson's Days* to York for its first performance on any stage in January 1922; in the cast were Hutchison, Alfred Bishop, Elsie Stranack and Marie Hemingway, and the scenery consisted of 7 heavy sets by Joseph Harker, Bruce Smith and Walter Johnstone. This year saw the visits of Iris Hoey in *Clothes and the Woman* and *Me and My Diary*; of Connie Ediss in *Lord Richard in the Pantry*; of Gerald Lawrence in the first performance of *Mr. Garrick*, and of Ena Grossmith in *Coming Through the Rye*. Notable new plays were *The Skin Game* and *A Bill of Divorcement*. Pinero's plays were being ransacked to make musical comedies and several of these came to York, including *My Nieces* from *The Schoolmistress*. An important innovation was that the summer drama season was in the hands of a repertory company from London which had been selected and rehearsed there by Hutchison himself. It specialised in the sentimental with such pieces as *The Story of the Rosary*, *East Lynne* and *Her Love Against the World*. Ralph Richardson returned with the Doran Shakespeare Company which had now also acquired as members Francis Sullivan, Cecil Parker, Barbara Everest and Norman Shelley.

Jack the Giant Killer was Bannister Howard's pantomime for 1923. We now enter the period of the depression when money was scarce, but the Theatre still had its successes, notably with pantomime, Gilbert and Sullivan, Carl Rosa opera and musical comedies such as *Sally* and *The Lady of the Rose*. *The Beggar's Opera*, then in its third year at the Lyric Hammersmith came in April; so did Bransby Williams, the Dickensian actor, in his famous rôle of Micawber. Hutchison himself inaugurated the summer drama season before his departure on another South African tour. The first play was *The Silver King* at reduced prices of stalls and dress circle 2/4, pit and upper circle 1/3, gallery 6d. After the summer cleaning, to meet the pressure of the times the normal prices were reduced to dress circle 3/-, stalls 2/6, plus tax. *Polly* followed *The Beggar's Opera*, the Macdona No. 1 company presented *Quality Street*, and *The Dover Road* came for one week. Benson varied his Shakespeare with Sheridan, himself performing Sir Anthony Absolute and Sir Peter Teazle. In the Doran Company Richardson had risen to principal rôles such as Orlando, Bottom and Mark Anthony, whilst Barbara Everest was the leading lady playing Desdemona, Rosalind and Lady Macbeth.

Bannister Howard's 8th and last Boxing Day pantomime was *Robinson Crusoe*, which was visited by nearly 8000 people in its first four days. There was a harlequinade in which Harlequin was danced by a girl.[42] During 1924 Mrs. Patrick Campbell revisited York in *The Second Mrs. Tanqueray* and *Magda*; Dennis Eadie in *The Eternal Spring*; Dennis Neilson Terry and Mary Glynne in *The Hon. Mr. Tawnish*; Eille Norwood in *The Return* and Ethel Irving in *Mrs. Dane's Defence*. A newcomer was Peggy O'Neil in *The Little Minister* with Robert Harris as Gavin Dishart. Plays of note were *At Mrs. Beam's*, *The Lilies of the Field*, *The Likes of 'Er* and *Our Betters*. Hutchison's lease expired in September and was renewed for seven years at a rent of £900, an increase of £250 from the original price. One stipulation was that the York Amateur Operatic and Dramatic Society or another was to have the Theatre the first week in March for £200. Twenty-five theatres in the country had closed down because they no longer paid, largely owing to the competition of the cinema.[43]

The Boxing Day pantomime was *Jack and Jill* written by J. Hickory Wood, who had been responsible for a long series at Drury Lane, and was produced by Harry Bistow.

Unemployment was rife and a concert was given at the Theatre one Sunday in March 1925 for the Lord Mayor's Fund for the Unemployed. York saw some of the outstanding dramas of the day this year including *Outward Bound, Anna Christie* and *St. Joan* with Dorothy Holmes-Gore as the Maid. In lighter vein there were the Co-Optimists Company which had been on tour for 2 years, and *Lilac Time* with the original Schubert, Courtice Pounds.

For the first time the Lena Ashwell players supplied the summer drama with a six weeks repertory season in which Esmé Church played the leads. Among their pieces were *The Importance of Being Earnest, Nan, The Truth about Blayds, Dandy Dick* and *The Country Wife*, in an adaptation of Garrick's adaptation with some of the deleted lines restored. As in most provincial theatres Monday nights were poorly attended, and Henry Tweedie, now acting manager, appealed to patrons to support them and thus encourage each company at its opening performance. Percy Hutchison returned from his 50,000 miles tour in U.S.A., Canada and South Africa and came to York in October with *The Man from Hong Kong*.

The pantomime, *Little Red Riding Hood*, was the first of a series brought by George Brydon Phillips, whose company was in its 34th year and claimed to be the oldest pantomime company on tour.

In 1926 George Clarkson became resident manager. In Benson's company Robert Donat was playing the 1st Witch, Osric and Guildenstern, and Slang in *She Stoops To Conquer*. The Lena Ashwell players had their second season during which they gave *The Witch, Wife To a Famous Man, What Every Woman Knows* and *The Silver Box*, and they were honoured with a Grand Civic Night. After their departure the Theatre was closed for decorating, and was re-opened by Violet Vanbrugh, in two new plays *The Second Blooming* and, for the first time on any stage, *The Duchess Decides*. The Macdona Players in a round of Shaw gave *Man and Superman* in its entirety, a 6 hour performance in which Esmé Percy sustained the exacting rôle of Tanner-cum-Don Juan. Zena Dare made her first appearance in York since her return to the stage in *The Last of Mrs. Cheyney* in which Terence de Marney played the footman George. Hutchison acted in *Cock o' the Roost* with Catherine Lacey his new leading lady, an occasion commemorated by a souvenir programme. The American drama *Sun-up* with Lucille La Verne, and *Hay Fever* with Eva Moore were other notable events. There was no pantomime as the Christmas weeks were devoted to *Rose Marie*.

Hutchison went on another South African tour in 1927 and took his leave of York in his old favourite *Brewster's Millions* which had not, however, been seen there for seven years. The programme in a 'Theatre Talk' stated that he had produced 78 plays, controlled 200 touring companies and 17 London theatres. Plays seen this year included *The Farmer's Wife, Escape, A Woman of No Importance* (brought by Vivian Edmond's repertory company),

Yellow Sands, in which Esmond Knight acted Arthur Varwell, and *And So To Bed* with Robert Morley in a small part. *The Terror* was tried out prior to its production at the Lyceum with Dennis Neilson Terry, Mary Glynne, Felix Aylmer and Franklyn Bellamy. Old friends were Julia Neilson and Fred Terry in *The Wooing of Katharine Parr*; Courtice Pounds in *Shavings*; the Lena Ashwell players, who in this third season gave *The Magistrate*, *The Little Minister*, *The Fugitive* and *The White Headed Boy* among other pieces, and the Birmingham Repertory in *Devonshire Cream* with Roger Livesey. Lydia Kyasht danced in a cabaret performance; Florence Smithson appeared in *The Gipsy Princess*, and Amy Augarde in *Just a Kiss*. Phillips's pantomime was *Jack and the Beanstalk*. The Theatre was doing so badly that the management at the end of the year resorted to distributing a slip begging for support as 'The Theatre is fighting for its very existence against the mechanical entertainments of the age.' The coming of the talking films was proving the death blow to numbers of theatres throughout the country and causing anxiety to most of the rest.

The year 1928 was uneventful. Perhaps the most famous of its plays was *The Constant Nymph* with André van Gyseghem as Lewis Dodd. Lena Ashwell returned with her players and was accorded a reception by local ladies. Their repertoire was rather lighter than usual including such pieces as *The Sport of Kings* and *Daddy Long-Legs*. Cecil Trouncer and Rodney Ackland, soon to be well known as a dramatist, acted in the company. Hutchison did not appear as he was in Australia, nor was there any opera, Shakespeare or pantomime. Instead of this last *The Desert Song* came for two weeks. Hutchison returned to York in April, 1929, with Renée Kelly and his new leading lady, Olive Sloane in *Looking for a Wife*. The Ashwell Players included plays that had been specially asked for by York audiences. In their repertoire was *I'll Leave It To You*, *The Enchanted Cottage* and *The Green Goddess*. *Journey's End* and *Young Woodley* were the best of the new plays. In September Hutchison tried out *Miss Adventure* with Renée Kelly and Morris Harvey, and in December he organised an All Star Matinée in aid of a home for aged members of the profession in which he, Margaret Bannerman, Annie Saker, Renée Kelly and the York Operatic Society appeared. Victor Stevens's pantomime *Puss in Boots* was produced on Boxing Day by the Brydon Phillips company.

The year 1930 saw the first attempt at local repertory in York. Hutchison, in an effort to recoup the Theatre's ebbing fortunes, got together and rehearsed a weekly repertory company which he called the Percy Hutchison Players. In the company were Arthur Burne, George Bellamy, Mary Brackley, Faith Liddle, daughter of the composer of *Abide With Me*, and two local actresses Mrs. Muriel Thorpe and Ann Benson who had started as an amateur in the Rowntree Players. The company opened on March 10 with *The Skin Game*. Hutchison appealed for support to help the Theatre over its period of depression: 'The York Theatre' he said 'has stood for 200 years or more. It is in danger of annihilation by the American talkies. Are you going to allow it to die, or will you back us up in our endeavour to save the theatre.'[44] The prices, he declared, were the lowest in England and he announced that he had the support of the clergy, the corporation, the military, the railway institute, Messrs. Rowntree, Terry and the workers of the city. In June, J.T. Grein came to see *Dear Brutus* and said: 'The Theatre Royal, York, is unique in the United Kingdom.'[45]

The weekly repertory ran until the middle of July and produced *The Admirable Crichton, The Great Adventure, Dear Brutus, Berkeley Square* and *General Post,* It was followed in September by the Birmingham Repertory who put on *The Apple Cart* with Marian Spencer as The Princess Royal. The only remarkable touring visit was the farewell of those old favourites Julia Neilson and Fred Terry in *Sweet Nell of Old Drury.* Brydon Phillips's panto- mime was *Aladdin* with Charles Danvers as the Widow Twankey. This was followed in January 1931 by *Cinderella* from Huddersfield and Newcastle, in which, for the last time, the revived harlequinade was seen on the York stage. On April 1 Jan Kubelik gave a concert at the Theatre playing on his famous Stradivari violin "Cremona". The Percy Hutchison Players returned in May 'for the production of English Plays to maintain the Traditions of York's Historic Theatre.' There were a few of the same performers as the previous year but a number were new; they included George Fearon, later a theatrical journalist, Douglas Vigors and K. Steuart West. Hutchison produced, and plays given included *Mr. Pim Passes By, The Dover Road, Mrs. Dane's Defence* and *A Butterfly on the Wheel.* Prices were from 3/6 to 6d and subscription tickets could be obtained at reduced rates. 'Gentlemen, you may Smoke, but no Pipes please' was an added attraction.

In a letter Lord Danesfort pointed out that 'owing to constantly growing competition of the cinemas, there is an actual danger of the historic York Theatre being closed down. This would be a real disaster.' He invoked the names of Kemble and Macready who had trod its boards and the 166 years of the Theatre's existence. At the end of the repertory season in September Hutchison announced 'our Historic Theatre has been saved from disaster by the Repertory movement, the loyalty of both Players and Public and a policy of moderate prices of admission.' Hutchison was actually already insolvent but, hoping that matters might mend, he hung on for over two years more. Another blow fell in November with the increase in the enter- tainment tax, for this was the year that England went off the gold standard, and the government crashed. Most of this burden had to be borne by the lessee though the pit was raised to 1/3. A new kind of seat called 'The Royal Stall' could be booked on the day of the performance for 2/6 instead of 3/6. The prices, Hutchison was careful to point out, were 50% lower than those at Leeds. Touring attractions included Annie Saker in *The Eternal Magdalene,* a drama about a prostitute which was pronounced 'very throb- bing stuff'; Martin Harvey in *The King's Messenger*; Renée Kelly and Gerald Lawrence in *The Marriage of Kitty*; Annie Croft, a Yorkshire star and the first musical comedy actress to go into management, in *The Chocolate Soldier*; and Violet Vanbrugh in *After All* supported by Rex Harrison.

This year's pantomime was a Limbert and Russell production of *Robinson Crusoe* with an under-the-sea ballet to the music of Coleridge Taylor of which the *York Gazette*[46] said that 'Some of the scenes stamp themselves on the mind through their sheer beauty.'

In February 1932 Hutchison renewed his lease for £900 and on February 8 he celebrated the 21st anniversary of his management by appearing once again as Arsène Lupin, the rôle in which he had opened it in 1911. The Repertory Players commenced their third season after this and ran right on into the middle of September with the exception of July when the Theatre was closed for cleaning. Prices were higher: boxes £1.6.6, stalls and dress circle 3/8, upper circle 1/10, pit 1/3 (early doors 1/10), gallery 6d (early doors 9d). To encourage patrons to attend Mondays, the stalls were obtainable that night for 2/6. Matters were going from bad to worse. The list of theatres converted into cinemas was growing apace and in Hull and Scarborough no first-class theatre now existed. The only hope was in the so-called repertory movement[47] which had obtained a firm foothold in many towns. Hutchison threw down his challenge: 'I would rather', he wrote, 'surrender my Lesseeship than be a party to turning York's historic Theatre into what would eventually mean an American Picture Theatre.' Galsworthy sent word of encouragement: 'Enterprises like the Repertory Theatre at York afford the best means of keeping life-blood flowing in the body of the British Drama.' Hutchison was now trying to establish a permanent repertory company in conjunction with the Nottingham Theatre to present new plays interspersed with classics. 'Whether', he declared, 'the Theatre Royal closes in four weeks depends entirely on the public.' The Theatre did not close but Hutchison lost £600 on it.[48]

The repertory presented, among other pieces, several by Galsworthy, *The Queen Was in the Parlour*, *The Cradle Song*, *Our Betters*, and *Rain* which it was the first repertory to give. In it Olive Sloane, who had been touring with Hutchison and was playing with the company for a few weeks, was Sadie Thompson. The touring companies returned in the autumn with *Bitter Sweet*, *The Geisha*, in which Leo Sheffield, a former York Minster song man played, and *Musical Chairs* with Basil Bartlett. The Pinder troupe, who had graced many a Drury Lane pantomime, came with Limbert and Russell's *Goody Two Shoes*.

In the early months of 1933 touring companies brought *The Good Companions*, *Dangerous Corner*, *The Barretts of Wimpole Street* and *Wonder Bar* for which the stage was built out with steps leading down into the stalls. Ruth Draper gave her inimitable sketches, Iris Hoey returned in *Intimate Relations* and the Irish Players presented St. John Ervine's *Mixed Marriage*. Then Percy Hutchison crashed. He filed a bankruptcy petition on March 27 and the first meeting of his creditors on April 14 revealed a deficit of £7697.[49] The next week the Theatre closed. In the proceedings which followed Hutchison averred that he had made a profit until 1929 but had lost on his Australasian tours. The York Theatre was at that present time just paying expenses.[50] He alleged that the causes of his failure were the economic depression, the competition of the talkies and the entertainment tax. Undoubtedly he had gone on much longer than he should have done with increasing liabilities. The scenery and office furniture at the Theatre were sold under distress for rent on which he owed £309. He had been unable to live or to work in a small way and he admitted to having entertained, for publicity's sake, 300 people at a time on the York stage. In his defence one must say that the times had been against him and that he had kept the flag flying for the drama to the bitter end.

In his rather tiresome autobiography *Masquerade* he has told us but little of his 22 years' management, though the list of stars whom he brought to York is fairly impressive. It is, however, in this volume that we first hear tell of the Theatre's ghosts. One haunted spirit was that of an actor killed in a duel in Blake Street who appeared to an understudy on the stage, staggering in the wings. More famous was the beautiful 'nun' who haunted one of the dressing rooms and who was said to have been walled up alive as a punishment. Lady Benson spent a night in the dressing room praying for the repose of her soul and she had not been seen since. But 'the Grey Lady' was not finally exorcised and Miss Pauline Letts writes that she and many members of the company had felt and heard her on several occasions, always during a costume play. Earlier she had appeared and spoken at a séance held in the haunted room and turned out not to be a nun at all. But every self-respecting old theatre should certainly have its ghost, though one might think it would rather be that of one of the many managers who had lost their money and broken their hearts over its failures.

The Theatre reopened on September 18 under S. Weetham Crawshay as lessee and managing director with N. Howard Pate as resident manager. The interior had been redecorated and lighting effects installed on more modern lines.[51] The pit and upper circle were bookable and the stalls and dress circle were reduced after a fortnight to 2/6. Musical comedies and crime plays constituted the fare, but a pantomime, *Cinderella*, in which the local topics of football and trams were made comic butts, was put on in December. In January 1934 *Jack and the Beanstalk* came, followed by a circus and by Carmo the conjurer. After a few succeeding engagements the Theatre shut once more.

York was only a No.2 town and could not command the best touring companies. The quality of those that came had deteriorated. Obviously, if the theatre was not to meet the fate of so many others and be converted into a cinema or closed down some drastic action would have to be taken to rescue it from the slough into which it had fallen.

CHAPTER NINE

The York Citizens' Theatre

ONCE again it was the men and women of York who saved their historic play-house and made possible the continuation of its long theatrical tradition. A group of prominent and public spirited citizens formed a company, which was registered on July 17, 1934, to take over the lease of the Theatre.[1] The directors of the venture, who gave their services, were W. G. Birch, J. N. Blenkin, H. E. Bloor, W. T. Crombie, Benjamin Dodsworth, W. H. Farrar, the Earl of Feversham, B. Seebohm Rowntree, Mrs. Edward Shaw, F. D. Stewart, Claude Thompson and K. E. T. Wilkinson. £2300 was subscribed in £1 shares on which returns above 5% were not to be distributed to the shareholders but to go to improvements in the Theatre. A lease was obtained for two years, with an option to extend for seven, at a rent of £800. The plan was to form a weekly repertory company in the spring of 1935, but in order to tide over the remainder of 1934 a series of No. 1 touring companies was engaged. The town was thus at once raised from No. 2 to No. 1 status. The Theatre re-opened under the new auspices on August 20, a great civic occasion which was attended by the Deputy Lord Mayor and the Sheriff and his Lady.

The next week Dodie Smith's *Touch Wood* had its first performance out of London with Marian Spencer and Percy Marmont. On October 5, H.R.H. The Princess Royal attended, accompanied by Princess Helena Victoria. This was the first time that she had been to the Theatre on an oc-casion other than a charitable benefit. The directors had previously sent a critic to Eastbourne to see the *Richard of Bordeaux* No. 1 Company and this was then specially engaged for the royal visit. Anthony Eustrel played Richard II, Patricia Bradfield the Queen, and Robert Morley the Duke of Gloucester.[2] Appropriately, H.R.H. was preceded by the city swordbearer wearing the cap of maintenance originally presented to the city by Richard II, which bore with it the privilege of being worn before royalty. A special illuminated programme of cream vellum, with a cover design which bore the royal arms and the York coat of arms, was prepared at the York School of Arts and Crafts.

Later in October, Florence Smithson returned in *First Episode* by two Oxford undergraduates, one of whom was the now noted playwright, Terence Rattigan. Some York amateurs acted *The Rose Without a Thorn* in December, their producer being E. Martin Browne. The weekly repertory company came into being in February 1935, an occasion which marked the Theatre's final transfer from the touring to the repertory system. Not that touring companies were altogether excluded, but the main dependence was once again on a local company. York came late to repertory when Liverpool had been going 25 and Birmingham 21 years. Every encouragement was given to the feeling that the effort was part of a widespread movement and programmes bore information as to what was being done in other repertory companies. E. Martin Browne, who had begun his work as a producer for the Shakespeare festivals of 1932, was one producer, and Roy Langford, who had directed *The Miracle*, the other. Among those in the permanent company were Joan Ingoldby, who had understudied The Madonna in Reinhardt's *Miracle*, Henzie Raeburn, who had the distinction of being the first woman stage manager in London, Mavis Edwards, who had visited Canada with Sir Barry Jackson, Betty Barton, Patricia Wilding, Robert Morley, who had recently been seen in *Richard of Bordeaux*, Hal Burton from the Birmingham Repertory, Christopher Casson, son of Sybil Thorndike who had had experience in America and in the Open Air Theatre, Julian Somers, who had started life as a jockey, Guy Spaull, Edward Sinclair, Anthony Bazell, Walter Pemberton and J. Massie-Griffiths.

A preliminary public meeting was held at the Theatre on February 4 to introduce the company who showed their paces in *Winsome Winnie*. An address was given by Iden Payne, then director of the Stratford-on-Avon Shakespeare Memorial Theatre.[3] The Archbishop of York sent a message of encouragement. Mr. Seebohm Rowntree, chairman of the York Citizens' Theatre, stressed that the venture was founded on the town itself and must be a natural growth fostered by the whole body of citizens. Mr. Roy Langford declared that what was being tried out at York was of national importance. £2300 had been subscribed and £200 more was needed for the cost was estimated at about £300 a week. To cut the expenses the orchestra had been dispensed with in favour of a gramophone. The house was packed and enthusiastic and the *York Gazette* jubilantly proclaimed 'The Gaiety tradition is broken but a York tradition lives.'[4] For the rest of the week Sherwood's *The Queen's Husband* was played. *London Wall* and *Wings Over Europe* followed. Then the musical touring companies returned, including Emile Littler's presentation of a musical *Alice in Wonderland* and *Through the Looking Glass*, and Tom Arnold's of *Wild Violets*. This latter introduced a revolving stage advertised as the theatre's answer to the challenge of the talkies, and 'the biggest scenic effort ever presented in the provinces'; six railway trucks were employed to convey the scenery, and a gang of workmen laboured day and night for the week prior to the opening; special lighting equipment was installed and the effects included real ice skating.

When the repertory returned in *Private Lives*, Sybil Thorndike came on the opening night to see her son act. During Holy Week, Langford produced a Passion play, entitled *Dark Hours*, in which the auditorium was used and a unit form of staging was seen for the first time on the York boards.

The Royal Jubilee was celebrated in May by a Crazy Week with a midnight matinée. Local interest in the Brontë family was catered for by Davison's *The Brontes of Haworth Parsonage* and by a dramatisation of *Wuthering Heights*.

Despite the initial enthusiasm the season was losing money. On May 10 application was made in the County Court for the conversion of the company into a non-profit making concern. The shareholders had agreed to forego their dividends, the directors were not salaried, and from the start the Citizens' Theatre had never been a purely business organisation. The application was granted and as a result the company was relieved of entertainment tax on plays considered partly or wholly educational. Later the regulations were altered and the privilege given, not to particular plays, but to non-profit making companies so that all their productions were free of the burden. In this way the government recognised the good work that the repertory companies were doing in keeping drama alive among the people.

In May the company obtained the concession of performing *Viceroy Sarah*, though the piece had not yet been on tour. This was a precedent as repertory rights were usually not granted until after plays had been toured. The season closed with *Clive of India* on June 15 and the Theatre then housed a school of acting.

The original £2300 had been lost but another £500 was raised for further trial. The director toured England to enquire into the success of other repertories. He found that Mr. Redvers V. Leech, the receiver of the bankrupt theatre at Coventry, had been running a successful season there and invited him to try his hand at York. Mr. Leech came, saw the Theatre, and agreed to do so. It was largely due to his efforts that the York Citizens' Theatre turned the corner to success. The new regime instituted twice nightly performances at 6.30 and 8.50 and a drastic reduction of prices which enabled the Theatre to compete with the cinemas. The old and new charges were as follows:[5]

93 dress circle first two rows	3/6d old	2/6d new
145 dress circle remainder	3/6d old	1/6d new
361 stalls	3/6d old	1/6d new
123 pit	1/6d old	9d new
268 upper circle	1/6d old	7d new
250 gallery	9d old	4d new

The result was that almost from the start attendances rose to 10,000 a week. A system of block booking by which twelve tickets could be purchased at a further reduction was also introduced.

331

The new concern had an authorised capital of £1000. Expense was not stinted, for as Mr. Rowntree had said, the watchword was how well, not how cheaply. A new company was carefully selected and extra artists were engaged when bigger casts were needed. Fresh sets were made and appropriate furniture hired for each play and an orchestra of six was engaged under the musical directorship of Edgar Matthews. William J. Carter came as resident manager and licensee. He had received his early training with the Daniel Meyer Company, had been for some time at the Lyceum, and had managed Sybil Thorndike's *St. Joan* tour. The opening play on September 16 was *Sweet Aloes*. It was produced by Osmund Willson who had been with the Birmingham Repertory, and the stage settings were by Bernard Miles. The reporter of the *York Gazette* said that 'the first night was a joy on both sides of the stage.' The whole atmosphere was subtly changed.[6] Indeed the Theatre had one of the best weeks it had enjoyed for years. After the first two plays Anthony John took over the producing and Hal Henshaw, who had worked with the Coventry and other repertories, became scene designer. Notable plays given up to the end of the season on December 21 were *Bird in Hand*, *The Circle*, *The Distaff Side*, *Eden End*, *The Silver Cord* and the evergreen *Charley's Aunt*. The policy of having touring or visiting companies during the Christmas holidays at raised prices was adopted from the start and this winter the attractions were all musical: *Waltzes from Vienna*, a revue, Harry Lauder, and *A Waltz Dream*.

The repertory re-opened on February 10, 1936, with *The Dominant Sex* and during the year included *The Black Eye*, *Candida*, *The Cathedral*, *The Venetian*, *The Farmer's Wife*, *Lady Precious Stream* and *The Constant Nymph*. Its success at popular prices was established; the Theatre had become a habit, and by July the original Citizens' Theatre Company Ltd., was wound up and the lost £2300 returned in full to the shareholders. During the summer £2000 was spent in alterations. Bad congestion had up till then accompanied the nightly change of house, but now new exits were made from the auditorium to relieve this. The foyer was reconstructed to almost double the size, a new refreshment bar was installed on the first floor, cloakrooms and electric fittings were improved.[7]

The first birthday of the new repertory was celebrated in September by a souvenir programme, and in November a Playgoer's Club was formed, and was addressed at its inaugural meeting by Maurice Browne.

On December 26, Harry Russell and Will Seymour's pantomime *Robinson Crusoe* in which the Yorkshire comedian Stan Jay appeared, was put on for a fortnight. This was followed by the Yorkshire Amateur Operatic and Dramatic Society in *San Toy* and then by *1066 and All That*.

When the repertory re-opened on January 25, 1937, Phillip Fellows had succeeded Henshaw as scenic artist. Plays this year included *Little Women*, *Anthony and Anna*, *Yellow Sands*, *Pride and Prejudice*, *The Last of Mrs. Cheyney*, *London Wall*, *Aren't We All?*, *To-night at 8.30*, *The Admirable Crichton* and *When Knights Were Bold*. It was not an experimental policy for there were no new or untried plays, but it was a safe one which yet afforded reasonable variety.

Once again during the summer there were extensive renovations. The stalls, pit and circles were reseated, the stalls foyer was panelled, the look of the auditorium was altered by complete redecoration, recarpeting and a new lighting system.[8] In addition there was a new drop curtain. The plays of 1938 were on the whole of better quality and included *The Importance of Being Earnest*, *I Have Been Here Before*, *Judgment Day*, *Laburnum Grove*, *Mrs. Warren's Profession*, *Night Must Fall*, *Our Betters*, *Parnell*, *Private Lives*, *Quinneys*, *Gallows Glorious*, and *Strange Orchestra*. Phyllis Calvert had joined the company from Coventry. She opened as Katharine O'Shea in *Parnell* and during the year she played 35 rôles. She then left to understudy Adrianne Allen. In August W. Stanley Moore succeeded Phillip Fellows as scenic artist.

The Boxing Day attraction was Harry Welchman in *The Desert Song*. This was followed by *Peter Pan* and *Victoria Regina*.

During 1939 the company performed, among other pieces, *The Young Idea*, *Arms and the Man*, *And So To Bed*, *Loyalties*, *Milestones*, *Windows*, *Spring Cleaning*, *The Wind and the Rain* and *Gaslight*. Among several newcomers to the company were Pauline Letts and Imelda (later Anne) Crawford.

War broke out just before the company celebrated its third birthday with 180 plays and 2152 performances to its credit. The audience was reminded, for A.R.P. purposes, that they were protected by the Theatre's original walls built of thick stone slabs.

The three opening weeks of 1940 brought a galaxy of stars since the London theatres were shut. That great comedienne, Marie Tempest, came in *Dear Octopus* with Leon Quartermaine, Valerie Taylor, Hugh Sinclair, Angela Baddeley and Una Venning. Phyllis Neilson Terry brought *The Corn Is Green* and Fay Compton and Owen Nares appeared in *Robert's Wife*.

The repertory re-opened with *Quiet Wedding* and included in its productions this year *A Bill of Divorcement*, *Pygmalion*, *The Apple Cart*, *The Barretts of Wimpole Street*, *The Silver Box*, *Sheppey* and *When We Are Married*. Michael Rennie had joined the company. A Bradford man, he had spent a year with the Wakefield Repertory and had already appeared in a film. Pauline Letts left in July and, after five years' service, Anthony John became a pilot officer and was succeeded as producer by William Sherwood.

The war caused some changes in the times of performance. There was only one performance on Mondays at 7.15 and on Tuesdays a matinée at 2.30 and evening performance at 7.15, otherwise twice nightly. Then after October the first three nights of the week were once nightly, the last three twice nightly with a Wednesday matinée. The paper shortage resulted in the reduction of programmes to four pages, and the consequent cutting out of information and gossip paragraphs about theatrical matters in general and the repertory company in particular which had enlivened them in previous years.

Visiting companies in the winter of 1940-1 included *On Approval* with Barry K. Barnes, Diana Churchill, Cathleen Nesbitt and Roland Culver; Vic Oliver and Sarah Churchill in variety, and Emlyn Williams and Angela

Baddeley in *The Light of Heart*. In the cast of this last was Osmund Willson who had produced the first two of the company's plays.

At the re-opening of the repertory season in 1941 Geoffrey Staines was the new producer. Plays this year included *Berkeley Square, Hay Fever, Mary Rose, Thunder Rock, Mr. Pim Passes By, The Marquise, The Man With a Load of Mischief, Sweet Lavender, See Naples and Die, The Millionairess*, and, for the first time on any stage, *Russian Salad* by Jack and Roy Forster. This year there was a star season in the summer too: Jack Hulbert and Cicely Courtneidge brought *The Hulbert Follies*; *Dear Brutus* had an all-star cast with Gielgud as Dearth, Muriel Pavlow as Margaret, Nora Swinburne as Mrs. Purdie, Mary Jerrold as Mrs. Coade, Ursula Jeans as Joanna, Zena Dare as Lady Caroline, Roger Livesey as Matey and Leon Quartermaine as Coade. This was followed by Marie Tempest, A. E. Matthews and Milton Rosmer in *The First Mrs. Fraser*. W.J. Carter went to the war in November and was succeeded as resident manager by John C. Turner.

The first piece of 1942 was *The Skylark* with Constance Cummings, John Clements, Hugh Sinclair and Valerie Taylor. This was succeeded by the first visit to York of the Old Vic Company who put on *The Merchant of Venice* with the Czech actor Frederic Valk as Shylock, Jean Forbes-Robertson as Portia, Renée Asherson as Nerissa, and van Gyseghem as Gratiano, the production being by Esmé Church. Their second piece was the Norwegian drama *The Witch* produced by van Gyseghem. The Sadler's Wells opera followed with *Rigoletto, Madame Butterfly, The Barber of Seville* and *La Traviata*; the first time for many years that opera had been heard in the Theatre. Next Priestley's *Good Night Children* was tried out with Leslie Banks, Gillian Lind and Lawrence Hanray, and lastly the D'Oyly Carte company returned with Darrell Fancourt.

The repertory opened rather later this year on February 9 and on March 2 gave the first performance anywhere of *Yellow Dog Dingo* by Jack and Roy Forster. Among other productions were *The Queen was in the Parlour, The Truth about Blayds, Blithe Spirit*, which had the distinction of being put on for two weeks, *Dangerous Corner, Geneva, Old Acquaintance, You Never Can Tell, Dandy Dick, The Anatomist* and *The Private Secretary*. For the first time too the company essayed Shakespeare. *Romeo and Juliet* was chosen and put on on November 16 with Owen Holder as Romeo, Pauline Letts, who had returned to the company, as Juliet and Geoffrey Staines as Mercutio. After October 3 the twice nightly programme was discontinued and performances started at 7 with matinées on Wednesdays and Saturdays. This meant a relief for the overworked actors but lower profits, so prices were increased to boxes 12/-, dress circle 3/-, 2/-, pit 1/, upper circle 9d, gallery 6d. In December York saw the Sadler's Wells ballet, whose home in London had been shut since the raids, for the first time. Robert Helpmann, Alexis Rassine, Margot Fonteyn, Beryl Grey and the full company danced. York had never before witnessed the great ballet classics, *Coppélia, Les Sylphides* or *Casse Noisette* (Act II) to which were added such modern ones as *Hamlet, The Rake's Progress* and *The Birds*.

Starring visits at the commencement of 1942 were *The Duke in Darkness* with Leslie Banks, Michael Redgrave and Mervyn Johns with settings and costumes by Ernst Stern; *The Watch on the Rhine* with Zena Dare, Ursula Jeans and Roger Livesey; the Old Vic Company in *Shirley* with Nova Pilbeam as Caroline Helston, Audrey Fildes as Shirley, Edward Robson as Robert Moore; the Sadler's Wells and the D'Oyly Carte operas.

The repertory started their 8th season with that well-tried favourite *Romance* in which Pauline Letts acted Madame Cavallini. The company had two Shakespeare productions to their credit this year, *The Taming of the Shrew* with Michael Warre and Pauline Letts as Petruchio and Catharine and *Hamlet* which was put on for two weeks in December with Michael Warre as the Prince, Lalage Lewis as Ophelia, Lester Barrett as Claudius and Enid Staff as Gertrude. *The School for Scandal* and *The Importance of Being Earnest* were revived. Several foreign plays were performed such as the American *Little Foxes* and *The Petrified Forest*, the Czech *R.U.R.* and the Russian farce *Squaring the Circle*.

Robert Bottomley succeeded Turner as resident manager at the end of May and Redvers Leech gave up the directorship in July remaining, however, as a Governor. Prices had to be augmented again to dress circle 3/6, circle and stalls 2/6, pit 1/3, upper circle 1/-, gallery 6d, but they were still able to compete with the cinemas.

At the end of the year the Sadler's Wells Opera Company returned with Peter Pears, Joan Cross and Victoria Sladen giving among other operas *Hansel and Gretel* and *La Bohème*. They were followed in January 1944 by Emlyn Williams in *Night Must Fall* and by the try-out of his play *The Druid's Rest* subsequently produced in London. Pantomime returned in the shape of Harry Benet's *Cinderella* from Hull. Benet was the pantomime king of the north who had been in the business nearly 40 years and produced 5 or 6 pantomimes a year.

Othello was the Shakespeare play chosen for two weeks' representation by the repertory this year with Richard Fisher as Othello, Norman Hoult as Iago and Elizabeth Kentish as Desdemona. Ibsen was represented by *Hedda Gabler* and *A Doll's House*, Shaw by *Major Barbara*, and Bridie by *Mr. Bolfry*. Other interesting plays were the Spanish *A Hundred Years Old* and the Irish *Shadow and Substance*. During Holy Week Drinkwater's Biblical play *A Man's House* was given. This was the last production for some time by Geoffrey Staines who left the Company owing to illness and was succeeded by Alexander Scott with Norman Hoult as stage director. In July a departure was made from the usual custom of having travelling companies only at Christmas in favour of Priestley's war play *Desert Rats* brought by a special company of service men.

In their visit at the end of the year the Sadler's Wells ballet company gave for the first time in York the full length ballets *Giselle* and *Lac des Cygnes* as well as *Promenade* and *Le Festin de l'Araignée*.

Harry Benet again brought his Hull pantomime, *Jack and the Beanstalk*, in 1945. A number of interesting plays were put on by the repertory company this year, their wide range covering *An Ideal Husband*, *The Bread-winner*, the Soviet comedy *Distant Point* by Afinogenev, Obey's *Noah*, *Ghosts*, *Quality Street*, *Six Characters in Search of an Author*, *The Long Mirror*, *They Came to a City*, *This Happy Breed*, and *It Depends What you Mean*, a series of which any company might well be proud.

A new but, unfortunately not very successful, experiment was tried this summer in the form of a three weeks' Drama Festival by a specially selected company. The three pieces chosen were *The Alchemist* with Baliol Holloway in the title rôle, Peter Bennett as Face, Althea Parker as Doll Common and Jean Forbes-Robertson as Dame Pliant, production by Geoffrey Staines; *The Confederacy* with Holloway as Brass, John Garside as Gripe and Jean Forbes-Robertson as Flippanta; and a hitherto untried modern play *The Spinster of South Street* by R. F. Delderfield, with Jean Forbes-Robertson as Florence Nightingale.

When James Agate[9] reviewed this last on its arrival at Hammersmith, in an article entitled 'York Leads the Way' he wrote 'The most significant thing about this production is that it is the work of the York Festival Company, presented by the York Citizens' Theatre Trust Ltd. I take this to be a sign that the work of decentralising the theatre has begun ... I am convinced that whereas what London hankers after is "an evening out", what the provinces hunger for is the art of the drama.' Nevertheless York did not hunger for the highbrow drama at augmented prices and the season was a failure.

Meanwhile the repertory company had gone on an E.N.S.A. tour and Sara Greenhalgh had become their new scene designer. Their 10th birthday was celebrated by a revival of *Trilby* with Elizabeth Kentish in the title rôle and Lester Barrett as Svengali. In October W. J. Carter returned from the army as resident manager.

The International Ballet came at the Christmas season with Mona Ingoldsby, Leslie French and Rovi Pavinoff. In their repertoire were *Aurora's Wedding*, *Prince Igor*, *Danses Espagnoles*, *Carnaval*, *Everyman* and *Twelfth Night* which were all new to York.

D'Oyly Carte paid its annual visit in January 1946 and was followed by Donald Wolfit with Rosalind Iden and Antony Eustrel in *Hamlet*, *The Merchant of Venice*, *Merry Wives of Windsor*, *King Lear* and *Twelfth Night*. Benet's pantomime was *Red Riding Hood*.

The repertory's first offering was *Emma*. Geoffrey Staines had returned to the company as director of productions, assisted by Alexander Scott and Norman Hoult. Plays included *The Enchanted Cottage*, *The Morning Star*, *On the Rocks*, *Robert's Wife*, *She Passed Through Lorraine*, *Skipper*, *Next to God*, *Trelawney of the 'Wells'*, *The Wind of Heaven*, *Heartbreak House*, *Hindle Wakes*, *The Switchback* and *Flare Path*.

In July 1946 the York Citizens' Theatre opened a second theatre, the Opera House at Scarborough, with another company, and at the start of 1947 the two companies became interchangeable playing each new piece for one week at York and one at Scarborough. This enabled each Company to have a fortnight in which to prepare a new play. Weekly repertory is a gruelling and unsatisfactory business, involving under-rehearsed plays, scamped performances and a worn-out company. It is a poor training for actors who are forced to resort to tricks to cover up deficiencies resulting from lack of rehearsals. With the new regime plays could be staged with more care and the company become a worthy training ground for new talent as the stock company used to be before it.

By October 1947 the York Citizens' Theatre had put on a total of 448 plays and 61 revivals. Outstanding pieces that year were *The Doctor's Dilemma, The Lake, The Man Who Came to Dinner, St. Joan, You Can't Take It With You* and *To What Red Hell*. The Shakespeare play was *Macbeth*. There was also a welcome tendency to put on entirely new plays. Of these *Hallowe'en* was by a local dramatist, Leslie Burgess; the others were *Strange Captivity* by Conrad Carter and John Stericker, *Burma Road* by Ian Hay and John Smyth and *The Boxer and the Ballerina* by Elizabeth Keen and John Macadam. The experimentation with new plays or with those unknown to the West End is of great value. Rising dramatists who would have little chance of seeing their work produced in London are enabled to learn their craft empirically by seeing it staged by the more adventurous repertories.

Since Mrs. Keregan erected her playhouse in Mint Yard in 1744 no year has passed in which the York Theatre has not opened its doors. This record of over 200 years is one of which the city may well be proud. As we look back over the procession of lessees and managers, good, bad and indifferent, and of great players to whom this Theatre gave their first chance or their early training, we draw strength and confidence for the future from the long and continuous tradition of the York stage.

The record will not end here, for York's theatrical history is still in the making. May we hope, therefore, that the Theatre will continue to thrive, so that the shade of Tate Wilkinson himself may look down upon it and nod approval.

APPENDIX A

List of Dramatic Companies in York
1565–1628

A. Secular

C.A.   =   Chamberlain's Accounts quoted from J. T. Murray,
           English Dramatic Companies
C.M.B. =   Corporation Minute Books quoted from notes
           kindly lent by the Reverend A. Raine

1565	Jan. 28.	Lord Scrope's	C.A.
	Feb.	Earl of Bedford's	C.A.
	April 6.	Lord Rich's	C.A.
	,, ,,	Earl of Leicester's	C.A.
1581	Sept.	Earl of Sussex's	C.M.B. Vol.28. f.26
	,,	Lord Hunsdon's	C.M.B. Vol.28. f.26
1584	March	Earl of Essex's	C.A.
	Aug.	Queen's Majesty's	C.A.
1585	March	Earl of Worcester's	C.A.
	June	Lord Oxford's	C.A.
1587	Feb. 27	Earl of Essex's	C.A.
	June	Earl of Oxford's	C.A.
	Sept. 9.	Queen's Majesty's	C.A.
	Oct. 6.	Lord Stafford's	C.A.
	–	Lord Chandos's	C.A.
	–	Lord Admiral's	C.A.
	–	Earl of Sussex's	C.A.
1588	Feb.	Earl of Essex's	C.A.
	June 20.	Earl of Sussex's	C.A.
	July 13.	Earl of Leicester's	C.A.
1590	Sept. 26.	Lord Beauchamp's	C.A.

List of Dramatic Companies in York 1565–1628

A. Secular *Continued*

1592	July	Queen's	C.M.B. Vol.30. f.339 v.
	Oct.	Earl of Newcastle's	C.A.[1]
1593	April	Lord Admiral & Lord Morden's	C.A.
	May	Earl of Worcester's	C.A.
	June	Earl of Pembroke's	C.A.
	Aug.	Earl of Sussex's	C.A.
	Sept.	Queen's	C.A.
	Nov. 30.	Lord Ogle and Darcy's	C.A.
1594	Oct.	Lord Burrough's	C.A.
1595	Nov.	Lord Willoughby's	C.M.B. Vol.31. f.141 v.
1596	July	Her Majesty's	C.A.
1597	June	Lord Chandos's	C.A.
1598	Aug.	Her Majesty's, no play	C.A.
1599	April	Earl of Worcester's, no play	C.A.; C.M.B. Vol.32. f.10
	Nov.	Lord Mounteagle's	C.A.
	–	Earl of Lincoln's	C.A.
	–	Queen's	C.A.
1600	Jan. 21	Earl of Pembroke's	C.M.B. Vol.32. f.63.
1601	July	Lord Chandos's	C.M.B. Vol.32. f.156 v.
1602	July	Queen's	C.A.
	Oct.	Earl of Lincoln's	C.A.
1603	April	Lord Dudley's at visit of James I	C.A.
	–	Lord Admiral's	C.A.
	Dec.	Lord Stafford's	C.A.
	,,	Lord Evers's	C.A.
1605	Aug.	Lord Dudley's	C.A.
	Dec.	Lord Berkeley's	C.A.
1606	–	Queen's	C.A.
1607	–	Lord Dudley's, no play	C.A.
	Sept.	Queen's Majesty's	C.M.B. Vol.33. f.90 v.
1608	–	Lord Evers's, no play	C.A.
1610	July	Lord Albany's, no play	C.A.
1611	–	Lord Albany's	C.A.
1625	Feb.	Two unnamed, no play	C.M.B. Vol.35. f.2 v.
1628	June	Unnamed	C.M.B. Vol.35. f.60 v.

B. Ecclesiastical

Reverend A. Raine, *Two Notes on the History of the Drama,* Yorks. Philosophical Society Papers 1926. Slightly emended (from Chamberlain's Books in the Zouche Chapel.)

1576		Earl of Essex's
		Lord Stafford's
		Lancashire men players
1581		Lord Strange's
1582		Lord Stafford's
1584		Queen's Majesty's
1587		Earl of Essex's
1592	July	Her Majesty's
1593	Sept.	Her Majesty's
1596		Her Majesty's
1597/8	Feb.	Players at Mr. Doctor Bennitt's
1599/1600	Feb.	Lord Sudder's

APPENDIX B

Some Rôles Played in York by Famous Actors whilst Members of the Company

Richard Suett

1773   Bolgolam (*Lilliput*), songs (*Timon of Athens*).

1774   –

1775   Paris (*Jealous Wife*), Guildenstern, Squire Richard (*Provok'd Husband*), Officer (*Coriolanus*), Silvius (*As You Like It*), Burgundy (*Lear*), Trappanti (*She Wou'd and She Wou'd Not*), Frederick (*Choleric Man*), Squire Gordon (*Love à la Mode*), Robin (*Waterman*), Jack (*Lame Lover*), Dick (*Minor*), Lucius (*Theodosius*), Sir Harry (*High Life Below Stairs*), Brazen (*No One's Enemy But His Own*), Harry (*Mock Doctor*).

1776   Jessamy (*Bon Ton*), Ralph (*Maid of the Mill*), Harlequin (*Theatrical Candidates*), Apprentice, Thomas (*Thomas and Sally*), Cadwall (*Cymbeline*), Tony Lumpkin, Marplot (*Busy Body*), Jarvis (*Runaway*), Acres, Launcelot Gobbo, Swab (*Coquette*), Barnardine (*Measure for Measure*), Peto (*Henry IV*).

1777   Trimwell (*Hotel*), Roderigo (*Othello*), Malvolio, Oxford (*Richard III*).

1778   Tom (*Conscious Lover*), Mercury (*Amphitryon*), Mungo (*Padlock*), Spanish Barber, Brush (*Clandestine Marriage*), Matthew (*Every Man in His Humour*), Toby Aircastle (*Cozeners*), Crabtree, Ali (*Alarm*), Hecate.

1779   Pistol (*Henry V*), Gradus (*Who's the Dupe?*), Dromio of Ephesus (*Comedy of Errors*), William (*As You Like It*), Gravedigger, Charles (*Know Your Own Mind*).

1780   Ralph (*Grenadier*), O'Kite & Splash (*Widow and No Widow*), Dogberry, Young Marlow, Skirmish (*Deserter*), Faulconbridge, Hardy (*Belle's Stratagem*), Muskato (*'Tis Well It's No Worse*), Booze (*Belphegor*), Apothecary (*Romeo and Juliet*), Scrub, Bowkitt (*Son-in-Law*).

John Philip Kemble

1779   Orestes (*Distress'd Mother*), Ranger (*Suspicious Husband*), Edgar (*Lear*), West Indian, Young Cape (*Author*), Earl Edwin (*Battle of Hastings*), Prince Edward (*Black Prince*), Tobeni and Prologue (*Suicide*), Perillus (*Bonduca*), Joseph Surface, Bireno (*Law of Lombardy*), Marcus[2] (*Belisarius*), Col. Manley (*School for Scandal Scandalis'd*), Modeley (*School for Lovers*), Athelwold (*Elfrida*), Douglas (*Percy*), Capt. Dormer (*Word to the Wise*), Lothario (*Fair Penitent*), Campley (*Funeral*), Moneses (*Tamerlane*), Exeter and Prologue (*Henry V*), Alonzo (*Revenge*), Jaffeir, Faulkland, Novel (*Plain Dealer*), Lord Mirror (*Touchstone of Truth*), Young Belmont (*Foundling*), Teribazus (*Zenobia*), Master (*Toyshop*), Sir Charles Easy (*Careless Husband*), Orlando, Sir George Airy (*Busy Body*).

1780   Col. Mountfort (*Times*), Almaimon (*Zoraida*), Mirabel, Don Carlos (*'Tis Well It's No Worse*), Romeo, Rivers (*Fatal Falsehood*), Henry (*Richard III*), Petruchio, Cromwell, Lord Newbery (*Separate Maintenance*), Lord Random (*Summer Amusement*), Benedick, Archer, Evander (*Grecian Daughter*), Col. Feignwell (*Bold Stroke for a Wife*), Shylock, Hastings, Edwin (*Mathilda*), Belville (*School for Wives*), Posthumous, Edward (*Earl of Warwick*), Oakley (*Jealous Wife*), Puff.

1781   Hamlet, Othello, Florizel, Prince of Wales (*Henry IV*), Sir Harry Glenville (*Generous Impostor*), Pharnaces (*Siege of Sinope*), Hyllus (*Royal Suppliants*), Lord Rentless (*Dissipation*), Grey (*Chapter of Accidents*), Contrast (*Lord of the Manor*), Frederick (*Miser*), Phocyas (*Siege of Damascus*), Theodosius, Atall (*Double Gallant*), Don Carlos (*Love Makes a Man*), Juba (*Cato*), Sir Giles Overreach, Valentine (*Love for Love*).

Stephen Kemble

1782   Nerestan (*Zara*), Hamlet, Omar (*Fair Circassian*), Clerimont sen^r (*Tender Husband*), Lord Wronglove (*Lady's Last Stake*), Douglas (*Percy*), Ribero (*Braganza*), Seyward (*Hypocrite*), Dauphin (*Silent Woman*), Charles Steady (*Variety*), Aubrey (*Fashionable Lover*), Aboan (*Oroonoko*), Minor, Mellefont (*Double Dealer*), Don Carlos (*Love Makes a Man*), Sir Charles Raymond (*Foundling*), Siffroy (*Cleone*), Portius (*Cato*), Drawcansir (*Rehearsal*), Duke (*Rule a Wife*), Henry (*Richard III*), Oakley (*Jealous Wife*), Count of Narbonne.

Dorothy Jordan

1782   Calista, Macheath, Hermione (*Distress'd Mother*), Arionelli (*Son-in-Law*), Rachael (*Fair American*), Priscilla Tomboy (*Romp*).

Dorothy Jordan *Continued*

1783   Queen Dollilolly (*Tom Thumb*), Euphrasia (*Grecian Daughter*), Adonis (*Poor Vulcan*), Amanda (*Love's Last Shift*), Arpasia (*Tamerlane*), Lady Davenant (*Mysterious Husband*), Queen Elizabeth (*Richard III*), William (*Rosina*), Almeria (*Mourning Bride*), Zara, Indiana (*Conscious Lovers*), Amelia (*Summer Amusement*), Lady Alton (*English Merchant*), Lady Racket (*Three Weeks After Marriage*), Countess of Rutland (*Earl of Essex*), Phillipo (*Castle of Andalusia*), Letitia Hardy, Lady Restless (*All in the Wrong*).

1784   Lionel (*Lionel and Clarissa*), Daphne (*Midas*), Mrs Ford, Poor Soldier, Cowslip (*Agreeable Surprise*), Patie (*Gentle Shepherd*), Araminta (*Young Quaker*), Sophy Pendragon (*Which Is the Man?*), Louisa (*Reparation*), Athenais (*Theodosius*), Old Maid, Victoria (*Bold Stroke for a Husband*), Coelia (*School for Lovers*), Catalina (*Castle of Andalusia*), Emilia (*Othello*), Adelaide (*Count of Narbonne*), Mrs Beverley (*Gamester*), Ophelia, Leonora (*Revenge*), Statira (*Rival Queens*), Country Madcap, Belvidera, Miss Bull (*Fontainbleau*), Fatima (*Cymon*), Ethelinda (*Royal Convert*), Allen à Dale (*Robin Hood*), Isabella (*Measure for Measure*), Miss Marchmont (*False Delicacy*), Andromache (*Distress'd Mother*), Juliet.

Miss Wilkinson (*later* Mrs Mountain)

1785   Patty (*Maid of the Mill*), Sylvia (*Cymon*), Celia (*Fontainbleau*), Victoria (*Castle of Andalusia*), Stella (*Robin Hood*), Rosina (*Spanish Barber*).

1786   Fanny (*Clandestine Marriage*), Country Girl, Perdita, Ophelia, Prince Edward (*Richard III*), Constantia (*Man of the World*), Prince Arthur, William (*Rosina*).

John Fawcett

1787   Douglas, Oroonoko, Romeo.[3]

1788   Sir George Airy (*Busy Body*), Pedrillo (*Castle of Andalusia*), Saville (*Belle's Stratagem*), Tinsel (*Double Disguise*), Young Cockney (*Romp*), Campley (*Inkle and Yarico*), Harcourt (*Country Girl*), Sultan (*Such Things Are*), Clodpole (*Fashionable Wife*), Col. Briton (*Wonder*), Lord Gayville (*Heiress*), Philip (*Brothers*), Rohlf (*Disbanded Officer*), Peeping Tom, Dick (*Confederacy*), Frankly (*Suspicious Husband*), Horatio (*Hamlet*), Moses (*School for Scandal*), Don John (*Much Ado*), Lennox (*Macbeth*), Oliver (*As You Like It*), Suffolk (*Earl of Warwick*), Launcelot Gobbo, Amber (*He Wou'd be a Soldier*), Don Manuel (*Barataria*), Bullock (*Recruiting Officer*), Dr. Druid (*Fashionable Lover*), David (*Rivals*), Young Wilding (*Citizen*), Jemmy Jumps (*Farmer*), Renault

(*Venice Preserv'd*), Surrey (*Henry VIII*), Nicholas (*Midnight Hour*), Simkin (*Deserter*), Southampton (*Earl of Essex*), Sir Shenkin ap Griffith (*Fontainbleau*), Jack Hastings (*Natural Son*), Jemmy Twitcher (*Beggar's Opera*), Diggory (*She Stoops to Conquer*), Twist (*Love in the East*), Buckingham (*Richard III*), Varland (*West Indian*).

1789　Scrub, Alscrip (*Heiress*), Muns (*Prisoner at Large*), Sir Anthony Absolute, Midas, La Nippe (*Lord of the Manor*), La Fleur (*Animal Magnetism*), King Arthur (*Tom Thumb*), Ruttekin (*Robin Hood*), Trinculo, Bourbon (*Henry V*), Isaac (*Duenna*), Apothecary (*Romeo and Juliet*), Young Clincher (*Constant Couple*), Muskato (*Pannel*), Shelty (*Highland Reel*), Gomez (*Regent*), Lysimachus (*Rival Queens*).

1790　Figaro (*Follies of a Day*), Jonas (*Iron Mask*), Jacob Gauky (*Chapter of Accidents*), Gregory Gubbins (*Battle of Hexham*), Francis (*Henry IV*), Metheglin (*The Toy*), Robin (*No Song No Supper*), Jobson (*Devil to Pay*), Jerry Sneak (*Mayor of Garratt*), Dogberry.

1791　Sir Samuel Sheepy (*School for Arrogance*), Lazarillo (*Two Strings to Your Bow*), Twineall (*Such Things Are*), Vincentio (*Bold Stroke for a Husband*), Whim (*Divertisement*), Young Philpot (*Citizen*), Vapid (*Dramatist*), Gregory (*Mock Doctor*), Edward (*Haunted Tower*), Florestan (*Richard Coeur de Lion*), Dashwood (*Know Your Own Mind*).

Robert William Elliston

1791　Don Carlos (*Revenge*), Belville (*Country Girl*).

1792　Young Marlow, Random (*Ways and Means*), Neville (*Dramatist*), Harry Dornton (*Road to Ruin*), Earl of Surrey (*Henry VIII*), 1st Spirit (*Comus*), Henry (*Next Door Neighbours*), Marquis (*Midnight Hour*), Dorilas (*Merope*), Lord de Courci (*Carmelite*), George Belville (*Cross Purposes*), Egerton (*Man of the World*), Raymond (*Widow of Malabar*).

1793　Theodosius, West Indian, Sir Harry Portland (*Duplicity*), Wingrove (*Fugitive*), Don Carlos (*Love Makes a Man*), Aimwell, Campley (*Funeral*), Frenchman (*Surrender of Calais*), Capt. Savage (*School for Wives*), Young Lovegame (*Miss in Her Pranks*), Capt, Crevelt (*He Would Be a Soldier*).

Andrew Cherry

1792　Shelty (*Highland Reel*), Lazarillo (*Two Strings to Your Bow*), Darby (*Poor Soldier*), Sir David Dunder (*Ways and Means*), Rover (*Wild Oats*), Robin (*No Song No Supper*), Leopold (*Siege of Belgrade*), Vapid (*Dramatist*), Dornton (*Road to Ruin*), Gripe (*Two Misers*), Scaramouch (*Don Juan*), Gardiner (*Henry VIII*), O'Cutter (*Jealous Wife*), Peeping Tom, Ruttekin (*Robin Hood*), Muns (*Prisoner at Large*), Joey (*Modern Antiques*), Edward (*Haunted Tower*), Linco (*Cymon*), Nicholas (*Midnight*

Andrew Cherry *Continued*

Hour), Bluntly (*Next Door Neighbours*), à la Greque (*Day in Turkey*), Irishman (*Jubilee*), Clod (*Young Quaker*), Bowkitt (*Son-in-law*), Zany (*Blue Beard*), Launcelot Gobbo, Isaac (*Duenna*), Lingo (*Agreeable Surprise*), Sturmwald (*Doctor and Apothecary*), Puff, Grub (*Cross Purposes*), Darby (*Darby in America*), Sir Pertinax MacSycophant (*Man of the World*), O'Whack (*Notoriety*).

1793   Murtogh Delany (*Irishman in London*), Sir Peter Teazle, Little Hunchback, Peregrine Forester (*Hertford Bridge*), Solus (*Everyone Has His Fault*), Tinsel (*Double Disguise*), Don Lewis (*Love Makes a Man*), Sir Andrew Aguecheek, Figaro (*Follies of a Day*), John (*Mogul Tale*), Lenitive (*Prize*).

1794   Walter (*Children in the Wood*), Nipperkin (*Sprigs of Laurel*), Sadi (*Mountaineers*), Harlequin (*Harlequin Shipwreck'd*), Steady (*Purse*), King Arthur (*Tom Thumb*), Grigsby (*World in a Village*), Mock Doctor, Metheglin (*Hampton Court*), Timothy (*Heigh Ho! for a Husband*), Gossip (*My Grandmother*).

John Emery

1795   Jabal (*The Jew*).

1796   Caleb (*He Wou'd Be a Soldier*), Gregory Gubbins (*Battle of Hexham*), Placid (*Every One Has His Fault*), Peter (*Romeo and Juliet*), Sir David Daw (*Wheel of Fortune*), Ralph (*Lock and Key*), Silky (*Road to Ruin*), Sands (*Henry VIII*), Dicky Gossip (*My Grandmother*), Ephraim Smooth (*Wild Oats*), Gunnel (*Netley Abbey*), Abel Drugger (*Tobacconist*), Old Kecksey (*Irish Widow*), Miser, Peter (*Apparition*), Record (*Adopted Child*), Jeremy (*Cherokee*), Project (*Speculation*), Caustic (*Way to Get Married*), Maj. Rampart (*Man of Ten Thousand*), Francis (*Henry IV*), Hodge (*Love in a Village*), Mat Medley (*The Woodman*), Peter (*Hertford Bridge*), Solomon (*Quaker*), Filch (*Beggar's Opera*), Watchman (*Upholsterer*).

1797   Trudge (*Inkle and Yarico*), Bobby Notice (*Bannian Day*), Tom Seymour (*Fortune's Fool*), Tony Lumpkin, Mungo (*Padlock*), Mawworm (*Hypocrite*), Darby (*Poor Soldier*), Gravedigger, Frank Oatland (*Cure for the Heart Ache*), Pantaloon (*Harlequin at Amsterdam*), Harry Hawser (*Shipwreck*).

1798   Realise (*Will*), Obadiah (*Honest Thieves*), Scrub, Freakish (*Poor Sailor*), Abram (*Harlequin's Invasion*), Edward (*Haunted Tower*), Dr. Last, Capt. Meadows (*Deaf Lover*), Bobby Pendragon (*Which is the Man?*), Torrington (*School for Wives*), Grime (*Deserted Daughter*), Young Testy (*Abroad and at Home*), Solus (*Every One Has His Fault*), Fulmer (*West Indian*), Crabtree, Wilford (*Iron Chest*), Steadfast and Zekiel

Homespun (*Heir at Law*), Motley (*Castle Spectre*), Nicholas Rue (*Secrets Worth Knowing*), Periwinkle (*Bold Stroke For a Wife*), Lingo (*Agreeable Surprise*), Fustian (*Sylvester Daggerwood*), Cymon (*Irishman in London*), Endless (*No Song No Supper*), Joe (*King and the Miller*), Jemmy Jumps (*Farmer*), Sturmwald (*Doctor and Apothecary*), Darby (*Darby in America*), Pan (*Midas*).

Maria Duncan (*later* Mrs Davison)

1797 Sophia (*Road to Ruin*), Statira (*Rival Queens*), Widow Belmour (*Way to Keep Him*), Perdita, Jessy Oatland (*Cure for the Heart Ache*), Winifred (*Zorinski*), Celia (*School for Lovers*).

1798 Jane Shore, Lady Contest (*Wedding Day*), Elinor Bloomly (*Cheap Living*), Emily Fitzallan (*False Impressions*), Agnes (*Raymond and Agnes*), Kathleen (*Poor Soldier*), Dolly Snip (*Harlequin's Invasion*), Polly, Miss Dorillion (*Wives as They Were*), Joanna (*Deserted Daughter*), Ellina de Rosalba (*Italian Monk*), Nell (*Devil to Pay*), Lady Eleanor Irwin, Adelaide (*Count of Narbonne*), Violante, Lady Teazle, Barbara (*Iron Chest*), Caroline Dormer (*Heir at Law*), Angela (*Castle Spectre*), Mrs Greville (*Secrets Worth Knowing*), Fanny (*Shipwreck*), Maria Delaval (*He's Much to Blame*), Anna (*Doctor and Apothecary*), Mrs Belville (*School for Wives*).

1799 Belinda (*All in the Wrong*), Lady Sadlife (*Double Gallant*), Dorothy (*No Song No Supper*), Mrs Haller (*Stranger*), Beatrice, Rosa (*Secret*), Mrs Mortimer (*Laugh When You Can*), Lilla (*Siege of Belgrade*), Miranda, Gangica (*Votary of Wealth*), Lady Macbeth, Grace (*Poor Vulcan*), Rosa (*How to Grow Rich*), Miss Plumb (*Gretna Green*), Ophelia, Agnes (*Mountaineers*), Cleopatra (*All for Love*), Cora (*Pizarro*), Irene (*Blue Beard*).

1800 Juliana (*Management*), Juliet, Elizabeth (*Count of Burgundy*), Winifred (*Zorinski*), Portia, Janette (*False and True*), Cordelia, Miss Hoyden (*Man of Quality*), Susan Ashfield (*Speed the Plough*), Rosalind, Maria (*Five Thousand a Year*), Lady Zephyrine Mutable (*What is She?*), Tasseni (*St David's Day*), Fanny (*Maid of the Mill*).

Charles Mathews

1798 Silky (*Road to Ruin*), Lingo (*Agreeable Surprise*), Theodore (*Raymond and Agnes*), Rundy (*Farmer*), Governor (*Chapter of Accidents*), Governor (*Critic*).

1799 Sir Anthony Absolute, Zekiel Homespun (*Heir at Law*), Shelty (*Highland Reel*), Caleb Quotem (*Review*), Stave (*Shipwreck*), Sir Matthew Maxim (*Five Thousand a Year*), Jabal (*The Jew*), Bonus (*Laugh When*

Charles Mathews *Continued*

You Can), Label (*Prize*), Verdun (*Lovers' Vows*), Metheglin (*Lie of the Day*), Nicholas Rue (*Secrets Worth Knowing*), Old Bromley (*Jew and the Doctor*), Record (*Adopted Child*), Ralph (*Lock and Key*), Fustian (*Sylvester Daggerwood*), Frank Oatland (*Cure for the Heart Ache*), Shacabac (*Blue Beard*), Old Peasant (*Mouth of the Nile*), Motley (*Castle Spectre*), Solomon (*Stranger*), Verges, Ralph (*Secret*), Dorus (*Cymon*), Leopold (*Siege of Belgrade*), Clown (*Fortunatus*), Autolycus, Trinculo, Pedrillo (*Castle of Andalusia*), Old Visorly (*Votary of Wealth*), Ennui (*Dramatist*), Freakish (*Poor Sailor*), Poor Vulcan, Tempest (*Wheel of Fortune*), Endless (*No Song No Supper*), Sadi (*Mountaineer*), Sir Solomon Sadlife (*Double Gallant*), Polonius, Lovell (*Henry VIII*).

1800   Crack (*Turnpike Gate*), Old Doily (*Who's the Dupe?*), Tubal, Count Benini (*False and True*), Sir Caustic Oldstyle (*What is She?*), Ephraim Smooth (*Wild Oats*), Allspice (*Way to Get Married*), Farmer Ashfield (*Speed the Plough*), William (*As You Like It*), Sir Peter Teazle, Old Philpot (*Citizen*), Habakuk (*Naval Pillar*), Scaramouch (*Don Juan*), Fluellen, Sancho (*Lovers' Quarrels*), Mist (*Management*), Apothecary (*Romeo and Juliet*), Witski (*Zorinski*), Murcia (*Child of Nature*), Sir Harry Sycamore (*Maid of the Mill*), Lord Mayor (*Richard III*), Sir Solomon Swallow (*Wandering Jew*), Thomas Filbert (*What D'Ye Call It*), Sapscull (*Honest Yorkshireman*), Owen (*St David's Day*), Chellingoe (*Ramah Droog*), Ferret (*Horse and the Widow*), Baron Duberley (*Heir at Law*).

1801   Frederick (*Of Age To-morrow*), Sir Solomon Cynic (*Will*), Kecksey (*Irish Widow*), Dashington (*What a Blunder*), Dominique (*Deaf and Dumb*), Cadi of Bagdad (*Il Bondocani*), Cymon Bumpkin (*Civilian*), Miser, Sir Francis Gripe (*Busy Body*), Timid (*Duplicity*), Trudge (*Inkle and Yarico*), Steinberg (*Point of Honour*), Nipperkin (*Rival Soldiers*), Gabriel Lackbrain (*Life*), Lovel (*High Life Below Stairs*), Brainworm (*Every Man in His Humour*), Periwinkle (*Bold Stroke for a Wife*), John Grouse (*Liberal Opinions*), Hale (*Bank Note*), Skirmish (*Deserter of Naples*), Hardy (*Belle's Stratagem*), Lord Priory (*Wives As They Were*), Sir Luke Tremor (*Such Things Are*).

1802   Sir Walter Wareing (*Woodman*), Falstaff, Dominique (*Paul and Virginia*), Obi Woman (*Obi*), General (*Midnight Hour*), Jobson (*Devil to Pay*), Shenkin (*Folly As It Flies*), Clod (*Young Quaker*), Tailor (*Catharine and Petruchio*), Don Pedro (*Wonder*), Solomon (*Quaker*), Sentinel (*Pizarro*), Capt. Meadows (*Deaf Lover*), Varland (*West Indian*), Drugget (*Three Weeks After Marriage*), Papillion (*Liar*), Timothy Starch (*Wise Man of the East*), Ollapod (*Poor Gentleman*), Sir Benjamin Dove (*Brothers*), Item (*Deserted Daughter*), Tinker (*Magic Oak*), Governor Harcourt (*Chapter of Accidents*), Sir Shenkin ap Griffith (*Fontainbleau*), Timothy (*Heigh Ho! for a Husband*), Apathy (*Children *in the Wood*), Scrub (*Beaux' Stratagem*), Sharp (*Lying Valet*), Sir David Dunder (*Ways and Means*), Bobby Pendragon (*Which is the Man?*), Filch (*Beggar's Opera*), Mock Doctor, Lingo (*Agreeable Surprise*), Sir Simon Flourish (*Abroad and at Home*), Ruttekin (*Robin Hood*).

1803   Prattle (*Deuce is in Him*), Sir Oliver Oldstock (*He Wou'd Be a Soldier*), Capt. Battledore (*Poor Sailor*), Don Jerome (*Duenna*), Puzzle (*Funeral*), MacScrape (*Netley Abbey*), Lord Ogleby (*Clandestine Marriage*), Dr Scarecrow (*Mad Guardian*), Croaker (*Good Natur'd Man*), Lenitive (*Prize*), Don Caesar (*Bold Stroke For a Husband*), Robin (*Waterman*), Whimsiculo (*Cabinet*), Proteus (*Family Quarrels*), Tipple (*Flitch of Bacon*), Hob.

John Liston

1803   Raw Recruit (*Everyone Has His Fault*), Chronicle (*Young Quaker*), Lord Priory (*Wives As They Were*), Abel (*Honest Thieves*), Lazarillo (*John Bull*), Farmer Woodland.

Sarah Smith (*later* Mrs Bartley)

1803   Lady Harriet (*Funeral*), Lady Bell (*Know Your Own Mind*), Maria (*Citizen*), Lady Bell Bloomer (*Which Is The Man?*), Mary Thornberry (*John Bull*), Young Lady (*I'll Tell You What*), Ellen Vortex (*Cure for the Heartache*), Young Norval (*Douglas*), Juliet, Statira (*Rival Queens*), Caroline (*Hear Both Sides*), Angela (*Castle Spectre*), Peggy (*Country Girl*), Clarissa (*Mad Guardian*).

Edward Knight

1803   Sampson (*Isabella*), Motley (*Castle Spectre*), Maj. Benbow (*Flitch of Bacon*), Dan (*John Bull*), Piero (*Tale of Mystery*), Frank Oatland (*Cure for the Heart Ache*), Dulcet (*63rd Letter*), William (*As You Like It*), Thomas (*Irish Widow*), Davy (*Bon Ton*), General (*Midnight Hour*), Gravedigger, Sim (*Wild Oats*), Sir Peppercorn Crabstick (*Family Quarrels*), Meshec (*House To Be Sold*), Crazy (*Peeping Tom*), Sir Abel Handy (*Speed The Plough*), Jeffrey (*Netley Abbey*), Simon Squeezum (*Mad Guardian*), Label (*Prize*), Joey (*Merry Mourners*), Sir Ralph Aspen (*Hear Both Sides*), Old Bromley (*Jew and the Doctor*), Prattle (*Deuce is in Him*), Blunder (*Honest Yorkshireman*), Solus (*Everyone Has His Fault*), Old Sapling (*Delays and Blunders*), Cuddy Pickwidgeon (*Trick upon Trick*).

1804   Dominique (*Paul and Virginia*), Sam (*Raising the Wind*), Tailor (*Catharine and Petruchio*), Baron Duberley (*Heir at Law*), Caleb

349

Edward Knight   *Continued*

Quotem (*Review*), Polonius, Ross (*Richard II*), Carrier (*Henry IV*), Record (*Adopted Child*), Sir David Dunder (*Ways and Means*), Muns (*Prisoner at Large*), Sir John Evergreen (*Invasion*), Don Pedro (*Wonder*), Silky (*Road to Ruin*), Crack (*Turnpike Gate*), Risk (*Love Laughs at Locksmiths*), Nicholas Rue (*Secrets Worth Knowing*), Ollapod (*Poor Gentleman*), Timothy Quaint (*Soldier's Daughter*), Sir Francis Wronghead (*Provok'd Husband*), Varland (*West Indian*), Squeezeall (*Counterfeit*), Caleb (*He Wou'd be a Soldier*), Tester (*Suspicious Husband*), Corsican Fairy (*Fairy*), Allspice (*Way to Get Married*), Sancho (*Lovers' Quarrels*), Billy Bustler (*First Love*), Autolycus, Sir Solomon Cynic (*Will*), Toppit (*Paragraph*), Drugget (*Three Weeks After Marriage*), Timothy Remnant (*Volunteers*), Timid (*Duplicity*), Adam Winterton (*Iron Chest*), Ralph (*Lock and Key*), Item (*Deserted Daughter*), Old Hairbrain (*Will for the Deed*).

1805   Old Mirable (*Inconstant*), Bobby Pendragon (*Which Is The Man?*), Sir Andrew Analyse (*Blind Bargain*), Frederick (*Of Age To-morrow*), Triangle (*Guilty or Not Guilty*), Miser, Jeronymo (*Hunter of the Alps*), Sir Adam Contest (*Wedding Day*), Jonathan Oldskirt (*Who Wants a Guinea?*), Don Manuel (*She Wou'd and She Wou'd Not*), Lord Mayor (*Richard III*), Osmyn (*Sultan*), Jacquez (*Honeymoon*), Timothy (*Out of Place*), Chimpanzee (*Perouse*), Flam (*Gay Deceivers*), Trudge (*Inkle and Yarico*), Cymon (*Jealous Wife*), Lord Danbury (*To Marry or Not to Marry*).

1806   Genl Tarragon (*School of Reform*), Briefwit (*Weathercock*), Isaac Mendoza (*Duenna*), King Arthur (*Tom Thumb*), Maj. Tornado (*Delinquent*), Robin Roughhead (*Fortune's Frolics*), Matthew Daw (*School for Friends*), Gardiner (*Henry VIII*), Delvo (*Travellers*), Solomon (*Quaker*), Ferret (*We Fly By Night*), Sir Peter Teazle.

1807   Lazarillo (*Two Strings to Your Bow*), Antoine (*Youth, Love and Folly*), Useph (*Siege of Belgrade*), Peter (*Stranger*), Darby (*Poor Soldier*), Dominique (*Deaf and Dumb*), Old Philpot (*Citizen*), Spriggins (*Five Miles Off*), Tinker (*Magic Oak*), Mungo (*Padlock*), Zekiel Homespun (*Heir at Law*), Bonus (*Laugh When You Can*), David (*Rivals*), Launcelot Gobbo, Walter (*Curfew*), Michael (*Adrian and Orilla*), La Fleur (*Animal Magnetism*), Philip (*Catch Him Who Can*), Antonio (*Follies of a Day*), Clod (*Young Quaker*), Prolix (*Man of Enterprise*), Plod (*False Alarms*), Bras de Fer (*Tekeli*), Faulconbridge (*King John*), Simkin (*Deserter*), Dicky Gossip (*My Grandmother*), Lingo (*Agreeable Surprise*), Verges (*Much Ado*), Steinberg (*Point of Honour*).

1808   Hawbuck (*Town and Country*), Molino (*Blind Boy*), Mustapha (*Forty Thieves*), Ruttekin (*Robin Hood*), Jacob Gauky (*Chapter of Accidents*), Don Caesar (*Bold Stroke for a Husband*), Richard (*Errors Excepted*), Hardy (*Belle's Stratagem*), Index (*World*), Squire Richard (*Provok'd Husband*).

1809 Young Cockney (*Romp*), Witch (*Macbeth*), Justice Greedy (*New Way to Pay Old Debts*), Sir Francis Gripe (*Busy Body*), Diggory (*All The World's a Stage*), Caper (*Who Wins?*), Humphry Grizzle (*Three and the Deuce*), Vincent (*Fortress*), Baron of Oakland (*Haunted Tower*), Jerry Sneak (*Mayor of Garrett*), Ponder (*Man and Wife*), Pierrot (*Touchstone*), Pedrillo (*Plot and Counterplot*), John (*Spoil'd Child*), Servitz (*Exile*), Hob (*Hob in the Well*), Nicholas (*Midnight Hour*).

1813 Ludovico (*Peasant Boy*), Somno (*Sleep Walker*), Dick (*King's Bench*), Larole (*Young Hussar*), Lubin Log (*Love, Law and Physic*), Philip (*English Fleet*), Mingle (*Bee Hive*), Suckling (*Education*), Fidget (*Boarding House*), 1st Plebeian (*Julius Caesar*), Dan (*John Bull*), Trap (*How to Lie for Love*), Trembello (*Aladdin*), Darby (*Poor Soldier*), Dory (*Maniac*), Flutterman (*Ella Rosenberg*), Tester (*Suspicious Husband*), Jaques (*Honeymoon*), Benedetto (*Venoni*), Periwinkle (*Bold Stroke for a Wife*), Cosey (*Town and Country*), Crabtree, Caleb Quotem (*Review*), Tony Lumpkin, Romeo Rantall (*At Home*), William (*Rosina*), Nicholas Rue (*Secrets Worth Knowing*), Varbel (*Lodoiska*), Muns (*Prisoner at Large*), Molino (*Blind Boy*), Launcelot Gobbo, L'Eclaie (*Foundling of the Forest*), Sambo (*Laugh When You Can*), William (*Rosina*), Risk (*Love Laughs at Locksmiths*), Launcelot (*Sleeping Beauty in the Wood*).

Joseph Leathley Cowell

1816 Francis (*Henry IV*), Baron Piffleberg (*Of Age Tomorrow*), Shears (*Love and Gout*), Martin (*Maid and the Magpie*), Bartholo (*Brother and Sister*), Dick (*My Spouse and I*), Motley (*Living in London*), Jeronymo (*Hunter of the Alps*), La Ruse (*Portfolio*), Paul Pounceby (*What's a Man of Fashion*), Whiskerandos, Squib (*Past Ten O'Clock*), Sir Benjamin Backbite, Dicky Gossip (*My Grandmother*), Barney (*Where to Find a Friend*), Endall (*Who's Who?*), Apothecary (*Romeo and Juliet*), Dominique (*Paul and Virginia*), Sir Simon Rochdale (*John Bull*), Chip (*Chip of the Old Block*), Sharp (*What Next?*), Flutterman (*Ella Rosenberg*), Bertram (*Lady of the Lake*), Nipperkin (*Rival Soldiers*), Patch (*Harlequin Hoax*), Hatcher (*King Charles I*), Lingo (*Agreeable Surprise*), Larole (*Young Hussar*), Pietro (*Bertram*), Marall (*New Way to Pay Old Debts*), Trot (*Town and Country*), Governor (*Frederick the Great*), Brisk (*Sharp and Flat*), Lubin Log (*Love, Law and Physic*), Acres, Myrtillo (*'Tis All a Farce*), Kecksey (*Irish Widow*), Juno (*Midas*), Dominie Sampson (*Guy Mannering*), Molino (*Blind Boy*), Thierry (*Charles the Bold*), Hecate (*Macbeth*), Goldfinch (*Road to Ruin*), Tiptoe (*Ways and Means*), Sambo (*Laugh When You Can*), Earl of Oxford (*Richard III*), Trudge (*Inkle and Yarico*), Lampedo (*Honeymoon*), Cecil Fitzharding (*Smiles and Tears*), Piero (*Tale of Mystery*), Darby (*Poor Soldier*), Crack (*Turnpike Gate*), Servitz (*Exile*), Orson (*Iron Chest*), Somno (*Sleep Walker*), Blunt (*George Barnwell*), Stephano (*Rugantino*),

Joseph Leathley Cowell *Continued*

Ithoruck (*Child of the Desert*), Squire Tallyho (*Fontainbleau*), Earl of Essex (*King John*), Arthur Maythorn (*Royal Oak*), Theodore (*Travellers Benighted*), Dr Pother (*Farmer's Wife*), Conrad (*Curfew*), Nicholas (*Midnight Hour*), Squire Richard, Varland (*West Indian*), Launcelot Gobbo.

Lionel Benjamin Rayner

1821   Dandie Dinmont (*Guy Mannering*), Lavigne (*Therese*), Bearward (*Modern Collegians*), Thomas (*Secret*), Jeremy (*Lady and the Devil*), Frank Oatland (*Cure for the Heart Ache*), Farmer Ashfield (*Speed the Plough*), M'Swill (*Vampire*), Tony Lumpkin, Nicol Jarvie (*Rob Roy*), Ralph Hempseed (*X.Y.Z.*), David (*Rivals*), Lissardo (*Wonder*), William (*Rosina*), Tyke (*School of Reform*).

1822   Fixture (*Roland for an Oliver*), Trick (*How to Die For Love*), Sam (*Raising the Wind*), Jocrisse (*Henri Quatre*), Robert Rafter (*Too Late for Dinner*), Murdoch (*Knight of Snowdoun*), Carronade (*Wife of Two Husbands*), Edward (*Haunted Tower*), Paddock (*My Spouse and I*), Ponder (*Man and Wife*), Dickory (*Spectre Bridegroom*), Zekiel Homespun (*Heir at Law*), 2nd Witch, Countryman (*Recruiting Serjeant*), Tester (*Suspicious Husband*), Sim (*Wild Oats*), Timothy Quaint (*Soldier's Daughter*), Timothy (*High Notions*), Sadi (*Mountaineers*), Geordy (*Robert the Bruce*), Jacky Hawbuck (*Town and Country*), Bearward (*Over the Bridge*), Yellowley (*Pirate*).

Samuel Phelps

1827   Lothair (*Miller and his Men*), Savile (*Belle's Stratagem*), Frank Rochdale (*John Bull*), Frederick (*Wonder*), Mat Muggins (*She Stoops to Conquer*), Seyward (*Hypocrite*), Welzien (*Exile*), Milford (*Road to Ruin*), Officer (*Slave*), Serjeant (*Guy Mannering*), Cassio, Matthew (*Warlock of the Glen*).

1828   Bates (*Gamester*), Everard (*Maid and the Magpie*), Louis (*Sergeant's Wife*), Oliver (*As You Like It*), Albany, Officer (*Illustrious Stranger*), Willoughby (*Dramatist*), Frederick Poppleton (*Too Late for Dinner*), Belville (*Laugh When You Can*), Clement (*Steward*), Danvers (*Love, Law and Physic*), Vernon (*Rob Roy*), Banks (*Wild Oats*), Homely (*Where Shall I Dine?*), Capt. Smith (*23 John Street*), Henry (*Speed the Plough*), Capt. Galliard (*X.Y.Z.*), Nokes (*Giovanni in London*), Sebastian (*Paul and Virginia*), Bertrand (*Foundling of the Forest*), Anhalt (*Lovers' Vows*), Murdock (*Lady of the Lake*), Marquis Lenoir

(*Father and Son*), Squire Chase (*Luke the Labourer*), Giaffer (*Child of the Desert*), George Barnwell, Starow (*Blind Boy*), Harcourt (*Country Girl*), De Courcy (*Haunted Tower*), Gesler (*William Tell*), Pizarro, Tom Swivel (*Robinson Crusoe*), Delpair (*Therese*), Lord Derwent (*Shepherd of Derwent Vale*), Smart (*Turnpike Gate*), Bayard (*Peter Smith*), Sir Lewis Beaumanoir (*Ivanhoe*), Somers (*Paul Pry*), Lovell (*Race for a Dinner*).

1830   Darnley (*Hypocrite*), Lively (*All at Coventry*), Albert (*Massaroni*), Douglas (*Wallace*), Arnaud (*Idiot Witness*), Rattlepate (*Sleep Walker*), Glanville (*Fifteen Years of a Drunkard's Life*), Frank Hardy (*Paul Pry*), Charles Franklin (*Sweethearts and Wives*), Aufidius, Bassanio, Crostree (*Black Ey'd Susan*), Manly (*Provok'd Husband*), Richmond, Lovejoke (*Wives by Advertisement*), Hans Hattock (*Inchcape Bell*), Vivid (*Daughter to Marry*), Marcus (*Green Ey'd Monster*), William Thompson, Caribert (*Bear Hunters*), Alfonso (*Masaniello*), Mayfly (*John Overy*), Duke of Argyle (*Heart of Midlothian*), Pilot, Juba (*Cato*), Rosambert (*Sonnambulist*), Hayston of Bucklaw (*Bride of Lammermuir*), Ambrose Gwinett, Burbage (*Shakespeare's Early Days*).

Frances Ternan

1845   Lady Teazle, Mrs Oakley, Lady Randolph, Rosalind, Maratina (*Don Caesar de Bazan*), Mrs Ferment (*School for Reform*), Lady Elinor Irwin (*Every One Has His Fault*), Bianca (*Spy of Venice*), Catharine (*Catharine and Petruchio*), Juliet, Charlotte (*Hypocrite*), Queen Elizabeth (*Richard III*), Ophelia, Cordelia, Desdemona, Lady Macbeth, Jessie Oatland (*Cure for the Heart Ache*), Amelia (*Hut on the Red Mountain*), Susan Greenwell (*Love's Frailties*), Juliana (*Honeymoon*).

Hermann Vezin

1850   Malcoff (*Wood Demon*), Jaques (*Cabin Boy*), Caithness (*Macbeth*), Juan (*Paul and Virginia*), Mayfield (*Flowers of the Forest*), Francis Bevil (*Cross Purposes*), Bishop (*Julian*), 2nd Traveller (*Henry IV*), Lord Ross (*Richard II*), Francisco (*Hamlet*), Mail Guard (*Box and Cox*), Col. Reichel (*Charles XII*), Sexton (*Much Ado*), John (*Haunted Inn*), Baptiste (*Leontine and Gerard the Pedlar*), Leonardo (*Merchant of Venice*).

APPENDIX C

List of Scenery and Properties Belonging to the Theatre

This list, among the Corporation records, is not dated but the mention of *Family Jars* puts it after 1822 when that piece was first brought out. It probably dates from John Wilkinson's new head lease in 1828.

Drop Scenery

   Green Curtain
   Act Drop
3 Grove Scenes
4 Chamber Scenes
2 Gothic Scenes
1 Saloon Scene
1 Library Scene
1 Prison
1 Garden
1 Cottage
1 Arch
1 Transparent Fire
1 Horizon
1 Illuminating Palace do.

Frame Scenery

1 Frame Chamber with Centre Doors
3 Frame Cottages
1 Frame Street
1 Frame Gothic with Centre Doors
1 Frame Chamber with Centre Windows
    & Fire Place
1 Panel Chamber with French Windows
    & Side Piece
1 Triumphal Arch
   Pizzaro Arches
   Castle Gates
2 Cut Woods
76 Wings
6 Sk. Borders

Set Scenery

1 Fancy Bridge
1 Rustic Bridge
4 Side Cottages
2 Stage Doors

Set Scenery

3 Short Planks
   Statue Horse
2 Set Pieces used in The Slave
   Boat Truck

Set Scenery Continued		*Set Scenery* Continued	
4	Balcony Houses		Grind Stone
2	Prison Doors		Joiners Bench
3	Rows of Waters		Paint Frame with Windlass
	Garden Walls	2	Pallet Boards
2	Open Caves	46	Paint Pots
8	Rock Pieces		Large Ship with rigging
2	Rows of Ground Pieces		Quarter deck
2	Waterfall Pieces		Set Tents
1	Row of Garden Palings		Dolphin
	Set Garden Pieces		Forum
6	Pair of Steps		
3	Ladders		
2	Long Planks		
3	Castle pieces		
2	Statue Figures		
3	Trap Covers		
5	Flower Trees		
2	Frame pieces for Family Jars		
	Horse Platform		

These scenes are in General Use

80 Pieces that are nameless
5 Drop Scenes with Lines to them

A List of Properties

	Rain Box and Thunder		
2	Thrones	1	Coffin
2	Banks		Roping and Iron Blocks
	Sofa		Large Bell
	Flap Screen		Sword Case
2	State Chairs		Great Drum
	Looking Glass		With sundry other properties
6	Common Chairs		
3	Gothic Chairs		

APPENDIX D

Lessees of the York Theatre

Mrs Thomas Keregan	1744
Joseph Baker	1744 – 1767
Tate Wilkinson	1767 – 1803
John Wilkinson	1803 – 1814
Robert J. Fitzgerald	1814 – 1818
Robert Mansel	1818 – 1820
Calvert for Mrs. Fitzgerald	1820 – 1821
Robert Mansel	1821 – 1824
Thomas Downe and Samuel Faulkner	1825 – 1826
Thomas Downe	1826 – 1827
Charles Cummins	1828 – 1829
Samuel Butler	1830
W. J. Hammond	1830 – 1832
O. E. Read	1833
Thomas Downe	1834 – 1839
Edward Hooper	1840 – 1842
John Langford Pritchard	1843 – 1850
John Caple	1850 – 1851
Henry Beverley	1851 August
John Caple	1852 – 1854
George Owen	1854 May
Sheridan Smith	1855 March
Edward Addison	1855 – 1856
Thomas Cooper Clifford	1856 – 1857
John Bellair	1857 – 1858
John Pritchard	1858 August
Frederick B. Egan	1859 – 1860
W. S. Thorne	1860 – 1864

Appendix D. Lessees of the York Theatre

John Coleman	1865 – 1875
William Alfred Waddington	1876 – 1883
Waddington and Sons	1883 – 1901
W. H. Waddington	1901 – 1910
Percy Hutchison	1911 – 1933
S. Weetham Crawshay	1933 – 1934
York Citizens' Theatre Company Ltd.	1934 – 1936
York Citizens' Theatre Trust	1936 –

NOTES

Prelude

1 The earliest reference to a performance is in 1378 but the plays are
thought to date from 1340-50.
2 L. Toulmin Smith: *York plays.* 1885.
E. K. Chambers: *Mediaeval stage.*
Records of Early English Drama: York,
ed. Alexandra Johnston and Margaret
Rogerson. Univ. of Toronto Press,
1979. 2 vols.
3 William Tydeman: *English medieval*
theatre 1400-1500. Chapter 4 gives alternative staging.
4 See Appendix A for list of visiting companies.
5 Rev. A. Raine: *Two notes on the History of*
the Drama in York. (Yorks Philosophical
Society Papers 1926). See Appendix A
for list of companies.
6 Minute Book, Vol. 27, f.116.
7 ibid., Vol. 28, f.26.
8 I owe all references to these Corporation Books to the kindness of the Rev.
Angelo Raine who generously lent me
his notes.
9 Minute Book, Vol. 28, f.40v.
10 J. P. Collier: *Memoirs of Edward Alleyn.*
1841, p.26. referred to in J. T. Murray:
English Dramatic Companies, 1558-1642.
Vol. 1, p.89.
11 Minute Book, Vol. 30, f.340.
12 ibid., Vol. 31, f.141v.
13 ibid., Vol. 32, f.10v.
14 ibid., Vol. 32, f.63.
15 ibid., f.156v.
16 ibid., Vol. 33. f.90v.
17 For Yarmouth *see* Glynne Wickham:
Early English Stages, II, i, p.166, and
Bristol K. M. Barker: *A Seventeenth*
Century Provincial Playhouse. (Theatre
Notebook, 1975.)
18 Minute Book, Vol. 33, f.173v, 187.
Printed by the Rev. A. Raine, op. cit.
19 Minute Book, Vol. 35, f.2v.
20 Cal. State Papers Dom. 1629-31, p. 59.
21 G. E. Bentley: *The Jacobean and Caroline*
Stage. Vol. I, p.273.

Chapter One

1 Cal. S. P. Dom. 1682, p. 536.
2 *Biographia Dramatica*, Vol. II, p.217.
3 Gent, *Historia Compendiosa Anglicana*,
1741, pref. p. viii.
4 Mention must be made too of John
Maxwell, a blind poet, who wrote several tragedies in verse which were not,
however, put on the stage.
5 The York production preceded that at
Lincoln's Inn Fields in April 1716.
6 Francis Drake, *Eboracum*, 1736, p. 324.
It was later used as a school and de-
molished in 1815.
7 *Biographia Dramatica*, Vol. 1, p. 178.
8 S. Rosenfeld, *Strolling Players* p.111,
and for his activities in Norwich and
Canterbury pp. 49 et seq., 218.
9 *Wandering Patentee*, 1795, Vol.II, p.202.
10 Though dated only T.15 it can safely
be assigned to 1727 since George II
came to the throne on June 11 and the
15 August fell on a Tuesday.
11 Edward Miller, player, was married to
Ellener Brown at St. Michael-le-Belfry
on Nov. 11, 1728. Register, p.159. Miss
Brunskill kindly gave me this reference.
12 Minster Library shown me by Miss
Brunskill.
13 *Archaeologia Aeliana*, 2nd series, Vol.
IV, p.236. Not the famous Henry
Woodward.
14 July 1732, p.871.
15 Vol. 42, p. 161.
16 *A Journey From London to Scarborough in*
Several Letters. [1736] 2nd ed., p. 42.
17 The tennis court is shown on *A New*
and Exact Plan of the City of York,
Haynes, 1748.
18 Temple Newsam rent books and papers, Leeds Library. Information
kindly supplied by the Archivist, Miss
Foster.
19 Op. cit., Vol. II, p.203.
20 The series in the *York Herald* office has
generously been put at my disposal.

21 Mention of King Charles's martyrdom gives the month as January and January 27 fell on a Tuesday in 1736.
22 Chetwood, *General History of the Stage*, 1749, p. 157.
23 Op. cit., Vol. I, pp.29-31.
24 Tom Davies, *Memoirs of the Life of David Garrick*, 1780, Vol. I, p. 36.
25 It was given at Covent Garden, April 1738.
26 Op. cit., Vol. 1, p.240.
27 *Wandering Patentee*, Vol. II, p.204.
28 Temple Newsam rent books cease after this year. Keregan had probably a ten years' lease which would have expired in 1744.
29 *York Courant*, Aug. 1, 1738.
30 Chetwood, op. cit., p. 196; see also *Biographia Dramatica*.
31 Ed. R. B. Cook, 1911.
32 Passages from this fragment are quoted in *Wandering Patentee*, Vol. 1. The original does not appear to be extant.
33 *Historical View of the Irish Stage*, 1788, Vol. I, p.213.
34 *Memoirs*, Vol. IV, p. 19.
35 *Dramatic Miscellanies*, 1784, Vol. III, p.136.
36 Publications of the York Parish Register Society, Vol. XI, p.255.
37 York Probate Office, Vol. 87, f.391.
38 When it is advertised as his in the *York Courant*, July 30.
39 Op. cit., p.255.
40 Her name does not appear in the Temple Newsam rent books until Michaelmas 1742.
41 Minster Library.
42 *A New and Exact Plan of the City of York*, Haynes, 1748.
43 *Hull Courant*, Aug. 21, 1744.
44 *Wandering Patentee*, Vol. I, p. 47.
45 Probably Henry Giffard, who had brought Garrick on the stage, and his wife who had been playing leads with Garrick at Drury Lane up till March 14. After that date they did not appear in London until September and may easily have spent a few weeks in York.
46 Minster bill, April 6.
47 *Leeds Mercury*, April 2, 1745.
48 Probably Downing's *Tricks of Harlequin; or, The Spaniard Outwitted*.
49 *Literary Anecdotes*, 1812. Vol. VI, p.421.
50 *Protestant York Courant*, York Public Library.
51 Wilkinson, *Memoirs*, Vol. IV, p. 36.
52 Welch, *Alumni Westmonasterienses*, 1852.
53 *York Courant*, October 28, 1768.
54 *Memoirs*, Vol. IV, p. 37.
55 *Wandering Patentee*, Vol. I, p.27.
56 Doran, *Annals of the English Stage*, Vol. II, p. 348; D.N.B. under Crawford.
57 *Account of the English Stage*, Vol. VII, p.353.
58 *Wandering Patentee*, Vol. I, p. 48.
59 *Memoirs*, Vol. II, p.10.
60 Morgan's version had appeared in 1754 at Covent Garden but was not printed until 1767; Garrick's at Drury Lane in 1756, printed 1758.
61 *Wandering Patentee*, Vol. I, p. 50.
62 ibid., p. 51.
63 *Wandering Patentee*.
64 George Benson, *The Theatre Royal and Drama in York*, 1911.
65 *York Courant*, Dec. 14.
66 York Public Library.
67 An actor in the Edinburgh Company.
68 Comedy by Frances Sheridan produced at Drury Lane, February 3, 1763.
69 Wilkinson, *Memoirs*, Vol. III, p.145.
70 *Wandering Patentee*, Vol. I, p. 50.
71 *Memoirs*, Vol. II, p. 6.
72 Op. cit., Vol. I, p.291.
73 *Retrospections of the Stage*, 1830, Vol. I, p.171.
74 *Memoirs*, Vol. III, p.135.
75 ibid., Vol. IV, p.24.
76 *York Courant;* Wilkinson gives the date as May 17.
77 *Wandering Patentee*, Vol. I, p. 33.
78 *The Itinerant*, 1808, Vol. I, p.217.
79 *Wandering Patentee*, Vol. I, pp. 34-6, 67.
80 *Gentleman's Magazine*, April 1764, p.190.
81 Minster Library playbill, May 19.

Chapter Two

1 Proceedings of the Committees on Leases, 1704-1813. The lease, among the Corporation records, is dated January 5, 1765. It is endorsed renewed to Metcalfe and Thos. Wilson.
2 *Memoirs*, Vol. III, p.224.
3 *Poems Chiefly Pastoral*, 1771, 2nd. ed., p.179; *York Courant*, Jan. 8.
4 *Memoirs*, Vol. IV, p.11.
5 *Memoirs*, Vol. IV, p. 59 et seq.
6 *Memoirs*, Vol. IV, p. 67.
7 *Wandering Patentee*, Vol. I, p. 45.

8 Actually Arne's version was given at Covent Garden.

9 *Wandering Patentee*, Vol. I, p. 52.

10 Winston, *Theatric Tourist*, p. 36.

11 Parker, *Who's Who in the Theatre*. A confusion with James Robertson has been straightened out by J. M. Bulloch, *Notes & Queries*, 1932, pp. 398, 418, 434.

12 Called *Alexander and Statira, or the Death of Bucephalus* in the *Biographia Dramatica*. Another *Death of Bucephalus* by Ralph Schomberg is listed as given at Edinburgh c.1765, so that Wallis may have merely adapted another burlesque.

13 *York Courant*, March 24.

14 Unless otherwise stated information is from playbills in the York Public or Minster Libraries or the British Museum.

15 Linnecar, *Miscellaneous Works*, 1789 says the comedy was brought out at Oram's benefit on February 6, 1769, but Oram's benefit was on February 4 in 1769 and no new play was given at it. The title, *The Double Marriage; or the Husbands Reform'd* is a suitable alternative one to the *Plotting Wives*, and must refer to this play.

16 *Wandering Patentee*, Vol. I, p. 58.

17 ibid., p. 68. Possibly the same Bryan who was prompter in 1762.

18 ibid., p. 61.

19 Where she became the first wife of John Palmer, lessee of the theatre and of mail coach fame. The D. N. B. article on him states that his first wife was unknown. Wilkinson, *Memoirs*, Vol. IV, p.19.

20 *Wandering Patentee*, Vol. I, p. 56; *Memoirs*, Vol. III, p. 64.

21 J. C. Dibdin, *Annals of the Edinburgh Stage*, p.172.

22 Public General Acts, 9 GEO. III, p.715.

23 *Wandering Patentee*, Vol. I, p.73.

24 ibid., p. 63.

25 ibid.; James Robertson, *Poems*.

26 *Wandering Patentee*, Vol. I, p. 63; *York Courant*, March 21.

27 *Wandering Patentee*, Vol. I, p. 65.

28 Op. cit., Vol. II, p.23.

29 *York Courant*, Aug. 15, 1769.

30 *Wandering Patentee*, Vol. I, p. 65.

31 ibid., p. 60.

32 ibid., p. 68.

33 ibid., p. 61.

34 York's Architectural Soc. T. P. Cooper, *Some Old York Inns*.

35 *York Courant*, Jan. 9.

36 *Biographia Dramatica*.

37 *Wandering Patentee*, Vol. I, pp.73-2.

38 York Probate Office, Will Vol.114, f.275.

39 *York Courant*, Apr. 3.

40 Odell, *Shakespeare from Betterton to Irving*, Vol. II, p.33.

41 *Wandering Patentee*, Vol. I, p.76.

42 *York Courant*, Dec. 25, 1770.

43 *Diary of Sylas Neville*, ed. Basil Cozens-Hardy, 1950, p.185.

44 *Wandering Patentee*, Vol. I, p.80.

45 ibid., p.77.

46 ibid., p. 96.

47 ibid., p. 91.

48 *York Courant*, Feb. 19, March 5.

49 *York Courant*, Apr. 9, 16.

50 D. N. B.; Clark Russell, *Representative Actors*, p.142.

51 *Memoirs of that Celebrated Comedian Thomas Weston*, 1776, p. 33.

52 *Memoirs* Vol. IV, p.259.

53 *Wandering Patentee*, Vol. I, p.81.

54 D. N. B.; Clark Russell, op. cit., p.119; Doran, op. cit., Vol. II. p. 363; *An Apology for the Life of George Anne Bellamy*, 1785, Vol. IV, p.206.

55 *York Courant*, Jan. 15; *Wandering Patentee*, Vol. I, p.236.

56 *York Courant*, Feb. 19.

57 This does not seem to be otherwise known.

58 *York Courant*, April 9.

59 ibid., March 19.

60 ibid., p.87.

61 He was subsequently prompter at the Haymarket and the Theatre Royal, Dublin. His wife and daughter were great favourites on the Irish stage. He died in 1809. See D. N. B.

62 ibid., p.86; *York Courant*, July 9, 16; Hitchcock, op. cit., Vol. II, p.225.

63 ibid., p.85; *York Courant*, July 9.

64 *Wandering Patentee*, Vol. I, p.103.

65 *York Courant*, Sept. 3.

66 *York Courant*, Dec. 24, 1771.

67 *Wandering Patentee*, Vol. I, p.117.

68 *Wandering Patentee*, Vol. I, p.122 et seq.

69 ibid., Vol. I. p.152; *York Courant*, May 12, 1772.

70 *Wandering Patentee*, Vol. I, p.119.

71 *York Courant*, Jan. 18, May 5.

72 Wilkinson says (*Wandering Patentee*, Vol. I, p.166) that it was first presented in 1778, but it is advertised in the *York Courant* Feb. 18 for performance on Feb. 22, 1772. It may have been postponed; on the other hand Wilkinson is often inaccurate.

73 Dalton's was brought out at Drury Lane. Nicoll gives 16/10/1773 for the date of Colman's version at Covent Garden and Genest 17/9/1772, but if it was given in York on 4/4/1772 it must have been seen there earlier.
74 *Wandering Patentee*, Vol. I, pp.163-5.
75 *Thespian Dictionary*.
76 ibid., under Charles Murray.
77 *Wandering Patentee*, Vol. I, p.173; Gilliland, *Dramatic Mirror*, Vol. II, p.822; Doran, op. cit., Vol. III, p.266.
78 *Wandering Patentee*, Vol. I, p.174; *York Courant*, May 7; Hitchcock, op. cit. Vol. II, p.239.
79 *Wandering Patentee*, Vol. II, p. 38.
80 Holograph letter dated May 11, 1773, Brander Matthews Dramatic Museum, Columbia University.
81 *Works* of William Mason, 1811, Vol. II, p.178.
82 *York Chronicle*, Mar. 12; *Wandering Patentee*, Vol. I, p.166.
83 *York Chronicle*, Jan. 29, Feb. 12.
84 *Wandering Patentee*, Vol. I, p.175.
85 Vol. I. p.167.
86 *York Chronicle*, Jan. 22.
87 ibid., Feb. 12.
88 ibid., May 7.
89 *York Chronicle*, Aug. 13.
90 *Wandering Patentee*, Vol. I, pp.175-6.
91 ibid.
92 ibid., p.188.
93 Copy in the Minster Library.
94 *York Chronicle*, March 11, April 22.
95 ibid., March 4.
96 D. N. B.
97 *Wandering Patentee*, Vol. I, p.174.
98 *York Chronicle*, Feb. 18.
99 *Wandering Patentee*, Vol. I, p.199.
100 ibid., p.202.
101 ibid.
102 ibid., pp.203-209. Minster Library playbills.
103 Powell became co-manager with Whiteley but soon left him to join Younger at Manchester and Liverpool.
104 *General Magazine and Impartial Review*, Nov. 1788.
105 See Appendix B for list of his rôles.
106 Minster Library playbill, Jan. 10.
107 *Biographia Dramatica*.
108 *York Chronicle*, April 7.
109 *York Chronicle*, Feb. 24.
110 Ante, pp.62-3.
111 *York Chronicle*, March 31.
112 Holograph letter from Leeds, July 11, in Harvard College Library, Theatre Collection.
113 *Wandering Patentee*, Vol. I, p.210. Wilkinson says she played Juliet but this rôle is given to Mrs. Hudson in the playbill.
114 ibid., p.212.
115 I have been unable to trace the advertisement.
116 *Wandering Patentee*, Vol. I, pp.218, 300.
117 *Wandering Patentee*, Vol. I, p.218; Minster Library playbills; *Memoirs of the Life of Mrs. Gumbel, later Wells*, 1811, I, 27.
118 *Wandering Patentee*, Vol. I, p.223.
119 ibid., p.224; original hand-bill in Minster Library.
120 ibid., p.219. She had formerly been Mrs. Vernon and was later to become Mrs. Bannister. For the strange story of her marriages, see *Theatrical Biography*, 1772, Vol. II, p.27.
121 ibid., p.227.
122 *Wandering Patentee*, Vol. I, p.209.
123 ibid., p.213; playbill Minster Library, Feb. 27.
124 *Memoirs*, Vol. II, p.230.
125 Malahide Papers, Vol. II, p.291.
126 *Wandering Patentee*, Vol. I, p.228.
127 ibid., p.229.
128 York Public Library.
129 *Wandering Patentee*, Vol. I, p.233. He went back to sea, then joined the Norwich company where he resumed his real name of Murray. He became a favourite in the comic line at Bath and was engaged at Covent Garden in 1796 where he specialised in old men.
130 ibid., p.243.
131 *Retrospections of the Stage*, Vol. I, p.175.
132 Oxberry, *Dramatic Biography*.
133 *Wandering Patentee*, Vol. I, p.244.
134 ibid., p.249.
135 ibid., p.253 et seq.
136 Wilkinson Account Book.
137 *Wandering Patentee*, Vol. I, p.246.
138 ibid., Vol. II, p.13; Wilkinson Account Book.
139 *York Courant*, March 18.
140 *Wandering Patentee*, Vol. I, p.248.
141 Minster Library bill, March 10.
142 ibid., Jan. 21, April 15; *York Courant* Feb. 4, May 13.
143 *Wandering Patentee*, Vol. I, p.251.
144 *Wandering Patentee*, Vol. I, p.257. Minster Library playbills.
145 Op. cit. Vol. I, p.178.

146 Wilkinson says Bernard was not engaged but Bernard himself and the playbills testify to the contrary.
147 Op. cit. Vol. I., p.168.
148 Op. cit. Vol. I., p.180.
149 *Wandering Patentee*, Vol. I, p.277.
150 ibid., pp.277, 303.
151 ibid., p.274.
152 ibid.
153 ibid., p.273.
154 ibid., p.275.
155 ibid., p. 304.
156 *Wandering Patentee*, Vol. I. p.299; *York Courant*, Feb. 21.
157 ibid., p. 300.
158 *Wandering Patentee*, Vol. II, p.12.
159 *York Courant*, April 14; *Wandering Patentee*, Vol. I, p. 303.
160 *Wandering Patentee*, Vol. I, p.236.
161 *York Courant*, March 10.
162 ibid., Feb. 3.
163 ibid., Mar. 3.
164 ibid., Jan. 20.
165 March 17, Minster Library.
166 There is however an additional item: Cash above 1st Sub. £6.17.6.
167 *Wandering Patentee*, Vol. I, p. 305.
168 Herschel Baker, *John Philip Kemble*, 1942; p. 37 from letter in Folger Library.
169 *Wandering Patentee*, Vol. II, p.11 gives 19th but see Minster Library playbill; Boaden, *Memoirs of the Life of J. P. Kemble*, 1825, Vol. I, p.20.
170 Oxberry, *Dramatic Biography*, Vol. I, p.109.
171 See Appendix B for list of his rôles.
172 *Wandering Patentee*, Vol. II, p.19.
173 ibid., pp.14, 34.
174 ibid., p.15.
175 *York Courant*, Jan. 12.
176 *York Courant*, Jan. 14; Minster Library playbill.
177 Minster Library playbills, Jan. 20, 26.
178 Printed in his *Fugitive Pieces*, 1780.
179 Minster Library playbill, March 6.
180 *Wandering Patentee*, Vol. II, p.12.
181 Op. cit. pp. 45-6.
182 Boaden, *Memoirs of the Life of J. P. Kemble*, 1825, Vol. I, p.24.
183 *New Monthly Magazine*, 1832; H. Baker, op. cit.
184 *York Courant*, March 30, February 9.
185 *York Courant*, April 13; Minster Library playbill, Aug. 28.
186 *Wandering Patentee*, Vol. II, pp. 56, 76.
187 *Memoirs of Mrs. Inchbald*, Vol. I, p. 95.
188 *Wandering Patentee*, Vol. II, p. 64.
189 Boaden, *J. P. Kemble*, Vol. I, p. 33.
190 *Wandering Patentee*, Vol. II, pp.71, 84-5.

Chapter Three

1 For their rôles see Appendix B
2 *Wandering Patentee*, Vol. II, p.80.
3 *Wandering Patentee*, Vol. II, p.77.
4 Mrs. Inchbald, ms. diary, Folger Library under Aug. 24, 1780.
5 ibid., p. 91; Ireland, *Records of the New York Stage*, 1866-7, Vol. I, p.168.
6 ibid., p. 92.
7 *Thespian Dictionary*.
8 *Wandering Patentee*, Vol. II, p.77.
9 Mrs. Inchbald, ms. diary, March 8-17.
10 May 16.
11 *York Courant*, April 11; Minster Library playbill, April 15. The event took place in 1778.
12 *York Courant*, May 2.
13 *Wandering Patentee*, Vol. II, p. 90.
14 ibid., pp. 96, 101.
15 ibid., p. 98.
16 *Wandering Patentee*, Vol. II, p. 97.
17 Boaden, *Memoirs of Mrs. Inchbald*, Vol. 1, p.105.
18 *Wandering Patentee*, Vol. II, p.102.
19 ibid., p.103.
20 ibid., p.101.
21 *The Itinerant*, Vol. I, p.261.
22 *Wandering Patentee*, Vol. II, p.11.
23 *York Courant*, March 27. For rôles see Appendix B.
24 *The Kembles*, Vol. I, p.81.
25 *Wandering Patentee*, Vol. II, p.105.
26 Wilkinson says that even the best actors could not claim attention for the last act, which only too easily aroused laughter.
27 *York Courant*, May 8.
28 ibid., April 10.
29 ibid., Feb. 6, 13; March 6; May 1.
30 Minster Library playbills, April 19, 24, 26.
31 *York Courant*, Jan. 2.
32 ibid., Jan. 9.
33 See *Yorkshire Magazine*. 1786, p.229 for a complete list of his parts in York.
34 Baker, op. cit., p. 62.
35 *Wandering Patentee*, Vol. II, p.118.
36 Minster Library playbills, Aug. 21, 29.
37 D. N. B. says he was first heard of as an actor at the Capel Street Theatre, Dublin. For rôles see Appendix B.

38 *Wandering Patentee*, Vol. II, p.126.
39 Minster Library playbill, April 30.
40 *York Courant*, Jan. 29, Feb. 12.
41 *Wandering Patentee*, Vol. II, p.125.
42 *York Courant*, March 26.
43 *York Courant*, April 23; Minster Library playbill, March 9.
44 Minster Library playbill, May 4.
45 ibid., May 18.
46 ibid., April 20.
47 Minster Library handbill, May 4.
48 *Wandering Patentee*, Vol. II, pp.131, 132.
49 ibid., p.142.
50 ibid., p.143.
51 ibid., Vol. II, pp.138, 143; D. N. B.
52 ibid., p.132 et seq.; Oxberry, *Dramatic Biography*, Vol. I, p.198.
53 Wilkinson is said to have suggested the name to her because she had crossed the water. Bernard, op. cit. I, 234.
54 ibid., p.141.
55 ibid., p.144.
56 *York Courant*, Aug. 20.
57 Account Books.
58 Inchbald letters, York Public Library.
59 Minster Library playbill, Jan. 23.
60 *Wandering Patentee*, Vol. II, p.149.
61 Minster Library playbill, March 10; Wilkinson says as Selima, *Wandering Patentee*, Vol. II, p.150.
62 For rôles see Appendix B.
63 *York Courant*, Feb. 18, April 1; Minster Library playbill, March 18; for the Stockwell Ghost, see Sacheverell Sitwell, *Poltergeist*, pp.132, 289.
64 Minster Library playbill, March 10.
65 Minster Library playbills, Jan. 28, 29.
66 ibid., March 15.
67 *Wandering Patentee*, Vol. II, p.151.
68 *Wandering Patentee*, Vol. II, p.155.
69 *York Courant*, May 11.
70 *York Courant*, Feb. 17, March 2, 9; Minster Library playbill, Feb. 19.
71 *Wandering Patentee*, Vol. II, p.164.
72 ibid., p.156.
73 *York Courant*, March 30.
74 For rôles see Appendix B.
75 *Wandering Patentee*, Vol. II, p.171.
76 *York Courant*, Feb. 24, Mar. 16, April 27.
77 A length was 42 lines.
78 *Harlequin Philosopher* according to the playbill.
79 *Wandering Patentee*, Vol. II, p.166.
80 *York Courant*, Aug. 31.
81 cf. List Appendix C.
82 *York Courant*, Nov. 9.

83 *Wandering Patentee*, Vol. II, p.181.
84 Minster Library.
85 *Wandering Patentee*, Vol. II, p.174 et seq.
86 *York Courant*, Jan. 25, says in her 15th year. D. N. B. says she was born about 1768.
87 See Appendix B.
88 *Wandering Patentee*, Vol. II, p.183.
89 Bernard, op. cit., Vol. I, p.117.
90 *Wandering Patentee*, Vol. II, p.187. *York Courant*, April 19, 26, May 3.
91 Minster Library playbill, May 3.
92 *Wandering Patentee*, Vol. II, p.182. Minster Library playbills, Feb. 5, 7, 8, 10, 12; *York Courant*, Feb. 15.
93 Minster Library playbill, Jan. 20.
94 ibid., May 21.
95 ibid., Feb. 22, May 12.
96 *York Courant* March 29; Minster Library playbill May 5; *Wandering Patentee*, Vol. II, p.178.
97 *Wandering Patentee*, Vol. II, p.192.
98 ibid., p.190.
99 ibid., p.192.
100 *York Courant*, March 22.
101 *Wandering Patentee*, Vol. II, pp.188, 193.
102 ibid., p.195.
103 ibid., p.199.
104 ibid., p.236.
105 ibid., p.248.
106 ibid., p.250 et seq.
107 ibid., p.255.
108 ibid., p.248.
109 ibid., p.246. For rôles see Appendix B.
110 ibid., p.258.
111 See ante, pp.27-9.
112 Minster playbill, May 20.
113 *Wandering Patentee*, Vol. II, p.259.
114 ibid., p.259; *York Courant*, May 30.
115 ibid., p.260; Minster Library playbill, May 27.
116 ibid., p.212
117 Minster Library playbill, Jan. 26.
118 *Wandering Patentee*, Vol. II, p.246.
119 ibid., Vol. I, p.238; Vol. II, p.249.
120 Minster Library playbills, Feb. 18, Mar. 9.
121 Bill, Society for Theatre Research.
122 York Library playbill, Aug. 24.
123 *Yorkshire Magazine*, 1786, p.255.
124 *York Courant*, Aug. 1.
125 *Wandering Patentee*, Vol. III, p.7.
126 D. N. B.; Wm. Dunlap, *Life of G. F. Cooke*, 1815, p. 40; *Wandering Patentee*, Vol. III, p.22.
127 *Dramatic Biography*, Vol. IV, p.20; post, p.214.

128 *Wandering Patentee,* Vol. III, p.23; letter in possession of Miss Warman.
129 ibid., p.14.
130 ibid., p.25.
131 ibid., p.22; D. N. B.
132 ibid., p.26.
133 ibid., p.20; A. E. Wilson, *Christmas Pantomime,* p.116.
134 ibid., p.31.
135 ibid., p.40.
136 Gilliland, op. cit., Vol. II, p.759.
137 *Wandering Patentee,* Vol. III, p.32.
138 ibid., p.40.
139 ibid., p.42.
140 ibid., p.44.
141 ibid., p.49.
142 Vol. I, p.307.
143 *Wandering Patentee,* Vol. III, p.53.
144 ibid., p.53.
145 Copy in the Minster Library.
146 Minster Library playbill, March 10.
147 ibid., March 25.
148 ibid., March 11.
149 *Wandering Patentee,* Vol. III, p.29.
150 For list see Appendix B.
151 *Wandering Patentee,* Vol. III, pp.54,56.
152 ibid., Vol. III, p. 55.
153 ibid., Vol. III, p. 58.
154 ibid., p. 67.
155 Wilkinson, *Memoirs,* Vol. IV, p.128.
156 *Wandering Patentee,* Vol. III, p. 67.
157 For rôles see Appendix B.
158 *Wandering Patentee,* Vol. III, p.73.
159 ibid., p.74 and Minster Library playbills.
160 ibid., p.75.
161 W. Clark Russell, *Representative Actors,* p.157.
162 *Wandering Patentee,* Vol. III, p.77; Minster Library playbills.
163 York Library playbill, April 2.
164 ibid., Apr. 28.
165 York Library.
166 *Wandering Patentee,* Vol. III, p.85.
167 Minster Library playbills; Wilkinson, *Wandering Patentee,* Vol. III, p.87 says his first appearance was as Mirabel so that it is possible he never appeared in *The Natural Son.*
168 Dibdin, *Annals of the Edinburgh Stage,* p.202.
169 *Wandering Patentee,* Vol. III, pp.85, 87.
170 ibid., p.90.
171 *Wandering Patentee,* Vol. III, p.93.
172 ibid., p.101.
173 ibid.
174 ibid.; Minster Library playbill, March 4.
175 ibid., p.102; Minster Library playbill, May 11.

176 *York Chronicle,* May 28; Minster Library playbill, Feb. 10, 1791.
177 ibid., April 16; *Wandering Patentee,* Vol. III, p.101.
178 Doran, op. cit., pp.211, 252.
179 *Wandering Patentee,* Vol. III, p.105.
180 Minster Library playbill May 20, says she was to act Lady Townly but this may have been altered at the last moment.
181 *York Chronicle,* May 2.
182 Minster Library playbill, April 18.
183 Minster Library playbill, Mar. 2.
184 *York Chronicle,* Mar. 26.
185 ibid., Mar. 5.
186 ibid., Mar. 19; Minster Library playbill, Mar. 11.
187 Minster Library playbill, April 20.
188 *York Chronicle,* April 2, 9.
189 *Wandering Patentee,* Vol. III, p.106.
190 ibid., p.110. Wilkinson is actually referring to her performance of these rôles in Pontefract but doubtless the same applied to her acting of them in York.
191 ibid., pp.111, 112.
192 ibid., pp.111, 113.
193 Ante, p.125.
194 ibid., pp.113, 124.
195 ibid., p.132.
196 ibid., p.126.
197 ibid., p.216.
198 ibid., p.127.
199 ibid., p.129.
200 *York Chronicle,* March 4.
201 Minster Library playbill, March 31.
202 *Wandering Patentee,* Vol. III, p.131.
203 ibid., p.218.
204 ibid., p.237.
205 ibid., p.262.
206 ibid., p.265.
207 *Reminiscences,* 1826, Vol. II, p.10.
208 Minster Library playbill.
209 *Wandering Patentee,* Vol. III, p.232.
210 Op. cit., Vol. II, p.8.
211 *Wandering Patentee,* Vol. IV, p.6.
212 ibid., p.15.
213 ibid., p.19.
214 See Appendix B. for Cherry's and Elliston's rôles.
215 G. Raymond, *Life of Elliston,* 1857, p.13.
216 *Wandering Patentee,* Vol. IV, p.17.
217 ibid., p.13.
218 ibid., p.19.
219 Minster Library playbill, March 22.
220 *Wandering Patentee,* Vol. IV, p.20; *York Chronicle,* April 6; Minster Library playbill April 12.

221 ibid., p.35.
222 ibid., p.18 referring to its presentation in Hull; *York Chronicle*, Mar. 2.
223 ibid., pp.113, 121.
224 *York Chronicle*, Mar. 21.
225 ibid., April 20.
226 *Wandering Patentee*, Vol. IV, p.60.
227 *York Chronicle*, April 6; Brit. Mus. playbill, April 17.
228 *Wandering Patentee*, Vol. IV, p.20. He played Wolsey again in 1796.
229 D. N. B.
230 *Wandering Patentee*, Vol. IV, p.38 et seq. He played it again in 1800.
231 ibid., p.42.
232 ibid., pp.111, 118.
233 ibid., p.49.

Chapter Four

1 *Wandering Patentee*, Vol. IV, p.63.
2 *York Courant*, Apr. 8.
3 Jan. 31.
4 *Wandering Patentee*, Vol. IV, p.55.
5 Op. cit., Vol. III, p.75.
6 *Wandering Patentee*, Vol. IV, p.64; York Library playbill.
7 ibid., Vol. IV, pp.57, 64.
8 York Library playbill.
9 ibid., May 4.
10 *Wandering Patentee*, Vol. IV, p.59.
11 York Library playbill, May 18; *York Courant*, May 27.
12 *Wandering Patentee*, Vol. IV, p.66.
13 ibid., p.67.
14 *York Chronicle*, Aug. 19.
15 *Wandering Patentee*, Vol. IV, p.145 et seq.
16 York Library playbill, Mar. 25.
17 *Wandering Patentee*, Vol. IV, p.164.
18 York Library playbill, Apr. 22.
19 *Wandering Patentee*, Vol. IV, p.151.
20 ibid., p.152 et seq.
21 ibid., p.164; York Library playbill, Apr. 24.
22 ibid., p.166.
23 ibid., p.168.
24 York Library playbill, Aug. 16.
25 *Wandering Patentee*, Vol. IV, p.170.
26 *York Courant*, Aug. 16.
27 *Wandering Patentee*, Vol. IV, p.178.
28 ibid., p.203; York Library playbill, May 9.
29 ibid., p.197.
30 ibid., p.199.
31 Minster Library playbills.
32 *Wandering Patentee*, Vol. IV, p.227.
33 York Library playbills, April 28, May 2.
34 ibid., March 14.
35 Minster Library playbills.
36 See ante, p.91.
37 For Emery's rôles see Appendix B.
38 G. Raymond, *Life of Elliston*, 1857, p.14.
39 Minster Library playbill, April 9. Unless otherwise stated information is from this collection.
40 Feb. 20.
41 British Museum playbill, Aug. 20.
42 For rôles see Appendix B; *Memoirs of Charles Mathews*, Vol. I, p.383.
43 May 1797, p.312.
44 York Library playbill, April 8.
45 *Monthly Mirror*, May 1797, p.312; D.N.B. under Davison; Oxberry, op. cit., Vol. I, p.52. For rôles see Appendix B.
46 *York Herald*, March 11.
47 Advertised in 1796 but evidently not played.
48 York Library playbill, March 4.
49 Autograph letter in the Garrick Club, kindly copied by Sir St. Vincent Troubridge, Bt.
50 August 1797, p.114.
51 For rôles of Emery and Maria Duncan see Appendix B.
52 Minster Library playbill, Apr. 22.
53 May 19.
54 *York Herald*, March 10.
55 ibid., July 1; *Monthly Mirror*, July 1798, p.49.
56 Holograph letters in Harvard College Theatre Collection; *Memoirs of Charles Mathews*, 1838, Vol. I, p.204 et seq.
57 *Monthly Mirror*, Dec. 1798, Jan. 1799.
58 ibid., October 1806.
59 ibid., Aug. 1798, p.119.
60 December, 1798, p.372. *Memoirs of Charles Mathews*, p.240.
61 *Memoirs*, p.371.
62 *Monthly Mirror*, Jan. 1799, p.49 with reference to his performances at Hull; Burton, *A Pasquinade on the Performers of the York Company*, 1801.
63 Dec. 1798, p.372.
64 ibid.
65 Benjamin Thompson was a native of Hull.
66 Minster Library playbill, March 9.
67 *York Herald*, March 2.
68 *Monthly Mirror*, Aug. 1799.
69 ibid.
70 Minster Library playbill, May 20.
71 *York Herald*, March 15.

72 York Library playbill, March 8.
73 Holograph letter, Harvard Library Theatre Collection.
74 D. N. B.; Oxberry, op. cit. Vol. IV, p.152.
75 See ante, p.107.
76 *Memoirs of the Green Room*, pp.244-5.
77 Dec. 1800.
78 *York Herald*, Feb. 19.
79 ibid., Mar. 7.
80 Dec. 1800; Jan. 1801.
81 *Memoirs*, Vol. I, p.312.
82 Denman married Eliza Close at Doncaster on Nov. 2, 1800. *York Herald*, Nov. 8.
83 *Memoirs*, Vol. I, p.380.
84 *Monthly Mirror*, April; Mathews, *Memoirs*, Vol. I, p.312.
85 *York Herald*, Feb. 28.
86 York bill, May 16.
87 July 25.
88 Feb. 1802, p.138; March 1802, p.205.
89 Mathews, *Memoirs*, Vol. I. p.337.
90 British Museum playbill.
91 Feb, March, 1802.
92 Playbill, Harvard Theatre Collection.
93 British Museum playbill, May 26.
94 D. N. B.; *Life and Reminiscences of E. L. Blanchard*, 1891, Vol. I, p.1.
95 *Memoirs*, Vol. 1, p.344 et seq.
96 Holograph letter, Enthoven Collection.
97 D. N. B.; *Memoirs of the Green Room*, p.138.
98 Holograph letters in Harvard Theatre Collection.
99 There is no record of his having played this rôle before May.
100 March 4, 1826.
101 Holograph letters, Harvard Theatre Collection.
102 For rôles see Appendix B.
103 March 5.
104 D. N. B.; holograph letter Harvard Theatre Collection. According to the *York Herald*, March 31, 1804, her sister was the daughter of Smith, Treasurer at Bath, and a former actor in the company 1780-6, and Wilkinson in his letter sends his compliments to Mr. Smith. Mrs. Bartley's maiden name is variously said to have been Williamson and O'Shaunessy, the Smith being adopted after her mother's second marriage with an actor in the Salisbury company. Sarah was probably Smith's step-daughter by his second wife. For rôles see Appendix B.
105 *Era Almanack,* 1892, p.41.

106 *York Herald*, April 30.
107 Oxberry, op. cit. Vol. II, p.112; *Monthly Mirror,* Sept. 1804, p.209.
108 Mathews, op. cit., p.415, et seq.
109 August 27.
110 York Probate Office, 148, f.87.
111 Mathews, op. cit., p.380.
112 Op. cit., Vol. I, p.291.
113 Delap, op. cit., p.177.
114 *The Itinerant*, Vol. III, p.112.
115 Bernard, op. cit., Vol. I, p.152.

Chapter Five

1 Ms. note on playbill.
2 June 9.
3 ibid., Mar 31; *Monthly Mirror,* Sept. 1804, p.209.
4 *Biographia Dramatica; York Herald,* March 28.
5 *York Herald*, April 2.
6 ibid., May 4.
7 ibid., Aug. 10.
8 Playbill, Aug. 19.
9 Enthoven Collection, Theatre Museum, Covent Garden, Oct. 2, 1805.
10 Hull Library Ms. *Lives of Actors.*
11 *York Herald*, Nov. 9, 16, 23.
12 ibid., April 5, June 14.
13 *York Herald*, April 5; *Monthly Mirror,* Dec. 1805, p.409.
14 *York Herald*, May 29.
15 ibid., April 5.
16 ibid., July 26, Aug. 9.
17 ibid., Aug. 30.
18 Oxberry, op. cit., Vol. II, p.113.
19 Harvard Theatre Collection playbills.
20 *York Courant,* May 11.
21 Cf. ante, p.178.
22 *York Herald*, July 18; playbills Harvard. She returned in 1809, 1812.
23 *York Herald*, Nov. 19.
24 *A Description of York*, p.69.
25 In Sotheran's *Guide for Strangers*, 1843, the height of the stage is given as 44 ft.
26 Oxberry, op. cit., Vol. II, p.114.
27 ibid., Vol. IV, p.152.
28 *York Herald*, Feb. 3.
29 *Monthly Mirror,* July 1810, p.78.
30 Ireland, op. cit., Vol. I, p.130; ante pp.171, 173.
31 July 1810, p.78.
32 March 23.
33 *York Herald*, Sept. 7. Holograph letters of Mathews in possession of Miss Hartnoll who kindly allowed me to see them.

34 *York Chronicle*, Oct. 16, 1824; *York Herald*, March 7, 1812.
35 He married Miss S. de Camp.
36 *Memoirs of the Green Room*, p.67. Stirling was an assumed name. She was really Mrs. Smith but had been deserted by her husband.
37 See Appendix B.
38 Ms. notes in Hull Library, quoting from a playbill of November 9, state that the owners of free tickets agreed to take it over and allow Wilkinson an annuity and free benefit.
39 *York Herald*, May 14.
40 Playbill, Harvard Theatre Collection.
41 J. L. Cowell, *Thirty Years Passed Among the Players;* the Rev. R. D. Clark writes that his middle name in the burial register of St. John's, Wakefield looks like Jerrold but may be Jerald.
42 *York Herald*, July 23.
43 Corporation Leases, 424.
44 House Books, 48, f.127.
45 May 20.
46 May 25.
47 Theatrical Fund instituted at the Theatre-Royal in York, July 22, 1815. Hull; printed by Myrton Hamilton, Silver-Street.
48 *Description of York*, 1816 and 1818.
49 *Thirty Years Passed among the Players*, 1845.
50 D. N. B.
51 Appendix B.
52 Minster Library playbill, April 16.
53 ibid., May 16.
54 March 13.
55 J. N. Ireland, op. cit., Vol. I, p.349.
56 *York Chronicle*, June 26; *York Herald* June 28.
57 March 21, York Library.
58 *York Herald*, April 19.
59 ibid., Aug. 23.
60 ibid., June 28.
61 J. N. Ireland, op. cit., Vol. I, p.375.
62 *York Herald*, May 9.
63 Senior, *Old Wakefield Theatre*, p.85; information kindly supplied by the Rev. R. O. Clark.
64 Minster Library bill, July 13.
65 *York Herald*, July 28.
66 Vol. II, p.465.
67 Op. cit., Vol. I, p.179.
68 Advertised on a playbill March 10, 1818 but presumably not performed.
69 *York Herald*, May 22.
70 B. W. Proctor, *Life of Edmund Kean*, 1835, Vol. I, p.156; H. N. Hillibrand, *Edmund Kean*, 1933, p.67.

71 *York Herald*, July 10, 24.
72 Letter to his wife, Aug. 14, in possession of Miss Hartnoll.
73 York Library bill, Apr. 25.
74 *York Chronicle*, Oct. 28, 1824.
75 *York Herald*, April 15, 1820.
76 June 3.
77 D. N. B.
78 *York Herald*, Sept. 9.
79 House Books, Vol. 48, p.441.
80 House Books, Vol. 48, pp.443, 448; *York Courant*, Aug. 21.
81 *York Chronicle*, July 12.
82 Playbill, Hull Library; the London theatres had been so opened by Royal Command.
83 See Appendix B.
84 Oxberry, op. cit., Vol. I, p.200.
85 *York Herald*, May 22, 1923. The sword is now in the Guildhall.
86 *York Courant*, Nov. 22.
87 ibid., Feb. 12.
88 York Library playbill, Feb. 14.
89 *A New Description of York*, 1825, p.93.
90 Corporation Records.
91 £200 according to the *York Directory* of 1823.
92 Feb. 19.
93 *York Chronicle*, Feb. 21.
94 *York Courant*, March 19.
95 D. N. B.
96 Playbill, April 8, in possession of Mr. Patrick Waddington. For Carew see D. N. B.
97 *York Chronicle*, May 2.
98 ibid., Aug. 1.
99 R. V. Taylor, *Leeds Worthies*, p.456.
100 *New Description of York*, 1825.
101 Ante, p.193.
102 York Library playbill, April 22; *York Herald*, April 26.
103 York Library playbill, March 31; probably Phil Phillips who later painted the dioramas for his uncle Davidge at the Surrey.
104 *York Herald,* May 10.
105 A term otherwise unknown to me.
106 *York Herald*, Sept. 13.
107 ibid., Sept. 27; *A New Description of York*, 1825, p.94.
108 *York Herald*, Jan. 17; Corporation House Books, Vol. 49, p.82.
109 Corporation Records.
110 Jan. 17.
111 D. T. R. Drummond, *Memoirs of Montague Stanley*, 1848. Dibdin, *Annals of the Edinburgh Stage* and the D. N. B. both twist Drummond's statement that he acted under Manby (i.e.

Mansel) into his adopting this as a pseudonym. He played under his own name.

112 See M. Willson Disher, *The Greatest Show on Earth,* 1937, p.207.

113 Playbill in the late Sir St. Vincent Troubridge's Collection.

114 D. N. B.

115 *York Chronicle,* Oct. 16, 28.

116 Information kindly supplied from the Parish Register by the Rev. F. E. Vokes.

117 Oxberry, op. cit., Vol. I, p.32.

Chapter Six

1 Holograph letter in my possession.

2 *York Herald,* April 8, 1826.

3 ibid., March 19, 1825.

4 House Book, Vol. 49, pp.109, 158.

5 May 7.

6 ibid., April 11.

7 September 17.

8 Date kindly supplied by the Rev. P. Cowley.

9 *York Herald,* April 8, 25.

10 Details of playbill kindly sent me by Mr. Stuart Brown.

11 *York Herald,* April 15.

12 Oxberry, op. cit., Vol. I, p.119.

13 W. May Phelps and J. Forbes-Robertson, *Life of Samuel Phelps,* p.35; J. Coleman, *Memoirs of S. Phelps,* 1886, p.65. For rôles, see Appendix B.

14 Oxberry, op. cit., Vol. I, p.25.

15 *York Herald,* Aug. 11.

16 Op. cit., Vol. IV, p.164.

17 House Book, Vol. 50, Mar. 4; Corporation correspondence, 143; Lease 434. James Chitty enquired for particulars of the proposed letting of the Yorkshire Theatres on April 24 (holograph letter in my possession).

18 See Appendix C.

19 Aug. 7.

20 March 26; April 16.

21 *York Chronicle,* April 2.

22 *York Herald,* May 16.

23 *York Chronicle,* Aug. 8.

24 ibid., July 23, Aug. 1, 8.

25 Corporation Records, Correspondence 413. *Memorial of John Wilkinson.*

26 T. Raymond of the Warwick, Leicester, Northampton, Stratford and Stourbridge theatres wrote for particulars of the lease of the York circuit on Jan. 14 but this evidently came to nothing (autograph letter in my possession).

27 *York Chronicle, York Herald,* Jan. 23.

28 *York Herald,* Feb. 3.

29 ibid., March 6.

30 Westland Marston, *Our Recent Actors,* 1888, Vol. I, p.26; Coleman, *Fifty Years of an Actor's Life,* 1904, p.156.

31 See Appendix B. Phelps's opening rôle was Hayston of Bucklaw in *The Bride of Lammermuir* on March 20, 1830, not, as Coleman states, the Sentinel in *Pizarro* on Easter Monday, 1828.

32 Newspaper cutting in York Library.

33 *York Herald,* May 1.

34 ibid., Oct. 2, 9; *York Chronicle,* Oct. 7.

35 *New Description of York,* 1830 (Todd).

36 *York Chronicle,* Jan. 20.

37 British Museum playbill, Mar 21.

38 *York Chronicle,* July 20, 28.

39 ibid., Nov. 3, 10.

40 House Book, Vol. 50, Nov. 9, 1831; Corporation Records, Correspondence 413.

41 See post, p.241.

42 *Fifty Years of an Actor's Life,* Vol. I, p.282.

43 House Book, Vol. 50, Nov. 22, 1832; Jan 22, 1833.

44 *York Chronicle,* March 14.

45 *York Chronicle,* May 23.

46 ibid., Aug. 8.

47 *York Chronicle,* April 8, 11, 18.

48 ibid., Aug. 15.

49 ibid., Sept. 26.

50 ibid., Oct. 10, 17.

51 ibid., Feb. 13.

52 May 15; Odell, *Annals of the New York Stage,* Vol. III, p.499.

53 J. C. Dibdin, op.cit., p.340; Davenport Adams, *A Dictionary of the Drama.*

54 W. Clark Russell, op. cit., p.277.

55 House Books, Vol. 50.

56 ibid., Feb. 3, 1835.

57 ibid., Dec. 24, 1835; *York Chronicle,* March 5; British Museum playbill, March 24.

58 *York Chronicle,* April 23.

59 March 26.

60 ibid., May 21.

61 ibid., April 23.

62 This piece is not listed in Nicoll or *The Stage Cyclopaedia.*

63 *York Chronicle,* April 30.

64 ibid., May 7.

65 ibid., May 28.

66 ibid., March 26.

67 *Memoirs of Henry Compton,* ed. C. & E. Compton, 1879.

68 ibid., May 21, July 30.

69 April 9.
70 Sept. 10.
71 Sept. 17.
72 March 5.
73 Westland Marston, *Our Recent Actors,* p.258.
74 See Ephraim Hardcastle (W. H. Pyne), *Wine and Walnuts,* 1823, Vol. I, p.281.
75 *York Courant,* April 21.
76 *York Gazette,* July 16.
77 See Parker, *Who's Who in the Theatre.* He does not include in his genealogy a daughter with this initial.
78 *York Gazette,* Oct. 8.
79 *York Courant,* Aug. 26; Davenport Adams, op. cit.
80 ibid., June 3.
81 ibid., April 15.
82 D. N. B.
83 *York Courant,* March 11, Apr. 13.
84 ibid., July 15.
85 ibid., Aug. 26.
86 ibid., Nov. 18, 25.
87 Edward Stirling, *Old Drury Lane,* Vol. I, p.21.
88 *York Gazette,* Jan. 6, 13, 20. There is a set of musical glasses in the Kirk Museum, York.
89 ibid., May 12, 19.
90 April 28.
91 Listed by Nicoll as anon, but ascribed to Barnett in a bill of Oct. 22.
92 Its first performance in York was on May 4.
93 Westland Marston, *Our Recent Actors,* p.288.
94 *York Gazette,* March 24, June 2.
95 ibid., July 14.
96 Sept. 15.
97 Corporation Minute Book, Vol. 2, p.106.
98 *York Gazette,* March 23, July 20.
99 Paul McGuire, *The Australian Theatre,* p.51.
100 *York Gazette,* May 4.
101 ibid., July 13, 20.
102 ibid., July 27.
103 The York-Leeds line opened in May this year.
104 *York Gazette,* July 27.
105 Hooper applied for the lease of the York circuit on October 14, 1839 stating that he had had twenty years' experience in the profession, fourteen of which had been in the London theatres. For six years he had been acting manager and treasurer at the Olympic under Mme. Vestris (holograph letter in my possession).

106 Holograph letter, Oct. 17, 1839 in my possession.
107 D. N. B. says his first professional experience was in the circuit at Hull in 1839.
108 *York Gazette,* March 28, Apr. 4, 25, May 2.
109 ibid., May 8.
110 Coleman, op. cit., Vol. I, p.83.
111 A. E. Wilson, *Christmas Pantomime,* p.107.
112 Also attributed to R. B. Peake, *Theatre Notebook,* Vol. I, p.29.
113 Playbill in possession of Mr. Patrick Waddington.
114 *Recollections and Wanderings of Paul Bedford,* 1864.
115 Information from Professor Glen Wilson from Kean Account Book, Houghton Library, Harvard University.
116 See D. N. B.
117 Information from Professor Glen Wilson, from Kean's Account Book, Houghton Library, Harvard University.
118 *Fifty Years of an Actor's Life.* Vol. II, pp. 556, 558.
119 *York Gazette,* Oct. 15.
120 Minute Book, Vol. 2, p.445.
121 April 3; *York Gazette,* Apr. 3.
122 See post, p.284; *York Gazette,* Sept. 22, 1866.
123 In Minster Library.
124 May 18.
125 Quoted in British Museum playbill, March 14.
126 March 25.
127 *York Courant,* March 18, June 1.
128 See post, p.296.
129 *York Gazette,* Apr. 13
130 Minute Books, Vol. 3, p.115, Aug. 5.
131 *Yorkshireman,* Apr. 16.
132 Other versions were by A'Beckett, Lemon and Stirling. Nicoll does not list this one.
133 ibid., Jan 24; information kindly supplied by the Vicar, the Rev. J. Spencer.
134 Probate office.
135 March 28.
136 May 9.
137 These two latter are not among the versions given by Nicoll.
138 *York Gazette,* Oct. 5.
139 Op. cit., p.227.
140 *York Gazette,* March 20.
141 ibid., March 27; Coleman, op. cit., Vol. II, p.361.
142 ibid., June 12.

143 ibid., Oct. 2.
144 ibid., Nov. 27.
145 Minute Book, Vol. 3, p.335.
146 April 1.
147 *Era*, Feb. 13.
148 Coleman, op. cit., Vol. II, p.406.
149 *York Gazette*, April 1.
150 ibid., Jan. 1. They had previously appeared at the Lecture Hall, Goodramgate.
151 ibid., Feb. 3.
152 ibid., Feb. 24.
153 ibid., March 17.
154 March 31; Coleman, op. cit., Vol. II, p.455.
155 ibid., April 21.
156 ibid., May 12.
157 D. N. B. gives autumn, 1850. For rôles see Appendix B.
158 *York Gazette*, June 15.
159 ibid., June 8, 15.
160 May 18.
161 Information from Professor Glen Wilson, from Kean's Account Book, Houghton Library, Harvard University.
162 *York Herald*, Aug. 10.
163 *York Gazette*, Aug. 3.
164 Coleman, op. cit., Vol. II, p.595.

Chapter Seven

1 Minute Book, Vol. 4, p.11.
2 *York Gazette*, Aug. 24.
3 Nov. 15.
4 *York Gazette*, Aug. 21.
5 *Yorkshireman*, Dec. 18.
6 Hanton's *York Guide*, 1853.
7 Minute Book, Vol. 4, p.581.
8 *York Gazette*, Nov. 13, 20, Dec. 18; Jan. 1, 1853.
9 Minute Book, Vol. 4, p.611; Lease in Corporation Records.
10 ibid., Vol. 4, p.628; Vol. 5, p.29.
11 *York Gazette*, April 23, 30.
12 ibid., Oct. 8.
13 ibid., Oct. 29.
14 ibid., Nov. 19, 26.
15 Op. cit., Vol. I, p.26.
16 *York Gazette*, Feb. 25.
17 ibid., April 29, May 13.
18 Op. cit., Vol. II, p.455.
19 He was in York again in 1863.
20 Coleman, op. cit., Vol. I, p.268.
21 ibid., Vol.II, p.577; Westland Marston, op. cit., p.308.

22 *York Gazette*, April 14.
23 ibid., Oct. 20.
24 John Coleman, op. cit., Vol. I, p.90.
25 *York Gazette*, April 12, 19.
26 He was to die in poverty in 1886. E. L. Blanchard, op. cit., Vol. II, p.594.
27 *York Gazette*, July 26.
28 ibid., Aug. 16, 23. She was born in 1823.
29 ibid., Jan. 24.
30 May 2.
31 Westland Marston, op. cit., p.308.
32 July 11.
33 *York Gazette*, Jan. 30.
34 ibid., Nov. 27, December 11.
35 ibid., May 21.
36 ibid., Feb. 18, 1860.
37 He died December 24, 1868. *Who's Who in the Theatre*.
38 *Era*, May 27.
39 *York Gazette*, May 12.
40 Further reduced to 2/- in June.
41 June 23.
42 ibid., Aug. 11.
43 ibid., Aug. 25.
44 ibid., Aug. 25, Sept. 1.
45 ibid., May 4, 18.
46 Neither is mentioned in Nicoll or *Stage Cyclopaedia*.
47 *York Gazette*, Oct. 5.
48 ibid., Nov. 30.
49 ibid., April 26, 1862.
50 ibid., April 5.
51 ibid., Sept. 20, 27.
52 E. L. Blanchard, op. cit., Vol. II, p.286.
53 ibid., p.500; *York Gazette*, Dec. 5; the piece had been played in Glasgow in August.
54 *York Gazette*, March 26, Apr. 9.
55 ibid., Jan. 28.
56 Corporation Records, 239.
57 *York Gazette*, May 20; Harvard Library playbill.
58 Coleman, op. cit., Vol. II, p.637.
59 *York Gazette*, May 27, June 3, 10.
60 ibid., July 1.
61 A. E. Wilson, *Pantomime Pageant*, p.117.
62 *York Gazette*, Dec. 2.
63 ibid., March 31, Apr. 7, 21.
64 ibid., July 2.
65 ibid., Aug. 18, 25.
66 ibid., Sept. 22.
67 ibid., Aug. 10.
68 ibid., Dec. 7.
69 ibid., Jan. 18.
70 ibid., Apr. 4, 18, May 2.
71 ibid., May 23, 30.
72 ibid., Oct. 23.

73 ibid., Jan. 15, 22.
74 ibid., Mar. 5.
75 ibid., June 4.
76 Op. cit., Vol. I, p.326.
77 *York Gazette,* Apr. 23, 30.
78 Corporation Minute Book, Vol. 12, p.39.
79 ibid., Vol. 12, p.117; *York Gazette,* Aug. 20.
80 Corporation Records, 239.
81 *York Gazette,* Aug. 20.
82 Perhaps the same as *The Gnome King; or, The Fairy of the Silver Mine* brought out at the Queen's in 1868.
83 *York Gazette,* March 23.
84 ibid., Apr. 13.
85 ibid., Aug. 3.
86 ibid., Nov. 23, Dec. 7.
87 ibid., Nov. 23.
88 ibid., Dec. 28.
89 See York Library collection from which information is taken unless otherwise stated.
90 ibid., Mar. 8.
91 ibid., July 26.
92 ibid., Aug. 30.
93 ibid., Nov. 29.
94 *York Gazette,* Oct. 17.
95 ibid., Nov. 28.
96 ibid., Oct. 31.
97 Corporation Minute Book, Vol. 15, p.65.
98 *York Gazette,* Mar. 27, Apr. 3, 24.
99 Coleman, op. cit., Vol. II, p.640; *York Gazette,* June 12.
100 *York Gazette,* June 26.
101 York Library playbill, Oct. 18.
102 *York Gazette,* Oct. 23.
103 *York Directory,* 1892.
104 Box plan, 1888, Corporation Records 3126, 172.
105 *York Gazette,* Dec. 11, Jan. 1, 1876; Corporation Minute Book, Vol. 15, p.494.
106 *York Gazette,* March 11.
107 Op. cit., Vol. II, p.651.
108 *York Gazette,* Jan. 29.
109 ibid., Jan. 22-29.
110 ibid., March 4.
111 Clipping, York Library.
112 ibid., Apr. 15, 22, May 6.
113 Minute Book, Vol. 15, p.494.
114 ibid., p.594.
115 *York Gazette,* Aug. 26.
116 ibid., Nov. 11.
117 Clippings in York Library volume of playbills etc.
118 *York Gazette,* Dec. 21; Corporation Records, 179.
119 ibid., May 12.
120 Minute Book, Vol. 16, p.407.

Chapter Eight

1 *York Gazette,* Sept. 15.
2 ibid., September 29.
3 ibid., Nov. 17.
4 Minute Book, Vol. 17, p.263.
5 Contracts are among the Corporation Records, 239.
6 Minute Book, Vol. 17, p.481
7 *York Gazette,* May 4.
8 ibid., May 25.
9 Minute Books, Vol. 17, p.58; Vol. 18, pp.31, 276.
10 *York Gazette,* Apr. 5, 19.
11 ibid., Sept. 27.
12 ibid., Oct. 25.
13 York Library clipping, Jan. 18.
14 Minute Book, Vol. 19, p.123.
15 Lease, Corporation Records 179.
16 Ante, p.243.
17 Erroll Sherson, *London's Lost Theatres of the 19th Century,* p.188.
18 *York Gazette,* Apr. 23.
19 *Dramatic and Musical Directory,* 1883.
20 *Reminiscences of J. L. Toole,* 1889, Vol. II, p.71.
21 Minute Book, Vol. 24, pp.108, 248, 252, 264, 317, 368, 447.
22 *York Directory,* 1892; but the figure is given as 2000 in C. H. Fox's *Dramatic and Musical Directory,* 1892, p.336.
23 Minute Book, Vol. 24., pp.482, 547.
24 *York Herald,* Sept. 24.
25 *York Gazette,* March 26.
26 Minute Book, Vol. 28, p.258; Lease No. 1114.
27 Opened Jan. 20, 1902.
28 Minute Book, Vol. 28, pp.417, 432, 459.
29 *York Gazette,* Feb. 15, March 1.
30 ibid., July 23.
31 Minute Book, Vol. 31, pp. 78, 79.
32 July 25.
33 ibid., July 29.
34 *York Gazette,* Oct. 10; *Herald,* Oct. 9.
35 Minute Book, Vol. 33, p.53.
36 ibid., pp.255, 259, 274.
37 July 29.
38 Minute Book, Vol. 33, p.430; *York Gazette,* July 29.
39 *York Gazette,* March 10.
40 ibid., Apr. 14, 21.

41 Minute Book, Vol. 39, p.293.
42 *York Gazette,* Jan. 7.
43 ibid., Sept. 17.
44 ibid., May 10.
45 ibid., June 21.
46 Dec. 26.
47 Real repertory consists of a nightly change of bill; these theatres provided a new play every week, or every two or three weeks.
48 *York Gazette,* Aug. 13, 1934.
49 ibid., Apr. 15.
50 ibid., May 12; Apr. 13, 1934.
51 ibid., Sept. 15.

Chapter Nine

1 Local Government Service, Oct. 1, 1943, p.453, article by B. Seebohm Rowntree; *York Gazette,* July 20, Aug. 10.
2 *York Gazette,* Sept. 14, Oct. 5.
3 Prospectus York Citizens' Theatre, York Public Library.
4 Feb. 8.

5 Local Government Service, op. cit.
6 Sept. 13.
7 Corporation Records, 1283; *York Gazette,* Aug. 14.
8 Programme June 28; *York Gazette,* July 30.
9 *The Contemporary Theatre,* 1944-5, p.211. I owe this reference to Mr. Geoffrey Staines.

Appendices

APPENDIX A

1 Under year 1593 as on 24 Oct. 1590, which year is presumably an error.

APPENDIX B

2 J. P. Collier, *New Monthly Magazine,* 1832, p.174, conjectures that this was Kemble's rôle. See also H. Baker, op. cit.
3 The two last according to Gilliland, *Dramatic Mirror,* Vol. II, p.759.

INDEX

Index

381

Index

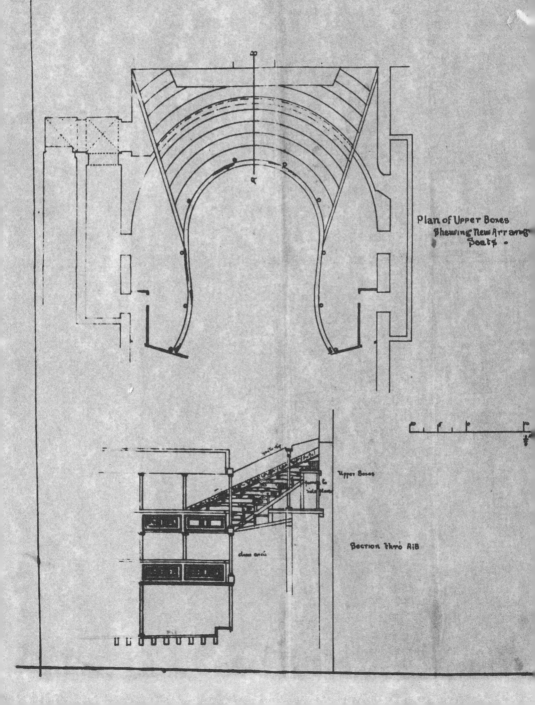

Plan of Upper Boxes
Shewing New Arrang
Seats -

Upper Boxes

Dress circle

Section Thro' A&B